Rural China, 1901–1949

Highlighting the interwoven relationship between Chinese rural society and larger historical forces, this book charts the evolution of China's rural society from 1901 to 1949, concentrating on the major changes of this period and the scenarios developed to modernize rural society during the half century leading up to the Revolution.

The modern history of rural China is one of sweeping institutional and structural transformation across many dimensions. As the first half of the twentieth century unfolded, against a backdrop of turbulent changes across a country that underwent industrialization, urbanization and modernization, China's agriculture, rural population and rural communities encountered many crises, but also showed remarkable resilience and capacity for adaptation and reform. In each of the six chapters, the author delves into one aspect or examines one period of this massive transformation, and identifies the social, economic, political and cultural significance of these tumultuous processes at work.

The book will appeal to both scholars and general readers interested in modern Chinese history and the transformation of rural China.

Wang Xianming is currently a professor in the History Department at Nankai University. His interests lie in the teaching and research of modern Chinese social history, cultural history and rural history, and he has received several national and ministerial achievement awards.

China Perspectives

The *China Perspectives* series focuses on translating and publishing works by leading Chinese scholars, writing about both global topics and China-related themes. It covers Humanities & Social Sciences, Education, Media and Psychology, as well as many interdisciplinary themes.

This is the first time any of these books have been published in English for international readers. The series aims to put forward a Chinese perspective, give insights into cutting-edge academic thinking in China, and inspire researchers globally.

Titles in sociology currently include:

Social Structure and Social Stratification in Contemporary China
Lu Xueyi

Social Construction and Social Development in Contemporary China
Lu Xueyi

Economic Transition and People's Livelihood: China Income Distribution Research
Zhao Renwei

Economic Transition and People's Livelihood: China Economic Transition Research
Zhao Renwei

Academic Experiences of International Students in Chinese Higher Education
Mei Tian, Fred Dervin and Genshu Lu

Rural China, 1901–1949
Modernization and Resilience
Wang Xianming

The Complexity of Rural Migration in China
The Story of a Migrant Village
Xiong Fengshui

Revisiting China's Rural Urbanisation
A Pearl River Delta Region Perspective
Daming Zhou

For more information, please visit www.routledge.com/China-Perspectives/book-series/CPH

Rural China, 1901–1949
Modernization and Resilience

Wang Xianming

LONDON AND NEW YORK

The publication of this book is sponsored by the Chinese Fund for the Humanities and Social Sciences

First published in English 2021
by Routledge
2 Park Square, Milton Park, Abingdon, Oxon OX14 4RN

and by Routledge
52 Vanderbilt Avenue, New York, NY 10017

Routledge is an imprint of the Taylor & Francis Group, an informa business

© 2021 Wang Xianming

Translated by Chen Qiang

The right of Wang Xianming to be identified as author of this work has been asserted by him in accordance with sections 77 and 78 of the Copyright, Designs and Patents Act 1988.

All rights reserved. No part of this book may be reprinted or reproduced or utilised in any form or by any electronic, mechanical, or other means, now known or hereafter invented, including photocopying and recording, or in any information storage or retrieval system, without permission in writing from the publishers.

Trademark notice: Product or corporate names may be trademarks or registered trademarks, and are used only for identification and explanation without intent to infringe.

English Version by permission of Social Sciences Academic Press (China).

British Library Cataloguing-in-Publication Data
A catalogue record for this book is available from the British Library

Library of Congress Cataloging-in-Publication Data
A catalog record has been requested for this book

ISBN: 978-0-367-63061-4 (hbk)
ISBN: 978-0-367-63067-6 (pbk)
ISBN: 978-1-003-11200-6 (ebk)

Typeset in Times New Roman
by Newgen Publishing UK

Contents

Preface	vii
1 From mass uprising to revolution: rural social changes before and after the Revolution of 1911	1
2 Replacement of the township system and social changes in rural areas	61
3 Rural social changes in the process of modernization	128
4 Historical changes in rural social structure and social stratification	164
5 Historical changes in the structure of rural power	271
6 Rural crisis in the 1930s and countermeasures	330
Index	424

Preface

Since 2000, issues related to agriculture, rural areas and rural population have been put in the spotlight. While these are very much current problems, they have origins in an earlier era. We can trace the emergence, development and evolution of these problems, with which the Chinese people have been preoccupied throughout the nation's modernization process, across a historical trajectory. There was a great deal of academic interest among thinkers and scholars in the 1930s in issues related to social changes in rural China against the backdrop of industrialization and urbanization. In addition, exploring and seeking answers to this issue from different perspectives also played an important part in the development of Chinese history since modern times. Looking back on our history, only if we consider this issue against the background of Chinese modern history can we figure out the underlying causes of its formation and the trends for its development, and understand its characteristics of the times in the dynamic process.

A theoretical debate over rural development in China that has waxed and waned since its beginning almost a hundred years ago has left its own historical imprint. Scholars with different social, political and academic backgrounds have different academic viewpoints and theoretical knowledge on the issue of how to observe rural society and choose a path for China's social development. However, they have a common goal, that is, to try to deepen their understanding of China's rural society and then modernize and revive the rural society based on their understanding. It is these various theories and different opinions that form the ideological premise for us today to re-examine the trend of rural development theory, because they may gather together to build social consensus or accumulate as rational resources.

1 From mass uprising to revolution

Rural social changes before and after the Revolution of 1911

At the turn of the twentieth century, there was a rising trend for supporting the revolution, and finally democratic republicanism replaced autocratic imperial power, which ushered in a new era in Chinese history. During this period, the change in the history of rural society didn't completely synchronize with the change in political revolutions or power at the upper levels. Instead, it has other historical characteristics. This chapter not only reveals the internal connection between revolutions and rural areas and the trend of development from the perspective of mass uprising in rural areas and changes in the rural public property system, but also discusses revolutions' in-depth impact on rural social change after the revolutions veered from modernity to tradition.

The gentry and mass uprisings in the late Qing dynasty (1840–1912) – historical trends and causes of conflicts between the gentry and plebs

Modern China entered the twentieth century after the Boxer Protocol was signed in 1901, which represented humiliation for China. Before returning to Beijing, the Qing government in exile announced the implementation of a political reform in Xi'an to promote the New Deal and change the political status quo for the purpose of winning popular support and getting through the crisis. However, social upheaval, together with various crises, not only showed deep social crises that were unique to the new century, but was also full of irony because the New Deal itself was also a cause for mass uprisings.

Mass uprisings flared up, which were not only a response to the political appeals of members from the organized revolutionary party and the constitutional party, and thus became one of the factors affecting the basic framework of Chinese historical trends, but also showed more apparent and salient conflicts between the gentry and plebs and highlighted underlying changes in the Chinese social structure. In the past, when conducting research on mass uprisings, scholars had paid more attention to the types of mass uprisings, the composition of participants, the role of mass uprisings in forming revolutionary conditions and other issues, but little attention was given to underlying changes in the social structure hidden behind mass uprisings. During

2 From mass uprising to revolution

the Great Revolution period (1924–1927), conflicts in the rural society broke out and a campaign was launched with the goal of overthrowing local tyrants and the evil gentry, which was not just caused by the political mobilization of the Kuomintang or the Communist Party. If there were no fairly long-term accumulative rural social conflicts and there was no structural imbalance in the interests among officials, the gentry and common people, how was the political slogan "those with lands are local tyrants, and all the gentry are bad people" revealed during the Great Revolution period? From the conflict of interest between the gentry and plebs triggered by the event of destroying schools and killing the gentry in the late Qing dynasty to the political appeal of overthrowing the gentry power during the Great Revolution period, all of these implied structural social changes along with a differentiation and recon-struction of interests on the basis of changing social systems. An accurate and in-depth understanding of the outbreak of significant historical events should depend more on an analysis of the long incubation process of those events.

Conflicts between the gentry and plebs in mass uprisings

The year 1900 marked the natural turning point of a century and, of course, a historical turning point rich in social and cultural connotations. Mary Wright believed that the year 1900 was the starting point of a series of revolutions for China in the twentieth century. The origins of revolutions that took place from 1919 to 1927 could be found at this time, and so could those of many revolutions that took place even after 1949.[1] It could be said that after 1901, mass uprisings continued to surge from the bottom of society, and they could be seen every-where and every minute. Mass uprisings, together with the so-called New Deal proposed by the imperial court, constituted an important factor that allowed both people at the upper levels and people at the lower levels to act on society in the late Qing dynasty. According to research findings, it is estimated that from the first lunar month of 1902 to the eve of the Revolution of 1911 in August, there were 1,028 mass uprisings nationwide[2] (Ma Ziyi counted the number of mass uprisings and it reached over 1,300[3]).

> The annual incidence of mass uprisings in the late Qing dynasty was dozens, hundreds and even thousands of times higher than that in the middle term of the Qing dynasty. Moreover, it also skyrocketed compared with that before and after the Sino-Japanese war from 1894 to 1895.[4]

In terms of year, mass uprisings occurred in 1986 (133 cases), 1907 (139 cases), 1909 (116 cases), 1910 (217 cases) and 1911 (108 cases). Conflicts accumulated at the bottom of society and aggressive forces mainly occurred in two periods – from 1906 to 1907 and from 1909 to 1911, with 1910 being the high-incidence year.

Different from the contradictions between officials and plebs in the old times when an oppressive government drove the people to rebellion was the general character in that mass uprisings in the new era presented a unique complexity and diversification of structural social contradictions at the beginning. First, there was extensive public participation in mass uprisings, showing the general trend of a severe differentiation of the social stratum. The results of existing research showed once again that major powers and the identity of their leaders in the last ten years of the Qing dynasty had quite different epochal characters from those in the middle term of the Qing dynasty. In the middle term of the Qing dynasty, "these participants were almost from poor or marginal areas, and they were surplus population without lands or necessary means of production".[5] To be sure, the major powers in mass uprisings were from the lower class of society, and among them "vagrants without means of production, also called marginalized people, accounted for a large proportion".[6] People of the middle and upper classes were "seldom involved in crimes", and even if involved in crimes, "they usually acted as receivers of stolen goods, protectors or assistants of bandits"/[7] However, "the gentry and the powerful and rich accounted for a large proportion of participants in mass uprisings in the late Qing Dynasty, and a larger proportion of leaders of mass uprisings".[8] In the local society with a terribly unstable social order, "the major forces consist of those who entered into official careers and those with a social status".[9] In the late Qing dynasty, "it is said that traditional intellectuals gave up their studies, most of them lost their jobs and then joined in the society party, for the government suspended the imperial examination and made the intellectual lose hope".[10] "Even scholars with official positions or a social status are tempted to join the society party".[11] "All people are involved in mass uprisings",[12] which was a unique epochal characteristic.

Second, in a world faced with conflicts in the form of mass uprisings, the interests of social groups were intertwined with each other. Social situations were complex and various. The increasing number of participants in mass uprisings indicated the intensity and universality of the differentiation of social interests, making the combination of power and the direction of the struggle more complex and changeable and creating a historical phenomenon of multi-mode contradiction and conflict, including the gentry and plebs against officials (a mass uprising in Xianju County, Taizhou City, Zhejiang Province in February 1910, a massing uprising in Mixian County, Henan Province in April[13] and another mass uprising in Mingshan County, Sichuan Province in 1911 when the county magistrate was ousted from power by the gentry and plebs[14]); officials and gentry against plebs (a mass uprising in Laiyang); officials and plebs against the gentry (officials adopted an attitude of connivance or neutrality when dealing with the incident in which common people attacked the gentry during an incident of destroying schools).[15] The differentiation of interests of the gentry class was also more prominent. The gentry class was divided into five groups and they all competed for power and benefits and refused to give in to each other.[16] The traditional social power structure model of the officials, the gentry and the people entered the historical process of decomposition and reconstruction.

4 *From mass uprising to revolution*

Table 1.1 Statistics on the incidents of conflicts between the gentry and plebs in the ten years before the Revolution of 1911

Year	1902	1903	1904	1905	1906	1907	1908	1909	1910	1911
Incidents of Conflicts between the Gentry and Plebs Cases (times)	5	2	9	8	31	44	14	38	97	59

A trend that was worth particular attention was the contradiction between the gentry and plebs in mass uprisings, which became increasingly frequent and intense. According to data, in the late Qing dynasty, the number of incidents of conflict between the gentry and plebs that could be directly pointed out or implied in the Chronology of the Mass Uprisings reached at least more than 300, and the number continued to increase year by year. This trend is shown in Table 1.1.

After 1906, the number of mass uprisings continued to increase, and the frequency of conflicts between the gentry and plebs also clearly increased. In 1910, the number of times mass uprisings happened reached its zenith during the historical period, and so did the number of times conflicts between the gentry and plebs appeared. But the two did not increase in equal increments, and the number of times conflicts between the gentry and plebs happened was far more than the number of times mass uprisings happened. In 1906, there were 133 cases of mass uprisings and 31 cases of conflicts between the gentry and plebs, while in 1907, there were 139 cases of mass uprisings and 44 cases of conflicts between the gentry and plebs. In 1910, although the number of mass uprisings rose to 217, the number of times conflicts between the gentry and plebs appeared, jumped to 97, close to half of the number of mass uprisings. This phenomenon clearly revealed the basic trend in which the contradiction between the gentry and plebs was becoming more and more intense.

According to statistics provided by each province, during the ten years in the late Qing dynasty mass uprisings happened most frequently in Jangsu Province with 275 cases, in Zhejiang Province with 178 cases, in Jiangxi Province with 69 cases, in Anhui Province with 64 cases and other provinces. In terms of geographical distribution, mass uprisings mainly happened in the vast southern areas of the Yellow River, and most of them were in provinces with a relatively developed economy. In the areas of Jiangsu and Zhejiang Provinces with the most developed economy, mass uprisings happened most frequently. What is more, the causes of mass uprisings can be classified into four kinds in terms of the 768 cases of mass uprisings that we can identify the causes of: the burden of taxation (262 cases), the issue of rice (199 cases), the issue of salaries (80 cases) and the contradiction between plebs and local powers (70 cases). With regard to proportion, mass uprisings with the burden of taxation as their cause accounted for one-third, and mass uprisings with the issue of rice as their cause accounted for one-fourth.[17] Compared with other causes, these two were the most important ones, and they were closely related to the role played by the gentry. "In recent years, there are two causes for mass uprisings: one is refusing to pay taxes and the other one is disturbing the process of education. Asking people to pay taxes and educating people are the tasks of the government". The epochal characteristics of the causes for mass uprisings were prominent:

> Today the so-called "paying taxes and educating people" never occurred before in Chinese history and was also never mentioned in books on politics by ancient people. For a decade or two, the performance of a county magistrate has been evaluated strictly according to his achievements in collecting taxes and educating people apart from his routine work. So three kinds of people would benefit from collecting taxes and educating people, including the government, local governors and magistrates of prefectures and counties. Only plebs were the victim.[18]

Refusing to pay taxes and disturbing the process of education embodied the crises of an era facing internal and external troubles, and revealed the degree of differentiation of social interests and the historical trend of social contradictions from a general viewpoint.

Disputes and conflicts of interest and power among all parties in the social strata were gathered together in mass uprisings. An article titled "On the Mass Uprisings in Shaanxi Province" states that in order to build railways, officials in some prefectures and counties collected taxes per mu (about 667 m2) grain yield from plebs, which caused mass uprisings. Then this situation spread to more than ten prefectures and counties and lasted for about four months. As a result, railways were not built because of the incorrect guidance of local officials. Local officials arbitrarily collected taxes on salt and land, and meanwhile there was competition between officials and the gentry because local officials tried to transfer the right to build railways from the gentry to themselves. Local officials wanted to take the opportunity to benefit from it and attempted to control everything in order to put their subordinates in certain positions. Given this, lots of bureaus were built. Those officials took advantage of the New Deal to do harm to plebs' well-being, and plebs bore the heavy burden of paying taxes for a very long time and did not know when to stop. There was no way for them to get rid of this burden.[19] Incidents of destroying schools and hitting the gentry emerged one after another in each place. For plebs, they had a personal stake in these incidents, though superficially these incidents had something to do with the values of "old and new

6 *From mass uprising to revolution*

ideas", "innovation" and "conservatism". "The cause of these incidents was nothing more than levying taxes". "Paying taxes to the officials did no good for plebs, and paying taxes to private schools also did no good for plebs".[20]

The evolution of history was sometimes very different from the expectations of what was predicted. The implementation of the New Deal did not eliminate social contradictions or address ruling crises, but triggered and expanded the surge of mass uprisings. In the meantime, the change in the gentry's roles and functions in the society had a significant influence on mass uprisings.

> Now the officials play the role the gentry originally played, so it is easier for us to unite to fight against the gentry. The so-called changes are caused by incidents of destroying private schools. Therefore, with regard to the causes for the incidents, we know that it was plebs that destroyed private schools, but they didn't make trouble in schools on purpose. In fact, since the officials always oppressed plebs, the latter wanted to give vent to their anger by destroying private schools.[21]

Obviously, this was quite different from the positions and functions of the gentry in the traditional society in which

> the officials had a distant relationship with plebs while the gentry had a close relationship with plebs. Plebs had more trust in the gentry than the officials [...] If there were talents in one place, they would help the officials to educate plebs.[22]

From this perspective, the original balanced power structure related to officials, the gentry and plebs, in which "the gentry trusted the officials, and plebs trusted the gentry. In this way, commands given by the upper level could be passed to the lower level and thus the decree could be carried out",[23] was gradually falling apart and finally became a thing of the past.

The gentry in mass uprisings: From the struggle against paying taxes in Laiyang to the rice riot in Changsha

Repeated outbreaks of mass uprisings had different causes and led to different opportunities, and the social powers who participated in mass uprisings played different roles. However, by analyzing cases of large-scale mass uprisings, we might observe the relationship between the local gentry and the brewing, triggering, developing and closing process of mass uprisings.

In May 1910, an anti-taxation campaign headed by Qu Shiwen broke out in Laiyang, Shandong Province. The immediate cause of this mass uprising was that natural disasters had led to crop failures. As a result, "the grain is so expensive and its price has reached the highest point in decades".[24] Peasants were unable to pay taxes in that year, so they wanted to use the grain stored in the grain stock for many years. At last, these peasants clashed with the gentry who were in charge of the grain stock. In fact, for a long time plebs had complaints against the gentry who were in charge of the grain stock. In 1880, after a bumper harvest of agricultural products in Laiyang County, plebs learned a lesson from the past (in 1876, a severe drought hit Laiyang County and a lot of people starved to death), and they stored up grain in grain stocks in case of famine. However, the gentry who were in charge of the grain stocks colluded with feudal officials to transport the stored grains to the county, and then sold the grain at a high price and recorded a low income in accounts, so as to fill their own pocket with most of the money obtained by selling grains. Privatizing the "public" interests of society through using the "public power" of society was a vexed problem of the social power structure at the grass-roots level in the tradition era and also a fundamental social cause of conflicts among the interests of officials, the gentry and plebs. In Laiyang County, Zhu Huaizhi, magistrate of the county, put all land taxes paid by plebs in the county into private banks run by the evil gentry like Wang Qi, Yu Zangyang and Wei Longzhang after resuming his old post. They took advantage of reforming systems to brazenly "privatize" the social public power, thereby causing benefit redistribution between the officials and gentry.

> When the gentry got 10,000 taels of silver, Zhu Huaizhi would take 1,500 taels of silver from them. The gentry like Wang Qi took coercive measures to force peasants to pay half of land taxes by specie and the other half by copper coins. This alone increased the burden on peasants by 25 percent.[25]

Miscellaneous taxes in Laiyang County included taxes on lands, contracts, dyers, registered residence and so on. Given this, those evil gentry like Wang Qi, Wang Jingyue, Yu Zanyang, Zhang Xiangmo and Ge Guixing enjoyed a bad reputation among people as "three pests and two moths".

The problem also lay in that the New Deal with the purpose of reforming political systems kept the social power structure at the community level and power subjects untouched, and the government allowed the traditional power to implement the New Deal with modern characteristics. The modern New Deal carried out by the Qing government did not try to solve these contradictions at all. Instead, the government made things even worse by letting the evil gentry run private schools and police stations and asking plebs to bear all the expenses of building private schools and police stations. The government would not part with even a cent! For this reason, the officials in Laiyang County levied a tax on many things or persons like contracts, registered residence, Confucian temples, oil workshops, cloth dyeing workshops, silk, flax, tobacco, livestock, the hooves of animals and blind people. Eventually, the

8 *From mass uprising to revolution*

burden on peasants had increased dozens of times. As was commented in the newspaper at that time,

> Since the local autonomy was carried out, the local gentry wantonly collected heavy taxes from people which were more than the taxes people were supposed to pay in the name of collecting funds. The gentry levied taxes on houses and registered residence and even requisitioned oxen and horses to prepare for a war. As a result, people lived in misery, and the gentry and people showed hatred for each other. When they decided to give vent to their anger, there was turmoil. Moreover, the officials didn't show solicitude for people, but were partial to the evil gentry. If people couldn't pay heavy taxes, the officials would put them to torture until they got what they wanted. This was the cause of turmoil.[26]

What was even more intolerable was that most of the taxes were embezzled by officials and the gentry. The annual expenditure of secondary schools was no more than 1,883 strings of copper coins, while the money collected from people by Wang Qi and his brother (two evil squires) was no less than 14,000 strings of copper coins. The annual expenditure of police stations was no more than 4,695 strings of copper coins, while the money collected from people by the evil gentry Wang Jingyue was no less than 7,800 strings of copper coins. The New Deal provided fairly convenient conditions for the evil gentry to commit evil deeds and bully the people. The gentry like Wang Qi and Yu Zanyang, who were in control of local power in Laiyang County, ran many old-style Chinese private banks and shops and availed themselves of the public power of the New Deal Reform to gain more profits for themselves. Therefore, private banks run by Yu Zanyang, just like the Yuanshun Private Bank run by Wang Qi, were places the government funds were stored.[27] The gentry who were in control of the social public power in rural areas

> oppressed people in the name of implementing local autonomy, made use of official authority to bully others, made profits for themselves under all sorts of pretexts, or even colluded with police officers and conspired with governors to make excuses for gaining profits.[28]

Therefore, people in Laiyang gathered together and asked the officials to use the grain stored in grain stocks to compensate for all kinds of taxes. It was not so much as a temporary measure in response to famine as the inevitable outbreak of people's historical grievances against the evil gentry. Later, before it was proved that the evil gentry in Laiyang "had already sold the grains in grain stocks and deposited only 4,000 strings of copper coins into an account, and there was nothing left",[29] this hearsay actually widely circulated among people and gradually became a sensitive catalyst to cause change at any time. Hence the mass uprising in Laiyang centered around anti-taxation was a fight against the evil gentry at the beginning. On April 21, 1910, peasants in every village, headed by Qu Shiwen, president of the Peace Society and Yu Zhu, president of the Yongzhuang Society, set up a village union and mobilized peasants from another 30 villages in the northwestern areas to take part in the struggle for getting stored grain back. On May 21, over 700 people gathered at the Temple of Guan Yu in the west of the county to argue with those evil gentry. "When people knew the evil gentry had hid away, Qu Shiwen led them into the county office",[30] and forced the magistrate to summon the evil gentry there and balance accounts within ten days. If the money did not match the account, they would ask for compensation. Thus, people's appeal for using stored grains to pay taxes turned itself into large-scale mass uprisings.

From cases of mass uprisings of different types, we can see that it was the officials whom people taking part in the rice riot in Changsha obviously intended to fight against when the rice riot happened, and that this rice riot presented another type of contradiction between the officials and plebs. But if we do not limit our perspective to the immediate cause of the outbreak of the rice riot, and do not just focus on the antagonistic situation that can be deduced between the officials and plebs when the incident went to the extreme, we can still find out the leading and irreplaceable role that the gentry played in the rice riot.

> Since the Taiping Rebellion occurred in Hunan Province, local officials asked the gentry to assist them when making preparations for anything. At the beginning, the officials and gentry could make concerted efforts through mutual cooperation, but later the officials usually showed preference and mercy towards the gentry when the latter were involved in troubles. Gradually, the drawbacks of the officials' practice had exposed that the gentry ignored the fact that the officials were their superiors and sometimes they even threatened the officials. People noticed that the gentry infringed on the power of officials, so they made use of this as a pretext for gathering a crowd and expressing their desires.[31]

The historical causes of the local power structure in Hunan Province offered unique conditions to expand of local gentry power and its resistance to the official power. "Hence it happened occasionally that a county office was besieged by a crowd of people, and thus rites and laws were totally abandoned".[32]

After this incident, Rui Cheng, governor of Hunan and Hubei Provinces, blamed the evil gentry for turmoil in Hunan Province. Though it seemed that officials shielded one another, what he said was not a groundless rumor: "I believe that turmoil in Hunan Province is certainly related to poor governance of local officials, but it is the evil gentry who cause turmoil".[33] Regarding this

10 *From mass uprising to revolution*

point, an article entitled "The Cause of the Turmoil in Changsha" made an analysis. The article states that

> in Hunan Province, people lived a tough life in recent years. The reasons for this were as follows: first, the government recklessly issued copper coins, resulting in rising prices of goods; second, people had no interest in workmanship and were fully engaged in agriculture; third, each provincial government recruited soldiers instead of conscripting them, so many soldiers returned back to their hometowns and lost their original jobs; fourth, the social education was poor and everything was in the control of the stubborn gentry [...] For this time, the immediate cause of the mass uprising was not banning rice, and it was the most direct one.[34]

As far as the immediate cause of the mass uprisings in Changsha was concerned, the gentry was still vaguely in a dominant position.

> Owing to a competition between the officials and gentry, the price of rice skyrocketed. Poor people couldn't stand it and were ready to revolt [...] unscrupulous merchants and despotic gentry didn't care about people's lives but took the chance to loot. People asked the local government to open grain stocks and sell grains at the state-fixed price, but the officials refused to do so. As a result, people automatically vented their hatred on Cen Chunming, a commissioner, and then the struggle started.[35]

When the relationship between the officials, the gentry and plebs was on the verge of breaking up, as far as the different groups' interests changed, the officials cared more about the interests of plebs and the gentry ignored them. In the first place, in order to solve the problem of hunger for victims,

> the government had intended to ask officials to raise money and then let the gentry do the rest of the work. But later it found that there weren't enough official funds, so it decided to persuade the gentry to donate money and then sold grain for free. Having heard about this decision, a gentry called Wang Xianqian opposed it and the plan for donating money was postponed.[36]

Right after the gentry and the rich people refused to donate money for selling grain for free, Cen Chunming became furious and put up a strongly worded notice twice, which stated:

> Both shops of the gentry and the rich and the houses of plebs should be checked by the security group in order to find out how much grain they have stored in stock. If the checker discovers that one has surplus grains or at least several hundred kilograms of grain except grain for personal use, that person would be accused of having bad intentions as

From mass uprising to revolution 11

far as curbing the sale of grain. Once this person is discovered by the general gentry during a pacification operation or is informed against by the group, then this person and the checker in the security group who didn't report this offense would be punished by the county government.

Moreover, Cen also demanded that the public grain should be sold as much as possible at the state-fixed price. If a manager of a grain stock refused to do as told, and once it was discovered, then the grain confiscated from the manager would be included in the public grain used for sales.[37] So in terms of the interest relationship between the officials, the gentry and plebs, Cen Chunming was inclined to take plebs' part, at least based on his subjective wishes and the measures he adopted at the beginning. "It was because the two measures adopted by Cen Chunming directly did damage to the interests of the gentry that the contradiction between the officials and gentry became increasingly intense".[38] The gentry did not care about people's lives or consider the stability of the social order, but rather they cautiously attempted to reorganize the power of the officials and the gentry.[39]

In fact, a sign of the contradiction between the interests of the gentry and plebs had been exposed. In June 1909, thousands of victims in Changde encircled the house of a gentry called Li Heng to force him to donate money for disaster relief.[40] In the spring of 1910, poor people in Xiangtan gathered together to ask for food in a queue and "those poor people in counties like Jinggang of Changsha, Hengzhou, Liling and Ningxiang gathered together to eat the food of rich families and destroy workshops for processing rice".[41] The contradiction between the interests of the gentry and plebs was a very common social problem, and the crux of the problem lay in the gentry's manipulation of the local economy. At that time, rice and firewood were expensive. A rich man called Ye Dehui "stored more than 600,000 kilos of grains in his house, but he refused to sell them at a reduced price. Hence people in the village despised him for his unkindness, meanness and shamelessness".[42] A gentry called Yang Gong "did everything for personal interests and possessed a lot of housing estates".[43] Moreover, Ye Dehui did the same as the evil gentry, though he took up a position as Inspector-General of the Rice Donation Bureau in Hunan and Hubei Provinces.

He also ordered that all the money gained by selling donated rice should be stored up in his Dechang private bank, and he often just kept a lot of money in his bank for making profits and did not give it to the county government.[44]

After the Revolution of 1911, thanks to their skillful political means, the experienced gentry cleverly turned the contradiction between the gentry and plebs in the rice riot into a direct confrontation between the officials and plebs.

In terms of the evolution of interests and power between the officials, the gentry and plebs, the mass uprisings in Laiyang and Changsha developed in

12 *From mass uprising to revolution*

different ways. The mass uprising in Laiyang developed with direct conflicts between the gentry and plebs. Plebs had once regarded local officials as intermediary agents who would adjust the interests of the gentry and plebs and discuss matters with the central government. A magistrate called Zhu Huaizhi also explained to plebs that "all exorbitant taxes were collected by the evil gentry like Wang Qi and Wang Jingyue". He also promised that "he would levy taxes according to regulations without surtaxes, repay stored grains and remove the evil gentry from office, including Wang Qi and Wang Jingyue".[45] However, the integration of the interests of the officials and the gentry caused Zhu to go back on his own promise, eventually resulting in the frequent occurrence of mass uprisings. On June 11, plebs burned the house and clothes of an evil gentry called Wang Jingyue. Conflicts between the gentry and plebs went to extremes, which immediately led to a breakup of the interest relationship between officials and the gentry. The gentry were obviously annoyed by the magistrate because the latter made plebs vent their anger on the gentry. Wang Jingyue, director of the police station, dispatched his son, Wang Tinglan, to follow the evil gentry called Wang Qi to handle affairs in Jinan, "and they carried a lot of money and bribed officials everywhere, so as to request the commissioner of Shandong to remove Zhu Huaizhi from office".[46] On June 24, Zhu was relieved of his post for poor performance in selling grains. But Kui Bao, the newly appointed magistrate, "took 3,500 taels of gold from the evil gentry in Laiyang as a bribe and canceled all agreements reached by Zhu Huaizhi", and used military forces to suppress plebs with the excuse "that plebs resisted the New Deal and formed a clique to cause turmoil". After that, this bad situation escalated. In early July, about 100,000 plebs assembled, shouting the slogan "killing all corrupt officials and evil gentry". Almost at the same time, people in Haiyang County, adjacent to Laiyang, also revolted on June 6, 1910, and attacked the county office. They made nine demands, such as "opening grain stocks for famine relief, abolishing a tax on contracts, levying an additional tax on grains, punishing policemen and so on". The magistrate explained to peasants that "extra money charged on grains was embezzled by the gentry in the village community". On June 8, people from the western area of Haiyang "waged a struggle against the gentry in the village community".[47] "They went to villages from different directions, fought against the gentry, distributed money earned by selling grains and launched a campaign of eating food in rich families". The struggle lasted for more than half a month and covered hundreds of miles, with tens of thousands of people participating in it, and the target of this struggle was always the gentry.

The cause of the mass uprising in Changsha was closely related to the gentry in Hunan Province.[48] But the development of mass uprisings was still in the control of the gentry. On the one hand, the gentry sent some people dressed like famine victims to "show their respect and support for Zhuang Gengliang", thus creating an atmosphere of supporting Zhuang in taking up the position of commissioner. On the other hand, Wang Xianqian, on behalf of seven gentry, sent a telegram to the governor of Hunan and Hubei Provinces to ask for the replacement of the commissioner in Hunan Province.[49] They attempted to maximize the rights and interests of the gentry through reorganizing the power structure of local officials and the gentry. The gentry in Hunan Province wanted to take advantage of a mass uprising to turn "the long-time fight" between officials and the gentry into a conflict between officials and plebs "that made things difficult for the commissioner".[50] On April 14, as the situation became worse, the government mobilized the gentry, who acted as the head of groups in counties, to hold meeting and find solutions to problems. Then the gentry used the situation as a bargaining chip to maximize their own interests, even at the cost of the New Deal. The gentry, headed by Kong Xianjiao and Yang Gong, held that only if the officials met their seven requirements could they cooperate with the officials, and the seven requirements included stopping building railways and schools, abolishing the police system, restoring the Bao-jia system, selling grains at the state-fixed price, opening the imperial grain stock and withdrawing the standing army.[51] The officials needed to bargain with the gentry and deal with plebs, so in the fight between the officials, the gentry and plebs, it seemed that the gentry and plebs united as one to fight against the officials. At least superficially such a situation had formed. However, as far as the interests the gentry cared about most and the seven requirements they raised were concerned, the gentry's demand for interests (like their resistance to selling grain at a fair price thanks to the gentry's donation) and rights (like seizing the right to carry out the New Deal) was expressed, but the basic needs of famine victims were not mentioned at all. The interests were basically consistent with the conflicts between the gentry and plebs over destroying private schools and refusing to pay taxes. In the rice riot, conflicts between the officials and plebs became increasingly intense and finally broke out in extreme ways, which had something to do with "the increasingly fierce struggle between the officials and gentry",[52] who hid for a long time. And the conflicts between officials and the gentry finally broke out in a mass uprising.

However, once a mass uprising erupted and it did harm to the interests of the gentry, the gentry would put it down directly instead of manipulating it secretively.

> On March 6th, rebels looted the houses of the gentry and rich people in the city. Terrified by them, the gentry gather in the ancestral hall of the Xi family to discuss solutions to putting down the rebellion and they began using severe punishment.[53]

Therefore, the results of a mass uprisings were still considered on the basis of conflicts between the gentry and plebs. "The gentry would ask the officials to punish the rebels severely immediately they heard that the rebels looted the houses of the gentry and rich people and bad things would befall them".[54] In the rice riot in Changsha, the gentry could manipulate the mass uprising

14   *From mass uprising to revolution*

in the dark, and put pressure on the commissioner and officials in the light, with the aim of gaining advantage from both sides. This complex situation indicated conflicts between the interests of the gentry and plebs, and the differentiation and reconstruction of the officials–gentry power structure.

Though the interest relationship between the officials, the gentry and plebs in the massing uprising in Laiyang showed different features from that in the rice riot in Changsha, both of them revealed that the fundamental conflict of interest on the part of the gentry and plebs was basically the same. It was the conflict of interest between the gentry and plebs and the worsening relationship between them that constituted one of the basic factors in the constant mass uprisings in local society since the late Qing dynasty.

The New Deal in the late Qing dynasty and institutionalization of the gentry's power

Since the late Qing dynasty, the local social order was often turbulent and out of control, and especially mass uprisings developed in the form of conflicts between the gentry and plebs. The gentry, as a main subject of local powers, could hardly absolve themselves of responsibility for this turmoil. Since then, the name of "evil gentry" was known to everyone and to an extent the evil gentry played an important role in causing rural social turmoil. For example, "the reason for the mass uprising in Laiyang was that the magistrate levied heavy taxes on people and the evil gentry held the candle to the devil".[55] Kui Bao "consulted with the evil gentry and merchants about everything after he took office, which caused turmoil".[56] However, the gentry were regarded as evil people, and conflicts between the interests of the gentry and plebs became increasingly intense in a general sense, which was closely related to changes in the public interest of rural society and the institutional nature of power, instead of to a difference in the morality of good gentry and evil gentry. In the process of institutional change, not only did the relatively balanced relationship between the interests of the officials, the gentry and plebs break up, but also the gentry class moved to the center of a reconstructed power dynamic. In the process of institutional changes taking place as part of the New Deal, the gentry became the ones who possessed all kinds of local power resources, so they were called "gentry with power".

Under the system of the "Old Deal" (given by the editor), the opposite term of the "New Deal", the interests of the gentry were certainly different from those of plebs because they were from different classes, but there were hardly frequent, severe conflicts between their interests. It is recorded in the *Annals of Liling County* that

> Liling County was once called Yan County. People there endured hardship and worked hard. There were no rich families but it was filled with poor people. Young men would be proud for themselves if they could gain an official position by taking the imperial examination and support their

From mass uprising to revolution   15

own needs. Poor men would make a living by writing essays and didn't go after fame and money [...] peasants were diligent in farming and common people and scholars had equal status [...] The elderly people taught the young that they should attach equal importance to farming and learning, and their values were similar to today's populism.[57]

At least, since people in the same village or of the same clan had common interests, the interest relationship between officials and plebs was less intense than that between officials and the gentry. During the reign of Emperor Tongzhi (1862–1875), officials collected taxes on tribute grains in the middle reach of the Yangtze River. With the help of clan organizations, the gentry and plebs in the rural society worked together to fight against the feudal government. In some areas a kind of situation formed in which in rural areas, people from clan organizations

> often gathered together to revolt against the officials, flaunt their superiority and bully the weak. Ancestral halls were the places they assembled and hid themselves. If one committed crimes like murder and theft and then fled into a village protected by powerful people, it was difficult to capture him.[58]

As indicated in Zhang Zhongli's study, the gentry shouldered the responsibility of promoting the development of and protecting interests of their own hometowns. In front of government officials, they spoke up for the interests of local areas. Under normal circumstances, the government's main interests were consistent with those of the gentry, and in order to keep the society functioning normally and maintain the status quo, both sides would cooperate with each other. If their interests were opposed, the gentry would criticize, and even resist the government's administration.[59]

In the structure of basic interests and power between the officials, the gentry and plebs of the traditional society, both plebs and the government, and the stability of the local order and the adjustment of interests usually relied on the gentry class.

> The rural system didn't change in a period of the Qing Dynasty [...] Baizheng (a leader of 500 families) was also called Xiangbao [...] the orders given by the administrative office of prefectures were passed on to village people, but they didn't know what rural governance was [...] so this was a period without rural governance.[60]

Both the maintenance of the rural social order and the operation of life depended on the gentry, and many public organizations in the rural society were also built thanks to the prestige of the gentry, such as the Water Board, the Association of the Elderly, the Dike Engineering Bureau and so on.[61] The gentry class, who enjoyed cultural authority and social authority, was the

16   *From mass uprising to revolution*

social foundation of this control system. However, the gentry did not win support of the system, though the influence or dominance of the gentry in local affairs cannot be underestimated. At the same time, the gentry handled public affairs with prestige and capability, which could not bring about the normalization and institutionalization required by modern administration.[62]

When the Taiping Rebellion occurred, local officials of the Qing dynasty realized that they must adjust the relationship between the folk gentry and themselves, so that they could fight against the Taiping army with the help of the gentry. In 1852, Zhang Liangji, the commissioner of the Hunan, insisted that "it was a top priority for the local gentry to be informed of all kinds of situations in local places".[63] What local officials felt deeply was that within the framework of the tripartite forces of the officials, the gentry and plebs, the gentry and plebs had more consensus about interests, and they could work together against the government. Therefore, in an era of crises, local officials must cooperate with the gentry to resist the Taiping army. Luo Bingzhang, the commissioner of Hunan, noticed that "the officials cannot connect with plebs, but the gentry could act as intermediary agent", and "it was essential to keep the officials, the gentry and plebs in touch with each other, so as to prevent officials of a lower rank from doing something bad".[64] The unity of interests between officials and the gentry was realized in group training.[65] The officials assisted the gentry. When the civil corps conscripted or dispatched people, "it should certainly be approved by the government, but in fact the practice was up to the gentry themselves".[66] In addition, "there were lots of directors of civil corps and gentry working in civil corps and all of them were powerful gentry at the upper level".[67] The appearance of the gentry working in bureaus or as directors indicated that the local power was transferred from the gentry class to the group of powerful gentry.[68]

The combination of the gentry and group training organizations, and the systematization of their power opened the process of the institutionalization of the gentry's power and transferring the gentry into powerful ones for the gentry class with scholars representing the cultural and social authority as a basic feature. "After the mid-19th century, the nature of traditional organizations in villages began to change". The change was not only reflected in the fact that the gentry began to become leaders of organizations in towns and villages, and that the functions of organizations in villages extended from dealing with official business to intervening in civil dispute mediation, collecting taxes and organizing local armed forces, but also "by the emergence of various clubs featured by modern local autonomy and different from traditional organizations in villages".[69] Some organizations were "under the leadership of the gentry and began to perform local public functions, although there were no obvious changes in themselves".[70] There were continuous changes in the New Deal or local autonomy in the historical process, and therefore the New Deal and local autonomy gained a greater space for power and a foundation of legitimacy. As Zhou Xirui said, "local autonomy and earlier gentry power continue to exist with great significance".[71]

From mass uprising to revolution 17

In modern times, the local government had more and more political affairs to handle. As far as a prefecture or county was concerned, all affairs about education, police, agriculture, industry and commerce needed to be handled. As the magistrate of a county, how could he be capable of dealing with everything on his own? In all countries, local officials were only responsible for handling affairs in his own jurisdiction. As a result, everything could be handled properly and local governance performed well. The officials appointed by the central government just acted as supervisors.[72]

Compared with the Old Deal, the New Deal and its supported local autonomy system laid a legitimate and institutional foundation for the increasingly expanding gentry power,[73] and made non-institutional gentry power based on customs and local situations in traditional times legitimate and institutional. "It was discovered that whether the gentry or the officials had jurisdiction over local bureaus in each was not specified at first, so their limits of jurisdictions were determined by their own power. If one side was defeated, it may regard the other side as an enemy and be incompatible as fire and water". Now, "the gentry was liable for management, while the officials played a leading role. Hence the plebs could rely on both of them, and then there was no turmoil".[74] Moreover, in the process of constructing modern systems, local economy and finance were also in the control of the gentry,

> Since local governments were unable to use national funds for implementing local autonomy, they had to find other ways of raising money, except for the public funds and property they already had [...] local autonomy means choosing local people to handle local affairs. Local people could easily make progress in management because they were familiar with local conditions, but there were obvious drawbacks. If local government did not choose the right person in an election, and then the elected person gained private ends in a public cause and had a monopoly on everything, there were only bad results and no benefits.[75]

Moreover, in some new fields, the social organizations also provided historical opportunities for the gentry to gain profits. For example,

> in recent years, if education associations and chambers of commerce were well-run, they would certainly promote the development of civilization every day; if not, they would even hinder the development of local places. Therefore, implementing the New Deal was not easy. Since then, sagacious people were afraid of damaging their own good reputation, so they did not want to participate in implementing the New Deal, whereas some people with a bad reputation took advantage of this chance to commit evil deeds, causing other people to despise them.[76]

18 *From mass uprising to revolution*

The comment of Yuan Shuxun was criticized by many critics, but it proved the control of the traditional gentry over power in new fields.

From the traditional system to the modern system, there was not only a transformation of the institutional framework or form, but also a transformation of the subject of power in its essence. "Before the reform was carried out in the early Qing Dynasty, those junior officers were all regarded as officials appointed by the imperial court..." "Since the Emperor Guangxu took the throne, many old officials were laid off and now most of the local gentry worked in educational institutions, police stations and so on".[77] In the late Qing dynasty, the bureaus of finance, industry, police and education, which were referred to as the "Four Bureaus" by Wei Guangqi, were "all in the charge of the gentry". Therefore, handling local public affairs (or public power) depended more on the powerful gentry who had authority over public organizations and organs of power than on the reputable gentry in traditional times. So the institutional transformation, initiated by the New Deal, "actually made the traditional practice institutional and organization that it was the gentry instead of the officials who handled local public affairs".[78] Different from the traditional times, "most of the written laws and regulations had provided basis for the gentry's handling local public affairs".[79] In the early twentieth century, the gentry who played an active role in the power center of rural society

> mostly took up a position in quasi-authority organs like the civil corps of the town as gentry working in the civil corps, as the director of the civil corps, as a member of the school board, as the deputy chief or director of county government organs, or as the district governor or director [...] at the same time, they were also clan leaders in control of clan power in civil society. They held the political and economic rights of the urban and rural society, representing a high degree of integration of land ownership, political rights, gentry power and clan power. So they were the special class in rural society.[80]

Relationship between the gentry and plebs: from identity difference to interest conflict

In the early twentieth century, mass uprisings spread across the country, but among them there were few large-scale ones with a lot of people gathering together. It can be seen from the record of mass uprisings in the *Oriental Magazine* that the immediate causes of mass uprisings were various, but those related to conflicts between the gentry and plebs were relatively concentrated, like incidents concerning household surveys. In 1909, in an essay titled "The Record of Household Surveys in Jiangxi ", it was stated that "mass uprisings occurred one after another" all over the area. "Rumors spread quickly and most of people lost their mind". In Shutansha, Xiangxi and other places in Nanchang County, local people "gathered together to make disturbances".

From mass uprising to revolution 19

Later "a local gentry came forward to intervene, but local people beat him hard without any reason and it is also said they destroyed the house of the gentry". The mass uprisings, triggered by household surveys, was aimed at fighting against the gentry, and incidents continuously happened in which the gentry "were beaten or sometimes killed by people".[81] On May 27 and 28, 1909, in Chongren County, "It was heard that people gathered together in the Statistics Division, and allied with people from other counties to search for and kill the gentry who handled affairs about the New Deal". In June, in Liudu of the Duchang County, "a squire called Zeng Tunan received orders from the county magistrate to do household surveys. Finally he was beaten by people and his house was destroyed". In Anyi County, "two squires named Yu Chengjie and Gong Jieshi won in the primary election and then they pretended to be the gentry who were responsible for household surveys, so they were hated by people" (Yu Chengjie was killed and Gong Jieshi was crippled). In Zhangshu Town, Xinchang County and Ningdu Prefecture, local people killed many squires and destroyed their houses.[82] In Xingan County, "local people had more and more violent actions. They beat the gentry, destroyed their houses and looted everywhere, so that the officials and gentry who fell victim to the violence fled into cities and dare not go home". "Local people wanted to kill the gentry". In Ningdu County, "several more squires were beaten and robbed".[83]

The incident involving the destroying of private schools was also a major cause of conflict between the gentry and plebs. It is reported in an article titled "News about a Mass Uprising in Yuanzhou of Jiangxi" that

> the affairs of education and donation for the New Deal were mostly handled by Lu Yuanbi, who then took advantage of this opportunity to abuse his power to levy all kinds of taxes on people and arbitrarily extract money from taxes without reporting details to the officials for the latter's deliberation and approval. [...] When it came to the New Deal, plebs suspected it was the gentry who made trouble out of nothing, and thus they hated the gentry and wanted to go into towns to destroy private schools and kill the gentry.[84]

On July 27, 1909, in Yizhou (today it is Yi County of Hubei), directly affiliated to the central government, "the gentry raised money and collected more taxes under the pretext of carrying out the New Deal like setting up private schools, patrol-police offices and the autonomy bureau". After the autonomy bureau was established, a squire with the surname Zhang, sold all stored grains in public grain stocks and then levied taxes on people to fill his own pocket in the name of raising money for implementing autonomy, triggering a mass uprising.[85] In 1909, the incidents in which plebs showed hatred for the gentry happened frequently in Zhejiang. In Cixi County, Shangyu County, Suian County, Jingning County and other counties, plebs burnt down private schools, because "some evil squires raised money to gain

20 *From mass uprising to revolution*

personal benefits in the name of establishing private schools, causing people to generated hatred for learning".[86] Many institutions in Shangyu County were destroyed, including private schools, the education association, the study encouragement office and the Statistics Division and Research Institute of Autonomy. "The local officials were not only unable to prevent incidents from happening, but also unable to solve problems after the incidents. As a result, many organs could not function normally".[87] In the prefectures and counties of Jiangsu, "the incidents that people gathered together to destroy private schools, houses and hurt the gentry happened almost everywhere". In ten areas, including Jiangjing County, Wu County, Changshu County and other counties, "it was the gentry that people mainly fought against".[88]

"The local gentry actively held and participated in activities concerning the implementing of the New Deal in local areas. Especially they were in charge of the establishment of private schools and the local police administration. They turned temples in towns into schools and collected a lot of taxes on rural people to raise money for the establishment of private schools and local police administration. Consequently, peasants in villages often showed hatred for the gentry, and in fights against implementing the New Deal in local areas, peasants often mainly fought against the gentry. Meanwhile, in mass uprisings, the situation in which people revolted against the gentry instead of the officials was also related to the instigation of the local government, owing to the contradiction between the gentry and officials in the activities of the New Deal".[89] In the mass uprising in Yichun in 1910, officials acted as provokers and agitators in increasingly intense conflicts between the gentry and plebs, causing such a situation that the officials and plebs worked together to revolt against the gentry. The officials said to plebs who besieged the town, "It was the gentry instead of the local government who raised money". "Hence when it came to the New Deal, plebs suspected it was the gentry who made trouble out of nothing, and thus they hated the gentry and wanted to go into towns to destroy private schools and kill the gentry".[90] According to statistics offered by Wang Shuhuai, during the year from the first lunar month of 1910 to February of 1911, people destroyed more than 50 private schools and 18 autonomous public offices in towns of Jiangsu.[91] In Cixi County, Shangyu County, Suian County and other counties of Zhejiang, many incidents involving the destroying of private schools happened successively in February 1911. The education association, the study encouragement office, institutes and the statistics division in charge of the gentry were destroyed, and the houses of the gentry were also destroyed and looted.[92] "People made up their minds to go into towns to destroy private schools and kill all the gentry in the academic circle".[93]

The incidents concerning household surveys and destroying schools were major parts of the New Deal issued by the imperial court, and thus those triggered mass uprising, apparently to show resistance towards the New Deal. "There were various causes of turmoil in Hunan Province and the root cause did not lie in the prices of rice and goods". As for the root cause, "the New

From mass uprising to revolution   21

Deal that the government invested money in was practical and realistic, but it also made troubles".[94] In the mass uprising of Laiyang, "the gentry and plebs had been hostile towards each other for a long time". Moreover, "recently the New Deal was carried out by the gentry and they didn't care about public opinions, so people had many complaints against the gentry".[95] However, this was obviously different from the distribution of interests and power between the new and old gentry who competed with each other.[96] As far as people were concerned, there was no new or old policy. A policy would be seen as a bad one as long as it damaged people's basic needs for survival. Therefore, superficially based on the New Deal, the conflicts between the gentry and plebs were actually caused by the overexpansion of the powerful gentry's interests affecting people's basic needs for survival.

First, in the traditional era of gentry governance, institutionalized regional and rural finance was out of the question. There was no standing organization for the gentry to deal with public affairs by financial means, "which were not compulsory taxes and fees based on public power and relevant systems". As for local public welfare undertakings, "all of them were handled by the local gentry before the government carried out autonomy in the early Qing Dynasty". "All public funds and property were raised by the gentry and the latter were in charge of revenue and expenditure and then reported it to the county office for the record".[97] In the changes made in local systems in the late Qing dynasty, the gentry dealt with local public undertakings and local finance in an institutional and routinized way. Some official affairs, which were originally handled by officials, were then handled by the gentry. For example, in the late Qing dynasty, the task of collecting taxes in Henan and Shandong provinces was handled by the gentry instead of petty officers or officials. The duty of providing food supplies by each *li* and *bao* was changed to paying officials a salary and collecting taxes according to the head count and each mu of lands. A bureau of justice was set up in Wuzhi, Henan, for offering carriages and horses.[98] The problem, however, was that it did not ease the burden on peasants but increased it after the gentry handled public affairs.

> As far as the disadvantages of apportioning charges, the gentry set up a bureau to offer carriages and people covered the costs. Then the gentry would squander the revenue collected by the bureau and lied about the expenditure. It was impossible to find out the truth.[99]

In the Official Business Bureau, many affairs were handled by the gentry instead of petty officers [...] Except for corruption and extortion, it was stipulated that the total amount of money used for handling public affairs reached 149,000 taels of silver annually.[100]

Therefore,

> with the change in political systems that the New Deal would be carried out immediately without preparing for its implementation for dozens

22 *From mass uprising to revolution*

of years", the fact that the officials and gentry conspired to gain profits was publicized, which meant "the officials and gentry raised all money from people through continuously increasing taxes and asking for more donations, but they made no achievements at all. It was just the officials pursuing profits who wanted to fill their own pockets.[101]

The rural regime was characterized by personal gain, which could be seen even more clearly without the guise of moral factors. "It could be regarded as the darkest days of the rural life in China".[102]

Second, the traditional gentry and plebs had different social statuses, but there were no direct conflicts of interest between them, because the gentry did not directly possess public power and resources. A county magistrate called Wang Huizu expressed his own opinion about the relationship between the interests among officials, the gentry and plebs, saying that

the officials kept a distant relationship with plebs, whereas the gentry maintained a close relationship with plebs. Plebs had more trust in the gentry than the officials. Since all the laws and regulations enacted by the imperial court cannot be understood by plebs, the gentry would explain them to plebs. An edict were given to the gentry and then the gentry passed it on to plebs, so that it was easy for plebs to understand principles and for the gentry to teach plebs.[103]

Since the late Qing dynasty, the evolution of the local political system had broadened the gap between interests of the gentry and plebs, leading to a direct conflict between the gentry, who possessed rural public power and public interests, and plebs, who pursued survival. For instance, in Yizhou (today it is Yi County of Hubei Province), which was directly affiliated to the central government, "the gentry raised money and collected more taxes for handling affairs like setting up private schools, patrol-police offices and the autonomy bureau, which made plebs detested the gentry terribly". "All matters about the New Deal were dealt with by a few evil squires, and they always filled their own pockets with public funds".[104] In Wukang County, Zhejiang Province,

plebs showed hatred for the policemen who handling relevant affairs, for the latter embezzled the donated money. On the New Year's day, annoyed by some trifles, plebs gathered together and then flooded into the county office, so that the lobby was destroyed, the officials beaten, the police station damaged, the policemen attacked and a squire surnamed Gu beaten.[105]

Consequently, "destroying private schools and killing the gentry" was used as a slogan to mobilize plebs.[106]

It seemed that the relationship between the gentry and plebs under the New Deal was completely different from that under the Old Deal. "In the

From mass uprising to revolution   23

past, the social elite had a strong local relationship and kept in touch with the rural society. They were somewhat concerned about some interests of the peasant class out of their respect for traditions".[107] The emerging evil gentry

> wore a long robe, walked around all rural areas and never had a rest all day in order to win respect among uneducated peasants. What they did in rural areas included fomenting troubles, intervening in legal cases, protecting landlords, bullying uneducated peasants, and blackmailing others all around.[108]

It was the institutional arrangement of the New Deal that changed the role of the traditional gentry so that a new pattern of interests formed in which "the gentry entered the government office at will and oppressed and exploited plebs, or availed themselves of this opportunity to pursue private ends. As a result, the gentry were despised by plebs".[109] The gentry with public power in local society only cared about the development of gentry power and the expansion of their own interests, leading to a situation in which "the gentry were more powerful than the county officials"[110]. The gentry and plebs turned from two classes with different statuses into two strata facing interest conflicts, and with in-depth institutional changes, the differentiation of interests between the gentry and plebs became more and more intense, making it hard to maintain a stable social order and adjust to accommodate these two groups' interests.

Therefore, the reverence of plebs for the gentry class that was based on differences in culture and social status changed into social hatred for the group of evil gentry who used their power to oppress others. Therefore, the intensifying social contradictions at the grassroots level were mainly demonstrated by fairly frequent conflicts between the gentry and plebs. The New Deal made it legitimate for the gentry to occupy public power and resources in rural society and made the gentry's interests directly opposite to plebs', to some extent changing the basic pattern of antagonism between the officials and plebs in the traditional era.

> For example, the gentry had no official position in the government and should be treated in the same way as common people, but they almost received the same treatment as the officials did, and even oppressed and exploited plebs more cruelly than the officials. Once constitutionalism was carried out, the evil gentry intervening in local legal cases would be elected as local councilors. It was the corrupt officials in the imperial court and the evil gentry in the wild rather than plebs who supported constitutionalism. It had nothing to do with plebs' well-being and did harm to plebs' interests.[111]

So, from an article titled "The Gentry Were Public Enemy",[112] published in *Henan Magazine* in 1908, the political mobilization with the slogan "all the

24 *From mass uprising to revolution*

landlords were rich, and all the gentry were evil" during the Great Revolution period was not just a kind of social ethos prevailing at the community level, but also an epoch content that reflected the complex and diverse institutional changes in the social structure and power structure. Although as far as plebs' interests were concerned, "it was no good for plebs to donate money to the officials and private schools", but the condition was fundamentally different in terms of plebs' benefits and the difficulty of achieving a counterbalance, for "now the officials play the role the gentry originally played, so it is easier for us to unite to fight against the gentry. The so-called changes are caused by incidents of destroying private schools".[113] Therefore, under the traditional system, an unconventional large-scale uprising caused by the contradiction that "the officials drove plebs to rebel" mainly manifested itself as universal social conflict with new characteristics reflected by a situation in which "the gentry drove people to death".[114]

The New Deal provided an institutional and legitimate basis for the traditional gentry to expand their power. In the process of gathering resources, there was a direct conflict between the powerful gentry's actions and the interests of plebs. In addition, a lack of new checks and balances of power[115] made the contradiction between the gentry and plebs and the interest conflicts between them increasingly intense without there being any timely and moderate adjustment. Consequently, conflicts broke out in the form of mass uprisings. In the late Qing dynasty, the "New Deal" formed an institutional basis for the "institutionalized" expansion of the gentry's power, while the "institutionalization" of the powerful gentry also constituted the institutional root of mass uprisings or conflicts between the gentry and plebs.

The Revolution of 1911 and rural public property based on historical study centering on Hunan and Hubei Provinces

Public property was a relatively special economic resource for rural areas and the donating, handling and use of public property were all dealt with by the gentry class, which meant the operation of public property was affected by changes in the rural power structure. From the Taiping Rebellion to the Revolution of 1911, the national regime changed a few times, and the rural power structure also gradually moved toward an imbalance. Thus the characteristics of public property operations and social functions also changed along with the times. These fundamental changes began with the Revolution of 1911 and triggered new revolutions. Conducting a historical study on the changing process[116] and analyzing the real effects and institutional causes of this change can help reveal the complex and profound relationship between the reform of the national political system and the trends in the development of the rural power structure.

From mass uprising to revolution 25

The historical track of public property operation

In traditional society, the gentry, as the leaders of villages, actively took the lead in participating in local public welfare affairs in order to gain prestige, authority and economic benefits. There were a lot of records in local chronicles indicating that the gentry donated money and property and did activities for charity. In Hunan and Hubei Provinces, there were many squires with a lower rank, but they were keen on local affairs and the public welfare of clans, and devoted themselves to building ancestral temples, purchasing clan property and compiling the pedigree of a clan, making the number of local public properties uncountable. Generally speaking, public property mainly included stored goods, lands and all sorts of public funds collected from people and used for the interests of people after the Taiping Rebellion.[117]

Various kinds of rural public property were managed in different ways with inherent consistency, which meant the gentry acted as managers and officials as supervisors, thus constituting an operational system featuring the gentry's management with the officials' supervision. For instance, the officials did not manage public grain stocks, but

> they were granted the right of supervision. The gentry would be punished according to the laws related to embezzlement and dereliction of duty after compensating for the loss, if they were corrupt. Officials would be ordered to compensate for others due to their malfeasance like coercion or embezzlement according to the law of abusing one's power to seek personal gains.[118]

In regard to the management of public funds, the government stipulated that

> those who were in charge of the local place and misappropriated public property shall be punished as thieves, and those who squandered public funds shall compensate for the loss. A person who refused to pay all fees asked shall be sent to the official court to call him to account for his behavior. A person who took advantage of one's power to threaten others shall be punished as a bandit. A person who lied about how many lands he owned or distributed lands unfairly would be punished after investigation.[119]

The public property of a clan would be protected by the government from "wayward clan members with designs on such property".[120] The head of a clan usually reported their family rules and regulations for the protection of public property to the government to gain the latter's support.[121] There were checks and balances between the official power and the gentry power, effectively making the public property function. Since the storing system functioned normally, the issue of crop failure could be addressed properly, so people "believed in" this system,[122] for it could ensure people's well-being. The relief

26 *From mass uprising to revolution*

offered by a clan also "exerted considerable influence on people's life".[123] The number of lands used for building charitable institutions was also steadily rising,[124] and the collection of public funds helped maintain the order of the civil corps. Moreover, the officials and gentry did not overtax the people.

However, when the government carried out the New Deal, the implementation of local autonomy made it possible for the rights of local administration and tax collection to be granted to the gentry, so that the balanced relationship between the power of the officials and the gentry was broken. In 1908, the Qing government asked the constitutional compilation bureau to formulate and issue the Constitution on Local Self-government in Cities, Towns and Villages, which provided that autonomous public offices might use local public houses or temples, and use local public funds, property and donations (surtaxes and special taxes), to cover the expenses of autonomy. The method of managing funds "shall be determined by the councils", and "the funds shall be managed by the board of directors of a town or village".[125] In fact, the collection and management of funds for autonomy were in the control of the gentry, because the gentry, working in councils or on boards of directors at all levels established by public offices in towns and villages, "were all local gentry with an official rank".[126] Although in the Constitution all kinds of supervisory mechanisms were designed for the implementation of local autonomy to manage funds carefully, the weakening central authority made it hard to put the design into practice. The gentry, free of institutional constraints, soon degenerated, and regarded autonomy as a good opportunity for seeking personal gain. As a result, the characteristics of public property operations turned from "using public property to serve the public" into "using public property to pursue private ends" after the gentry were in control of the public property. Autonomous institutions "issued various regulations to deceive the public, and these regulations served as an excuse to infringe upon common people's rights and levy heavy taxes on people".[127] Public property operations only extracted resources from local areas. Though superficially public property was owned by the public, it did not actually serve the public.

> What the gentry truly did for the public only included lighting up street lamps, spraying water on streets, or building a few newspaper offices and preaching institutions. But the public funds used by orphanages, old people's homes, private schools charging no tuition, grain stocks and so on, and spent on distributing medicine and tea to the poor and storing were all squandered.[128]

From "using public property to serve the public" to "using public property to pursue private ends", the social functions of public property weakened greatly, but the mode still existed that officials acted as supervisors and the gentry as managers. The Revolution of 1911 completely broke this mode and forced the characteristics of public property operation to go through an essential change from "using public property to pursue private ends" to

From mass uprising to revolution 27

"turning public property to private property". This revolution resulted in the gentry power no longer being subject to the constraints of previous systems, and the expansion of the gentry's power got out of control. With regard to this situation, people living at this time sighed with emotion, "the gentry power expanded so rapidly and largely that it was not easy to control its expansion".[129] At the same time, "the expanding power of local autonomous groups, including the power of collecting land taxes and other local taxes, was transferred to the gentry of each county".[130] After 1912, public funds bureaus were built on a large scale in Hubei Province, and

> they were mainly responsible for managing local revenue, expenditure and special donations of the county. The local gentry were mostly appointed to work in the bureaus as officials who were not officially recognized by the imperial court. These bureaus were run by local people and their operations were supervised by the officials. The director of a bureau would be elected by the local gentry and then the latter would report the election results to the county magistrate for his approval.[131]

In 1924, the Department of Finance of Hunan issued the "Regulations of Local Financial Lists in Various Counties of Hunan Province", specifying that local property depository departments were run by the gentry and they were in charge of tax collection and the handing over of taxes to their superiors.

> Local property depository departments should be set up in the county magistrate's office and the magistrate selected a wealthy and righteous squire to manage the department and report details to the Department of Finance and the government at the prefecture level for the record. [...] The county magistrate entrusted to a wealthy and righteous squire in towns or villages the duties of collecting taxes and additional taxes based on local conditions and reporting details to the county office.[132]

Obviously, after the founding of the Republic of China, the gentry were entirely in control of public property operations. Since the behavior of using public property to seek private gain became increasingly common, public property was gradually being "privatized". "In each town and village, temples, confiscated property, school-owned lands, public grain stocks and other public industries were either possessed by someone for personal interests or abandoned".[133]

> The gentry shall bear the duty of levying taxes on all organs including the Likin Bureau, Bureau for Public Sale, Printing Bureau and Bureau for Collecting Taxes on gambling. Moreover, the gentry in charge of collecting taxes on lands and population incited small local warlords to borrow money gained through tax collection. In each county, some

28   *From mass uprising to revolution*

> people still borrowed money even in 1929 or 1930. The gentry were the ones to blame for this, for they want to gain profits![134]

As a whole, public property operations were always restricted by the checks and balances between the officials (government) and gentry. From the Taiping Rebellion, to the implementation of the New Deal, to the founding of the Republic of China, public property operations changed from "using public property to serve the public", to "using public property to pursue private ends", and then to "turning public property into private property". The main reason for this lay in the imbalanced allocation of rural power caused by the change in the political system.

Institutional causes of public property operations

The traditional pattern in which officials acted as supervisors and the gentry as managers restricted public property operations to checks and balances of power between the officials and gentry. If they were balanced, the operations were effective; otherwise, they were ineffective. In local society, "the officials worked together with the gentry to govern an area",[135] but after the Taiping Rebellion, this situation changed. In Hunan and Hubei Provinces, a large number of group training organizations emerged, and Hunan Province "ranked first" in the number of this kind of organizations.[136] The gentry played an increasingly important role in group training. The number of the gentry involved in the group training accounted for 9 percent to 13 percent of the total number. Hubei ranked first in the country, with the number of the gentry accounting for 10 percent to 14 percent.[137] The gentry in Hunan and Hubei Provinces not only took charge of the armed forces for group training, but also were granted the right of tax collection. "They made great progress in increasing the number of their members and gaining power".[138] Though the expansion of the gentry's power made "all scholars in Hunan try their best to make things difficult for the local officials",[139] and this resulted in some conflicts with officials, "these conflicts were not serious enough to bring about changes in power structure and the existing social political order".[140] At the time, the gentry generally tended to pursue local interests and rights, and endeavored to maintain the existing ruling order and make the management and operations of public property function smoothly. As a result, public property played a prominent role in being "us[ed] … to serve the public".

When the New Deal was carried out in the late Qing dynasty, the government decided to promote autonomy in local areas so as to transform the regime, absorb local power and pander to the "public opinion"[141] trend of implementing autonomy. From the perspective of the government, the first step in implementing local autonomy was dividing the scope controlled by the government and by the local people respectively, and it was in essence a redistribution and allocation of power. "The aim of this move was obviously to specify the balance of power between bureaucrats and Local interest groups".[142] The appointment of gentry to official positions offered an opportunity for the gentry to expand their power. According to statistics, among the known 72 directors of autonomous public offices, 49 of them were squires, accounting for 68 percent; among the known 32 directors of local autonomous institutes, 22 were squires, accounting for 6.8 percent. Moreover, those taking up the post as a director of the board in public offices or as a lecturer in local autonomous institutes everywhere were generally squires who had graduated from local autonomous institutes or came from the local gentry.[143] In 1908, the Autonomous Bureau was set up in Hubei Province to take charge of local autonomy, and autonomous public offices were also established in places below the county level including towns and villages, but "local affairs were actually handled by the local gentry".[144] The implementation of autonomy endowed the gentry with the right to collect taxes and manage old and new local affairs in the form of a system, which offered a legitimate and reasonable basis for the expansion of the gentry's power. Through their control of local autonomy, the gentry "gradually used the public domain as a main base for social political activities". Additionally, "some state power was also transferred to the local gentry".[145]

Although lots of power was delegated to the gentry in terms of the New Deal, the New Deal still followed the principle of equilibrium and restriction. The purpose of designing the system was to centralize power through decentralization.

> Local autonomy stemmed from national sovereignty. Autonomy could only be implemented with the approval of the nation. Hence the statues of autonomy shall not contradict national laws, and the affairs of autonomy shall not resist the supervision of the officials. Therefore, autonomy ran parallel to governance of the officials, and the former was not independent of the latter.[146]

When the Qing government delegated power to the gentry, it also had concerns that "if the gentry did not carry out autonomy in the correct way, such as oppressing and exploiting plebs or using their power to tyrannize them, it might have bad effects".[147] So the government designed many systems for supervision in order to realize the balance of power. For example, with regard to the collection of funds, "the system of collection and donation was specified in the Constitution. Standards had been set for reference and the gentry could report relevant information to the local officials for their checks",[148] so as to prevent the gentry from becoming corrupt. After the national crisis in 1990, the authority of the Qing government fell into decline so quickly that the situation was completely out of its control. The so-called supervision and restraint had not been put into practice, and moreover, some officials abandoned their right of supervision and conspired with the evil gentry to seek private gain.[149] The situation with decentralization but no

30 *From mass uprising to revolution*

effective limitation on power caused by the absence of a supervisory system led to an imbalance in the rural power structure. In Hunan Province,

> since the Taiping Rebellion occurred, local officials asked the gentry to assist them when making preparations for anything. At the beginning, the officials and gentry could make concerted efforts through mutual cooperation, but later the officials usually showed a preference and mercy towards the gentry when the latter were involved in trouble. Gradually, the drawbacks of the officials' practice had been exposed such that the gentry ignored the fact that the officials were their superiors and sometimes they even threatened the officials.[150]

The local gentry turned into powerful actors in control of institutional rights from having been the ones with moral authority.[151] As a result, the phenomenon of "using public property to pursue private ends" could be seen everywhere. For instance,

> the gentry took advantage of the officials' power to seek their own profits in handling public affairs. The so-called autonomy was in fact "no self-discipline", because the gentry only embezzled public funds without donating money, and only bullied the poor without showing solicitude for the poor.[152]

From the Taiping Rebellion to the New Deal, local governors who had certain power and the gentry at the bottom of society were gradually "getting away from the Qing government in their mind",[153] the spread of "localism" led to a growing rift between the central government and local areas, and the construction of national political power would certainly lead to a struggle between the central government and local areas based on resources, and the reconstruction and distribution of interests. The force that restricted public property operations changed from the traditional relationship between the officials and gentry to a clash between the efforts to advance the construction of state political power and the power of local forces. After the imperial court was overthrown during the Revolution of 1911, the construction of a new type of nation and state political power became a historical theme in the whole period of the Republic China. The construction of state political power meant the expansion of the national administrative system to the local society and the control of local resources, and most importantly it emphasized the counterbalance to all social forces resisting the control of society by the state. But the effect depended on the response of state political power to the local society's capacity for infiltration and resistance.[154]

In the late Qing dynasty, changes in the political system as a result of the New Deal led to local public property and power being completely controlled by the powerful gentry. For example, in Hubei Province, "public property of rural areas like stored grains, temples, lands and local public property was in

From mass uprising to revolution   31

the charge of the local tyrants and evil gentry who exploited peasants".[155] After the founding of the Republic of China, the new type of state political power would certainly meet explicit or hidden resistance from the local gentry if it attempted to control rural resources like public property and integrate rural society. For example, the gentry in Liling County used a temporary expedient to prevent the government from achieving its goal of unifying financial power.

> Until April 1920, when the Study Encouragement Office was established, land rent worth 600 tons was in the control of the Educational Property Office. The Bureau of Finance was established in 1929 to handle local financial affairs and take charge of the local property depository department. People in towns were afraid that the financial power was entirely in the hands of the government, so they allocated land rent worth over 300 tons, which originally belonged to the Depository Department, to the Bureau of Education, and the Bureau of Finance only had land rent worth over 60 tons.[156]

The gentry's action of preventing the government from extracting local public property was written about in local annals, commending them.[157] It was fully indicated that the gentry showed resistance to the interference of state political power in local affairs. This phenomenon was especially prominent in Hunan Province where "the gentry had much power".[158] What is more, owing to frequent changes in the regime and the confused fighting between the warlords in Hunan and Hubei Provinces, the government focused their attention on military expenditure and tax collection, so they had no time to spare for political power construction and had to adopt the system of local autonomy in the early Qing dynasty[159] and rely on the gentry to extract local resources. "Local organizations in many places below the county level had few changes compared with those in the late Qing Dynasty".[160]

In addition, the elimination of imperial power led to the abolition of privileges given to the gentry based on their traditional status in the social hierarchy. The gentry had to "make new connections with formal institutions in control of state political power"[161] if they wanted to maintain power. The continuous implementation of local autonomy offered an opportunity to maintain and expand influence to the gentry. In the early Republic of China, local councils and other institutions were still "almost in the control of the local gentry".[162] After the Revolution of 1911, banditry happened frequently in Hunan and Hubei Provinces, leading most group training organizations to enhance their capabilities. Some local group training organizations merged with local autonomous institutions. For example, in Yidu County,

> over 60 branches of civil corps were built up in various counties, the autonomous association was regarded as the head office of the civil corps in towns and villages, and the county council was regarded as the head office of the civil corps in counties.[163]

32 *From mass uprising to revolution*

In June 1913, the head office of the civil corps was set up in Yingshan County, and the seven villages and three towns originally set up in the late Qing dynasty were turned into ten districts in Guangji County. A district was not only a civil corps but also an administrative division. The establishment of *li* and *jia* was kept in places below the level of district.[164] In general, the gentry "had full control over rural clan society below the county level centering around the civil corps of districts".[165]

After the Revolution of 1911 came to an end with ferocious speed, we could see the change in the national regime, and the continuation and expansion of local power. The gentry power had been steadily moving toward expansion since the Taiping Rebellion, leaving the rural power structure imbalanced but not completely broken. Since the imperial court was overthrown during the Revolution of 1911, the local gentry did not need the systems and institutions offered by the imperial court to endow them with legitimate rights. Through military force, capital accumulated since the Taiping Rebellion, and the control of local autonomous institutions the nature of the gentry power fundamentally changed. The abolition of the challenge system established by law not only reduced the government's restrictions on the gentry, but also led to a regime characterized by collusion between the officials and gentry, just as was sung in a ballad: "The Qing dynasty ends, the Republic of China is founded, but both of them are the same by their nature. Plebs live in the hell, whereas the officials and gentry live in heaven".[166] Consequently, "the balance between the political authority and the social authority that had been maintained up to the present day collapsed".[167] Finally, all public property, an important local resource, was possessed by the evil gentry, who turned it into "private property", and laid an economic foundation for plutocrats to take control of rural politics.

> The gentry in a village were like warlords, and those local tyrants and squires handled all local affairs in rural areas, forcibly occupied the lands and property of ancestral halls and temples and charitable organizations, oppressed village people and exploited tenant peasants.[168]

When the historical trend of political modernization started with the New Deal, the allocation pattern of rural power moved toward differentiation, reconstruction and imbalance. The practical function and symbolic significance of public property also changed, continuously intensifying conflicts within rural areas and constituting an endogenous force in rural areas to trigger mass uprisings and even great revolution in the late Qing dynasty.

The realistic effects caused by changes of functions of public property

Public property belonged to the public and had a double meaning: in terms of a symbolic meaning, it was shared by the public; in terms of real functions, it was used by the public. The operation of public property was originally a two-way flow of resources. In the traditional society, officials and the gentry had similar interests. "In order to keep the society functioning normally and maintain the status quo, both sides would cooperate with each other".[169] The local gentry gained authority and economic benefits from the local people by taking the lead in handing local affairs,[170] and then they donated public property to bring benefit to the local people, achieving the goal of the return of resources. The two-way flow of resources, to some extent, eliminated the social contradictions brought about by polarization between the rich and the poor, and maintained social order and stability. However, since modern times, the gradual imbalance of the rural power structure, especially the fundamental changes in the gentry's power after the Revolution of 1911, led to all rural public property being controlled by the evil gentry. The operation of public property only became a monopoly and a one-way extraction of local resources. In public property, "most of the taxes on land revenue were certainly under the control of local tyrants, the evil gentry and even local ruffians and hoodlums. They had the absolute right to control it but in the name of public property".[171] The real function for which public property was intended to be used by the public had gone with the wind. "From the late Qing dynasty to the early period of the Republic of China, all the originally stored public property was sold and embezzled by the despotic gentry and evil officials. It was just a mess".[172] In Hanshou County, there were "a lot of public property and funds" at first, but after 1912, several institutions had jurisdiction over the county, and thus "its public property and funds were privatized and squandered by anyone. Some people formed a clique to take control of and even embezzle public property and funds. This was the financial situation of Hanshou County before".[173]

The nature of the redistribution of interests regarding public property reflected an axiom that public property was shared by the public and that it represented fairness, justice and morality. Public property should bring benefit to everyone, and it meant that peasants' basic living conditions could be met and they had the right to this guarantee. "Since clan fields were public property, as a member of the clan, they had a share of the fields".[174] Furthermore, peasants believed that the rich "should bear a duty to help those from the same clan or hometown".[175] According to the historical trend in the late Qing dynasty, the expansion of the gentry power and the degradation of the gentry's quality made it impossible to ensure that public property should be shared by the public. Once the moral sense was lost, peasants' basic needs for life could not be met and they felt no sense of security. Under such circumstances, they would experience more pain than if they were faced with a decrease in the standard of living. The gentry, once acting as protectors of a village, were even protected by the people by use of force.[176] Now, they became "local tyrants and the evil gentry", who took control of rural public property, so that peasants were not only unable to obtain the living security provided by public property in the past, but also were exploited. The gentry and plebs,

34 *From mass uprising to revolution*

who had similar interests, began to antagonize each other, and consequently conflicts inevitably broke out and mass uprisings happened frequently.

> The local gentry wantonly collected heavy taxes from people which were more than the taxes people were supposed to pay in the name of collecting funds. They collected taxes on various items, so that people lived in misery, and the gentry and people showed hatred for each other. When they decided to give vent to their anger, there was turmoil. Moreover, the officials did not show solicitude for people, but were partial to the evil gentry. If people could not pay heavy taxes, the officials would put them to torture until they got what they wanted. This was the cause of turmoil.[177]

The change in the real functions of public property was also reflected in the fact that public property laid an economic foundation for the evil gentry to take charge of rural politics.

> Those who possessed public property spent it in organizing the civil corps and had military force to keep order and rule rural areas, thus dominating rural people. Hence a minority of people who were able to take control of public property could manipulate the economic and political institutions in a rural area.[178]

In Hunan and Hubei Provinces, the gentry mainly expanded their power by means of organizing a civil corps, but different kinds of people joined these groups. "The leaders of these groups did something obscene, and self-respecting group members refused to do such things. Only ill-behaved local tyrants and scholars did something bad".[179] The change in the quality of the gentry in the civil corps and expansion of power (especially power of tax collection) left the civil corps a personal tool for the gentry to wantonly oppress people, levy taxes on people and collect public funds. In Baling County, "the gentry in each li formed a clique to collect money, so they were criticized by people".[180] Many initiatives of the New Deal "had been taken by those civil corps, and they turned into a kind of organization that exploited peasants once again".[181] From the Taiping Rebellion to the Republic of China, the "civil corps always existed",[182] and the continuous change in the quality of the gentry in the civil corps and the expansion of power offered an opportunity to the civil corps to move toward separatist rule along with the elimination of imperial power.

After the Revolution of 1911, there were no constraints on imperial power, and people did not show any expectations for a republican regime. The gentry "could not rely on the power of the government to protect the safety of their life and property, so they had to train their own peasant organizations into self-defense groups, namely, a civil corps, to safeguard their life and property. Therefore, there was no need for the gentry to show obedience to the political authority of the government".[183] The gentry forcibly occupied public property,

From mass uprising to revolution 35

usurped public power and then collected public funds to train henchmen for self-defense under the pretext of group training. The civil corps completely became an organ with military force by which the gentry controlled the rural politics. In Xinhua County, the expenditure of the civil corps

> cost the most. The funds for each bureau were neither distributed by the head office, nor paid by the Department of Finance. As a result, the gentry arbitrarily collected taxes on people with no fixed tax rate and people bore a heavier burden.[184]

In Huangmei County, the gentry also collected taxes on paper and firewood except on lands. They collected taxes on all goods as well, and "peasants had to pay fifty or sixty and even a hundred copper coins for the hay they decided to sell in the town".[185] The tax revenue was possessed by the civil corps. There was no regulation for tax collection, so the gentry wantonly collected taxes from people. If someone refused to pay taxes, he would be arrested by the Bureau of the Civil Corps. Hence peasants "showed more fear and hatred for rural autonomous organs resorting to violence than for the county government and tax-collection organs full of corrupt officials".[186]

The leader of the civil corps became a local tyrant or a plutocrat for his control of all kinds of resources in rural areas, especially through military force. What was different from the situation in the late Qing dynasty was that plutocrats at that time neither agreed with nor relied on any political power, and that they occupied an area on their own. Thus a situation occurred in which "provinces were under the control of warlords and counties were under the control of plutocrats in the early Republic of China".[187] After the Republic of China was founded in 1912, the head office of the civil corps was set up in Anxian County, and branches of the civil corps were set up in each district, with the director of each branch elected by the gentry in each district. In addition to controlling the armed forces of the civil corps, each branch took charge of civil and criminal proceedings, and formulated their own policies to oppress local people without obeying the orders given by the head office. "Among the people, eight directors of eight districts were called 'eight dukes'. Just imagine how arrogant they were at that time".[188] Though the bureaus of the civil corps in other counties and districts "were somewhat different from each other, they did not perform their duties in a correct manner indeed. So people just regarded the bureaus of the civil corps as a government of rural warlords".[189] After 1920, the Kuomintang regime encountered strong resistance and even sanguinary conflicts when it tried to establish a local power system in places where the local gentry took power. In most counties,

> all leaders of organizations below the county level were elected by a minority of people, and the election had nothing to do with the government, so it was difficult for the government to carry out its decree without the help of these leaders or directors.[190]

36 *From mass uprising to revolution*

As people of the time said,

> Local tyrants and the evil gentry made use of their official positions, wealth and power to collude with the officials, cover up the crimes committed by bandits, take control of bureaus of the civil corps and rural politics, embezzle public funds and oppress the common people. What they did was similar to feudal separation.[191]

In the late Qing dynasty, issues of public property and public power reflected peasants' demands for their own interests to be recognized in conflicts between the gentry and plebs. The reason for destroying private schools and resisting household surveys was that "local people believed that what the gentry did caused damage to their basic conditions for survival".[192] After the Revolution of 1911, the change in the real functions of public property not only aggravated the interest conflicts between the gentry and plebs, but also brought about a confrontation between the government and the local gentry at the top level of power. "Previous autonomous organizations completely turned into a tool for the landlord class to play up to warlords and rule local people".[193] To construct a unified nation-state power structure in rural areas, "the privileges granted to the gentry and the notables should be revoked, and the gentry meeting should be canceled to prevent local tyrants and the evil gentry from monopolizing rural politics".[194] In addition, a campaign should be launched to struggle against local tyrants, the evil gentry and wayward landlords who represented feudal forces. Finally, a revolution was also a choice the times offered to people.

> In rural areas, big changes must take place. The activities of local tyrants, the evil gentry, wayward landlords and all anti-revolution parties must end under the power of peasants; the rural regime must be transferred to peasants from local tyrants, the evil gentry, wayward landlords and all anti-revolution parties.[195]

When the concise theory of political parties combined political power with the interests of the people, there was an upcoming revolution.

During the period of the Great Revolution, public property was related to political ideals and was endowed with new connotations in the context of the revolution. Public revolution, which was used to maintain the social order, now became a means of revolutionary mobilization in a new era and was used to reconstruct the national-state power. Since the gentry made use of their military forces and wealth to oppress local people, "public property in rural areas like stored grains, temples, lands and local public lands should be used to meet the interests of peasants, but in the past public property was actually pocketed by local tyrants and the evil gentry!"[196] Therefore, in order to overthrow the special class and realize a democratization of politics, all

From mass uprising to revolution 37

sorts of public property had to be taken back to destroy the economic base of the separatist regime set up by the evil gentry.

In rural areas, civil corps, defending groups, local bureaus and protection bureaus took away a lot of public funds, but these funds were usually used by the gentry and the landlord class to oppress peasants. So we should take back all public funds and store them in our association under our management and control.[197]

Peasants might have some concerns when they fought against landlords, but if they overthrew the gentry on the grounds of their embezzlement of public funds, they "would participate in the fight without hesitation".[198] In Hubei Province, peasants

fought against local tyrants and the gentry in the name of checking all kinds of public funds, and then used a hemp rope to attach a cloth on which was written the slogan "local tyrants and the evil gentry" to the hats of local tyrants and the evil gentry, and at last let them walk around the villages".[199]

In 1927, the "Interim Regulations on Punishment of Local Tyrants and the Evil Gentry in Hunan Province" defined those who damaged or obstructed local public welfare and embezzled public funds as local tyrants and the evil gentry.[200] When fighting against local tyrants and the evil gentry, they could either resort to revolutionary means or confiscate their assets to destroy the gentry power, and most of the local tyrants and the evil gentry were overthrown in the fight were charged with embezzling public funds.[201] Although overthrowing the gentry in the name of public property clearing had less deterrent effects than that in the name of anti-revolution, it was still characterized by legitimacy and the power of mobilization.

Recently, there were a lot of peasant movements. Peasants struggled against anyone who destroyed the agricultural association or embezzled public funds before, but most of the struggles were revolutionary actions by the poor peasants and the punishment for local tyrants and the evil gentry was not appropriate.[202]

During the period of the Great Revolution, peasant movements in Hunan Province were more aggressive than those in other places. "These movements were just like a storm, and those who obeyed peasants' orders would survive, while those who disobeyed their orders would die. They wiped out the privileges of feudal landlords which had lasted for thousands of years";[203] thus, the rural power order was rearranged to some extent. The main reason lay in the expansion and disorderly operation of the gentry power caused by

38 *From mass uprising to revolution*

the change in the power structure for a long time, which intensified the contradiction between the gentry and plebs, and the conflict between the officials (government) and the gentry. These conflicts showed different characteristics in different phases: in the late Qing dynasty, the conflicts between the gentry and plebs caused by the implementation of the New Deal and intensified by using public property to pursue private ends were just a kind of confrontation for economic benefits, which was represented by widespread mass uprisings; the change in the political system triggered by the Revolution of 1911 provided the evil gentry with an opportunity to control public property and set up a separatist regime, thus causing the interest conflict to escalate into a revolution and the reconstruction of national and state power. So there is a need for us to discuss why the Revolution of 1911 advocating the Three Principles of the People (namely nationalism, democracy and the livelihood of the people) led to an imbalance in the rural power structure, and to comprehend the influence of the reform of the regime on the rural power structure in terms of public property.

Power reconstruction and public property management

The traditional pattern of public property operations in which officials acted as supervisors and the gentry as managers can be comprehended from the perspective of political systems. In the Qing dynasty, a centralized feudal monarchy, reached its peak. In order to prevent power from being transferred into the hands of others, such a political system was designed in which the emperor took control of the monarchical power and there was system of checks and balances between the government organs. For example, the central administrative body consisted of six ministries and local governments with diversified leadership systems, so that they could supervise each other and prevent one from arrogating all the power to itself.[204] The political idea of checks and balances was not only reflected in the operation of the bureaucracy, but also guided the design of all kinds of local systems; however, the people to whom power was delegated shifted from the officials to the gentry.

From the view of local society, the gentry were the local authority, but from the perspective of the officials, the gentry assisted them in expanding their dominion. "Many officials found that it is much easier to give orders to the people through the gentry than through normal government channels", and it would overcome the weakness of relying on officials if the gentry handled local affairs.[205] Hence, delegating formal administrative power to the local elite would be "seen as a reform measure".[206] Nevertheless, the distribution of power to the gentry was not simply delegating power to lower levels, but also reflected the intention of constructing a supervision system. For example, when dealing with the affairs of likin collection, the gentry took actions, while officials showed consideration for the overall situation. Under such a circumstance,

From mass uprising to revolution 39

if the gentry did something bad, the officials had the right to punish them, and if the officials did something bad, the gentry would inform against them secretly. So the two sides supervised each other, and there were also eyes and ears around them. As a result, the gentry and officials made few mistakes that would exert a bad influence on the society. It was a must for the officials and the gentry to supervise each other.[207]

In Hunan Province, Luo Bingzhang asked both the officials and the gentry to work together. The appointed gentry were born into a wealthy or distinguished family, and did not care only for money as the petty officers did, so they would do their job of supervising well to achieve a good result. The measure did work, because in terms of handling affairs of likin, compared to other provinces, Hunan Province did the best. At that time, both Chinese and foreign people argued that its success should be attributed to the appointment of the gentry to the job.[208] It was based precisely on the political idea of checks and balances, and the design of government institutions so that public property operations were also implicitly or explicitly included in the institutional framework in which officials acted as supervisors and the gentry as managers. In this way, the officials still had the right to rule the gentry. When the central government's authority was strong, the gentry "dared not defy the officials".[209] Moreover, they would also invite the other gentry to be involved in local affairs. Through the checks and balances between the power of the officials and the gentry, the stability of the rural power structure could be maintained to further ensure that public property would perform its function of stabilizing the social order.

In response to the crisis in governance created by the Taiping Rebellion, the imperial court and local high-ranking officials of the Qing dynasty encouraged the low-ranking gentry to organize a civil corps.

> The successful candidates in the civil and military imperial examinations at the provincial level were encouraged to work with jinshi, a successful candidate in the highest imperial examinations. The intellectuals were encouraged to work with the successful candidates in the imperial examinations at the provincial level.[210]

A large group of the gentry with military exploits emerged in Hunan and Hubei Provinces, and their power was not only limited to handling general local public welfare affairs, because they also had power over armed forces and the right to recruit and dispatch soldiers. "They took control of official business, handled affairs arbitrarily and intervened in the collection of land taxes and other affairs beyond the call of duty in the name of organizing civil corps".[211] Under such a circumstance, the gentry power expanded. Later the instability of the local order in Hunan and Hubei Provinces enabled those civil corps to play an increasingly important role in the society. In many places, the Bao-jia system was replaced by the establishment of a civil corps, or the two

40 *From mass uprising to revolution*

were integrated into a new social control system in rural areas. For instance, the Huanggang civil corps and its armed forces began to turn themselves into permanent bodies and quasi-authority organizations between the local officials and the rural society,[212] while the gentry in the civil corps "played a major part in controlling local society".[213] In the early twentieth century, the government and the society chose to implement local autonomy, in view of both traditional thinking and reality, the gentry should be appointed to carry out local autonomy. The implementation of the New Deal needed a lot of money, but the government treasury had no money left. In this case, the government had no choice but to rely on temporary bureaus, responsible for raising money like bureaus of likin collection, military supplies and relief when the Taiping Rebellion happened, to collect funds. "Once the government started to do so, it would become a habit".[214] These bureaus were not formal institutions of the government and were under the control of the gentry who acted as a member of them. If "they took control of these Western-style bureaus, they were able to completely control rural areas",[215] but at the same time it meant that only if they controlled and manipulated those new public authorities could they make the gentry's power legitimate and reasonable. From the Taiping Rebellion to the New Deal, the expansion of the gentry's power resulted from the Qing imperial court's initiative to delegate power and it could be done within the established institutional framework, just as people of the time said: "The government was just like a hunter and the gentry were its lackeys; the government was just like a butcher and the gentry were like shape knives in its hands".[216] The situation reflected that, though the operation of public property was under the control of the gentry and the system in which officials acted as supervisors and the gentry as managers began to break up, the gentry's abuse of public property and public power could only be justified in the name of the New Deal. As a result, the phenomenon of using public property to pursue private ends was "still not uncommon".[217] The expansion of the gentry's power was reflected in the operation of public property, from "using public property to serve the public" to "using public property to pursue private ends". The only difference was in the degree, but in the change from "using public property to pursue private ends" to "turning public property into private property", the expansion of power led to fundamental changes, which indicated that the political change brought about by the Revolution of 1911 resulted in the transformation of the power structure at the grassroots level in rural areas.

Although royal rule ended owing to the Revolution of 1911, the gentry's power still expanded. After the revitalization, in Hunan and Hubei Provinces, the new regime was in the hands of the gentry. As far as Sichuan, Hubei, Jiangsu, Zhejiang and Guangdong Provinces were concerned, among people with political power at all levels, revolutionary party members accounted for 47.8 percent of the total number, the local gentry 23.9 percent, the former officials and military officers 13 percent, people in the new regime that integrated officials, the gentry and revolutionary parties 15.2 percent.[218]

According to the statistics offered by Li Kan, in 38 prefectures and counties of Jiangsu and Hubei Provinces of the new regime, a total of 57 persons were appointed to main administrative and military posts, including 23 squires (including constitutionalists), and 21 old bureaucrats (including new military officers). The two groups of people accounted for 77 percent of the total number, while there were only ten revolutionary party members.[219] After the mansion of the governor was set up in Changsha, Hunan Province, "the gentry group that was dormant for a long time began to thrive",[220] and the magistrate of Xinhua County had limited ability, so "his power was transferred to the hands of a squire, and people in this county said in jest that there were two magistrates".[221] The gentry gradually "became arrogant again and returned to power in rural areas",[222] as the poem has it: "Woe is the Chinese people, who for all the lives lost and blood spilled, ended up with but a counterfeit republic". In the drastic changes in the political systems, the gentry had the initiative and "dominated all the political activities of the county".[223] However, the New Deal and the constitutional movement "doubtlessly pointed out the central government's objective of wanting to control local society".[224] Furthermore, in the early Republic of China, the theme of the times behind the seemingly chaotic society was also the construction of state power. "Almost all the governments of the Republic of China tried to create a strong regime, which could strictly exercise the power of supervising, intervening in and controlling local affairs".[225] The main difference was that the centralization of state power was realized by checks and balances in the process of implementing the New Deal, whereas the centralization of state power was realized by retaking the power during the period of the Republic of China. However, when the local power was strong, retaking the power would inevitably result in a growing rift between the state power and the local power. "Since the founding of the Republic of China in 1912, the Beijing government made repeated efforts to restore centralization, but the local regime created by military forces and the gentry was becoming more and more consolidated".[226]

This rift led to fundamental changes in the rural power structure and also influenced the operation and functions of public property.

First, the phenomenon in which the gentry set up a separatist regime by force was common. The elimination of imperial power led to the abolition of authority given to the gentry through their traditional status in the social hierarchy. In order to maintain their social status, the gentry "had reached consensus that obtaining power depended on the control of a civil corps. Therefore, they aimed to struggle for the command of a civil corps, and once they achieved success, they would declare themselves the leaders of a true community".[227] In the early Republic of China, the identity of the three "new squires" in Dongjin Town, Xiangyang County, Hubei Province, showed that a powerful force had replaced social status and fame as the source of local authority.[228] In Hunan and Hubei Provinces, the establishment of a civil corps prevailed for a long time. From the late Qing dynasty to the early Republic of China, a "civil corps with a solid foundation had been organized all over the

42 *From mass uprising to revolution*

middle reaches of the Yangtze River. The armed forces of the civil corps and the gentry power based on them constantly developed".[229] After the revitalization, "police stations were built up in four villages and acted of their own free will",[230] and the gentry in the civil corps controlled everything in rural areas. Consequently, plutocrats set up separatist regimes in counties and villages, and public property, as an important source of revenue for maintaining group defense, naturally fell into the hands of the gentry.

Second, the division of the whole gentry class led to the seizing of grassroots power by people in rural fringe groups such as bullies. The abolition of the imperial examination system in 1905 and the collapse of the political system of the Qing dynasty in 1911 destroyed the foundation of survival and development for the gentry class, and become a fundamental turning point in its historical destiny. The gentry had formerly been leaders of the common people, but now "they lost their job and had no way to earn a living",[231] and were forced to receive education in all kinds of new educational institutions in conformity with policies. "The imperial examination system might be abolished, and the scholars under thirty years old could study in private schools until graduation".[232] In Hubei Province, in the last 20 years of the Qing dynasty, about at least 20,000 squires received education again, accounting for 43 percent of the total number. Among them, squires engaged in the field of education and culture, law and politics, military administration and industry accounted for 40 percent, 15 percent, 8 percent and 5 percent respectively.[233] A large number of squires who received modern education took up various social occupations, such as teachers, military officers, clerks and so on, which led to an unprecedented scale of social mobility. Not only was succession to the social status of the gentry class interrupted, but also the local elites left rural areas for cities because most of the new occupations could be obtained in cities. Those who stayed in rural areas were also unwilling to take up their posts because of the poor political and economic environment.

> The officials in charge of pacification operations randomly levied higher taxes and imposed a fine on people and arrested innocent people, and similar cases were numerous. If the local gentry addressed inquiries to the officials, they would be accused of sheltering bandits or bullies.[234]

Villagers looked at those officials with angry eyes: "it was common for the gentry to leave from their villages and for those who stayed in villages not to step forward to manage local affairs",[235] so "only the gentry who were not qualified for their jobs were left behind, and marginal figures like bullies and ruffians began to seize power at the bottom of the society".[236]

The collapse of the national regime led to such a situation that the gentry of good character resigned their positions and the evil gentry came to power. From 1911 to 1920, Hunan Province was ruled by northern warlords successively, including Tang Xiangming, Fu Liangzuo and Zhang Jingyao, and it was locked in tangled fights.

> Over the past year, the north and south were in turmoil. As long as one side waged a war, there was a pile of dead bodies. Once troops and horses approached a village, the villagers would run away. Business was in decline, scholars and plebs were compelled to leave their homes and roam about, farmlands were derelict and private schools were overgrown with weeds.[237]

Several years of warfare led to a continuous increase in the government's military expenditure and donations, which gradually destroyed what Prasenjit Duara called a "protective brokerage", and it was clearly reflected in the operations of local property depository departments.

The gentry took the lead in setting up local property depository departments to safeguard their own and local rights.

> Cases in which the gentry and scholars in each county charged their magistrate or guardians of departments with absconding with money were very common. These were brought about by not setting up depository departments in conformity with regulations, not handling affairs in conformity with regulations, mishandling affairs or employing the wrong persons. So the gentry and plebs would make use of these drawbacks to accuse their magistrate or guardians of malpractice. Local areas would suffer a great loss in property, and thus public funds were not used in a prudent way. If officials in some places did not set up the local property depository department within ten days after they received the edict, they should choose the gentry of good character to take charge of the establishment of the depository department and report details to the central government.[238]

Later, the staff of the depository department were "worried that they would be threatened, so they resigned their position".[239] In Ningxiang County,

> the provincial government ordered the county to establish a branch in charge of pacification operations and appointed the county magistrate, named Wang Danian, as director of the branch. Wang Danian, greedy, vulgar and brutal, levied heavy taxes on lands and endlessly blackmailed local people. Wang Hongze, director of the depository department, and Xiao Zhiqing, a guardian, wanted to resign their position to oppose Wang Danian. Plebs in this county also went to the provincial capital to accuse Wang Danian of misconduct.[240]

All of these phenomena fully indicated that under the pressure of endless donations and tax collection, there was no room for protective brokerage to

44 *From mass uprising to revolution*

retreat. The implementation of tax farming made protective brokerage thrive. For example, when Zhang jingyao governed Hunan Province, in order to raise money,

> he fixed a price for each vacant post and allowed people to bid for it. As a result, bandits and thieves traded what they got through extortion and theft with an official post. Once they took office, they would exploit people for more personal gain, causing people to live a hard life.[241]

In Xiangtan, the county office was in urgent need of military supplies and decided to pledge against a loan.

> A squire was appointed to raise money, and he did not take into consideration that people lived a hard life after a disaster. Instead, he stepped up his efforts to collect heavier taxes and more donations from people. If a person delayed paying taxes or handing in donations, the squire would dispatch his men to collect the taxes and donations at the person's home. Consequently, people suffered a lot from this situation.[242]

Like North China, the growing seepage of pressure from the state caused the grassroots power to fall completely into the hands of profit brokers. "Local tyrants seized the opportunity to occupy all kinds of official positions, which became the mainstream of rural regime".[243] With regard to this, it was known to people that the operation of public property had become a means of pursuing private ends.

As China's traditional political system became modernized, the normal practice of "using public property to serve the interest of the public" was quickly replaced with that of "using public property to pursue private ends", especially by members of the local gentry. The escalating conflicts between the gentry and plebs, and the emerging mass uprisings gave birth to the Revolution of 1911. However, the purpose of the Revolution of 1911 was to achieve what was declared in the Three Principles of the People and the Constitution of Five Powers.[244] The new national regime brought by the revolution only had the form of democratic republicanism, but it was not endowed with the spirit of freedom, equality and fraternity. During the Revolution of 1911, "the old structure was replaced with a new structure and the old order was replaced with a new order".[245] However, the weakening central authority made the division between the state and local power increasingly prominent, like the differences in culture and economy between the urban and rural areas. As a result, this "new order" not only failed to address the issues of the people, but abolished various systems that "once maintained social unity and stability",[246] which led to changes in rural grassroots power. Public property became the economic foundation of a separatist regime set up by the gentry through drastic changes in the regime. However, more than a decade later, the foundation of democracy changed into that of "abolishing the group security

From mass uprising to revolution   45

system by revolutionary means in rural areas, so that local tyrants, the evil gentry and landlords could not continue to monopolize rural political power in rural areas".[247] At last, the interests of people intersected with the principle of parties, and the replacement of rural grassroots power and the reconstruction of national state power were realized in the form of "revolution" again. The complex and profound relationship between the reform of the national political system and the trends related to the rural power structure could be vividly displayed in the various characteristics of public property operations and social functions in different times.

Notes

1 Mary Wright, "Introduction: The Rising Tide of Change", in *China in Revolution: The First Phase 1900–1913*, ed. Mary Wright (New Haven, CT: Yale University Press, 1968), 1–19.
2 Zhang Zhenhe, Ding Yuanying. "Chronicle of Mass Uprisings in the Late Qing Dynasty". Editorial Group of Modern Historical Documents in Institute of Modern History of Chinese Academy of Social Sciences: *Documents about Modern History*, the 3rd or 4th issue of 1982; The first Historical Archives of China and Department of History in Beijing Normal University selected and edited: *Historical Documents about Mass Uprisings in the Ten Years before the Revolution of 1911* (2 vols.) (Beijing: Zhonghua Book Company, 1985); Du Tao, "A Review of the Research on Mass Uprisings in the Ten Years of the Late Qing Dynasty", *Fujian Forum*, July 2002, 70–74.
3 Ma Ziyi, "Unprecedented Peak of Mass Uprisings – Analysis of Mass Uprisings in the Ten Years before the Revolution of 1911", *Journal of Shanghai Jiaotong University* (Philosophy and Social Science Page), 5 (2003): 66.
4 Ma Ziyi, "Unprecedented Peak of Mass Uprisings", 66.
5 See relevant research results: (America) Robert Antony, "The Social and Economic Origin of Bandits: A Study of Guangdong in the Early 19th Century", in *A Study on Regional Social Economy in the Qing Dynasty* (vol. 1), ed. Ye Xianen, 534–543; Qin Baoqi, "The Origin of the Heaven and Earth Society Recorded in Historical Documents", *Historical Archives*, 2 (1982); Liu Ping, "The Relationship between Folk Culture, Code of the Brotherhood and the Society Party", *A Study on the History of the Qing Dynasty*, 1(2002), 71–78.
6 Liu Ping, "The Relationship between Folk Culture", 71–78.
7 (America) Robert Antony, "The Social and Economic Origin of Bandits", 536.
8 Ma Ziyi, "Unprecedented Peak of Mass Uprisings", 69.
9 *Shun Pao*, May 24, 1876, qtd. in Ma Ziyi, "Unprecedented Peak of Mass Uprisings", 70.
10 "A Memorial to the Emperor submitted by Supervisor Li Zhuohua in which he mentioned that schools were difficult to run and imperial examination should be carried out", in *Historical Documents about Preparation for Implementing Constitutionalism in the Late Qing Dynasty* (vol. 2), ed. Department of Ming and Qing Archives of the Palace Museum (Beijing: Zhonghua Book Company, 1979), 995.
11 Zhao Erfeng, "A Memorial Mentioning that an Alliance of Parties led by Zhang Zhixiang Advocated Reform", The First Historical Archives of China and

46   *From mass uprising to revolution*

Department of History, Beijing Normal University, selected and edited: *Historical Documents about Mass Uprisings in the Ten Years before the Revolution of 1911* (vol. 2) (Beijing: Zhonghua Book Company, 1985), 774.

12 Ma Ziyi, "Unprecedented Peak of Mass Uprisings", 66.

13 According to the results of mass uprisings in Taizhou, not only common people but also the gentry were bullied and oppressed by feudal officials for no reason. See "A Detailed Account of Mass Uprisings in Taizhou", *Oriental Magazine*, March 1910, 69. The county magistrate of Mixian County carried out the New Deal, and the gentry and plebs felt displeased with it. As a result, thousands of angry gentry and plebs gathered together to destroy the county office. See "Chronicle of Events in March, 1910", *Oriental Magazine*, April 1910, 55.

14 "Records of the New County of Mingshan", in *Historical Documents about the Revolution of 1911 in Sichuan* (vol. 2), ed. Yv Yingtao (Chengdu: Sichuan People's Publishing House, 1982), 158–160.

15 Before 1964, the actors who made trouble in schools or destroyed schools were mostly students, whereas after 1964, the actors were mostly common people. Though it was common people who destroyed schools, the officials were the ones who were blamed for this. See "Does Destroying Schools Become a Common Practice?", *Oriental Magazine*, October 1910, 78. In the mass uprising in Cixi City, the gentry blamed the county magistrate for his connivance in violent actions and hatred for learning. See *The Revolution of 1911* (vol. 3), ed. Association of Chinese Historians (Shanghai: Shanghai People's Publishing House, 1957), 454–455.

16 *Collection of Documents about the Revolution of 1911* (vol.1), ed. Cunsui Society (Hong Kong: Hong Kong Dadong Book Co., 1980), 169.

17 Du Tao, "A Review of the Research on Mass Uprisings in the Ten Years of the Late Qing Dynasty", *Fujian Forum*, 2004, pp. 70–74.

18 "On the Large Number of Mass Uprisings in Recent Days", *Oriental Magazine*, November 1904, 270–271.

19 Ha Xiao, "On the Mass Uprisings in Shaanxi Province", *Oriental Magazine*, March 1907, 38–42.

20 "Does Destroying Schools Become a Common Practice?", *Oriental Magazine*, November 1904, 78.

21 "Does Destroying Schools Become a Common Practice?", *Oriental Magazine*, November 1904, 78.

22 Li Yanguang, "The Political System in the Qing Dynasty", in *Proceedings of the International Symposium on the History of the Ming and Qing Dynasties* ed. Group of Papers of the Secretariat of the International Symposium on the History of the Ming and Qing Dynasties (Tianjin: Tianjin People's Publishing House, 1982), 257.

23 Yao Ying, "A Reply to an Official whose Surname was Fang", in *A Compilation of the Classics of the Imperial Dynasty* (Volume 23) edited by He Changling, administration, *Modern Chinese History Series* (Part 1, Volume 74) (731) edited by Shen Yunlong, Wenhai Publishing House, photocopy in 1966, p. 856.

24 *Shun Pao* on May 15, 1910, quoted from *Anti-taxation Campaign in Laiwu, Haiyang and Zhaoyuan and the Revolution of 1911*, ed. Liu Tongjun and Dong Ligang (Beijing: Beijing Institute of Technology Press,1994), 15.

25 *Anti-taxation Campaign in Laiwu, Haiyang and Zhaoyuan and the Revolution of 1911*, 15.

From mass uprising to revolution 47

26 Chang Xing, "On the Mass Uprisings in Laiyang County", in *Selected Works of Comments in the Ten Years before the Revolution of 1911* (vol. 3), ed. Zhang Zhan and Wang Renzhi (Beijing: Sanlian Bookstore Press, 1977), 653.

27 "A Field Survey on the Incident of Laiyang Done by Shandong People Association in Modern Beijing", *Modern Historical Documents of Shandong Province* (vol. 2) (Shandong: Shandong People's Publishing House, 1958), 9–11.

28 *Historical Documents about Preparation for Implementing Constitutionalism in the Late Qing Dynasty* (vol. 2), ed. Department of Ming and Qing Archives of the Palace Museum, p. 757.

29 "A Field Investigation Report on the Incident of Laiyang Done by Shandong People Association in Modern Beijing", quoted from *Anti-taxation Campaign in Laiwu, Haiyang and Zhaoyuan and the Revolution of 1911*, 15.

30 "A Field Investigation Report on the Incident of Laiyang Done by Shandong People Association in Modern Beijing", quoted from *Anti-taxation Campaign in Laiwu, Haiyang and Zhaoyuan and the Revolution of 1911*, 16.

31 "A Memorial to the Emperor Submitted by Rui Cheng, Governor of Hunan and Hubei Provinces", in which he mentioned the registered gentry who caused trouble for personal interests should be punished respectively, in *A Compilation of Historical Documents about the Rice Riot in Changsha*, ed. Rao Huaimin and Koetsu Fujiya (Changsha: Yuelu Press, 2001), 95.

32 "A Memorial to the Emperor Submitted by Rui Cheng, Governor of Hunan and Hubei Provinces", in which he mentioned the registered gentry who caused trouble for personal interests should be punished respectively, in *A Compilation of Historical Documents about the Rice Riot in Changsha*, 95.

33 "A Memorial to the Emperor Submitted by Rui Cheng, Governor of Hunan and Hubei Provinces", in which he mentioned the registered gentry who caused troubles regarding people's personal interests should be punished respectively, in *A Compilation of Historical Documents about the Rice Riot in Changsha*, 97.

34 "Recent News in Hunan Province", in *A Compilation of Historical Documents about the Rice Riot in Changsha*, 225.

35 "A Report on Hungry People Opposing Tyranny in Changsha in 1910", in *A Compilation of Historical Documents about the Rice Riot in Changsha*, 284.

36 "A Memorial to the Emperor Submitted by Rui Cheng, Governor of Hunan and Hubei Provinces", in which he mentioned the registered gentry who caused trouble for people's personal interests should be punished respectively, in *A Compilation of Historical Documents about the Rice Riot in Changsha*, 96.

37 "The Notice Issued by Cen Chunming, a Commissioner in Hunan Province", quoted from "The Officials, Gentry and Plebs in the Rice Riot in Changsha", Yang Pengcheng, *Modern Chinese History Studies*, 3(2002): 116.

38 Yang Pengcheng, "The Officials, Gentry and Plebs in the Rice Riot in Changsha", 112.

39 The gentry in Hunan Province devoted themselves to restructuring the power in that province and replacing the commissioner with another one in the rice riot. (Author's note)

40 Editorial Committee of Local Chronicles in Hunan Province, *Chronicle of Events in Hunan Province* (Changsha: Hunan People's Publishing House, 1999), 179.

41 "A Notice Issued by Cen Chunming, a Commissioner in Hunan Province", quoted from Yang Pengcheng, "The Officials, Gentry and Plebs in the Rice Riot in Changsha", 116.

48 *From mass uprising to revolution*

42 Yang Pengcheng, "The Officials, Gentry and Plebs in the Rice Riot in Changsha", 111.

43 "A Memorial to the Emperor Submitted by Rui Cheng, Governor of Hunan and Hubei Provinces", in which he mentioned the registered gentry who caused troubles for personal interests should be punished respectively, quoted from Yang Pengcheng, "The Officials, Gentry and Plebs in the Rice Riot in Changsha", 111.

44 "A Poem about the Rice Riot in Changsha", quoted from Yang Shiji, *The History of Hunan before and after the Revolution of 1911* (Changsha: Hunan People's Publishing House, 1982), 177.

45 *Anti-taxation Campaign in Laiwu, Haiyang and Zhaoyuan and the Revolution of 1911*, 17.

46 *Anti-taxation Campaign in Laiwu, Haiyang and Zhaoyuan and the Revolution of 1911*, 17.

47 *Anti-taxation Campaign in Laiwu, Haiyang and Zhaoyuan and the Revolution of 1911*, 21.

48 "A Letter to Commissioner of Hubei Province", in *A Compilation of Historical Documents about the Rice Riot in Changsha*, 73.

49 "Preface", in *A Compilation of Historical Documents about the Rice Riot in Changsha*, 13.

50 "Preface", in *A Compilation of Historical Documents about the Rice Riot in Changsha*, 13.

51 "Preface", in *A Compilation of Historical Documents about the Rice Riot in Changsha*, 12.

52 "Preface", in *A Compilation of Historical Documents about the Rice Riot in Changsha*, 3.

53 "A Memorial submitted by Rui Cheng, governor of Hubei Province and Yang Wending, commissioner of Hunan Province in which they mentioned that rebels in Hunan Province caused trouble and the officials there did not handle it well", in *A Compilation of Historical Documents about the Rice Riot in Changsha*, 93.

54 "A Memorial to the Emperor Submitted by Rui Cheng, Governor of Hunan and Hubei Provinces", in which he mentioned the registered gentry who caused troubles for personal interests should be punished respectively, in *A Compilation of Historical Documents about the Rice Riot in Changsha*, 96.

55 *Shengjing Times*, quoted from *Anti-taxation Campaign in Laiwu, Haiyang and Zhaoyuan and the Revolution of 1911*, 26.

56 *Shengjing Times*, *Anti-taxation Campaign in Laiwu, Haiyang and Zhaoyuan and the Revolution of 1911*, 26.

57 "Annals about Etiquette and Custom", in *Annals of Liling County* (vol. 4) (Publishing house and publication date unknown), 8–9.

58 Tao Shu, "Details on the Situations in Various Regions of Jiangxi Province and on the Situations of Bandits", quoted from *Studies of the Officials, Gentry and Merchants in the Modern History of China*, ed. Zhang Kaiyuan, Ma Min and Zhu Ying (Hubei: Hubei People's Publishing House, 2000), 388.

59 Zhang Zhongli, *Chinese Gentry* (Shanghai: Shanghai Academy of Social Sciences Press, 1991), 50, 51, 67.

60 "Annals of Towns", *Annals of Ji County* (vol. 3), 1. See relevant research in Wei Guangqi, *Official Governance and Autonomy China's County System in the First Half of the 20th Century* (Beijing: The Commercial Press, 2004), 50–53; Wu Jianren, *Bizarre Happenings Eyewitnessed over Two Decades* (Beijing: People's

From mass uprising to revolution 49

Literature Publishing House, 1959), 439. Qiu Jie, "Local Government and Social Control in the Late Qing Dynasty and the Early Republic of China – A Case Study of Guangzhou as an Example", *Journal of Sun Yat-sen University* (Social Science Edition), 6 (2001): 46–58.

61 Wei Guangqi, *Official Governance and Autonomy – China's County System in the First Half of the 20th Century*, 53.

62 Wei Guangqi, *Official Governance and Autonomy – China's County System in the First Half of the 20th Century*, 72.

63 Li Hanzhang and Zeng Guoquan, eds., *Annals of Hunan Province* (vol. 108), "Chronicles of Famous Officials" (17), "Dynasties" (6) (Yangzhou: Yangzhou Ancient Books Publishing House, 1986) photocopy, 16.

64 "An Edict of Merging Towns into Stockaded Villages and Forts for Defense Issued by Minister Luo Bingzhang", Zhang Yanqi, *County Annals of Changsha*, block-printed edition in 1874, vol.15, Military Defense.

65 See relevant research in Zhang Kaiyuan, Ma Min and Zhu Ying, *Studies of the Officials, Gentry and Merchants in the Modern History of China*, 395.

66 See relevant research in Zhang Kaiyuan, Ma Min and Zhu Ying, *Studies of the Officials, Gentry and Merchants in the Modern History of China*, 405.

67 He Yuefu, *Gentry in the Late Qing Dynasty and the Changes of Modern Society Compared with the Japanese Scholars* (Guangzhou: Guangdong People's Publishing House, 1994), 55.

68 (Japan) Takeshi Sasaki, *Secret Associations in the Late Qing Dynasty*, 35–37, quoted from Zhang Kaiyuan, Ma Min and Zhu Ying, *Studies of the Officials, Gentry and Merchants in the Modern History of China*, 414.

69 Wei Guangqi, *Official Governance and Autonomy – China's County System in the First Half of the 20th Century*, 79.

70 Wei Guangqi, *Official Governance and Autonomy – China's County System in the First Half of the 20th Century*, 79–80.

71 (America) Joseph W. Esherick, *Reform and Revolution in China – The 1911 Revolution in Hunan and Hubei*, trans. Yang Shenzhi (Beijing: Zhonghua Book Company, 1982), 111.

72 "A Memorial Submitted by a General from Shengjing Called Zhao Erxun about the Situations of Pilot Local Autonomy Bureau in Mukden", *Historical Documents about Preparation for Implementing Constitutionalism in the Late Qing Dynasty* (vol. 2), 717.

73 "A List of Regulations on Local Autonomy in Cities, Towns and Villages" defines the scope of local autonomy as follows: "First, as for affairs about education in the cities and towns, it involves primary and middle schools, nursery schools, education associations, education board, preaching institution, libraries, newspaper offices and other matters about education; second, as for affairs about hygiene in the cities and towns, it involves cleaning streets, removing dirt, medicines agency, hospitals, parks, associations of quitting smoking and other matters about hygiene; third, as for affairs about road projects, it involves mending roads, repairing roads, building bridges, dredging ditches, constructing common premises and street lamps and other matters about road projects; fourth, as for affairs about agriculture, industry and commerce, it involves advancing crop production, animal husbandry, fishery, craft factories, industrial schools, improving workmanship, put business in order, opening up markets, protecting young crops, carrying out water conservancy projects, clearing up farmlands and other affairs about

50 *From mass uprising to revolution*

agriculture, industry and commerce; fifth, as for affairs about charity, it involves alleviating poverty, providing relief for widows, defending reputation, bringing up babies, distributing clothes, providing food for the hungry, storing rice in grain stocks, craftsmanship of poor people, life-saving association, fire-fighting association, famine relief work, offering coffins and tombs for free, preserving historical sites and other affairs about charity; sixth, it involves affairs about public utilities; seventh, it involves affairs about raising money to implement these regulations; eighth, other affairs with no disadvantages were dealt with by gentry board according to local customs". *Historical Documents about Preparation for Implementing Constitutionalism in the Late Qing Dynasty* (vol. 2), 728–729.

74 "A Memorial submitted by the Constitutional Compilation Chamber of Regulations on Local Autonomy in Cities, Towns and Villages and Regulations on Election for Deliberation and Approval", *Historical Documents about Preparation for Implementing Constitutionalism in the Late Qing Dynasty* (vol. 2), 726.

75 "An Edict Issued by the Emperor on December 27, 1908", *Historical Documents about Preparation for Implementing Constitutionalism in the Late Qing Dynasty* (vol. 2), 727.

76 "A Memorial Submitted by Yuan Shuxun, the Commissioner of Shangdong Province", in which, to implement local autonomy according to regulations, he mentioned the local governments' establishment of autonomous research institutes, and respectfully beseeched the emperor to confirm the work, *Historical Documents about Preparation for Implementing Constitutionalism in the Late Qing Dynasty* (vol. 2), 741–742.

77 *A List of Officials as Assistants*, in *New Annals of the Dongming County* (vol. 9) in the Republic of China.

78 Wei Guangqi, *Official Governance and Autonomy –China's County System in the First Half of the 20th Century*, 118.

79 Wei Guangqi, *Official Governance and Autonomy – China's County System in the First Half of the 20th Century*, 136.

80 Zhu Ying, *The Revolution of 1911 and the Social Changes in Modern China* (Wuhan: Central China Normal University Press, 2001), 686.

81 "The Record of Household Surveys in Jiangxi Province", *Oriental Magazine*, July 1909, 223.

82 "The Record of Household Surveys in Jiangxi Province", *Oriental Magazine*, July 1909, 223.

83 "A Sequel to the Record of Household Surveys in Jiangxi Province", *Oriental Magazine*, August 1909, 275.

84 "News about a Mass Uprising in Yuanzhou of Jiangxi Province", *Oriental Magazine*, October 1909, 366.

85 "Current Affairs", *Oriental Magazine*, 6, no. 8, quoted from Zhang Zhenhe, Ding Yuanying, *Chronicle of Mass Uprisings in the Late Qing Dynasty* (vol. 2). Editorial Group of Modern Historical Documents in Institute of Modern History of Chinese Academy of Social Sciences: *Documents about Modern History*, 4 (1982), 102–103.

86 "News about Plebs in Zhejiang Province Destroying Private Schools", *Oriental Magazine*, May 1910, 27.

87 "An Addendum to the Record of the Great Events in China", *Oriental Magazine*, in June 1910, 49.

From mass uprising to revolution   51

88 "An Addendum to the Record of the Great Events in China", *Oriental Magazine*, June 1910, 48–51.

89 Zhu Ying, *The Revolution of 1911 and the Social Changes in Modern China*, 650.

90 *The First Historical Archives of China: Historical Documents about Mass Uprisings in the Ten Years before the Revolution of 1911* (vol. 1), 353–355; Association of Chinese Historians, *The Revolution of 1911* (vol. 3), 419–422.

91 Wang Shuhuai, *Regional Research on China's Modernization – Jiangsu Province*, Institute of Modern History (Taipei: Taiwan Academia Sinica, 1984), 205–206.

92 Association of Chinese Historians, *The Revolution of 1911* (vol. 3), 454–455.

93 Association of Chinese Historians, *The Revolution of 1911* (vol. 3), 416–419.

94 Liang Qichao, "Thoughts on Turmoil in Hunan Province", in *A Compilation of Historical Documents about the Rice Riot in Changsha*, 247, 251.

95 "An Addendum to the Record of the Great Events in China", *Oriental Magazine*, August 1910, 61.

96 In Hunan Province, "the evil gentry, surnamed Yang and Kong, always opposed the New Deal, so they made use of this chance to order potters and carpenters to burn down all churches, schools, wharves and Fuzhong school". See "A Report on Details about Turmoil in Hunan Province submitted by People there", in *A Compilation of Historical Documents about the Rice Riot in Changsha*, 230, 237.

97 "A Detailed List of Surveying Autonomy in 34 Counties of Shangdong Province like Licheng", *Files of the Ministry of Internal Affairs of the Beiyang Government*, file number: 1001/969, quoted from Wei Guangqi, *Official Governance and Autonomy – China's County System in the First Half of the 20th Century*, 138.

98 The Republic of China, *A Sequel of Chronicle of Wuzhi County* (vol. 6), "Chronicles of Food and Goods".

99 "The Financial Statement of Hunan Province", quoted from Zheng Qidong, "Apportioned Charges of North China in Modern Times (1840–1937)", *Modern Chinese History Studies*, 2(1994): 84.

100 Xiong Zuyi, "A Letter to Officials Who Were in Charge", quoted from Zheng Qidong, "Apportioned Charges of North China in Modern Times (1840–1937)", 85.

101 "Warnings about Turmoil in Hunan Province", in *A Compilation of Historical Documents about the Rice Riot in Changsha*, 245.

102 Li Dazhao, "The Youth and Rural Areas", in Tong Fuyong, *A Compilation of Documents about Modern Chinese Education History* (Shanghai: Shanghai Education Publishing House, 1997), 949–953.

103 Li Yanguang, "The Political System in the Qing Dynasty", in *Proceedings of the International Symposium on the History of the Ming and Qing Dynasties*, ed. Group of Papers of the Secretariat of the International Symposium on the History of the Ming and Qing Dynasties, 257.

104 "The Record of the Great Events in China", *Oriental Magazine*, August 1910, 99–101.

105 "Chronicle of Events in March, 1910", *Oriental Magazine*, April 1910, 51.

106 Zhang Zhenhe, Ding Yuanying, *Chronicle of Mass Uprisings in the Late Qing Dynasty* (vol. 2). Editorial Group of Modern Historical Documents in Institute of Modern History of Chinese Academy of Social Sciences: *Documents about Modern History*, 4(1982): 85.

52 *From mass uprising to revolution*

107 (France) Jacques Gernet, *Le Monde Chinois*, translated into Chinese by Huang Jianhua and Huang Xunyu (Beijing: Chinese People's Publishing House, 1995), 542.

108 Zhou Gucheng, "New Perspective on Rural Society", in *A Collection of Historical Essays of Zhou Gucheng*, ed. Zhou Gucheng (Beijing: People's Publishing House, 1983), 403.

109 "The Record of the Great Events in China", *Oriental Magazine*, November 1909, 164.

110 "On the Gentry and Scholars", in *Historical Documents Reported during the Last 40 Years of the Qing Dynasty*, ed. Xu Zaiping and Xu Ruifang (Beijing: Xinhua Publishing House, 1988), 242.

111 Wang Zhaoming (pen name: Jingwei), "On the Trend of Revolution", in *Selected Works of Comments in the Ten Years before the Revolution of 1911* (vol. 3), 536.

112 The article titled "The Gentry were Public Enemy" stated that the so-called constitutionalism and local autonomy were not based on the people's interests. Instead, they were just used by the gentry for their own private ends in the name of the New Deal. The government was just like a hunter and the gentry were its lackeys. See *Selected Works of Comments in the Ten Years before the Revolution of 1911* (vol. 3), 302–305.

113 "Does Destroying Schools Become a Common Practice?", *Oriental Magazine*, November 1904, 78.

114 Plebs sent hundreds of people holding bamboo-made boards, on which was written, "the officials drove plebs to rebellion and the gentry drove people to death", to take the officials in charge of pacification operations to the provincial capital under escort and accuse them of disturbing residents. See Zhang Zhenhe and Ding Yuanying, *Chronicle of Mass Uprisings in the Late Qing Dynasty* (vol. 2), *Documents about Modern History*, 4(1982): 103.

115 Earlier studies suggested that the scope of local activities administered by the gentry had never been clearly separated from that imposed by the government. The cowardliness of the government would inevitably lead to ultra vires of notable figures; otherwise, it would lead to endless controversy. Specifying the scope of local affairs administered by the local people could lead to the active participation of local celebrities and official repression within an appropriate range. See R. Keith Schoppa, *Chinese Elites and Political Change: Zhejiang Province in the Early Twentieth Century* (Cambridge, MA: Harvard University Press, 1982), 31–33. Regarding details of autonomous institutions in Shandong and Jiangsu Provinces, see the essay by Zhang Yufa and Wang Shuhuai, in *Collection of the Institute of Modern History of the Academia Sinica* (6th series), 1977, 159–184, 313–328.

116 Relevant studies: Lin Ji, *Clan Society and Its Changes in the Middle Reaches of the Yangtze River – Case Study on the Situation of Huangzhou (From the Ming and Qing Dynasties to 1949)* (Beijing: China Social Sciences Press, 1999), 210–225; Liu Yongtai, "Issues of Public Property and Tribunals during the Period of National Revolution – A Comparison between the Peasant Movement of Hunan and Hubei Provinces and of Guangdong Province", in *Studies on Republican China*, ed. Center for the History of Republican China of Nanjing University, 5(1999); Zhang Kaiyuan, *Studies of the Officials, Gentry and Merchants in the Modern History of China* (Wuhan: Hubei People's Publishing House, 2000), 387–415; Zhu Ying, *The Revolution of 1911 and the Social Changes in Modern China*

From mass uprising to revolution 53

(Wuhan: Central China Normal University Press, 2001, 634; Wang Xianming, *The Gentry in the Times of Uncertainty – The Gentry and the Change of Rural Social Structure (1901–1945)* (Beijing: People's Publishing House, 2009), 109–145. Most earlier relevant studies regarded the operation of public property as the embodiment of the expansion of the gentry's power, and analyzed how the gentry were in control of public property and pointed out its effects, but few of them focused on analyzing the situation in which the characteristics of public property operations and social functions changed along with the times, discussing real effects and the institutional causes of this change and revealing the complex and profound relationship reflected by the change in public property between the reform of the national political system and the trend in the development of the rural power structure in particular.

117 Regarding what Philip Alden Kuhn suggested, the changes in the Chinese traditional social order started "the year when the Taiping Army was put down". ((America) Philip Alden Kuhn, *Rebellion and Its Enemies in Late Imperial China*, trans. Xie Liangsheng into Chinese (Beijing: China Social Sciences Press, 1990), 8). Rural public property operations also underwent remarkable changes in this period. In order to cope with the crisis of the regime, a form of internal tariff called likin emerged, which fundamentally destabilized the centralized financial system of the Qing dynasty. Hence, a situation resulted in which the Ministry of Revenue had less and less power, while local officials governing an area had more and more power. Against this background, local governments began to adopt "a new idea that local people provided funds" for organizing group training (Kuhn, 90.), which meant local governments obtained funds by collecting taxes or apportioning charges according to grain yield. In 1859, the donated money accounted for nearly 90 percent of the total expenses of local group training in Hunan Province (*Annals of Counties of Hunan Province from 1874* (1), vol. 5, "Military Defense", *Collection of Chronicles about China's Local Areas* (Jiangsu Ancient Books Publishing House, Shanghai Bookstore, Bashu Publishing House, photocopy of 2002), 366). A fund for military defense (public funds) was raised in the name of collecting taxes (public power) to protect the local people, and all kinds of public funds for tax collection were derived from it after that. Since the people did not trust petty officials (Li Huaiyin, *Village Governance in North China, 1875–1936*, trans. Sui Yousheng and Wang Shihao into Chinese (Beijing: Zhonghua Book Company, 2008), 304. (Other scholars, like Philip Alden Kuhn, Huang Zongzhi and Qu Tongzu, held similar opinions.) The gentry in local troops were in charge of collecting taxes with the help of group training organizations. For example, in Jingshan County, "officials who were in charge of grains were replaced with local gentry, and the latter worked with the Bao-jia group to collect taxes on grains" (*Annals of Jingshan County from 1871 to 1908* (vol. 8), "Chronicles about Officials", quoted from Yang Guoan, *A Study on Grassroots-Level Organizations and Rural Society in Hunan and Hubei Provinces during the Ming and Qing Dynasties*, 313.). Since that time, the gentry and group training organizations were legally granted part of the right to collect taxes. As a result, one of the major factors in the change in the rural power structure in modern times was hidden here. (Author's note)

118 Li Hanzhang, *General Annals of Hunan Province* (vol. 55), "Chronicles of Food and Goods·Storing", *Revision of The Siku Quanshu – Volume*

54 *From mass uprising to revolution*

> *662 – History·Geography* (Shanghai: Shanghai Ancient Books Publishing House, 2002), 636.

119 *Annals of Counties of Hunan Province from 1874 (1)*, vol. 5, "Military Defense", 358–359.

120 "A Study on the Protection of Public Property According to the Law", in *A Study on the Rituals of the Official Family* (vol. 4), "A Study on the Sacrificial Ceremony of the Official Family", ed. Lin Botong, *The 3rd Revision of a Collection of Series* (vol. 25), ed. Wand Deyi (Taipei: Xinwenfeng Publishing Co., Ltd., 1997), 439.

121 Yang Guoan, *A Study on Local Organizations and Rural Society in Hunan and Hubei Provinces during the Ming and Qing Dynasties*, 286.

122 Zhou Rong, *The Social Security System of the Ming and Qing Dynasties and the Local Society of Hunan and Hubei Provinces*, 440.

123 Zhang Yan, *Clan Fields and Local Social Structure in the Qing Dynasty* (Beijing: China Renmin University Press, 1991), 226.

124 "Chronicles about Politics", *Annals of Liling County* (1) in the Republic of China, *Collection of Chronicles about China's Local Areas* (Nanjing: Jiangsu Ancient Books Publishing House, Shanghai: Shanghai Bookstore, Chengdu: Bashu Publishing House, photocopy of 2002), 550.

125 Department of Ming and Qing Archives of the Palace Museum, *Historical Documents about Preparation for Implementing Constitutionalism in the Late Qing Dynasty* (vol. 2), 738.

126 Wang Xianming, *The Gentry of Modern Times – The Destiny of a Feudal Class* (Tianjin: Tianjin People's Publishing House, 1997), 301.

127 Ming Sun, "Discussions on Local Autonomy", in *Selected Works of Comments in the Ten Years before the Revolution of 1911* (vol. 3), 407.

128 Department of Ming and Qing Archives of the Palace Museum, *Historical Documents about Preparation for Implementing Constitutionalism in the Late Qing Dynasty* (vol. 2), 757.

129 Zhou Qiuguang, *Collected Works of Xiong Xiling* (vol. 1) (Changsha: Hunan Publishing House, 1996), 351.

130 "A Report on Trade by the Customs", quoted from (America) Esherick, *Reform and Revolution in China – The 1911 Revolution in Hunan and Hubei*, 298.

131 Local Chronicle Compilation Committee of Hubei Province, *Chronicles of Hubei Province·Regime* (Wuhan: Hubei People's Publishing House, 1996), 136.

132 "Regulations of Local Financial Lists in Various Counties of Hunan Province", *Hunan Monthly Finance Journal*, 72 (April 1924): 4.

133 "A Development Scheme of Rural Areas in 13 Counties of Western Hunan Like Fengma", *Monthly Journal of Peasant Construction in Western Hunan*, October 1934, 55.

134 Bu Luan, "The Gentry Class Should Be Overthrown", *China Youth*, June 1926, 666.

135 Wu Han and Fei Xiaotong, *Imperial Power and Gentry Power* (Guahgzhou: Observation Society, 1948), 50.

136 *Annals about Counties of Hunan Province from 1874* (1), vol. 5, "Military Defense", 366.

137 He Yuefu, *Gentry in the Late Qing Dynasty and the Changes of Modern Society Compared with the Japanese Scholars*, 54–55.

138 Yang Xinsheng, *A Study on the Gentry Class in Modern Hunan Province* (Changsha: Yuelu Press, 2010), 73.

139 "A Memorial in Which Zhuang Gengliang, Chief Secretary of Hunan was Impeached", in *Rough Drafts of Tuilu* (vol. 2), ed. Hu Sijing, *A Sequel of Series* (vol. 47) (Shanghai: Shanghai Bookstore Publishing House, 1994), 39.

140 Qu Tongzu, *Local Governments in the Qing Dynasty* (Beijing: Law Press. China, 2003), 329–330.

141 Mu Xiangyao, "Lectures of Shanghai Local Autonomy Research Association", *Constitutional Magazine*, 2nd issue, quoted from Ma Xiaoquan, *State and Society: Local Autonomy and Constitutional Reform in the Late Qing Dynasty* (Kaifeng: Henan University Press, 2000), 42.

142 (America) Kuhn, *Rebellion and Its Enemies in Late Imperial China*, 222–223.

143 Yang Xinsheng, *A Study on the Gentry Class in Modern Hunan Province*, 236.

144 Local Chronicle Compilation Committee of Hubei Province, *Chronicles of Hubei Province Regime*, 6.

145 Wang Di, "The Development of the Public Domain in the Upper Reaches of the Yangtze River in the Late Qing Dynasty", *Historical Research*, 1(1996): 14.

146 Department of Ming and Qing Archives of the Palace Museum, *Historical Documents about Preparation for Implementing Constitutionalism in the Late Qing Dynasty* (vol. 2), 725.

147 Department of Ming and Qing Archives of the Palace Museum, *Historical Documents about Preparation for Implementing Constitutionalism in the Late Qing Dynasty* (vol. 2), 718.

148 Department of Ming and Qing Archives of the Palace Museum, *Historical Documents about Preparation for Implementing Constitutionalism in the Late Qing Dynasty* (vol. 2), 726.

149 Department of History, Yangzhou Normal University, *Historical Documents of Jiangsu Province during the Revolution of 1911* (Nanjing: Jiangsu People's Publishing, 1961), 12.

150 "A Memorial to the Emperor Submitted by Rui Cheng, Governor of Hunan and Hubei Provinces", in which he mentioned that the registered gentry who caused trouble for personal interests should be punished respectively, in *A Compilation of Historical Documents about the Rice Riot in Changsha*, 95.

151 Wang Xianming, *The Gentry in the Times of Uncertainty – The Gentry and the Change of Rural Social Structure (1901–1945)*, 117.

152 Quoted from (America) Esherick, *Reform and Revolution in China – The 1911 Revolution in Hunan and Hubei*, 133.

153 Liu Wei, *Governor Politics of the Late Qing Dynasty – A Study on the Relationship between the Central Government and Local Areas* (Wuhan: Hubei Education Press, 2003), 394.

154 (America) Zhang Xin, *The Evolution of Chinese Society in the Early 20th Century – Local Elites in the Country and Henan Province, 1900–1937*, trans. Yue Qianhou and Zhang Wei into Chinese (Beijing: Zhonghua Book Company, 2004), 235.

155 "Resolutions on Rural Public Property", in *Documents of Peasant Movement during the First Civil Revolutionary War*, 492.

156 "Chronicles about Politics", *Annals of Liling County* (1) in the Republic of China, 528.

56 *From mass uprising to revolution*

157 "Chronicles about Figures", *Annals of Liling County* (3) in the Republic of China, 38–39.

158 Pi Xirui, *Essays Written in Shifu Hall (1898–1900)*; See Editorial Office of *Historical Documents of Hunan Province, Historical Documents of Hunan Province* (vol. 2) (Changsha: Hunan People's Publishing House, 1981), 169.

159 "An Edict about Political Affairs in Prefectures and Counties and Autonomous Public Offices"; See Association of Chinese Historians, *The Revolution of 1911* (vol. 5) (Shanghai: Shanghai People's Publishing House, 2000), 139.

160 Local Chronicle Compilation Committee of Hubei Province, *Chronicles of Hubei Province·Regime*, 12.

161 (America) Kuhn, *Rebellion and Its Enemies in Late Imperial China*, 228.

162 Local Chronicle Compilation Committee of Hubei Province, *Chronicles of Hubei Province·Regime*, 134.

163 "A Reply to the Autonomous Council in Yidu County", Hubei Provincial and Wuhan Municipal Committee of the Chinese People's Political Consultative Conference, *Anthology of Archival Data about Wuhan Uprisings* (Wuhan: Hubei People's Publishing House, 1982), 121.

164 Local Chronicle Compilation Committee of Wuxue City, Hubei Province, *Annals of Guangji County* (vol. 3), "Establishment" (Shanghai: Chinese Dictionary Publishing House, 1994), 39.

165 Zhu Ying, *The Revolution of 1911 and the Social Changes in Modern China*, 681.

166 Committee for a Study of Cultural and Historical Documents of the National Committee of the Chinese People's Political Consultative Conference, *Memoirs of the Revolution of 1911* (vol. 5) (Beijing: Zhonghua Book Company, 1963), 180.

167 Chuzo Ichiko, "The Gentry and the Revolution of 1911", in *A Study on the Modern History of China Abroad* (vol. 18), ed. editorial department of publisher (Beijing: China Social Sciences Press, 1991), 176.

168 China Modern Economic History Section of Institute of Economics of Chinese Academy of Social Sciences, *Anthology of Historical Documents about Struggles for Land during the First and Second Civil Revolutionary War* (Beijing: People's Publishing House, 1981), 102–103.

169 Zhang Zhongli, *Chinese Gentry*, 73.

170 Wu Han and Fei Xiaotong, *Imperial Power and Gentry Power*, 123.

171 Deng Wenyi, "A Study on the Issue of Lands", *Chinese Peasants* June 1927, 24.

172 Chen Zuiyun, "Disaster Relief Policy and Warehouse System", *A Monthly of Cultural Development*, March 1936, 62.

173 Zeng Jiwu, *Note on an Investigation in Various Counties of Hunan Province* (vol. 2), a printed copy by Changshahejian Printing Company, 1931, 38.

174 Zhang Yan, *Clan Fields and Local Social Structure in the Qing Dynasty*, 293.

175 Zhou Xiaohong, *Tradition and Change – The Social Psychology of Peasants Jiangsu and Zhejiang Provinces and Its Evolution since Modern Times* (Shanghai: SDX Joint Publishing Company, 1998), 70.

176 Xu Zaiping and Xu Ruifang, *Historical Documents Reported during the Last 40 Years of the Qing Dynasty* (Beijing: Xinhua Publishing House, 1998), 175.

177 "On the Mass Uprisings in Laiyang County", *National Customs Newspaper*, October 1910, 2.

178 Liu Yongtai, "Issues of Public Property and Tribunals during the Period of National Revolution – A Comparison between the Peasant Movement of Hunan and Hubei Provinces and of Guangdong Province", in *Studies on Republican*

From mass uprising to revolution 57

China, ed. Center for the History of Republican China of Nanjing University, 5(1999): 6–7.

179 *Annals of Shanhua County from 1871 to 1908* (vol. 32), "A Sequel of Art and Literature" (Nanjing: Jiangsu Ancient Books Publishing House, Shanghai: Shanghai Bookstore, Chengdu: Bashu Publishing House, photocopy of 2002), 661.

180 *Annals of Baling County from 1871 to 1908* (2) (vol. 31), "Chronicles about Figures (4)" (Nanjing: Jiangsu Ancient Books Publishing House, Shanghai: Shanghai Bookstore, Chengdu: Bashu Publishing House, photocopy of 2002), 133.

181 (America) Esherick, *Reform and Revolution in China – The 1911 Revolution in Hunan and Hubei*, 71.

182 Fu Jiaojin and Liu Lansun, *Civil Corps of Hunan Province* (Hunan provincial government, 1934), 13.

183 (Japan) Chuzo Ichiko, "The Gentry and the Revolution of 1911", in *A Study on the Modern History of China Abroad* (vol. 18), 176.

184 Zeng Jiwu, *Note on an Investigation in Various Counties of Hunan Province* (vol. 2), 14.

185 "A Report from Cao Dajun, an Inspector of Eastern Hubei Province", *Documentation of the Revolutionary Base Areas of Hunan, Hubei and Jiangxi Provinces* (vol.1) (Beijing: People's Publishing House, 1985), 120.

186 "The Situation of the Peasant Movement in Hunan Province", in *Documents of Peasant Movement during the First Civil Revolutionary War*, 383.

187 Wang Qisheng, *Revolution and Anti-revolution: The Politics of the Republic of China from the Perspective of Social Culture* (Beijing: Social Sciences Academic Press, 2010), 336.

188 Zeng Jiwu, *Note on an Investigation in Various Counties of Hunan Province* (vol. 2), 23.

189 "Resolutions on Peasants at the Second Congress of the Party Headquarter of Hunan Province of the Kuomintang", in *Anthology of Documents about Peasant Movement in Hunan Province*, ed. Chinese Revolutionary Museum and Hunan Museum (Beijing: People's Publishing House, 1988), 199.

190 Statistics Office of Hunan Provincial Government Secretariat, *An Almanac of Hunan Province* (Changsha: Dongting Printing House, 1936), 113.

191 "An Important Declaration of the Provincial Peasants' Association", in *Anthology of Documents about Peasant Movement in Guangdong Province*, ed. Memorial Hall of the Site of Institute of Peasant Movement in Guangzhou (Beijing: People's Publishing House, 1986), 421.

192 Wang Xianming, "Historical Memory and Social Reconstruction – A Study on the Change in the Gentry Power of the Early Republic of China", *Historical Research*, 3(2010), 11.

193 "Resolutions at the First Peasants' Congress in Hunan Province", in *Documents of Peasant Movement during the First Civil Revolutionary War*, 406.

194 "Resolutions on Issues of County Administration", in *Documents of Peasant Movement during the First Civil Revolutionary War*, 486.

195 "A Declaration Pledged to Peasants by the third plenary session of the Second Central Executive Committee of the Chinese Kuomintang", in *A Collection of Important Declarations of the Kuomintang of China over the Years*, ed. Party Headquarters of Zhejiang Province, Kuomintang of China (Publishing house unknown, 1932), 298.

58 *From mass uprising to revolution*

196 "Resolutions on Issues of Rural Public Property", in *Documents of Peasant Movement during the First Civil Revolutionary War*, 492.

197 "Important Resolutions at the First Peasants' Congress in Guangdong Province", in *Documents of Peasant Movement during the First Civil Revolutionary War*, 270.

198 Liu Yongtai, "Issues of Public Property and Tribunals during the Period of National Revolution – A Comparison between the Peasant Movement of Hunan and Hubei Provinces and of Guangdong Province", in *Studies on Republican China*, ed. Center for the History of Republican China of Nanjing University, 5(1999), 15.

199 (Japan) Tadao Tanaka, *National Revolution and Rural Issues* (vol. 2), trans. Li Yuyun into Chinese (Nanjing: Village Governance Monthly, 1932), 155.

200 "Interim Regulations on Punishment of Local Tyrants and the Evil Gentry in Hunan Province", *Ta Kung Pao* (Changsha), January 29, 1927, 6th ed.

201 Department of Modern History, Hunan Academy of Social Sciences, *Anthology of Historical Documents about Peasant Movement in Hunan Province During the First Civil Revolutionary War* (5), in *Historical Data of Hunan Province* (vol. 2 of 1981), 44–87.

202 Li Weihan, "On the Peasant Movement in Hunan in January", in *Selected Works of Li Weihan* (Beijing: People's Publishing House, 1987), 26.

203 The Ministry of Peasants of the Party Headquarter of Zhejiang Province of the Kuomintang of China, *The Situation of Peasant Movement in China Sixteen Years Ago* (Publishing house and publication date unknown), 45.

204 Bai Gang, *History of Chinese Political System* (vol. 2) (Tianjin: Tianjin People's Publishing House, 2002), 817.

205 Qu Tongzu, *Local Governments in the Qing Dynasty*, 306–309.

206 (America) Kuhn, *Rebellion and Its Enemies in Late Imperial China*, 220.

207 "A Comment by the Emperor Guangxu on the Memorial submitted by Supervisor Xu Shujun on July 14, 1889", quoted from Luo Yudong, *History of Chinese Likin System* (vol. 1) (Beijing: The Commercial Press, 1936), 49–50.

208 Luo Yudong, *History of Chinese Likin System* (vol. 1), 87.

209 Luo Yudong, *History of Chinese Likin System* (vol. 1), 35.

210 Yin Futing, *Chronology of the History of the Qing Dynasty* (vol. 9) (Beijing: China Renmin University Press, 1998), 130.

211 *Annals of Counties of Hunan Province from 1874* (1), vol. 5, "Military Defense", 366.

212 Lin Ji, *Clan Society and Its Changes in the Middle Reaches of the Yangtze River – Case Study on the Situation of Huangzhou (From the Ming and Qing Dynasties to 1949)*, 182.

213 Wang Xianming, *On the History of Social Culture in Modern China* (Beijing: People's Publishing House, 2000), 47.

214 "A Memorial in Which the Treasury Department Reported the Financial Situation of Each Province to General Office of Finance", *Political Official Newspaper*, April 8, 1909.

215 (America) Guy Salvatore Alitto, *The Last Confucian: Liang Shu-ming and the Chinese Dilemma of Modernity*, trans. Wang Zongyu and Ji Jianzhong into Chinese (Nanjing: Jiangsu People's Publishing,1996), 229.

216 "The Gentry Were Public Enemy", See *Selected Works of Comments in the Ten Years before the Revolution of 1911* (vol. 3), 305.

217 "Warnings to My Fellow Villagers", *Zhejiang Tide*, February 1903, 10.

218 He Yuefu, *Gentry in the Late Qing Dynasty and the Changes of Modern Society Compared with the Japanese Scholars*, 246.

219 Li Kan, "On the Victory and Defeat of the Revolution of 1911 from the Perspective of the Recovery of Several Prefectures and Counties in Jiangsu and Hubei Provinces and on the Relationship between the Bourgeois revolutionaries and Peasants", in *Proceedings of the Symposium to Commemorate the 70th Anniversary of the Revolution of 1911*, ed. editorial office of Zhonghua Book Company (Beijing: Zhonghua Book Company, 1983), 470.

220 Committee for a Study of Cultural and Historical Documents of the National Committee of the Chinese People's Political Consultative Conference, *Memoirs of the Revolution of 1911* (vol. 2) (Beijing: Literary and Historical Documents Publishing House, 1981), 207.

221 "Important News of Xinhua", *Ta Kung Pao* (Changsha), on February 8, 1917, 7th ed.

222 Committee for a Study of Cultural and Historical Documents of the National Committee of the Chinese People's Political Consultative Conference, *Memoirs of the Revolution of 1911* (vol. 2), 365.

223 Zhu Ying, *The Revolution of 1911 and the Social Changes in Modern China*, 660.

224 Wang Xianming, *The Gentry in the Times of Uncertainty – The Gentry and the Change of Rural Social Structure (1901–1945)*, 126.

225 Zhang Xin, *The Evolution of Chinese Society in the Early 20th Century – Local Elites in the Country and Henan Province, 1900–1937*, 299.

226 Chen Zhirang, *The Local Regime Created by Military Forces and the Gentry – The Warlord Period in Modern China*, 59.

227 Zhang Xin, *The Evolution of Chinese Society in the Early 20th Century – Local Elites in the Country and Henan Province, 1900–1937*, 92.

228 Wang Qisheng and Wang Qisheng, *Revolution and Anti-revolution: The Politics of the Republic of China from the Perspective of Social Culture*, 331.

229 Zhang Kaiyuan, *Studies of the Officials, Gentry and Merchants in the Modern History of China*, 407.

230 Zeng Jiwu, *Note on an Investigation in Various Counties of Hunan Province* (vol. 2), 39.

231 Liu Dapeng, *Diaries Written in Tuixiang Study* (Shanxi: Shanxi People's Publishing House, 1990), 149.

232 "A memorial in which educational ministers suggested that the imperial examination system should be abolished and the government should attach importance to private schools", *Oriental Magazine*, January 1904, 124.

233 Su Yunfeng, *Regional Research on China's Modernization – Hubei Province from 1860 to 1916*, Institute of Modern History (Taipei: Taiwan Academia Sinica, 1981), 467.

234 Yuan Lan, "The Inside Story of the Officials in Charge of Pacification Operations", *Hunan*, September 1919, 2.

235 Department of Civil Affairs of Hubei Provincial Government, *An Overview of County Administration of Hubei Province·Introduction* (vol. 1) (Publishing house unknown, 1934), 10.

236 Xu Jilin, "Social Groups in the Vicissitudes of Modern China", *Social Science Research*, 1992, 87.

60 *From mass uprising to revolution*

237 Party History Committee of Hunan Province of the Communist Party of China, *History of Hunan People's Revolution during the New Democratic Revolution Period* (Changsha: Hunan Publishing House, 1991), 12.

238 "A Report on Setting up the Local Property Depository Department in Each County", *Ta Kung Pao* (Changsha), on February 16, 1917, 7th ed.

239 "The Staff of the Depository Department Resigned", *Ta Kung Pao* (Changsha), on February 28, 1927, 7th ed.

240 *Annals of Ningxiang County* (vol. 1), "County Chronicles", *Annals of Ningxiang County in the Republic of China* (2) (Nanjing: Jiangsu Ancient Books Publishing House, Shanghai: Shanghai Bookstore, Chengdu: Bashu Publishing House, photocopy of 2002), 589.

241 "A Story of the Governor of Hunan Province Persecuting the Gentry", *Hunan* (Vol. 1), no. 3, (Publishing house and publication date unknown): 3–4.

242 "An Appeal made by Rural People in Xiangtan", *Ta Kung Pao* (Changsha), January 28, 1926, 7th ed.

243 (America) Prasenjit Duara, *Culture, Power, and the State: Rural North China, 1900–1942*, trans. Wang Fuming into Chinese (Nanjing: Jiangsu People's Publishing, 1996), 238.

244 Bei Hua, *The History of Chinese Revolution, in A Sequel of Modern Chinese History Series* (vol. 86), ed. Shen Yunlong (Taipei: Wenhai Publishing House, photocopy in 1981), 211.

245 Liang Shuming, *The Main Idea of Chinese Culture, Complete Works of Liang Shuming* (vol. 3) (Jinan: Shandong People's Publishing House, 2005), 224.

246 (America) Esherick, *Reform and Revolution in China – The 1911 Revolution in Hunan and Hubei*, 309.

247 Soldier Weekly Newspaper Office, *A Collection of Essays on the Issues of Peasant Movement in Hunan Province*, Soldier Weekly Newspaper Office, 1927, p. 45.

2 Replacement of the township system and social changes in rural areas

China's rural society in the early twentieth century underwent extensive and volatile changes. Most of all, chain institutional changes led to structural change in rural society. In the historical process where a new system replaced an old system or a system transformed, the rural society did not accept all changes passively, nor did it simply resist them. Its complex, various forms and multiple choices and trends also enriched our knowledge about history.

From autonomy to the Bao-jia system: historical trend of the reconstruction of the township system

This part focuses only on the historical development process of modern autonomy and the traditional *Bao-jia* system from substitution to integration in the transformation of rural systems. It aims to show what actually happened in rural social changes and interpret the historical reasons why rural systems turned back to tradition,[1] and attempts to reveal the underlying historical theme in the trend of "*Bao-jia*-autonomy-*Bao-jia*" with paradoxical representation.

In Hunan and Hubei Provinces, traditional controlling power and mechanisms in rural society were well developed. Not only were squires in both provinces the most active all around China, but also the *Bao-jia* system and local troops or organizations also developed very well and had a long-term impact on the building and the operation of rural power. In the process of modernization since the late Qing dynasty, the development of modern power and the adoption of New Deal measures in Hunan and Hubei Provinces were also more salient than other provinces and regions. In these two provinces, the society's traditional power and modern power were prominent, and collision and accommodation had their own distinguishing features in social transformation and rural social reform. Therefore, all of them were of typical significance for analysis. Moreover, these two provinces possessed analyzable specific information related to carrying out the *Bao-jia* system in rural areas; therefore, this book's research perspective is limited to the society in Hunan and Hubei Provinces.

62 *Replacement of the township system*

Institutional reform and abolishment of the **Bao-jia** *system*

From the year 1683 when Emperor Kangxi, the fourth emperor of the Qing dynasty, revised the *Bao-jia* law, to the early twentieth century before reform of the rural power system in China was carried out, the *Bao-jia* system had still been the basic system directly controlled by state power in the rural society. However, in the rural social power structure of Hunan and Hubei Provinces in the late Qing dynasty, the *Bao-jia* system, which was directly dependent on the official system, was being undermined. The *Bao-jia* system in both provinces was weakening to varying degree.[2] But its functional decline did not mean the system had collapsed, and as a formal organizational unit constitutive of an institution, Bao-jia continued to be a hallmark of a distinct period in the history of rural society.

In 1901, the Qing government launched the New Policy, which brought the transformation of rural systems into local self-government characterized by its modern political form. The *Bao-jia* system was criticized for its ineffectiveness and the troubles it brought to people, and the government intended to replace it with a police system. Later, the Qing government implemented the *Constitution on Local Self-Government in Cities, Towns and Villages*, in which the traditional system of dividing *Bao-jia* areas was abolished and the system of dividing police districts was advanced. This meant that cities, towns and villages must be divided by the police into each department, prefecture and county. If a special case occurred, officials in each prefecture and county were to divide this area in the proper way, and then report on their move to their superiors for deliberation and approval.[3] There was no doubt that diverse models of rural life and regional history and culture made it difficult to clarify the imbalance in the transformation of rural systems and the complexity of the course of development, but its historical direction of transformation was clear and recognizable. In the trend of reforming local political systems, remarks on local self-government could be heard every day in the early twentieth century[4] and had become the discourse of this era, which was familiar to almost everyone nationwide.[5] In addition, replacing the traditional *Bao-jia* system with a modern police system was a main point for local self-government.

The historical stage of evolution of the rural political system from the late Qing dynasty to the Republic of China can be summarized as follows: the Libao system in the nineteenth century, the system of district sheriff from 1900 to 1928, and the system of district governor after 1929.[6] Though their organizational forms were different from each other, the historical trend was on the whole to replace the old system (the *Bao-jia* system) with the new system (the police system), and the rural political system was always established under the modern banner of local self-government. From the time the New Deal was implemented in the late Qing dynasty, the village-level organizations based on the *Bao-jia* system was being dismantled and replaced with police districts, school districts and autonomous regions. Although self-government was not put into practice in general, the new police system was established by and large. The sheriff not only maintained social order but also had administrative powers such as collecting taxes on farm lands and passing government decrees on to the folk people. The new police system did not completely separate itself from the original *Bao-jia* system, which involved public security and finance.[7] Hence, replacing the *Bao-jia* system with the police system became a major point of the reform of rural systems in the early twentieth century and also an important part of the "modernization" campaign launched in the rural society. It is recorded that during the reign of Emperor Xuantong, the last emperor of the Qing dynasty, the new police system was being established while the *Bao-jia* Bureau in each province was being dismantled. Once the organ responsible for carrying out the *Bao-jia* system was dismantled, the *Bao-jia* system was not mentioned in government decrees anymore.[8]

The decline of the traditional *Bao-jia* system and the rise of modern self-government and the police system constituted the historical content of the rural reform in the early twentieth century. From the late Qing dynasty to the Republic of China, the local political system of Hunan Province had experienced a sudden collapse of the old system and a sudden rise of the new system, such as a change in the Security Bureau and the *Bao-jia* Bureau in the Hundred Days Reform, a failed 103-day national, cultural, political and educational reform movement that spanned from June 11, 1898, to September 21, 1898, in the late Qing dynasty. However, in conformity to the historical trends of the times, the postmodern police system began to be advanced in each prefecture and county after 1903. Dazhou County and areas around lakes gained better results in the change of local political systems, while there was no significant progress in promoting the police system in Hunan Province.[9] Nonetheless, the trend of advancing the system of local autonomy and replacing the *Bao-jia* system with the police system did not change. The emergence of this system fundamentally changed the dual social control model of "the government setting up the *Bao-jia* system" and "squires conducting group training". The system of old rural political organizations in each county of Hubei Province was generally divided into three levels. For example, the Quzhen factory of Huangmei County, Fantuan District of Huanggang, Qutuan Town in Bamboo Mountain, Hanchuan, Xiakou, Xiangyang and other counties were all below these three levels. There were also *jia* and *pai*, but no significant political power. The organization at each level was the ruling government in that area.[10] These changes in rural institutions in Gongan County of Hubei Province would inevitably leave one with a deep sense of wistfulness about how different things are now from what they were yesteryear.[11]

However, the trend of changing rural systems in the early twentieth century was reversed in the 1930s. In order to address the issue of social order, the government of the Republic of China shifted its focus from modern local autonomy to the traditional *Bao-jia* system again in the reconstruction of local political systems.

64 *Replacement of the township system*

Resilience of the **Bao-jia** *system*

In the middle of the 1930s, after decades of operation of a modern rural political system, which started at the beginning of the century, the national government used the *Bao-jia* system to control rural society once again. The so-called combining the *Bao-jia* system and autonomy meant keeping the original autonomous system on the whole and "grouping people in villages and towns into *jia* and *bao*".[12] Hence, at the level of the grassroots organizations used for social control in rural areas, the *Bao-jia* system replaced the *Lv-lin* system, grouping 25 families into an *lv* and five families into a *lin* in autonomous organizations.

Hubei Province was among the first pilot areas to carry out the *Bao-jia* system. The book *China's Bao-jia System*, by Wen Juntian, gave a brief description of the implementation of the *Bao-jia* system in Hubei, explaining that "at that time, no written law was available for reference, so everything could be done according to traditions".[13] Many counties and districts finished drawing up a plan in one year. Statistics about the arrangement for implementing the *Bao-jia* system in each county are shown in Table 2.1.

Moreover, the fund for implementation of the *Bao-jia* system had been included in current expenditure of local finance and also accounted for a considerable proportion of it, which indicated that the traditional system had become the most basic grassroots system in local politics. However, the reconstruction of the *Bao-jia* system in the Republic of China, especially the selection of *Dibao* working for the government and serving as middlemen between officials and plebs, did not directly depend on the personnel resources of the traditional *Bao-jia* system. For example, in Hankou, "*Dibao* was an important

Table 2.1 Statistics of the arrangement for implementing the *Bao-jia* system of each county in Hubei Province

Districts of Administration and Supervision	The Number of Bao	The Number of Jia	Households	An Average of People in Each Household
The 1st District (11 counties)	6,065	59,564	705	5
The 2nd District (11 counties)	7,976	78,982	832	6
The 3rd District (10 counties)	9,177	88,880	948	5
The 4th District (9 counties)	7,416	72,409	777	5
The 5th District (7 counties)	4,367	41,958	449	5
The 6th District (8 counties)	3,318	33,191	360	5
The 7th District (8 counties)	2,187	21,631	226	6
The 8th District (6 counties)	2,838	27,468	285	6
Hankou City			155	6

Data source: Hubei Branch of China Statistical Society, Summary of Statistics of Hubei Province, 1937

Replacement of the township system 65

position before 1926. At that time, many county offices in Xiakou County asked *Dibao* to assist them in governing people, and all tasks involving explaining edicts to the public were undertaken by *Dibao*". However,

> after the revolutionary army arrived in Wuhan, they regarded the position of Dibao as a remaining evil element of feudalism and believed it was of little importance. Later, the local government cut some officials jobs in Xiakou, so *Dibao* stopped playing a role in local administration. Now, most *Dibao* were idle and had no work to do, and some found another job. Since they lost their function as a middleman, the government therefore paid little attention to them.[14]

The situation in Hunan Province was more complex. "The local government of Hunan Province had worked out a plan to carry out local autonomy by stages and designated 14 counties, including Changsha, to implement autonomy in advance". However, when the autonomous system had not been established completely, "in 1934, the local government acted under orders of the administrative judgment institute to carry out the *Bao-jia* system for the purpose of laying a foundation for autonomy".[15] Therefore, those who had political power in counties and districts were not well prepared to face the change in rural political system, and there was also no organizational resources, so it was inevitable for them to encounter a lot of difficulties during the operation of the *Bao-jia* system. It was not until around 1941 that *Bao-jia* organizations were completely reestablished in Hunan. The basic situation is shown in Table 2.2.

The construction of a rural political system in Hunan and Hubei Provinces indicated that the reconstruction of the *Bao-jia* system after the founding of the Republic of China made the political system of the grassroots society, "in which people were nearly unorganized at one time and people at the upper levels often knew little about people's well-being", at least formally unified.

> For this time, people were grouped into a *bao* or *jia*. First, the local government would unify organizations below the level of counties and cities, and then set up public offices in districts, as was stipulated in autonomous laws and regulations. Counties, villages and towns below the level of district were set up, with counties consisting of villages and towns, and *fang* consisting of urban areas. Public offices were set up in all *fang* of villages, and a *bao* was below the level of *fang*, and consisted of ten *jia*. For the head of each *bao*, a bureau would be set up to deal with public affairs. A *jia* would be organized below the level of *bao*, and consisted of ten families. For the head of each *jia*, a bureau would be set up to deal with public affairs.[16]

Underpinned by the system, the state power got a chance to go deeper in rural areas.

Table 2.2 Statistics of Bao and *jia* in villages and towns of Hunan from 1937 to June 1942

Year	The Number of Villages and Towns					The Number of Bao					The Number of Li
	Total Number	First Class	Second Class	Third Class	No Class	Total Number	First Class	Second Class	Third Class	No Class	
1937	2,842				2,842	41,652				41,652	457,711
1938	1,644				1,644	39,183				39,183	1,046,452
1939	1,608	453	661	308	183	22,159				22,159	270,912
1940	1,607	449	674	315	169	19,783				19,783	251,322
1941	1,607	550	788	271		20,136	7,649	9,341	2,506	640	289,376
By the end of June, 1942	1,612	559	782	271		20,428	8,053	9,547	2,828		287,538

Data source: *Statistics of Administration in Hunan for Six Years*, p. 10.

Replacement of the township system 67

Table 2.3 A Comparison between the *Bao-jia* system from 1638 to 1661 in the Qing dynasty and that of the Republic of China

Time	Establishment	Content
The *Bao-jia* system of the Republic of China	The *Bao-jia* system took a family as a unit and there was a householder in a family. A *jia* was composed of ten families and a *bao* was composed of ten jia. Hence people were grouped into a *jia* or *bao* in accordance with order. If the rest of people could not constitute a *jia* (*bao*), 6 families (*jia*) and above could be regarded as a *jia* (*bao*). If there were fewer than 5 families (*jia*), they could be incorporated into the neighboring *jia* (*bao*).	The leader of a *bao* was responsible for checking residence cards and reporting this to the local government, supervising the training of conscripts and assisting military police in keeping order. The leader of a *jia* took orders from the leader of a *bao* to check residence cards, selected conscripts from among the people, investigated violations of law and discipline, and reported unusual situations of households to the leader of *bao*.
The *Bao-jia* system from 1638 to 1661 in the Qing Dynasty	In terms of the *Bao-jia* system, in urban and rural areas of prefectures and counties, ten families could be regarded as a *pai*, and there was a leader in each *pai*. Ten *pai* could be regarded as a *jia*, and there was a leader in each *jia*. Ten *jia* could be regarded as a *bao*, and there was a leader in each *bao*.	An imprinted card would be given to each family, on which was written the names of family members. If a person went out, he or she should note where he or she was going, and if a person came back, he or she would be questioned about where he or she came from.

From the perspective of the form of organizational structures, the *Bao-jia* system advocated by the national government was not that much different from the traditional *Bao-jia* system. We can illuminate this point through a comparison between the "Amendment to Regulations of the *Bao-jia* System" of the Republic of China and the *Bao-jia* system from 1638 to 1661, as shown in Table 2.3.[17]

From the above table, it can be seen that, though the two systems were slightly different from each other (for example, as with the Bao-*jia* system of the Republic of China, it did not mention the level of *pai*), there was no big change in the basic system, because both of them regarded *jia* as their basic unit, and their organizational chain was still centered on *jia*. With *jia* as an intermediary, families, the cell of social organizations, were connected with administrative organs in villages, towns, districts and counties. However, the principle of the system that "a *jia* was composed of ten families and there was a leader in each *jia*, and a *bao* was composed of ten *jia* and there was a leader

68 *Replacement of the township system*

in each *bao*",[18] was just empty talk and not completely consistent with the real situation. For instance, people in Hengshan County were classified into a *bao* or *jia*, but even if some people were classified into the same group, they did not necessarily come from the same family. Eighty families in Yuecun were classified into 20 groups. There were only two *jia*, and more than 160 people in each *jia*.[19] It can be seen that *jia* was the entity unit of social organizations. Through the establishment of *jia*, the scattered people and households were integrated into one social unit, and the organizations at all levels of villages, towns, districts and counties knew exactly over which they should exercise their power. However, what was different from the situation in which the state power of the Qing dynasty did not extend below the county level, was that the national government brought the *Bao-jia* system into its administrative power system; constructed a mechanism with county governments, public offices of districts, towns, *bao* and *jia*, and families involved; and the 24 rules of the *Bao-jia* system would be issued by the Ministry of Military Affairs and Ministry of Internal Affairs.[20] In addition, even the right to elect a leader of a *jia* or *bao* of the grassroots organizations was delivered to the county government, and the leader of a *jia* or *bao* would be elected by organizations at the lower level.[21] For the national government, *bao* and *jia* organizations were considered to be the basic factor in activating the whole rural power mechanism.

Autonomy as the foundation, the Bao-jia *system for practical application*

It was undeniable that although the reform of China's rural system surged, the traditional system taking root in rural society was not completely overthrown as the new trend advanced. Going deep into the rural society, we can see how complicated and diverse the power structure was.

First, at the institutional level, the reform of replacing the *Bao-jia* system with police system was basically only implemented in provincial capitals, important cities or commercial ports. "But in rural areas, few police stations were set up. The imbalance of police distribution in urban and rural areas was one of the most prominent problems in the development of local police administration in the late Qing dynasty".[22] Although the Revolution of 1911 had an influence on the rural system in terms of the political superstructure, "there was little innovation for grassroots organizations of the society. And people belonging to a *li* or *jia* were still in control of power". This left a large space for the reconstruction of the power system in rural society.

Second, both the police system and autonomy absorbed the characteristics of the traditional system to a considerable extent in the process of implementation. Police organizations, when entering the rural society, had to look carefully to achieve a balance between the exclusion and the use of traditional power organizations, in view of the differences in the situation. Before 1932, "the grassroots organizations still adopted the system of the Qing dynasty".[23] Not long after the New Deal was put into operation, local officials in some areas just dissolved the police group and replaced it with *bao* and *jia*, reappointed officers of the security regiment as committee members of *bao* and *jia*, and leaders of the regiment as leaders of *bao* and *jia*, or integrated police groups with *bao* and *jia*. In Hunan Province, with the exception of 14 counties, including Changsha, "most of the other counties were unorganized".[24] Obviously, local officials in many places seemingly implemented the police system, but in fact it was of the same kind as the *Bao-jia* system.[25] On the whole, it was a mere formality that brought little substantive progress. The traditional *Bao-jia* system still played a role in some parts of Hubei Province until the Northern Expeditionary Army came there in 1926.[26]

Third, there was no change in the traditional mode of life in rural areas, which constituted the basic premise the old system depended on.

> The rural social organizations and structures experienced complex and volatile changes, but the changes at the bottom of society were often not as violent and turbulent as what it seemed, because it was a mere formality with no change in its essence.[27]

As far as the social structure was concerned, "more than half of Chinese villages followed the feudal system and still played a role as an economic organization carrying out systems".[28] The rural social structure still preserved the characteristics of the traditional mode of life because of its stability. These characteristics provided practical conditions for the implementation of the *Bao-jia* system: first, a highly dispersed living pattern increased the possibility that "the state power could organize the public and divided them into a certain number of groups to form an organized regime in a certain way";[29] second, there was a lack of social mobility in rural society, so residents there were familiar with each other, and then a society of acquaintances was formed. In such a society, outsiders were often excluded by local residents, which laid a foundation for the implementation of horizontal surveillance by *Bao-jia* system in the way of "implicating". Only in such a society where people were familiar with each other could local governments control the means to reach the goal of "ruling a household by strengthening controls over one person around it and ruling a village or town by strengthening controls over a household in it".[30] Therefore, when social crises arose, the national government noticed the weakness of modern systems and thus resorted to the traditional *Bao-jia* system, "which turned passive autonomy into active autonomy, and an administration of enslaving and keeping an eye on people into one of protecting and educating people".[31]

However, though elements of the *Bao-jia* system were latent in society and came into play within limits and to some extent, this fact only made it possible for the national government to seek traditional organizational resources, but cannot fully explain why the national government would adopt the *Bao-jia* system again. The reconstruction of the formal system eventually rested with the political demands of state power, but the expansion of demands and

70 *Replacement of the township system*

the necessity of path choice still depended on the relationship between the existing rural system and state power. The transformation and intensification of this relationship was a prominent and typical phenomenon in Hunan and Hubei Provinces.

Since the late Qing dynasty, the reform of rural systems in Hunan and Hubei Provinces had moved along a path to modern local autonomy. During the process, the traditional scholar-gentry became the power-gentry, so that the local gentry grabbed all the power, all of them gave their own orders and none of them were subordinate to the other. The rural power developing from the system of local autonomy not only went beyond reasonable limits set for state power, but also strongly restricted the county power. For example, Sangzhi County was

> divided into eight villages and the head of every village possessed dozens and even hundreds of guns. All of them governed a village in their own way and none of them were subordinate to the other. Moreover, they neglected orders given by local officials. Therefore, some years ago, people in this county jokingly said that heads of eight villages were eight dukes. Just imagine how arrogant and imperious they were![32]

In most counties, the rural political system changed from one of local autonomy into "one of no democracy".[33] The situation of Hubei Province was similar to that of Hunan Province.

> The system of old rural political organizations in various counties of Hubei Province was divided into three levels. An organization at each level was a ruling government in the local place. Everything was under the control of the landlords and the representatives of landlords, namely, local tyrants and the evil gentry.[34]

Originally, the decline of state (central) power and the development of social (local) public power were part of the trend in the evolution of the political system since the late Qing dynasty. However, with the founding of the Republic of China, the sharp decline of state authority caused by the collapse of the Qing dynasty did not stop, and state authority was not fully reconstructed. Instead, due to the construction of the political system of "local autonomy", the public resources and public power in rural society fell into the hands of the despotic gentry. "Public property in rural areas stored grains, and temples, lands and local public lands became the private coffers of local tyrants and the evil gentry".[35]

In the twentieth century, the rural power structure of Hunan Province was so surprisingly similar to that of Hubei Province that villagers during the period of national revolution used the same words to describe rural politics: in Hubei Province, peasants showed hatred for these organs and called them "old government office[s] in feudal China" or "iron threshold". Moreover, they called

Replacement of the township system 71

those individuals working in those organs "Tiger", "Kong Kim", "Taibao" and "Emperor".[36] In Hunan Province, "peasants also described those organs in the same way".[37] As a result, the national government occasionally met with resistance from rural social power like the Bureau of the Civil Corps and defense groups[38] in each county, as it attempted to construct its state authority and make it penetrate into the grassroots society nationwide. "So after all government decrees were delivered to county officials, they became just an idea on the paper and could not be put into operation".[39] The conflicts within rural society were intense and the rural society was in disarray. Whether rural political power in Hunan and Hubei Provinces was a three-level, two-level or four-level structure, "those who had the power took control of rural politics and oppressed the villagers as before".[40] Villagers in Hubei Province felt that

the gentry were so tyrannical, for they often beat others for no reason, distributed others' property at their will. If a widow got married, she needed to give her dowry to the gentry, and if one wanted to sell his property, he needed to give a part of the money to the gentry. Poor justice, and extortion and nonfeasance of local officials provided the gentry with an opportunity of bullying peasants.[41]

Therefore, contradictions in rural areas were becoming more and more acute, and the focus of conflicts was ultimately on the political monopoly of rural regimes. "People showed more fear and hatred for the gentry's power than county governments and all government revenue-collecting organs".[42] The operation of rural political power under the system of "local autonomy" in the previous 20 years revealed the issue of county administration that needed to be addressed at present that "the privileges granted to the gentry and the notable should be revoked, and the gentry meeting should be canceled to prevent local tyrants and the evil gentry from monopolizing rural politics".[43]

The need to expand state power into the grassroots society and eliminate of internal contradictions in rural society, the reality of latent *Bao-jia* organizational resources and other factors explained why the institutional structure of the grassroots society of the national government turned back to the traditional *Bao-jia* system once again. But the *Bao-jia* system of the Republic of China was "revived" in modern times, and how could it match the autonomous political system that had been carried out for more than 30 years, although the authorities found the traditional *Bao-jia* system more effective in performing a control function than the existing autonomous system? Or how could the traditional system and the modern system be integrated? It was both a useful choice for promoting the *Bao-jia* system and an issue the authorities needed to consider and address if they wanted to maintain the modern system. The Kuomintang Central Committee abolished autonomy in the provinces, including Hubei, Henan and Anhui Provinces first, and after implementing the *Bao-jia* system, it put forward the "Proposal of

72 *Replacement of the township system*

Reformulating Laws and Regulations for Organizations in Counties, Districts and Towns and Implementing the *Bao-jia* System in Districts, Villages or Towns" at the second National Internal Affairs Conference in December 1932. After the meeting, many provinces such as Shanxi Province, Fujian Province and Zhejian Province began to carry out the *Bao-jia* system.

The *Bao-jia* system appeared as opposite to the autonomous system, so from the perspective of the people of that time, there were fundamental differences between the two. As Chen Baixin pointed out, the *Bao-jia* system was implemented to keep order in the society, while the implementation of the autonomous system was to make it possible for local people to participate in government and political affairs, and it could be referred to as a transformation of the whole local government system. The implementation of the *Bao-jia* system aimed at assisting the government administration, and though the personnel involved in the *Bao-jia* system were selected by the head of a household or a *jia*, the right to appoint someone fell into the hands of the government, while an autonomous organization was a grassroots one in the whole constitutional system and the personnel involved in autonomy were chosen by the people.

> Generally speaking, implementing the *Bao-jia* system was a negative measure just for coping with an emergency, whereas the autonomous system was a positive measure crucial for generations to come. With regard to this point, they could not be mentioned in the same breath.[44]

Since the late Qing dynasty, replacing the *Bao-jia* system with local autonomy had become the first choice for the state and local governments in establishing political systems. However, the development of history was often inevitable because the results of the choice would meet severe challenges when faced with reality. In 1929, it was recorded in the "Summary of the First Civil Affairs Conference of the Ministry of the Interior of the Republic of China" that

> in the late years of the Qing dynasty, the national government issued the *Constitution on Local Self-Government in Cities, Towns and Villages* in the name of constitutional reform. But the appointed personnel were the local despotic gentry. Since the influence of feudalism was not eliminated, there was no hope of expanding civil rights. Local officials abused their power in the name of implementing autonomy. After the founding of the Republic of China, Shanxi Province was the first province to establish the autonomous system. When examining the regulations issued by various provinces and cities, one will find that except for Tianjin, which defined the establishment of four rights [the right to vote, the right of recall, the right of initiative and the right of referendum], other provinces and cities only defined the right to vote and the right of recall. When it came to local autonomy, it was still under the control of despotic people.[45]

Replacement of the township system 73

The academic analysis of all social problems should finally indicate the value of social utilitarianism. In this regard, there was no absolute opposite and alternative relationship between tradition and modernity. In November 1935, the Kuomintang reached a consensus on the relationship between *bao*, *jia* and autonomous organizations.[46] Soon, the Kuomintang officially decided to "incorporate the *Bao-jia* system into autonomy and divide villages and towns into a *bao* or *jia*".[47] Based on legislative interpretation, the original antagonism was transformed into realistic integration.

First, the national government regarded the defects and malpractices in the operation of local autonomy as requirements for the revival of the *Bao-jia* system. The implementation of local autonomy was originally a trend in social change in the late Qing dynasty and early years of the Republic of China, and also an achievement of the democratic Republican revolution. Later, "after the *Bao-jia* system was abolished, county offices began to build police stations". In view of this point, people believed that "it brought a new atmosphere that local government performed their duties well and put an end to malpractices"[48]. However, a moment of joy brought about by the new atmosphere failed to address constant rural crises, and the problem of rural autonomous power itself was already prominent. Local autonomy, which had been put into operation in rural areas for decades, did not bring new changes to the rural society, and worsening rural situations aroused people's dissatisfaction with the rural autonomous system. By the early 1930s, "local autonomy had been carried out for over 20 years, but there were no outcomes at all".[49] As a result, "most affairs of autonomy were under the control of local tyrants and the evil gentry".[50] Obviously, the rural power controlled by "local tyrants and the evil gentry" could not be simply attributed to local autonomy itself, but the situation was able to serve as a reason for the national government to reconstruct rural political systems.

Second, a practical strategy of "autonomy as the Foundation, the *Bao-jia* system for practical application"[51] was adopted to reconstruct the grassroots power. In order to make good use of the control function of the traditional *Bao-jia* system, and retain the authority of the existing local autonomy, the national government, on the one hand, would continue to execute the planning of rural autonomous regions, designate autonomous regions and identify the level of autonomous organizations in villages, towns and districts. On the other hand, it would further advance autonomy combined with the *Bao-jia* system, just as was recorded: "the *Bao-jia* system was a part of autonomy, and the establishment of *bao* and *jia* laid a foundation for implementing local autonomy".[52] Moreover, it emphasized that "local governments should make use of *bao* and *jia* to promote autonomy and combine affairs of autonomy with the *Bao-jia* system".[53] The adopted measure was aimed at integrating the existing autonomous units like districts, villages and towns with the *Bao-jia* system, and by doing so, the government could unify and administrate these organizations based on the premise of keeping autonomous planning, and thus exercise its power over rural people directly.

74 *Replacement of the township system*

Thirdly, the functions of the *Bao-jia* system in the Republic of China, different from the defense function of the traditional *Bao-jia* system, were various. "The land tax of each county was collected by the leader of *bao* or *jia*". This was absolutely not an expedient, but "it was not easy for the county to set up an independent organization in charge of land tax collection and it needed the help of the administrative organs, or *bao* and *jia*".[54] Therefore, in Hunan Province, organizations like *bao* and *jia* were regarded as ones that urged people to "pay their debts year by year". "County bureaus conveyed messages to each district, and then leaders of each *bao* and *jia* were informed to urge people to pay debts door to door".[55] The so-called implication of the *Bao-jia* system in modern times still lay in state power and status, and was not based on the interests of communities or villagers.

> It was an obligation for people to pay taxes to the state, and leaders of local autonomous organizations like *bao* and *jia* shall bear the responsibility of urging or persuading people to pay taxes. Especially, the responsibility of collecting taxes on slaughter shall be shouldered by the personnel involved in the autonomous system or the *Bao-jia* system; otherwise, the revenue would not be managed properly or increased.[56]

In many villages of Hunan Province, the function of forest protection performed by the association of closing a mountain pass was also included in functions of the *Bao-jia* system.[57]

Hence, a rural power structure model was formed in which autonomy and the *Bao-jia* system merged into one, which established a connection between the traditional system and the modern system. They were uniform not only at the theoretical level but also in practical operation.

Difficulties faced by both traditional and modern systems

"*Bao* and *jia* were democratic organizations, which were different from other civil corps. Unifying people as one to prevent the revival of feudalism depended on the *Bao-jia* system".[58] The traditional *Bao-jia* system in the national revolution was interpreted as the basic system of great importance in modern times in terms of the reconstruction of the rural political system by the national government, while local autonomy, which was once revered, was called a tool for implementing feudalism. This was really a sarcastic historical evolution.

Theoretically, the establishment of *bao* and *jia* might be completed in accordance with the provisions of the national government. Nevertheless, it also met many challenges in its operation. In Hunan Province,

> the *Bao-jia* system should be carried out according to the original time schedule. Household-registration documents should be checked in each county and city, and the establishment of *bao* and *jia* would have been

Replacement of the township system 75

completed by the end of May this year [1935] [...] However, the establishment of *bao* and *jia* and the check on household registration documents required a fund, but if the province was hit by a natural disaster frequently and people suffered a lot from it, it was quite difficult to raise a fund. Furthermore, progress was also impeded by other factors. For example, banditry could not be put to an end, autonomous regions below the county level might change their plan for any reason and leaders of *bao* or *jia* were less educated. Officials in many counties submitted a memorial in which they requested an extension to the deadline, so it can be seen from this that things did not go smoothly as scheduled.

Half a year passed after their request was approved, "but the establishment of a *bao* or *jia* was still not finished in some counties. It was particularly difficult to check household registration documents, and a majority of counties did not finish the task".[59]

According to the data presented by each region, the difficulty of establishing the *Bao-jia* system was first reflected in the conflict between existing regions (including autonomous regions and traditional regions) and regions consisting of *bao* and *jia*. For instance, it was recorded in *Local Chronicles of Liling in Hunan Province in the Republic of China* that the civil corps in Liling were actually similar to a *bao* and *jia*.

The local government adopted the measure of dividing neighboring households into a civil corps. Ten neighboring households were grouped into a *pai*, and there was a leader in each *pai*; several *pai* were grouped into a *jia*, and there was a leader in each *jia*; several *jia* were grouped into a civil corps, and there was a leader in each civil corps. At night, a *jia* would be dispatched to go on patrol, and if there was an emergency, people in a *jia* would be gathered together. A connected door plate would be attached to the door of a house, on which family members' names and occupations would be noted. If someone was ill-behaved in daily life, then no one would wish to connect with him. Consequently, he was unable to get a door plate and would be expelled from the place or imprisoned by local government office.[60]

Some counties like Changsha, Anren and other counties carried out the plan of dividing autonomous regions. "After the implementation of the *Bao-jia* system, the original districts, villages and neighborhoods turned into districts, townships, *bao* and *jia*".[61] However, since the functions performed by the civil corps or autonomous organizations were similar to those of a *bao* and *jia*, and the civil corps and autonomous organizations had merged into the society, it was troublesome to reorganize and readjust the *Bao-jia* system promoted by the government and the original organizations and regional divisions. For example, Liling County merged "the original 15 districts and 165 regions into 5 districts", "turned the old villages and towns into 49 villages

76 Replacement of the township system

and 6 towns" and "completely reorganized organizations below the level of villages and towns". "In Liling County, there was a total of 11,200 *jia*, 1,125 *bao*, 55 villages and towns and 5 autonomous regions. Organizations below the level of county were divided into five levels: district, village and town, *bao*, *jia* and household".[62] In Hengyang County,

> local officials received the order to establish *bao* and *jia*. In view of local conditions, they decided to turn the original neighborhoods into *bao* and *jia* and check household registration documents, but now they had not put this into operation. On the one hand, local officials made requests for extending the deadline, and on the other hand, they urged the leaders of each district, village and town to check household registration documents, so as to make preparations for the establishment of *bao* and *jia*.[63]

The government tried to make the *Bao-jia* system become the basic system of state power for controlling its grassroots society, indicating that it was a compulsory administrative act that strove to fundamentally change the original power structure. Therefore, the penetration of state power into the rural society was bound to encounter resistance from the existing power system of the rural society.

> In the Ningyuan autonomous region, all organs, corporations and district governors gathered together to hold a meeting. At the meeting, a plan was proposed that the original regions would be divided into five districts and one village directly under the districts in terms of three principles of population, taxes and terrains. The gentry from the sixth and seventh districts had different opinions and strongly opposed merging, so the establishment of the *Bao-jia* system was postponed for a long time.[64]

Second, the difficulty lay in the dispute between the local society and the government over the expenditure for establishing the *Bao-jia* system. In Hunan Province, "From 1850 to 1875, local governance system went through changes according to circumstances. In order to prevent theft from happening, local officials divided villages into civil corps, and then divided civil corps into districts when the system of autonomy was carried out".[65] Its rural political system could be divided into levels of townships, *du* (*tu*) and *jia*, or townships, civil corps and villages, or townships, *yu* and *jia*. When local people established the political system, they just followed local customs.[66] Since the right to control rural areas fell into the hands of the local society, the funds for the operation of local organizations would be raised by the local gentry and public organizations themselves. After the implementation of the *Bao-jia* system, not only were the funds under the control of local power, but the taxes were also levied by *bao* and *jia*.

Replacement of the township system   77

If someone owed money to the government, he would be asked to pay back the money when a new round of tax collection started. The bureau of each county would paste up a notice to inform people that they should pay taxes within a time limit. If people did not do as told, their names would be on the list. Then county bureaus conveyed messages to each district, and then leaders of each _bao_ and _jia_ were informed to urge people to pay debts door to door.[67]

With the transfer of economic rights, the promotion of the _Bao-jia_ system would face many obstacles set up by the rural power. In Xiangyin County of Hunan Province, "each party had a dispute over the funds for _bao_ and _jia_, and leaders of some villages and bao were incapable of raising funds and thus showed a negative attitude".[68] In Chen County, Guiyang County and other counties, "the local government decided to collect a tax of 77 cents for each silver ingot" to address the issue of funds for _bao_ and _jia_, but the original "group funds" could not be completely canceled, so it split the difference. "The local government kept the original group funds and also reduced a tax of 80 cents for each silver and took 45 cents of each silver as the funds for establishing the _Bao-jia_ system".[69] Therefore, there were 42 counties in Hunan Province whose budget documents for the regular expenses had been approved.

For those counties whose budget documents had not been approved yet, some of them had such a high budget that the government asked them to readjust it, some had not finished the task of dividing organizations into groups and others were unable to raise a fund.[70]

The resistance to promoting the _Bao-jia_ system came from the local society, so "most of people were unwilling to take up the post as head of a village or town, for they had to bear a heavy burden".[71]

One of the intentions of the national government in setting up the _Bao-jia_ system was to destroy the traditional local social power. "The local government merged townships, abolished the original system of establishing all kinds of civil corps and set up public offices in districts and townships"[72] so as to directly extend state power to local society. But the social power rooted in local communities had not faded because of the expanding power of the government. What is more, local society with a bond of kinship (ties of blood and geography) shielded itself from the impacts of official power, which detracted from the display of the government's administrative function. In Linwu County, while the local government

appointed the leaders of villages or _bao_ living near tree farms as forest rangers and made an inspection tour in those farms in turns every week [...] an association for closing a mountain pass was set up in rural areas of Linwu County and it clarified the responsibilities of each member,

78 *Replacement of the township system*

including planting trees and preventing thieves from cutting trees and animals from treading on grasslands. Peasants in each village voluntarily set up such an association and made strict rules, and they helped each other for many years and had no disputes between them. Until today, this kind of powerful association still exists.[73]

There were about 140 associations of this kind in Anhua County.

There were several associations of this kind in each district of Xinhua County, which were voluntarily set up by owners of mountains in the village. Those owners made regulations and rules for each one to observe, and finally they achieved a good result in protecting forests.[74]

This function entrusted by the government to *bao* and *jia* was resisted by local social organizations. Therefore, the *Bao-jia* system was quite hard to implement in Hunan Province because of the lack of funds.

Moreover, progress was also impeded by other factors. For example, the banditry could not be put to an end, autonomous regions below the county level might change their plan for any reason and leaders of *bao* or *jia* were less educated. So things did not go smoothly as scheduled. [...] It was particularly difficult to check household registration documents, and a majority of counties did not finish the task.[75]

The specific situation of operation of the *Bao-jia* system varied from county to county in Hubei Province, but on the whole, "they reported to the local government that they had finished the task, and according to an investigation, all those counties just slightly revised the old traditional *Bao-jia* system implemented in townships and neighborhoods before".[76] According to the data on the implementation of the Bao-jia system reported by each county, it could be divided into several categories, as shown in Table 2.4.

It can be seen that the *Bao-jia* system, which was viewed as an important political solution to crises by the national government, was implemented only through the establishment of organizations, and "then the results were reported to each county, but the system offered no real use in society".[77] The national government had difficulty in effectively controlling the rural society.

The national government had no confidence in local autonomy and then relied on the traditional *Bao-jia* system to attempt to win its power back. The *Bao-jia* system had dramatically changed from an old system into a new one established for emerging groups and organizations. However, the system was implemented perfunctorily and most organizations were not mature. Thus arises a question: why was the *Bao-jia* system unable to help the national government achieve good results?

In fact, the system on which power depended, whether traditional or modern, provided only one basic form. It substantive content and impacts

Replacement of the township system 79

Table 2.4 Implementation of the *Bao-jia* system in each county of Hubei Province

The Implementation of the Bao-jia *system*	*Scope*
1. The following counties finished the implementation of the system, but some households did not have a door plate, or some door plates were broken.	Zaoyang County, Gucheng County, E'cheng County, Jianli County, Enshi County, Weifeng County, Yidu County, Wufeng County, Huangpi County, Anlu County, Xiaogan County, Yingshan County, Yunmeng County, Yingcheng County, Mianyang County, Jingshan County, Qianshan County
2. The following counties slightly adjusted the old *Bao-jia* system.	Badong County, Xiangyang County
3. The following counties had perfect regulations, but they did not record the unusual mobility of households.	Zhijiang County, Gong'an County, Zaoyang County, Gucheng County, E'cheng County, Jingmen County, Jianli County, Tongcheng County, Wuchang County, Enshi County, Hefeng County, Lichuan County, Weifeng County, Dongfeng County, Yidu County, Wufeng County, Changyang County, Nanzhang County, Yichang County, Yuan'an County, Qichun County, Xishui County, Huangmei County, Guangji County, Huangpi County, Lishan County, Anlu County, Yunmeng County, Yingcheng County, Jingshan County
4. The following counties did not make regulations for the implementation of the system.	Chongyang County, Hanyang, Enshi County, Hefeng County, Wufeng County, Nanzhang County, Yuan'an County, Lishan County, Sui County, Anlu County, Jingshan County
5. In the following counties, leaders of a *bao* or *jia* were illiterate, so the system was difficult to implement.	Zhijiang County, Gucheng County, Xiangyang County, E'cheng County, Tongcheng County, Wuchang County, Hefeng County, Lichuan County, Weifeng County, Dongfeng County, Yidu County, Xingshan County, Zigui County, Changyang County, Nanzhang County, Yichang County, Yuan'an County, Huangmei County, Guangji County, Macheng County, Lishan County, Anlu County, Zhongxiang County, Qianshan County
6. The following counties had a lack of funds for the implementation of the system.	Jianli County, Xianning County, Wuchang County, Badong County, Yuan'an County

Data of Source: *An Overview of County Administration of Hubei Province*

80 *Replacement of the township system*

depended on the recognition of the subject of power and the related stakeholders. The *Bao-jia* system was unlikely to be recognized by people in rural areas, because

> both the system of setting up *bao* and *jia* and the local organizational system were promoted by the government. People always haggled over the regulations and rules of the *Bao-jia* system, but after their regulations and rules were made identical, they could not put them into practice.[78]

In Hengshan County of Hunan Province, for leaders of a *jia* in the grassroots society,

> many people were unwilling to take up the post. Many old people in Yue Village recalled that the leader of a *jia* was appointed in turns. If it was someone's turn to do the job and he did not wish to do it, he might spend money hiring others to do it for him. At the beginning, it was a one-year rotation and then it was a three-month rotation.[79]

The leaders of a *bao* or *jia* who had been included in the quasi-administrative system "held few meetings except those for assigning work and had no work except for urging people to pay taxes".[80] Therefore, though people resisted the implementation of the *Bao-jia* system,

> organizations like a *bao* or *jia* under the control of the government were set up everywhere. [...] Peasants showed no interest in those organizations, because they still thought those organizations were as same as those from a century of rule by warlords. The key reason was that such organizations just gave orders to peasants or asked peasants to obey their orders and had no connection with peasants' life.[81]

More importantly, the operation and function of the traditional *Bao-jia* system depended to a large extent on the recognition and effective support of the local social power like the gentry, and on a proper balance and good interaction between the interests of officials, the gentry and plebs being maintained.[82] As a connection had been established between the autonomous system and the *Bao-jia* system, the scholar-gentry, who originally controlled the power of districts and townships (in the form of election), was transformed into the power-gentry. This meant that "the righteous scholar-gentry would be selected to be appointed as district governors or mayors of a town",[83] so that "the gentry began to abuse their power and became a force of evil based on violence and power, and thus people refused to obey their orders".[84] A part of the local gentry directly entered the state power system through formal administrative channels to make sure local people controlled local power. For example, among county magistrates of all counties in Hunan and Hubei Provinces, more than 70 percent came from the two provinces.[85]

Replacement of the township system 81

"A non-native person was unlikely to be elected as a district governor, and even if he was elected, the job was not easy for him to undertake. So at that time all district governors were local people".[86] A majority of the gentry were "unable to rely on others and the scholar-gentry were incompetent. Righteous people were invited by many parties to take part in dealing with affairs of the county".[87] Lots of the gentry left the rural areas, and "in recent years, most of the outstanding people lived in cities. The righteous scholar-gentry did not want to intervene in county affairs, for those leaders of a *bao* or *jia* were mostly less educated and of low moral quality".[88] By the 1940s, according to statistics from 12 counties in Hubei Province, the illiterate leaders of *bao* accounted for 20 percent to 30 percent.[89] In this way, on the one hand, the traditional balance of power among officials, the gentry and plebs in rural society had been disturbed, so the rural society lacked a center of gravity; on the other hand, most of the leaders of a *jia*, selected by the government, were illiterate, so "the *Bao-jia* system was difficult to implement".[90]

From the *Bao-jia* system to autonomy, and then from autonomy to the *Bao-jia* system, the changes in the rural system showed the operation of China's rural political system in the early twentieth century, and also indicated the rise and fall of Western culture in the process of the construction of the Chinese system. In a sense, it can be said that the transformation and changes in Chinese rural areas over the past half century was a process of introduction to and development of various new forms of economic and political organizations and other forms of mass organizations. However, once all kinds of economic and political organization forms originating from Western society were separated from their cultural matrix where they had come into being and developed, and they were put into the rural society from top to bottom by powerful administrative forces, their political structures and operating systems would undergo amazing changes. A set of concepts and behaviors should be matched with various kinds of organizational forms to make the latter function normally.

> But those organizational forms were introduced into the new regime for the purpose of meeting the government's political and economic needs by gathering peasants scattering across rural areas together. Those peasants, who had no time to learn and adapt themselves to the regulations made for the normal operation of new organizations, had to bring into the newly established organizations the traditional ideas and behaviors hidden behind what Prasenjit Duara called the "cultural network" and what Li Peilin called the "social invisible web".[91]

The government only introduced the organizational form of modern autonomy, and it would still be transformed by the old social authority and power.

Moreover, local autonomy did not mean the local society was governed by local people, and it was an operation system of modern power on the

82 *Replacement of the township system*

premise of the proper division of state power and local social power. The correlation and interaction between the two constituted basic conditions for the normal operation and development of society. At the beginning, when the local autonomy was put into trial use in the late Qing dynasty, attention was paid to the division of state power and local social power. Just as Zhao Erxun mentioned in his memorial, "in all countries, local officials were only responsible for handling affairs in his own jurisdiction. As a result, everything could be handled properly and local governance performed well. The officials appointed by the central government just acted as supervisors".[92] However, in late Qing dynasty, such a regulation for the division of power had not been made such that "the government carried out local autonomy because officials at court were unable to govern all areas, and all those matters within the jurisdiction of officials were not within the scope of autonomy", and therefore there were a lot disputes over this regulation.

It was discovered that whether the gentry or the officials had jurisdiction over local bureaus in each province was not specified at first, so their limits of jurisdictions were determined by their own power. If one side was defeated, it might regard the other side as an enemy and be incompatible as fire and water. There were only bad results and no benefits.[93]

In fact, since the late Qing dynasty,

the construction of state power in modern times had not been completed in China. It did not constitute a strong binding force to regulate the authority at the grassroots level, and the villagers were still in the control of authoritative autonomy to a large extent. Therefore, the reason for the slow development of civil rights was that there were deficiencies in autonomy, but also in the construction of state power, for the latter did not protect the basic conditions for the existence of the former – the exercise of civil rights.[94]

Therefore, local autonomy in modern times was not an institutional change under the normal function of strong state power, and there was surely no proper division between the two. At the same time, the reasonable supervision and checks and balances of state power and social power (authority) were also gone. As a result, a bad result came about in which each side governed people in their own way.

The revival and promotion of the *Bao-jia* system indicated the national government's attempt to weaken arbitrary rural social power. "Since the 1930s, the administrative system of the local government had directly been extended to villages, making villages the most grassroots administrative units. The previous township autonomy meant actually that the local gentry governed local areas in their own way".[95] The national government had issued many regulations and rules for governing townships and villages,[96] but most of these

Replacement of the township system   83

rules and regulations were limited by the central government's authority in their implementation in various regions and local areas. As a result, those rules and regulations were just an idea on paper and not put into operation in an all-around way.[97] In fact, a new type of relationship between the public and public authority had to be based on the establishment of modern citizenship and public institutions. Without this, the modern development and rational operation of the system were out of the question. Therefore,

> although the construction of state power gained momentum by expansion of its own power, its success could not be achieved without relying on the establishment of new administrative relations, administrative principles and rules, and the advancement of development recognized by new political units (the state).

However, the limitations of authoritative autonomy in villages could not promote the transformation of the relationship between citizens and the authority. In this sense, we say that it was necessary for the state power to participate in creating this relationship.[98] Although the strongly expanding state power was able to break up the rural social power that had been forming in Hunan and Hubei Provinces for a long time, the weakened local social power could only perform inefficiently in cooperation with and as part of the checks and balances of the state power. Therefore, though the cost of rural power construction by the national government increased, its effect was far from its goal of institutional design.

It seemed that the government was unlikely to solve complex social problems only through institutional reform. The two results of the changes in the rural system in the early twentieth century might seemingly be different, but the underlying reasons were the same: both the autocracy of the local gentry formed in the implementation of autonomy and the arduous process of forcefully promoting the *Bao-jia* system resulted from the abnormal construction of a power system in modern times. As early as 1939, Fei Xiaotong critically described the local administrative system in the Republic of China in his book titled *The Economy of Jiang Village*, and pointed out that the system was established on the pretext of "planned social change" and that it was essentially an extension of control over communities.[99]

> The establishment of modern local administrative system was indeed a major part of social changes, but it was by no means a social evolution carried out independently by the society and it was closely related to the efforts to establish the modernity of state power.[100]

Its positive momentum originated from the operation or reconstruction of state power or quasi-state power (which did not follow the orders of the central local warlords or provincial governments and so on), while the negative momentum was the expansion of rural society and a response to the erosion of

84 *Replacement of the township system*

external forces. However, since there was no clear division or norms between state power and local social power, the uncertain orientation in institutional change depended on the growth and decline of both sides, and the disorder and turmoil caused by it were doomed to be inevitable.

Apparently, the construction of state power meant not only expanding the control power of the state (cracking down on the power of separatist autonomy), but also, more importantly, regulating changes in the role of the regime itself and administrative rules at all levels through forceful implementation of new rules to make it a real public institution. Only when autonomy (local) and official governance (*bao* and *jia*) were not opposite to each other, and the government and local areas divided power in a reasonable way and cooperated with each other could they move toward modernity through institutional innovation.

The seemingly circumflex historical process of replacing the *Bao-jia* system with autonomy and of promoting autonomy by reviving the *Bao-jia* system deeply reflected the complex and exploratory characteristics in the reconstruction of the modern national state and social structure after the collapse of the traditional imperial court and its social structure. The variability and repetition of the modern rural system resulted from the fact that different power subjects continued to carry out practices to satisfy their own needs under the dual function of Chinese traditional institutional cultural resources and Western modern institutional cultural resources. Meanwhile, it also revealed that, whether for the construction of modern system or traditional system, the essence of constructing a power mechanism lay in the moderate division and normative definition of the interests of power subjects, and not just in simple institutional reform.

Changes in the land relations and social structure of the Jin-Sui Border Area – case analysis about social changes in rural areas in the 1930s and 1940s[101]

In modern times, the economy in Chinese rural areas continued to decline and social crises became even more severe. The land reform movement led by the Communist Party of China is one of the revolutionary movements to realize the transformation of rural areas and then the transformation of Chinese society. The regional characteristics of rural society in China were obvious, and its historical conditions, social environment and social structure were quite different, so the process and characteristics of land reform were not the same. The Jin-Sui Border Area was "the hub of the anti-Japanese base areas in North China, a vital transportation line for soldiers who went to the front and stayed in base areas and one of the five strategically important areas in North China".[102] It was also "a testing ground for the Communist Party of China to mobilize farmers, intellectuals and the local gentry during wars".[103] This chapter attempts to take the reform of land relations in Jin-Sui Border Area as an entry point to conduct a case analysis of rural society, in order to

Replacement of the township system 85

show the real situation of land relations in rural areas and social structure changes, and the efforts and experiments made by the Communist Party of China on the reform and development of rural society in the 1930s and 1940s, and tries to reveal the historical trends and characteristics of social change in China's rural areas (implied in cases).

Social structure in rural areas

It was mainly based on the social and historical conditions and the social structure of the Jin-Sui Border Area that the anti-Japanese democratic regime of the Communist Party of China engaged in rural social reform, adjusted land relations and implemented its own strategies and policies. According to investigations and statistics (of hundreds of administrative villages and nearly a thousand natural villages in 18 counties of the Jin-Sui Border Area in 1941), landlords, accounting for 2.85 percent of the total population, occupied 14.6 percent of total land; rich peasants, accounting for 5.5 percent, occupied 12.5 percent of total land; middle peasants, accounting for 31.6 percent, occupied 45 percent of total land; poor peasants, accounting for 51 percent, only occupied 25.5 percent of total land.[104] In terms of land concentration and class structure differentiation, compared with the statistics of provinces in the South China and Central China areas, about 10 percent of landowners and rich peasants took up more than 70 percent of land, with differences among regions being quite obvious. It can be said that this area was less affected by external social changes. "In the late Qing Dynasty and the early Republic of China, it still maintained the feudal self-sufficient lifestyle, and the residents had little contact with the outside world".[105] "With regard to this, it can said that it still had a feudal landlord economy".[106] Its traditional social economy and structure had the following features:

1. The rural social economy had a strong feudal nature. Although there were no big landlords, the trend of land concentration was also very obvious. According to an investigation of 17 natural villages in four counties, which were Xing County, Hequ County, Baode County and Ningwu County, "Landlords rented 80 percent of their own land, and rich peasants rented one-third", and "there was a tenancy relationship for one third of total land". With the land as a bond, the main social relation structure of the country was shown by the tenancy relationship (between landlords and the tenant farmers), the employment relationship (between rich peasants and farm laborers) and the cooperative relationship (among land-holding peasants themselves). The local land rent rate was as high as 60 percent for flat land and paddy fields, and even for slightly lower mountainous areas, the rate was also between 30 percent and 40 percent on average. "A large part of the peasants' harvest would be handed over to landlords in the form of land rent, so peasants could only maintain a state of semi-hunger".[107] Peasants lived an extremely hard life and "their demand for

86 Replacement of the township system

Table 2.5 The number of peasant households in debt in five villages such as Dongli Village in Dingxiang County in Shanxi Province[183]

Villages	Total Number of Peasant Households	The Number of Peasant Households in Debt	Percentage (percent)
Dongli Village	132	89	66.66
Zhi Village	213	187	87.79
Nanwang Village	187	123	65.77
Shijiagang Village	67	51	76.12
Shenshan Village	143	97	67.83

the high-interest loan was great", so a large number of peasants were in debt. According to an investigation of five villages such as Dongli Village in Dingxiang County, about 70 percent of total households were in debt (See Table 2.5).

Therefore, "peasants had no choice but to yield to more harsh conditions",[108] and their living standard was going from bad to worse.

2. The scale of family farms was not big, and owners of family farms could not manage them well and their technological level for production was low. Reflecting an investigation of 7,142 peasant households in 26 administrative villages of Xing County, the general situation of peasants' farms is shown in Table 2.6.[109]

As far as the number of acres of land was concerned, each household owned a considerable amount of land, but their land productivity was very low. The reasons for this were as follows: first, the land of each household was part wasteland, and the mountain land of Xing County was of poor quality and the yield produced on ten acres of mountain land was even lower than that produced on one acre of flat land; second, with regard to the number of bulls, landowners had an average of 1.5 bulls per household, rich peasants 1.25 bulls, middle peasants 0.86 bull and poor peasants only 1 bull for 4 households. The productivity of family farms was quite low, and "their management mode was out of date. Until today, their farming tools are mainly ploughs, and the plowshare is so small that it can only enter the soil for five or six inches".[110] For most land-holding peasants, "they even did not own a bull to assist them to plow. For example, it could often be seen that four or five peasants used a plough to plough the land".[111]

3. There was a great fluctuation in land price and the ownership of land continued to change. Because of the influence of wars, an opposite flow of land transfer formed. Before wars broke out, the land in the Jin-Sui

Table 2.6 Management scale of rural households

Stratum	Average Land Per Household	Average Land Per Household Rents	Average Land Per Household Rents out	Average Farm Area Per Household
Rich Peasants	213	6.3	48	171.3
Middle Peasants	76.5	28.5	8.1	96.9
Poor Peasants	38.4	15.9	0.54	53.76
Farm Laborers	7.8	3.9	0.45	11.25

Border Area began to fall into some people's hands. "More and more land was transferred from the hands of poor peasants to those of landlords and rich peasants". However, after the outbreak of wars, "the rich ran away and had no time to attend to the accumulated land, so the land price plummeted suddenly". Then the land began to fall into the hands of peasants. According to a sampling survey of villages in four counties, which were Xing County, Lin County, Xin County and Baode County in 1941, of those people who sold their land, 77.9 percent were rich peasants, 14.3 percent were middle peasants and 7.5 percent were poor peasants. Of those people who purchased land, 10 percent were landlords and rich peasants, and 86.3 percent were middle and poor peasants.[112] Land in rural areas began to be owned by a lot of people instead of by certain people, although the transfer process was slightly low. This situation was basically consistent with Zhang Wentian's investigation of rural areas in Shanxi and Shaanxi provinces in Yan'an. To be specific, at that time, in Xing County, "except for landlords and the tenancy relationship they represented, the changes in social economy were shown by specific division of land rights and an increasing number of well-educated land-holding peasants".[113] As a result, the overall situation of rural society in this area was "agriculture was in decline, handicraft workshops went out of business, and the economy in the whole rural areas was in recession".[114]

The democratic government in the Jin-Sui Border Area adjusted the ownership of land and class structure in rural areas in such a specific historical context. Moreover, it needed to finish two major tasks: the first one was to mobilize and gather the masses in order to consolidate and broaden the united front in rural areas; the second one was to adjust rural relations of production, improve the productivity of people from all walks of life and help the masses live a better life. The two tasks were closely related to the basic policy for solving land issues. In terms of the historical process, the basic policy was mainly implemented in two stages: reduction of rent and interest during the War of Resistance against Japan, and land reform during the War of Liberation.

88 *Replacement of the township system*

After the outbreak of the War of Resistance against Japan, the Communist Party of China (CPC) Central Committee published the "Ten Guiding Principles for Resisting against Japan and Saving the Nation", and proposed that the confiscation of landlords' land should be changed into rent and interest reduction, which would be regarded as the basic policy for solving the peasant problem during the War of Resistance against Japan, so as to further consolidate and expand the anti-Japanese national united front. In the autumn of 1938 and in the summer of 1939, under the leadership of the CPC, the Revolutionary League of self-sacrifice for national salvation and a peasant association for anti-Japanese national salvation mobilized the masses to launch a campaign of rent and interest reduction in Shilou, Lingxi (Jiaokou County today), Fangshan County (now in Lvliao Prefecture) of the Jin-Sui Border Area. After the Incident of Jinxi in December 1939, a democratic regime was established in each county. The anti-Japanese democratic government, led by the Communist Party, began to further launch the rent-and-interest-reduction movement on a large scale in the Border Area from the beginning of 1942. After the victory of the War of Resistance against Japan in 1945, 72 percent of the villages in Shanxi's anti-Japanese base areas reduced rent and interest rates, of which 51.12 percent villages thoroughly carried out a rent-and-interest-reduction movement. Seventy-three percent of the villages in the marginal areas launched a campaign to fight for rent and interest reduction.[115] Jin-Sui Anti-Japanese Base areas actively implemented the series of decisions of the CPC Central Committee on rent and interest reduction. On the one hand, it helped peasants reduce rent and interest, weaken feudal exploitation, improved people's living standard and increased their enthusiasm for the anti-Japanese war and production. On the other hand, after the reduction of rent and interest, peasants still needed to pay rent and interest to protect the landlord's ownership of land and property, and also guarantee the relative stability of tenancy rights. On April 20, 1940, the administrative office of the northwest Shanxi issued the "Specific Regulations of Rent and Interest Reduction in the Second Guerrilla Area of Shanxi Province", and it is stipulated in the Specific Regulations of Rent and Interest Reduction in the Second Guerrilla Area of Shanxi Province that the land income of landlords should be reduced by 25% according to the original rent, regardless of renting out land to tenants and farming annually (including co-farming), and all additionality shall be cancelled; rent and profit deduction was strictly prohibited; and interest exploitation and usurious loans were strictly prohibited. In the process of implementation, the Commission reflected that some regulations were not practical. The reason for this was that during the War of Resistance against Japan, the actual output of the mountainous areas in northwest Shanxi fell by about 30 percent, so many peasants paid rent at their own discretion according to their harvest and handed in seven *dou* of grains per *dan*. But in accordance with the regulations of rent reduction, they had to hand in 7.5 *dou* of grains per *dan*, and thus they were unwilling to accept those regulations.[116] As a result, on April 1, 1941, the administrative office of the northwest Shanxi issued the amended "Provisional Regulations of Rent and Interest Reduction in the Second Guerrilla Area of Shanxi Province", and it stipulated that the rent reduction was 25 percent, and the land rent would not exceed 37.5 percent of the total harvest of main products of cultivated land; both the annual and monthly interest of money or grain would not exceed 15 percent, and profit deduction, usurious loans and gambling were prohibited.[117]

Based on results of the movement of rent and interest reduction, on September 20, 1942, the administrative office of the northwest Shanxi issued the "Regulations of Rent Reduction and Tax Collection in the Northwest Shanxi", and it stipulated that the rent for mountainous areas would be reduced by 50 percent on the basis of the original rent before the outbreak of the war; there was no rent reduction in the investment of leasers who engaged in group farming, and the investment would be removed from the total output at first and then the share of the leasers would be reduced by 25 percent based on the original share before the outbreak of the war; for a small number of widowers, widows and the childless who were not part of the labor force and rented a small amount of land to support themselves, and for the landlords living a hard life whose family members were anti-Japanese martyrs or sacrificed themselves in the War of Resistance against Japan, their tenancy relationship should be treated differently and their rent would be slightly reduced or not reduced.[118] The regulations guaranteed the land rights of landlords or peasants, stabilized the tenancy relationship, and increased peasants' enthusiasm for production. On November 6 of the same year, the Northwest Shanxi Provisional Senate amended and passed the "Regulations on Rent reduction and Tax Collection in Northwest Shanxi" and the "Regulations on Interest Reduction in Northwest Shanxi", so the movement for rent and interest reduction was universally carried out. According to statistics in northwest Shanxi Province in 1941, the rent for 20,987 tenants in 17 counties was reduced by 17,716 *dan* of grains in total, with an average rent reduction of more than eight *dou* per household, and 12 of those counties cut interest rates by 8,842 *yuan*.[119] With the development of the situation, a campaign of rent and interest reduction was not only carried out in old base areas but also gradually in the newly developed areas and guerrilla areas.

The policy of adjusting the land relations in rural areas based on rent and interest reduction was carried out on the premise of ensuring peasants' tenancy rights and improving their living standard. Although it did not overturn feudal landlords' ownership of land, it brought about profound social and economic changes:

First, poor peasants lived a better life and their basic living needs were satisfied. According to statistics of 20 administrative villages in Hequ County, the tent had been reduced for a total of 602 leasers, with landlords accounting for 33 percent, rich peasants 30 percent and other peasants 37 percent. The tent had been reduced for a total of 1,535 tenants, with landlords accounting for 2.5 percent and peasants 97.5 percent. Among those peasants, 80 percent

90   *Replacement of the township system*

were poor peasants.[120] The rent and interest reduction in the Jin-Sui Border Area "focused on tenancy relationship between landlords and peasants", and its principle was to "weaken feudal exploitation and improve peasants' living standards". The improvement of peasants' living standard is shown in Table 2.7.

The movement for rent and interest reduction adjusted the tenancy relationship to a certain extent, so that the basic living needs of poor peasants were satisfied and their living standard was improved.

Second, since land relations had been adjusted, land relations and even class structure also changed to a certain extent. Based on an investigation of two villages in Xing County and three villages in Lin County in June 1944, the land changes for each class are shown in Table 2.8.[121]

For the five villages shown in Table 2.11, the change in the proportion of land occupied by various classes before and after the rent reduction and interest movement was that before rent production, landlords possessed 30.3 percent of land, rich peasants possessed 24.8 percent of land, middle peasants possessed 27.5 percent of land, poor peasants possessed 16.3 percent of land and farm laborers possessed 0.85 percent of land; after rent production, landlords possessed 9.0 percent of land, rich peasants possessed 17.5 percent of land, middle peasants possessed 49 percent of land, poor peasants possessed 23.5 percent of land and farm laborers possessed 0.4 percent of land[122] (the year before rent reduction refers to 1940 and the year after rent production refers to 1944). According to an investigation of 13 villages in three counties, which were Lin County, Linan and Lishi, in comparison with the situation of land occupation by various classes in the year 1942 when the movement of rent reduction was first carried out, the change in land procession by various classes was such that the proportion of land occupation by landlords dropped from 23.4 percent to 6.5 percent, the proportion of land occupation by rich peasants dropped from 19.9 percent to 13.5 percent, the proportion of land occupation by middle peasants rose from 35.5 percent to 51.15 percent, the proportion of land occupation by poor peasants rose from 20.9 percent to 26.5 percent, and the amount of land each household possessed increased from 14.7 *mu* to 31.3 *mu*.[123]

In a place where the movement of rent reduction was conducted more thoroughly, the feudal land system had not been in a dominant position, land became more decentralized and middle and poor peasants benefited a lot from this. Surely, in a majority of places, although the situation of land occupation had been improved, it did not overturn the feudal land system. However, due to the change in land relations, clear changes took place in the rural class structure, which was mainly shown by the narrowing gap between the rich and poor in rural areas and the increasing number of middle peasants. According to an investigation of five villages in Xing County and Lin County of the Jin-Sui Border Area, the change in the proportion households of each class accounted for the total number of rural households (before and after rent production): the proportion landlords accounted for dropped from 3.8 percent

Table 2.7 The benefit peasants gained through rent and interest reduction (Unit: *dan*, ten thousand *yuan*, *mu*, *kong*)

Region Project	Withdrawal of Grain Tent	Withdrawal of Paper Money Tent for Peasants	Tent of Land Reduced than before	Redemption of Land	Withdrawal of Cave Dwelling	Peasants who regained land	Others
Xing County	4,841.9	27.728	50 percent	2,890	52	125,366	Reduced prices for other returned items: 12.20 million *yuan*; old contracts: 11,990; account books destroyed: 292. It also included 122,760 *dan* of grains, silver dollars worth 85,313, 888,489 *diao* copper coins, and 1,738.5 taels of silver.
The 6th District, 52 Villages County	8,434	46.7	50 percent	18,680	436	127,930	Returned silver dollars worth 3,500 *yuan*; reduced prices for other returned items: 28.368 million *yuan*; old contracts: 3,389; account books destroyed: 386.
Lin County	100				1,909		Adjusted land: 1,118 *mu*; borrowed grains: 30 *dan*.
The 4th District, Xiaoxiang Village	362.25		50–68 percent			400	165 new and old contracts were signed, guaranteeing tenant rights for 111 peasant households, raising the income of 15 hired peasant households by 25 percent to 30 percent and reducing the number of peasants in debt from 60 percent to 70 percent.

(*continued*)

Table 2.7 Cont.

Region Project	Withdrawal of Grain Tent	Withdrawal of Paper Money Tent for Peasants	Tent of Land Reduced than before	Redemption of Land	Withdrawal of Cave Dwelling	Peasants who regained land	Others
Jiaodong County (a part of Jiaocheng County)	313	1,313		1,040.5 *shang*	67		The government announced that the debts owed before 1921 and rent in arrears before 1941 would be canceled, and that the pledged title deeds for a house or land would be returned. There was rent reduction and debt relief for 2,928 debtors of 1,173 peasant households. Items withdrawn: 17,613 *yuan*, 156 cattle and horses, 38 items of clothing; landlords whose property was confiscated: 329; debtors: 721.
Wenshui County (15 villages, including Yongle Village, Xiaqu Village and other villages)	279.3			3,585	17		120 new and old contracts were signed, the amount of land rented for 3 to 5 years reached over 3,000 *mu*, and the income of 49 tenants would increase, and the grains they got would increase by 97.4 *dan*.

Notes

1. Since each county was unable to provide complete data, we could not compile statistics, but those examples can still reflect the general situation of the district.
2. Data Sources: *Annals of Lvliao Prefecture*, p. 112; *Annals of Lin County*, p. 129; *Annals of Jiaocheng County*, p. 163; *Annals of Xing County*, p. 106; *Annals of Fengyang County*, pp. 139–140.

Table 2.8 Changes in land occupation by various classes in the Jin-Sui Border Area in 1944 (Unit: *mu*)

Land Changes of Each Class	Landlords	Rich Peasants	Middle Peasants	Poor Peasants	Farm Laborers	Others
Sold	5,606	2,310	1,284	642	49	66
Pawned Items Sold	2,583	554	164	90		
Redeemed	415	157	118	98		
Total	8,604	3,012	1,566	830	49	66
Purchased	30	739	1,963	6,535	280	162
Pawned Items			357	2,239	396	32
Redeemed		62	60	578	191	
Total	30	801	2,380	9,352	867	194

to 2.4 percent, the proportion rich peasants accounted for dropped from 10.8 percent to 4.2 percent, and the proportion farm laborers accounted for dropped from 5.2 percent to 2 percent.[124] According to an investigation of 13 villages in three counties, which were Lin County, Linnan and Lishi, in comparison with the proportion households of each class accounted for in the total number of households in the year 1942 when the movement for rent reduction was first carried out, the change in the proportion households of each class accounted for of the total number of rural households: the proportion landlords accounted for dropped from 3.9 percent to 2 percent, the proportion rich peasants accounted for dropped from 6.7 percent to 7.1 percent, the proportion middle peasants accounted for rose from 17.6 percent to 51.2 percent, and the proportion poor peasants accounted for dropped from 61 percent to 40.3 percent.[125]

> The property relations in the Jin-Sui Border Area experienced profound changes, and the general trend was a surge in the proportion of middle peasants (land-holding peasants) accounted for in rural areas and a drop in the number of people of other classes, including landlords, rich peasants and farm laborers.[126]

As far as middle peasants were concerned, "the number of middle peasants increased by 73 percent, and they became the largest group in rural areas".[127]

What is more, the policy of rent reduction was implemented on the premise of consolidating and developing an anti-Japanese national united front, so as to properly take care of rural people of all classes and arouse their enthusiasm for production. "After the victory of the fight for rent reduction, all peasants felt so delighted that they gathered together to discuss matters about production and made up their minds to increase production".[128] Surely, not

94 *Replacement of the township system*

only did poor peasants who achieved success in the movement of rent production have enthusiasm for increasing production, but the rich in rural areas also had confidence in increasing production. "With the thorough implementation of the policy, not only poor peasants but also landlords and rich peasants participated in production activities with great enthusiasm".[129] These developments reached a crescendo after December 1940. Thanks to timely and effective efforts by the Border Area political authority to tamp down on leftist radicalism, and its commitment to the anti-Japanese united front policy, "social order was restored, and people of all social classes could once again devote themselves to economic production". In addition, political power bridged the gap between peasants and landlords, so landlords took part in production work with great enthusiasm". According to an investigation of nine scholar-gentry in the second district of Xing County, those scholar-gentry tilled 342 *shang* of land in 1940 and 779 *shang* of land in 1941. A majority of landlords and rich peasants who had fled, returned to base areas and engaged in production work.[130] In some areas, landlords who rented their land also gradually became rich peasants who hired others to do farm work. Therefore, in comparison with the situation in which a large number of farm laborers were dismissed in the early days of the anti-Japanese war,

> with economic development under the leadership of the new political power, the number of farm laborers began to increase. For instance, the number of farm laborers hired by the year in three districts of Linbei in 1941 increased by 64.8 percent over that in 1940.[131]

In 1942, there was a recovery in the agricultural economy in the Jin-Sui Border Area, which had been in recession before the war, that prompted the development of production activities in base areas and made great progress in the development of industrial production. The once impoverished Jin-Sui Border Area became a place where people were gradually well fed and well clothed.[132] All of these conditions laid a relatively favorable economic and social foundation for the construction of a democratic regime and a military struggle in the anti-Japanese war.

Three types of land reform

The policy of rent and interest reduction was implemented by the CPC in the anti-Japanese war to adjust rural land relations and "completely eliminate the feudal and semi-feudal system of exploitation that had lasted for several thousands of years in China". Tillers would have their own land through the equal distribution of land. "The emancipation of thousands of Chinese peasants" was a fundamental objective of the CPC to start the land revolution.

After the victory in the anti-Japanese war, with the development of the war of liberation and the spreading of the movement for rent and interest

Replacement of the township system 95

production, peasants in each liberated area would directly obtain land from the hands of landlords in the struggle against Japanese spies, of liquidation and of rent and interest reduction, reaching the goal that tillers would have their own land,[133] so land was in great demand. In order to meet the needs of peasants to conduct a mass movement and guide the movement, on May 4, 1946, the Central Committee of the Communist Party of China issued the "Instructions on Issues of Liquidation, Rent Reduction and Land" (also called "May 4th Instructions"), in which it was stipulated that the policy of rent and interest reduction was changed to the policy of confiscating landlords' lands and distributing them to peasants without land or with less land. On May 12, 1946, the suboffice passed on the May 4th Instructions to units above the county level, and on June 19, a one-month meeting was held by key personnel above the county and district levels and in armies. A decision was made at the meeting that while the movement of resistance against Japanese spies and liquidation was promoted in new liberated areas, the movement of rent and interest reduction was transformed into land reform in old liberated areas. After the meeting, the suboffice sent a working group to investigate rural class relations and land occupation, formulated a document on "how to divide the rural class components", and trained a number of cadres in a planned way. Subsequently, a large number of cadres working in government organs and troops were selected by the suboffice to form a land reform group, and then went to rural areas one after another to carry out the pilot work of land reform. The pilot area chosen by the Party Committee of three prefectures of the Jin-Sui suboffice was Sanlian Village in Haojiapo of Lin County, and villages chosen as a pilot area for land reform included Caijiaya Village of Xing County, Ganquan, Guimao, Anye, Zhangjiawan, Baiwen, Nanzhuang, Chengjia Village of Lin County, Eastern xiangwang Village and Western xiangwang Village of Lishi County, Mijiata, Gaojiazhuang Village of Fangshan County, Jinluo and Shangqiao Village of Zhongyang County and Xiepo Village of Lan County.[134] Later, the Jin-Sui suboffice issued the "Summary of Mobilizing the Masses to Address Land Issues" and "Follow-up Instructions" one after another, which provided solutions to questions such as what peasants should get in land reform.

From the beginning of the land reform to the spring of 1947, the main task was to eliminate feudal exploitation, requiring that landlords' land and property be confiscated, and that surplus land and property be handed over by rich peasants. With regard to ideas and thoughts and working methods, some officials dared not mobilize the masses and let land reform working groups and cadres take care of everything. When distributing land and property, some officials showed more concern about solving the problem of a minority of landless peasants, and arranged everything without discussing matters with the masses, resulting in an unequal distribution of land and property. Later, under the repeated guidance and supervision of Liu Shaoqi, secretary of the Working Committee of the CPC Central Committee, the Jin-Sui suboffice corrected the right-wing approach. However, then under

96 *Replacement of the township system*

the specific guidance of Kang Sheng and Chen Boda, the left-wing approach appeared, and the left-wing error was further enlarged. They set the wrong class division standard, raised the proportion of landlords, and unrestrictedly expanded the power of the peasant association so that the party's leadership over the grassroots regime was replaced. After the publication of "A Letter to Peasants" on September 24, 1947, it was proposed that "the peasant association could completely replace the regime", so that the land reform work in Jin-Sui liberated areas seriously deviated from the leadership of the Party, thus causing infringements on the interests of middle peasants, industrialists and businessmen, and even extreme cases appeared in some places, such as the arbitrary use of brutal corporal punishment and random killings.

From December 1947 to February 1948, with the guidance and help of the CPC Central Committee, Mao Zedong and Ye Jianying, the Jin-Sui suboffice consecutively issued six instructions in 1948, which helped quickly correct the left-wing errors. By the end of 1948, the Jin-Sui suboffice had basically completed the land reform of the old and semi-old base areas, and issued land certificates.

Seven counties in the Lvliang Prefecture, involved in the land reform of old base areas, included Xing County, Lin County, Lan County, Fangshan, Lishi, Zhongyang and Shilou. The land reform was conducted in some villages of four counties, which were Fenyang, Wenshui, Jiaocheng and Xiaoyi. According to the "Report on the Completion of the First-Phase Land Reform in Old and Semi-old Base Areas of the Second District in Jinzhong on February 16, 1949", there were 856 villages in old base areas of three counties, which were Fenyang, Jiaocheng and Xiaoyi, 566 of these villages had undergone thorough land reform in the winter of 1947, and the land had been thoroughly adjusted in 236 villages, and not adjusted in 50 villages.[135]

The land reform in old and semi-old base areas consisted of three types: areas where the land reform was thoroughly conducted, areas where the land reform was conducted halfway and areas where the land reform was barely conducted. Different land reform projects had been adopted according to the characteristics of different areas. For the first two categories of areas, they mainly adopted the method of confiscating land and property from landlords, rich peasants (including old and new rich peasants), some middle peasants and cadres who occupied more land and property, so that poor peasants and peasants could increase their land and property. For the third category of areas, the policy of "distributing land equally and completely eliminating feudal land system" was just adopted. According to statistics at the end of 1946 in the Jin-Sui liberated areas, millions of peasants received 3.7 million *mu* of land, and people who received land accounted for one-third of the total population, with an average of 3.9 *mu* per person. Among them, since July 1946, 1.06 million acres of land were transferred to farmers, with an average of nearly two acres per person.[136] The practice of land reform in old and semi-old base areas had provided many maturing experiences and

Replacement of the township system 97

profound lessons and laid a foundation for the successful completion of rural land reform in new base areas.

The land reform in the new area was carried out from December 1948 to March 1950. Four counties in the Lvliang Prefecture, which were Fenyang, Xiaoyi, Jiaocheng and Wenshui, participated in land reform, and carried out the reform according to the "Decisions on Land Reform in the Middle Shanxi" approved by the North China Bureau. In the areas where the land relations had been disturbed by the "Army and Agriculture Union", only the distribution of land would be carried out in accordance with population. In the areas where the "Army and Agriculture Union" had not been implemented, it would be carried out in accordance with the "Outline of the Land Law of China" (hereinafter referred to as "Outline"). The land reform in new base areas was carried out under the guidance of the mature experience of the old base areas, and there were no left-wing or right-wing thoughts, and it went on faster and more smoothly. By the end of 1952, combined with making an exact measurement of land, land certificates had been issued and then the land reform in new base areas was completed. Thus, the land reform in this region was brought to an end.

The institutional object of land reform was the land ownership of landlords in rural society for a long time. The contents of land reform were so profound, the subjects of interest adjustment so extensive, the conflicts of interests between social organizations so intense, and the specific situations so complex that the land reform was unprecedented. Due to the differences in economic, social conditions and historical customs among villages and counties, it was difficult to harmonize the process and the specific operations of land reform. In view of these differences, we selected the documents of land reform conducted in Tianjiahui Village in the fifth district of Lishi County and in the whole fourth district of Lishi County to make an comparative analysis, in order to understand and determine the specific process and practical situation of the rural land relations and social structure changes from different levels.

Tianjiahui Village was a large-scale administrative village in the fifth district of Lishi County in the Jinsui Border Area, including three natural villages, with a total of 1,330 people from 374 households. Before the land reform, the village "went through two liquidation struggles and rent and interest reduction". Although land relations changed, the land transfer was weak, "the feudal land system still existed", and "a disparity in land occupation among all strata had basically not changed".[137] (See Table 2.9)

The landlords and rich peasants, who accounted for 9.8 percent of the whole population of the village, occupied 22.4 percent of the land in the whole village, and the land they occupied was of good quality, so the output of their land was higher, accounting for 27.5 percent of the total output of the village. Therefore, peasants were strongly willing to deprive the rich of their land. The land reform of Tianjiahui Village began on February 11, 1948. Since the land reform of the village started after the correction of the left-wing thoughts by the central government and "immediately after correcting

98 Replacement of the township system

Table 2.9 Land Occupation by people of all strata in Tianjiahui Village before the land reform[184]

Strata	Land (mu)	Per Capita (mu)	Output (dan)	Per Capital Output (dan)
Landlords	428.8	12.61	144.649	4.254
Rich Peasants	891.7	9.29	258.742	2.695
Middle Peasants	3,724.4	6.03	865.881	1.403
Poor Farm Laborers	746.65	1.71	138.573	0.318
Poor Businessmen	118.1	0.8	58.515	0.4

the wrong ingredients", the mature experience made the land reform of the village smoother and more stable. Its basic procedures were: first, the masses should be mobilized, the evaluation and distribution committee should be elected and it should be determined that the work of the committee was under the leadership of the administrative village representative committee, and the method of land distribution should be discussed by the representative meeting and approved by the peasants' congress; second, the land should be measured and its output assessed; third, land should be selected and distributed; fourth, the results of distribution should be revised, supplemented and adjusted. The land reform of Tianjiahui Village ended on March 5, and the focus of the whole work would be on spring ploughing. This violent reform lasted for one month.

Land was not only the basic resource for the life and survival of rural residents, but also a main symbol of villagers' social status or a primary condition for obtaining membership in rural communities. Land reform was related to the vital interests of all social strata in rural areas, and conflicts between interest groups were inevitable. However, since landlords and rich peasants were identified as "revolutionary objects", in the face of deterrence of the strong revolutionary regime and the great mass movement, landlords and rich peasants were only passively obedient to the needs of "history". In the process of land reform in Tianjiahui Village, the main conflicts and entanglements were not (at least not openly) manifested in class antagonism between landlords, rich peasants and poor peasants, but between different groups of village communities.

First, land reform involved interest conflicts and adjustment between villagers and nonnative people and businessmen. "In determining the number of businessmen and poor peasants who should receive land, it aroused a heated discussion". Although businessmen had lived in a village for a long time, most of them were nonnative people and just lived there, so it was difficult for them to integrate into village communities and become a real part of the villagers. Tianjiahui was a small town with a lot of nonnative businessmen and there were about 40 or 50 households. Thus, it was a quite common phenomenon in Tianjiahui that villagers ejected nonnative people from this village.[138] Though

Replacement of the township system 99

working groups talked with villagers several times, poor peasants and farm laborers were adamant that nonnative businessmen should be ejected. "The Council of Agriculture even wrote an introduction letter to 11 nonnative businessmen without authorization to ask them to leave the village". Even for those nonnative businessmen who had been elected as a member of the evaluation and distribution committee, "villagers still wanted to drive [...] away". Therefore, there was antagonism between villagers and working groups for land reform.[139]

Second, land reform involved interest conflicts and adjustment between natural villages. Tianjiahui Villages consisted of three natural villages, which were Tianjiahui, Shanglouqiao and Wangjiata. Owing to the geographical environment with mountains and valleys, there were mountain land, flat land and paddy fields that were scattered, so it was hard to measure land and evaluate the output of the land. In order to finish land measurement as soon as possible and properly, "most of them adopted the method of evaluation", that is, "taking three liters of wheat seed as the standard of one *mu* of land at the time of planting", and carried out an evaluation and calculation. As a result, people in natural villages had quite different opinions on land measurement, and considered that "Tianjiahui did not measure the land in accordance with the right standard, and we should deserve more land". Therefore, Tianjiahui also met some difficulties in carrying out land reform.[140] In order to resolve conflicts between natural villages, the working group of land reform invited representatives of the nearby villages involved in land issues of Tianjiahui to attend the congress of all administrative villages. Because of the working group's mediation, conflicts were finally resolved.

The one-month land revolution had brought about fundamental changes in land occupation in Tianjiahui Village. See Table 2.10.[141]

The amount of land that landlords and rich peasants occupied, greatly dropped from 12.61 *mu* per person to 3.43 *mu* per person and from 9.29 *mu* per person to 4.72 *mu* per person respectively after land reform. Among all strata, middle peasants occupied the most land. Although the amount of land occupied by poor peasants was not as much as that of middle peasants, their land quality was better, and thus the output was obviously higher than that

Table 2.10 Land occupation by people of all strata after land reform in Tianjiahui Village (Unit: *mu, dan*)

Strata	Landlords	Bankrupt Landlords	Rich Peasants	Middle Peasants	Poor Farm Laborers	Businessmen and Poor Peasants
Land Per Capita	3.43	4.52	4.72	5.48	4.88	0.72
Output Per Capita	0.968	1.577	1.142	1.286	1.38	0.33

100 *Replacement of the township system*

of middle peasants, so the pattern of land occupation after land reform could be described as an "inverted pagoda" compared with that before land reform. After the fierce land revolution, the social structure of Tianjiahui Village would help form an inverted new society.

The whole process of land reform in the fourth district of Lishi County, from publicity and mobilization to determination of land rights, lasted for half a year (from early January to mid-July in 1948). There were 14 administrative villages, 118 natural villages, 7,159 households and 28,967 residents in the district, and there were 12,814 *mu* of paddy fields, 12,213 *mu* of dry fields, and 180,834 *mu* of mountain land, all of which added up to 205,861 *mu* of land.[142] The social and historical conditions varied from one village to another in the fourth district. Among those villages, ten administrative villages belonged to semi-old base areas and four administrative villages belonged to old base areas, so rural land occupation and class structure were also different for different types of villages. The land relations in semi-old base areas were rarely adjusted by the democratic regime, and land occupation varied greatly among people of different social strata. "The average amount of land occupied by landlords was eight times more than that of poor peasants, and the average amount of land occupied by rich peasants was eight times more than that of poor peasants". There were also lots of people living in abject poverty.[143] The villages in old base areas had established a democratic regime since 1940. After the struggle of rent and interest reduction and liquidation, land relations had been adjusted. "Therefore, a lot of land and property of landlords and rich peasants were transferred".[144] However, the average amount of land occupied by landlords was still nearly double that of poor peasants and farm laborers, and the amount of land occupied by middle peasants was about the same as that of poor peasants and farm laborers. The overall situation in the region was the following:

1. The feudal forces in old base areas were weakened, and the land of landlords and rich peasants was transferred to middle and poor peasants and the process lasted for a long time, and the land rights were also identified. The transfer of land occupied by landlords and rich peasants in semi-old base areas was limited, the process lasted for a short time and most of the land was adjusted, and peasants had no land rights.
2. Peasants in old base areas obtained land earlier, and many poor peasants were indeed emancipated and were identified as "new middle peasants". Few peasants in semi-old base areas were emancipated and there were no "new middle peasants".
3. There were no landless peasants in old base areas, and about one-tenth of peasants in semi-old base areas had no land or very little land.

Therefore, according to principles of the land reform adopted by the party organization at a higher level, the fourth district carried out different policies

Replacement of the township system 101

of "land extraction and compensation" and "equal distribution of land" for different types of villages in old and semi-old base areas.

After more than half a year of hard work, including review and repeated error correction, the land reform movement in the fourth district ended in mid-July. Although specific plans for the implementation of land reform in each village were different due to different social and historical conditions, the final results were basically the same. That is, based on the premise that people of each class occupied land basically in an equal manner, priority should be given to protecting the interests of poor peasants and farm laborers by depriving the interests of landlords and rich peasants and extracting the interests of middle peasants, so as to achieve the purpose of getting the poor emancipated. In the whole district, the households that land was extracted from accounted for 35.4 percent, the households that gained supplementary land accounted for 56.8 percent, and the households with a fixed amount of land accounted for only 6.3 percent. With regard to

Table 2.11 Land occupation by people of all strata after land reform

Class Status		*The Situation before Land Reform*		*The Situation after Land Reform*		*For Reference*
		Land	*Per Capita*	*Land*	*Per Capita*	
	Landlords and Rich Peasants	10,757	10.5	10,703	6.63	
	Middle Peasants	88,357	8.5	78,337	7.5	
	Poor Peasants and Farm Laborers	36,737	5.2	58,073	8.2	
	Others	1,068	2.6	718.3	1.7	subsidiary business
	Total	142,919	7.34	147,831.3	7.6	
	Landlords and Rich Peasant	5,632	8.5	4,523	6.4	
	Middle Peasants	29,045	5.7	29,157	6.4	
	Poor Peasants and Farm Laborers	12,391	4.7	16,951	6	
	Total	47,068	6.3	50,661	6.3	
For Reference	There was lack of data on the land of Pingtou Village before land reform; there was a difference in the amount of land in semi-old base areas before and after land reform; in some places the land was not measured according to a standard; there was a lack of data about two natural villages.					

102 *Replacement of the township system*

these, the social strata involved in land reform were considerably extensive. Land occupation by people of all strata in the district, after land reform, is shown in Table 2.11.[145]

As shown in the table, land reform had bridged the wide gap of land occupation between each class, and the land occupation of all strata had basically reached a balance. "There were no landless peasants in the whole district, and peasants were likely to get emancipated".[146]

The land reform and social structural changes of Tianjiahui Village and the fourth district of Lishi County were not only meaningful for case analysis, but they also represented the whole social structural changes at different levels in the Jin-Sui Border Area. Social changes in villages, counties and districts might have their own characteristics in terms of specific operation, but the goals and development trends were in conformity to the overall characteristics of social changes in the whole Jin-Sui Border Area.

Land reform was a revolutionary movement of the CPC, which aimed at abolishing feudal landlords' ownership of land and eliminating landlords as a class, and reaching the goal that each peasant had his own land. The rural social changes it led to were also violent and profound:

First, the traditional rural land system of the Jin-Sui Border Area had been completely overturned, and land relations had undergone fundamental changes. After land reform, landlords' land was distributed equally, and the surplus land of rich peasants was expropriated. The peasants who had no land or less land obtained adequate land, and their living needs were basically met. According to statistics, there were about 700,000 to 1.05 million landless peasants in the old and semi-old base areas with a population of about 2.1 million in the northern part of the third division. That is, 33.4 percent to 50 percent of the population had obtained about 2.7 million *mu* of land and their need for land was filled. In land reform, the transferred land accounted for 9.5 percent of the total area.[147] Due to a lack of complete information, the sampling statistics can be taken to show land occupation by people of all strata in old, semi-old and new base areas after land reform, as show in Table 2.12 and 2.13.[148]

In old and semi-old base areas, due to the great and long-term impacts of the democratic regime on the change in land relations, more poor and middle peasants became new middle peasants and new rich peasants. Therefore, the interests of middle peasants and rich peasants had been guaranteed in the process of land reform. In terms of per capita land occupation, middle peasants and rich peasants had obvious advantages. According to the situation of the new base areas shown in Table 2.13, although the amount of land occupied by landlords and rich peasants was higher than that of middle peasants, poor peasants and farm laborers (7.40 *mu* per capita for rich peasants, 6.60 *mu* per capita for landlords, 6.60 *mu* per capita for middle peasants and 6.35 *mu* per capita for poor peasants and farm laborers by order of amount), the land quality of the former was obviously lower than that of the latter (1.23 *dan* for middle peasants, 1.21 *dan* for poor peasants and farm

Table 2.12 Results of sample surveys on land occupation by people of all strata in old and semi-old base areas after land reform

	Land Occupation by People of All Strata in Old Base Areas after Land Reform				Land Occupation by People of All Strata in Semi-old Base Areas after Land Reform			
	Landlords	*Rich Peasants*	*Middle Peasants*	*Poor Peasants and Farm Laborers*	*Landlords*	*Rich Peasants*	*Middle Peasants*	*Poor Peasants and Farm Laborers*
Land (*mu*)	4,436.8	11,837.6	106,755.7	75,174.6	2,013	4,501.4	39,942.9	31,435.7
Per Capita (*mu*)	7.50	12.70	11.50	11.40	2.60	5.20	5.40	4.34
Percentage (percent)	2.21	5.91	53.40	37.50	2.50	5.20	5	40
Output (*dan*)	620.10	1,416.7	15,066.60	10,763	712.60	1,012.8	9,772.8	9,021.50
Per Capita (*dan*)	1.05	1.52	1.62	1.63	0.92	1.16	1.32	1.24
Percentage (percent)	2.20	5	53	38	3.45	4.87	47.20	43.70

Notes

1. This was the statistics of seven counties, ten administrative villages and three natural villages in old base areas. In the table, rich peasants also include new rich peasants, and middle peasants also include new middle peasants.
2. These was statistics of eight administrative villages and three natural villages in semi-old base areas. The statistics of a few villages might not be accurate.

104 *Replacement of the township system*

Table 2.13 Per capita land occupation by people of all strata in six villages of Fencheng County in new base areas before and after land reform[185]

	Before Land Reform					After Land Reform				
	Landlords	Rich Peasants	Middle Peasants	Poor Peasants and Farm Laborers	Total Amount in the Whole Village	Landlords	Rich Peasants	Middle Peasants	Poor Peasants and Farm Laborers	Total Amount in the Whole Village
mu	10.60	10.70	6.87	2.80	6.75	6.60	7.40	6.6	6.35	6.56
Output (*dan*)	3.55	2.37	1.26	0.44	1.23	1.05	1.18	1.23	1.21	1.19
Total Percentage	15.80	7.20	45.60	18.80	100	6.50	4.87	45.60	42.50	100
(percent)	18.50	8.70	4.60	15.70	100	5.50	4.40	45.30	44.60	100

Notes
1. The given data was completely in conformity to the raw materials, and a few data might not be accurate.
2. The amount of land and output in the whole village before land reform included that of communities.

laborers, 1.18 *dan* for rich peasants and 1.05 *dan* for landlords). Therefore, the property and land of landlords and rich peasants were confiscated, the social status of poor peasants and farm laborers was greatly improved, the status of middle peasants was maintained, and the land relations and social structure of the whole rural society had been completely changed. "By 1948, the vast rural areas in Jinsui had taken on a new look". In an area with a population of 2.1 million, "landlords' ownership of land and property was completely abolished, the feudal and semi-feudal land system of exploitation was eliminated, and land issues were truly resolved".[149]

Second, poor peasants gained a dominant position in the rural society, and the rural social-class structure underwent drastic changes.

> The purposes of land reform were to maximize the benefits of poor peasants, to make sure every peasant who had no land and little land could get land, to solve land problems, and meet peasants' need for land to the maximum extent, to liberate peasants from the feudal exploitation of landlords.[150]

Because of land reform, structural changes took place in land occupation at all levels of rural society, and an inverted pagoda-shaped structure formed, which was different from that of the old era. For example, in Lin County,

> when distributing land, the working groups in each village would care more about poor peasants and farm laborers by giving them land of good quality or near their home, and the amount of land distributed to people of all strata also presented an inverted pagoda-shaped structure. That is, the amount of land occupied by each poor peasant and farm laborer was the largest, then followed by middle peasants and rich peasants (The gap in output of land occupied by people of each class was about three *dou*). Landlords and bankrupt landlords had too little land to support themselves.[151]

Though it was later found to be a left-wing mistake, it was a real change in social class relations in rural land reform at that time. Table 2.14 shows the statistics of land allocation in five villages in Jin-Sui old and semi-old base areas, the proportion of land confiscated from each class to the original amount of land and the proportion of people who gained supplementary land to total population of the class.[152]

After the distribution of land, the average amount of land per capita was 1.13 *mu*. The amount of land occupied by each person of all strata was as follows: 0.82 *mu* of land for each landlord, 1.09 *mu* of land for each rich peasant, 1.29 *mu* of land for each middle peasant, 1.17 *mu* of land for each poor peasant and farm laborer, and 0.5 *mu* of land for a person of other strata.[153]

106 *Replacement of the township system*

Table 2.14 The proportion of confiscated land and occupied land in each stratum

Strata	Landlords	Rich Peasants	Middle Peasants	Poor Peasants and Farm Laborers	Others
The proportion of land confiscated from each class to the original amount of land	44 percent	42.5 percent	8.63 percent	2.06 percent	12.3 percent
The proportion of people who gained supplementary land to total population of the class	10.6 percent	6.15 percent	19.2 percent	80 percent	41 percent

Poor peasants and farm laborers were the biggest beneficiaries in the land reform movement. "All peasants were jubilant, and during the Spring Festival, they did the Yangko dance in the streets, with a smile on each one's face".[154] As Li Jingquan said at the peasants' representative meeting in the second district of Xing County,

> Poor peasants and farm laborers used to be looked down upon by others. But for this time, they fought against landlords and set up poor peasant unions, so they dared to speak and give their opinions. Poor peasants and farm laborers were treated with scorn in the old society, but after the new regime was founded, they gained property and land, and had courage to give their own opinions. Some peasants were even appointed as an official or representative to lead the peasant association. This was good.[155]

Poor peasants who got emancipated economically began to occupy the core position of the rural society politically. "Rural poor peasant unions or poor peasant groups played an important role in the movement. In many places, they were even in the vanguard of revolutionary change".[156] There were also fundamental changes in the rural social power structure.

> Even if people of poor peasant unions were not in a majority, they were at the core of leadership. All work in the countryside, especially all issues related to land reform, must be put forward and approved by poor peasant unions first, otherwise they cannot be done.[157]

The structural changes in social rural class and power relations with the "poor peasant class as the core" would have a lasting and far-reaching impact on the direction of rural social development in China.

Class division and influence of leftism

In the rural society, land relations were always the most basic ones among the social structure relations. "All strata in rural areas were not separated from land relations", and "agricultural production was a main factor in determining the living standard of people of all strata".[158] Adjusting and reforming land relations was a social revolutionary movement of great significance to transform the rural society and reconstruct rural class relations, and the problems it faced were extensive and profound. In the historical process of land reform in the Jin-Sui Border Area, of all the issues that were not only related to the overall situation, but also affected the direction of rural social development in China in the future, at least two major issues deserved special attention: the division of rural class status and how to protect the interests of middle peasants.

The first issue concerned the division of rural class status. After receiving the May 4th Instructions in 1946, the Jin-Sui Border Area formulated the document titled "How to Divide the Rural Class Status" in September, which specifically determined three criteria for dividing rural class status: the first criterion was in accordance with exploitative relationship and nature; the second one was in accordance with the amount of wealth and property, the living standard and the degree to which one exploited others or one was exploited; the third one was in accordance with one's background and past records. In view of the complexity, diversity and imbalance of the class structure in rural society, the document pointed out that the three criteria were "not of equal importance" and "the most important one was, of course, the first standard". In view of the mistakes often made in the division of rural class status, the document also gave special examples of the division of "rural class status". In terms of social class or social class structure, there were two major classes (landlords and peasants) and 18 strata (landlords, managing landlords, bankrupt landlords, rich peasants, middle peasants, poor peasants, farm laborers, workers, industrial workers, artisans, apprentices, handicraftsmen, factory owners, merchants, freelancers, poor people, lumpen-proletariat and others).[159] Later practices repeatedly proved that this was a feasible guidance document that conformed to the rural social class structure. However, the basic principles of this document had not been truly implemented, and the land reform movement in the Jin-Sui Border Area quickly went to the extreme of leftism six months after its launch.

On May 7, 1947, the Jin-Sui suboffice held a land reform experience exchange meeting attended by the secretary of the prefectural party committee and directors of local land reform groups in Haojiapo of Lin County. It was

108 *Replacement of the township system*

suggested at the meeting that the land reform in the previous stage was of too much rightism and failed to mobilize the masses, and that there was an idea of supporting rich peasants, so the meeting redefined the division of class status according to standards like family background, family property and political attitudes and ideas, and pointed out that attention should be paid to landlords who were not involved in land management and "whether one was identified as a landlord should be determined by the masses, and working groups should accept the masses' opinions instead of asking the masses to obey their orders". After the meeting, the booklet on how to divide the rural class status was collected and destroyed.[160] According to the ultra-left spirit of the meeting, the division of the rural social class status in each district was seriously out of control, causing great damage to the work at that time and later. According to the data of Caijiayya administrative village cited in Ren Bishi's report titled *Several Problems in Land Reform*, there were 552 households (except Quechaershang administrative village), of which 124 households were identified as landlords and rich peasants, accounting for 22.46 percent. After a new review by the suboffice, the number of landlords and rich peasants (of 579 households including Quechaershang) was reduced to 71, accounting for 12.26 percent of the total number of households (Many landlords and rich peasants lived in Caijiaya).[161] According to the statistics of the first district of Lishi County, of the 2,356 households in the district, 73 households were originally identified as landlords, 55 households were bankrupt landlords and 151 households were rich peasants. After redefining the class status, there were 32 landlords, 10 bankrupt landlords and 91 rich peasants.[162] In Xing County, 21 percent of households were identified as landlords and rich peasants in the first district, 27.6 percent in the second district, and 24.5 percent in the fifth district. Of 58,400 households in Lin County, 9,557 households were identified as landlords and rich peasants, accounting for 16.3 percent of the total number of households; and 4,844 were wrongly identified, accounting for 8.3 percent of the total number of households.[163] The wrong division of class status resulted in a negative consequence in which a large number of people were forced to leave the camp they should belong to, which led to a fuzziness of class status and ideological confusion.

In 1948, the CPC Central Committee promptly discovered the ultra-left behavior in the land reform of the Jin-Sui Border Area, and issued the "Instructions on the Division of Class Status" on January 12. It pointed out that the division of class status should be determined according to the difference in people's relations with the means of production. The relationship of exploitation and being exploited was the only criterion for dividing class status according to whether people owned the means of production or not, how many they possessed, what they possessed and how they used them.[164] According to the instructions, the Jin-Sui suboffice quickly corrected the misclassified class status and returned the misconfiscated property, so that the land reform could be carried out smoothly.

Replacement of the township system   109

The second issue was about a policy of protecting the interests of middle peasants. The Outline stipulated that

> the land and public land of all landlords in villages shall be confiscated by the rural peasant association. These lands, together with other land in villages, shall be distributed uniformly and equally according to the total population of a village, regardless of men, women, the old and children.

In the process of implementing this policy, many areas in the Jin-Sui Border Area failed to correctly carry out the equalitarian policy, that is, confiscating the surplus land to make up for those who had no or little land, not touching the land of middle peasants and keeping a balance between people at both ends, with the result that they paid too much attention to absolutely equal distribution of land and infringed upon the interests of middle peasants.

According to the statistics of three counties in old base areas, including Lin County, a total of 359,478 *mu* of land was confiscated, of which 49 percent of land was confiscated from landlords and rich peasants, 20.8 percent of land was from various public land and 29.6 percent of land was confiscated from middle peasants, among whom 37.5 percent of the land was confiscated from middle peasants in Lin County. In three counties, including Xing County, which focused on the absolutely equal distribution of land, of all confiscated land, the land confiscated from middle peasants accounted for over 45 percent. According to statistics of eight counties, including Fangshan, in semi-old base areas, 957,913 *mu* of land was confiscated, of which 54 percent of land was confiscated from landlords and rich peasants and 36.1 percent of land was confiscated from middle peasants.[165] Some villages in the fourth district of Lishi County adopted a method of equal difference of distribution between each class status. There was a gap of one or two *dou* of land between landlords, rich peasants, middle peasants, poor peasants and farm laborers. Since the land landlords and rich peasants gained so little and what they gained was of such poor quality, they were unable to support themselves and the interests of middle peasants were terribly damaged.[166] The absolutely equal distribution of land resulted in land cut into pieces and caused excessive cost of land management, so many people were dissatisfied with this method of distributing land.[167] Of all confiscated land, 5,481 *mu* of land was confiscated from eight administrative villages, including Xixiangwang, in semi-old base areas, of which 33.2 percent of land was confiscated from landlords and rich peasants, and 61.5 percent of land was confiscated from middle peasants. In eight natural villages like Chongli in old base areas, 1,445 *mu* of land was confiscated, of which 22.4 percent of land was confiscated from landlords and rich peasants, and 70 percent of land was confiscated from middle peasants.[168]

Middle peasants, that is, land-holding peasants, were the main forces in the society of this region, and especially after the movement for rent and interest reduction, many poor peasants and some rich peasants became middle peasants in the adjustment of land relations, which led to middle peasants becoming

110 *Replacement of the township system*

the main body in the rural social structure. Documents of land reform in the fourth district of Lishi County indicated that "Middle peasants belonged to a special class in distributing land", and "a large number of rural people were in the class". "Take the fourth district of Lishi as an example. Middle peasants accounted for 54.2 percent of the total population".[169] Middle peasants not only had overwhelming superiority in terms of elements of social structure, but also played a significant part in many aspects like agricultural production and government administration. The statistics of five administrative villages' output in the fourth district of Lishi are helpful in explaining the impact of middle peasants on production, as shown in Table 2.15.

According to the statistics of the five villages, the production of the middle and middle peasants accounted for 60 percent of the total production of all strata in rural areas, which determined that middle peasants naturally became the main force for providing public grains in base areas. According to the statistical table of providing public grains in 1948, middle peasants provided 56.4 percent of public grains, as shown in Table 2.16.[170]

In addition, middle peasants also provided more than 60.5 percent of supplies for military service and more than 50 percent of supplies for troops.

In the whole Jin-Sui Border Area, the proportion of middle peasants was even higher. Middle peasants accounted for more than 90 percent of the rural population and more than 92 percent of the total number of households.[171] Therefore, the phenomenon of the violation of middle peasants' interests to meet the requirements of poor peasants and farm laborers in the land reform of the Jin-Sui Border Area caused panic and dissatisfaction among middle peasants and also made it quite difficult to maintain an in-depth and smooth development of land reform. This obviously deviated from the direction of abolishing feudal and semi-feudal exploitation and protecting the interests of peasants. What is more, this also triggered a contradiction between poor peasants, farm laborers and middle peasants, weakened the revolutionary force and imperiled the stability of the rural social order.

2.2.4 *Historical lessons learned from the land reform in rural areas*

In fact, both the division of class status and the infringement on the interests of middle peasants resulted from leftism. Leftism always accompanied land reform in old base areas of the Jin-Sui Border Area and caused much damage to land reform in the Border Area. In the Jin-Sui Border Area, in addition to the influence of false leadership at higher levels, there were also some other reasons for leftism.

First, those leaders were not qualified to guide the work of land reform. The implementation of land reform required the guidance of leaders who were quite familiar with land reform, so as to control the direction of and carry out proper policies. Among working group members who were assigned to carry out land reform on the front line, few senior officials had been engaged in land reform before, and, influenced by the idea of achieving good results as soon

Table 2.15 The output of middle peasants in five administrative villages[186]

Administrative Villages	Total Households	Total Population	Total Output	Middle Peasants		The Output of Middle Peasants	
				Households	Population	Output (dan)	percent
Dawu	657	2,447	2,630	212	998	1,440	54.8
Dianping	504	2,071	2,368	288	1,298	1,565	66.2
Baijiashan	567	2,255	2,662	309	1,259	1,840	69
Chongli	499	2,108	2,400	169	769	7,100	45.8
Xiangdang Village	138	501	642	75	327	441	68.7
Total	2,359	9,382	1,072	1,053	4,681	6,389	59.6

Notes
1. The output was the amount of whole grains;
2. Xiangdang Village could represent the documents of an administrative village.

112 *Replacement of the township system*

Table 2.16 Public grains middle peasants provided

Administrative Villages	Total Amount of Required Public Grains	Total Amount of Public Grains Middle Peasants Provided	The Proportion of Public Grains Middle Peasants Provided
Dawu	209	101.4	48.5
Dianping	194	120.5	62.1
Baijiashan	178	113	63.5
Chongli	119	61	51.3
Xiangdang Village	50	27	54
Total	750	422.9	56.4

as possible and being revolutionary, they made some mistakes in conducting land reform.

In February 1947, the central government dispatched Kang Sheng and Chen Boda to the Jin-Sui Border Area to guide the land reform work. Kang Sheng did pilot work in Haojiapo administrative village in the fifth district of Lin County, and in the process he identified industrialists and merchants who were once landlords as hidden landlords, and proposed to investigate an individual's past records and family property. As a result, the implementation of land reform fell into disorder, so that some people were criticized and denounced for no reason and even beaten by others. At a meeting where experiences were shared held in Haojiapo, Kang Sheng, the minister of social affairs of the Central Committee of the CPC, boasted about his experience with "uncovering all the assets of the landlords and rich peasants", and the land reform task force in Mulangang of Xing County, which worked under the direction of the head of the Jin-Sui office, put forward the wrong criteria for class division. This meeting caused land reform to move toward leftism. Later, at the meeting held by Kang Sheng and Chen Boda in Caijiaya, they insisted that the landlord class should be eliminated by completely crushing landlords. The meeting even gave recognition to leftism, and led it to spread and become legalized.

Second, there were omissions in implemented policies represented by the Outline. Compared with the May 4th Instructions, the Outline thoroughly abolished the feudal and semi-feudal land system, but it, as a guidance document for the large-scale land reform, had its own shortcomings. First, the Outline did not specify the standards for dividing class status. Although the CPC had issued the document "How to Analyze the Rural Classes" in 1933 and accumulated some experience in the land revolution, the land reform in 1947 was carried out after the implementation of the land policy of reducing rent and interest rates and the May 4th Instructions a year earlier. The Outline faced different historical conditions and rural social conditions, so it was necessary to specify how to divide rural classes. However, with regard to this point, the Outline did not give clear definitions and explanations. Under the

Replacement of the township system 113

guidance of Kang Sheng and others, the Jin-Sui Border Area divided classes of people, determined class status, and took a person's past records and other aspects as a standard according to their interpretation of leftism, which led to confusion about the division of class status and classes. According to statistics, under the influence of "the experience of post Muganglan" in Xing County, 21 percent of households were identified as landlords and rich peasants in the first district, 27.6 percent in the second district and 24.5 percent in the fifth district. Of 58,400 households in Lin County, 9,557 households were identified as landlords and rich peasants, accounting for 16.3 percent of total households; and 4,844 were misidentified as landlords and rich peasants, accounting for 8.3 percent of total households.[172]

Second, the Outline did not clearly define the interests of middle peasants, and this was another important reason for the occurrence of leftism in implementing policies. The CPC always adhered to the policy of protecting middle peasants' interests, but the Outline did not mention this point. Article 6 of the Outline stipulated the policy of uniformly and equally distributing land according to total rural population, which inevitably infringed upon the interests of middle peasants. For example, in three counties of northwest Shanxi Province, including Lin County, the land confiscated from middle peasants and used to distribute accounted for 30 percent of all land.[173]

Then, "A Letter to Peasants" put forward many ultra-left slogans, which made the land reform go the extreme of "mass movements". "A Letter to Peasants", issued by the interim committee of the peasant association in the Jin-Sui Border Area, proposed that land should be thoroughly and equally distributed, that democracy should be promoted and the masses had the right to examine any organizations and officials, that all matters should be handled according to what the masses wished, and that military and political organs of the Party at all levels should be supervised by peasant associations, which led to a misconception that a one-sided line of poor peasants and farm laborers had replaced the Party's class line. This strongly provocative idea spread quickly and caused many people to be denounced for no reason.[174] The land reform work became seriously separated from the leadership of the Party, and infringed on the interests of middle peasants and industrialists and merchants, and in some places there were also violent crimes such as fighting and killing people without discrimination. According to the statistics of Xing County, on June 22, 1948, 1,151 people were killed as a result of land reform, including 384 landlords, 382 rich peasants, 345 middle peasants and 40 poor peasants and farm laborers.[175]

The land reform in the Jin-Sui Border Area triggered a deep change in the rural social structure. Whether for revolutionaries or those who had been transformed, its lasting and far-reaching influence was far from an adjustment of economic interests and a change in the system. Violent land reform, especially the leftist movement, cast an indelible shadow on peasants' minds in terms of its economic development and social structural orientation. For

114 *Replacement of the township system*

example, "some people were very cautious and afraid that they were essentially different if they became rich peasants [Poor peasants became rich]",[176] and some people even showed more concern about their social status or believed "it was better to be poor than rich". A typical idea spread among peasants that "they should live in a small house, till a small piece of land and feed an old ox". "In the rural economic development after land reform, was it allowed to become outstanding? The so-called outstanding referred to a new type of rich peasant economy, and it was allowable in the stage of the new democratic revolution. [...] This statement was actually a reflection of the thought of agricultural socialism".[177] However, how to dispel peasants' concerns was obviously not just a matter of ideological understanding.

Leftism in land reform was a tendency that appeared repeatedly and lasted for a long time, and even after land reform, it still had a strong impact on rural people of all social strata.

> The influence of leftism in land reform still lingered, regardless of its extent and state of existence. If the problem was not solved, it would be difficult to arouse peasants' enthusiasm for production and the combination of labor, land and capital would be hindered.[178]

Until March 1949, the Party's economic and fiscal policy was still difficult to implement, and one of the reasons for this was that the harm caused by leftism to peasants was difficult to eliminate.

> Peasants showed concern about the Party's policies of living a better life through production and hard work, such as "would the land be distributed later?", "would people be attacked if they became rich through hard work?", "would people be identified as landlords or rich peasants if they rented their land?", "would people be fought against if they employed others to till land?", "was it a usurious loan if people borrowed money?" and so on.[179]

As a result, a social mentality formed that "being poor was honorable and being rich was dangerous".[180]

In fact, these issues were both simple and profound. They were simple because they were directly related to peasants' daily life like their survival and development, and each peasant (including poor peasants, landlords and rich peasants) had to face these issues; they were profound because they were major theoretical and practical issues related to the development of rural areas and peasants in China. Eliminating the exploitative system in rural society through the equal distribution of land created relatively equal living conditions for peasants at the starting point. However, even if the starting point was the same, the complexity of the development process and differences in factors involved in the process also resulted in inequality. The emergence of new rich peasants in the Border Area had fully predicted that the rural social structure would inevitably move toward polarization. This historical development was not unexpected. Therefore, on April 17, 1949, the CPC Central Committee issued the "Instructions on the Division of New and Old Rich Peasants", and pointed out particularly that the Jin-Sui Border Area should be different from the Shaanxi-Gansu-Ningxia Border Area in the standards of dividing the class of new rich peasants because of the former's special historical conditions. It was believed that

> Only after the establishment of the democratic regime, farm laborers, poor peasants and middle peasants who rose up as new rich peasants as a result of the implementation of the policies by the democratic regime were identified as new rich peasants.[181]

The class of new rich peasants belonged to a new class of rural society, which grew up under the condition of equal distribution of land after the land reform implemented by the CPC, and it was a result of the vertical social mobility of workers at all social levels. Therefore, deeper questions it brought about were as follows: when the CPC came into power, could the polarization between the rich and the poor be allowable in rural economic development? Now that farm laborers were regarded as the ones who were exploited by landlords, how was the land management scale to be expanded without farm laborers? Obviously, the party organizations in the Border Area had begun to take these questions into consideration in the summary and review of land reform. They proposed that

> any form of large-scale business should be encouraged and organized, and it should be allowed to develop smoothly if it did not violate laws and policies, and that if peasants had money to hire a few farm laborers, it was a good thing and progressive, and that rich peasants should also be rewarded at exhibitions if they reaped an especially bountiful harvest. Those who turned from poor peasants to middle peasants or from middle peasants to rich peasants should be greatly rewarded for their efforts.[182]

The historical process in the future repeatedly proved the rural social structure would inevitably move toward this direction at a very high cost.

The Jin-Sui Border Area was a typical rural social region in North China. The process of land concentration in this area was relatively slow. The polarization and class conflicts (as well as class consciousness) in rural society were not as sharp and prominent as those in rural areas of South China and Central China. Before the CPC entered the Jin-Sui Border Area, the rural social culture was less influenced by the outside world and it developed in a relatively closed social living environment. In the rural society, which lacked a cultural foundation, especially the momentum of social modernization, it is not difficult to imagine the difficulty of launching the land system revolution, which aimed to overturn the traditional land system for thousands of years.

116 *Replacement of the township system*

The CPC in the Jin-Sui Border Area was faced with not only the problem of how to mobilize peasants to form a social force to completely eliminate the feudal land exploitation system, but also the problem of how to bring it into the correct track and maintain the proper direction of the land revolution once the peasants were mobilized. The more important problems were after the land reform of equal distribution of land, how to face and guide the uneven development of rural social classes, and how to liberate and develop productive forces to the maximum extent within an institutional framework, and only by addressing these problems could peasants live a better life and the rural society move toward modernization. The land reform movement in the Jin-Sui Border Area showed repetitive fluctuations, and even caused some serious consequences, and all of these had something to do with the understanding of this direction by the party organizations in the Jin-Sui Border Area. The understanding of the correct direction of the social revolution could not be obtained in advance, nor could it be obtained through copying an established model; rather, it could only be obtained in the tortuous course of practices (experiments) in social revolutions.

The land reform in the Jin-Sui Border Area was a rural land revolution led by the CPC based on the special situation of China in a specific historical period, and during the revolution the Party had experienced many hardships. However, the land reform changed the rural land relations from feudal landlord ownership to peasant ownership (that is, each peasant had his own land). The completion of land reform reached one of the goals of the rural social revolution, that is, each peasant had his own land. It also improved peasants' productivity, met peasants' basic demands for grains, aroused peasants' enthusiasm for production and participation in political affairs, and facilitated the smooth progression of the Anti-Japanese War and the War of Liberation. What is more, it provided preliminary conditions and useful experience for the socialist transformation in rural areas and the development of a large-scale planned economy, and resulted in profound historical lessons of social philosophical significance.

Notes

1 *China's Bao-jia System*, written by Wen Juntian and published in 1935 by the Shanghai Commercial Press, and *New Edition of Trial of the Bao-jia System in China*, written by Huang Qiang and published in 1936 by the Zhengzhong Publishing House, both discuss the issue of the *Bao-jia* system implemented in the 1930s, but they just give a general description of regulations and rules, or the historical evolution of the system itself, and thus ignore any discussion on the implementation of the *Bao-jia* system under modern political systems and the relationship between them. Some books that appeared in modern times like *Villages in Hebei, Shandong and Henan Provinces in Modern Times*, by Cong Hanxiang (published in 1955 by the China Social Science Publishing House), and *Chinese Rural Systems*, by Zhao Xiuling (published in 1998 by the Social Sciences Academic Press), place emphasis on cross-sectional studies on modern economy and society in rural areas or on vertical development of political systems, and

do not discuss much about the implementation of the *Bao-jia* system in modern times. Zhang Jishun once conducted an in-depth study on the *Bao-jia* system put into place in Shanghai in the 1940s (see his article "Shanghai's *Bao-jia* System during Its Fall", *Historical Research*, 1(1996)), but his study only focused on special measures adopted in the occupied area during the war and the role of urban resources in the *Baoj-jia* system, and its understanding of the nature of Shanghai's *Bao-jia* system (between nation and society) was different from the characteristics of the *Bao-jia* system in rural areas in the 1930s. *A Study on the System of the Bao-jia System in Eastern Hebei and Henan Province in the 1930s and 1940s*, by Zhu Dexin, published in 1996 by the China Social Science Publishing House, mainly discusses the issue that state power delegated its power to the lower levels and also does not further discuss relevant issues about the modern trend of rural system reform and the traditional *Bao-jia* system. The necessity of the integration of modern autonomy and the traditional *Bao-jia* system at both the academic and operational levels, as well as the historical theme implied by the political orientation, is still valuable for further discussion. (Author's note)

2 Zhang Pengyuan, *Early Progress Made in Hunan's Modernization (1860–1916)* (Changsha: Yuelu Press, 1994), 205; Su Yunfeng, *Regional Research on China's Modernization – Hubei Province from 1860 to 1916* (Institute of Modern History, Taiwan Academia Sinica, 1981).

3 Gan Houci, *A Sequel of Official Documents Collected from the Northern Region – Self-government* (vol. 2) (Wenhai Publishing Co., 1997), 15.

4 Gong Fazi. "Warnings to My Fellow Villagers", *Zhejiang Tide*, 2 (February 1903), 23.

5 "Declaration of the Political News Association", *The Revolution of 1911* (vol. 4), 113.

6 Cong Hanxiang, *Villages in Hebei, Shandong and Henan Provinces in Modern Times* (Beijing: China Social Sciences Press, 1995), 57–58.

7 Cong Hanxiang. *Villages in Hebei, Shandong and Henan Provinces in Modern Times*, 57.

8 Wen Juntian. *China's Bao-jia System*, 224.

9 Zhang Pengyuan, *Early Progress Made in Hunan's Modernization (1860–1916)*, 209.

10 "Resolutions on Rural Political Issues", quoted from *Data on Peasant Movement during the First Revolutionary Civil War* (Beijing: People's Publishing House, 1983), 487.

11 *Annals of Gongan County* in the Republic of China, "Introduction".

12 Hu Ciwei, "The 'New County system' during the Period of Reactionary Rule of the Kuomintang", *Selected Collections of Literary and Historical Materials* (vol. 29) (Beijing: Chinese Literature and History Publishing House, 1995), 200.

13 Wen Juntian, *China's Bao-jia System*, 401.

14 Wen Juntian, *China's Bao-jia System*, 403.

15 Statistics Office of Hunan Provincial Government Secretariat, *An Almanac of Hunan Province*, 6th ed., "Politics" (Hunan Provincial Government Secretariat, 1936), 111.

16 Statistics Office of Hunan Provincial Government Secretariat, *An Almanac of Hunan Province*, 6th ed., "Politics", 113.

17 Fan Yang, *Administration of Wars and Military Affairs by the Police*, ed. Political Department of the Military Commission of the National Government, 80; *A General Study of the Documents of the Qing Dynasty* (vol. 19), "Registered Permanent Residence" (1); See 5024.

118 *Replacement of the township system*

18 Yu Jianrong, *Politics of Yuecun Village* (Beijing: The Commercial Press, 2001), 175.

19 Yu Jianrong, *Politics of Yuecun Village*, 176.

20 "Organization System Table of the National Regiment", in Attachment 1 of *Outline of County-Level Organizations and References for Local Autonomy* (printed and distributed by Central Training Mission, publication date unknown), p. 1940.

21 Statistics Office of Hunan Provincial Government Secretariat, *An Almanac of Hunan Province*, 6th ed., "Politics", 113.

22 Han Yanlong, Su Yigong, *Modern Chinese Police History* (vol. 1) (Beijing: Social Sciences Academic Press, 2000), 143.

23 *Annals of Hengshan County* (Yuelu Press, 1994), 1999, quoted from Yu Jianrong, *Politics of Yue Village – The Change of Chinese Rural Political Structure during the Period of Transformation*, 137.

24 Statistics Office of Hunan Provincial Government Secretariat, *An Almanac of Hunan Province*, 6th ed., "Politics", 113.

25 "A Memorial of Improving the Police System of Shanxi Province submitted by Commissioners of Shanxi", *Oriental Magazine*, August 1905,128.

26 Wen Juntian, *China's Bao-jia System*, 403.

27 Cong Hanxiang. *Villages in Hebei, Shandong and Henan Provinces in Modern Times*, 101.

28 "Resolutions of the Fifth National Congress of the Communist Party of China on Issues of Land", in *Henan Peasant Movements during World War I*, ed. Party History Working Committee of the Henan Provincial Party (Committee of the Communist Party of China, 1985), 69.

29 Wen Juntian, *China's Bao-jia System*, 4.

30 Wen Juntian, *China's Bao-jia System*, 14.

31 Huang Qiang, *New Compilation of Bao-jia Experiment in China* (Zhengzhong Press, 1935), 5.

32 Zeng Jiwu, *Note on an Investigation in Various Counties of Hunan Province* (vol. 1), 44.

33 Zeng Jiwu, *Note on an Investigation in Various Counties of Hunan Province* (vol. 1), 36.

34 "Resolutions on Rural Political Issues", quoted from *Data on Peasant Movement during the First Revolutionary Civil War* (Beijing: People's Publishing House), 487.

35 "Resolutions on Issues of Rural Public Property", in *Documents of Peasant Movement during the First Civil Revolutionary War* (Beijing: People's Publishing House), 492.

36 "Resolutions on Rural Political Issues", quoted from *Data on Peasant Movement during the First Revolutionary Civil War* (Beijing: People's Publishing House), 487.

37 "Resolutions on Issues of Rural Autonomy", in *Historical Data of Hunan Province* (vol. 2), 13.

38 "Resolutions on Issues of Rural Autonomy", in *Documents of Peasant Movement during the First Civil Revolutionary War*, 408.

39 Zhang Fukang, *Chinese Local Governments*, p. 95, quoted from Huang Ziyu and Huang Huawen, *General History of Hubei Province* (Volume: The Republic of China) (Hangzhou: Huazhong Normal University Press, 1999), 278.

40 "Resolutions on Issues of Rural Autonomy", in *Documents of Peasant Movement during the First Civil Revolutionary War*, 406.

41 Yan Zhongda, "Rural Areas in Northwest Hubei Province", *Oriental Magazine*, August 1927, p. 44.

Replacement of the township system   119

42 "The Situation of the Peasant Movement in Hunan Province", in *Documents of Peasant Movement during the First Civil Revolutionary War*, 383.

43 "Resolutions on Issues of County Administration", *Republic Daily of Hankou*, March 23, 1927, in *Documents of Peasant Movement during the First Civil Revolutionary War*, 486.

44 Chen Baixin, "Implementation of Local Autonomy", *Local Autonomy*, March 1936, 8.

45 Secretariat of the first Civil Affairs Conference of the Ministry of the Interior, "Summary of the First Civil Affairs Conference of the Ministry of the Interior", in Shen Yunlong, *The Second Series of Modern Chinese History* (vol. 53) (Taipei: Wenhai Publishing House, 1989), 71–72.

46 Central Committee of Local Autonomy, "The Evolution of the System of Local Autonomy in China", *Local Autonomy* (vol. 2), June 1936, 131–136.

47 Hu Ciwei, *History of County System in the Republic of China* (Shanghai: Dadong Press, 1948), 116.

48 *Annals of Ding County*, vol. 8, "Chronicles of Politics and Institutions·New Policy".

49 Liang Shuming, "The Issue of Local Autonomy in China", *Complete Works of Liang Shuming*, vol. 5, 309.

50 Long Fajia, *An Introduction to Rural Education* (Shanghai: The Commercial Press, 1937), 100.

51 Long Fajia, *An Introduction to Rural Education*, 100.

52 Long Fajia, *An Introduction to Rural Education*, 101.

53 Chen Guofu, *Summary of Politics of Jiangsu Province*, in Shen Yunlong, *A Sequel of Modern Chinese History Series*, volume 97 (Taipei: Wenhai Publishing House, 1983), 32.

54 Jiang Shijie, *A Study on the Li-jia System* (Chongqing: Commercial Publishing House, 1944), 69.

55 Statistics Office of Hunan Provincial Government Secretariat, *An Almanac of Hunan Province*, 21st ed., "General Situation of Cities and Counties·Anxiang County", 996.

56 Jiang Shijie, *A Study on the Li-jia System*, 74.

57 Statistics Office of Hunan Provincial Government Secretariat, *An Almanac of Hunan Province*, 21st ed., "General Situation of Cities and Counties·Anhua County", 810–811.

58 Huang Qiang, *New Edition of Trial of the Bao-jia System in China*, 278.

59 Statistics Office of Hunan Provincial Government Secretariat, *An Almanac of Hunan Province*, 6th ed., "Politics", 111.

60 *Local Chronicles of Liling in Hunan Province in the Republic of China*, Chapter 3, "Politics", Chapter 6, "Group Defense", 40.

61 Statistics Office of Hunan Provincial Government Secretariat, *An Almanac of Hunan Province*, 20th ed., "General Situation of Cities and Counties", 704.

62 Statistics Office of Hunan Provincial Government Secretariat, *An Almanac of Hunan Province*, 20th ed., "General Situation of Cities and Counties", 665.

63 Statistics Office of Hunan Provincial Government Secretariat, *An Almanac of Hunan Province*, 20th ed., "General Situation of Cities and Counties", 692.

64 Statistics Office of Hunan Provincial Government Secretariat, *An Almanac of Hunan Province*, 21st ed., "General Situation of Cities and Counties·Ningyuan County", 764.

120 *Replacement of the township system*

65 *Images of Jiahe County in the Republic of China* (vol. 1), 1–2.

66 *Images of Lantu Coutnty* (vol. 9), (Four) "A Table of Villages, *Yu, Du* and *Jia*".

67 Statistics Office of Hunan Provincial Government Secretariat, *An Almanac of Hunan Province*, 6th ed., "Politics", 996.

68 Statistics Office of Hunan Provincial Government Secretariat, *An Almanac of Hunan Province*, 21st ed., "General Situation of Cities and Counties", 648.

69 Statistics Office of Hunan Provincial Government Secretariat, *An Almanac of Hunan Province*, 21st ed., "General Situation of Cities and Counties", 729 and 735.

70 Statistics Office of Hunan Provincial Government Secretariat, *An Almanac of Hunan Province*, 6th ed., "Politics", 114.

71 Statistics Office of Hunan Provincial Government Secretariat, *An Almanac of Hunan Province*, 21st ed., "General Situation of Cities and Counties", 831.

72 Statistics Office of Hunan Provincial Government Secretariat, *An Almanac of Hunan Province*, the 21st edition, "General Situation of Cities and Counties", p. 790.

73 Statistics Office of Hunan Provincial Government Secretariat, *An Almanac of Hunan Province*, the 21st edition, "General Situation of Cities and Counties", p. 794.

74 Statistics Office of Hunan Provincial Government Secretariat, *An Almanac of Hunan Province*, 21st ed., "General Situation of Cities and Counties", 818.

75 Statistics Office of Hunan Provincial Government Secretariat, *An Almanac of Hunan Province*, 6th ed., "Politics", 111.

76 Department of Civil Affairs of Hubei Provincial Government, *An Overview of County Administration of Hubei Province* (vol. 4), Xiangyang County, 1934, 1076.

77 Department of Civil Affairs of Hubei Provincial Government, *An Overview of County Administration of Hubei Province* (vol. 3), Tianmeng County, Hanchuan County, 752 and 777.

78 Huang Qiang, *New Edition of Trial of the Bao-jia System in China*, 212.

79 Yu Jianrong, *Politics of Yue Village – The Change of Chinese Rural Political Structure during the Period of Transformation*, 177–178.

80 *Cases of Leaders of a Bao in Counties, Villages and Towns*, collected in Hubei Archives, File No.: LS3/2879.

81 Long Fajia, *An introduction to Rural Education*, 101.

82 Wang Xianming, "The Historical Change of the Social Status of the Gentry in the Late Qing Dynasty", *Historical Studies*, 1(1996), 28.

83 Statistics Office of Hunan Provincial Government Secretariat, *An Almanac of Hunan Province*, 21st ed., "General Situation of Cities and Counties·Guzhang County", 871.

84 Yu Jianrong, *Politics of Yue Village – The Change of Chinese Rural Political Structure during the Period of Transformation*, 140–141.

85 Editorial Committee of the Annals of the Ministry of the Interior, *Annals of Internal Affairs*, 1934, p. (B) 833; Hunan Provincial Civil Affairs Department, *Statistics of Hunan Provincial Civil Affairs Department in the 29th Year*, 1941, 30; *List of County Governors of Hubei Province* (September 1939), collected in Hubei Archives, File No.: LS2/1/11.

86 *The Situation of All Counties in Hubei in 1940*, Archives of the Department of Civil Affairs of Hubei Province in the Republic of China collected in Hubei Archives, File No.: LS3/1/642.

87 Department of Civil Affairs of Hubei Provincial Government, *An Overview of County Administration of Hubei Province*, Zhijiang County, 1039.

88 Ministry of the Interior, Statistics of *Bao* and *Jia*, printed by the Statistical Department of the Ministry of the Interior, 1938, 8.

89 "Hubei Provincial Government's Examination Form for the Results of Civil Affairs Work in the First Phase of the 32nd Year", Archives of the Department of Civil Affairs of Hubei Province in the Republic of China collected in Hubei Archives, File No.: LS3/1/655.

90 Department of Civil Affairs of Hubei Provincial Government, *An Overview of County Administration of Hubei Province*, Xiangyang County, 1104.

91 Ma Rong, Liu Shiding and Qiu Zeqi, *A Study on the Change of Organizations in Chinese Townships* (Beijing: Huaxia Publishing House, 2002), 334.

92 "A Memorial Submitted by a General from Shengjing Called Zhao Erxun about the Situations of Pilot Local Autonomy Bureau in Mukden", *Historical Documents about Preparation for Implementing Constitutionalism in the Late Qing Dynasty* (vol. 2), edited by the Department of Ming and Qing Archives of the Palace Museum, 717.

93 "A Memorial Submitted by the Constitutional Compilation Chamber of Regulations on Local Autonomy in Cities, Towns and Villages and Regulations on Election for Deliberation and Approval", *Historical Documents about Preparation for Implementing Constitutionalism in the Late Qing Dynasty* (vol. 2), edited by the Department of Ming and Qing Archives of the Palace Museum, 727.

94 Zhang Jing, "Village Autonomy and the Construction of State Political Power – Case Analysis of West Village in North China", in Huang Zongzhi, *A Study on the History of Chinese Villages* (vol. 1) (Beijing: The Commercial Press, 2003), 216.

95 She Xiaoye, *Village Reconstruction* (China Social Science Publishing House, 1997), 9.

96 Wu Chenghu, *Laws and Regulations of the Local Autonomous Village System* (Publishing Department of the Central Village System Research Society, 1929); Lin Wenfu, *A Compilation of Local Autonomous Decrees* (Shuntian Printing Press, 1934); Dong Xiujia, *Issues of Chinese Local Autonomy* (The Commercial Press, 1937); Hao Zhaogong, *History of Chinese County System* (Hongye Publishing House, 1970).

97 Guo Baoping, *An Overview of the Political System in the Republic of China* (Taiyuan: Shanxi People's Publishing House, 1995), "Introduction", 9.

98 Zhang Jing, "Village Autonomy and the Construction of State Political Power – Case Analysis of West Village in North China", in Huang Zongzhi, *A Study on the History of Chinese Villages*, 215.

99 Ma Rong, Liu Shiding and Qiu Zeqi, *A Study on the Change of Organizations in Chinese Townships*, 55.

100 Ma Rong, Liu Shiding and Qiu Zeqi, *A Study on the Change of Organizations in Chinese Townships*, 55.

101 The Jinsui Border region is one of the main base areas created by the Communist Party of China during the War of Resistance against Japan, which was called the Jin-Sui Liberation Area during the War of Liberation. It included the northwest and southwest areas of Shanxi Province, and the Daqingshan Mountain Area of Suiyuan. (Author's note)

102 "Jin-Sui Border Area in Battles (1944)", in Writing Group of Financial and Economic History of Jin-Sui Border Area and Shanxi Archives, *Documents*

122 *Replacement of the township system*

Compilation of the Financial and Economic History in the Jin-Sui Border Area (General ed.) (Taiyuan: Shanxi People's Publishing House, 1986), 16.

103 Feng Chongyi, *Peasants, Intellectuals and Democratic Construction in Jin-Sui Anti-Japanese Base Area*, in Feng Chongyi, Goodman, *Anti-Japanese Base Areas and Social Ecology in North China* (Beijing: Contemporary China Publishing House, 1998), 193.

104 Wei Wen, "Land Issues in Northwest Area of Shanxi Province", in Writing Group of Financial and Economic History of Jin-Sui Border Area and Shanxi Archives, *Documents Compilation of the Financial and Economic History in the Jin-Sui Border Area* (agriculture), 63; Shanxi Historical Annals Research Institute, *General Annals of Shanxi·Annals of Land* (Beijing: Zhonghua Book Company, 1988), 218.

105 Feng Hefa, *Data of Rural Economy in China* (Shanxi Province) (Shanghai: Liming Book Company, 1933), 884.

106 Li Xiangqian, *The Anti-Japanese War and the Rural Social Changes in the Northwest China – A Comment on Zhang Wentian's View of "New Capitalism"*, in Feng Chongyi, (Australia) Goodman, *Anti-Japanese Base Areas and Social Ecology in North China* (Beijing: Contemporary China Publishing House, 1998), 42.

107 "The Economic Situation and the Change of Land Relations in the Early Stage after the Establishment of Jin-Sui Revolutionary Base Area", in Writing Group of Financial and Economic History of Jin-Sui Border Area and Shanxi Archives, *Documents Compilation of the Financial and Economic History in the Jin-Sui Border Area* (agriculture), 84–85.

108 Bi Renyong, "Shanxi Agricultural Economy and its collapse", *Chinese Villages*, 1935, 62.

109 Wei Wen, "Land Issues in Northwest Area of Shanxi Province", in Writing Group of Financial and Economic History of Jin-Sui Border Area and Shanxi Archives, *Documents Compilation of the Financial and Economic History in the Jin-Sui Border Area* (agriculture), 65.

110 Wei Wen, "Land Issues in Northwest Area of Shanxi Province", in Writing Group of Financial and Economic History of Jin-Sui Border Area and Shanxi Archives, *Documents Compilation of the Financial and Economic History in the Jin-Sui Border Area* (agriculture66.

111 "A Survey of Peasants' Life in Three Counties along the Frontier of Northwest Shanxi Province", *New Villages*, May 1935, 35.

112 Wei Wen, "Land Issues in Northwest Area of Shanxi Province", in Writing Group of Financial and Economic History of JIn-Sui Border Area and Shanxi Archives, *Documents Compilation of the Financial and Economic History in the Jin-Sui Border Area* (agriculture), 68–69.

113 Zhang Wentian, *Zhang Wentian's Collection of Investigation Reports in Shanxi and Shaanxi Provinces* (Beijing: History of the Communist Party of China Press, 1994), 95.

114 "The Economic Situation and the Change of Land Relations in the Early Stage after the Establishment of Jin-Sui Revolutionary Base Area", in Writing Group of Financial and Economic History of Jin-Sui Border Area and Shanxi Archives, *Documents Compilation of the Financial and Economic History in the Jin-Sui Border Area* (agriculture), 83.

Replacement of the township system 123

115 Shanxi Historical Annals Research Institute, *General Annals of Shanxi·Annals of Land*, 218.

116 Shanxi Historical Annals Research Institute, *General Annals of Shanxi·Annals of Land*, 214.

117 Jia Weizhen, *Chronicles of Xing County* (Beijing: Encyclopedia of China Publishing House, 1993), 567.

118 Shanxi Historical Annals Research Institute, *General Annals of Shanxi·Annals of Land*, 217.

119 Shanxi Historical Annals Research Institute, *General Annals of Shanxi·Annals of Land*, p. 218.

120 "Rent Reduction and Tax Collection in Hequ County", in Writing Group of Financial and Economic History of Jin-Sui Border Area and Shanxi Archives, *Documents Compilation of the Financial and Economic History in the Jin-Sui Border Area* (agriculture), 45.

121 Shanxi Historical Annals Research Institute, *General Annals of Shanxi·Annals of Land*, 219.

122 Shanxi Historical Annals Research Institute, *General Annals of Shanxi·Annals of Land*, 220.

123 Local Annals Compilation Committee of Lvliang Prefecture, *Local Annals of Lvliang Prefecture* (Shanxi People's Publishing House, 1989), 112.

124 Shanxi Historical Annals Research Institute, *General Annals of Shanxi·Annals of Land*, 220.

125 Local Annals Compilation Committee of Lvliang Prefecture, *Local Annals of Lvliang Prefecture*, 112.

126 Li Weisen, "Peasants in Liberation: Changes in Rural Class Relations in Liberated Areas", *The Masses*, 10, no. 19.

127 This is the result of an investigation of five villages in Xing County and Lin County. See Research Room of the Jin-Sui Suboffice, "Changes in Class Relations and Land Occupation", in Writing Group of Financial and Economic History of Jin-Sui Border Area and Shanxi Archives, *Documents Compilation of the Financial and Economic History in the Jin-Sui Border Area* (agriculture), 107.

128 *A Movement of Rent Production Conducted in Xing County*, December 21, 1943.

129 Lin Feng, "Base Areas of Northwest Shanxi Province in the Backstage Battlefield", *Liberation Daily*, July 8, 1943.

130 "An Investigation of Agricultural Production", in Writing Group of Financial and Economic History of Jin-Sui Border Area and Shanxi Archives, *Documents Compilation of the Financial and Economic History in the Jin-Sui Border Area* (agriculture), 694.

131 Wei Wen, "Land Issues in Northwest Area of Shanxi Province", *Liberation Daily*, April 20, 1942.

132 "Jin-Sui Border Area in Battles (1944)", in Writing Group of Financial and Economic History of Jin-Sui Border Area and Shanxi Archives, *Documents Compilation of the Financial and Economic History in the Jin-Sui Border Area* (General Edition), 25–26.

133 "Instructions of the Central Committee of the Communist Party of China on Issues of Clearing, Rent Reduction and Land", in Writing Group of Financial and Economic History of Jin-Sui Border Area and Shanxi Archives, *Documents*

124 *Replacement of the township system*

      Compilation of the Financial and Economic History in the Jin-Sui Border Area (agriculture), 320.

134 Local Annals Compilation Committee of Lvliang Prefecture, *Local Annals of Lvliang Prefecture*, 113.

135 Peng Ming, *Selected Collections of Modern Chinese History* (vol. 6 supplement), (Beijing: China Renmin University Press, 1993), 439.

136 Shanxi Historical Annals Research Institute, *The History of Shanxi Province of the Communist Party of China* (Beijing: Central Party Literature Press, 1999), 684.

137 "Report on the Distribution of Land and Identification of Land Rights by Tianjiahui in the 5th District of Lishi County", collected in Liulin County Archives, File No.: 1/15/12.

138 "Report on the Distribution of Land and Identification of Land Rights by Tianjiahui in the 5th District of Lishi County", collected in Liulin County Archives, File No.: 1/15/12.

139 "Report on the Distribution of Land and Identification of Land Rights by Tianjiahui in the 5th District of Lishi County", collected in Liulin County Archives, File No.: 1/15/12.

140 "Report on the Distribution of Land and Identification of Land Rights by Tianjiahui in the 5th District of Lishi County", collected in Liulin County Archives, File No.: 1/15/12.

141 "Report on the Distribution of Land and Identification of Land Rights by Tianjiahui in the 5th District of Lishi County", collected in Liulin County Archives, File No.: 1/15/12.

142 "Summary of Land Reform Issues in the 4th District of Lishi County", collected in Liulin County Archives, File No.: 1/9/8.

143 "Summary of Land Reform Issues in the 4th District of Lishi County", collected in Liulin County Archives, File No.: 1/9/8.

144 "Summary of Land Reform Issues in the 4th District of Lishi County", collected in Liulin County Archives, File No.: 1/9/8.

145 "Summary of Land Reform Issues in the 4th District of Lishi County", collected in Liulin County Archives, File No.: 1/9/8.

146 "Summary of Land Reform Issues in the 4th District of Lishi County", collected in Liulin County Archives, File No.: 1/9/8.

147 "Summary of Jin-Sui Suboffice of the CPC Central Committee on Land Reform and Party Work" (January 30, 1949), in Writing Group of Financial and Economic History of Jin-Sui Border Area and Shanxi Archives, *Documents Compilation of the Financial and Economic History in the Jin-Sui Border Area* (agriculture), 495–496.

148 "A Statistical Table on Land Occupation in Some Villages in Old and Semi-old Base Areas of the Jin-Sui Border Area before and after Land Reform", in Writing Group of Financial and Economic History of Jin-Sui Border Area and Shanxi Archives, *Documents Compilation of the Financial and Economic History in the Jin-Sui Border Area* (agriculture), 429–430.

149 *The Jin-Sui Liberated Areas in 1948*, in Writing Group of Financial and Economic History of Jin-Sui Border Area and Shanxi Archives, *Documents Compilation of the Financial and Economic History in the Jin-Sui Border Area* (General ed.), 652.

150 "A Principle of Distributing land in an Average, Fair and Reasonable Way", *Jin-Sui Daily*, April 5, 1947.

Replacement of the township system 125

151 "Several Problems in Distributing Land Recently", *Jin-Sui Daily*, January 24, 1948.
152 Shanxi Historical Annals Research Institute, *The History of Shanxi Province of the Communist Party of China* (Central Party Literature Press, 1999), 698–699.
153 Shanxi Historical Annals Research Institute, *The History of Shanxi Province of the Communist Party of China*, 1999, 698–699.
154 "Some Experiences of Land Reform in Donghu", *Jin-Sui Daily*, February 20, 1947.
155 *Land Reform Communications*, the 9th issue, in Writing Group of Financial and Economic History of Jin-Sui Border Area and Shanxi Archives, *Documents Compilation of the Financial and Economic History in the Jin-Sui Border Area* (agriculture), p. 469.
156 "Summary of Jin-Sui Suboffice of the CPC Central Committee on Land Reform and Party Work", in Writing Group of Financial and Economic History of Jin-Sui Border Area and Shanxi Archives, *Documents Compilation of the Financial and Economic History in the Jin-Sui Border Area* (agriculture), p. 497.
157 "Instructions Given to the Jin-Sui Suboffice by the Central Working Committee on the Establishment of the Leadership of Poor Peasants and Farm Laborers in Land Reform and the Convening of Representative Meetings at All Levels", in Writing Group of Financial and Economic History of Jin-Sui Border Area and Shanxi Archives, *Documents Compilation of the Financial and Economic History in the Jin-Sui Border Area* (agriculture), 382.
158 "Summary of Mass Work in Northwest Shanxi Province", in Writing Group of Financial and Economic History of Jin-Sui Border Area and Shanxi Archives, *Documents Compilation of the Financial and Economic History in the Jin-Sui Border Area* (General ed.), 172.
159 "How to Divide the Rural Class Status?", in Writing Group of Financial and Economic History of Jin-Sui Border Area and Shanxi Archives, *Documents Compilation of the Financial and Economic History in the Jin-Sui Border Area* (agriculture), 329–339.
160 Jia Weizhen, *Chronicles of Xing County* (Beijing: Encyclopedia of China Publishing House, 1993), 571.
161 Peng Ming, *Selected Collections of Modern Chinese History* (vol. 6 supplement), p. 437.
162 "Summary of the Issues of Class Status Division and Party Work in the First District of Lishi County Committee of the Communist Party of China", collected in Liulin County Archives, File No.: 1/9/12.
163 Shanxi Historical Annals Research Institute, *General Annals of Shanxi·Annals of Land*, 234.
164 Peng Ming, *Selected Collections of Modern Chinese History* (vol. 6 supplement), 432–434.
165 Shanxi Historical Annals Research Institute, *General Annals of Shanxi·Annals of Land*, 223.
166 "Summary of Land Reform Issues", collected in Liulin County Archives, File No.: 1/9/14, p. 11.
167 "Summary of Land Reform Issues", collected in Liulin County Archives, File No.: 1/9/14, p. 17.
168 "Summary of Land Reform Issues", collected in Liulin County Archives, File No.: 1/9/14, p. 34.

126 *Replacement of the township system*

169 "Summary of Land Reform Issues in the 4th District of Lishi County", collected in Liulin County Archives, File No.: 1/9/12, p. 21.

170 "Summary of Land Reform Issues in the 4th District of Lishi County", collected in Liulin County Archives, File No.: 1/9/12, p. 21.

171 "Summary of Jin-Sui Suboffice of the CPC Central Committee on Land Reform and Party Work", in Writing Group of Financial and Economic History of Jin-Sui Border Area and Shanxi Archives, *Documents Compilation of the Financial and Economic History in the Jin-Sui Border Area* (agriculture), 503.

172 Shanxi Historical Annals Research Institute, *General Annals of Shanxi·Annals of Land*, 113.

173 Shanxi Historical Annals Research Institute, *General Annals of Shanxi·Annals of Land*, 113.

174 Jia Weizhen, *Chronicles of Xing County*, 573.

175 Shanxi Historical Annals Research Institute, *General Annals of Shanxi·Annals of Land*, 235.

176 "Meeting Summary of Production in the Jin-Sui Border Area", in Writing Group of Financial and Economic History of Jin-Sui Border Area and Shanxi Archives, *Documents Compilation of the Financial and Economic History in the Jin-Sui Border Area* (General ed.), 723.

177 "Meeting Summary of Production in the Jin-Sui Border Area", in Writing Group of Financial and Economic History of Jin-Sui Border Area and Shanxi Archives, *Documents Compilation of the Financial and Economic History in the Jin-Sui Border Area* (General ed.), 723.

178 "Meeting Summary of Production in the Jin-Sui Border Area", in Writing Group of Financial and Economic History of Jin-Sui Border Area and Shanxi Archives, *Documents Compilation of the Financial and Economic History in the Jin-Sui Border Area* (General ed.), 826.

179 "Review of Financial Work in 1948 and the Tasks and Principles of Financial Work in 1949", "Meeting Summary of Production in the Jin-Sui Border Area", in Writing Group of Financial and Economic History of Jin-Sui Border Area and Shanxi Archives, *Documents Compilation of the Financial and Economic History in the Jin-Sui Border Area* (General ed.), 815.

180 Shanxi Historical Annals Research Institute, *General Annals of Shanxi·War of Liberation*, 392.

181 "Instructions on the Division of New and Old Rich Peasants", in Writing Group of Financial and Economic History of Jin-Sui Border Area and Shanxi Archives, *Documents Compilation of the Financial and Economic History in the Jin-Sui Border Area* (agriculture), 404.

182 "Meeting Summary of Production in the Jin-Sui Border Area", in Writing Group of Financial and Economic History of Jin-Sui Border Area and Shanxi Archives, *Documents Compilation of the Financial and Economic History in the Jin-Sui Border Area* (General ed.), 723.

183 Bi Renyong, "Shanxi Agricultural Economy and Its Collapse", *Chinese Villages*, 1, no. 7(1935): 63.

184 "Report on the Distribution of Land and Identification of Land Rights by Tianjiahui in the 5th District of Lishi County", collected in Liulin County Archives, File No.: 1/15/12.

185 Writing Group of Financial and Economic History of Jin-Sui Border Area and Shanxi Archives, *Documents Compilation of the Financial and Economic History*

in the Jin-Sui Border Area (agriculture), 431. *The Jin-Sui Liberated Areas in 1948*, in Writing Group of Financial and Economic History of Jin-Sui Border Area and Shanxi Archives, *Documents Compilation of the Financial and Economic History in the Jin-Sui Border Area* (General ed.), 652.

186 "Summary of Land Reform Issues in the 4th District of Lishi County", collected in Liulin County Archives, File No.: 1/9/12, p. 21.

3 Rural social changes in the process of modernization

Since the twentieth century, the process of China's modernization has gone beyond one-way development and begun to expand in such fields as politics, economy, culture and society. However, industrialization and urbanization were the main trends of modernization, thus leading to rural social changes different from those in traditional times. The geographical and regional features were quite different, and the breadth, depth and degree of those changes also greatly varied. This chapter only focuses on the impact of certain modern elements on rural social changes to reflect the whole situation.

The development of urbanization and modernization in modern China

Urbanization appeared as a product of the modern industrial revolution. It referred to the process of people in a society moving to cities or towns, and the historical process had different historical characteristics in different historical stages. China is a large country with an ancient urban civilization, but ancient Chinese cities and towns were mainly established as administrative centers or for military defense, and there was a lack of cities with thriving industry and commerce. "It was not until five spots opened to the outside world in the middle 1800s that urbanization entered a new phase in its development. Major commercial ports along coasts opened successively, and modern industry gradually thrive". China's urbanization heralded the beginning of a new chapter.[1] In the process of China's modernization and urbanization, the Westernization Movement also played an important part.

Since the 1860s, the Westernization Movement had been launched. The westernizationists in the Qing government established a group of military industries and civil enterprises, which gave rise to capitalist productive forces in China. However, those new productive forces mainly arose in cities and thus some Chinese cities took a step towards modernization.[2]

The inchoation of urbanization and modernization in China

One of the structural changes in modern Chinese history was the initial launch of urbanization, which was featured by the birth and growth of cities that thrived with the development of industry and commerce, the construction of roads and the opening of ports. In those cities, industrialization gradually took the place of agricultural civilization and then those cities became semicolonial and semifeudal ones with a certain degree of modernization. The Westernization Movement played an active part in promoting the urbanization and modernization of cities. For example, the building of industrial and mining districts, the revitalizing of commerce and trade, and the building of railways and private schools all had a direct impact on the initial launch of urbanization like expanding ancient cities and towns and transforming some villages into cities. As a result, a part of the rural people were attracted to work and earn their living in cities, accelerating the speed of population agglomeration in urban areas.

After the Westernization Movement came about, cities in modern China began to step into a new developing stage. As far as the development of modern urbanization was concerned, it basically followed two main paths: one was modernizing cities and the other was urbanizing rural areas. From the 1860s to 1894, before the Sino-Japanese War, 21 military enterprises and 40 civil enterprises were set up. After the war, the westernizationists also established some industries. In Wuhan, 20 enterprises were set up by the government or merchants but supervised by the government, most of which were established after the war. From the point of view of the development characteristics and pattern of modern cities, the modernization of cities or modern urbanization was often accompanied by the process of industrialization. Urban industry began to come into being and developed rapidly, which became the main symbol of urban modernization. From 1840 to 1894, Western countries set up 103 industrial enterprises in China, and those enterprises were mainly located in port cities like Shanghai, Tianjin, Hankou, Guangzhou, Xiamen[3] and so forth. In the 1860s when the westernizationists began to implement the New Deal, Chinese began to set up enterprises. Both government-operated enterprises and civil enterprises were mainly located in port cities like Shanghai, Guangzhou, Wuhan, Hangzhou, Wuxi, Tianjin and so forth.[4] The westernizationists also presided over or took charge of the construction of Tangshan-Xugezhuang Railway, Jinghan Railway, Jingu Railway, Keelung-Taipei Railway and the Daye-Yangtze River and explored coastal lines along the Yangtze River. In Tianjin, the Telegraph Office was set up, and telegraphic lines in many provinces were established. Before 1894, a national telecommunications network was formed, which had a bearing on the formation of urban networks in modern China. Of the 207 cities in modern China, more than one-fourth benefited directly from the Westernization Movement, and the latter had an indirect impact on all cities. Newly emerging cities in modern China could be classified into the following types:

130 *Rural social changes*

The first type was port cities. Since five ports were opened to the outside world, 34 trading ports had been opened nationwide before the outbreak of the Sino-Japanese War. In general, those ports were opened passively, but some were opened voluntarily like Wuchang. Port cities such as Shanghai, Tianjin, Guangzhou, Hankou and Qingdao all developed with foreign trade as the forerunner. This could be regarded as a new path for the development of modern Chinese cities. Shanghai's foreign trade, from 1864 to 1910, accounted for about half of the value of the country's foreign trade, with the highest proportion up to 65.64 percent. The rise and growth of port cities were closely related to the increase in foreign trade volume and the import of mechanized vehicles. "The level foreign trade reached in late imperial China was unprecedented (though it was impossible in the Middle Ages), and mechanized vehicles were, of course, playing a new role in it".[5] As a result, in half a century, a group of modern cities began to rise.

New port cities like Hong Kong and Shantou are rising, but Shanghai and Tianjin attract the most attention. The urban system in the lower reaches of the Yangtze River has been rebuilt, and significant changes have also taken place in the other three coastal areas.[6]

The second type was industrial cities. There were three sorts of factories across China: foreign-funded factories, government-operated factories or factories jointly operated by the government and merchants, and national capitalist factories. Although the number of factories sponsored by the westernizationists was not large, those factories had a large scale and a lot of imported equipment and capital, so that they greatly promoted the construction of the infrastructure and economic development of cities where they were located. Those cities had gone through a transformation from an agricultural civilization of feudal towns to a modern industrial civilization. Later, a lot of site areas, service industries, work sheds and related transportation and telecommunications facilities emerged. Factories run by the westernizationists were mainly located in Shanghai, Tianjin, Wuhan, Nanjing, Fuzhou, Xi'an, Guangzhou, Jinan, Changsha, Chengdu, Jilin, Beijing, Hangzhou, Kunming, Taiyuan and Taipei, and they promoted the development of those cities. Key cities where the Westernization Movement mainly took place in particular, like Shanghai, Tianjin, Wuhan and so on, all became important industrial bases in old China. The early industrialized movement in Tianjin in modern times was also triggered by the Westernizationist Movement and it started with the military industry. In 1866, the Qing government decided to set up bureaus in Tianjin. The Tianjin Machinery Bureau was set up four years later, and large-scale modern military industrial enterprises had gradually been established. Modernization soon brought about chain effects, and driven by modern enterprises' demands, corresponding modern means of communication like telegrams, telephone and railways began to be put into use. Until

Rural social changes 131

1892, Tianjin was reputed to be one of the largest information centers in the Far East.

China invented electric wires ten years before and recently it has been widely used thanks to a relatively liberal climate. It can reach Jilin and the boundary between Heilongjiang and Russia northeastward; it can reach Gansu and Xinjiang northwestward; it can reach Fujian, Guangdong and Taiwan southeastward; and it can reach Guangxi and Yunnan southwestward. It covers over 22 provinces and even Korea, and though people are far apart, they still can keep in contact with each other. It is so convenient,

said Li Hongzhang proudly, a Chinese general and statesman of the late Qing Empire.[7] Obviously, industrialization was closely related to the process of urbanization, which, to a certain extent, revealed the different characteristics of traditional urban development and modern urbanization. "It was negligible that large-scale modern industry had stimulated the growth of cities in Tianjin. The establishment of the Tianjin Machinery Bureau helped create a new city among all the traditional cities in Tianjin".[8] At least in the late nineteenth century, with the driving force of industrialization, the development of Tianjin had come out of the traditional track. Finally, Tianjin became an important industrial city in the north that was in the process of restructuring and integrating the military industry and a number of light industries.

The third type was mining and metallurgy cities. The westernizationists also mined iron, coals, copper and gold. According to incomplete statistics, there were six government-operated coal mines, nine government-supervised and merchant-managed coal mines, three government-operated metal mines, and 18 government-supervised and merchant-managed metal mines. Mining and smelting led to the emergence of a number of mining and metallurgy cities. Wilderness areas became downtown areas and settlements. Tangshan, Anyuan and Jiaozuo grew prosperous due to coal mining; Lengshuitan in Hunan Province became thriving due to stannaries; and Yumen in Gansu Province developed well due to oil. Anyuan was originally sparsely populated in the western Jiangxi. Due to mining coal, tens of thousands of miners and merchants were assembled and a number of long streets are formed. At that time, Anyuan was called "Small Nanjing". Li Hongzhang approved the building of the Tangshan Coal Mine in 1878 and it was constructed in 1881. The Tangshan Coal Mine was the first modern mine to put machines into use in China. After that, Tangshan turned from a countryside into an industrial city.

The fourth type was cities with ports and docks. Among these, there were riverside and coastal ports and docks along rivers or along railways. Someone analyzed 207 cities in old China, and 176 of them were located on land and water communication lines, especially close to railways, rivers and seas. Not only was the development of Shanghai, Beijing, Tianjin, Wuhan and other

132 *Rural social changes*

cities closely related to docks along rivers or railways, but some cities like Shijiazhuang, near the Jinghan Railway, Hengyang, near the Yuehan Railway, and Pukou and Bengbu, near the Jinpu Railway, were also thriving thanks to railways. Bengbu was also located at the junction of railways and the Huaihe River, so it was beneficial to expanding business and trade and people also gathered there. In 1914, the number of people living there increased to 100,000, and in 1926, it reached 260,000.

The rise of modern cities and changes in their geographical conditions and functions fundamentally changed the relationship between rural and urban structures in traditional society. Since the middle of the Ming dynasty, many ever prosperous cities along the canal in the Ming dynasty (1368–1644) no longer developed along a normal track and gradually tended to decline, and some of them even became a remote county. As for the immediate cause of this, the following two reasons must be mentioned: "one was social turmoil, and the other one was changes in economic and geographical conditions".[9] However, the process of industrialization initiated by the opening of ports for trade and the New Deal proposed by the westernizationists was the result of the times.

Due to the historical joint force formed by the Westernization Movement and other factors, the development of urbanization in modern China had gotten rid of the stagnant and closed state of traditional cities, and the process of building modern cities had been initiated. Hard as it was, a modern urban system had been basically established in the late Qing dynasty, including an urban network with Shanghai and Beijing as the center and each region with an urban network: an urban system in North China with Tianjin as the center; an urban system in Central China with Wuhan as the center; an urban system in South China with Guangzhou as the center; an urban system in Southwestern China with Chongqing as the center; an urban system in Northeast China with Shenyang as the center; and an urban system in Northwest China with Lanzhou as the center. This had a lasting and far-reaching impact on the changes in the social structure of modern China.

Rapid development of industrialization and urbanization

Generally speaking, so-called industrialization referred to modern industrialization. It meant vigorously developing modern industry to ensure that it could occupy a dominant position in the national economy.[10] China's modern industry started with the military industry set up by Zeng Guofan, Li Hongzhang and others from 1862 to 1874, and it also embarked on the process of industrialization.[11] In 1862, Zeng Guofan set up an armory in Anqing to make steamers, and it became the first modern military industrial enterprise in China. That same year, Li Hongzhang established a firearms bureau in Shanghai. Later, with the launch of the Westernization Movement, many military industrial enterprises were successively established like Jiangnan General Administration of Manufacturing in 1865, the Fuzhou Shipping

Bureau in 1866, the Tianjin Machinery Bureau in 1867 and so on. In the same period, civil industry also developed, among which there were some relatively important enterprises like Gansu General Administration of Wool in 1878, Shanghai Mechanical Textile Bureau in 1890, Hubei Spinning and Weaving Official Cloth Bureau in 1893 and so forth. Since then, the number of industrial enterprises in modern China was increasing day by day, and the scale was also expanding. Take the enterprises of national capital in the textile and flour industries as an example. The number of modern cotton mills increased by 10 from 1895 to 1899; there were more than 190,000 spindles; and the total amount of capital reached over 5 million *yuan*. Each household had an average of 19,000 spindles with the capital of 500,000 *yuan*. The number of modern cotton mills increased by 9 from 1905 to 1910, and each household had an average of 14,000 spindles with the capital of about 556,000 *yuan*. The number of modern cotton mills increased by 44 from 1914 to 1922, and each household had an average of about 26,000 spindles. There were 38 modern flour mills before 1911, and their number rose by 20 from 1912 to 1913 and by 105 from 1913 to 1921. The total production capacity reached 203,585 packages of flour. Moreover, the total capital of 85 flour mills whose capital was available reached 23.18 million *yuan*, and the average capital per mill was 289,000 *yuan*.[12]

The above analysis of modern Chinese industries from 1895 to 1922 was only based on enterprises of national capital in the two most important industries – textile and flour. Those figures indicated that China's modern enterprises of national capital made great progress in more than 20 years.[13] However, after 1922, since civil wars occurred frequently and foreign capitalism made a comeback, China's modern enterprises of national capital suffered major setbacks and this situation lasted until 1927.

After 1927, with the founding of the Nanjing Kuomintang government and the gradual unification of the whole country, the Kuomintang formulated a series of policies for developing industry while establishing its dominant position in the country, exerting a positive influence on the process of industrialization. In February 1928, the Fourth Plenary Session of the Second Central Executive Committee of the Kuomintang declared that further efforts should be made to develop agriculture and industry to lay a foundation for prosperity of the country. In July 1929, the Second Plenary Session of the Third Central Committee of the Kuomintang emphasized that industry and commerce should be protected and encouraged and that state-operated industry should be advanced. As for state-operated industry, the old state-operated industry should be reorganized and basic industrial manufacturing factories should be set up. In March 1930, the Third Plenary Session of the Third Central Committee of the Kuomintang mapped out the "Recent Construction Policy". The main contents of the Recent Construction Policy included: first, unexplored mines of coal, iron, oil and copper were owned by the state and foreigners were, to a certain extent, allowed to invest or participate in a joint venture; second, other special mines shall be "handled in

134 *Rural social changes*

accordance with the approved rent and private contract established by the Prime Minister"; third, within the scope of the government's promotion of agriculture, an increase in raw materials, a reduction in raw material prices and the implementation of protection taxes, ordinary industries were allowed to develop on their own; fourth, a new factory for special industries would be established according to the government plan, and using foreign capital and personnel would be permitted; fifth, the government should set up large-scale iron-making and steelmaking factories, shipyards and motor factories within two years, and using foreign capital to do this was permissible; sixth, Kuomintang members should do their best to help and promote the development of industry and agriculture, and assist the government in prohibiting all acts that undermined the development of industry and agriculture. In May 1931, the First Interim Plenary Session of the Third Central Committee of the Kuomintang decided that basic industries like water conservancy, electrical engineering, steel and iron, kerosene and automobiles should be actively advanced by the national government, and that those who advanced basic industries through private investment should be rewarded and assisted by the national government. In December 1932, the third Plenary Session of the Fourth Central Committee of the Kuomintang passed a resolution on industrial construction, in which many measures were proposed, including arrangement, production, transportation and marketing, holding a national conference on industrial production and enacting an organization law of industrial groups and so on. In January 1934, the Fourth Plenary Session of the Fourth Central Committee passed a resolution to protect emerging industries by introducing the dumping of duties as soon as possible. In December of that same year, the Fifth Plenary Session of the Fourth Central Committee passed a resolution to try to relieve the panic of national yarn mills and promote the marketing of local cloth in five ways by the government. In November 1935, the Sixth Plenary Session of the Fourth Central Committee adopted the measures of striving for production and construction in order to save the country. Among those measures, related to industrial development, were the promotion of establishing heavy industry, the rationalization of industry and so on. In all declarations and resolutions passed by the Fifth National Congress of the Kuomintang held in the same month, there were some rules of industrial development: all undertakings that were closely related to the national economy and the people's livelihood should be owned by the state, while general industries should be privately owned, and the government should actively support and protect them. In December 1937, it was stipulated in the resolution passed by the Third Plenary Session of the Fifth Central Committee that all industries related to the national plans like heavy industry, basic chemical industry, basic mining industry and industries requiring advanced technology were operated by the central government in principle; local public industries were operated by local governments in principle; and ordinary light industry and various agricultural product processing industries were operated by the people in principle.[14]

Rural social changes 135

The Kuomintang and national government put some of the above policies into practice: in order to meet the demands of civil wars and national salvation, the promotion of basic and military-related industries should be taken as the first step in the development of national industrial production capacity; highway construction, transportation, water conservancy and strategic industries should be supported by the government; the national government should run various kinds of businesses while encouraging and supporting private enterprises; and it seemed to follow a mixed economic model of state-owned and private enterprises advocated by Sun Yat-sen, but in fact it did not draw a clean line between public and private enterprises. Basic industries the government made investment in and preparations for, except individual projects put into production, all were interrupted by Japan's aggression against China. Some preferential policies were adopted that private industries which were of strategic significance for developing national defense industry should be rewarded and supported; some private industrial production that met the needs of national interest and people's livelihood should be given varying degrees of supervision and control; and a negative response should be given to the ever-declining cotton and textile industry.[15] Although these measures and actions were quite different from what the Kuomintang and the national government had expected, they still had certain positive impacts on industrial development and the process of industrialization in this period.

In this period, modern industries developed quickly. The proportion of modern industry in the total output value of industry and agriculture increased from 4.9 percent in 1920 to 10.8 percent in 1936.[16] Among those industries, some developed more quickly, including the mechanical, electronics, electric power, chemical and textile industries.

In this period, the categories of the mechanical industry increased from the shipbuilding industry to the production of a variety of power machines, railway vehicles, machine tools, spinning machines, farm machinery and other light industrial food machinery. The government planned to invest the most money in building large-scale machinery factories like Central Machinery Factory (which moved to the inland after the outbreak of the Anti-Japanese War), which produced seamless steel tubes, cast steel and iron tubes and so on. The number of private machinery factories was remarkably rising. From 1927 to 1936, the number of machinery factories nationwide increased by 377 and doubled. By 1936, public and private machinery factories amounted to 753 (not including railway vehicle factories) in 44 cities across the country with total capital of 7.863 million *yuan* and an annual output value of over 22.39 million *yuan*.[17] As for the electronics industry, in 1929, out of military needs, the Kuomintang set up a telecommunications workshop in Nanjing Military Transportation Machinery Repair Factory, which was attached to the General Headquarters of the Army, Navy and Air Force, and the workshop specialized in the installation and maintenance of 5-watt and 15-watt radio receivers and telephones. In 1935, the resource committee set up an electrical research room at the crystal station of Zhujiang Road, Nanjing,

136 *Rural social changes*

and research groups working on telephones, telegrams and electron tubes formed to use American parts to assemble complete machines. In 1935, this research room invented China's first 30-type amplifier tube, which was a landmark in the development of the electronics industry in China.[18] As for the electric power industry, except in northeast China, in each province inside Shanghaiguan Pass in 1932, there were 452 power plants with an installed capacity of 479,000 kilowatts, and those plants generated electric power of 1.2 billion degrees throughout the year with a total investment of 282 million *yuan*. In 1936, there were 461 power plants with an installed capacity of over 631,000 kilowatts, and they generated electric power of 1.72 billion degrees throughout the year with a total investment of 308 million *yuan*. Within five years, the installed capacity increased by 32 percent, and the generated power rose by 44 percent and the total investment increased by 10 percent.[19] Compared with the situation in 1928, the installed capacity rose by 76 percent and the generated power by 74 percent in 1936.[20] Regarding the basic chemical industry, though acid-making factories had been set up for several years, most of them were attached to arsenals in Dezhou, Hanyang, Shanghai and other places, and there were few independent acid chemical factories. Yongli Sulfuric Acid Factory was built in 1936 with four sets of production equipment for the production of synthetic ammonia, sulfuric acid, sulfur ammonia and nitric acid. Moreover, it annually produced 18,700 tons of "Red Triangular" dithallium sulfate, 11,500 tons of sulfuric acid and 1,520 tons of nitric acid. In 1937, eight major acid-making factories in China had an annual output of 410,000 loads of sulfuric acid, over 60,000 loads of nicotinic acid and 32,650 loads of nitric acid. The total amount of acid was 502,650 loads. In the same year, seven soda ash factories in China had an annual output of 631,000 loads of sodium carbonate, 73,500 loads of caustic soda and 132,200 loads of sodium metasilicate and sodium sulfide. The total amount of these producers was 818,700 loads. In 1936, there were ten alcohol plants in eight places, which were Shanghai, Guangzhou, Hunan, Jinan, Qingdao, Tianjin, Tangshan and Shaanxi, with an annual output of more than 2 million gallons of alcohol.[21]

Concerning the textile industry, in 1927, there were 119 cotton mills across China with 3,531,588 spindles and 29,788 looms. Among them, 73 cotton mills were run by Chinese businessmen with 2,033,588 spindles and 13,459 looms. By 1937, there were 148 cotton mills in China with 5,102,796 spindles and 58,439 looms. Among them, 96 cotton mills were run by Chines businessmen with 2,746,392 spindles and 25,503 looms.[22] Compared with the situation in 1927, the total number of cotton mills nationwide in 1937 grew by 29, an increase of 24 percent; the total number of spindles grew by 1,571,208, an increase of 44 percent; the total number of looms grew by 28,651, an increase of 96 percent. The number of cotton mills run by Chinese businessmen grew by 23, an increase of 32 percent; the number of spindles grew by 712,804, an increase of 35 percent; and the number of looms grew by 12,044, an increase of 89 percent, as shown in Figure 3.1.

Rural social changes 137

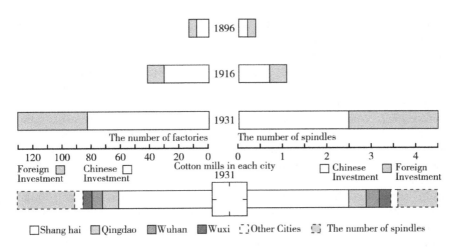

Figure 3.1 The development of the textile industry in China
Picture Source: Wu Bannong, *Statistical Map of China's Economic Status* (Peiping Publishing House, 1931).

With the development of various industries, some cities like Shanghai, Tianjin, Wuhan, Qingdao, Wuxi and so on became important industrial centers. As the biggest industrial center in China, Shanghai possessed 1,781 large and small factories in 1929 and over 2,000 factories in 1930. Among them, 676 factories met the requirements of the Factory Law. In 1932, there were about 4,000 factories, of which 1,229 factories met the requirements of the Factory Law.[23] Up to the eve of the outbreak of the War of Resistance against Japan, the gross domestic product of ten industries including Shanghai's national capital cotton textile industry, the wool textile industry, flour industry, cigarette industry, papermaking industry, matches industry, machinery industry and shipbuilding, electricity industry, etc. was 375.341 million *yuan* and the gross domestic product of other industries reached 432.055 million *yuan* (including a small part of the output value of foreign capital). Then the total output value would reach 807.376 million *yuan*. In 1936, the total modern industrial output value (including all foreign capital output value) in Shanghai was 1.182255 billion *yuan*.[24] Tianjin's industrial development showed two major characteristics from 1927 to 1937: on the one hand, national industry sharply declined and even was in recession in the early 1930s and developed slowly after 1935; on the other hand, foreign capital industry developed rapidly. Japanese-funded industry, in particular, could not catch up with American and European industry at the end of the 1920s, but surpassed other countries' industry by 1936, with its industrial investment accounting for over 56 percent of the total foreign capital industry. According to a survey carried out by the Japanese in 1938, Tianjin possessed 850 industrial enterprises with capital

138 *Rural social changes*

of 138.25 million *yuan*. Among those enterprises, there were 724 national enterprises with capital of 17.37 million *yuan* accounting for 12.57 percent of the total capital; there were 86 Japanese-funded enterprises with capital of 76.07 million *yuan* accounting for 55.02 percent of the total capital; there were other 36 foreign-invested enterprises with capital of 38.08 million *yuan* accounting for 27.54 percent; there were 4 Sino-foreign joint ventures with capital of 6.73 million *yuan* accounting for 4.87 percent of the total capital.[25] Before 1927, Wuhan possessed more than 600 national enterprises (including large semi-handicraft and handicraft workshops) in more than 20 industries including textile, rice milling, printing, machinery and so on. Later, Wuhan's industrial development was stagnant due to the political situation. Until 1933, there were 300 to 400 factories that met the requirements of the Factory Law, and if some small factories were counted, there were a total of over 500 factories with capital of about 30 million *yuan*. By 1936, the number of factories rose to 516 with capital of more than 51.48 million *yuan* and an annual output value of about 190 to 200 million *yuan*. Among all major cities in China, Wuhan ranked only second to Shanghai and Tianjin.[26] Before 1926, there were more than 90 modern factories in Qingdao. Japanese-funded factories accounted for a large proportion of these and factories run by Chinese businessmen only accounted for one-fourth. In 1932, there were 49 foreign-invested factories (the total capital of 40 factories reached over 76 million *yuan*), and 125 factories run by Chinese businessmen (the total capital of 118 factories reached over 17 million *yuan*).[27] In 1929, there were 129 factories in Wuxi with capital of over 14.04 million *yuan*. In February 1930, there were 211 factories with capital of over 11.77 million *yuan*. Among those factories, 153 of them met the requirements of the Factory Law with capital of over 12.17 million *yuan*. Before 1933, there were 7 spinning mills, over 20 textile factories, 49 silk mills, over 50 sock factories, 4 flour factories, 5 or 6 oil-pressing factories, over 10 rice mills, over 10 mills and 60 or 70 iron factories, as shown in Table 3.1.[28]

With the development of industry and improvement in the level of industrialization, the urbanization level in this period was also greatly improved. As we all know, an important index for measuring the level of urbanization is the change in the proportion of the total urban population to the total population of the whole country. However, it is surely difficult to do so without accurate demographic data. Under such a circumstance, it is an effective way to reveal the change in the urbanization level by observing the change in the number of cities a different times and with a different population scale. This is shown by relevant statistics indicating that before 1924, 3 cities had a population of 1 million to 2 million, which were Shanghai, Guangzhou and Beijing; 6 cities had a population of 500,000 to 1 million, which were Hangzhou, Tianjin, Fuzhou, Hong Kong, Suzhou and Chongqing; 41 cities had a population of 100,000 to 500,000, and 83 cities had a population of 50,000 to 100,000.[29] Before 1937, only one city had a population of over 2 million, which was Shanghai; 4 cities

Table 3.1 Comparison of industry in 12 cities across China in 1933

Places	Number of Factories	Percentage	Amount of Capital (ten thousand yuan)	Percentage	Number of Workers	Percentage	Net Products (ten thousand yuan)	Percentage
Nationwide	18,676	100	48,468	100	789,670	100	138,662	100
Shanghai	3,485	19	19,087	40	245,948	31	72,773	46
Tianjin	1,224	7	2,420	5	34,768	4	7,450	5
Beijing	1,171	6	1,303	2.6	17,928	2	1,418	1
Guangzhou	1,104	6	3,213	6.6	32,131	4	10,157	6
Wuhan	787	4	2,086	4	48,291	6	7,330	5
Nanjing	687	3.6	748	1.5	9,853	1	2,344	1.7
Chongqing	415	2	734	1.5	12,938	1.6	1,049	0.8
Fuzhou	366	2	261	0.5	3,853	0.5	777	0.4
Wuxi	315	1.7	1,407	3	63,764	8	7,726	5
Shantou	175	1	219	0.5	4,555	0.6	408	0.3
Qingdao	140	0.7	1,765	4	9,457	1	2,710	2
Xi'an	100	0.5	16	0.03	1,505	0.2	41	0.03

Data Source: Wei Yingtao, *History of Chongqing City in Modern Times*, Sichuan University Press, 1991, p. 209. Among them, the number of industrial capital in Guangzhou seems to be wrong, and the figures have been corrected according to the original table.

140 *Rural social changes*

had a population of 1 million to 2 million, which were Beijing, Guangzhou, Tianjin and Nanjing; 5 cities had a population of 500,000 to 1 million, which were Hankou, Hong Kong, Hangzhou, Qingdao and Shenyang; 66 cities had a population of 100,000 to 500,000, an increase of 61 percent; and 112 cities had a population of 50,000 to 100,000.[30] In contrast, the number of cities with a population of 1 million to 2 million increased by 33 percent; the number of cities with a population of 500,000 to 1 million dropped by 17 percent; the number of cities with a population of 100,000 to 500,000 increased by 61 percent; and the number of cities with a population of 50,000 to 100,000 increased by 35 percent.

Among those cites mentioned above, Shanghai, Tianjin, Wuhan, Chongqing, Qingdao, Zhengzhou, Shijiazhuang, Tangshan and other cities had become typical representatives of rapid population growth in trade port cities, emerging transportation hub cities and emerging industrial and mining cities during this period. Shanghai had a population of 2.641 million in 1927, and its population increased to 3.145 million in 1930 and to 3.702 million in 1935.[31] Its population in 1935 increased by 40 percent compared with that in 1927. The Tianjin Urban Area had a population of 1.122 million in 1928, and its population increased to 1.237 million in 1935 and to 1.254 million in 1936.[32] Its population increased by 3 percent in 1936 compared with that in 1928. The urban areas of three towns in Wuhan had a population of 850,000 in 1928, and their population exceeded 1 million in 1930 and reached 1.29 million in 1935.[33] Their population increased by 52 percent in 1935 compared with that in 1928. Chongqing had a population of 208,000 and its population increased to 253,000 in 1930 and to 471,000 in 1936. Within ten years, its population could more than double.[34] Urban areas in Qingdao (only including the first and second police stations and the Haixi police station of large and small ports) had a population of more than 920,000 in 19,615 households. In 1932, urban areas in Qingdao (including the first, second, third and fourth police station) had a population of more than 241,000 in over 49,000 households.[35] Its population increased by 162 percent in 1932 compared with that in 1927. Zhengzhou had a population of 81,360 in 20,513 households in 1928, and its population increased to 95,482 and the number of its households increased to 22,433 in 1930. In 1934, its population increased to 124,377 and the number of its households increased to 27,892.[36] Its population increased by 53 percent in 1934 compared with that in 1928. Shijiazhuang had a population of about 40,000 (including that of Xiumen Town) in 1926, and its population increased to 63,000 in 1933.[37] Its population increased by 58 percent in 1933 compared with that in 1926. Tangshan had a population of about 48,000 in 1926, and its population once reached 150,000 in 1931 and about 78,000 before 1937.[38] Its population increased by 63 percent before 1937 compared with that in 1926. The above figures were not exactly correct; however, there is no doubt that urbanization in this period developed rapidly.

With the rapid development of urbanization, China owned its first group of designated cities after 1927, which was an eye-catching event in the history of

Rural social changes 141

urban development in modern China. China's modern city system originated in the late Qing dynasty and began in the Republic of China. In 1908, the Qing government issued the *Constitution on Local Self-government in Cities, and Villages*, and its second article stipulated that

> urban areas governed by government offices, and governments at the prefecture and county level were designated as cities, and as for other places like towns and villages, if more than 50,000 people lived in a place, this place would be designated as a town, and otherwise it would be designated as a village.[39]

In 1921, the Beijing government published the "Municipal Self-government System", which stipulated that "municipal autonomous groups still belonged to their original cities or towns, but for those groups with a population of less than 10,000, they should be handled according to the right of autonomy of townships".[40] Meanwhile, cities were also classified into a special city and an ordinary city. At this time, those cities had autonomous jurisdiction. On July 3, 1928, the Nanjing National Government released the *Organic Law of the Special City* and *Organic Law of City*. The former law stipulated that the capital of the Republic of China, cities with a population of more than one million and other cities with special conditions were special cities, and the latter law stipulated that "cities with a population of more than 200,000 could be established as a city on the basis of their application to their provincial government for their consideration and the national government's special permission".[41] The publication of those two documents marked that the "city" had officially became China's first-level local administrative system. In 1930, the national government issued and revised the *Organic Law of City*, and the second article stipulated that

> a place where people lived and met the conditions listed in the left column should be established as a city and directly under the jurisdiction of the administrative department. The conditions were as follows: 1. the capital; 2. cities with a population of more than one million; 3. cities with political and economic conditions. If a place met Condition 2 or 3 and belonged to a provincial government, it should be under the jurisdiction of the provincial government.

The third article stipulated that

> a place where people lived and met the conditions listed in the left column should be established as a city and directly under the jurisdiction of the provincial government. The conditions were as follows: 1. a place with a population of more than 300,000. 2. a place with a population of more than 200,000 with its business tax, license tax and land tax accounting for more than 1/2 of the total income of the place each year.[42]

142 *Rural social changes*

After the publication of the *Organic Law of City*, the government designated Nanjing, Shanghai, Tianjin, Qingdao and Hankou as municipalities under the administrative department. In 1933, Xi'an was designated as a municipality under the administrative department. Peiping, Guangzhou and other cities were designated as a municipalities under the provincial government, as shown in Figure 3.2.[43]

The new development of economic form in the early twentieth century

With the rapid development of industrialization and urbanization, new progress had been made in China's economic form, which could be shown in many aspects like industry, handicraft industry, commerce and agriculture.

State-owned and private enterprises had made remarkable progress in advancing rapid industrial development in this period. As for state-owned enterprises, after the founding of the Nanjing national government in 1927, the government, on the one hand, nationalized some industrial and mining enterprises. For instance, in April 1928, the government placed the Jinling Power Plant under the jurisdiction of the Construction Committee. Before 1937, this plant's business area expanded from Nanjing to three counties, which were Jiangning, Jurong and Liuhe; its capital amounted to 13 million *yuan* from 500,000 *yuan*; and the number of its users increased to 44,000 households from 3,000 households. On the other hand, the government made great efforts to develop heavy industry. In 1936, many plants and factories were built, including the Central Iron and Steel Plant, Chaling Iron Plant, Jiangxi Tungsten Iron Plant, Peng County Copper Mine, Yangxin Daye Copper Mine, Central Machinery Manufacturing Factory, Central Electrical Appliances Factory, Central Electric Porcelain Factory and Gangkeng Coal Mine. In 1937, Xiangtan Coal Mine, Tianhe Coal Mine, Sichuan Coal Mine, Lingxiang Iron Mine, Central Copper Factory (later called Kunming Copper Factory) and Chongqing Temporary Copper Factory had been established. Meanwhile, a group of state-owned enterprises were also set up in each province. For instance, before 1937, some factories had been built in Guangdong Province like Tumin Soil (Cement) Plant, a paper-making factory, a textile factory, a fertilizer factory, a sulfuric acid factory, a beverage factory, a hemp paper factory, an electric power plant, and all of them had capital of 35 million *yuan*.[44] As for private industries, except for the industries mentioned above like textile and flour, some private enterprises also made further progress. Some relatively famous private enterprises included an enterprise group of Shenxin, Fuxin Maoxin Enterprises founded by Rong Zongjing and his younger brother, Rong Desheng; an enterprise group founded by Liu Hongsheng; Yong'an enterprise group founded by Guo Le and Guo Shun; and Minsheng Company, founded by Lu Zuofu. Rong Zongjing and his younger brother, Rong Desheng, started their business in the flour industry, and then established Maoxin Flour Factory, Fuxin Flour Factory and Shenxin Textile Factory consecutively. By 1931, Shenxin also owned nine affiliated factories with 500,000

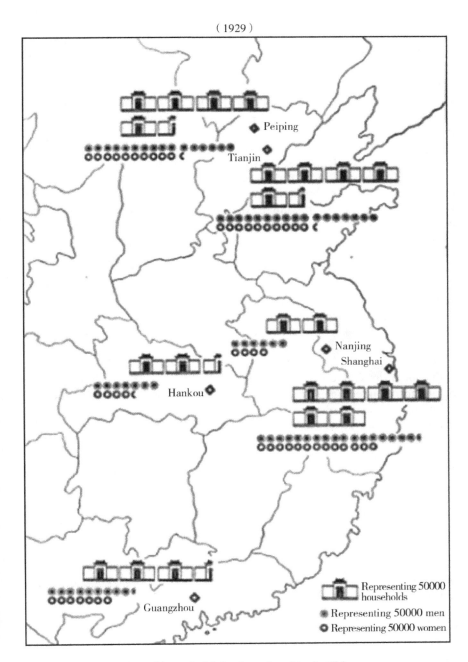

Figure 3.2 The number of households in six major cities in China
Picture Source: Wu Bannong, *Statistical Map of China's Economic Status* (Peiping Publishing House, 1931).

144 *Rural social changes*

spindles and 3,000 looms. Before 1937, Rong Zongjing and Rong Desheng had 12 flour factories with capital of 9.01 million *yuan*, accounting for 30.5 percent of the total capital of flour factories in 16 provinces inside Shanhaiguan Pass. There were 363 steel mills, accounting for 28.6 percent of the total steel mills of 16 provinces, inside Shanhaiguan Pass, and they produced 92,660 bags of flour per day, accounting for 31.4 percent of total daily production of 16 provinces inside Shanhaiguan Pass.[45] Among all the enterprises founded by Liu Hongsheng, Dazhonghua Match Company was the largest. The company was formed through a merger between the Rongchang Match Company, Hongsheng Match Company, Zhonghua Match Company and other match companies in 1930. Before 1937, each affiliated factory of this company had a daily production of more than 700 cases of matches. Dazhonghua Match Company's sales areas covered Jiangsu, Zhejiang, Fujian, Anhui, Jiangxi, Hubei, Henan, Guangdong, Guangxi, Sichuan, Shandong, Hebei and other provinces. It also set up sales agencies in Nanchang, Hankou, Jiujiang, Wuhu, Nanjing, Zhenjiang, Suzhou, Shantou, Fuzhou, Xiamen and other places.[46] In Yong'an enterprise group, Yong'an Textile Company was larger. Before 1937, the first Yong'an textile factory had 44,160 spindles, 4,000 wirebars, 1,200 looms and 3,000 workers. The second and fourth textile factories had 120,000 spindles. The third textile factory had more than 50,000 spindles and more than 200 looms.[47] Mensheng Company, founded by Lu Zuofu in 1926, had capital of 50,000 *yuan* and a 57-foot long, 14-foot wide and 90-horsepower boat. In 1929, this company had another three ships; in 1931 it merged with seven other companies and obtained another 11 ships; in 1932, it merged with four other Chinese shipping companies and one British shipping company and obtained seven ships; in 1933, it merged with three other Chinese shipping companies, obtained three ships and purchased two ships; in 1935, it obtained five ships from American Jiejiang Company. Within five years, from 1931 to 1935, it merged with a total of 15 shipping companies, obtained 42 ships and added nine new routes with a total tonnage of 24,000. By 1936, Mensheng Company ranked first in the number of built ships compared to other shipping companies in Shanghai.[48]

From 1927 to 1937, the handicraft industry showed different states of development. Before 1929, the industry had made steady progress, but after 1929, it began to decline day by day. However, in the 1930s, the production value of the handicraft industry accounted for 70 percent of the total production value of the manufacturing industry and for 25 percent of the total production value of the mining industry.[49] In these ten years, the rapid development of the semi-industrialization of the handicraft industry was one of the most notable indications of the development of handicraft industry.[50] As far as the cloth weaving industry in Gaoyang, Baodi, Ding County and Wei County in North China was concerned, the period from 1927 to 1937 was of great significance to the industry's development. The cloth weaving industry in Gaoyang underwent up and down in Gaoyang, Qingyuan, Li County, Anxin, Renqiu and other counties from 1927 to 1937. The industry thrived again from 1925 to

Rural social changes 145

1929, and major changes took place in the cloth weaving industry in Gaoyang like the increasing cotton cloth sales, the increasing popularity of man-made silk cloth, prosperous family factories, the prevailing credit system of hemp and prosperous machine calendering factories. After 1930, the cloth weaving industry began to decline and transform, and some changes took place. For example, there was no market for native cloth; the input of raw materials and cloth production dropped markedly; looms remained idle and unemployment rose; and most weavers tried to improve their products by weaving striped cloth and dyeing it. Moreover, most weavers tended to set up factories and collect cloth in Wei County in Shandong.[51] The cloth weaving industry in Baodi, Xianghe and other counties experienced a transition period from 1899 to 1909, during which its market expanded, technology became more advanced (the use of iron turbines), the division of labor became clear and a system of merchants and customers emerged, and there was a period of great prosperity from 1900 to 1923, during which firms flourished, the system of merchants and customers prevailed and cloth quality was improved. However, after 1924, the industry began to decline.[52] From 1927 to 1937, the cloth weaving industry in Baodi underwent up and down, and it was unable to achieve what it did in 1923. From 1926 to 1927, Yongxing cloth enjoyed popularity among people and its annual production was about 100,000. It was sold in local areas, Ningxia, Suiyuan, Rehe and northeast China. In 1928, the sales of Yongxing cloth decreased and its annual production was only 20,000 to 30,000. Later, its production dropped day by day, and in 1934 its annual production was only 2,000 to 3,000.[53] Before 1926, machine-made yarns produced by Yufeng Yarn Factory in Zhengzhou and Daxing Yarn Factory in Shijiazhuang began to be used in the cloth weaving industry in Ding County; and the newly modified wood machine (hand-operated machine) was used most frequently and the iron machine took the second place. It could be sold in Zhangjiakou, Feng Town, Guihua City, Baotou Town and other places.[54] Before 1937, the households engaged in cloth weaving in Ding County accounted for 20.22 percent of total households in the county. In 1927, Ding County sold 810,650 pieces of cloth to Chahaer, Shanxi, Suiyuan, Hebei and other places, which were worth 891,716 yuan. In 1930, it sold 1,220,240 pieces worth 1,464,288 *yuan*.[55] The cloth weaving industry in Wei County centered around Wei County but also covered its neighboring counties like Changyi and Changle. Before 1926, there were about 10,000 households engaged in cloth weaving, and more than 40,000 new-type wooden looms, and its daily production was about over 40,000 pieces of cloth.[56] After 1926, the cloth weaving industry went beyond the border of Wei County, and expanded to Changyi, Shouguang and Changle. Before 1934, there were more than 60,000 wooden and iron looms, its annual production was about 3.9 million pieces of cloth, and they were sold to Yunnan, Sichuan, Guizhou, Fujian, Hebei, Henan, Suiyuan and other provinces.[57]

From 1927 to 1937, and especially from 1931 to 1936, agricultural production was restored and progress was also made in agricultural development.

146 *Rural social changes*

From 1931 to 1936, the yield per unit area of rice, except for a drop in 1934, increased from 336 *jin* (=0.5 kilogram) per *mu* of land in 1931 to 355 *jin* per *mu* of land in 1936; the per unit yield of wheat, except for a drop in 1935, increased from 146 *jin* per *mu* of land in 1931 to 151 *jin* per *mu* of land in 1936; the per unit yield of sorghum increased from 165 *jin* per *mu* of land to 209 *jin* per *mu* of land.[58] During the same period, rice production, except for that in 1934, showed a curve increase from 974.369 million *dan* in 1931 to 1.034125 billion *dan* in 1936, an increase of 6.1 percent. Cotton production, except for a drop in 1935, increased steadily from 7.513 million *dan* in 1931 to 17.357 million *dan* in 1936, an increase of 131 percent.[59] With the increasing production of grains and other agricultural products, the total agricultural output also rose gradually to 19.922 billion *yuan* by 1936, an increase of 15 percent compared to 17.346 billion *yuan* in 1920.[60] In these ten years, the new progress made in agricultural development was mainly indicated by managing the landlord economy, the rich peasant economy, farming companies, the development of farms and other aspects. First, managing landlords occupied more land, invested more money, employed workers and took part in commodity production, which helped promote the growth of productive forces, commercializing and socializing the production process, and representing a trend toward progress. Within the ten years, management of the landlord economy did not develop steadily. Some landlords suffered a failure in their management due to family division, migration to cities or towns or external factors, and other landlords rented their land and thus a lot of small farmers became managing landlords. According to a study, among 131 managing landlords in Shandong Province, 59 of them were peasants, accounting for 45 percent; and 64 of them also ran a business, accounting for 49 percent. Among managing landlords in Hebei Province, two-thirds of them became rich through farming, one-third of them became rich by doing business or hiring laborers, and one-sixth of them could keep their fortune until their third generation.[61] Second, the rich peasant economy had become one of the important economic components before 1937. In South China, "a majority of tenant peasants occupying tidal land had become agricultural capitalists" in the Pearl River Delta; a new type of rich peasants appeared who occupied farms of 100 to 300 *mu* and employed a lot of laborers in Anxiang County near the Dongting Lake. In Jilin, Heilongjiang and other places in north China,

> a lot of new type rich peasants occurred. The number of rich peasants was the same as that of people who owned land, and sometimes the former was more than the latter. As for economic power, many rich peasants were wealthier than many small landlords.[62]

Third, farming companies were a newly emerging organizational form in modern Chinese agriculture. This organizational form stemmed from the late Qing dynasty, and there were 171 farming companies by 1912. From 1912 to 1920, farming companies made great headway with an annual growth rate

Rural social changes 147

of capital of 6.9 percent. After 1920, farming companies still achieved some results, but after 1931, owing to a drop in the price of agricultural products and frozen financial markets in rural areas, farming companies were greatly affected. Statistically, seven new farming companies were registered and established in 1929, six companies in 1930, four companies in 1931, two companies in 1932, four companies in 1933 and three companies from January to June 1934.[63]

With the development of industry, the handicraft industry and agriculture, progress was also made in commercial development from 1927 to 1937. It could be reflected in the following aspects: first, domestic markets expanded. From 1920 to 1936, the value of products in domestic markets increased by 82.1 percent with an annual growth rate of 3.8 percent. If the impact of rising prices was not taken into consideration, its value increased by 54 percent with an annual growth rate of 2.7 percent. Second, the commodity structure showed some changes. As far as imported goods were concerned, the proportion of imported cotton yarn and wool products by all provinces inside the Shanhaiguan Pass in net import value from 1920 to 1936 dropped from 32.4 percent to 1.7 percent, while the proportion of imported steel and iron, machines and transportation equipment increased from 14.1 percent to 25.2 percent. The top five imported goods changed from wool products, cotton yarn, kerosene, sugar and tobacco, to steel and iron, machine tools, transportation equipment, chemical products and dyestuff and pigment. As far as all commodities produced domestically were concerned, in 1936, agricultural products accounted for 49.4 percent (not including imported commodities, the same below), handicrafts accounted for 28.8 percent, modern chemical products accounted for 18.6 percent and mining goods accounted for 3.2 percent. Third, there was a change in the flow of commodities. By the 1930s, small markets in local areas had similar characteristics with domestic and even international commodity distribution centers. As far as local products produced domestically in interport trade were concerned, in 1936, the total value of exported local products by each customs office reached 1.1847 billion *yuan*, of which the value of cloth accounted for 16.2 percent; the value of cotton yarn accounted for 10.8 percent; the value of Chinese wood oil, grains, cigarettes and cotton accounted for less than 10 percent; and the value of flour, coal, tea and sugar accounted for less than 5 percent. They would be sold to several big ports like Shanghai, Hankou, Tianjin, Qingdao and Guangzhou. Fourth, commercial capital increased. The total amount of commercial capital was 2.3 billion *yuan* in 1920 and 4.2 billion *yuan* in 1936. The latter increased by 1.9 billion *yuan*, an increase of 82.6 percent, compared to the former. In terms of comparable prices, the latter increased by 54.3 percent with an annual growth rate of 2.7 percent.[64]

From 1927 to 1937, the Chinese economy experienced different degrees of development in industry, the handicraft industry, agriculture, commerce and other aspects, which marked the development of a new economic form in this period. Although there was a major imbalance in economic development

148 *Rural social changes*

between regions, the economic development in those regions reached a peak on the whole.[65]

Old-style private schools and new-style schools: mistakes in the modernization of rural education

In the early stage of the twentieth century, new-style schools were brought into rural society against the background of the country's urgent need for talent and a modernization of education. Unfortunately, new-style schools were unable to fit into rural society, and rejected and resisted by rural people, while old-style private schools were favored by rural people because of their good adaptability and flexibility. Rural people's different attitudes toward old-style private schools and new-style schools were their response to mistakes in the modernization of education and reasonable resistance against the deprivation of their right to education.

Raising questions

When it came to the educational model in rural society in the early part of the twentieth century, most scholars observed a dual structure in which old-style private schools and new-style schools coexisted with each other. Moreover, though new-style schools were strongly supported by the central educational authority, they were not recognized by rural people, who had different thoughts from the government's. Scholars believed there were three reasons for this situation: the first reason was that rural people did not fully recognize the advantages of new-style schools because they lived in a backward environment and were restricted by traditional ideas. Since traditional beliefs had internalized old-style private schools as a part of folk customs and habits, it was hard to change the situation; the second reason was that local government set up new-style schools and imposed new taxes on peasants, so that peasants felt overwhelmed by pressure and loathed new-style schools; the third reason was that old-style private schools had good adaptability and flexibility compared to new-style schools, so rural people favored old-style private schools.

From the perspective of rural people who favored old-style private schools, we may find a different opinion to explain why new-style schools could barely survive in rural areas but old-style private schools developed well. Pragmatic Chinese peasants pursued real interests and tried to maximize those interests. If they found new-style schools were beneficial to them, they were unlikely to devote themselves to resisting government decrees in the long term. However, the fact was that, though old-style private schools went through twists and turns, they still survived in rural society thanks to the strong support of rural people, but new-style schools were put into an awkward position. "The number of old-style private schools and its students were several times more than the number of new-style schools and its students".[66] Rural people's

Rural social changes 149

stubbornness and traditional ideas could not completely account for this phenomenon. New added taxes and good adaptability and flexibility certainly can explain why new-style schools were in a weak position. However, the new education taxes and new-style schools were not quite the same thing. Among the peasants, resentment toward the former did not necessarily entail rejection of the latter. In fact, new added taxes and new-style schools were two different concepts. Furthermore, why was it difficult for new-style schools to fit into rural society with their adaptability and flexibility? What was the root cause? This book will fully explore the reasons for the different positions of old-style private schools and new-style schools in rural areas and consider mistakes made in the modernization of education in the early twentieth century.

Old-style private schools and new-style schools from the perspective of rural people

Old-style private school education started from Confucius's establishing private schools and it was a traditional educational mode. For thousands of years, Chinese people embarked on or finished their education in private schools. In the late nineteenth century, the Qing government, faced with internal crises and external threats, was forced to implement the New Deal. Some far-sighted scholars gave top priority to abolishing the imperial examination system and establishing new-style schools in a political reform to make China strong. "Preserving the losing civilization, revitalizing neglected causes, cultivating benighted and weak people into wise and strong ones, all lie in school education".[67] "If the imperial examination system was not abolished and schools were not set up, then scholars would not remain steadfast in political reforms, common people would not open their minds and it would be hard for the country to advance".[68] Old-style private schools, focusing on esteeming Confucius and reading classics, and regarding participation in the imperial examination as the highest goal, were seen as backward in the context of modern educational reform, and also impeded revolutions and development. A good solution to saving the country could not be found in *The Four Books* and *The Five Classics*, and reciting articles and poems could not provide practical knowledge. Someone wrote in a newspaper and sighed,

> I learn about nothing after receiving education in private schools for a dozen years. Moreover, I also don't fully understand what my tutor is talking about. The old education system should be abolished so as not to waste young people's life.[69]

Some far-sighted scholars also gave a description of private schools:

> When it comes to private schools, I will associate them with a funny scene: a dark room, desks with missing legs, an old tutor with a long-stemmed Chinese pipe in his mouth, a few young children with disheveled

150 *Rural social changes*

hair and dirty faces, a teacher's desk, a thick and heavy ruler, a wall with lime falling off and sprinkled with ink. In a word, it is not exaggerated if we compared it to a hell on earth or a cage for children.[70]

If abolishing the imperial examination was taken as the most important task in eliminating the fixed values of traditional culture, then improving and replacing private schools in the late Qing dynasty and the Republic of China was the last shot. The late Qing government, the Beiyang government and the national government all intervened in and remolded private school education while promoting the building of new-style schools. Their final goal was to abandon the backward mode of private school education and modernize the teaching content of private school education.

Though traditional private schools regarded participation in the imperial examination as the highest goal, the teaching content of private schools in rural society did not purely focus on providing talent for the imperial examination. In fact, old-style private schools could be classified into schools of higher education and lower-level primary schools. The former schools helped young people pass the imperial examination, while the latter schools helped children learn to read. Teaching content directly and closely related to the imperial examination was taught by schools of higher education, while lower-level private schools, similar to primary schools, taught students pragmatic and basic cultural knowledge about rural areas, like Chinese characters frequently used in daily life, sprinkling water, sweeping flour and dealing with guests, simple calculation and doing accounts and educating rural people, which had little relation to eight-part essays that are harmful to people's minds. However, modern educational reform was carried out so forcefully and quickly that all the teaching contents of old-style private schools were totally abandoned instead of differentiating the teaching contents of private schools at different levels, which was not exactly the same. Even those improved private schools emerging in the Republic of China finally evolved into modern schools, because there was no reason for their existence.

New-style schools emerged in modern times and they were naturally accepted by the elites for their legitimacy, but the elites thought old-style private schools were a symbol of an anti-education model and hindered the modernization of education. However, from the perspective of rural people, private schools were of incontrovertible legitimacy, and during several decades when new-style schools originating from Western industrial society attempted to survive in rural society, new-style schools were barely recognized and strongly resisted by rural people, which surely drew the public's attention. Why did rural people have a strong sense of identity with private schools, which was the opposite of modern education, and why did they reject new-style schools that represented civilization and progress? It would be biased if one only explained this situation from the following aspects: rural people's conservativeness, backwardness and ignorance. In fact, rural people had their own wisdom for existence and judgment ability for their interests. Therefore,

Rural social changes 151

we will answer this by contrasting and analyzing o private schools and new-style schools in rural areas.

First, compared to new-style schools, the tuition collected by private schools was low, and its way of collecting tuition and its teaching hours were adaptable to agricultural society. New-style schools conformed to a normalized, institutionalized school-running model of cities and towns, which was not adaptable to rural society.

Most traditional private school education was free or charged a small fee, and books, writing brushes and inks cost little. Much money was spent on making preparations for taking the imperial examination periodically. For ordinary rural people, they mostly took part in examinations about basic knowledge and seldom took a high-level imperial examination. New-style schools collected tuition all at once, while private schools did so at three intervals, namely, the Dragon-boat Festival, the Mid-autumn Festival and the Spring Festival, which conformed to peasants' habit of cash flow. What is more, how much tuition a student should pay depended on the student's family financial situation: poor families paid less and wealthy families paid more. Thus, parents of those students in private schools bore little burden. As described below,

> as for books and stationery, students in private schools only needed to buy a book, a writing brush, an inkstone, a copybook printed with red Chinese letters, and when they used them up, they bought them again. Some books like *The Three-Character Classic* and the *Book of Family Names* might be first used by elder brothers and then by younger brothers and sisters. A son or grandson might use their grandfather's old books. But in new-style schools, students had to buy many textbooks about the national language, arithmetic and so on. If a student failed to go up to the next grade, he or she had to buy new books again. Apart from textbooks, students had to buy writing brushes, pencils, flagstones and several exercise books. Ordinary rural families were unlikely to pay so much money. As for tuition collection, private schools collected tuition according to the seasons, so they collected it at the Qingming Festival, the Dragon-boat Festival, the Mid-autumn Festival and the Winter Solstice Festival, when rural people had much money at hand. In addition, private schools asked parents to pay tuition by installments, so the amount was small and it was easier for parents to pay it. But for students in new-style schools in cities and towns, they were to pay their tuition when a new term began after a summer or winter holiday. For students in new-style schools in rural areas, they were to pay their tuition at the end of a summer or winter holiday when rural people had little money at hand.[71]

The Guimao education system specified that "except primary schools and high-class primary normal college, other kinds of schools should ask students to pay their tuition".[72]

152 *Rural social changes*

The south of the lower reaches of the Yangtze River was famous for its contribution to national revenues, but few students there could finish their five-year education in primary schools because most families were unable to make ends meet, let alone other financially disadvantaged provinces.[73]

Private schools collected not only lower tuition but also fewer miscellaneous fees than new-style schools. Apart from basic tuition, new-style schools also collected fees for gym suits, sports and so on,[74] and ordinary poor families could not cover such expenses.

The teaching hours of private schools was synchronized with the timetable of the Chinese lunar calendar, which showed that private schools had better flexibility and adaptability than new-style schools.

Private schools designated the period from the 20th day of the first lunar month to Minor Heat as the first semester, and the period from Start of Autumn to December 20 as the second semester. The teaching hours lasted for 70 days with annual vacation and summer holiday included. Most students in villages were about 12 years old, and they could participate in agricultural activities. According to the calendar of agricultural activities, people were at leisure from January to April and from July to September. But during the two periods, students in new-style schools were taking a holiday, and when people were busy breeding silkworms and farming, students in new-style schools should attend class.[75]

Furthermore, according to the strict regulations of new-style schools, students was not permitted to take a day off at will.

Students shall not ask for leave for no reason except for holidays required, and supervisors of all schools were required to submit their roll books. If a student did not attend all classes, some points would certainly be deducted from his or her graduation score according to the regulation.[76]

"If a student missed classes for one or two weeks, it was hard for him or her to make up those lessons. Therefore, it was inconvenient for students in rural areas".[77]

However, private schools set public holidays according to the Chinese lunar calendar, such as the Qingming Festival, Dragon-boat Festival, wheat harvest and Mid-autumn Festival. What is more, rich and poor students in private schools had their own vacations. For example, after the Dragon-boat Festival, poorer students were required to help their parents do farm work for two or three weeks. The individual teaching method of private schools minimized negative impacts of irregular holidays. Students' school work would not affect their families' farm work and vice versa.[78]

Rural social changes 153

Under such a circumstance, there was no doubt that rural people would choose private schools.

> Students from ordinary families were able to help their father and brother do farm work at the age of six or seven, but once they got to school, they would pay for tuition and could not help their family members do farm work. There was a clash between the teaching hours of new-style schools and farming time. Some schools could not adjust their teaching hours and make use of the slack season to accomplish their teaching tasks. Moreover, peasants were not willing to suffer a loss, so they did not allow their children to go to school.[79]

Second, rural people believed that the teaching content of private schools and the students they cultivated met more of their demands, while the teaching content of new-style schools and the students they cultivated could not meet the needs of rural society and were separated from rural life.

In rural people's common life, Chinese characters could be used on four occasions: weddings and funerals, technology, business and lawsuits.[80] Rural people had realistic thoughts about education in that they did not expect their children to become a government official and just wanted them to know how to deal with the above four occasions. Students in rural areas would use what they learned to do farm work or go outside their area to do business. Most private schools were low-level primary schools and their teaching objectives were simply in conformity with rural people's daily needs. From the point of view of the actual situation of farming, a primer called *A Collection of Daily Words* mostly used rhythmical language combined with items for daily use in rural areas, so it was practical. For example,

> Farming is the most important task for a person and if a man wants to do the accounts, he should learn about *A Collection of Daily Words* first. After the land unfreezes, one should use a hoe and shovel to plough the land and then put manure into it.

Such textbooks related to rural life enjoyed popularity among people. In private schools in Wenshang County, Shandong Province, "reading and writing were necessary tools for one to enter an official career, but students also learned some practical knowledge like abacus calculation, letter writing, invitation cards, obituaries, couplets, banners and so on".[81] From the perspective of doing business, ordinary merchants and owners attached much importance to whether young apprentices knew how to read, write articles and calculate with an abacus, which were strong points of students studying in private schools. If a student graduated from a private school, he often did well in writing and calculation. For instance, he had beautiful handwriting, and knew how to write letters and other practical articles (plain classical language) and how to use an abacus to do accounts. All those skills could meet

154 *Rural social changes*

the needs of rural society, and they were important skills for rural students who went outside the area to learn about how to do business. Some scholars investigated private schools in Xiliu Village, Shanxi Province, and found that one of the reasons why rural people sent their children to private schools was that they wanted their children to learn how to write and do accounts and then go to cities to carry out business.[82]

From the perspective of rural people, the knowledge taught by new-style schools was far away from their real life. This kind of new knowledge met the needs of students who were making preparations for further education and conformed to interests of urban people, but they were separated from the reality of rural life and became so-called foreign stereotypes. "The textbooks used in primary schools in rural areas were completely related to urban life and did not meet the needs of rural people".[83] "The current curriculum of primary schools was vague, general and unpractical".[84] "The textbooks used in primary schools were not related to people's daily life, so students graduating from those schools were unable to use what they learned to fit into society".[85]

> The new-style education in modern times originated from Western countries, and both its teaching content and school-running model were products of urban life. The government-approved textbooks were all published by publishing houses in Shanghai, and they mostly presented urban life in south China and had nothing to do with rural life in north China.[86]

In addition, the basic abilities in reading, writing and calculating, valued by rural people, had declined among students graduating from new-style schools. Among students who took the graduation examination of Beijing higher primary schools in 1909, no one "got a good score on the tests of Confucius classics and Chinese language", and "few of them passed the two tests".[87] Some scholars also argued that "the most important reason why new-style schools should be blamed was that students graduating from those schools were unable to recite articles, and they wrongly wrote a lot of Chinese characters and were bad at calculation".[88]

Students graduating from new-style schools could not play their parts in rural society, and their behavior and ideas were quite different from the traditional values of rural areas. As a result, they were barely respected and recognized by rural people. "Once children were sent to school, they would not be willing to help their father and brother do farm work".[89]

> After children from rural areas were sent to higher primary schools in urban areas, they were not accustomed to their simple rural life anymore and were unwilling to eat plain food or wear old clothes. They looked down upon everything in rural areas. Moreover, they did not equip themselves with knowledge and abilities that rural society required, and just learned some subject knowledge like English, physics and chemistry,

which were relevant to rural life. They also did not know how to do farm work, but became lazy and developed a habit of doing gymnastics and playing ball games.[90]

Under such circumstances, it was reasonable for rural people to choose private schools. "Most advanced new-style schools were denounced by the society, and some honest children did not go to those schools".[91]

Third, from the perspective of rural people, a tutor was an important part of rural society. Tutors and rural people lived in the same environment with the same social order, so there was a natural closeness between them. However, teachers in new-style schools were from the outside world and could not adapt to rural society.

A tutor was a literate peasant and had almost the same values and beliefs as rural people. Tutors were a part of the rural society, unlike foreign students or teachers who were strange to and alienated from rural people. As Liang Shuming stated, "in China, studying and farming, scholars and peasants are related to each other rather than separated from each other".[92] Therefore, tutors were totally integrated into rural areas, and often regarded as the central person of local society. In addition, they bore certain responsibilities that were especially related to rural people's spiritual life like culture, rituals and so on. For example, in rural areas,

if someone celebrated his birthday, he would request a tutor to write a couplet for him; if someone passed away, his family members would request a tutor to write an elegiac couplet or make a memorial speech. Rural people also asked a tutor to observe "fengshui" for a funeral, choose a propitious day to go on a long journey or build a house, feel a pulse and make a prescription.[93]

Another example was tutors of private schools in Yangqu County, Shanxi Province. "Tutors there knew a little about superstitious things like anecdotes, the horoscope and choosing a propitious day. If rural people did not understand something, they would turn to tutors for help. So tutors were seen as a sage of a village".[94]

Teachers in new-style primary schools of rural areas were unable to fit into the rural society. From the perspective of rural people,

in the early years, most rural teachers would be cautious with their own words and actions, and always polite to others, with a mustache and a long-stemmed Chinese pipe in their mouths, which made a deep impression on peasants' minds. Those peasants were dissatisfied with young teachers' performance because the latter could not choose a propitious day for a wedding or observe "fengshui".[95]

156 *Rural social changes*

Tutors in private schools occupied a dominant position in rural people's life of culture and etiquette, and they mastered all kinds of culture, knowledge and skills for holding a ceremony rural people valued so much. However, teachers in rural primary schools "just ignored such kinds of knowledge and skills because they thought they were not important, or objected to them because they thought they were superstitious. As a result, rural people had a lot of complaints about those young teachers".[96] What is more, "those young teachers could not play a positive role in the construction of new villages and rural production, so that rural people were good for nothing and then showed their respect for tutors in private schools".[97] Furthermore, those young teachers "treated peasants with an unfriendly attitude. They were not helpful for peasants, and were loathed by peasants".[98] Therefore, it was no wonder that teachers in rural primary schools were not popular among rural people. According to an investigation of rural education in Shangxi in 1934, more than half of teachers in primary schools were not popular among local people.[99]

Some scholars argued, "It was a pity that graduates from rural normal schools were often unwilling to go back to rural areas. Some might stay in rural areas but their hearts flew to cities".[100] However, rural teachers absolutely did not want to cause such a result. A social structure was composed of certain elements and an element could perform its functions in a social structure that the element fitted into. Rural primary schools teachers graduating from standardized normal universities were born in an industrialized and urbanized social environment and lived in modern society. They could not adapt to rural areas or maintain a harmonious relationship with rural people, which resulted from a mutual repulsion between a social structure and inharmonious elements and the adverse effect of a mismatch between a social organization and its components. In fact, those teachers were also frustrated, for their talents were not recognized by society. It was no wonder that some scholars stated that "rural teachers wanted to go back to cities not all for high salaries. They actually did not miss or love rural areas at all".[101]

Mistakes made in the history of rural educational reform

Based on what has been discussed above, we can see that rural private schools were a part of rural society in essence. In the three thousand years of Chinese history, lower-level private school education had been rooted in rural society and integrated into agricultural society. Private schools developed along with agricultural society and were organizations full of vigor in the traditional social structure. Fei Xiaotong said in the introduction to the article "Private Schools in Wenshang County",

the development, existence and change of an educational system took place in coordination with the whole society. In the traditional Chinese society, private schools worked well with other social systems due to their long history of development, from which we could truly understand the real functions of a private school. If we did not know about private schools and borrowed an educational system from other social organizations and compulsively matched the borrowed one with a rural society full of traditional Chinese organizations, the result would certainly not be good. So far, scholars in the circle of modern education are still not fully aware of the important question.[102]

From tutors to students, from teaching method to teaching content, from teaching hours to fees, private schools were tightly bound with and inseparable from the rural society's farming methods, rural etiquette culture and rural values. The close relationship between private schools and rural society is not a creation made by the government decree in a short time, but an organism formed during the natural evolution and development of rural society, which can't be synthesized by any high-tech means.

New-style schools were products of industrial society in essence and adaptable to industrialized and urbanized society. The professions, values and lifestyles of talented people cultivated by those schools were a link to and an element of the industrial society. As contemporary people commented, "the Achilles heel of rural education was that new-style schools had similar features with those in cities, and they could not meet the needs of rural people".[103] When this kind of educational system was implanted into the agricultural society, the essence of the system was still influenced by the industrialized and urbanized society. It was inevitable that it was incompatible with agricultural society. Liang Shuming sighed, "it did not bring any success but caused trouble to the society. It can be said new-style schools cultivated talented people for another society".[104] As scholars argued,

> we should find answers to the following questions: Which teaching method in rural primary schools was suitable for the poor? Which one was adaptable to rural areas? Why did rural students in primary schools not take vacations in the rural busy season and need to take holidays according to regulations? Why did the teaching content not meet the demands of rural people and instead stay the same as that of urban schools? Why did the course arrangement help a minority of students enter a higher-level school and not care about most students' demands? Why did schools ask students to pay for a school uniform instead of just letting them wear clean and tidy clothes? Why did schools help students develop a habit of bearing hardships and working hard but spoil them? What is more, students had to wear shoes and socks in school, use the same utensils and live at schools. All of these were not suitable for rural life, so many students from a poor family did not choose to go to these schools.[105]

Under certain circumstances and in a certain period, modernization did not necessarily benefit everyone. For peasants in modern times, the process

158 *Rural social changes*

of modernization was mostly demonstrated by the deprivation of interests, marginalization, immiseration and a more miserable life. As Liang Shuming asserted, the main problem for modern China was not poverty but more and more people living in poverty.[106] The reform of rural education did not avoid such a fate, and peasants possessed fewer and fewer educational resources. Peasants who were wise and pursued real interests suffered a lot in the trap of modern education. They found that "new-style schools caused people to leave the countryside and flood into cities, not grow rice or cotton, not plant trees, but go after a luxury life and look down on peasants, share interests instead of creating benefits, turn peasants into bookworms, rich people into poor people, strong people into weak people, and weak people into weaker ones".[107] Rural people's strong resistance against new-style schools and the resilience of private schools might hinder the development of modern education, but it would be more reasonable if we held that the embedding of modern education or new-style schools triggered the educational crisis in rural society and deprived students from poor families of their right to education. They resisted and struggled against the deprivation of the right to education, and they absolutely did not reject progress or civilization in favor of their conservative and stubborn attitudes. They fought for themselves in the survival crisis and made a rational choice to pursue their maximum interests when faced with the social reality. Moreover, they expressed their own reactions to the damage to their survival system caused by modernization and adjusted to the situation and made a response to the mistakes in the state's efforts to achieve modernization.

"Rural areas would follow their own path and find their own way to making progress",[108] Liang Shuming said firmly in his later years. The responses of peasants to educational modernization in the early twentieth century gave a warning to the public that on the way to achieving modernization, civilized progressives should show their respect for peasants' rational attitudes and notice their wisdom for survival and put their feet into peasants' shoes when attempting to transform backward, stubborn and benighted peasants. Only by doing so could the society really make progress in its development. The result would just be the opposite of their wish, and peasants would be overwhelmed by pain.

Notes

1 Zhao Gang. "On the Urban History of China from a Macro Perspective", *Historical Research*, 1(1993): 16.
2 Wang Shouzhong, Guo Dasong. *The History of Urban Changes in Shandong Province in Modern Times* (Jinan: Shandong Education Press, 2001), 684.
3 Sun Yutang. *Documents of the History of Modern Chinese Industry* (vol. 1) (Beijing: Science Press, 1957), 234–241.
4 Wang Jingyu, *Documents of the History of Modern Chinese Industry* (vol. 2) (Beijing: Science Press, 1957), 654.
5 (America) G. William Skinner, *The City in Late Imperial China*, translated by Ye Guangting (Beijing: Zhonghua Book Company, 2000), 262.

Rural social changes 159

6 (America) Skinner, *The City in Late Imperial China*, 262.

7 Association of Chinese Historians, *The Westernizationist Movement* (vol. 6) (Shanghai: Shanghai People's Press, 1961), 446.

8 Luo Shuwei, *The History of Modern Tianjin Cities* (Beijing: China Social Sciences Press, 1993), 223.

9 Wang Shouzhong and Guo Dasong. *The History of Urban Changes in Shandong Province in Modern Times*, (Jinan: Shandong Education Press, 2001), 99.

10 Li Bozhong, *The Early Stages of Industrialization in the Regions South of the Yangtze River* (1550–1850) (Beijing: Social Sciences Academic Press, 2000), 2.

11 Liu Dajun, *The Study of the Industrialization in Shanghai* (Beijing: Commercial Press, 1940), 13.

12 Wang Jingyu, *Modern Chinese Economic History from 1895 to 1927* (Beijing: People's Publishing House, 2000), 1609–1663.

13 Wang Jingyu, *Modern Chinese Economic History from 1895 to 1927*, (Beijing: People's Publishing House, 2000), 1596–1619.

14 Zhu Zishuang, *Industrial Policy of the Kuomintang of China*, (Chongqing: National Book Publishing House, 1943), 45–70.

15 Zhu Baoqin, *On the Industrial Policies of the Nanjing Government* (1927–1937), in *A New Discussion about the History of the Republic of China·Volume of Economy, Society, Ideology and Culture*, ed. Chen Hongmin (Beijing: SDX Joint Publishing Company, 2003), 3–15.

16 Wu Chengming, *Chinese Capitalism and Domestic Market* (Beijing: China Social Sciences Press, 1985), 135.

17 Lu Yangyuan and Fang Qingqiu, *Social and Economic History of the Republic of China* (Beijing: Economic Press China, 1991), 368–369.

18 Lu Yangyuan and Fang Qingqiu, *Social and Economic History of the Republic of China*, 369.

19 Tan Xihong, *China's Economy in the Past Ten Years* (1936–1945), in Shen Yunlong, *A Sequel of Modern Chinese History Series* (vol. 9: 83–85) (Wenhai Publishing House, a photocopy of 1974), 388–390.

20 Lu Yangyuan, Fang Qingqiu, *Social and Economic History of the Republic of China*, 371.

21 China Association for Cultural Construction, *China Ten Years before the War of Resistance against Japan*, 171–174. Lu Yangyuan and Fang Qingqiu, *Social and Economic History of the Republic of China*, 372–374.

22 Gong Jun, *Outline of the Development History of China's New Industry* (The Commercial Press, 1933), 123–133; Tan Xihong, *China's Economy in the Past Ten Years* (1936–1945), in Shen Yunlong, *Modern Chinese History Series*, 78.

23 Liu Dajun, *Investigation Report on China's Industry* (vol. 1), Outline of the Industrial Division (Part 3), 1933, p. 10.

24 Xu Xinwu and Huang Hanmin, *History of Modern Industry in Shanghai* (Shanghai Academy of Social Sciences Press, 1998), 212–213.

25 Luo Shuwei, *The History of Modern Tianjin Cities* (China Social Sciences Press, 1993), 505–510.

26 Pi Mingxiu, *History of Wuhan City in Modern Times* (China Social Sciences Press, 1993), 413–419.

27 Gong Jun, *A Statistical Analysis of the Development of Industrialization in China* (The Commercial Press, 1934), 162; Liu Dajun, *Investigation Report on China's Industry* (vol. 1), Outline of the Industrial Division (Part 3), p. 15.

160 Rural social changes

28 *A Statistical Analysis of the Development of Industrialization in China*, 107–111; Liu Dajun, *Investigation Report on China's Industry* (vol. 1), Outline of the Industrial Division (Part 3), p. 20.

29 Ruan Xiang et al., *The First Chinese Yearbook* (Beijing: The Commercial Press, 1926), 54–55.

30 Gu Chaolin et al., *Urban Geography in China* (Beijing: The Commercial Press, 1998), 76.

31 Xin Ping, *Observing History from Shanghai: Shanghai People and Their Social Life in the Process of Modernization from 1927 to 1937* (Shanghai: Shanghai People's Publishing House, 1996), 40.

32 Luo Shuwei, *The History of Tianjin Cities in Modern Times*, 457.

33 Pi Mingxiu, *History of Wuhan City in Modern Times*, 660.

34 Wei Yingtao, *History of Chongqing City in Modern Times* (Chengdu: Sichuan University Press, 1991), 398.

35 The Republic of China, *Annals of Jiao'ao* (Chengwen Publishing House, a photocopy of 1968), 231–276; International Trade Bureau of Industrial Department: *Annals of Industrial Department* (Shandong Province) (Third), 9–10.

36 Liu Yanpu, Appendix: "Note on the Urban Construction of Zhengzhou City", in *The Construction of the Contemporary Zhengzhou City* (Beijing: China Architecture & Building Press, 1988), 336; Chen Gengya, *Records of Northwest Inspection* (Shanghai: Shunpao Building, 1937), 472.

37 Jiang Pei and Xiong Yaping, "Railway and the Rise of Shijiazhuang City from 1905 to 1937", *Modern Chinese History Studies*, 3(2005), 170–197.

38 Wang Xianming and Xiong Yaping, "Railway and Development of New Inland Cities in North China from 1905 to 1937", *Research in Chinese Economic History*, 3(2006); Cheng Changzhi, "Brief Description of Tangshan Town", *Municipal Review*, 3, no. 14 (July 1935); Beining Railway Administration Bureau: *Economic Investigation Report along Beining Railway*, 1937 ed., 1247.

39 *Historical Documents about Preparation for Implementing Constitutionalism in the Late Qing Dynasty* (vol. 2), edited by the Department of Ming and Qing Archives of the Palace Museum, 728.

40 Editorial Board of the Summary of the History of the Republic of China, *Summary of the History of the Republic of China* (from July to September 1921), 29.

41 Editorial Board of the Summary of the History of the Republic of China, *Summary of the History of the Republic of China* (from July to October 1928), 9–19.

42 Editorial Board of the Summary of the History of the Republic of China, *Summary of the History of the Republic of China* (from April to June 1930), 615–616.

43 Xu Mao, *The History of the Political System of the Republic of China* (Shanghai People's Publishing House, 1992), 415–417.

44 Chen Zhen, *Documents of the History of Modern Chinese Industry* (vol. 3) (Beijing: SDX Joint Publishing Company), 1961, 774–839, 1171.

45 Sun Yutang. *Documents of the History of Modern Chinese Industry* (vol. 1), 372–389.

46 Sun Yutang. *Documents of the History of Modern Chinese Industry*, the 1st volume, p. 410.

47 Sun Yutang. *Documents of the History of Modern Chinese Industry*, the 1st volume, pp. 425–426.

48 Sun Yutang. *Documents of the History of Modern Chinese Industry* (vol. 1), 431–433.

Rural social changes 161

49 Xu Dixin and Wu Chengming, *History of the Development of Capitalism in China* (vol. 3) (Beijing: People's Publishing House, 2003), 187.

50 Semi-industrialization means the rise and development of a market-oriented, professional handicraft industry in rural areas with more advanced technology and a clear division of labor against the background of industrialization. See Peng Nansheng, "Semi-industrialization: A Description of the Development of Handicraft Industry in Rural Areas in Modern Times", *Journal of Historical Science*, 7(2003).

51 Wu Zhi, *A Study on the Cloth Weaving Industry in Rural Areas* (Beijing: The Commercial Press, publication date unknown), 31.

52 Fang Xianting and Bi Xianghui, *Observing the Evolution of the Industrial System through the Handicraft Industry in Baodi*, in *Collected Works of Fang Xianting* (vol. 3), ed. Fang Xianting (Beijing: The Commercial Press, 2013), 155–157.

53 Yin Mengixa and Li Qiang, *A Collection of Investigation Reports on Economy along Railways in the Republic of China* (vol. 2), 591–592.

54 "Cotton and Native Cloth of Ding County", *Chinese and Foreign Economic Weekly*, December 1926.

55 Zhang Shiwen, *An Investigation of Industry in Rural Areas of Ding County*, 82, 115.

56 "The Cloth Weaving Industry in Wei County, Shandong Province", *Industry and Commerce Semimonthly*, 6, no. 1(January 1934); "Recent Economic Situation in Wei County, Shandong Province", *Chinese and Foreign Economic Weekly*, 187 (November 1926).

57 The Traffic Department of Jiaoji Railway Administration Bureau, *An Investigation Report of Jiaoji Railways* (vol. 3) (Wei County), 1934, p. 14.

58 Yan Zhongping, *A Selection of Statistical Data of Modern Chinese Economic History*, 361.

59 Zhou Danning, *A New Discussion about Modern Chinese Economic History* (Nanjing University Press, 1991), 251.

60 Wang Yuru, "China's Economic Development between Two World Wars", *Research in Chinese Economic History*, 2(1987).

61 Xu Dixin and Wu Chengming, *History of the Development of Capitalism in China* (vol. 3), 313–321.

62 Xu Dixin and Wu Chengming, *History of the Development of Capitalism in China* (vol. 3), p. 337; Zhou Danning, *A New Discussion about Modern Chinese Economic History* (Nanjing University Press, 1991), 252–253.

63 Xu Dixin and Wu Chengming, *History of the Development of Capitalism in China* (vol. 3), 348.

64 Xu Dixin and Wu Chengming, *History of the Development of Capitalism in China* (vol. 3), 226–248.

65 Some scholars see this period as a "golden decade" for economic development and some believe the economic development of old China reached its peak in 1936. Wang Yuru, "China's Economic Development between Two World Wars", *Research in Chinese Economic History*, 2(1987); Zong Yuhai, "A Review on the Economic Construction by the Nanjing National Government from 1927 to 1937", *Republican Archives*, 1(1992). (Author's note).

66 Huang Zhicheng, "The Status of Old-style Private Schools in the Movement of Universal Education", *Chinese Education*, 22, no. 7(January 1935): 94.

67 Liang Qichao, *Discussion of Political Reforms·Schools*; Chen Xuexun, *Selected Works of Chinese Modern Education* (Beijing: People's Education Press, 1983), 130.

162 *Rural social changes*

68 Shu Xincheng, *Documents of the History of Chinese Modern Education* (vol. 1) (Beijing: People's Education Press, 1981), 363.

69 "A Good Method Should Be Adopted For Education", *Ta Kung Pao* (9th ed.), May 5, 1911.

70 Huang Zhicheng, "The Status of Old-Style Private Schools in the Movement of Universal Education", *Chinese Education*, 22, no. 7(January 1935), 93.

71 Huang Zhicheng, "The Status of Old-Style Private Schools in the Movement of Universal Education", *Chinese Education*, 22, no. 7(January 1935), 93.

72 Zhu Youhuan, *Documents about Modern Chinese Educational System* (vol. 2) (East China Normal University Press, 1989), p. 95.

73 "School Department of the General Educational Society of Jiangsu's Request for an Amendment to the Constitution of Primary Schools", *Government Newspaper of Yunnan Education* June 1909, 175.

74 "Reasons for Slow Development of Chinese Schools", *Shun Pao* (4th ed.), May 24, 1909.

75 "School Department's Request for Revising General Principles of Managing All Schools", *Shun Pao*, February 21, 1910.

76 "A Ban on Students' Asking for Leave", *Shun Pao* (11 ed.), March 28, 1909.

77 Liao Taichu, "Private Schools in Wenshang County", *Social Welfare Tientsin*, Tianjin (12th ed.), August 12, 1935.

78 Liao Taichu, "Private Schools in Wenshang County", *Social Welfare Tientsin*, Tianjin (12th ed.), August 12, 1935.

79 Deng Zhunshan, "Causes of Failure in Rural Education and Approaches for Improvement", *Social Welfare Tientsin*, Tianjin (12th ed.), February 27, 1937.

80 Gilbert Rozman, *The Modernization of China*, trans. research group of comparative modernization of National Social Sciences Fund (Jiangsu People's Publishing House, 1995), 189.

81 Liao Taichu, "Private Schools in Wenshang County", *Social Welfare Tientsin*, Tianjin (12th ed.), August 12, 1935.

82 Liu Rongting, "A Study on Rural Farms in Three Villages of Yangqu County, Shanxi and its Educational Situation", *New Villages*, June 1935.

83 Mao Zedong, "An Investigation Report on Hunan Peasant Movements", in *Selected Works of Mao Zedong* (vol. 1), ed. Mao Zedong (People's Publishing House, 1991), 40.

84 Jiang Wenyu, "Rural Education", *Chinese Education*, 18, no. 4(April 1930).

85 "An Education Program drawn up by the Ministry of Education" (December 1914), in *Documents about Modern Chinese Educational System* (vol. 3), ed. Zhu Youhuan (Shanghai: East China Normal University Press, 1989), 34.

86 "Records of the First Annual Meeting of Rural Education Research Association", *Rural Education*, 26th issue and 27th issue, 1935.

87 "An Admonition of an Official whose Surname was Meng to Primary Schools", *Ta Kung Pao*, March 19, 1909.

88 Yu Ziyi, "A Clash between Old and New Teaching Methods in Primary Schools", in Dong Yuanqian, *Selected Works of Education Theory Proposed by Yu Ziyi* (Beijing: People's Education Press, 1991), 54.

89 Deng Zhunshan, "Causes of Failure in Rural Education and Approaches for Improvement", *Social Welfare Tientsin*, Tianjin (12th ed.), February 27, 1937.

90 Liang Shuming, *Selected Academic Papers of Liang Shuming* (Beijing: Beijing Normal University Publishing House, 1992), 451.

Rural social changes 163

91 Zhuang Yu, "Primary Education", *Education Magazine*, February, 1909, 22.

92 Liang Shuming, *The Essence of Chinese Culture* (Shanghai: Xuelin Publishing House, 1987), 156.

93 Wang Kaiyuan, "Private School Life before and after the Revolution of 1911", Committee of Cultural and Historical Documents, *A Series of Chinese Literature and History* (vol. 17) (Beijing: Chinese Cultural and Historical Press, 1996), 22–24.

94 Liu Rongting, "A Study on Rural Farms in Three Villages of Yangqu County, Shanxi and its Educational Situation", *New Villages*, June 1935.

95 Wu Tengxiao, "Reasons for Rural Primary Schools Making No Progress", *Social Welfare Tientsin*, Tianjin (12th ed.), February 7, 1937.

96 Liu Rongting, "A Study on Rural Farms in Three Villages of Yangqu County, Shanxi and its Educational Situation", *New Villages*, June 1935.

97 Liu Rongting, "A Study on Rural Farms in Three Villages of Yangqu County, Shanxi and its Educational Situation", *New Villages*, June 1935.

98 Mao Zedong, "An Investigation Report on Hunan Peasant Movements", 40.

99 Song Zhenhuan, "An Investigation on Rural Education in Shanxi", *New Villages*, 13th issue and 14th issue, in June 1934.

100 Jiang Wenyu, "Rural Education", *Chinese Education*, 18, no. 4(April 1930).

101 Wang Shuhuai, "The Achilles Heel of Rural Education", *Social Welfare Tientsin*, Tianjin (3rd ed.), September 28, 1936.

102 Fei Xiaotong, "The Preface of 'Private Schools in Wenshang County'", *Social Welfare Tientsin*, Tianjin (12th ed.), August 12, 1936.

103 Wang Shuhuai, "The Achilles Heel of Rural Education", *Social Welfare Tientsin*, Tianjin (3rd ed.), September 28, 1936.

104 Liang Shuming, *Selected Academic Papers of Liang Shuming*, 451.

105 Wu Ke, "The Crisis of Chinese Rural Primary School Education", *New Villages*, June 1935, 14.

106 (America) Guy Salvatore Alitto, interviewer; Liang Shuming, interviewee; Yi Dan editor, *Will the World Become Better? – The Oral Account of Liang Shuming in His Later Years* (Beijing: Oriental Press, 2006), 183.

107 Tao Xingzhi, *Selected Works of Tao Xingzhi's Educational Thoughts* (Beijing: Educational Science Publishing House, 1981), 57.

108 (America) Alitto as interviewer; Liang Shuming as interviewee; Yi Dan as editor, *Will the World Become Better? – The Oral Account of Liang Shuming in His Later Years*, 266.

4 Historical changes in rural social structure and social stratification

The historical changes in the Chinese rural social structure and its stratification since the twentieth century not only became an essential issue for people at that time to think about and understand the nature of Chinese society, but also the starting point for the recognition of various sociopolitical forces to choose, reform and plan the development path of China. In particular, there are still many issues that are worth further questioning, inquiry and exploration regarding the judgment and cognition of the rural social class structure and the main rural social force.

Rural hired laborers in the early twentieth century: an investigation centered on the rural areas of Shanxi

The theoretical significance of exploring the generation and evolution of capitalist relations of production according to the development of the employment relationship has been verified by the typical Western European capitalist history. Meanwhile, only in the "reasonable" historical process can the rationality of historical understanding exist. Previous studies on modern Chinese rural hired laborers also regarded it as a product of agricultural production relations with a capitalist tendency, which was aimed at demonstrating the thesis of class opposition and class differentiation. Research in recent years has begun to break through this model of thinking. Some commentators pointed out that "There is little relationship between the employment relationship and the development of the commodity economy and social division of labor", and "It is a challenge to the classic theory which holds that commercialization that has been prevalent for many years inevitably leads to capitalism".[1] A commentator thinks that,

> From the perspective of world history, the rise of the employment relationship does not equal the germination of capitalism. And the germination of capitalism and the rise of the commodity economy are not equal to the transition to capitalism. In Western Europe, where labor is firmly attached to the land, the emergence of a free labor force is definitely one of the preconditions for the development of a capitalist economy.

Historical rural social structure changes 165

However, in China, where the rural labor force is overpopulated and the grassroots structure is loose, there is no shortage of labor with relative personal freedom.[2]

Some scholars identified rural hired laborers as "semi-feudal wage labor", "with traces of pre-capitalism"[3] and without a modern nature. This certainly helps clarify the dogmatic disorientation of the inevitable connection between hired laborers and the commodity economy or capitalism, but it does not help us understand the characteristics of the hired laborer group and how the era influenced its generation, nor is it sufficient to explain the historical connection between the evolution of the times and the rural hired laborer group. However, in-depth studies on the social relations of the hired laborer group are even much rarer. Obviously, in transcending the dual value judgment of "progress and backwardness" and "feudalism and capital", and in understanding deeply the social relations and social stratification of rural hired laborers in the early twentieth century, there is much more to be explored and excavated.

This chapter focuses on the Shanxi countryside in the early twentieth century as the scope of research. On the one hand, this is because the author obtained relatively concentrated local documents and materials on Shanxi to provide the context for in-depth analysis. On the other hand, this choice is due to the lack of previous relevant research involving Shanxi (even if "North China")[4], and there is still no research on Shanxi's hired laborers from the perspective of social history. Of course, although this chapter is based on the Shanxi countryside, the scope and even the application of data in this chapter is not completely limited to Shanxi. The author believes that by comparing relevant materials or data of other provinces and districts with Shanxi, not only the characteristics of rural laborers in Shanxi can be confirmed, but also the homogeneous structure and convergence behind the regional differences (even the differences based on customs, cultural inheritance and even economic levels) can be brought out.

Overview of rural hired laborers

In previous studies, the standard for identifying hired laborers was not consistent. It could be identified according to the occupation of the householders and those who were long-term hired laborers should be regarded as hired laborers. Either hired farm laborers who owned no land, or peasants who sold their labor to make a living without managing land (including landless households and those who rented out the land) could be called hired laborers. There was also a standard that used farm tools to identify hired laborers: "The tenant peasants themselves have no arable land, and the hired farmers do not even have farm tools".[5] The hired laborers discussed in this chapter include "hired farmers who sell their own labor and do not own land, farm animals or farm tools, and land-holding peasants who own a small amount of land, farm

166 *Historical rural social structure changes*

tools and some other things, work on their own land, and at the same time sell part of their labor".[6] Since sold labor is not necessarily used for farming, the research scope of this chapter specifically refers to the rural hired laborers described in the old literature as "the hired farmers [...] called long-term hired laborers, the day-serving workers are called long-term hired laborers".[7] That is, in Mao Zedong's words, agricultural hired laborers "refer to the long-term hired laborers, monthly laborers and part-time laborers and so on. These laborers do not have land, farm tools or money, so they have to sell their labor to make a living".[8] As for the large number of long-term or short-term hired laborers in villages or small towns who were employed to feed livestock, keep accounts, and work in oil mills, paper mills and other handicraft and service industries, they are not included in this study.

Previous studies have shown that "the number of rural hired laborers has increased since the Sino-Japanese War and the speed accelerated after the twentieth century".[9] In the process of the drastic changes in Chinese society in the early twentieth century, accompanying the trend of "rural bankruptcy", one phenomenon that occurred was the generalization of the employment relationship and the activation of hired groups. "With the reduction of land-holding peasants [...] the number of landlord increases gradually [...] rural hired laborers are increasing accordingly".[10] The significantly increasing employment relationship became one of the most basic social relationships in the countryside. Xu Dixin estimated that there were about 30 million rural hired laborers in the 1930s.[11] In North China,

> Most of the people who have less than 400 or 500 *mu* of farmlands manage their own fields and do not rent out their farmlands. They usually employ ordinary annual hired laborers and short-term hired laborers, so they can run large-scale operations. In this way, on the one hand, operations of hired laborers account for a large proportion in North China. And at the same time, the proportion of agricultural hired laborers in various rural classes is more than that in the central and southern regions of China.[12]

According to an estimate made in the 1930s, the percentage of hired laborers in the Yellow River, the Yangtze River and the Pearl River areas accounted for 11.4 percent, 9.3 percent, and 8.1 percent of the rural population respectively.[13] Recent studies have suggested that the employment relationship in Qingyuan, Hebei Province, is

> the most basic exploitative relationship in rural areas and it is far more common than the tenancy relationship. In surveyed villages, landlords may not rent out their land, but rarely do not hire laborers. And of course, rich peasants rely on hired laborers to exploit. Among the various classes of peasants, some middle and poor peasants also hire laborers during the busy farming season.[14]

Historical rural social structure changes 167

Table 4.1 Proportion of land-holding peasants, semi-land-holding peasants, tenant peasants and farm laborers in each county in Shanxi in 1928

County	Land-holding Peasants	Semi-land-holding Peasants	Tenant Peasants	Farm Laborers percent
Jiaocheng	49.25	31.10	9.81	9.80
Wenshui	64.19	22.45	8.73	4.52
Lanxian	43.36	27.89	14.87	13.78
Xingxian	49.48	24.1	13.8	12.58
Fenyang	30.11	21.69	32.53	18.67
Xiaoyi	62.6	14.77	15.9	6.73
Linxian	38.84	20.33	20.5	10.78
Shilou	62.46	17.53	17.04	3.17
Lishi	57.38	30.62	5	7
Fangshan	80.01	5.98	6.99	7.01
Zhongyang	28.85	32.69	17.31	21.15
Average	51.5	21.15	15.22	10.48

Source: Remake according to "Chorography of the Lvliang Prefecture", ed. Lvliang District Chorography Compilation Committee (Shanxi People's Publishing House, 1989), 109.

Statistics on the employment survey of 11 counties in Shanxi in 1928 are shown in Table 4.1.

Table 4.1 indicates that in 1928, the average proportion of hired laborers in Shanxi was 10.48 percent. Certainly, due to the difference in the scope of statistics, the average proportion of hired laborers may be slightly different. For example, in a survey by Nanjing Zhongshan Cultural Museum in 1933, the average proportion of hired laborers in 43 counties of Shanxi was 10.29 percent of the total number of peasants.[15] According to "China Industrial History" (Shanxi Province), "In 1935, there were 1,829,836 households in Shanxi Province, among which 170,803 were peasants who sold labor, accounting for 9.33 percent of the total households".[16] Therefore, only based on statistics, the number of hired laborers in Shanxi seems to have been decreasing. But this is only a theoretical average (and there is no direct comparability due to the scope of the survey), and is only of a reference value. In fact, influenced by multiple factors, the proportion of hired laborers in rural households varies greatly from region to region. "Before the Revolution of 1911, land-holding peasants in Yanggao, Shanxi Province had the highest superiority. As for the number of rich landlords, extremely poor farm laborers and tenant peasants, it was almost negligible". However, by the early 1930s, "tenant peasants and farm laborers accounted for 41.9 percent of the total rural households, of which farm laborers accounted for 15 percent".[17] In the three counties in north Shanxi (Tianzhen, Datong, Yanggao), "landless tenant peasants and farm laborers unexpectedly accounted for 31 percent of the total households".[18] In the late 1930s, farm laborers accounted for more than

168 *Historical rural social structure changes*

20 percent in 11counties in Shanxi. Most of these counties were cotton and wheat rotation areas or land reclamation areas. For example, farm laborers in Yongji County, a cotton and wheat rotation area, accounted for 34.24 percent of total households. And in Jingle County, where there was more land reclamation, farm laborers accounted for 23.72 percent of the total households.[19]

It should be noted that the growth is evident in the short-term hired laborers group, and although it is the main component of the rural employment relationship, it may not be fully included in the statistics (most of them are included for land-holding or tenant peasants). For example, in Heiyukou Village, Xing County, northwest of Shanxi, "rich peasants here often employ some short-term hired laborers, which are not counted in".[20] Tenant and poor peasants in some villages in Baode County also "sell part of their labor usually".[21] A comparative survey of villages in northern and southeast Shanxi showed that "The land of semi-land-holding peasants is not enough to support them. So they have surplus labor to plant other people's land to subsidize households, there will be fewer people that hired long-term hired laborers, and worker-peasant households will also reduce naturally".[22] "Worker-peasant households" here refers to "long-term hired laborers" rather than short-term hired laborers. Data from a survey in Henan also showed that the number of poor peasants who went out to work as short-term hired laborers was "almost three times more than that of purely farm laborers. There are more poor peasants serving as farm laborers at the same time in Hui County [...] Compared to the twelve pure hired households, the ratio is almost four to one".[23] Social turbulence and helplessness in life caused the mobility among poor peasants, tenant peasants and farm laborers. "Poor peasants have the possibility to become tenant peasants or farm laborers at any time, and tenant peasants may become farm laborers as well".[24] Therefore, the number of candidates to become rural hired laborers was increasing. For example, in Duanjiagou Village, Baode County, "before 1937, the proportion of farm laborers accounted for 13.63 percent of the total households in the village, and by 1942 it was 7.46 percent ".[25] However, the number of short-term peasants in the village increased continually: there were 7 households in 1936, 9 households in 1938, and 10 households in 1942. Most of the short-term farm laborers were poor peasants or land-holding peasants.

> Most of the hired laborers here are poor peasants. Besides working for themselves, they have a lot of surplus labor (the land is not enough to farm), so they make time to do short-term work for others (except for the people who go out of Shahukou and Zhangjiakou to engage in business).[26]

Moreover, most of the "small businessmen" in the village are hired laborers who return from places outside of Shahukou and Zhangjiakou. "They are very envious of the people who have lands, so they will plant some lands if

Historical rural social structure changes 169

possible, because agriculture is more reliable than business".[27] But these "hired laborers" are only included in the statistics of poor peasants and businessmen. In addition, some villages do not "declare the employment relationships. Most of the hired laborers (no matter whether it is long term or short term) are relatives of employers. They are nominally guests or helpers, but in reality there are employment relationships between them".[28] Such cases are also difficult to include in a count.

In addition to general long-term hired laborers (also called annual workers) and short-term hired laborers (commonly known as temporary workers), there were many other forms of hired laborers who were active in rural society of Shanxi. For example, "a laborer hired by season ", also known as "a laborer hired by month", was commonly known as monthly laborer: "If the work is enough for one month, a monthly laborer may be hired", "the duration of hired laborers in each stage is one or two months to three months [...] It's not more than five or six months in total". Its nature is similar to that of long-term hired laborers, but it is shorter in time and is intermittent. Generally speaking, monthly laborer is "temporarily hired in the busy farming season, such as the hoeing, intercropping and harvesting period".[29] There was also a saying at that time, that is, "the laborer who works more than half a month is a monthly laborer, and less than half a month is a daily laborer".[30] For example, "long-term work and short-term wage calculation" refers to short-term hired laborers who work for a long time. The nature and the work are the same as those of short-term hired laborers, and they work day by day. But the duration of working is longer than that of short-term hired laborers and it is only applicable to local villagers. If employers want to hire laborers, both employers and hired laborers will fix a time and they will start to work at any time. The remuneration is the same as or slightly higher than for the short-term hired laborers. Employers often adopted special forms of short-term hired laborers when times were turbulent, and it was difficult to hire people.[31] Another example is "winter laborers", who were long-term hired laborers working in the winter for three months. They usually worked at raising farm animals (mostly cattle), carrying coal, doing miscellaneous tasks around the home, running errands, carrying and splitting firewood, encircling and hunting down animals and so on. They were generally hired by wealthy and influential families, and their wages were to be half of their ordinary wages. In addition, there was the "half-time laborer" (who worked for half of the long-term laborer's time, also called a single part-time laborer), a "part-time laborer" (double-time laborer) and so on.[32]

Most of these types of hired laborers were generally active around the 1930s, showing the expanding trend of rural hired groups in general. There is no doubt that only focusing on the proportion of hired laborers (employees) in the statistical sense of household registration is far from enough to reflect

170 *Historical rural social structure changes*

the reality of rural social life. "However, it cannot be concluded that there were no hired peasants in worker-peasant households".

> In a peasant family, if there are more man forces than land, it will be necessary to leave some of them to farm at home and several of them to work as hired laborers at other people's homes. But in this phenomenon, the family in which only part of the people are hired laborers is not a pure worker-peasant household.[33]

According to this situation, the number of rural hired laborers is actually much greater than the household registration statistics.

The proportion of hired laborers in agricultural labor, although influenced and restricted by various factors, is closely related to the scale of agricultural operations. After the 1920s, the development of reclaiming and cultivating in Shanxi increased the demand for hired labor. However, due to the small scale of agricultural operations and the weak economic capacity of peasants, the number of employed laborers was generally not too large. "The number of hired laborers is generally two to three. In addition, there are some short-term hired laborers".[34] Among the hired laborers in Dayan Village, Zuoquan County,

> The strongest laborer can plant 15 *mu* of land, with an average of 10 *mu* of land per person, and the lowest laborer can plant 6 *mu* of land, with an average of 5 *mu* of land. With farm animals a laborer can plant 17 *mu* of land and without farm animals a laborer can plant 9 *mu* of land.[35]

According to the saying "seven is tight, eight is slow, and nine is free and happy" in rural Shanxi (meaning that seven to nine laborers are needed per *mu* of land), "If calculated by the workload that one laborer works for eight months every year in the field, it is sufficient for a person to plant 30 *mu* of land (except farm animals) on average".[36] "In Shenchi County, every strong peasant can cultivate 100 *shang* of land, and in Yonghe County, every strong peasant can cultivate 120 *mu* of land".[37] In addition, the proportion of peasant households that hired laborers not only varied regionally, but also depended on the economic conditions of the peasant households. Because of the scale of operations that was determined by the farming abilities and living needs of family members in most peasant households, the extensive existence of small-scale agriculture, the fact that there are more people and less land, the shortage of funds and other reasons, the number of hired laborers used by ordinary peasant households was also very limited.

According to a comprehensive study by academic circles, in the 1930s, "about 20 percent–30 percent of the land in the north was wholly or mainly operated by hired laborers".[38] And according to a survey conducted by the Department of Agricultural Economics of Jinling University from 1929 to

Historical rural social structure changes 171

1933, hired laborers accounted for 15 percent–20 percent of the total agricultural laborers in Shanxi. Compared with other provinces and autonomous regions, Shanxi was considered to be at a medium level in the surveyed provinces.[39] "According to statistics from Wuxiang and Wutai and other counties, the proportion of hired laborers in agricultural operations is 27 percent and 26.5 percent, which is slightly higher than the national average of 25 percent".[40]

The active employment relationship in rural areas was also embodied in the active employment market. In the north, the labor market was called "labor market", "work market" and "Kung Fu market", and the objects of transaction were usually daily laborer and monthly laborer. Short-term employment had a strong timeliness. A survey of 65 counties in Shanxi in 1934 showed that there were 35 counties that had relatively stable employment markets,[41] accounting for 53.84 percent of the total, and the 30 counties without markets accounted for 46.15 percent of the total.[42] Most of the short-term hired laborers were smallholders who farmed their own fields at the same time and could not be far away from home. Due to the constraints of time and space of the market, labor markets are seasonal markets and local markets. Labor markets were usually held in comparatively large villages regularly, and "gathered in a certain place at a certain time". Some labor markets appeared earlier. It is recorded that during the reign of Emperor Qianlong, "peasants come to the city to look for work in Yanggao County, Shanxi Province".[43] The labor market existed from the Ming and Qing dynasties to 1937 in Xiyan Town, Yu County. In ordinary villages, labor markets usually opened in the morning, and dispersed at noon at the latest. "At around five o'clock every morning, the employer will arrive at the place where the short-time laborers are gathered. And then, they come to an agreement".[44] *Liu Dapeng's Dairy* stated, "The reason why laborers arrive at the village to harvest wheat before sunrise may be that they will not be hired when they are late".[45] Markets with larger market towns sometimes lasted the whole day because of the requirement of continuous employment until the end of the season, so at noon and in the afternoon, agricultural workers made contracts with the employers, and then started to work the next day.

A short-term labor market could supply the needs of the ten or so surrounding villages. Depending on the size of the village, the season and the harvest situation, the size of the market could vary from a few hundred agricultural hired laborers to 20 or 30. In the labor market of Xiyan Town,

> During the period of hoeing sprouts and harvesting in autumn, there are more than 2,000 short-term hired laborers in the market every day, and people from everywhere come here in an endless stream. Except for the poor peasants in Xiyan Town and the villages of it, most of them come from the neighboring counties: Shouyang and Yangqu in the south, Wutai and Dingxiang in the north, Yangquan and Pingding in the east, and Xin and Guo in the west.[46]

172 *Historical rural social structure changes*

Even in small markets, there were short-term hired laborers and employers from nearby villages. According to Liu Dapeng, "Yurang Bridge in the county is the location of the labor market, and all of the laborers are in it".

> The wheat and sorghum are ripe and have already been harvested. Today, there are many people who are carrying sickles and poles and looking for employers to hire them to reap the wheat. It is clear that they are people from outside counties.

The labor market was sometimes prosperous but sometimes not: "Today, more than 200 people are hired by peasants in Xizhen, Huata, Yingdi and other villages and no one is left". But sometimes there were no laborers in the market: "This day, there are no laborers in the market, and all of the employers are troubled by the situation that no one works for them in fields [...] so they hire three people from elsewhere".[47] Although there is only a sporadic record in Liu Dapeng's diary, it provides vivid illustration for research on the rural labor market.

The price of labor in the market was generally higher before sunrise and lower after sunrise. The wages were negotiated by the employer and the employee. According to an investigation by Chen Zheng Mo, in the 65 counties of Shanxi, there were no intermediaries to bargain. Some employers called out the type of agricultural work and wages to hire laborers. And if no one applied, they would increase their wages. There were also hired laborers asking for prices. Prices of labor were affected by supply and demand, as well as by food prices and climate. "Daily wages in Xiaoyi, Zuoyun and other counties in Shanxi also change with the price of food".[48] In some labor markets where negotiation about wages between hired laborers and their employers was prohibited, the daily wages, which were mostly decided by the head of the village where the hired labor market is located or by the monks, were marked in the market every day. In this way, a unified price of labor was gradually formed in the labor market. However, there were still some employers who controlled the market and made it impossible for hired laborers to bargain. Like the words sung in folk songs, "do short-term work, do not bargain, do what the employers ask we do; reach an agreement, do not worry, wages in every household are the same".[49]

The hired labor market was quite widespread in Shanxi, but that did not mean that the labor force had to be traded in labor markets. In places far from the market or where there was no labor market, laborers usually visited door to door in groups to seek employment or a reservation. For example, in Yi County, Shanxi Province, "there is a labor organization in which ten rural laborers made a group, and in each group there was one foreman".[50] The foreman helped the laborers find jobs. There were "groups of rural laborers" that consisted of dozens of people in Fenxi, and there was a foreman to contact the employers for work and wages. This was actually a situation of the "labor market-to-be". The employment of short-term hired laborers had

Historical rural social structure changes   173

rarely been restricted. Although there were intermediaries in short-term transactions in some places, this was neither common nor systematic. It was only a custom, and its binding force only worked when the employer and the hired laborer could not come to an agreement.

The above are the trading places and methods of short-term hired laborers. As for long-term hired laborers, they were hardly employed through the labor market like short-term hired laborers. The employment of long-term hired laborers was conducted, either through direct negotiation between the employer and the employee, or through the introduction of intermediaries. There were many personal relationships involved. And long-term hired laborers could hardly find jobs without the introduction and matchmaking of intermediaries. After being recommended by others, the laborer negotiated the wage and other conditions at the employer's home as the place of employment and came to an oral agreement with the employer. Some hired laborers turned to the surety for guarantee.

The widespread existence of the "labor market-to-be" and the situation of "no market for long-term hired laborers" indicated that the labor market in the rural society of Shanxi was relatively underdeveloped and limited in space.

Analysis of rural employment relationships

The existence of employees, employers and the employment market together constitute the elements of a rural employment relationship. From the perspective of the tendency of employment, the selection of long-term and short-term hired laborers mainly depended on economic conditions or the demand for labor of both sides, and was not obviously subject to the mandatory role of "system" or "identity". A survey in 1936 showed that 52.46 percent of employees chose to be long-term hired laborers and 19.67 percent of employees intended to do short-term work. Moreover, 27.87 percent of them chose "changes with the environment".[51] To a certain extent, this shows the tendency of laborers to be hired, but it cannot completely prove that there were definitely more laborers who were willing to be long-term hired laborers rather than short-term hired laborers, but it is just a performance in a certain period. It depended on the specific situation of whether the laborer chose to do long-term or short-term work. The statistics from a sample survey at that time showed the main reasons for being willing to become a long-term laborer were having no family (2 cases), having no land (11 cases), and a stable lifestyle (31 cases), a total of 44 cases. The main reasons for being willing to become a short-term laborer were having a family (2 cases), having lands (28 cases), and earning more money (7 cases), a total of 37 cases.[52] Obviously, the main factors that determined laborers choice of long-term or short-term work were the possession of lands and life stability, of which the factor "life stability" that provided stable employment opportunities was obviously the most dominant reason.

174 *Historical rural social structure changes*

The living conditions and economic valuation of hired laborers were also constraints:

> It is easy to save a total amount of money rather than spending the money little by little when people work as a long-term laborer. While people are working as a short-time laborer, little bits and pieces of money can be easily splurged. Although the average annual salary of long-term hired laborers is less than that of short-term hired laborers, they earn money no matter whether it is a busy time or not. In contrast, although short-term hired laborers earn a lot of money in the busy time, when it turns to the idle months, they have no employers. Therefore, people are unwilling to be short-time laborers.[53]

Moreover,

> In peasants' opinion, working outside is something uncertain, and whether they can make money and get rich is still a problem. If they are just doing some short-term work in nearby villages, there will be few opportunities, so people are mostly more willing to be a long-term laborer. In this way, they can not only earn money reliably, but also do housework and cultivate their own lands.

This shows that the reasons for choosing to be long-term hired laborers were "when there are natural and man-made disasters, rural bankruptcies, oversupply of laborers and unstable wages [...] because of the sable wages, long-term work can insure life".[54] Another group of people chose to be long-term hired laborers because they had less land and more labor, and their labor was unduly left unused. The reason for choosing to be short-time laborers was that they were freer. Employers often treated long-term hired laborers unequally, and long-term employment made it impossible for hired laborers to cultivate their lands. Therefore, hired laborers dared not make a long-term agreement and they would prefer to do short-term work day by day.[55] Most long-term hired laborers had too many debts to make a living, but short-term hired laborers could make a living.[56]

From the perspective of the employer, the reason for choosing to hire a long-term laborer was that, first,

> short-term hired laborers cannot suffer as much as long-term hired laborers. Long-term hired laborers get up before dawn, while short-term hired laborers go to work late and get off early. They only suffer in the fields and never do housework.[57]

Second, "short-term hired laborers are not stable. Maybe there are laborers to do the work today, but there is no one to be hired the next day". "Long-term

Historical rural social structure changes 175

hired laborers are responsible. Short-term hired laborers and short-term-paid laborers are not responsible". "There are no toilsome members in the family, and all the livelihoods will be arranged by long-term hired laborers, who suffer all the year round and do almost everything".[58] Therefore, employers have nothing to worry about. Liu Dapeng once stated,

> Wang Laowu works as a long-term laborer for my family and this year is the fourth year. He knows all of the agricultural affairs and he can do everything I ask him to do immediately, so I do not have to go to the fields for many days.[59]

Of course, there were also benefits of hiring short-term hired laborers: hiring laborers only when it was too busy would not waste wages and money for food, and would increase work efficiency. That is,

> a day and a half's work can be done by a short-term laborer in one day (if a short-term laborer were hired, one laborer's five-day work of hoeing lands would be done in three days).[60]

However, due to the limited assets of employers and other reasons, far more peasant households hired short-term hired laborers rather than long-term hired laborers. A survey and statistics of 61 counties in Shanxi in the 1930s by Fei Jingshi showed that 26 counties employed more long-term hired laborers, accounting for 42.62 percent; 35 counties employed more short-time laborers, accounting for 57.38 percent.[61]

The seasonality of agricultural production caused an urgent need for labor part of the time and left laborers idle for part of the time. This caused a contradiction between the supply and demand of labor. In the best farming seasons, "there are few hired laborers everywhere, so although the wages are high, it is not easy to find a laborer". Liu Dapeng noted,

> There is an extraordinary shortage of hired laborers, although the wages are very high, I cannot hire a long-term laborer. [...] There are no laborers. I want to plant some millet between the wheat ridges. And last night, I looked for a laborer but I failed. Why there are so few laborers to do the farming work?

Especially in the "busy farming time of winter and spring",

> because of the ban on opium-smoking and the opium trade, half of the suffering laborers flee to other places, and half of them are in custody. Therefore, there is a tremendous shortage of laborers and the peasants are affected by this. However, people in charge do not take this situation into account.[62]

176 *Historical rural social structure changes*

According to a survey in the 1930s, the supply and demand situation of the agricultural labor force in counties of Shanxi was roughly as follows: 20 counties (36 percent) were in excess; 11 counties (20 percent) were in a moderate situation and 24 counties (44 percent) were in a situation of a lack of labor.[63] Laborers were still the dominant party in the rural labor markets in Shanxi. Therefore, in the employment relationship, the choice of employees seems to be more active.

> As long as there are valid reasons, dismissal and resignation are arbitrary. Generally, the employees resign from work more often than the employers fire laborers. If the food is not good, hired laborers will resign, and when summer comes, after three months' work, some laborers resign to earn more money. The employers are more unwilling to fire laborers because if not, they will have to hire new long-term hired laborers, but the salary is too high and laborers are too hard to hire.[64]

Then, in the employment relationship that occurs in rural society, or in other words, between the employers and the employees, has there formed a relatively stable, stratified, and clearly defined social relationship that marks the different statuses, identities and roles of employees? This is one of the basic prerequisites for helping us correctly understand the structure of rural society.

First, it is about the employer. In general, rich peasants and farm laborers are two opposite poles in the employment relationship.

> However, in the tense season of rural economy and labor, not only the majority of land-holding peasants, but even some tenant peasants and poor peasants, also temporarily play the part of employers [...] At the same time, in terms of employers, absolutely excluding landlords is practically impermissible.[65]

So almost anyone who was looking for work could be hired, and almost anyone who could afford to pay a wage could hire a laborer. Rich peasants and landlords were certainly in the class of employers. The reason for middle peasants to hire laborers was mainly the limited manpower in the short term. "Those who hire long-term hired laborers usually do so because there is a shortage of labor force in their families. Some of them run a business, but most of them are people whose families' labor forces go out to join the army or work, so they often complain of the lack of laborers".[66] Poor peasants hired laborers because of the lack of labor. Moreover, they had to pay wages. The employment of this class was mainly due to the urgency of farming. Tenant peasants, "because of the lack of family labor, or because of illness [...] or because the size of the agriculture they run exceeds the limit that the family labor may cultivate, they hire laborers to solve the problem".[67] However, it is rare for tenant peasants to hire laborers.

Historical rural social structure changes 177

Most of the employers of long-term hired laborers were from the class of rich peasants and landlords. According to relevant survey materials, in Dayou Town, Wuxiang County, there was one squire, employing nine long-term hired laborers; one landlord, employing five long-term hired laborers; twenty rich peasants, employing twenty-four long-term hired laborers; seventeen businessmen, employing two long-term hired laborers; seventy-eight other households such as middle peasants, poor peasants, farm laborers, and craftsmen, employing no long-term hired laborers.[68] "In Shouyang, Ying County, Zuoyun, Pingding, Wuxiang, etc. of Shanxi, only rich households can employ long-term hired laborers and non-rich households cannot. And in Anyi, Jincheng, Lingshi Counties, households higher than middle class can employ long-term hired laborers".[69] The number of long-term hired laborers was basically determined by the amount of land that was under management. Limited by the economic situation, in each village in Shanxi, the number of long-term hired laborers employed by the landlord household was generally two to three, and one to two in the rich peasant household. A few middle peasants employed at most one long-term laborer, while some employed less fewer one laborer (with others). In Xing County (before the War of Resistance against Japan), each peasant household (rich peasant) employed fewer than one and a half laborers. According to a survey on the employment relationship in eight v of Shenfu County and Xing County, the distribution of employers in all strata (26 households in total) was as follows: one rich peasant, twelve rich middle peasants, ten middle peasants, two poor peasants, and one small merchant.[70] Thus, the composition of rural short-term employers was more extensive, but the poor did not employ as many as the rich, nor for the length of time (rich middle peasants and middle peasants employed the most laborers and for the longest time). According to survey data of hired laborers in Yangjiapo, northwestern Shanxi in 1941, among the ten households that hired short-term laborers, landlords and middle poor peasants each accounted for five.[71] Of course, in general areas, the landlords had the most employment days, while rich peasants, middle peasants and poor peasants were decreasing in order. "The total annual average number of short-term laborers employed by various employers is 59–68 days, which is equal to two months or a little more".[72] "The average number of short-term laborers being employed was 40–50 days per year".[73]

Second, it is about hired laborers. Peasants who lost their land were naturally targets of employment in the countryside, but the hired labor was not limited to "rural proletarians". Poor peasants generally sold a small part of their labor force. See Table 4.2 about the reasons for different classes to become hired laborers:

Table 4.2 shows that although the causes were different, the main bodies of the long-term and short-term laborers were farm laborers, but there were also middle peasants, poor peasants and poor people. It should be noted that the amount of land that poor peasants occupied was much less than that of middle peasants. They could not make a living if they did not find

178 *Historical rural social structure changes*

Table 4.2 Analysis of reasons for different classes to become hired laborers

	Farm Laborers	Poor Peasants	Middle Peasants	Poor People
Work as Long-term Hired Laborers	have no possession, work for a long time	have not enough land to farm, have surplus labor	have surplus labor, work to make money, buy land and cattle	
Work as Short-term Hired Laborers*	cannot find a long-term job; lazybones	cannot find a long-term job; for freedom; have no food; have no cattle; have slight surplus labor	have surplus labor, have no cattle, work to buy clothes, hats and so on	carpenters, stonemasons and so on
Work as Monthly Laborers	resign from long-term job	cannot find a long-term job; have no cattle; have not enough food; have surplus labor	have surplus labor, have no cattle, work to buying clothes, hats and so on	
Work as Half-time Laborers	farm land in passing (rented); lack of food or have no food; cannot find a long-term job; together with renting land; together with planting land	farm own land in passing, have not enough land; lack of food or have no food; cannot find a long-term job; for freedom; together with planting land; rent land	have surplus labor; for freedom	
Work as Winter Laborers	hard-working; have no other ways	hard-working; have no food or clothes	hard-working	
Work as Short-term Hired Laborers for a Long Time / Work as Double Half-time Laborers	cannot find a long-term job; for freedom; farm rented land in passing; together with planting land; cannot find a long-term job; lack of food	cannot find a long-term job; for freedom; farm own land in passing; farm rented land in passing; together with planting land; lack of food; cannot find a long-term job		

Source: Remake according to "Fragmentary Materials of Hired Laborers" of Shanxi Provincial Archives (Shanxi Provincial Archives, file number: A88 / 3/34/ 6.). Basically, most of the short-term laborers were local ruffians, rogues, and they did short-term work to make money and did not like to suffer.

Historical rural social structure changes   179

other work, so doing short-term work was very common for them. On the one hand, they complained that "the land is not enough to plant" or "there is no land to plant". On the other hand, they had to find another job to make a living. "These are also the people who do short-term work, fluff cotton, roll and make felts, and even do long-term or double long-term work".[74] Because they had a small piece of arable land, they could neither make a living far from home nor seek a livelihood, so they had to sell their labor to supplement the family income. Therefore, in fact, there were far more poor peasants who were also hired laborers than pure hired laborers. "Poor peasants are the main suppliers of labor in the market".[75] Because of the shortage of land, the labor force was almost universally surplus, and the land could not support people's life, so they had to sell their labor and do some hard manual work. "In many families, fathers farmed at home while their sons worked as long-term laborers, or older brothers farmed at home while their younger brothers worked as long-term laborers".[76]

In terms of the composition of the hired laborer group, long-term laborers were basically from the class of farm laborers; poor peasants were more often hired as short-term laborers. The "constituent elements of short-term laborers are very complex and may include all classes of the whole laboring peasantry".[77] The distinction between tenant peasants and farm laborers was not very clear particularly. Tenant peasants "have no land at all, and their income is partly from the compensation of renting and planting farmland, which is equivalent to a wage, and partly from the earnings of selling labor or engaging in handicrafts".[78]

> The income of Chinese tenant peasants is not enough to support their families. Therefore, in addition to planting land, they have to take part in the employment of hired laborers or start careers in handicrafts and as hawkers to make up for their deficiency in life.[79]

According to the stipulation *How to Divide the Composition of Rural Class?* made by the Communist Party of China in 1946, farm laborers were "the rural proletariat". They had no land, and "they lived mainly by finding short-term work, selling their labor and suffering for others on the land". But in fact, in the three cases of hired laborers mentioned in the literature, there are also different forms of land management (such as rental planting and joint planting, own-land planting, full commission, etc.).[80] Therefore, in fact "farm laborers generally also have families and private property. If they have nothing, I am afraid that they will no longer stay in the countryside and will drift to metropolitan cities".[81]

Among the short-term laborers, the poor peasants were the largest group, followed by the middle peasants, poor people and farm laborers. Middle peasants and poor peasants often had the dual roles of both employers and hired laborers, but they were hired far more often than they hired laborers. It can be seen that every major class of rural society was involved in the

180 *Historical rural social structure changes*

social composition of the employment relationship, and that the roles of employers and employees were not completely fixed. Middle peasants, poor peasants, a few tenant peasants and farm laborers could play the roles of hired laborers and employers at the same time. The continual reciprocal translocation of hired laborers and employers formed a kind of circular interactive employment.

In family-oriented agricultural operations, those totally based on hired labor were still extremely rare, and ordinary hired laborers only supplemented family labor. "Small-peasant households have almost twice as many laborers per *mu* of land as large households".[82] Most poor peasants, owing to the shortage of arable land, had surplus labor and they were often hired temporarily in the busy farming season and took selling labor as one of the important family subsidiary businesses. In this way part-time wage laborers gradually formed. So there was a lack of pure hired laborers in the countryside, but there were vast numbers of seasonal part-time hired laborers. It can be seen that the universalization of the employment relationship in rural society was realized through the unfixed identities of hired laborers or the interchangeability of roles in employment.

Wage and food: the issue of employees' benefits

Paying wages to hired laborers by employers was also one of the important elements of an employment relationship. During the period of the Republic of China, the issue of hired laborers' wages was trivial and complicated, and it was difficult to generalize the forms of payment and regional differences. But there were two general trends, of which the formation and evolution were closely related to the social status and role of hired laborers.

The first one is the convergence in regional differences. According to *History of Chinese Industry* (Shanxi Province, 1935), the annual salary of a male laborer in the northwest of Shanxi was slightly different among different counties: it was 50 *yuan* in Jiaocheng, Wenshui and Xiaoyi; 40 *yuan* in Xing and Fenyang; 30 *yuan* in Lin, Shilou and Zhongyang; 24 *yuan* in Lan; 22 *yuan* in Fangshan; and 20 *yuan* in Lishi.[83] The factors that caused such regional difference were "working with bare hands, methods of agricultural working, decentralized land use and underdeveloped labor markets".[84] The relative average annual salary of hired laborers was about 40 *yuan*, because at that time, purchasing power was also calculated by 40 *yuan* (the annual wage of hired laborers was 40 *yuan*, which could buy 1,000 catties of wheat, 1,600 catties of millet, 2,000 catties of sorghum, 1,800 catties of corn, 7,000 catties of potato or 400 catties of egg).[85] The annual wages of male laborers in Yuci, Yangqu and Taiyuan before and after 1937 were 40 *yuan*, 36 *yuan* and 36 *yuan* respectively. This also illustrated the same problem. In addition, the level of job skills was also a main factor affecting wages. For long-term hired laborers in Ji County,

Historical rural social structure changes   181

the wages are negotiated by the two parties, the laborers who can rock a drill barrow in planting, send grass to the entrance when weeding and do all the work in the factory and field are highly skilled peasants and get the highest price,

but their wage also seemed to fluctuate around 40 *yuan*. "The highest wage before the War of Resistance was not more than 50 *yuan*, the next was 40 *yuan*, and then there were also 30 or 20 *yuan*".[86] Survey data of hired laborers in Yangjiapo also showed that the wages of hired laborers were "the highest 50 *yuan*, the lowest 30 *yuan*, and in general 35 *yuan* before the war".[87]

A survey in Qingwan County, Hebei, produced by Chinese scholars and South Manchuria Railways Co. showed that the average annual wage of local hire laborers in the 1930s was also set at about 40 *yuan*;[88] and according to the survey results of the National Bureau of Statistics, not only the average wage of hired laborers of 92 counties in Hebei was 43 *yuan*, but the average annual wage of hired laborers of 679 counties in 22 provinces nationwide was 41.7 *yuan*.[89] In a comparison of the data, it can be found that this wage level is quite general in Shanxi Province.[90] No matter how the specific wage amount varies among regions, the force of its market checks and balances will find a basic equilibrium in fluctuations. As Gurnot puts it,

The market, in economists' words, does not refer to any particular place where goods are traded, but the whole region in which interactions between buyers and sellers are free, and in this way, the prices of same commodity tend to equalize quickly.[91]

Regional differences in the wages of laborers cannot be freed from the "rapid equalization" rules of the labor market, and show a generally equal or similar trend in fluctuations. This rule of "salary price" "equal quickly" was actually constrained by the average living standard of peasants, because at the time "in terms of north China, one person only has about four *mu* of land on average, and earns about 40 *yuan* all year round".[92]

The second one is the low value in the growth trend.

Recently, the wages of hired laborers seem to have doubled on the surface, but the price of grain, homespun and daily expenses have more than doubled in these years. The price of wheat […] increases not only two or three times in 20 years. Therefore, the increase of wages in recent years is only in nominal terms, while real wages tend to decrease.[93]

Shi Zhihong's research also shows that

from a vertical perspective, the overall level of wages tends to increase gradually: taking selling labor and employing labor together to calculate, the total wages for long-term hired laborers were 60.79 *yuan* in 1930,

182 *Historical rural social structure changes*

62.32 *yuan* in 1936, and 71.78 *yuan* in 1946. Compared to 1930, wages of 1946 increased by about 18.1 percent. This change should be mainly related to inflation, not necessarily to the increase in real wages.[94]

The situation in the rural areas of Hebei Province and Shandong Province described by Ma Ruomeng was also similar: from 1901 to 1925,

> average annual wages of agricultural laborers have increased at about the same rate as prices of commodities [...] It can be seen that there was a sharp rise in wages in the late 1920s, which was because of the lack of laborers caused by the civil war. Prices of draft animals and ages of laborers tended to change in the same degree [...] land prices were rising at about the same trend and pace as rural general prices.[95]

The gentry Liu Dapeng from Jinzhong City gave a detailed account of the changes in the wages of hired laborers (mainly short-term hired laborers) from 1903 to 1941 in his diary.[96] According to this, it can be seen that the wages of hired laborers have increased significantly in the past 40 years, and although there was a great contrast in the fluctuations, it did not affect the overall growth momentum. However, the skyrocketing prices of food and other necessities was the main factor influencing the increase in the wages of hired laborers. In 1930, the provincial currency depreciated sharply, and "one silver dollar can be exchanged for the twenty *yuan* of 'provincial banknotes'", which resulted in "the accelerated decline in the purchasing power of the people of Shanxi".[97] Liu Dapeng's diary shows that wages increased with the highest rate in 1931, but in this year, the amount of increase of local food prices also reached the highest point in history.[98] Even as an employer, Liu Dapeng was deeply troubled by the soaring prices. He said (in September 1931) that "everything is expensive and reaches the maximum", which resulted in the "high wages" paid to hired laborers. Therefore,

> I work as a farmer temporally since I do not hire many laborers. Although it is not possible for me to work as a full-time laborer, I am able to be half a laborer [...] At a time when all things are expensive, even a grain of rice was difficult to gain.[99]

Even if the absolute volume increased significantly, wages paid to hired laborers could only passively move with the curve of food prices which were subject to fluctuations. The same was true of the three counties of northern Shanxi: "it is true that for this year and last year, the wage base has generally increased to twenty cents a day on average; but on the other hand, the price of food has risen above the wage bases".[100] As a result, the living standards of hired laborers, whose "nominal wages increased but real wages decreased", were still declining.

Historical rural social structure changes   183

"There was an advisable admonishment in ancient times that cut one's coat according to one's cloth. However, the income of hired laborers is limited while the output is numerous".[101] So, what was the support capacity of the income of hired workers according to the basic standard of living at that time? "The salary of a good laborer was not enough to support one and a half people (except for his own clothes)".[102] According to the survey data from five counties, which were Baode, Xing, Shuo, Lin, and Hequ,

before the War of Resistance against Japan, the wage of an annual laborer could support more than two people except for himself; the wage of a monthly laborer could support two people except for himself; the daily wage of a day laborer could support half to one person except for himself whose food was provided by the employer.[103]

But in general, in northwestern Shanxi, long-term laborers

usually are employed for eight to ten months each year. So the annual wages, no matter in the form of money or in kind, must be subsidies for the two-or-four-month time of unemployment (sometimes they do other work to make money for meals, such as carrying coals in winter, hawking goods, etc.), and in fact, they can only support about one person without taking their own living expenses into count.[104]

Generally, there were four or five members in a hired labor's family; some were seven; and some were two to three. "Most of the hired families in Wuxiang have five or six members in their families. There are many such families".[105] Undoubtedly, hired laborers "provided the largest labor force and some basic farm tools but got the basic salary, which was insufficient to maintain their most destitute family life".[106]

Of course, "the increase or decrease in wages means the increase or decrease in unpaid labor".[107] But for an agricultural society that is not dominated by capital, "hired laborers are not or are not primarily used as labor goods here, but as natural forms of labor". For employers, of course,

in this case laborers will not be considered as cost factors in the "check computation" of farm households, and the use of laborers will not be restricted by the principle of marginal remuneration diminishing and comparative benefits. As long as the rough output is more than zero within hired laborers' margins of tolerance of the "sense of hard labor", the laborers will be hired.[108]

The trend of low wages and low actual support capacity made it difficult for labor payment in the form of wages to fully develop in rural society. Therefore, for the survival of hired laborers, the payment method of food was not inferior to the payment method of wages.

184 *Historical rural social structure changes*

Generally speaking, long-term hired laborers were provided with food and accommodations, and the food for short-term hired laborers was also an important part of their labor payment.[109] Statistics on food and accommodations provided for hired laborers in counties of Shanxi from 1933 to 1934 are as follows, as shown in Table 4.3.[110]

It appears that most areas of Shanxi provided food and accommodations for hired laborers, especially long-term laborers. As a result, the relationship between long-term laborers and employers was more complicated than short-term laborers. The quality of food varied depending on the living conditions of employers and the living facilities and supplies provided to laborers. For example, bedding was different; some were customary while some were different from employer to employer. There was no fixed standard.

Money and food were both payment for labor, but hired laborers had different rights to use them. Monetary wage, which "was an agreed amount negotiated by employers and hired laborers",[111] was entirely discretionary for hired laborers. Food was provided by employers, and the quantity and quality of the food also depended mainly on them, while hired workers could only accept it relatively passively. There was no certain standard for long-term laborers' food and it depended on employers: In Liaoxi County, hired laborers generally ate well, and "must eat before employers", because employers knew how to "coax the belly".[112] Long-term laborers in Shouyang were provided with meals by their employers and "the main foods were bean flour, steamed corn bread and millet".[113] In Gaojia Village, Xing County,

the food for laborers was usually the same as employers'. Three-legged steamed corn bread, fried flour[114] or porridge were provided for breakfast, steamed corn bread or porridge for lunch, and porridge or fried flour for dinner. But it was different at good times.[115]

Before the war (before 1937) in Xiangyuan,

employers and hired laborers ate different foods, while medium employers usually ate the same as hired laborers, but they ate alone in small pots. Half of hired laborers ate bad food when the employers came and good foods when they left. Those laborers who were relatives of the employers had the same food as them.[116]

Regarding the food in Ji County,

the more generous little landlord ate the same meals as long-term laborers and sometimes there was a steamed bun that weighed half a catty for breakfast, white noodles and bean noodles etc. for lunch. Long-term laborers' meals provided by harsh landlords were mainly miscellaneous grain crops. But no matter the meal was good or bad, the laborers would be full.[117]

Table 4.3 Number of counties about food and accommodation supply for hired laborers

	Number of Counties	Categories of Laborers	Provide Food and Accommodations (counties)	Provide Food and No Accommodations (counties)	Provide Accommodations and No Food (counties)	Not Quite Clear (counties)
Laborers	60	Long-term laborers	55	3	\	2
Laborers		Monthly laborers	52	5	\	3
Laborers		Day laborers	33	18	\	9
Laborers	37	Long-term laborers	24	3	\	10
Laborers		Monthly laborers	27	5	\	5
Laborers		Day laborers	21	14	\	2
Laborers	55	Long-term laborers	50	1	\	4
Laborers		Monthly laborers	44	5	\	6
Laborers		Day laborers	29	15	\	11

Source: *Statistics of the Republic of China* (1936) compiled by the Statistics Bureau of the National Government's Accounting Office. Remake according to the table on pages 496 to 503.

186 *Historical rural social structure changes*

Laborers were also awarded with food because of farming, and sometimes they got consolations when they were "hoeing", "ploughing" and "harvesting". Sometimes, because short-term laborers "suffer a lot when doing hard work, they often eat solid food". Because of the whole day's labor in the summer and autumn when the farming was busy, the original amount of food was not enough to support it, so the three meals a day "mostly should be much better and not mixed with extra bran or even not bran at all". "Using wheat flour and rice for lunch instead of coarse grains such as corn and sorghum was a generous treatment".[118] The number of meals in a day varied with the seasons. Generally, three meals were eaten in the busy farming season, and two meals were eaten in the slack season.

The food condition of short-term laborers was generally determined by the employers and the employees together, and was relatively better. According to the content recorded by Liu Dapeng, in the area of Jinci in Taiyuan, "(October 1926) three meals for breakfast, lunch and dinner must be worth 700 *wen* per person" (and each person's monthly salary was 1,000 *wen* at that time). "(May, 1927) Regardless of the meals of morning and evening, there must be deep-fried cakes, liquor and meat for lunch".[119] This phenomenon was not uncommon, but in general, short-term laborers had better food than long-term laborers.

The share of wage in the payments of hired laborers was very limited. Research done by Huang Zongzhi proves that, even in the villages of the Yangtze River Delta, food and wage were equal in payments to hired laborers.[120] Therefore, analyzing wages alone is not enough to explain the economic status of hired laborers, let alone to reveal the complex and diverse social relationships and characteristics between employers and hired laborers.

Hired laborers often said, "Whether earn money or not, you'll have a round belly".[121] When food prices were rising continually, the price of food was often not lower than or even higher than the price of wages. "Rice and flour are expensive and three meals a day for each person must spend fifty or sixty cents on rice or flour". (The daily wage was sixty cents.)[122] If the reason for middle peasants to do short-term work is that "there is surplus labor to earn extra income". Then "the poor peasants do short-term work because of 'awful hunger'".[123] Some "poor peasants have to make their own land idle and go out to do short-term work for others because of hunger". Even "the land they got" in the land reform "is not a source of happiness, but a great burden for them".[124]

> Every year the average food cost of peasants from all parts of China accounts for about 60 percent of all the expenses, plus fuel costs, which are more than 10 percent; the sum total is about 70 percent. They work hard all year round almost completely for the problem of "eating".[125]

Historical rural social structure changes 187

This condition determined that the choice of "food" was better than the choice of wages. Even "work harder, eat more" would become a reason for hired laborers to "work not so hard".[126] Therefore, the requirement of "food" for the hired laborers to maintain the "labor force" was often greater than the requirement of "wage".

For the same reason, even in the payment of wages, even though it was agreed to be silver dollars, hired laborers were more willing to receive material objects such as food, oil, salt and cloth. "Wages are paid in large part by food provided by the employer or by cloth and other commodities bought from the shop".[127] Employers were more willing to pay in currency, while hired laborers were willing to receive millet. Because of the political instability and severe currency devaluation, such as the bankruptcy of the bank in 1930, after which the employer still paid the same banknotes as before,

> hired laborers suffer a big loss, which is equivalent to a year's hard work for nothing. Moreover, hired laborers who are willing to be paid in money also have to buy food, and because they cannot delay their work in other to buy grain in the city or the market, they have to buy from employers.

Therefore, "although the rural hired laborers have a certain income, they have not become consumers who rely entirely on the market to buy their daily necessities".[128] More than half of the necessities of hired laborers and their families were bought from their employers. "The employer seemed to be a consumer's cooperative for hired laborers and they deducted wages to buy foods and other things at the market price at the time. Grain was expensive in spring and cheap in autumn. Employers were reluctant to provide grain in autumn and they were willing to provide food in spring. But poor people needed grain in spring exactly, so they could do nothing except suffer the losses". As the folk song goes, "work in autumn, make a price in spring, you can buy three liters of grain in autumn, and you can only buy half a liter in spring".[129]

Purely from the perspective of the price system, some employers "converted the goods for hired laborers into higher prices than market prices [...] but the laborers still had to buy from the sole employer". On the surface, this seemed to be an expansion of the family relationship with a mild sense of nostalgia between employers and employees. In fact, the dominant constraint for the hired families was still the "economically reasonable calculation", because "buying things at the market meant delaying work and the salary could not be advanced".[130] Therefore, under severe living pressure, naturally, the choice of labor time is better than the calculation of market commodity prices. "Hired laborers are closely related to the market-oriented economy and the price system determines both their labor wages and the purchasing power of their wages".[131]

188 *Historical rural social structure changes*

At the same time, the form of labor payment by food would inevitably weaken the market attributes of both employers and employees and strengthen the personal dependence between them.

> Although they sell their labor nominally, they actually sell their bodies. There is a common saying, "eat a bowl of rice from others, then work for them [assign at will], eat a bite of food from others, shouted at by them" and that being a long-term hired laborer is "being a servant".[132]

However, this dependency was economic dependency under survival pressure rather than a feudal identity dependency. "Laborers always stayed in employers' homes, and it was not because they were in the legal position of serfdom, or out of consideration for the economic rationality of the farm,; rather, it was just a matter of custom. For laborers, it was more of a kind of protection than a restraint, but this situation has gradually receded in modern times".[133] Moreover, in most interaction involving employment relationships, employers "treat laborers as friends, because both the hired laborers and the employers are tenant peasants".[134] On the one hand, the wages or the food in the form of quasi-wages, in fact, reflected the contractual relationship between employers and hired laborers, which was the exchange of "ownership" between employers and hired laborers in the commodity society. That was, "expenditure was the transfer of ownership and income was the acquisition of ownership".[135] On the other hand, there was "no strict difference between employers and hired laborers [...] employers treated farm laborers equally, completely different from the way of treating slaves".[136] This apparent equality in human dignity at least showed that status or institutional restraint was not the normal rural employment relationship of the Republic of China. Such a fact was discovered by Zhang Wentian in his investigation (May 1949): Even after the land reform, hired laborers had their own land, "a part of the poor farm laborers [...] still want to stay in the countryside as hire laborers".[137]

It was precisely the food for work that maintained the basic needs for their own survival that became an important reason for the widespread existence and development of hired laborers under low wages. At the same time, it is actually a "mutually beneficial" economic factor in the interchange relationship between employers and employees.

Hired laborers in social stratification

Some researchers pointed out that

> farm laborers are the group with the lowest social status and the most miserable life in the countryside. In terms of income, they are busy enough with their own affairs and find it difficult to marry wives and start families. In fact, many farm laborers live a lonely life all their lives.[138]

"Tribulation and the lack of food and clothing all day long" is the normal state of the material life of a hired laborer's family. In the past, people mostly used the "polarization theory" to explain the emergence of a large number of rural laborers and their deteriorating living conditions, which was considered to be the result of a high concentration of land and polarization. "As long as there are small commodity producers, there will be differentiation, and there will be rich and poor people, employers and hired laborers generated from small commodity producers".[139] But since modern times, "segmentation of warlords has intensified the annexation and concentration of land [...] forcing overburdened tenant peasants to become farm laborers".[140] Historical facts invariably put such "gray" theoretical presuppositions in an awkward position. According to an analysis of a group of cadastral files from the Kangxi period of the Qing dynasty to the Republic of China, some scholars found that "although the distribution of land has varied from time to time and from place to place over the past two to three hundred years, the feature of the decentralization of land ownership is very obvious".[141] Even in the Jiangnan region,

> From the early years of the Kangxi Period (5–15 years) to 1949, the ratio of landlords' land to land-holding peasants' land was almost stable at 65: 35 during the 270–280 years. It seems that the supposed inevitability of the increasing concentration of land rights under the ownership of landlords has not been proven here.[142]

According to a detailed analysis of the land occupation from 1925 to 1949 based on a large number of different statistical data by Guo Dehong, he confirmed that "by either way, land occupation in the old China for decades tended to be scattered rather than concentrated".[143] Compared with the national trend of land occupation, "Shanxi's land was not as concentrated as that in other provinces, and the landlords' power was still small".[144] As a statistic during the War of Resistance against Japan (before and after 1937) showed,[145] in all districts and counties, the proportion of land occupied by landlords and rich peasants in northwestern Shanxi was the highest, at 60.8 percent, reaching or slightly higher than the above-average level of the country. In other areas, the highest average proportion of land occupied by landlords and rich peasants was 31.5 percent (Pingding, Yu County), and the lowest was 15.5 percent (Taigu, Qi County, etc.), which is far lower than the above national level of land concentration. Therefore, in fact, even in Xingxian County, Northwestern Shanxi and other places where the land was relatively concentrated, "the ownership of land has changed" before the land reform, and the "definite and inevitable trend" of the change was exactly "the decrease of the total amount of the land occupied by landlords and the increase of the land owned by middle and poor peasants".[146] This can be concluded in a certain sense in that "the transfer of land rights was achieved through superficial free trade in areas without agrarian revolution".[147] As Zhang Wentian found

190 *Historical rural social structure changes*

in a survey in the same year, "The changes of the entire social economy were also developing in the direction of subdivision of land rights, increase of both quantity and quality of land-holding peasant groups".[148] The fact is clearly far from the "polarization theory" caused by "land concentration".

From the perspective of a comparison of material life, the "polarization theory" is interpreted from the basic point of the strong contrast between the rich and the poor in social classes and its expanding trends. However, archival data shows that the "polarization" trend of the material life differences of all walks of life in the countryside is not significant.[149] For example, in Lin County, in terms of the total consumption of grain, oil, salt, meat and other necessities, the living standard of a hired laborer's family was identical to that of the poor peasant's family, was slightly different from that of the middle peasant's family and was quite different from the consumption of the landlord's and the rich peasant's family, but it was only a difference in degree. In terms of the quality of their consumption (that is, the type of staple food), the differences in material life between rural social strata were obvious (such as Baode, Linsui, in western Shanxi and Wuxiang in southeastern Shanxi).[150] However, the differences were mainly reflected in coarse food grain or refined grain, or with or without meat (the landlord's family only occasionally ate meat on New Year's Day or other festivals) and salt. The daily life of the landlord's family was undoubtedly better, but according to survey data, special features were reflected in two aspects: the landlord himself had white flour to eat at ordinary times (but his wife ate steamed cornbread); and had dumplings made of white flour to eat on New Year's Day or other festivals.[151] The material life of most households in rural Shanxi was "extremely simple and extremely economical, reaching the level of being very pale".[152] Investigation data from a survey conducted by the party committee of the Western Shanxi District of the Communist Party of China in Zhao Village, Xing County, shows that the daily life of the various classes in the rural areas was not so different. "The masses did not eat dishes at ordinary times. When they ate, they would make a large pot of a dish and eat as much as possible (both the rich and the poor –original note)".[153] In terms of clothing, the expenditure for clothes and quilts was not large. From a comparison of the consumption of cloth of various classes throughout the year, the difference between the annual cloth consumption of farm laborers and middle peasant families was small, with a difference of only two feet per capita; and there was a difference of seven feet among rich peasants.[154] Before the War of Resistance against Japan, there were not very prominent differences in the clothing consumption of landlords, rich peasants, middle peasants, poor peasants and farm laborers in Donggou Village of Wuxiang County.[155]

There was little difference in the use of clothes between a hired laborer household and a middle peasant household; landowners and rich peasants were relatively wealthy, but they only had two sets of clothes for each season a year on average. For most villagers, they "only change clothes twice a year, no more than three times".[156]

Historical rural social structure changes 191

Clothing and food, as the most basic living necessities for human beings, constitute the basic premise for social members to share their social status. The difference in quantity and quality of clothing and food consumption and its special trends are one of the main indicators for judging whether the society is differentiated or not and the degree of differentiation. But difference is not differentiation. Data shows that there are no considerable differences between the various classes of rural society. Although there are large differences among landowners, rich peasants and poor farm laborers, they have not formed a huge contrast of "polarization". What it presents is a scene of "universal impoverishment" in rural life. A 1936 issue of *Chinese Countryside* described the situation of villages in the middle area of Shanxi, saying, "Heaps of ruins and barren hills will be presented in your field of vision".

According to a survey, there were 1,300 households and 36 large or small business houses in the village of Beibao in Taigu County sixty years ago. A small part of the houses were tile-roofed houses, and the rest were mostly storied houses. The street was lined with houses on both sides [...] Now! Households can only be found in the ruins. There are only sixty households in all.

In another village surveyed by the author, "there are more than three hundred households. In the Jiaqing period, the number of households was originally more than five thousand".[157] This situation is almost the same as the decline of Man Village in Taigu County recorded in Liu Dapeng's diary:

In the past [...] there were many wealthy households in the village, with a total of 2,000 families, and the high-rise buildings were brilliant [...] the village declined, and now there are only a hundred or so households, and most of them are poor. There are 80 percent to 90 percent of the people who live on selling houses and pavilions, and there is no rich household.[158]

Obviously, this kind of overall "dismal sight" of decline was more concentrated in wealthy "large households".

In recent years [...] the number of peasants fleeing from their villages is increasing continually, and the barren land has a tendency to expand every year [...] This has caused a general stagnation in the economic life of the whole province, and it has made the impoverished farmers more and more unable to deal with it.[159]

In his petition (1935) to the nationalist government, Yan Xishan also described the following: "the entire rural economy of Shanxi has been bankrupted in the past year [...] as a result, nine of ten villages have difficulties and nine of ten families are poor".[160] In the same year, Liu Dapeng described the tragic scene of the decline of the local village in his diary:

192   *Historical rural social structure changes*

The phrase "rural bankruptcy" is a new term now, which means that a peasant family declines and cannot conserve its property. When this happens, the people will be extremely poor with wealth reaching its lowest extreme, and agriculture will be weak, there will be no way out.

One thing that is particularly worthy of deep thought is, Liu sighed, "Even though you want to go bankrupt and sell what you own, there are no buyers. Thus the extreme poverty of the rural areas is easily to see".[161] The phenomenon of "no one buys properties" fully reveals that this is not the concentration of "wealth transfer" shown by "polarization", but a decline in the overall sense. "Universal impoverishment"[162] and the "polarization" of overall decline are obviously two different evolutionary trends, although both can lead to the worsening living conditions of the rural disadvantaged group –hired laborers.

In the early twentieth century, the rural society in China was not sufficiently differentiated, which directly led to the "impurity" of rural laborer groups.

Most of the hired laborers here are poor peasants. They have a lot of surplus labor besides working for themselves, so they work for others when they have time. [...] So the number of households that hire short-term laborers [...] is still increasing.

Therefore, the total number of "part-time laborers" is far greater than the number of purely farm laborers.[163] As mentioned above in this chapter, "the universalization of the employment relationship in rural society is realized through the non-solidification of hired laborers or the interchangeability of roles in employment", which is obviously also a historical result of the evolution of the trend of "universal poverty". This is naturally also related to the social stratification of rural laborer groups.

First, the rural society was not sufficiently divided, so rural laborers did not constitute a relatively independent social class. Some rural social survey data at that time pointed out that there was no drastic class differentiation in rural China, and there were not many large landlords. The current situation is that "although there are few large landlords, the number of small and middle landlords is large".[164] Similarly, "farm laborers can be said to be as scarce as 'large landlords', and most of them are divided from tenant peasants [...]" Therefore, " 'day laborers' [...] [were] often counted in the percentage of tenant peasants listed above".[165] And in many places, the distinction between farm laborers, tenant peasants and land-holding peasants was not clear and was subject to change.

A farm laborer can change into a tenant peasant, a tenant peasant can change into a semi-land-holding peasant, a semi-land-holding peasant can change into a pure land-holding peasant, and at the same time, a land-holding peasant can change sequentially. There is a local proverb

Historical rural social structure changes 193

that says, "there are 800 masters of a piece of field in a thousand years", how fast the speed is of the change is conceivable from this.[166]

So, "sometimes farm laborers can be tenant peasants, sometimes tenant peasants can also become farm laborers, it is not permanent, and their boundaries are very imperceptible".[167] Especially for short-term laborers, "the constituents of day laborers are very complicated, which can include all members of different classes of the working peasant masses".[168] There even appeared some households with multiple identities in some villages,

> a middle peasant becomes a hired laborer and at the same time a rich peasant. Sends one person of his family out to be an annual laborer and hires a half-year laborer, then he can cope with others and increase his income at the same time.[169]

In Jingjing, Hebei Province, which is adjacent to Shanxi Province,

> the peasants who have absolutely no property in this county are the most in the minority. Those who have a property that is not enough for a family to plant, will become long-term laborers for others, rent out their own land or take their land to do long-term work and become a worker. Some people rent land from others because they have little land, and then they become tenant peasants. Or they do not do long-term work or become tenants; they just finish their work quickly in the busy farming season and help others "find jobs", which is also a kind of speculation.[170]

The transformation of the different roles and identities of long-term laborers, tenant peasants and job seekers not only shows the "free" characteristic of villagers' identity, but also the "inseparable" character between the role of hired laborers and other roles. This is actually the main reason why "rural social investigators" were unable to confirm the identity and number of "hired laborers" at that time.[171]

There were also the so-called

> semi-tenant peasants and tenant peasants – they were actually 'farm laborers who worked on the land of the employers' family, and they kept 25 to 50 percent of their harvest for themselves, and the remaining 50 to 75 percent were for landlords – masters. The best indicator of the situation of farm laborers was their wages: masters provided food for them and they earned 20 to 50 *yuan* per year.[172]

Therefore, from the change in the roles of hired laborers in Jiong Yuantou village, Pingbei County, in the late 1930s, it can be observed that: poor peasants rented out their land and became hired laborers; middle peasants became hired laborers and at the same time rich peasants. They sent a

194 *Historical rural social structure changes*

member of his family to work as an annual laborer and hired a half-year laborer.[173] Similarly, the transformation of hired laborers into poor peasants does not necessarily mean that their economic status rose.[174] Therefore, merely relying on the "employment relationship" may not be sufficient to develop an effective explanation for the nature of rural social relationships. We often find that for some typical land-holding peasants (middle peasants), "the main reason to hire laborers" was just the labor shortage, so these "developments of middle peasants to rich peasants were only changes of mode of operation in the case of labor famine, rather than new expansions of economy".[175] In the early twentieth century, rural hired laborers were a social group that was undergoing rapid evolution and had not yet formed a relatively independent class.

Second, the structure of social relationships between hired laborers and employers was complex, and the "polarized" mode of class relationships of "landlords and rich peasants – farm laborers" – could not adequately reflect the reality of rural social relationships at that time. In fact, the employment relationship was not limited to landlords and rich peasants, and farm laborers were often "employed by land-holding peasants and tenant peasants".[176] As relatively free labor sellers in rural society, the farm laborers were all "attached to the landlords and land-holding peasants". Although it was common for large landlords to hire laborers to cultivate the land, "many land-holding peasants who have a bit more fields hire one or two or three perennial male or female laborers, and many of them are hired from tenant peasants". Because of this relationship, it is "actually not easy" to accurately formulate the proportion of rural households' distribution.[177] Land-holding peasants hired laborers to manage their land, and it was a logical historical process of both the generalization of rural employment relationships and the evolution of widespread poverty in rural societies: "Since land owned by land-holding peasants cannot be fully farmed, it is necessary to hire laborers. Therefore, most of the farm laborers are employed by land-holding peasants".[178] As a consequence, "land-holding peasants have a close relationship with farm laborers [...] none of such land-holding peasants hire laborers".[179]

In some areas of central Shanxi, the so-called landlords who hired laborers to cultivate their land were actually small households that lacked male labor, or even large tenant peasants: "Landlords are almost small households of which the men go out for business or of which there are only women and children, while the peasants that rent land are local large landlords".[180] A similar situation also occurred in Songjiang, Jiangsu.[181] Therefore, the social relationship that occurred with hired laborers did not simply appear as a "polarized" situation of class opposition. "Generally speaking, the tenancy relationship – the confrontation between landlords and tenant peasants was very vague in that area".[182] Not only "employers treated farm laborers extremely equally, completely different from the way of treating slaves", but also "there was no strict difference between land-holding peasants and landlords".[183] The differentiation between the classes of employers and hired laborers was not clear.

Historical rural social structure changes   195

Although rural investigators at that time were lost in their subjective thinking, class division between employers and hired laborers had not yet been clearly demarcated, and this was an objective existence. "Therefore, some of the land-holding peasants are landlords, some are farm laborers. Some of the farm laborers are land-holding peasants, some are tenant peasants. Some of the tenant peasants are either land-holding peasants or farm laborers".[184] Thus, the social relationship that occurs by employing hired laborers is a multiple and complex reticular structure, rather than a simple bipolar structure. Just as the people of that time analyzed,

> "peasant" is just a general term. They can be divided into four groups: landlords, land-holding peasants, tenant peasants and farm laborers. In terms of landlords, they mostly belong to wealthy people and merchants with large capital. Farm laborers, on the other hand, belong to the scope of land-holding peasants and tenant peasants,

and have direct relationships with landlords, land-holding peasants, tenant peasants, those who are both landlords and land-holding peasants concurrently, and those who are both tenant peasants and land-holding peasants concurrently, and become the intersection point of rural social relationship network.[185]

Therefore, although "farm laborers have a kind of bitterness toward their employers", "there are no class rifts".[186] Even the children of hired families in traditional societies were once "cultivated and educated by landlords" and become successful candidates in the imperial examinations at the provincial level.[187] At least, "in the employment relationship here, the phenomenon is complicated and confused, and it is really difficult to grasp and easy to get lost".[188] Hierarchy and antagonistic conflict between employers and hired laborers were not very clear. For instance, Liu Dapeng, a local gentry, was quite concerned about the funeral of the hired laborer who had left their home for more than ten years, saying that "if I happen to hear the laborer's death, I will take part in his funeral procession".[189] Some old long-term laborers who had been hired for a long time "once received meager preferential treatment of the host family, ate the same food as that of the family rather than a separate meal", so that "the minds of the old laborers were the same as that of the host".[190] The employment relationship in rural society is actually a reticular structure with the intersection of multiple identities, status and roles, presenting the operating characteristic that attaches equal importance to the principles of interest and emotion:

> If the hired laborers have kinship with the employers, they call each other according to the kinship. If there is no kinship between them, the employers call the laborers by name and the laborers call the employers uncle or brother, depending on the age. There is no rich or poor class, nor master or servant, so they treat each other with sincerity.[191]

196 *Historical rural social structure changes*

The employer and the employee "can dismiss or resign at any time when there is a reason or the relationship between the two is not compatible".[192] Here, "the criterion of reciprocity and the right to subsistence" are also "solidly embedded in the social models of peasants' life", and "these social models attribute their strength and continuity to the morally recognized power that peasants can exert".[193]

In the early twentieth century, the Chinese rural society experienced unprecedented changes driven by mandatory institutional changes and social changes influenced by industrialization and urbanization. The deterioration of the living conditions of the rural hired laborer group was just one superficial phenomenon of the entire process of rural social change. However, this superficial phenomenon was actually intertwined and glued together with many relationships in rural society. Its complex and multiple social connections clearly showed the basic characteristics of the evolution of this era. Contemporary understanding of the employment group should only be reflected in the fact that rural society was generally impoverished at that time rather than the development model of agricultural capitalist or the tendency of "land concentration" and "polarization". However, "insufficient social differentiation" is not only the cause of the generalization of employment relationship and the non-solidification of employment status, but also the fundamental reason why the hired laborer group cannot constitute a relatively independent class.

An analysis of the social mobility of the rich peasants – centered on the countryside of North China in the 1930s and 1940s

In the dynamic research of social structure or social stratum, the theory and method of social mobility[194] is undoubtedly an important and effective analysis dimension. Social mobility refers to the changes in the social status of individuals or groups in society, that is, the process of their transformation from an existing status to a new status; it is a basic index that can be measured both absolutely and relatively in the process of social structural change. "The former refers to the ratio of those flowing from any class to another class, while the latter refers to the relative opportunity for members of one class to move to another class".[195] In this chapter, the social mobility of rich peasants in rural areas is taken as the research basis. It is mainly based on two considerations:

First, in the process of modern social changes, the status of the rich peasant class and its theoretical cognition has always been a focal issue. As early as the beginning of the twentieth century, there was cognition that rich peasants were both the "rural bourgeoisie" and the feudal "landlord".[196] In early revolutionary theory, rich peasants were regarded as the objects of revolution. For example, "there is no doubt that the petty peasant class should be united to fight against the landlord class and the rich peasants". "These rich peasants, inevitably, become the worst exploiters", while among the petty peasants, "the

Historical rural social structure changes 197

masses are half-starved, living on a small land". "The rich peasants in China, most of which are small landlords, exploit the main masses of peasants in a harsher and more brutal way". "The issue of rich peasants is one of the main theoretical points of contention at present, and this issue is very important, so it deserves our special attention". "Some people advocate that the rich peasants should be united in the Chinese Revolution [...] The status of the rich peasants is oppressed by the landlord class, so the rich peasants must rebel against the landlord class". Those who object argue that "the Chinese rich peasants have their special nature, which makes them the destined enemies of the proletariat".[197] Therefore, the breakthrough in any aspect that is "tangled" by this issue is an effort of great academic value and theoretical significance.

Second, there are a number of research results about the rich peasant class in modern times, but most of them are solid-state studies based on social stratification (i.e., the discussion on their class attributes, historical status and function, and the research on the policy changes of the Communist Party of China in different historical periods etc.)[198] There is no academic discussion from the perspective of social mobility. Actually, as early as in the Republic of China, Liao Shiyi had already written about this issue and put forward the climbing theory of e "agricultural ladder" (i.e., another expression of social mobility). According to the theory of American scholars at the time, he proposed the following: The so-called agricultural ladder was to explain a typical peasant, who first started working as an agricultural laborer and earned wages on his father's or someone else's farm. When he had saved capital that could run a farm on his own, he climbed to the second level of the agricultural ladder and became a tenant peasant. When he continued to cultivate for some time, he got enough capital to buy a farm, and he became a land-holding peasant. He believed that

> it is a kind of class society with the nature of mobility; its rate of change depends on the socio-economic system. Many agricultural sociologists and agricultural economists often use this concept to describe the social and economic status of farmers and the changing situation, and thus to describe the socio-economic system of an agricultural society.

And based on this, he summarized the dynamic characteristics of the rural social structure in China at that time: that is, there was a 7 percent possibility of rising from farm laborer to tenant peasant, a 1.6 percent probability of rising to semi-land-holding peasant, and only a 0.6 percent possibility of rising to land-holding peasant sequentially. "It can be seen that it is very difficult for Chinese peasants to climb the agricultural ladder".[199] However, this research orientation did not continue or was not carried forward. There are many reasons for this, but the main factors maybe the expansion of class theory and that the research orientation based on the interpretation of realpolitik choices occupied a dominant position, making this pure academic path disappear without a sound. Therefore, by means of the analysis path of

198 *Historical rural social structure changes*

social mobility, perhaps the dynamic characteristics and general situations of the rich peasant class in a specific historical period can be further revealed, so as to provide a new perspective for the theoretical study and historical positioning of the rich peasant class.

The lack of systematic data is obviously one of the biggest difficulties in studying the social mobility of the rich peasant class. We have attempted to make a dynamic analysis of the social mobility of the rich peasant class in the countryside of China in the 1930s and 1940s by using the family registration table (hereinafter referred to as the "registration table") collected in the archives of Ci County, Hebei Province during the period of the "four cleans" movement as reference,[200] combining this with other rural social survey data. According to the time recorded in the "registration form" to calculate, the generation of householders is in their 40s to 60s, the father generation should be around their 30s to 50s, and the grandfather generation in their 20s to 40s. Of course, this is only an approximate time frame. For the convenience of analysis, we selected 120 rich peasant families in 50 production brigades of eight communes in Ci County as analysis samples. It should be noted that the term "rich peasants" mentioned here refers to the class division of peasant households during the land reform, which is not necessarily exactly consistent with the "rich peasants" involved in academic research. However, it is undeniable that a very important basis for the class division during the land reform is the economic status of the family, so the economic level of a family before land reform can be roughly grasped through class composition. Therefore, the "rich peasants" in the class division are relatively wealthy peasant households that occupy a certain amount of land, and own houses, farm animals and other living tools in rural society. These registration forms

> can show the changes in the population and economic conditions of each specific family in different periods since the early 1940s before the land reform and even the 1930s. From this, it can provide a historical picture of the evolution of a family from the 1920s to the mid-1960s.[201]

Among the 120 sample households presented in the data, according to the age of the householder, there are 10 households under 20 years old, 20 households between 21 and 30 years old, 20 households between 31 and 40 years old, 20 households between 41 and 50 years old, 20 households between 51 and 60 years old, 20 households between 61 and 70 years old, and 10 households over 71 years old. According to the educational level of the householder, it can be classified into illiterate, lower primary, higher primary, junior high, and senior high school. According to the farmland area of rural households, it can be roughly classified into: less than 30 *mu*, 31–50 *mu*, 51–100 *mu* and more than 100 *mu*, as shown in Table 4.4:

With the analysis of 120 sample families, taking the householder as a generation, the scale and status of social mobility of the four generations of grandfathers, fathers, householders and children can be known. This also

Historical rural social structure changes   199

Table 4.4 Sample table of 120 rich peasant families in 50 communes of 8 communes in Ci County, Hebei Province

Sampling Households		Number of Samples (household)	Proportion (percent)
Gender	Male	107	89.2
	Female	13	10.8
Age	Under 20	10	8.2
	21–30	20	16.7
	31–40	20	16.7
	41–50	20	16.7
	51–60	20	16.7
	61–70	20	16.7
	Over 70	10	8.3
Educational Level	Illiterate	32	26.7
	Lower Primary School	50	41.7
	Higher Primary School	26	21.7
	Junior High School	10	8.3
	Senior High School	2	1.6
Area of Occupied Arable Land	Under 30 *mu*	22	18.3
	31–50 *mu*	35	29.2
	51–100 *mu*	31	25.8
	Over 100 *mu*	32	26.7

Source: According to the statistics of "Registration Form of Class Composition" (Hebei Ci County Archives Collection, Class Archives, file number: 95 / 12-13 / 7-8)

helps to illustrate, albeit perhaps indirectly, the general trajectory and period features of social mobility.

Trend of intragenerational mobility of the rich peasant class

Intragenerational mobility is the social mobility condition expressed by the change of social status in an individual's life. Because of the short time span, there are certain limitations in reflecting the changing trend of social structure, but intragenerational mobility can minutely show the distribution of opportunity structure of individuals with different backgrounds and characteristics and the operation of social selection mechanisms. In a given social class structure, if the direction of flow is from lower social status to higher social status, it can be called upward or rising mobility, and in contrast, the direction of flow from higher social status to lower social status is called downward or dropping mobility.

Upward mobility

In the small-scale peasant economy society, the pursuit of wealth and development is the driving force of peasants or rural social and economic

200 *Historical rural social structure changes*

development. Being hardworking and good at management has become one of the conditions for peasants to become rich, which is summarized in the traditional agricultural society and its literature as "work hard (in the fields) to get rich". For example, Gu Yong and his brother in NuanShuitun of Hebei did long-term work, suffered 48 years of hard work and sprinkled their blood and sweat on the barren land. Because they were not discouraged and still worked hard, they gradually got some land and raised their heads on the land",[202] and became rich peasants in the village. The 120 sample households in Ci County show that it was not uncommon for villagers to become rich peasants, as shown in Table 4.5.

Statistics show that compared with the father generation, the intragenerational mobility of the grandfather generation is relatively open, and post-generation factors play a certain role, which is mainly reflected in the fact that long-term laborers and other classes can gradually reach a degree of affluence through hard work and continuous accumulation, and thus flow to a higher class. The intragenerational mobility of the grandfather generation accounted for 58.9 percent of the sample number. This generation laid the foundation for rising through hard work and accumulation. For them, the most common reasons (or ways) to enter the rich peasant class were farming and doing short-term work. They cultivated a small amount of land by themselves and also worked as short-term laborers

Table 4.5 Situation of 120 households rising to rich peasants

Reason for Upward Mobility	*Grandfather Generation (90 Sampling Households)*		*Father Generation (120 Sampling Households)*	
	Number of Samples (household)	*Proportion (percent)*	*Number of Samples (household)*	*Proportion (percent)*
Do Long-Term Work	8	15.1	1	2.2
Farm Land and Do Short-Term Work	33	62.3	17	37.8
Farm Land and Do Business	4	7.5	3	6.7
Farm Land and Parergon	6	11.3	19	42.2
Adopted by Rich Peasants	2	3.8	1	2.2
Lend Money for Interest	--	--	4	8.9
In Total	53	100	45	100
Upward Households/ Number of Sampling Households	58.9 percent		37.5 percent	

Source: Compiled according to the statistics of the "Registration Form of Class Composition" (Hebei Ci County Archives Collection, Class Archives, file number: 95 / 12-13 / 7-8).

Historical rural social structure changes 201

in the busy farming season. They pinched and scraped, saved money to buy land and gradually became rich. The grandfather of Zhang Bao in Nankaihe Township was very poor when he was young. He could only do short-term work to make a living, and then gradually bought land to plant. He became rich after age 40.[203] The second way is to do long-term work and improve the family situation through the accumulation of work. The grandfather of Yao Guojun from Beilai Village brought the whole family to that village by begging, and worked as a long-term laborer to maintain his living. Then there was gradually some savings in the family.[204] The two ways together accounted for 77.4 percent of the households rising to rich peasant households. In addition, farm land and parergon accounted for 11.3 percent of the rise. For ordinary farmers, farming and concurrently operating sideline businesses, mainly household industries such as textiles, opening tofu shops, cotton ginning and so on, can increase opportunities to improve their families' life. Only 7.5 percent of the households farmed and did business at the same time. The grandfather of Liang Shuangye from Lintanxiang had a little savings by farming, so he went to Pengcheng, Libingzhuang and other places to engage in business for more than ten years, and his living standard then rose. In addition to the above-mentioned ways, there were still a few people who relied on being adopted by rich peasants, or being the foster son of them. The grandfather of Hu Changchun from Beilai Village had a poor family and had only 2 *mu* of arable land. Then he was adopted by a rich peasant household in the village and improved the production situation.[205] The grandfather of Xin Qiufang from Balipu, Beilai Village, fled from Shandong. He first worked as a long-term laborer for the rich household in the village, and later became the foster son of the rich household. Then he got 13 *mu* of land, and his livelihood was guaranteed, and since then continuous development continued to rise.[206]

In the father generation, the reason for the upward mobility of peasants was to develop sideline businesses, especially the profit from the cultivation of cash crops, which accounted for 42.2 percent of the rising households. Those who farmed and at the same time did short-term work accounted for 37.8 percent of the rising households. In addition, those who profited through money lending accounted for 8.9 percent. On the basis of the accumulation of the previous generation, there appeared some peasant households of the second generation that expanded their income by lending for interest, while a small number of peasant households moved upward through farming and doing business.

In the upward mobility of peasant households, in addition to ascribed factors such as property inheritance, personal achievement factors mainly include farming and short-term work, or a sideline business, or doing business, and all of these were ways to rise to the status of rich peasants. For example, among five villages in Xing County and Lin County, there were only nine households that rose to rich peasant households, of which three were active in labor, four planted cotton specialties, and two developed sideline

202 *Historical rural social structure changes*

businesses.[207] It can be seen that personal diligence and hard work and thriftiness was one of the main ways for peasants to rise. "It is not impossible for a few lucky land-holding peasants and even tenant peasants to rely on their hard work and careful calculation and strict budgeting to have a surplus, and gradually rise to become more prosperous peasants".[208] Therefore,

> there is no such thing as extreme poverty or extreme wealth in the Chinese countryside. Naturally, there is no great disparity in class, and the class of the peasants cannot be fixed. A peasant household may be well-off today, and be in bankruptcy the next day; or a poor peasant household in abject poverty today, may be a middle or rich household after some years. This is very common in rural China.[209]

Downward mobility

From the 1920s to the 1930s, with the deepening of the rural social crisis, the downward movement of rich peasants tended to accelerate. The downward mobility of rich peasants in Ci County is shown in Table 4.6.

Among them, the downward mobility of the grandfather generation was 11 percent, and factors such war and gambling led to the downward mobility of some households and they fell to the poor peasant class. The downward mobility of the father generation was about 15 percent and squandering

Table 4.6 Analysis table of the reasons for the downward mobility of 120 sample households of rich peasants in Ci County

Reason for Downward Mobility	Grandfather Generation (90 Sampling Households)		Father Generation (120 Sampling Households)	
	Number of Samples (household)	Proportion (percent)	Number of Samples (household)	Proportion (percent)
Gambling	--	--	2	11.1
Opium-Smoking	2	20	6	33.3
Divide up Family Property and Live Apart or Bad Management	--	--	3	16.7
Wars and Natural Disasters	8	80	7	38.9
In Total	10	100	18	100
Downward Households/ Number of Sampling Households	11.1 percent		15 percent	

Source: Compiled according to the statistics of the "Registration Form of Class Composition" (Hebei Ci County Archives Collection, Class Archives, file number: 95 / 12-13 / 7-8).

Historical rural social structure changes 203

Table 4.7 Table of downward mobility of rich peasants in Rural Henan and Shanxi in the 1920s–1930s.

Region	Number of Rich Peasants in 1928 (household)	Number of Rich Peasants in 1933 (household)	Percentage of Falling Households of the Original Number of Rich Peasant Households (percent)
5 Villages in Xuchang County	22	19	13.6
4 Villages in Hui County	39	31	20.5
6 Villages in Zhenping County	19	16	15.8
4 Villages in Weinan County	15	8	46.7
5 Villages in Fengxiang County	15	5	66.7
4 Villages in Suide County	9	8	11.1

Source: Rural Rehabilitation Committee of the Executive Court: "Survey of Villages in Henan Province" (Commercial Press, 1934), 18–20; Rural Revival Committee of the Executive Court: "Survey of Villages in Shaanxi Province" (Commercial Press, 1934), 4, 43, 80.

funds, such as by gambling and opium-smoking, was the main reason for downward mobility. Free mobility (or individual mobility) was still the main reason. Obviously, this was not just a regional issue. The situation of the downward mobility of rich peasants in rural Henan and Shanxi can be a reference (see Table 4.7).

The downward mobility of rich peasants in different regions was not the same, but overall, the trend of downward mobility still accounted for a large proportion. The statistics in the table above show that the least number was the four villages in Suide County, and about 10 percent of the rich peasants moved downward; the highest number was the five villages in Fengxiang County, and nearly 70 percent of the rich peasants fell to middle peasants, poor peasants and even went bankrupt. Among the four villages in Weinan County, there were 15 rich peasants in 1928, and by 1933 they divided into 20 households. All of them moved downward except eight, who were still rich peasants, (six households became middle peasants, four households were poor peasants and one household was other). In the past five years, more than 80 percent of rich peasants in Weinan County showed a tendency of downward mobility. In addition, one household became a landlord to earn rent, "because the householder is a woman, and the son and daughter-in-law were young and incompetent, the land was rented out". This so-called "rising" was just a change in the mode of production from a labor-hiring operation to a land-renting operation, and did not mean economic growth and wealth

204 *Historical rural social structure changes*

increase. Behind this transformation of production modes were the absolute reduction of family productivity and the loss of decision-making power in agricultural production, so it cannot be regarded as an increase. On the contrary, it was essentially downward mobility. In fact, in the villages of North China, if peasants with more than 100 *mu* of land "live[d] on [the] rent of land", it is not prosperity but a symbol of failure. For example, in Jinzhong, Shanxi,

> The farming is close to extensive agriculture, the cost and labor costs are relatively small, but the tax burden is large. So it will be more advantageous to run the farm on your own rather than renting it to others. Except for the households that lack strong males, no one is unwilling to be rent the land to others.

Here, "Landlords are almost small households in which men go out to do business or in which there are only women and children, while the peasants that rent land are local large landlords".[210]

Intergenerational mobility of the rich peasant class

Intergenerational mobility is mainly a study of changes in the social status of the parental generation and offspring at two time points. Like intragenerational mobility, peasants can realize their dreams of becoming rich through hard work and accumulation. In his investigation in Houjiaying Village, Changli County, Hebei Province, Man Tie found that

> in 1900, there were several large landlords in the village with 200–300 *mu* of land, but by 1942 these families had become poor and a new land group with 100–180 *mu* of land emerged. Most of these large landlords earned their income by doing short-term work in the northeast or running shops outside their villages. After saving a sum of money, they went back to the villages in their hometown to buy land.[211]

They accumulated wealth by working or doing business, and by buying land they accumulated and increased their wealth. Table 4.8 shows the specific situation of households that rose to rich peasant households through intergenerational mobility in Houjiaying Village, Li County, Hebei Province:

It can be seen that going out to work was another way for poor peasants to get rich. This "gold rush" type of method could help them accumulate a sum of money in a short time, thus quickly completing the upward movement between generations. A certain person in Shandong went to a county in Siping, Liaoning, in 1901 to do business. When he first arrived in the county, he set up a small shop with 13 *yuan* in cash; after that he developed his business step by step, he sold sundries and coarse grain in 1915, and had purchased more than 1,800 *mu* of land. In 1920, he also engaged in the oil industry

Historical rural social structure changes 205

Table 4.8 Table of intergenerational upward mobility in Houjiaying Village, Changli County, Hebei Province

Name	Father Generation	Reason for Intergenerational Upward Mobility	Family Property in 1941
Hou Qingchang	poor peasants with only 10 *mu* of Land	work in the northeast, go back the village to buy land	have 180 *mu* of land and rent out 100 *mu*
Hou Baolian	poor peasants	work in the northeast, go back the village to buy land	have 117 *mu* of land and rent out 6 *mu*
Hou Yuanwen	live in poverty	work in the northeast, go back the village to buy land	have 30 *mu* of land and rent out 10 *mu*
Hou Quanwu	live in poverty	save some money when serving as an attendant of an official in the past, buy land gradually	have 30 *mu* of land and rent out 10 *mu*
Hou Yuanhong	live in poverty	stay in the northeast for many years, save some many and buy land	have 30 *mu* of land and rent out 10 *mu*
Hou Yuanlai	poor peasants and packman	work in the northeast, go back the village to buy land	become rich and rent out the land
Hou Yunzhong	medium assets	stay in the northeast for many years, save some many and buy land, and increase the land through the agricultural income	cultivate own land
Liu Bingkui	rich household	do business and buy land gradually	have 170 *mu* of land and rent out 30 *mu*

Source: Remake according to the original table in: Ma Ruomeng, "Chinese Peasant Economy – Agricultural Development in Hebei and Shandong (1890–1949)", trans. Shi Jianyun (Jiangsu People's Publishing House, 1999), 262

206 *Historical rural social structure changes*

and his land had increased to 3500 *mu*; in 1922, he converted to run a grain store that also served as a pawnshop. By the time of the investigation in 1939, he had bought 13,663 *mu* of farmland in 21 villages in the county and had a very important position in the county.[212] Of course, in reality, there may not be so many such rich and powerful people, but going out to work was a relatively fast way for peasants to move upwards. "Farming is not the way to make money, and ambitious villagers must make their fortunes outside agriculture".[213] In Man Tie's survey, among the 20 rich households in nine villages in Hebei and Shandong, except for five households that inherited their ancestral business, the rest started to become rich by themselves or in their father's generation. Among them, a few accumulated money by doing business outside Shanhaiguan Pass, and most of them gained profits through hard work at farming.[214] The details are shown in Table 4.9.

Generally, the amount of land owned by a family is a standard to measure its economic status. "The prosperity of rural families is mainly achieved by buying land, and the decline is also triggered by emergencies of being forced to sell land".[215] Therefore, a change in land owned by peasants can be regarded as a quantitative standard for rising or falling mobility. Among the 12 rich peasant households listed above, upward mobility began to accumulate in the first generation, and by the second generation, most of them had developed, while a small number of families at least maintained the scale of the previous generation. In the third generation, families continued to purchase land, expand business and became rich peasants in the countryside. And the main reason for their continuous rise was hard work and continuous accumulation.

According to Man Tie's survey, Huang Zongzhi made a table of the intergenerational downward mobility of 14 rich peasant households and regarded separation as the main reason for this.

As shown in Table 4.10, the rich households of the first generation had been reduced to less than half by the time of the second generation, and by the third generation, none of the rich households had more than 100 *mu* of land and were basically in decline. There are two points in Huang Zongzhi's analysis that are debatable: First, it is a standard of the researcher to regard peasant households with 100 *mu* of land as rich households, which is different from the rich peasant households in real life and does not correspond to reality; second, further discussion is needed to completely determine the reasons for the downward mobility of the rich households in the village to separation. Huang Zongzhi believes that the so-called rich of rich households is only relative to the surrounding petty peasants struggling for survival. The limited accumulation of agricultural production can hardly resist the pressure of dividing up family property and living apart. The characteristics of rich peasants' separation are as follows: First, the economic conditions of the rich peasant households before the separation were rich. Compared with ordinary peasants, rich peasants had a relatively solid economic situation before the separation. In other words, the amount of capital available for distribution was large enough to basically guarantee the

Table 4.9 Table of intergenerational upward mobility of 12 rich households in 5 villages in Hebei and Shandong

| Village | 1890–1900 | | 1910–1920 | | 1930–1940 | | Unit: (mu) |
	Family Name	Have Land	Family Name	Have Land	Family Name	Have Land	Reason for Upward Mobility
Dabeiguan			Zhang	86	Zhang	145	gain profits from farming
			Zhang	150	Zhang	243	gain profits from farming
			Zhang	150	Zhang	218	gain profits from fanning
Shajing			X		Zhang	110	work in the city
Michang	Dong	46	Dong	86	Dong	130	gain profits from farming
	Dong	20	Dong	150	Dong	157	gain profits from fanning
	Dong	93	Dong	120	Dong	109	gain profits from farming
Qianlianggezhuang			Fu	90	Fu	118	gain profits from farming
	Wang	40	Wang	40	Wang	104	work in the three northeast provinces of China
Houjiaying			X		Hou	150	do business in the three northeast provinces of China
			X		Hou	114	do business in the three northeast provinces of China
			X		Hou	160	serve under officials

Source: Huang Zongzhi, "Small-Scale Peasant Economy and Social Changes in North China", 75–77.

Table 4.10 Downward mobility of 14 rich peasants in 6 villages in Hebei and Shandong

| Village | 1890–1900 | | 1910–1920 | | 1930–1940 | Unit: (mu) |
	Family Name	Have Land	Family Name	Have Land	Have Land	Reason for Downward Mobility
Houxiazhai	Wang	500	Wang	100		separation, 3 brothers
			Liu	140		separation, himself and two sons
	Wang	150	X			separation, 5 brothers
Dabeiguan	Guo	160	X			separation, 3 brothers
	Guo	230	X			separation, 3 brothers
	Zhang	172	X			separation, 2 brothers
	Zhang	180	X			separation, 2 brothers
Shajing	Li	200	Li	100		separation, 5 brothers
	Yang	270	X			separation, 3 brothers
Sibeichai	Xu	200	Xu	100		separation, 3 brothers
Michang	Dong	150	X			separation, 2 brothers
	Dong	165	X			separation, 3 brothers
Wudian	Yu	100	X			separation, 3 brothers
	Zhao	200	X			separation, 4 brothers

Source: Huang Zongzhi, "Small-Scale Peasant Economy and Social Changes in North China", 75–77.

living standard of their offspring above the medium level. After separation, the small families still had a certain scale of production and operation. Based on this scale, the state of operation of the offspring determined the economic basis on which the family would separate again. And in fact, as the saying goes, "three years after separation show the level of high and low". It is clear that after the separation there is high-level and low-level development of small families because personal abilities, business environment and other factors can continue to develop after the separation. Therefore, the purpose of separation is to provide a basis for future generations to survive and develop. If they only decline to the end of extinction after separation, then it is fundamentally against the original intention of separation. Second, there is no difference between the wealth of a large family before the separation and the sum of the wealth of small families after the separation. This is especially true from a per capita perspective. The difference in wealth brought about by the separation of families is mainly due to the fact that, though the offspring's wealth is evenly distributed from their parents, the difference in the number of children in the offspring's small family results in the difference in the average wealth level of the small families. Third, in terms of the absolute size of family wealth, it is true that after the separation, the family's wealth class or level in the village is decreased, such as the reduction of land, farm animals and other means of production. But at the same time, household expenditures will correspondingly decrease with the decrease of population. After separation, due to various reasons such as the differences in hardworking and lazy, and different management methods, although the property is evenly distributed to the brothers, their respective economic conditions may change after the separation. The brothers who are good at management can not only maintain the original standard of living, but also ulteriorly accumulate wealth and improve living standards. In contrast, for those who are not good at management, the wealth will be depleted and the household will move downward. Therefore, the rise and fall in the quality of life of small families after separation is not absolute.

From the analysis of the intergenerational mobility of 120 rich households in Ci County, Hebei, it can be seen that nearly 60 percent of the peasant households whose parents were rich peasants maintain the class and status of rich peasants and their original property was basically inherited from their parents. Among the 22 rich peasant households of which the land occupied by their parents is clearly recorded, 3 households had 35–50 *mu* of land, 11 households had 51–100 *mu*, 8 households had more than 100 *mu*, and the largest one was 300 *mu*. A father can hold his sons together while he is alive. In families with relatively affluent economic conditions before separation,

> maybe the brothers of these more affluent families have higher expectations of separation that they can become the heads of the family without reducing living conditions. Therefore, the death of a father is often an opportunity to push the separation between brothers.[216]

210 *Historical rural social structure changes*

After big families were separated, the total amount of wealth went from large to small after dividing the property, which led to changes in the production methods of each family and changes in family economic conditions. Some families rose rather than fell. Li Guangzhi's family in Shajing Village occupied 84 *mu* of arable land. There were five labor forces in the family, which equaled to everyone should cultivate 17 *mu* of arable land. But he slacked off on his father's farm and especially liked to go to the market, or go to the local temples to watch the bustling scene among the crowds. But later the brothers separated and each person got 27 *mu* of land. At this time, Li Guangzhi did his best to work. He recalled with pride that he cultivated 27 *mu* of land and only needed to hire 20 laborers per year, and the yield was no less than anyone in the village.[217] Zhu Zhengsheng's family in Qingyouzhuang Village, Ci County, had 110 *mu* of land, a horse and a donkey. They mainly cultivated the land by themselves and employed short-term laborers in the busy farming season. After the three brothers separated, Zhu Zhengsheng got 34 *mu* of land and a donkey, and he gradually developed to buy 23 *mu* of land. Then he began to hire laborers to cultivate, and lent money for interest, making his life more prosperous.[218] When Zhang Wanqin's father was alive in Lintan Village, Ci County, there were more than 300 *mu* of land, two mules, a cattle and a donkey. There were six brothers and seven labor forces in the family. They mainly cultivated the land by themselves and employed short-term laborers in the busy farming season. After the separation, each family got 50 *mu* of land. After several years of development, Zhang Wanqin's family bought 30 *mu* of land, bought a large cart, hired long-term laborers and expanded production.[219] It can be seen that after family separation and dividing the property, some small families with better conditions chose relatively reasonable methods of operation, spared no effort, worked hard and developed after years of accumulation. Some even expanded the farm area to many times the number when they separated.

In fact, most rich peasants can basically guarantee the living standard of their children over the middle level after separation. In a certain sense, separation increases the autonomy of small families over property and management. Because the capabilities and conduct are different among family members, some families will develop into a larger, wealthier family. Therefore, it does not seem complete enough to attribute the downward mobility of rich peasants to family separation.

Through his research on Taitou Village, Shandong Province, Yang Maochun summarizes the mobility of a family over several generations.

> Usually, a family works hard, lives frugally and then begins to buy land; members of the second generation continue to work hard so that the family has more land and becomes a wealthy family; the members of the third generation only care about pleasure, spend more and earn less, do not buy land anymore and gradually begin to sell land; the fourth

Historical rural social structure changes 211

generation sells more land until the family ends up in poverty. The circulation of this cycle is less than 100 years.[220]

In terms of the trend of mobility, Yang Maochun's estimate is generally right, but there is an obvious problem with the oversimplification of attributing the reason for a family's prosperity to declining to "only care about enjoyment, spend more and earn less". A wealthy family may encounter various factors that hinder the accumulation and development of the family. External causes include policies, wars, natural disasters and other factors, while internal causes include their own efforts and operating conditions. More often, the decline of rich peasant households was the result of both internal and external forces.

The above is the intergenerational vertical mobility of rich peasant households. What about the intergenerational horizontal mobility of rich peasant households (that is, horizontal mobility within the same social occupational stratum, and also the mobility between different working groups or organizations in the same region)? We take 120 rich peasant households in Ci County, Hebei Province, as the analysis samples, centering on the householders, tracing back in both directions from the status changes between the grandparents – parents, parents – householders to householders – children, so as to analyze the characteristics and scale of the mobility in four generations, as shown in Table 4.11.

The table above shows the different strata of paternal status, among which middle peasants and rich peasants are the most numerous. For rich peasants and middle peasants, they were often the backbone of village social life. They worked hard, arranged everything reasonably and were constantly frugal. If there was no major change, they could move upward and became the "rich men" that villagers long to be.[221]

For those offspring whose father generation was from a lower class of hired laborers and poor peasants, status was often obtained through their own diligence and effort, showing a characteristic of upward mobility as a whole. Among those offspring whose father generation were middle peasants, 25 percent of them kept their original status, 58.3 percent rose to become rich peasants; another three people became a teacher, doctor and businessman, and only one household declined and became poor peasants. The downward mobility of the generation whose fathers were rich peasants accounted for 16.7 percent; 59.6 percent basically maintained their original status; 11 households became other occupations, including government functionaries, teachers, doctors and businessmen. The above table shows that the inflow rate of rich peasants was 42.9 percent and the outflow rate was 40.4 percent. In this period, more than 80 percent of intergenerational mobility was within the peasant class, and about 10 percent of the mobility was due to occupational changes.

Most of the rich peasants did not break away from agricultural work when they were engaged in business, or as teachers or doctors. In this sense, this is

212 *Historical rural social structure changes*

Table 4.11 Table of intergenerational horizontal mobility of 120 sample households in Ci County

The Status of the Father Generation	Sample (house-hold)	Percentage (percent)	The Status of the Children							
			Occupation Mobility					Agricultural Ladder		
			Government Functionary	Teacher	Doctor	Crafts-man	Businessman	Rich Peasant	Middle Peasant	Poor Peasant
Hired Laborer	8	9.4	--	--	--	1	--	2	5	--
Poor Peasant	5	5.9	--	--	--	1	--	4	--	--
Middle Peasant	24	28.2	--	1	1	--	1	14	6	1
Rich Peasant	47	55.3	2	5	2	--	2	28	3	5
Businessman	1	1.2	--	--	--	--	--	1	--	--
In Total	85	100	2	6	3	2	3	49	14	6

Note: Rich peasants, middle peasants and poor peasants are not concepts in class division, but are distinguished by their living standards and are roughly divided into three levels: rich, middle and poor.

not an exactly horizontal mobility. The more affluent peasants are, the less able they are to abandon their own land. One or more members in a family may leave farming to do business or do other non-agricultural work, but the family is still rooted deeply in the land. After doing business or engaging in other occupations, most rich peasants would invest in buying land in their hometown. More accurately, they were leaving ground for retreat for themselves rather than exploiting the rents of tenant peasants. Once business fails and work was not guaranteed, they could return to the countryside, live on the land and even reaccumulate assets. In fact, many rich peasants returned to the countryside after moving outward.

Types and characteristics of social mobility in the rich peasant class

The "Sample Table" (Table 4.12) shows that the epochal difference in intergenerational mobility among generations is significant. The upward mobility rate of the grandfather generation is 52.2 percent, that of the father generation is 29.2 percent, and that of the householder is 26.7 percent. Both the mobility rate and the upward mobility rate show a downward trend, and the ratio of the upward mobility rate to the downward mobility rate also decreases generation by generation. This seems to indicate the overall decline of the rich peasant class. We can also further analyze the types and characteristics of the mobility of the rich peasant class from Table 4.12, which shows changes in 120 sample households.

First, intragenerational mobility is a historical process, which reveals the historical characteristics of the times in a certain sense. The intragenerational mobility of rich peasants in North China formed several stages: The first stage was before the mid-1930s. During this period, the intragenerational mobility of rich peasants had the following characteristics: First, a high mobility rate. Overall, the mobility rate was higher than the non-mobility rate. Among the 90 sample households, the mobility rate was 58.9 percent, indicating that the grandfather generation was mostly in a state of mobility. The second is that the upward mobility rate was higher than the downward mobility rate. The upward mobility of rich peasants was just a directional trend, manifested in the increase in wealth and social status. According to the statistics of the sample households, the upward mobility rate was 52.2 percent and the downward mobility rate was 6.7 percent, with the ratio of the two being 7.79. Upward mobility was significantly higher than downward mobility. This shows that the households tracing upward to the grandfather generation had begun to accumulate wealth and become the starting stage of a family business. Of course, it is undeniable that quite a few peasants, with a sample statistic of 41.1 percent, acquired their wealth from an earlier generation. The third is the combination of ascribed factors and post-causative factors, which determine the intragenerational mobility of rich peasants. On the one hand, part of the status of the rich peasants was obtained due to the existing family economic status. On the other hand, the post-causative factors

Table 4.12 Intragenerational mobility of 120 sample households in Ci County

Number of Samples		Grandfather	Father	Household		Offspring
		90 households	120 households	120 households		105 households
				Before Land Reform	After Land Reform	
Total Mobility	Sample (household)	53	45	41	0	0
	Percentage (percent)	58.9	37.5	34.2	0	0
No Mobility	Sample (household)	37	75	77	120	120
	Percentage (percent)	41.1	62.5	65.8	100	100
Upward Mobility	Sample (household)	47	35	32	0	0
	Percentage (percent)	52.2	29.2	26.7	0	0
Downward Mobility	Sample (household)	6	16	24	120	120
	Percentage (percent)	6.7	13.3	20	100	100
Rate of Upward Mobility/Rate of Downward Mobility		7.8	2.2	1.3	0	0

Source: Compiled according to the statistics of "Registration Form of Class Composition" (Ci County Archives, Class Composition, 95 / 12-13 / 7-8).

Historical rural social structure changes   215

played a more important role in intragenerational mobility. Through the post-causative factor, that is, through individual hard work, it was possible to upward mobility to a higher level of social status. Among the 90 sample families with upward mobility of grandfathers, except for 37 households who inherited the property of the older generation and 2 households adopted by other or became foster son, the remaining 51 households moved upward through personal effort, accounting for 56.7 percent of the total number of the sample households. The greater the role of the post-causative factor, the more it shows that the mobility of society is relatively open, and that individuals can rise through their own struggle, which objectively contributes to the development of social production. Compared with the upward mobility of the grandfather generation, the intragenerational mobility of the father generation was reduced and the upward mobility was reduced, while the downward mobility rate was increased.

In the second stage, before the land reform from the mid-1930s to the mid-1940s, the characteristics of the intragenerational mobility of the rich peasants mainly showed that mobility reduced and the non-mobility rate increased. In the acquisition of the economic status of rich peasants, the ascribed factors played a more important role than post-causative factors, and nearly two-thirds of the rich peasants achieved it because of their parents' economic status.

In the third stage, from the land reform to the early period of the founding of the People's Republic of China, the intragenerational mobility of the rich peasant class showed an overall downward trend and even stagnation. After the land reform, the downward mobility rate of both the householders and their offspring was 100 percent. This overall downward mobility can be called a mandatory mobility. In the land reform, rich peasants were deprived of land and other production tools without compensation, which reduced the overall economic power of rich peasants in rural society. At the same time, with the immobilization of the label of class identity, the political status of rich peasants plummeted, and their economic power could not even be compared with the poor peasants in rural society. Family members in "Registration Form of Class Composition" of Ci County were mainly adults over the age of 16. Children below 15 were only counted as family population and were not filled in separately. However, this did not affect a basic grasp of the mobility of "offspring". In the late 1950s, except for agricultural work, the children of rich peasants had no room for development in other nonagricultural fields. Among the 120 selected sample households, most of the offspring were engaged in agricultural production. Although the class composition was labeled "rich peasants", their living conditions were not rich in economy, so there was an overall decline, and intragenerational mobility basically stagnated.

In the first half of the twentieth century, there were some differences between the social differentiation of the rich peasant class and the actual state of the mobility process. In general, the scale of intragenerational mobility

216 *Historical rural social structure changes*

of the rich peasants changed from small to large, from the individual to the whole; the factors of policies and institutions gradually became prominent in the causes of mobility, and the nature of mobility shifted from free mobility to structural mobility.[222]

Second, upward mobility was characterized by diversity and complexity. How do we understand the meaning of upward mobility of rich peasants? Rich peasants referred to the peasants who were wealthy. If the upward mobility of rich peasants was understood from this broad concept, it should include two aspects: First, rich peasants developed into operational farmers with larger production scales. The larger production scale mentioned here referred to the possession of more means of production, including land, farm animals, farm tools and so on. And on this basis, the employment of hired labor by rich peasants expanded and became a larger operation. The second is the upward mobility of rich peasants, leaving the peasant class and becoming government functionaries. As urban-rural relationships continued to expand, the urban-rural relationship had in fact become the relationship between depriving and being deprived. Peasants were at the bottom of society, so as a more affluent class in rural society, it should be an upward development to leave the countryside and enter a relatively stable or income-expanding class.

An operational farmer is equivalent to the "operational landlord" in class division. The Communist Party's understanding of this class, like the rich peasants, also changed: In 1942, it was pointed out that "operational farmers" should be regarded as capitalist and should be classified as a category with rich peasants; in the *Land Reform Act* enacted in 1950, it was explicitly decided to merge the "operational farmers" into the landlords. Class division is mainly aimed at whether the possession of the means of production of a class is an exploiting class or an exploited class. But in terms of the amount of means of production, both operational farmers and rich peasants belong to the rich peasant class in rural society. In his study of the small-scale peasant economy in North China, Huang Zongzhi found that "those wealthy peasant households are actually not landlords but what I call 'operational farmers' – they employ 3 to 8 farm laborers to cultivate 100 to 200 *mu* of land (this should be distinguished from rich peasants who only employ 1 or 2 people)".[223] Huang Zongzhi distinguishes rich peasants from operational farmers and emphasizes that they are not the same. The fundamental difference is that the former is farm-based production, while the latter is family-based production. In the modern Chinese countryside, the so-called operational landlords still take the family as the management unit. From the statement of Huang Zongzhi, the distinction between the two is based on the number of hired laborers. It is not impossible to define qualify by quantity, but it is impossible to determine the prescriptive difference between the "quality" of a farmer hiring two laborers and three laborers. In the author's opinion, the similarities of the two lie in that, first, both take family as the basic business unit; second, they have broken the limit of family members' operations and adopted a labor-hiring management; third, although there is

Historical rural social structure changes 217

a gap in the scale of their development, it is not enough to break through the qualitative difference, and they are both far from the "rural bourgeoisie". So instead of emphasizing the different nature of the two, it is better to regard them as different stages of rich peasants in the process of quantity accumulation. Therefore, the expansion of the scale of rich peasants' operations must first be reflected in the increase in the number of hired laborers. Of course, not only in agriculture do rich peasants also need a certain number of hired laborers because they are engaged in sideline work, industry and commerce. Therefore, the difference between rich peasants and operational landlords is only a quantitative distinction, not a qualitative one. The upward mobility of the rich peasant class may not reach the extent of crossing the "class" boundary, but it is precisely this rising space that gives each peasant household the hope of rising.

In some rural survey materials, the process of change from rich peasants to landlords is regarded as upward mobility, but this is not comprehensive. Of course, this question inevitably involves a fundamental question: what is a "landlord"? This chapter is not intended to discuss the title of landlord here. Analyzing from the mode of operation, there are two basic modes of which land can be completely rented out and managed by hired laborers. That is, the "landlord" as indicated in the class division includes the landlord for rent and the landlord for business. It is still debatable whether the landlords who operate land by means of tenancy are rich peasants who go up a stratum. However, from rich peasants to larger operational farmers, the scale of operation has been enlarged, and it is regarded as the rise of rich peasants.

Third, it changed suddenly from free mobility to structural mobility. If a simple stage is set for the scale of the mobility of rich peasants, taking the time before and after the War of Resistance as the boundary, it would be roughly divided into two stages: centering on free mobility (or individual mobility) and centering on structural mobility. Before the War of Resistance against Japan, the mobility of rich peasants in North China was dominated by individual mobility. Traditional rural society recognized the gap between the rich and the poor, and therefore had its own understanding of the mobility of peasants. They owed the rich peasants' personal mobility to hard work, thrift, protection by ancestors and even good luck, and regarded it as the direction of their own efforts, or an example of educating their children. Peasants in Taitou Village, Shandong, likened successful people to winter wheat, which was better than other cereals because it had experienced the coldest winters. So when a person achieved success and good fortune through hard work and self-restraint, he would be compared to wheat and admired by everyone who knew him.[224] At the same time, these rich peasants also became role models. Farmers educated their children "if (they) did not work hard, the whole family would not have enough to eat". They

> tried hard to imitate the behavior of rich households in the village, who worked hard and saved money to buy land and livestock [...] People

218 *Historical rural social structure changes*

educated their children that hard work and frugality were strongly associated with the accumulation of wealth, and trained them not to accept destiny or be content with poverty, but to compete for the same status and wealth as the wealthy households in the village.[225]

Peasants in Lincheng County, Hebei Province, considered the families whose wealth was left by their ancestors as being "because their ancestors had accumulated with diligence and left behind some money for them".[226] In the view of the peasants, "rich man" and "master" were not synonyms of a corrupt life, as they were in the eyes of the revolutionaries. The more land and wealth, the more it became "a proof of noble morality".[227] And the fall and decline of peasants were more often attributed to splurging or to the failure to operate. Liu Fenglan, a villager in Langwuzhuang Village, Hebei, said,

> It was not easy at that time. I would rather beg for a meal than borrow a liter or a bowl from others. They fought the landlords, distributed the food, carried it to my family, and I returned it to him, I did not want to take even a thread residue from others. I could not leave a subject for ridicule for the children, saying that it was from harming others. Our family was poor because the old householder (husband's father) was keen on food and gambling with money. The rich were the ones who lived on their own.[228]

The economic stability of the rich peasants was poor, and there were constantly some individual peasants who rose through hard work or good opportunities, or declined due to disasters, personal capabilities and other factors. Since modern times, the general poverty of rural society has led to the continuous downward mobility of rich peasants to lower classes. Therefore, the scale of upward mobility is small.

After the War of Resistance, the CPC gradually carried out land reform in the liberated areas. Under the leadership of the revolution, social reform movements aimed at reforming the social structure and power structure arose one after another, resulting in the structural mobility of the rich peasant class. During the process of land reform, rich peasants were deprived of their surplus or even all of their land, houses and other means of production (see below for details). The influence of the father generation on the status of their offspring was negative. The offspring inherited the status of the "rich peasants" of the previous generation, and their political and economic status were the lowest in rural society. The ascribed factors had a decisive effect on the social status of the offspring, while the post-causative factors basically had no effect on changing this situation.

Historical destiny of rich peasants: thinking about history

After the twentieth century, there were still frequent wars and disasters in the rural areas of North China. In addition, the society continued to be unstable,

Historical rural social structure changes 219

the economy was severely bankrupt and peasants' lives tended to be generally impoverished.[229] It was not easy for rich peasants to maintain the existing production scale and living conditions, but there was still room for development. Generally, the intergenerational mobility of rich peasants is frequent, but the general trend of intergenerational mobility is downward. There were very few records about the upward mobility of rich peasants into government functionaries. In traditional society, the imperial examination was an important way for peasants to rise. The abolition of the imperial examination system in 1905, however, severed the institutional connection between rural society and the bureaucratic country, and the new school education system also had similar functional substitution to some extent, as shown in Table 4.13.

From the table showing the education background of some peasants in the 120 sample households in Ci County, it can be seen that in the intergenerational mobility of 11 rich peasant households, the mobility of peasants to other occupations had a certain relationship with their education background, with the degree related to the economic situation of the family. Among the 11 households, except for 1 household with poor economic conditions and 4 households without records, the economic conditions of the 6 households were all wealthy, and the time and degree of their children's education were relatively high, which had an important impact on occupational mobility. The education level of rich peasant family members was often higher than that of other classes, and they had then the ability to expand their operations. Therefore, in a certain sense, education provided them a channel for rising. Two of the 120 sample households in Ci County had this record. Xin Shipu was a scholar in the imperial examination, and later "became an official in the city and was in charge of water conservancy work". In another household, Fan Ailian's father also joined the work force after studying in school. He worked in a city bank, and later became the bank president.[230] Education provides a most basic path for the social differentiation and mobility of peasants, and plays a catalytic role in the formation of an open mobility mechanism of rural society. But in general, for rich peasants, the lack of institutional channels to move up to government functionaries makes such upward development scarcely impossible. In the social changes dominated by the "revolution", it is not enough to simply observe and analyze the social mobility of the rich peasant class in the twentieth century by the rules of ascribed factors and post-causative factors. Through analysis of the intergenerational and intragenerational mobility of the rich peasant class, it can be seen that in addition to the ascribed factors and post-causative factors proposed in previous sociological studies, the significance of political or institutional factors is particularly prominent. In the Communist Party's reform of the rural society guided by class theory, the reasons for the mobility of all classes changed from ascribed and post-causative factors to political and institutional factors.

220 *Historical rural social structure changes*

Table 4.13 Table of education background of some peasants in the 120 sample households in Ci County

Name of Offspring	Occupation of Father Generation	Family Situation of Grandfather Generation	Education Background of Father Generation
Fan Ailian	Bank staff, later promoted to bank president	hired long-term laborers and hired short-term laborers in the busy farming season.	went to school at an early age and then joined in work
Xin Quanxiang	Water conservancy department functionary	--	went to school at an early age; became a scholar in the imperial competitive examination and then became an official in the city
Hu Quanxing	Teacher	had 90 *mu* of land and 50 houses	went to school at an early age and worked as a teacher for decades
Ma Geibo	Teacher	had 61 *mu* of land and rented all the land out to tenant peasants	went to school at an early age and then became a teacher
Yang Yongfang	Teacher	hired 2 long-term laborers	went to school at an early age and then became a teacher
Yue Zhenyuan	Teacher	had a *qing* of land: over 50 houses and hired 2 long-term laborers	went to school at an early age and worked as a teacher for over 10 years after graduating from higher primary school
Xue Mingxuan	Teacher	--	went to school at an early age and then became a teacher after graduation.
Yuan Rongshou	Doctor	--	went to school then did agricultural work and became a doctor after 40 years old
Hu Gnangxing	Veterinarian	had almost 100 *mu* of land and over 50 houses	went to school at an early age and then joined in work
Yang Ying	Businessman	--	went to school from 8 to 24 and then opened a flower shop
Miao Shenghua	Businessman	had a bad life	opened a shop and then built up a family fortune

Downward mobility of rich peasants before land reform

Before the land reform, some base areas in North China had already been engaged in the struggle to reduce rent, lower the interest rate and increase capital. Because of the levy of progressive taxes, some wealthy households had to reduce the amount of land by selling or other means, or reduce their hired laborers to escape the burden. Their economy or living standards had shown a downward trend, as detailed in Table 4.14:

For the rich peasants who were mainly engaged in farming, the reduction of land meant the reduction of property and a decline in life. As shown in Table 4.11, at least 20 percent of rich peasants declined, even in the seven villages of Yanjiachuan, and 90 percent of rich peasants showed a declining trend.

Table 4.14 Downward mobility of rich peasants in Parts of Shanxi-Chahaer-Hebei border region in the 1940s

Year	Area	Original Rich Peasant (Household)	Downward Mobility (Household)	Percentage (percent)
1941	32 villages in 12 counties of Shanxi-Chahaer-Hebei Border Region	355	152	42.8
	4 villages in Pingshan County	71	16	22.5
1942	5 villages in Wuxiang, Liao County	102	21	20.6
	5 villages in Licheng, Pingshun County	76	19	25
1944	5 villages in Xing, Lin County	56	15	26.8
1945	9 counties in Jin-Sui Border Area	101	48	47.5
1945	7 villages in Yanjiachuan	11	10	90.9
1946	Baoding District, Hebei Province	173	40	23.1

Source: Wei Hongyun, "Draft of Financial and Economic History of the Shanxi-Chahar-Hebei Anti-Japanese Base Area" (Archives Press, 1990), 187; "Preliminary Collection of Land Issues in Taihang Base Area" (September 10, 1942), Archives of CPC Taihang District Party Committee, Shanxi Provincial Archives, file number: A 1/9/3. Jin-Sui Suboffice Investigation and Research Office, "Changes of Class Relationships and Land Occupation in Jin-Sui Suboffice" (October 1944), in Liu Xin and Jing Zhankui, *Financial and Economic History of Jin-Sui Border Area* (Shanxi Economic Press, 1993), 107.; Jin-Sui Suboffice Investigation and Research Office, "Materials of Changes in Rural Land and Class" (June 1946), Shanxi Provincial Archives, Archives of the Jin-Sui Suboffice of the CPC Central Committee, file number: A 21/3/14/1; "Research Materials of Land Investigation in Yihe and West District of Yanjiachuan" (February 29, 1948), Shaanxi Provincial Archives, Archives of Shaanxi-Gansu-Ningxia Border District Government Construction Department, file number: 6/3/30. Chen Hansheng et al., "Rural Economy in Wuxi and Baoding before and after Liberation (1929–1957)", Materials about the History of Agricultural Cooperation in China, 1988 (Supplement 2), p. 104.

222 *Historical rural social structure changes*

The file of "four cleans" was filled in the early 1960s, and it can be roughly estimated that the generation of the householders was in their 40s to 60s. This period was a time of great changes in rural society, and land reform became a major event affecting the flow of the rich peasant class. Before the land reform, the rich peasant class was still dominated by individual mobility. Although this analysis was based on the selected sample households being "rich peasants" according to the class composition of householders, through analysis, the number of households with downward mobility can be found. Because the file information was a "brief family history" filled out in the form of a table, there were only a few records on the reasons for the changes in the economic status of families. Some families did not state the reason for their decline, but it could be analyzed through the time of the householders from 1940s to 1960s in which the implementation of the policy of reducing rent and lowering the interest rate, the separation of families to escape the burden, wars and other factors should be the main reasons for the decline of rich peasants in this period.

This was confirmed by the changes in rich peasants in nine counties of Jin-Sui from 1939 to 1945.[231] In 1939, there were 101 rich peasants in the nine counties, accounting for 13.5 percent of the population and 22.8 percent of the total land. By 1945, it had decreased to 48 households, accounting for 6 percent of the total population and about 10 percent of the land. Specifically, the reasons for the reduction of land owned by rich peasants are shown in Table 4.15.

It can be seen from the above table that the land transferred out by rich peasants in six years was nearly 2,000 *mu*. The main reasons were: overburden,

Table 4.15 Reasons for the decline of rich peasants in 20 villages of 9 counties in Jin-Sui

Time	Number of the Reduced Land (mu)	Reason for the Reduction of Land (percent)				
		Overburden	Rent Reduction	Debt Clearance	Capital Increase	Domestic Reason, Operation and Other Reasons
1939	200	50	--	--	--	50
1940	6				100	
1942	12		100			
1943	405	46.4	16.9	--	3.7	33
1944	329	47.9	24.8	2.9	6.1	18.3
1945	1056.5	29.3	28.8	13.4	9.8	18.7

Source: Jin-Sui Suboffice Investigation and Research Office, "Materials of Changes in Rural Land and Class – Based on a Survey of Twenty Villages in Nine Counties in the Old Base Areas" (June 1946), Shanxi Provincial Archives, Archives of the Jin-Sui Suboffice of the CPC Central Committee, file number: A21/3/14/1.

accounting for nearly half of the total amount transferred out in six years; rent reduction, debt clearance and capital increase together, accounting for nearly one-third of the total number of transfers; domestic reasons, including change of production, management and living in other places. If the cause of the domestic reasons is considered to be due to rich peasants' own factors, the main reason for the reduction of land and the downward mobility of rich peasants is caused by external factors, that is, the restriction of the policy to reduce rent and lower the interest rate on the rich peasants' economy to some extent.

The reasons for the decline of rich peasants in central Hebei in the 1940s can be roughly classified into the following categories:

> The reasons for the decline are caused by many aspects. First, the impact of the war is major; second, liquidation and land donation; third, in order to shrink the target, quit the long-term laborers, reduce the operation or separate the family; fourth, pawn the land; fifth, some impacts of the policies, such as the burden policy and the rent reduction policy.[232]

Before the mid-1940s, policies such as liquidation and increasing burdens became a major factor in the downward mobility of rich peasants. In addition, the war caused social unrest and widespread poverty, which led to the slow economic development of rich peasants. The policy of reducing rents and interest rates increased the burden on rich landlords. For example, the burden of public grain for peasants in Fangshan County was reduced from 70 percent to 30 percent, while that of landlords and rich peasants was increased from 30 percent to 70 percent.[233]

The implementation of the rent and interest reduction policy and debt increase and capital increase policy by the CPC accelerated the reduction of rich peasants' land. In rural society, land is a natural yardstick of peasants' wealth. The decrease of land year by year, on the one hand, explains the trend of the upward mobility of the rich peasant class; on the other hand, it also indicates that mandatory external forces play a leading role in this mobility. The burden policy of the liberated area, which imposed a progressive tax of more than 35 percent on rich peasants, made rich peasants tired of land and reduced their land.

Downward mobility of rich peasants after land reform

In July 1947, the *Outline of the Land Law of China* was established to bisect the land completely, stipulating that it was necessary to "abolish the land ownership of all landlords",

> all the land of landlords and public land in the village shall be received by the rural peasant association, together with other land in the village, will be uniformly distributed according to the entire population of the village,

224 *Historical rural social structure changes*

both male and female, old and young. In the amount of land, more land is taken to supplement less land, and in the quality of land, fertile is taken to supplement barren land, so that all people in the village have equal land and the land is owned by them.

This marked the transition of the party's land policy in rural areas from paid land transfers to equal division of land. The government used compulsory powers to completely transfer the land and property of landowners, rich peasants, including new rich peasants, for free. Taking 35 counties in central Shanxi as an example, the rich peasant class accounted for about 3.84 percent of the total number of households before the land reform and only 1.97 percent after the land reform. Among them,

the original rich peasants that still maintained the rich peasant composition accounted for 9.69 percent, and the proportion of them that declined to rich middle peasants was 55.15 percent, 25.45 percent declined to general middle peasants, 7.88 percent to poor middle peasants, 0.67 percent to poor peasants, and 1.16 percent become solitaries.[234]

It can be seen that only about 10 percent of rich peasants could still be called "rich peasants", but their living conditions were not as good as they used to be due to the gratuitous deprivation of land and other means of production, while more than 90 percent of the rich peasants declined to middle and poor peasants.[235] According to the statistics after the land reform in nine villages, seven counties in central Hebei and Ji-Jin in 1946, among the original rich peasants, only 9.7 percent of them remained rich, 80.6 percent were reduced to middle peasants, 8.5 percent to poor peasants, and 1.2 percent to solitaries.[236] In Wuxiang County, Shanxi, the number of landlords and rich peasants dropped by 55 percent to 852 households from 1,894 households in 1935.[237] With the in-depth development of land reform, the "rich peasant economy" in the countryside had basically disappeared. Rich peasants were no longer wealthy peasants in the economic sense, nor were they a stratum in social stratification (but only left as "elements").

In the period of social change, institutional factors can reshuffle the status of all social members. After the 1930s, with the implementation of the Communist Party's policies in rural North China, in order to alleviate their burdens, most rich peasants reduced their production scale, stopped lending, laid off hired laborers and even sold land. In the late 1940s, land reform aiming at "equalization", especially the cooperative movement after the founding of the People's Republic of China, deprived the rich peasants of land and other means of production, which meant an overall decline. The same is true for upward mobility. Most of the new rich peasant groups that emerged after the Land Revolution and Land Reform were the result of the upward mobility of poor peasants. In a few years, poor peasants rose to rich peasants precisely because these poor peasants participated in the land revolution and benefited from it. In other words, the fruits of the revolution provided a platform for their upward mobility, so they did not have to be like the poor peasants in other regions who often had to pass through the accumulation of several generations to achieve upward mobility; instead, it could be done in a generation. Of course, one of the basic facts is that the peasants' hard work and hard management are the fundamental reasons for the upward mobility.

Social mobility can be divided into upward mobility and downward mobility in terms of its flow direction. There are two basic forms of upward mobility: one is the infiltration of individuals from a lower social class into an original higher class; the other is that these individuals construct a new social group that enters a higher social class, replaces the original group of this class or becomes a group parallel to the original group of this class. The former, such as poor peasants or farm laborers, move upward into the rich peasant class, while the latter, such as new rich peasant groups emerges. There are also two forms of downward mobility: one is that individuals fall from a higher social position to an original lower position, but the higher group they belong to does not fall or disintegrate; the second is reflected in the overall decline of a social group. As a class, compared with other classes, its status declines and even disintegrates. In the former, for example, some rich peasants decline from the higher economic class to poor peasants or tenant peasants with low economic status due to natural disasters, man-made disasters, poor management or other factors. Most typical of the latter is the overall decline of the status of the rich peasants as a whole after the land reform. Pitirim A. Sorokin made a rather vivid metaphor about this: the "sinking" of the first case refers to a person falling off a ship; the second case refers to the ship itself and all the people on board drowning, or because of the accident, the ship itself breaks apart.[238]

In fact, it is difficult to exactly define the rich peasants in the countryside. "Not to mention that it is unreasonable to simply divide the class according to the amount of land occupation, especially to adopt the same standard regardless the regional differences".[239] This is true even in the logical system of "revolutionary" discourse. For example, Mao Zedong mentioned in the conclusion written for the Second Plenary Session of the Seventh Central Committee of the Communist Party of China in 1949 that the Communist Party "has different understandings of what a 'middle peasant' is and what a 'rich peasant' is".[240] Obviously, the economic levels of rich peasants vary greatly,[241] and there is no uniform standard for the basis of stratification. In reality, it is difficult to clearly differentiate the rich peasants from rich middle peasants, or even from the landlords. Chen Hansheng wrote in *Land Issues in Modern China* that: "Rich peasants in China have become part of the landlords. But because of the fragmentation of land, the heavy taxation, and the sharp fall in grain price, they cannot move towards capitalism. In Wuxi, 58 rich peasant households rented out 18.76 percent of their land to poor peasants". In the Yangtze River Basin, "most rich peasants rent out land for land rents". In the north, "rich peasants often rent a lot of land from poor peasants".[242] This is

226 *Historical rural social structure changes*

especially true for policy provisions, such as the *Decision on Some Issues in Land Reform* in 1933, the new rules on the boundaries of rich peasants and rich middle peasants in 1948, and "supplementary decisions" in 1950 and so on.[243] However, as a social existence "entity", it is undoubtedly a relatively wealthy group in a rural community, of which the economic and production levels are above the average level of the same rural community: "Those whose living standards are better than middle peasants or who hire laborers to cultivate land or who have more farm animals".[244] For the rural society and even the whole society, its formation and existence is always an internal driving and leading social force. In 1909, the prosperity of the agricultural and the rural cotton weaving handicraft industry in Gaoyang, Hebei, was facilitated by the "dispersed and random intermediaries", and their identities were "mostly rich peasants or landlords in the countryside and each of them had its own close families who could be directly controlled and instructed by them".[245] In the 1930s, in the rural areas of Jiangsu with a relatively developed economy, not only

> the rich and the petty peasants had reached a not mutually exclusive but interdependent position: that is, the petty peasants are proletarianized, and because of the limitations of their small private or tenanted land, they had to rely on rich peasants; rich peasants had to keep petty peasants in the countryside because of their lack of labor and the need for commodity markets. Rich peasants and petty peasants depended on each other through agricultural operations, industrial operations, commerce and usury.[246]

At that time, various professional cooperative organizations in the rural areas of Jiangsu and Zhejiang showed that "one of the rich peasants' businesses that had separated from the old form, such as cooperatives, was ostensibly composed of petty peasants, but its economic function was actually dominated by rich peasants".[247] This operation of "rich peasants' management that inevitably develops in accordance with the development of the city and industry", "creates cooperative operation outside of large and small operations",[248] which not only reflects economic progress but also contains the trend of social progress.

Even in the base areas that had gone through the "revolution", the "new rich peasant" class still rose after the 1940s. "Most of the newly rising social elites are born in poverty, but they rise to new rich peasants or rich middle peasants through hard work to get rich". The emancipated peasant Wu Manyou "employed two long-term laborers and a shepherd boy, and in the busy farming season also hired short-term laborers", which became the "Wu Manyou direction" – the direction of rich peasants.[249] This rural development path of "accumulating capital by agriculture" – the economic form of "rich peasants manag[ing] their own land and employ[ing] long-term laborers"[250]

Historical rural social structure changes   227

still stubbornly presents the necessary rules of historical development under the conditions of "revolution". For villagers in the rural society, rich peasants are their most realistic direction of mobility (development). "Rich peasants are the 'flags' for middle peasants, especially rich middle peasants". "The middle peasants say that rich peasants have the so-called 'Three Good' (good livestock, good farming tools and good management), and the so-called 'Three Can' (they can speak, can write and can calculate)".[251] "Rich peasants", or peasants who are becoming rich, are undoubtedly the most realistic and direct choices and yearnings of rural people. Therefore, the development motivations of peasants to "support their families with agricultural production, develop their sideline production to get rich and make their fortune" in history have natural consistency with the development motivations and paths of most peasants in today's villages. "The purpose of promoting the 'rich peasant economy' on the basis of poor rural areas is to create an affluent countryside"; this kind of affluence is "average affluence" and "is the 'affluence' that does not go against the principle of 'equality', which is the realization of the Principle of People's Livelihood, that is, the realization of socialism".[252]

In the historical course of hundreds of years, the fate of the rich peasant class in the countryside has had ups and downs. It profoundly interprets the direction and track of the sociopolitical evolution of modern China from a side aspect. Although against the background of great institutional changes and social changes, the fate of rich peasants appears to be "passive" and "submissive". Once the society returns to normal, the rich peasant class naturally rises and becomes the guiding force for the development of rural society, which silently reveals the general rules and trends of social or economic evolution. A deep exploration of history will help us gain more and more sober rational understanding.

Landlords: the historical transformation from real right concept to class concept – construction and development of modern Chinese history

Modern Chinese history is essentially a revolutionary movement or a process of social reconstruction around "landlords" and their classes. It can constitute almost the main content – though not the whole – of this thrilling history. Even today, when the title of "landlord" has become a relatively distant term in people's real life, in the historical texts on land reform, it is still the central topic of disputes and the core concept that arouses ideological disputes and conflicts over positions.[253] It is history, but it is more than history.

It is not difficult to find discover in historical studies that using the concept of landlords as a class, or the class category of landlord-peasant, to refer to Chinese rural society and even the entire Chinese social structure, is only a fact formed along with the modern historical process. Previously, in general

228 *Historical rural social structure changes*

or in daily life, people did not use the paired category of landlord-peasant to refer to rural social groups, even during the Republic of China. For example:

> Therefore, if there are only petty peasants and no large peasants in China's agricultural management, there will be no hope of development of agriculture [...] It should be strongly advocated that large peasants and petty peasants should help each other achieve development. This is because if we do not advocate large peasants, we will not get the provision of farming steam turbines and irrigation works, thus cannot achieve the effect of improvement; if we do not maintain petty peasants, the life and property of the petty peasants will be absorbed by the large peasants, and gradually, the rich will become richer and the poor will become poorer, and the national livelihood will be out of control.[254]

The stratification of rural society in the traditional era is usually divided into large peasants, middle peasants and petty peasants based on living standards or the degree of wealth possession. In fact, the historical construction of the concept of taking landlords as a center was rather late. Until the 1930s, many cadres within the Communist Party were not clearly about the boundaries of the rural classes. Mao Zedong once pointedly explained,

> Among the questions given to me by my comrades, some ask what a rich peasant is. I think the landlord is mainly to collect rent; the rich peasant is mainly to hire laborers and participate in the labor himself; the middle peasant is mainly not to sell the labor force and to operate his own land; the poor peasant must sell his labor force and only living on his own land is not enough; the farmer laborer completely sells his labor force and has no land. Of course, this refers to their main indicators.[255]

Therefore, systematically sorting out the history of the landlords as a class concept and forming the history of its category is not only an important theoretical issue in our understanding of modern Chinese history, but also an academic topic with theoretical depth that needs to be summarized and refined urgently.

Landowner and proprietor

Traditionally, the so-called class division in China was based either on the feudal hierarchical system of the Wei and Jin dynasties in which powerful families had monopolistic control of the political apparatus or on the Master-Servant system of the Ming and Qing dynasties. To realize "equality in legislation, there is no better way than abolishing the titles of master and servant and giving the economically and materially deprived the freedom to become gainfully employed as they see fit".[256] The term "class" here refers to a hierarchy of status, not a concept of class in the modern sense. In fact, before the

Historical rural social structure changes 229

introduction of Marxist class theory to China and its acceptance, the discourse of the landlord class had not been formed in social life. People usually distinguished the entities existing in society by gentry households and civilian households, as Ding Richang said: "In the area north of the Yangtze River, the price of canal transportation was always different between gentry households and civilian households, and between urban households and rural households".[257] During the reign of Xianfeng, Feng Guifen also said in the "Persuade the Gentry with the Theory of Average Rich" that rural residents were divided into gentry households and civilian households, or large households and small households,[258] and that there was no such title as landlord or peasant. The occupiers of land were generally called landowners and proprietors. After the Boxer Rebellion, Jiangxi implemented a surcharge on each *mu* of land for payment of compensation. "Landowners could not support it so they gradually transferred or pawned their land to avoid paying grain as tax. Tenant peasants could not support it so they fled away with others and operated other businesses".[259]

In official documents, people are classified into civilian households, military households, salt producer households, fisherman households and other categories,[260] while civilians often used upper households and lower households or rich households and poor households to distinguish. Gong Zizhen described the social situation during the Daoguang period in the following way: Since the Qianlong period, the officials and the civilians were in distress.

> From the capital to places almost from all sides, people generally changed from rich to poor and from poor to hungry. Life at the top of the four kinds of households fell, and the general situation of all provinces was too precarious to support a month or even a day.[261]

Bao Shichen said regarding the difference between households that

> The family that has six *mu* of land per person on average is the upper household, the family that has four *mu* of land per person is the middle household, and the family that has two *mu* of land per person is the lower household. Those who have less than one *mu* of land are poor households.[262]

This approach also used the amount of land occupation to divide upper, middle and lower households, without special subdivision as the landlord. Until the Guangxu period, people still used this kind of discourse generally:

> Sunjiazhuang [Wangdu County, Zhili] has a total of more than 40 civilian households and over 1,000 *mu* of land. Among them, each of the upper households has land of 60 or 70 *mu*, the lower households, 3 to 5 *mu* of land.[263]

230 *Historical rural social structure changes*

In the Guangxu period, *Shun Pao* recorded the condition of the people in Jiangsu:

> some of the extremely poor households, renting land and planting, do not have grain to pay the tax; some tenant peasants and landowners both complete a half, this is the so-called field bottom of the land and surface of the land. Different provinces have different methods, and those who pay more money and grain for tax are listed on the upper household, this is same as the whole world. [...] None of the upper households are unable to pay, while the number of lower households is limited, but if there is good weather for the crops, it will be more than sufficient for them.[264]

In the contractual document with certain legal norms, the owner who transferred the land ownership was usually called the original owner, the owner of lost property, the abandoner or recipient, buyer, proprietor, and so on.[265] Landlords, or a set of concepts centered on the landlord, had not entered people's thought process. Even landowners with a considerable number of fields did not have the kind of domineering style that was alleged in later revolutionary discourse. For example, the Boxer Indemnity exacerbated the strain on the common people:

> recently, the government wanted to repair the Xi'an-Tongguan Railway but there was a lack of funds, so it reconsidered increasing the surcharge on each *mu* of land. Therefore, the people in the prefectures and counties of Weibei were in a panic and regarded the land as an encumbrance. They scrambled to sell the land at a low price, and there were even some who were willing to give people a large amount of land to cultivate and did not ask for any money. The suffering of the people of Qin can be seen from this.[266]

The suffering and decline of the landlords described in *Annals of Li County* in the Republic of China (1912–1949) also offers one piece of evidence for this:

> Recently, landlords and peasants have endured unspeakable hardships. Regardless of how much is produced in a year on the land, the landlord takes one-third. And since they can only fetch very low prices for whatever is left after all the wages have been paid, they inevitably fall into arrears. Divesting themselves from land ownership is therefore imperative [...] Landlords have no other source of income besides rents received from those who manage their land. Whatever the size of their household, its annual budget must at a minimum make allowance for [the operating costs associated with] the land it owns, which is also the reason why they racked up a great deal of debt for which they are harassed by debt collectors. Yet using land as collateral to borrow money in order to pay down debts has only led to the gradual depletion of a landlord's fortunes,

Historical rural social structure changes   231

something few if any land-owning households have managed to avoid. In fact, all the well-known grain farmers in Li County have been reduced to a shadow of their past financial glory.[267]

Along with the generation and evolution of modern revolutionary discourse, the concept of landlords began to emerge and gradually became popular. Sun Yat-sen mentioned the issue of average land rights in "The Revolutionary Strategy of the Chinese Alliance (1906)", saying that "The current land price is still owned by the original owner; the increased price of the social improvement and progress after the revolution belongs to the state and the people".[268] What was discussed here was also called the original owner rather than the title of landlord. Since then, Sun Yat-sen repeatedly emphasized the Principle of People's Livelihood and preached the proposition of the equalization of land ownership. In the "Speech in Tokyo *Newspaper of Civilian*'s Anniversary Celebration Conference" in December of the same year, he used the word "landlord" when he talked about the issue of land price again. But here "land-owner" did not refer to a specific class. He further explained that some people said that the Principle of People's Livelihood was "grabbing the land of rich people as their own. This was because he did not know the reason and spoke casually". Since after the land price is fixed, the increase in price belonged to the public and did not belong to the landlords.[269] Obviously, the concepts of landlord and rich people are basically synonymous here.

After 1912, the frequency of the concept of "landlord" in Sun Yat-sen's revolutionary discourse system gradually increased. He believed that after the success of the national civil rights revolution, the social revolution had to be carried out to prevent the suffering from the polarization between the rich and the poor. His basic strategy was "if the equalization of land ownership can be achieved, then the social revolution will be achieved 70 percent to 80 percent". At the beginning of the implementation of the equalization of land ownership,

the main contract of each place must be changed. This is the thing that should be done in the reform of every dynasty [...] In the past, taxes on the land owned by the people were paid according to the area and were divided into three classes: top, middle and bottom. In the future, the law should be changed to collect taxes based on the price. The higher the land price, the higher the tax, and the lower the land price, the lower the tax. The expensive land must be located in a prosperous place, most of the land is owned by the rich, and taxing more on them is not excessive. While the cheap land must be in a remote and backward place and mostly owned by the poor, so the tax must be taken lightly.[270]

Landowner here refers to the owner of the land in the sense of ownership, though there is a difference between rich and poor. In the ideological system of the People's Livelihood of Sun Yat-sen, the landlord does not have a clear

232 *Historical rural social structure changes*

class designation, but has a relatively broad sense of ownership of property rights.

First, it is a concept equivalent to the proprietor. Sun Yat-sen believed that after the success of the revolution, implementing the People's Livelihood, resuming the land, and levying a tax on the spot, "then the country becomes a large owner, which is very rich".[271] In view of these proprietors of land who deliberately quote and seek windfall profits, the countermeasure is

> to prevent the proprietors from quoting a higher price than the real price, the provincial capital should set a condition, such as when the country is to open a railway, road, build a large workshop and other things, the land can be nationalized at any time. Then the behavior of quoting a higher price than the real price will not be worrying.[272]

Second, there is no special class distinction between landlords and capitalists, and they are both so-called rich people. The difference lies in the different ways of profiting.

> And the landlords often inherited the legacy of their ancestors; many of them became extremely rich without plowing or weaving or thinking. These landlords increased their wealth by land and became capitalists and the capitalists made profits through industry and then became big landlords. Then the land of the city was monopolized by these people [...] The more advanced the industry and the more developed the business, the greater the benefits of capitalists and landlords, and the poorer the workers.[273]

Third, there were no big landowners in the sense of polarization in China, but only small landlords (i.e., petty peasants) who were diligent and frugal.

> Chinese industry is underdeveloped and land prices have not yet increased. Therefore, there are still few big landlords [...] So the method of checking and determining land price should be used to avoid the pain of the polarization between the rich and the poor. [...] The pricing method is determined by the price quoted by the owner, but the scope should be based on two conditions: First, based on the quoted price, the land should pay tax as 1 percent or 2 percent of the quoted price in the future. Second, if the government uses the land in the future, it will always be bought at this price and cannot be increased; if someone buys and sells the land privately, it will be returned to the public at the increased price. The landowner can only get the original land price, and the new landowner pays the tax at the new land price.[274]

Therefore, "the land issue in China has not changed much since the abandonment of the well-field system to the present day". It has always been a society in which petty peasants are the mainstays. As the saying goes, "everyone can be a small landlord; the diligent and thrifty peasants all have the hope to become small landlords, and so the road to people's livelihood is not exhausted".[275] As Liang Qichao put it, "Since there are no noble landlords in China, the small-scale peasant system has always been implemented"[276] This is a completely different social structure from that in Europe and the United States: "whereas in Europe and the United States, it is impossible for petty peasants to become small landlords and small workers to be small capitalists".[277]

Landlords during the Great Revolution

With the surge of the "Great Revolution", the peasant movement became the center of revolution. "The peasant problem is at the center of China's current social problems; most of the revolutionary theoretical struggles also take the peasant problem as the starting point of the struggle".[278] The Kuomintang used to call on the peasants to engage in the National Revolution to fulfill their political demands: "Therefore, the national revolutionary movement must rely on the participation of peasants and workers of the whole country, and then it can win decisively, without doubt". Based on this, "on the one hand the Kuomintang assisted the peasants' and workers' movement, and on the other hand, it made efforts for the peasants and workers to participate in Kuomintang",[279] so as to promote the national revolutionary movement. The first National Congress of Kuomintang clearly stated its purpose:

> The peasants are the majority of our Chinese people. If the peasants do not participate in the revolution, we have no basis for the revolution. The Kuomintang is to be reorganized, to join the peasant movement, and the aim is to use the peasants as the foundation, the peasants must be the foundation of our party.[280]

And it proclaimed that

> the National Revolution, in essence, is the Peasant Revolution. In order to consolidate the foundation of the National Revolution, our party must first liberate the peasants; political or economic movements should be based on the peasant movements. The party's policy, first of all, should focus on the interests of peasants themselves; the government's actions must also be based on the interests of peasants to seek their liberation. Because if the peasants have achieved liberation, that is, the completion of most of the National Revolution, it is the basis for the realization of the Three Principles of People of our party.[281]

Then, in the National Revolution movement that required a "big change in the countryside", did landlords became the object of the "Great Revolution"? Not really!

234 *Historical rural social structure changes*

In the second declaration of the Kuomintang in 1926, it was clear that the objects of the National Revolution were warlords, bureaucrats, compradors and local tyrants. They "were both tools of imperialism and forces to suppress the peasant-working class". Therefore, the objects of the revolution were "first the warlords, and then bureaucrats, compradors and local tyrants".[282] This is basically consistent with the "Resolution of the First Peasant Congress of Hunan Province (December 1026)", which listed corrupt officials, local tyrants and evil gentries as the objects of the revolution.[283] In the discussions on the peasants and the National Revolution in the first to fifth issues of *Chinese Peasants*, sponsored by the Peasant Department of the Central Executive Committee of the Chinese Kuomintang, the concentrated presentation of revolutionary objects did not point to the specific class of "landlords", but instead aimed at fighting the focus on the gentry: "Since the gentry and the peasant have become deadly enemies",[284] and the gentries were the foundation of all the evil forces in China, namely, warlords, bureaucrats and corrupt officials, the reason why the Chinese revolution failed after the second and third times was that "The local tyrants and the evil gentries in the lower classes still have not been shaken".[285] Although there is no shortage of landlords among the gentries, the two are in fact not equal because the composition of the gentry group is far beyond the scope of landlords and their attributes. It is a hybrid: "most of the urban gentries are frustrated soldiers, politicians, elders of former Qing dynasties or compradors". And as for rural gentries, "their compositions are probably: evil landlords, inferior local ruffians and boring semi-intellectuals".[286] In the context of the National Revolution, the revolutionary objects marked by the Kuomintang are "special classes with exploitative nature: evil gentries, local tyrants, bureau directors, heads of regiments, patriarchs and corrupt officials".[287]

Slightly different from before, the third declaration of the Kuomintang listed the "feudal landlord class" as the object of the National Revolution. That is,

the feudal landlord class is the true foundation of the imperialist warlords and corrupt officials and all counter-revolutionaries [...] On the part of the peasants, they have been ruled by the feudal landlord regime for thousands of years. Without overthrowing the feudal landlord's regime in the countryside, all economic struggles, such as rent reduction and interest reduction are simply impossible to talk about.[288]

This formulation is obviously related to the position of the CPC,[289] and its formulation is almost identical to the views of Mao Zedong at that time. At the Guangzhou Peasant Movement workshop in 1926, Mao Zedong put forward the following:

The peasant problem is the central issue of the National Revolution. If the peasants do not rise to participate in and support the National

Historical rural social structure changes   235

Revolution, the National Revolution will not succeed; the peasant problem will not be solved until the peasant movement is carried out quickly; if the problem of peasants is not solved quite well in the current revolutionary movement, peasants will not support this revolution.

Therefore, the Great Revolution with the Peasant Revolution as the main body "targeted the rural patriarchal feudal class (the landlord class)". This rural patriarchal feudal class is the only solid foundation for the domestic ruling class and foreign imperialism.[290] It is worth noting that the "feudal landlord class" referred to here is not the landlord in the general sense, but specifically the local tyrants, evil gentries and corrupt officials.

> The situation of the Chinese revolution is just like this: either the basis of imperialism and warlords – local tyrants, evil gentries and corrupt officials suppress the peasants, or the basis of the revolutionary forces – the peasants rise to suppress the local tyrants, evil gentries and corrupt officials.[291]

In fact, this is not fundamentally different from the revolutionary objects that the Kuomintang has repeatedly emphasized: "first the warlords, and then bureaucrats, compradors and local tyrants".[292]

Undoubtedly, in the context of the National Revolution, with the focus of "knock down the gentry class" and "knock down the feudal system in the countryside",[293] landlords and their "class" in the general sense were not constructed as antagonistic forces of the Great Revolution. In fact, throughout the period of the National Revolution, the concept of landlords did not form a specific class category, although the Kuomintang and the Communist Party had different understandings and distinctions of landlords.

First, in the discourse system of the Kuomintang around 1927, the landlord did not exist as a specific class, but only as a part of the overall composition of the "peasant". The "National Land Occupation Overview" issued by the "Report of the Land Commission of the Ministry of Farmers of the Central Executive Committee of the Chinese Kuomintang" (published in June 1927) clearly states: "there were 56,000,000 peasant households (including landlords) nationwide, with an average of six people, a total of 336,000,000 people; among the 336,000,000 peasants, the number of peasants with land (ranging from one *mu* of land to even a large landlord) ranges from 120,000,000 to 150,000,000; the total number of peasants is 336,000,000, minus 150,000,000 peasants with land and 30,000,000 farm laborers without land, minus 20,000,000 nomads and bandits, and the remaining 136,000,000 are tenant peasants who do not have land and rent others' land".[294] That is, the landlord family belongs to the peasant household, and the landlord belongs to the peasant – the meaning is the owner of the land – regardless of the number of *mu*; and the specifically marked peasants with land (landlords), account for 45 percent of the total number of peasants.

236 *Historical rural social structure changes*

Second, the landlord was only a stratum of the peasant class, not an independent class, especially the hostile class. "What we should pay attention to is the division of the peasant class. This division can be roughly divided into five types: landlords, land-holding peasants, semi-land-holding peasants, tenant peasants, farm laborers or coolies".[295] It was listed in the "Methods of the Peasant Movement" that in the division of "the number of analysis of peasants in different regions", they were only distinguished according to the four categories of large peasants, middle peasants, petty peasants, and bitter peasants,[296] and there were no special allegations of landlords. At this time, "the term so-called 'peasant'" is a collective concept that "includes large peasants, petty peasants, land-holding peasants, tenant peasants and farm laborers, etc.".[297]

In fact, the Communist Party at this time did not separate the landlords and the peasants into opposing class forces.

> At present, the organization of the peasant association cannot be class-like (such as separately put a farm laborer organization or a tenant peasant organization forward), and it cannot be clearly pointed out that those who have a few *mu* of land cannot join (because it is not easy to set an appropriate standard). It can only be generalized to point out the following two kinds of people who are not allowed to join the peasant association: The first kind, who do not cultivate and own most of the land; the second kind, the exploiters.[298]

Even in general, landlords were the objects of solidarity in the peasant movement:

> Our policy is to use the slogan of the unity of all peasants to unite tenant peasants, land-holding peasants, small landlords and middle landlords, neutralize big landlords who do not actively do evil and only attack reactionary landlords, such as those who become evil gentries and local tyrants. Do not simply propose the slogan of defeating landlords and do not use the slogan of defeating evil gentries and local tyrants to actually defeat big landlords.[299]

Landlords in the context of class revolution

Under the premise of the greatest common divisor in the cooperation between the Kuomintang and the Communist Party, the landlords in the National Revolution were neither constructed as a class, nor could they be constructed as the enemy of the revolution.

> Both parties failed to incorporate the "interests" of the peasant class into the political strategy of treating the landlord class as a national enemy.

Historical rural social structure changes   237

In the strategic thinking of early Communists, the excessive rent of the landlord class, its abuse of customary power, and its unfettered local authority were far less important than their potential value in another aspect, namely, to unite their tenant peasants against the warlord.[300]

Not only the Kuomintang "was still confused about the exact meaning" of the class or landlord class,[301] but the COC also emphasized:

The class relationships in the countryside are extremely complicated, so it is not necessary to propose the term "peasant classes". At this time, we only propagandize the slogan of "All peasants stand up against corrupt officials, local tyrants and evil gentries, against the heavy taxes and the compulsory donation of warlord government.[302]

However, there were inherent factors of division in the violent National Revolution. "Revolutions before 1925 were considered mainly political, while the revolutions after the May 30th Movement increasingly showed a social dimension".[303] The distinction between the "class revolution" advocated by the Communist Party and the "national revolution" insisted on by the Kuomintang is not only increasingly obvious with the continuous development of the Great Revolution, but also inevitably led to a split with the reduction of the bipartisan conventions.

It is precisely the development of this dimension that finally led to the split of the Kuomintang and the Communist Party and caused the Chinese revolution once more to fall into the "political dimension" – the struggle between the two major political parties.[304]

"The beginning of the social revolution or 'class struggle' in the National Revolution in the 1920s marked a split between the lines of the Kuomintang and the Communists".[305]

Zhu Zhixin, a theorist during the Revolution of 1911, once commented on the difference between political revolution and social revolution: "The subject of any political revolution is the civilian, and the object is the government. The subject of social revolution is the civilian, and its object is the rich and powerful family".[306] This indicated that the opposition between the government and the people in the political revolution was different from the class opposition in the social revolution. Therefore, when the Communists led the Chinese revolution to a social revolution dominated by class revolution after the national revolution, the landlord marked by private ownership of land would inevitably become the "object of the revolution".

It was also in the discourse of "class revolution" that landlords became the focus of historical construction in this era. "The introduction of class struggle led the Chinese revolution to a new orientation".[307] In May 1927, *The*

238 *Historical rural social structure changes*

Fifth National Congress of the Communist Party of China on the 'Resolution of Land Issue' began to specify that

> The economic life of rural areas in China is still largely based on the feudal relationship. Most of the land (about 66 percent) is occupied by big landlords who collect rents. Only 34 percent of China's land belongs to peasants [...] The well-field system has long been eliminated. But the management system of the so-called public land is still left in the countryside as the basis of the patriarchal social power in the countryside. The ownership of the land has been usurped by the gentry and the cultivators lost their rights of ownership, and when gentries or others become landlords, they even use this right to exercise the authority and domination of their patriarchal society.[308]

Under the guidance of the "class revolution", the conference proposed that

> the land must be completely redistributed under the principle of equalization of land ownership to solve the land issue. To achieve this step, the land must be owned by the nation [...] Land nationalization is indeed the basic principle of the Communist Party's party platform on peasant issues.[309]

"The main feature of the new stage of the Chinese revolution now" is the class revolution, and it is a revolution beyond the attributes of the National Revolutionary and has the nature of "class struggle of which peasants in the countryside struggle against rich gentries and big landlords"[310] in the new historical stage.

"Class is a red line connecting various political phenomena. If politics and class are observed separately, then no real understanding of political phenomena can be obtained by any means".[311] In the discourse of "class revolution" (instead of the general "revolutionary discourse"), class struggle has become the main line of historical construction and the starting point of China's road choice. "In fact, the inherent role of class contradiction is precisely the mechanism that drives history and the driving force for social development".[312] Therefore, in the course of modern Chinese history with the peasant revolution as the main body, landlords and their classes were inevitably constructed as the antagonistic classes of the revolution. "The contradiction between the landlord class and the peasant class was the cause of the stagnation of society and the backwardness of the nation of China. The peasants had shown great power in previous revolutionary movements".[313] Redefining and dividing the peasants and the landlords into opposing class forces became the theme of the era of the "class revolution" (or communist revolution) that continued to advance after the national revolution.

Historical rural social structure changes   239

The peasant class refers to the laborers engaged in land production. Those landlords and farm owners who profit by other people's toil are excluded. [...] Especially in the land where the feudal system and the big landlord class have not been eliminated, the so-called peasant movement and peasant revolution almost exclusively refer to the land movement and the land revolution.[314]

Particularly after the "August 7th" meeting of the CPC, the Communist Party combined peasants with armed defense regimes, and made a clear declaration: "Landlords' land, peasants collect crops, do not pay off debts, do not send rent".[315] Landlords and their classes began to become hostile forces of the Chinese revolution.

The theoretical understanding of taking the landlord class as the primary enemy of the revolution was also formed late in the process of the Chinese Communist Party's revolutionary appeal. We found that although Li Dazhao clearly stated in his book *My View on Marxism* that he "accepted the thought of class struggle", insisted that "every history that existed before is a history of class competition" and regarded Marx's class theory as a content of historical materialism, he had doubts about the theory of class struggle. He said, "Marx classified the activities of the class within the natural changes in the economic itinerary. However, despite this statement, there is something farfetched and contradictory".[316] In the theoretical system of Li Dazhao, there was no class consciousness of sharp opposition between peasants and landlords, but only a vague, general concept of class (in fact, stratification):

In the past, mental workers were noble, manual workers were lowly; gentlemen were noble, savages were lowly; aristocratic families were noble, civilians were lowly; males were noble, females were lowly; it was a vertical organization. The modern manual worker class unites as a horizontal organization, resisting the mental worker class, the savage class against the gentleman class, and the female class against the male class.[317]

In the *Selected Works of Chen Duxiu*, there are only "The Cry of the Poor and Workers' Awareness – A Speech at the Shanghai Shipbuilding and House building Industry Association" and other essays that respectively talked about the relationship between the polarization of the rich and the poor and the social revolution in Chinese society, as well as the problem of the working class. It still expresses the concept of social stratification of "mental workers" and "manual workers" with traditional cultural characteristics.[318] There is no clear-cut theory of class, let alone of the landlord and his class.

In the history of the CPC, Mao Zedong was the earliest leader who formed the theory of class struggle and took landlords as revolutionary objects. In an article titled "On Rural Investigations", he said that in the 1920s, after reading *Class Struggle* by Kautsky for the first time, the

240 *Historical rural social structure changes*

Communist Manifesto translated by Chen Wangdao and *The History of Socialism* written by an Englishman, he "just knew that human beings have had class struggle from time immemorial. Class struggle is the driving force of social development. And a methodology for understanding issues is initially obtained".[319] Even so, a clear understanding of the class structure and stratification of Chinese society had not yet been formed. He said that the classic theory of Marxist class struggle had not been implemented in the practice process of Chinese social revolution; because "these books do not include China's Hunan and Hubei, nor China's Chiang Kai-shek and Chen Duxiu. I only took four words from it: 'Class struggle' and then began to study the actual class struggle in a down-to-earth way". Thus, he began to investigate and analyze the social class situation in rural China. "The central government asked me to manage the peasant movement. I went to Hunan and investigated five counties: Changsha, Xiangtan, Xiangxiang, Hengshan and Liling".[320] It was exactly on the basis of a large number of investigations, especially through the "Xunwu Investigation" and "Xingguo Investigation" in the 1930s, that there was creatively constructed a class analysis model of Chinese society, especially rural society, which formed the theoretical system of the Chinese revolution, and finally "determined which classes are the main forces of revolutionary struggle, which classes are our allies, and which classes are to be overthrown".[321] The landlord – a social stratum that originally belonged to the peasants in the realm of property rights – was constructed as a hostile class of peasants, and even small landlords (that is, semi-rich peasant landlords) were identified as "the worst enemy class in the countryside. In the eyes of the poor peasant, there is no reason not to defeat him".[322]

In the context of class revolution, the concept of landlord has only been interpreted by the times, and it has almost become an important word of an era. Thus, the historical process of "class revolution" with peasants, especially poor peasants as revolutionary pioneers and landlords as revolutionary objects, had begun. "Where history begins, where should the ideological process begin, and the further development of the ideological process is merely an abstract, theoretically consistent form of the historical process".[323]

The construction of modern history

> In the morning, he was a peasant who worked in the field, and at evening he already became the minister in the court and worked for the emperor. The noble and powerful were not born by nature. Good boys should have the ambition to work hard and keep improving.[324]

Liang Shuming believed that China's social class differentiation and opposition were not strong and fixed, "there is no class at all. (Only the concept of family, but not the concept of class)".[325] This was the basic gist for his

Historical rural social structure changes 241

argument with Mao Zedong's "class revolution" theory when he visited Yan'an in early 1938. With the victory of the CPC many years later, Liang Shuming acknowledged that the "class revolution" theory was "remarkable and clear", and that "a nationwide unified and stable government was established from the class struggle and stood in the east of the world".[326] Therefore, constructing the concept of the landlord of the property right as a class concept with unique significance has become the fundamental premise of the history of the Chinese Communist Party's class revolutionary movement.

"Once a theory has mastered the masses, it will become a material force".[327] Mao Zedong understood this well and constructed the revolution's primary problem in a simple and popular way through the judgment of "who is our enemy and who is our friend". Based on the investigation of the current situation of Chinese society, from the complicated class and stratum structure, he positioned the enemies of the Chinese Communist Party's revolution on landlords and their classes: "The object of China's current revolution is 'imperialism and feudalism'", specifically, "is the bourgeoisie of the imperialist countries and the landlord class of our own country.[328] Mao Zedong further argued that

> the landlord class is the main social foundation for imperialism to rule China. It is the class that exploits and oppresses peasants with the feudal system. It is a political, economic and cultural obstacle to the advancement of Chinese society without any progressive effect. Therefore, as a class, the landlord class is the object of revolution.[329]

Thus, the history of the modern Chinese revolution (class revolution) led by the CPC has obtained a clear direction.

Indeed, for the theoretical study and behavioral practice of landlords and their classes, there are also uncertain swings (such as the "left" or right adjustment from time to time) and even misjudgments in the continuous history of the CCP revolution. "Where the land struggle has deepened, a 'leftism' perspective will occur, giving many middle and even poor peasants the hats of landlords and rich peasants, and harming the interests of the masses".[330] What is more extreme is that in 1929, the Soviet regime in Huang'an, Hubei, stipulated:

> A peasant household of more than five *mu* of land is considered a rich peasant and must be confiscated, so there are many peasants who abandon their fields. Xianbei Township changed the shape of the fields, removed the original boundaries and remerged the fields to implement the so-called policy of land equalization. On the one hand, the peasants were forced to abandon their original land. On the other hand, they did not make efforts for the fields under public management due to the relatively low interest […] the fields were mostly deserted.[331]

242 *Historical rural social structure changes*

How to accurately define the landlord has obviously become an extremely important and complex and difficult subject in the course of the revolutionary movement. Of course, the confusion often appearing in practice is not only a matter of the boundary of policy control, but about the canonical interpretation of theoretical concepts.

> According to the number of households in the countryside, landlords and rich peasants only account for about 8 percent, and middle peasants, poor peasants and farm laborers together account for 90 percent. This front cannot be confused, and many comrades have no clear idea about this.[332]

However, no matter what statistical criterion is used to estimate the number of landlords,[333] in the agricultural-based Chinese society, the number is always a minority or a small minority. In Mao Zedong's words, "80 percent of the population in China is peasant. This is the common sense of elementary school students". This determines the revolutionary goal of overthrowing the "landlord class" and has a natural basis for mobilizing the vast majority of peasants to join the revolution. "So the peasant problem has become the basic problem of the Chinese revolution. And the power of the peasants is the main force of the Chinese revolution". Thus, "the deprivation of landlords' property and the eradication of the landlords' classes have become the prerequisites for evoking the class revolution among the masses".[334] This is because it determines that "this revolution can be supported and sponsored by more than 80 percent of the people".[335]

As a practical operation of the revolutionary theory, the historical practice of eliminating landlords also has strategic room for adjustment at any time, because the standards of landlords and their classes are difficult to clearly indicate, even if Mao Zedong's own understanding was based on investigations. "This is a kind of historical material, some of which are opinions at that time but change later".[336] Although this change has certain theoretical cognition, it is obviously more prominent in targeted strategies. "As a whole class, landlords are to be eliminated, but as individuals, they must be treated differently according to the situation".[337] Promoting the property right attribute of the landlord into a class attribute and constructing it as a revolutionary object of the era itself contains the strategic direction of mobilizing the majority of peasants to engage in class struggle with very few enemies – landlords.

> The main method of our investigation is to dissect the various social classes. Our ultimate goal is to understand the relationships between the various classes, get the correct class estimates, and then determine our correct strategy for struggle and determine which classes are the main forces of revolutionary struggle, which classes are our allies and which classes are we going to bring down. Our purposes are all here.[338]

Historical rural social structure changes 243

The elimination of landlords' private land ownership is a necessary historical stage in this revolutionary process. "The purpose of our struggle is to shift from nationalism to socialism". "The development of this struggle will be followed by the tasks of the socialist revolution".[339] In the stormy revolutionary practice, the revolution of landlords and their forms of land possession was carried out in the simplest and most effective way:

> As for the declaration of the confiscation of land, there is no longer any need to declare it in written form [...] The word "equalization" includes the two meanings of confiscation and distribution.[340]

The problem is that this theoretical interpretation and historical practice not only fit the ultimate purpose of the CCP revolution – the elimination of private ownership[341] – but also had a relatively consistent appeal with the "concept of equality" that has always existed in Chinese history:

> In the past dynasties of China, the socialist policy was always carried out by the agricultural administration. This is because preventing the gap between the rich and the poor and eliminating the disadvantages of mergers are the only points that the managers of government's affairs in China should focus on. And its spirit can be described as the cultivation of the well-field system.[342]

Zhu Zhixin also once put forward that

> regarding the state ownership of land, this concept has also existed in China since ancient times. Land tax to the Tang dynasty was called rent, which showed the meaning that the country is the owner of the land. And they were called owners of the land only because they had a permanent farming right.[343]

In a sense, this theoretical construction has a historical and cultural basis to gain social recognition and wide understanding.

However, even though a particular understanding of landlords and a class interpretation of this group can be supported by and valid within a logical framework for analyzing revolutions, within a broader context, that is, outside this framework, such understanding and interpretation do not hold. "The opposition of 'landlords' and 'peasants' cannot explain the basic social division that under the systems of the Qin and Han dynasties in China".[344] That is to say, landlords out of the context of "class revolution" are only social existences in the sense of land ownership, that is, the peasants who occupy the land. "What we should pay attention to is the division of the peasant class. This division can be roughly divided into five categories: landlords, landholding peasants, semi-land-holding peasants, tenant peasants, farm laborers, or coolies".[345]

244 *Historical rural social structure changes*

It was still the common sense of social cognition at that time that landlords belonged to one of the peasant classes. The statistics of landlords and their social stratification in the "Tianjin Agricultural Investigation Report" in 1931 are listed in Table 4.16.[346]

The survey data show that within the scope of its literature, not only does the landlord not constitute a class, but there is also no systematic exploitation and oppression for peasants (tenants); in the various shares of rents, the landlord has obtained an even lower amount than renters. From an academic standpoint, people have realized the confusion of the content of the concept of the landlord class:

> If the landlord class refers to people who have hundreds of *mu* or thousands of *mu* of land, then after hundreds of years of huge population pressure, the landlords are mostly disappeared naturally. The households remaining are too few to constitute a class.[347]

In Chinese rural society in the twentieth century,

> strictly speaking, there are few big landlords in China, farmland is scattered among small and medium-sized owners, and more than 70 percent of the farmland is cultivated by the owners themselves [...] Rural areas in China are becoming increasingly poor, and this poverty is widespread, as is the case of tenant peasants, as well as of land-holding peasants.[348]

Therefore, the book *Peasants in the Unconventional Period* states that in fact, the landlord is a class of peasants, even an oppressed class: the economic aggression of the great powers, "causes the accumulation of capital and the differentiation of the entire peasant class", "whether for landlords or peasants, under the manipulation and slaughter of imperialism, there is only one way, that is to perish together".[349]

The usual social survey statistics still identify the landlord in the sense of property ownership. For example, as recorded in *The Situation of Agriculture in Jiangxi*,

> although the peasants' living standard is low, the tax is heavy, and they cannot bear the hardships. When the landlord has one *mu* of land, the amount of harvest is evenly divided with tenant peasants. Except for the grain tax of canal transportation, the actual harvest is one-fourth. Because of this, compelled by the livelihood, many people from Jiangxi have to go to various provinces to do business to make a living. Recently, due to a lack of labor, the land is barren and there is even a trend that the landlord is unable to find tenant peasants. At the moment, if the tax reform is not started, peasants will have nothing to live on.[350]

Table 4.16 The statistics on landlords and their social stratification

Village	Land Occupation of Peasant Households	Social Stratification	Tenancy System or Share of Tenant Peasants
Dongyuwang zhuang		Most people of this village are land-holding peasants and there is no distinction between landlord and tenant peasant.	Even if there are people who cultivate other people's fields, the fields are mostly graveyards. They get something from cultivating the borrowed land, but have the cost of looking after the graves. They do not pay rents, and the taxes are paid by the owners of the land.
Xuhuquan Village	Among the 14 peasant households, the largest owns 5 *mu* of land, while the least owns 1 *mu* of land.	1 landlord, 9 land-holding peasants and 4 tenant peasants.	Share: landlord: 20 percent, tenant peasants: 80 percent.
Balitai Village and Wuyao Village	the largest owns 50 *mu* of land, while the least owns 2 *mu* of land. No landlords.	20 households, 5 land-holding peasants and 15 tenant peasants.	Tenant peasants have emphyteusis and non-emphyteusis. The so-called emphyteusis is because the lands of the landlords are all wastelands, and the lands are automatically reclaimed by the tenant peasants, so they can get emphyteusis, the land price cannot be changed optionally and the land cannot be rented to others. On the tenant peasants' side, they can rent the land to another person, so the landlord has the right to collect the rent, and the tenant has the property right.
Xiaoliuzhuang	The tenant peasant Liu Guilin has 227 *mu* of land	Hire laborers to manage the land, the annual wages of long-term laborers are 50–60 *yuan*, while that of short-term daily labor is 80 cents to 1 *yuan*	

(*continued*)

Table 4.16 Cont.

Village	Land Occupation of Peasant Households	Social Stratification	Tenancy System or Share of Tenant Peasants
Tangjiakou			The relationship between the landlord and the tenant peasants is commonly referred to as the "three big piles", that is, the landlord gets one-third and the tenant peasants get two-thirds.
Qiangzishang, Gongyuanhou		There is 1 land-holding peasant and the rest are all tenant peasants.	One of the tenant households cultivates the land with the landowner and does not need to pay rent. The farming costs will go fifty-fifty and their harvest will both account for half of the total.
Jinzhong River Bank, Paotaizhuang	On average, peasants can have more than three *mu* of land for every household. The harvest in previous years has been very profitable. The annual crops per *mu* can be worth hundreds of *yuan*. In addition to about 30 *yuan* for seed, fertilizer and hired laborers, there are still more than 70 *yuan* left.	There are 326 main households, more than 700 deputy households, and 24 peasant households among them. Most of the peasants are tenant peasants and there is only one land-holding peasant.	Tenant peasants pay rents twice a year, ranging from 6 *yuan* to 13 *yuan* per *mu*, and the general price is about 7 *yuan*. If planting vegetables, it can be worth 20 to 50 *yuan* per *mu*. When harvest is rich, it may still double the amount.

Historical rural social structure changes 247

In this case, the peasant group includes landlords.

In such statistics of rural social surveys, landlords do not exist as a class, especially as a class of exploitation and oppression. For example, *The Situation of Agriculture in Hubei* describes the peasant class in this way:

> It can be divided into three categories: small-scale peasants, land-holding peasants and sharecroppers. Among the three, small-scale peasants are the majority, followed by land-holding peasants, and then sharecroppers [...] the farming costs and other expenses are all borne by the tenant peasants, and there is no rental fee. At the time of harvest, landlords and tenant peasants share the harvest equally.[351]

In the survey data of the National Government Administration Executive Court system, the statistics on peasants or peasant households are usually divided according to "the force of wealth". In this classification, landlords also basically belong to the meaning of owners of the land, such as in Hui County, Henan,

> land owned by landlords concentrates to the high stage (the absolute number of households with over 30 *mu* of land increased from nine to thirteen, and the relative number also increased by 12.17 percent) [...] the number of rich peasants with over 50 *mu* decreased by 12.41 percent. In the stage of 30–49.9 *mu*, there is a particular increase. The number of middle peasant households under 50 *mu* are generally increased, especially at this stage of 10–19.9 *mu*, with an increase of 3.54 percent; there were originally 13 households above 50 *mu*, which is now reduced to ten households, a decrease by 4.19 percent. The number of poor peasant households with less than 20 *mu* increases by 3.65 percent, and the number of poor peasant households with more than 20 *mu* decreases by 3.65 percent.[352]

According to the situation of land possession, landlords are said to have more than 30 *mu*, the rich peasants more than 50 *mu*, and some middle peasants also have more than 50 *mu*. This cannot be explained from the class attribute; the landlord here is only one type of peasant. "If the landlord is a land-holding peasant – one land-holding peasant who employs tenant peasants because of his weak ability, – eighty percent of the relationships between the tenant peasant and the landlord are equal relationships".[353]

In the *Investigation of Rural Areas in Lanxi*, edited by the sociologist Feng Zigang, the economic living conditions of landlords are recorded as follows:

1. Housing situation. The average number of the houses owned by those who are landlords and concurrently land-holding peasants is about 12 houses per household, about 7 houses per landlord household on average, about 6.5 houses per land-holding peasant household on average, about

248 *Historical rural social structure changes*

5 houses per semi-land-holding peasant household on average, about 3 houses per tenant peasant household on average, about 2.5 houses per tenant peasant and concurrently farm laborer household on average and only 1.5 houses per farm laborer household on average.[354]

2. Land capital. The highest average number is 5,211 *yuan* per landlord and concurrently land-holding peasant household. The next is 2,446 *yuan* per landlord household on average, 1,437 *yuan* per land-holding peasant household on average, and an average of 589 *yuan* per semi-land-holding household. The average of per tenant peasant household is 23 *yuan*, 18 *yuan* per tenant peasant and concurrently farm laborer household on average, and each farm laborer household 17 *yuan* on average, this is the least.[355]

3. Income situation. Most landlords do not operate agriculture on their own, so there are very few planting products. The average income of 30 landlords is 3.96 *yuan* for each household; the land rent income, plus the money rent income 190.09 *yuan*. Adding livestock products, sideline businesses and others, the average annual income of landlords is 263.97 *yuan*, and the income from land rent accounts for 72.01 percent.[356]

After the calculation of the comprehensive income and expenditure, the survey data show that

the landlords have almost no surplus, and each household has a loss of 67.58 *yuan*. Except for the average landlord and concurrently land-holding peasant household with a surplus of 62.19 *yuan*, all classes are in deficit. The losses of landlords, land-holding peasants, semi-land-holding peasants, tenant peasants, tenant peasants concurrently farm laborers and farm laborers are 67.58 *yuan*, 12.61 *yuan*, 95.70 *yuan*, 59.62 *yuan*, 18.21 *yuan* and 11.17 *yuan* respectively.[357]

The landlords and poor peasants here do not reflect a polarized class opposition relationship, and under the subcategories of peasants, it is obvious that it includes landlords, land-holding peasants, tenant peasants, farm laborers and other agricultural-related subclasses – there is no division of the landlord class based on class attributes.[358]

Through deep study of the process of modern Chinese history, we should clearly clarify a basic fact: the theoretical construction of the landlord and his class attributes only gained specific significance for the era in the revolutionary discourse system, and the historical process of a new era was constructed in the process of putting it into practice. However, its inherent property right of land cannot be wiped out, especially "the concept of social class has also been brought up seriously for discussion today, and this concept is increasingly torn between realism and nominalism".[359] This has led to occasional conflicts and tensions in history and reality with their class attributes. What we need to think about is that, when the class attributes

Historical rural social structure changes 249

are gradually receded and dissipated, and the real property attribute returns to the landlord – the owner of the land, there will be enough room for the exploration of this thesis, both in academic theory and practical value. This is an epochal topic based on history, which also originates from history, and will eventually transcend history.

Notes

1 Related studies include Huang Zongzhi, *Small-Scale Peasant Economy and Social Changes in North China* (Beijing: Zhonghua Book Company, 2000); *Small-Scale Peasant Family and Rural Development in the Yangtze River Delta* (Beijing: Zhonghua Book Company, 1992); Liu Kexiang, "Research on Quantity of Agricultural Employed Labor in China in the 1920s and 1930s", *Research on Chinese Economic History*, 3(1988); Qin Hui, "'The Guanzhong Mode' in Feudal Society – One of the Studies on the Guanzhong Rural Economy before the Land Reform", *Research on Chinese Economic History*, 1(1993); Qian Xiaohong, "A Comparative Study of the Relationship between Agricultural Employment and Tenancy in Shaanxi in the Early Period of this Century", *Research on Chinese Economic History*, 3(1999).

2 Luo Rongqu, "A New Theory of Modernization – The World's and China's Modernization Process" (Beijing: The Commercial Press, 2004), 261. (Author's note)

3 Zhang Youyi, "A Trivial Discussion on the Historical Materials of the Germination of Agricultural Capitalism in China", in *Anthology of Agricultural History in Ming Dynasty, Qing Dynasty and Modern Times* (Beijing: China Agriculture Press, 1997), 281–282.

4 See also: (America) Huang Zongzhi, *Small-Scale Peasant Economy and Social Changes in North China* (Beijing: Zhonghua Book Company, 2000); (America) Du Zanqi: Culture, Power and the State-North China in 1900–1942 (Nanjing: Jiangsu People's Publishing. Ltd, 1996); (Japan) Masao Uchiyama: "Research on the Social Economy of North China in the twentieth Century", translated by Li Enmin and Xing Liquan (Beijing: China Social Sciences Press, 2001).

5 Qi Zhijin, "The Second Volume of villages' Ownership of Land – Rural Areas in Northern Shanxi", *National News Weekly*, March 1934, 24.

6 Ren Bishi, "Several Issues in Land Reform", in Financial and Economic History Compilation Group of Jin-Sui Border Region, *Selected Materials of Financial and Economic History in Jin-Sui Border Region* (Taiyuan: Shanxi People's Publishing House, 1986), 444.

7 Qi Zhizao, "Annotations to the Agricultural Things in Mashou" (Beijing: China Agriculture Press, 1999), 79.

8 "Analysis of Various Classes in Chinese Society", in *Selected Works of Mao Zedong* (vol. 1) (Beijing: People's Publishing House, 1991), 8.

9 Xu Dixin and Wu Chengming, eds., *The History of the Development of Capitalism in China* (vol. 3), 299.

10 Wang Shifu, "A Survey of the Situation of Peasants in Different Places of Jingjiang, Jiangsu", *The Eastern Miscellany*, August 1927, 119.

11 Xu Dixin, "The Livelihood of the Middle and Lower Class in Henan in Rural Bankruptcy", *The Eastern Miscellany*, January 1935, 45.

250 *Historical rural social structure changes*

12 Tao Zhifu, "A Study of the Nature of China's Rural Economy at The Present Stage", in *On China's Rural Economy*, ed. Feng Hefa (Shanghai: Dawn Publishing House, 1934), 200.

13 "Encyclopedia of China · Economics" (Beijing: Encyclopedia of China Publishing House, 1992), 1327.

14 Shi Zhihong, "Tenancy and Employment Relationships of Villages in the North China Plain in the 1930s and 1940s: Take Four Villages in Qingyuan County, Hebei Province for Example", *Research in Chinese Economic History* (vol. 1), 50.

15 Chen Zhengmo: "Employment Customs and State Between Supply and Demand of Agricultural Hired Laborers in Different Provinces", 58, adapted from Yan Zhongping, *Selected Data of Modern Economic History Statistics of China* (Beijing: Science Press, 1955), 263.

16 Edited by Party History Study Office of Shanxi Provincial Committee of the Communist Party of China and Shanxi Provincial Archives, *Selected Data of Land Issues in Taihang Revolutionary Base* (Taiyuan: Shanxi Provincial Archives, 1983), 7.

17 Fan Yuwen, "A Bird's Eye View of Yanggao's Rural Economy at This Stage", *New Countryside*, 20 (January 1935): 9.

18 Fan Yuwen, "Overview of Peasants' Life in Three Counties in the Border of North Shanxi", *New Countryside*, 24 (May 1935): 8.

19 Edited by Party History Study Office of Shanxi Provincial Committee of the Communist Party of China and Shanxi Provincial Archives, *Selected Data of Land Issues in Taihang Revolutionary Base* (Taiyuan: Shanxi Provincial Archives, 1983), 7.

20 "Land Use of Heiyukou" (September 1942), Shanxi Provincial Archives, file number: A141 / 1/99/2.

21 "Changes in Class Relations since the War of Resistance against Japan", "Investigation Report of Duanjiagou Natural Village in Baode County" (July 1942), Shanxi Provincial Archives, file number: A137 / 1/3/1.

22 Liu Rongting, "Comparison of Survey of Sixteen Villages in Gaoping County, Lingchuan County, and Shenchi County, Shanxi Province", *New Countryside*, 9 (February 1934): 9.

23 Xi Chao, "Wage Labor in Rural Areas of Henan", *The Eastern Miscellany*, 18, no. 31 (September 1934): 68.

24 Zhou Gucheng, "Modern Economic History of China" (Shanghai: Fudan University Press, 1987), 110.

25 "Investigation Report of Duanjiagou Natural Village, Baode County", *Table of Changes in Class Relationships* (vol. 1), July 1942, Shanxi Provincial Archives, file number: A137 / 1/3/1.

26 "Investigation Report of Duanjiagou Natural Village, Baode County", "Lend Commodity and Land as Collateral" (July 1942), Shanxi Provincial Archives, file number: A137 / 1/3/1.

27 "Allocation and Development of Land Occupation and Use", "Investigation Report of Duanjiagou Natural Village, Baode County" (July 1942), Shanxi Provincial Archives, file number: A137 / 1/3/1.

28 "Collected Materials of the United Front's Policy", "Classes in Northwestern Shanxi" (December 1941), Shanxi Provincial Archives, file number: A21 / 3/37.

29 Fan Yuwen, "Overview of Peasants' Life in Three Counties in the Border of North Shanxi", *New Countryside*, 24 (May 1935): 13.

Historical rural social structure changes 251

30 "Chorography of the Lvliang Prefecture", edited by Lvliang District Chorography Compilation Committee, 110.

31 "In Order to Appropriately Improve the Lives of Hired Laborers and Promote the Production of Hired Laborers, We Propose to Implement One-Fifth Dividend", "Archive Materials of Northwestern District of Shanxi" (1942), Shanxi Provincial Archives, file number: A88 / 3/23/3.

32 "In Order to Appropriately Improve the Lives of Hired Laborers and Promote the Production of Hired Laborers, We Propose to Implement One-Fifth Dividend", "Archive Materials of Northwestern District of Shanxi" (1942), Shanxi Provincial Archives, file number: A88 / 3/23/3.

33 Liu Rongting, "Comparison of Survey of Sixteen Villages in, Gaoping County, Lingchuan County, and Shenchi County, Shanxi Province", *New Countryside*, 9 (February 1934): 9.

34 Editor-in-Chief of Department of Agricultural Economics, Renmin University of China, *History of Modern Agricultural Economy in China* (Beijing: China Renmin University Press, 1980), 9.

35 "Investigation of Hired Laborers in Dayan Village, Zuoquan County by Federation of Workers, Peasants Youths and Women to Save the Country" (April 1943), Shanxi Provincial Archives, file number: A7 / 1/12/9.

36 Li Changyuan, editor-in-chief, "Selection Data of Agricultural History of Taiyue Revolutionary Base" (Taiyuan: Shanxi Science and Technology Press, 1991), 442.

37 Chen Zhengmo, "Investigation and Research on the Employment Habits of Agricultural Hired Laborers in Different Provinces", *Zhongshan Cultural Education Museum*, August 1934, 365. Note: the area of mountain and land is calculated by shang (垧), and the pronunciation is "shǎng"(赏, award). When peasants write it, they either use (垧) from "soil", or (晌) from "day". According to the meaning of "soil", it is the name of land, and as for the meaning of "day", the speaker thinks that there is a need for one manpower per day, that is, the area of land that each person works per day is one *shang*. The number of *mu* per *shang* varies from place to place, or by the area of lands that each man works per day, which varies from place to place. The land in the northwest of Shanxi is barren. If it is calculated by *mu*, it is quite different. This is because the yield of one *shang* of land in the northwest can only reach the yield of one *mu* of land in other counties. Labor is also saved. The labor required for one *mu* of land in another place is enough to operate a *shang* of land in the northwest. The area of farmland in Shenchi County is generally calculated on the basis of five *mu* equals to one shang. (Author's note)

38 Wang Jingyu, editor-in-chief, "Modern Economic History of China" (vol. 2), (Beijing: People's Publishing House, 1997), 1021.

39 (Britain) Dai Leren et al., "The Study of Chinese Rural Economy", compiled by Li Xizhou (Peiping: Peiping Peasant Movement Research Association, 1928), 123, 170, 120.

40 Xu Songrong, editor-in-chief, "Modern Agricultural Economy of Shanxi Province" (Beijing: China Agriculture Press, 1990), 272.

41 Chen Zhengmo, "Investigation and Research on the Employment Habits of Agricultural Hired Laborers in Different Provinces", *Quarterly Journal of Zhongshan Cultural Education Museum*, August 1934, 333.

42 Zhang Youyi, "Modern Agricultural History of China" (vol. 3) (Beijing: SDX Joint Publishing Company, 1957), 771.

252 *Historical rural social structure changes*

43 Li Wenzhi, Wei Jinyu, Jing Junjian, "Seeds of Agricultural Capitalism in the Ming and Qing Dynasties" (Beijing: China Social Sciences Press, 1983), 66, "Asiha reported on December 20, the 16th year of the reign of Emperor Qianlong in the crime case reports"

44 Edited by Research Committee on Literature and History Materials of Yu County in Shanxi of Chinese people's Political Consultative Conference, "Cultural and Historical Materials of Yu County" (vol. 1), 89.

45 Liu Dapeng, "Liu Dapeng's Diary", 263, 398.

46 Edited by Research Committee on Literature and History Committee of Yu County in Shanxi of Chinese people's Political Consultative Conference, "Cultural and Historical Materials of Yu County" (vol. 1), 89.

47 Liu Dapeng, "Liu Dapeng's Diary", 263, 456, 477.

48 Chen Zhengmo, "Investigation and Research on the Employment Habits of Agricultural Hired Laborers in Different Provinces", *Quarterly Journal of Zhongshan Cultural Education Museum*, 1(August 1934): 332.

49 Editorial Board of the History of Taihang Revolutionary Base, "The Fifth Volume of Historical Materials of Taihang Revolutionary Base – Land Issues" (Shanxi People's Publishing House, 1987), 159.

50 Chen Zhengmo, "Investigation and Research on the Employment Habits of Agricultural Hired Laborers in Different Provinces", *Quarterly Journal of Zhongshan Cultural Education Museum*, 1(August 1934): 334.

51 Fei Jingshi, "Statistics and Analysis of Wages for Farm Laborers", *Quarterly Journal of Internal Statistics*, 1(1936): 111–112.

52 Chen Zhengmo, "Investigation and Research on the Employment Habits of Agricultural Hired Laborers in Different Provinces", *Quarterly Journal of Zhongshan Cultural Education Museum*, 1(August 1934): 362.

53 "Records of the Meeting of Research on Hired Laborers of Yangjiapo" (1942), Shanxi Provincial Archives, file number: A88 / 3/32/1.

54 Chen Zheng Mo, "Investigation and Research on the Employment Habits of Agricultural Hired Laborers in Different Provinces", *Quarterly Journal of Zhongshan Cultural Education Museum*, 1(August 1934), 359, 360.

55 "Fragmentary Materials of Hired Laborers" (1942), Shanxi Provincial Archives, file number: A88 / 3/34/6.

56 Chen Zheng Mo, "Investigation and Research on the Employment Habits of Agricultural Hired Laborers in Different Provinces", *Quarterly Journal of Zhongshan Cultural Education Museum*, 1(August 1934): 360.

57 "Records of the Meeting of Research on Hired Laborers of Yangjiapo" (1942), Shanxi Provincial Archives, file number: A88 / 3/23/1.

58 "Hired Laborers of Yangjiapo" (1942), Shanxi Provincial Archives, file number: A88 / 3/32/2.

59 Liu Dapeng, "Liu Dapeng's Diary", 322.

60 "Fragmentary Materials of Hired Laborers" (1942), Shanxi Provincial Archives, file number: A88 / 3/34/6.

61 Fei Jingshi, "Statistics and Analysis of Wages for Farm Laborers", *Quarterly Journal of Internal Statistics* 1(1936): 110–111.

62 Liu Dapeng, "Liu Dapeng's Diary", 308.

63 Fei Jingshi, "Statistics and Analysis of Wages for Farm Laborers", *Quarterly Journal of Internal Statistics*, 1(1936): 108–109.

64 "Hired Laborers of Yangjiapo" (1942), Shanxi Provincial Archives, file number: A88 / 3/32/2.

Historical rural social structure changes   253

65 Fan Yuwen, "Overview of Peasants' Life in Three Counties in the Border of North Shanxi", *New Countryside*, 24 (May 1935): 12.

66 "Population, Labor Force, and Wage Labour in Renjiawan (Four)" (1943), Shanxi Provincial Archives, file number: A141 / 1/118/1.

67 Edited by Xu Dixin, Wu Chengming, *The History of the Development of Capitalism in China* (vol. 1) (People's Publishing House, 1985), page number unknown.

68 "Summary of Land Survey Materials of Dayou Town, Wuxiang County" (September in 1942), Shanxi Provincial Archives, file number: A181 / 1/44/1.

69 Chen Zhengmo, "Investigation and Research on the Employment Habits of Agricultural Hired Laborers in Different Provinces", 363.

70 Zhang Wentian, "Survey of Villages in Shenfu County and Xing County" (Beijing: People's Publishing House, 1986), 46.

71 "Classes in Northwestern Shanxi" (1943), "Collected Materials of the United Front's Policy", Shanxi Provincial Archives, file number: A88 / 3/32/3.

72 Shi Zhihong, "Tenancy and Employment Relationships in the North China Plain in the 1930s and 1940s – A Case Study of 4 Villages in Qingyuan County, Hebei Province", *Research in Chinese Economic History* (vol. 1), 55.

73 (America) Huang Zongzhi, "Small-Scale Peasant Economy and Social Changes in North China", 80.

74 "Population, Labor Force, and Wage Labor in Renjiawan (Four)" (1943), Shanxi Provincial Archives, file number: A141 / 1/118/1.

75 Chai Shufan, Yu Guangyuan and Peng Ping, "Preliminary Study on Land Issues of Suide and Mizhi County" (Beiing: People's Publishing House, 1979), 111.

76 Xi Chao, "Wage Labor in Rural Areas of Henan", *The Eastern Miscellany*, September 1934, 68.

77 Fan Yuwen, "Overview of Peasants' Life in Three Counties in the Border of North Shanxi", *New Countryside*, 24 (May 1935): 14.

78 Zhai Ke, "Study on Rural Issues in China" (Guangzhou: Publishing Department of National Sun Yat-sen University, 1933), 91.

79 Akira Nagano, "Research on Chinese Land System", trans. Lu Yi (Shanghai: New Life Publishing House, 1933), 39.

80 Financial and Economic History Compilation Group of Jin-Sui Border Region, Shanxi Provincial Archives, *Selected Materials of Financial and Economic History in Jin-Sui Border Region* (Agricultural ed.) (Taiyuan: Shanxi People's Publishing House, 1986), 337. Freeman's research on Wugong Village, Raoyang County, Hebei Province, showed that in 1936 "33 villagers were employed as long-term laborers" and "95 villagers were employed as short-term laborers, almost all of them were peasants who had their own land". See (United States) Freeman et al., "Chinese Village, Socialist Country", trans. Tao Heshan (Beijing: Social Sciences Academic Press, 2002), 40.

81 Li Shuqing, "The Levels of Poverty of Chinese Peasants", *The Eastern Miscellany*, 32, no. 19 (October 1935), 73.

82 (United States) D. H. Perkins, "Agricultural Development in China (1368–1968)", trans. Wu Dange (Shanghai: Shanghai Translation Publishing House, 1984), 140.

83 See "Chorography of the Lvliang Prefecture", p. 111.

84 (Hungary) Mazayar, "Research on Chinese Rural Economy", translated by Chen Daiqing and Peng Guiqiu (Shanghai: Shenzhou Guoguang Publishing House, 1934), p. 403.

254 *Historical rural social structure changes*

85 See "Chorography of the Lvliang Prefecture", p. 111.
86 Liu Cunren and Lv Qi, "Land Tenancy and Usury in the Old Society of Ji County", in *Shanxi Cultural and Historical Materials* (vol. 42), ed. Research Committee on Literature and History Materials of Shanxi Committee of Chinese People's Political Consultative Conference, 152.
87 "Investigation of Hired Laborers in Yangjiapo" (1942), "Collected Policy Materials of United Front", Shanxi Provincial Archives, file number: A88 / 3/32/4.
88 Wu Zhi estimated that in the 1930s, the average salary of long-term laborers in Qingwan was about 40 yuan. See Wu Zhi, "A Study of the Rural Textile Industry" (Beijing: The Beijing: The Commercial Press, 1936), 142; Gan Qiansun, "Affairs about Qingwan County, Hebei Province", Central Command of New People Society", 1938, 156.
89 "Employment Customs and State Between Supply and Demand of Agricultural Hired Laborers in Different Provinces"; see also, Hou Jianxin, "Population Migration and Labor Employment in Central Hebei Province in the 1930s and 1940s", *Journal of Northeast Normal University*, 3(2002): p. 59.
90 See "A Survey of the Situation of Peasants in Different Areas", *The Eastern Miscellany*, 24, no. 16 (August 1927). It can be seen that the wages of rural laborers from Dangtu County in Anhui, Jingjing County in Hebei, and Wujin County in Jiangsu were all around 40 *yuan*. (Author's note)
91 (British) Marshall, "Principles of Economics", trans. Chen Biliang (Beijing: The Commercial Press, 1965), 19.
92 Li Jinghan, "The Structure and Problems of Rural Population in North China", *The Social Community*, 8 (June 1934), 12.
93 Yin Tianmin: "The Life of Agricultural Hired Laborers in Su County, Anhui Province", *The Eastern Miscellany*, 32, no. 12 (June, 1935): 108–109.
94 Shi Zhihong, "Tenancy and Employment Relations in the North China Plain in the 1930s and 1940s – A Case Study of 4 Villages in Qingyuan County, Hebei Province", *Research in Chinese Economic History* (vol. 1), 2003, 4.
95 (United States) Ma Ruomeng, "Chinese Peasant Economy – Agricultural Development in Hebei and Shandong (1890–1949)", trans. Shi Jianyun (Nanjing: Jiangsu People's Publishing. Ltd, 1999), 157–158.
96 Liu Dapeng, "Liu Dapeng's Diary" records the salary paid to hired laborers (short-term laborers) over the years: 1903, 110 wen; 1916, 180 wen; 1917, 350 wen; 1918, 200 wen; 1919, 150 wen; 1926, 600 wen; 1927, 700 wen; 1929, 450 wen; 1930, 1500 wen; 1932, 850 wen; 1939, 600 wen; 1941, 1200 wen. This is the evolution of the average daily wage of the agricultural laborers hired by Liu's family during the busy farming season, which can reflect the long-term trend of wage evolution. (Author's note)
97 Bei jia, "Shanxi Politics and Rural Areas on the Eve of Turmoil", *Chinese Country*, 2, no. 6 (1936): 63, 65.
98 According to Liu Dapeng's Diary, the rice prices in each year are: 2000 wen in 1916, 1800 wen in 1917, 2500 wen in 1918, 2700 wen in 1921, 1700 wen in 1923, 3360 wen in 1926, and 1.9 yuan in 1930, 3 yuan in 1931, 1 yuan in 1932, 1.1 yuan in 1933, 3.5 yuan in 1934 and 1.5 yuan in 1936. According to the parity rate at that time, the rice price after 1930 was converted from yuan into wen for comparison. (Author's note)
99 Liu Dapeng, "Liu Dapeng's Diary", 430, 431.

Historical rural social structure changes   255

100 Fan Yuwen, "Overview of Peasants' Life in Three Counties in the Border of North Shanxi", *New Countryside*, 24 (May 1935): 14.

101 Feng Hefa, "On China's Rural Economy" (Dawn Publishing House, 1935), 507.

102 "Comprehensive Category of Western Shanxi District Party Committee, Survey Materials of Gaojia Village, Xing County (II)" (1942), Shanxi Provincial Archives, file number: A22 / 1/18.

103 "Collected Materials of United Front Policy of Western Shanxi District Party Committee (II) Concluding Remarks" (1941), Shanxi Provincial Archives, file number: A22 / 4/3/2.

104 "Collected Materials of United Front Policy of Western Shanxi District Party Committee (II) Concluding Remarks" (1941), Shanxi Provincial Archives, file number: A22 / 4/3/2.

105 "Investigation Materials of Hired Laborers in Wuxiang" (1943), Shanxi Provincial Archives, file number: A7 / 1/12/5.

106 Fan Yuwen, "Overview of Peasants' Life in Three Counties in the Border of North Shanxi", *New Countryside*, 24 (1935): 14.

107 Marx, *Das Kapital* (vol. 3) (Beijing: People's Publishing House, 1953), 679.

108 See also: Xia Mingfang, "A New Probe into the Nature of Rural Market Development in North China in Modern Times", in *Rural China* (vol. 3) (Social Sciences Academic Press, 2005), 88.

109 Most of the short-term laborers recorded in Liu Dapeng's Diary were provided with food. (Author's note)

110 Compiled by the Statistics Bureau of the National Government's Accounting Office, "The Statistical Summary of the Republic of China" (Commercial Press, 1936), 496–503.

111 Xu Dixin and Wu Chengming, eds., *The History of the Development of Capitalism in China* (vol. 1) (Beijing: People's Publishing House, 2003), 75.

112 "Summary of Survey on Land Issues in Changcheng Town of Liaoxi County", (1943), Shanxi Provincial Archives, file number: A166 / 1/59/1.

113 Liang Nong, "Depletion of Yanzhu Village, Shouyang County, Shanxi", *New China*, 2, no. 9 (1934), 78.

114 Fried flour: First fry the sorghum and beans and grind them into flour. It is better to grind dried dates with fried sorghum and beans into powder, then grab a handful of the flour into water and porridge. It can be eaten. It is sometimes eaten with vegetables. Fried flour is the most convenient food and keeps people full. Therefore, when the peasants are busy, they take fried flour to the field for lunch. (Author's note)

115 "Comprehensive Category of Western Shanxi District Party Committee, Survey Materials of Gaojia Village, Xing County (II)" (1942), Shanxi Provincial Archives, file number: A22 / 1/18.

116 "A Survey of Agricultural Workers of the Jin-Ji-Yu District Federation of Trade Unions" (1943), Shanxi Provincial Archives, file number: A7 / 1/11/1.

117 Liu Cunren and Lv Qi: "Land Tenancy and Usury in the Old Society of Ji County", in *Shanxi Cultural and Historical Materials* (vol. 42), ed. Research Committee on Literature and History Materials of Shanxi Committee of Chinese People's Political Consultative Conference, 153.

118 Huang Zongzhi, "Small-Scale Peasant Family and Rural Development in the Yangtze River Delta" (Beijing: Zhonghua Book Company, 1992), 64.

256 *Historical rural social structure changes*

119 Liu Dapeng, "Liu Dapeng's Diary", 21, 353, 341.
120 Huang Zongzhi, "Small-Scale Peasant Family and Rural Development in the Yangtze River Delta", 65.
121 Chai Shufan, Yu Guangyuan and Peng Ping, "Preliminary Study on Land Issues of Suide and Mizhi County" (Beijing: People's Publishing House, 1979), 120.
122 Liu Dapeng, "Liu Dapeng's Diary", 558.
123 Zhang Wentian, "Anthology of Zhang Wentian's Investigation into Shanxi and Shaanxi", 47.
124 Zhang Wentian, "Anthology of Zhang Wentian's Investigation into Shanxi and Shaanxi", 48, 61.
125 Yan Xinzhe: "A Survey of Rural Families", in *Social Survey Series of the Republic of China* (Rural Society Volume), ed. Li Wenhai, Xia Mingfang and Huang Xingtao (Fuzhou: Fujian Education Press, 2005), 603.
126 Yang Runan, "Social Survey of General situations of the Sixty-four Villages in Xixiao, Beiping", in *Social Survey Series of the Republic of China* (Rural Society Volume), 282.
127 Fan Yuwen, "Overview of Peasants' Life in Three Counties in the Border of North Shanxi", *New Countryside*, 24 (May 1935): 13.
128 Yan Wanying and Yin Yinghua. "History of Agricultural Development in China" (Tianjin: Tianjin Science and Technology Press, 1992), 167.
129 Editorial Board of the History of Taihang Revolutionary Base, "The Fifth Volume of Historical Materials of Taihang Revolutionary Base – Land Issues" (Taiyuan: Shanxi People's Publishing House, 1987), 159.
130 "Investigation of Hired Laborers in Yangjiapo" (1942), Shanxi Provincial Archives, file number: A88 / 3/32/2.
131 (America) James·C. Scott, "The Moral Economics of Peasants: Rebellion and Survival in Southeast Asia", 77.
132 "Summary and Study of the Materials for Rural Workers" (1940), Shanxi Provincial Archives, file number: A7 / 1/2/1.
133 Yang Nianqun, editor-in-chief, "Space, Memory, Social Transformation" (Shanghai: Shanghai People's Publishing House, 2001), 330.
134 (Hungary) Mazayar, "Research on Chinese Rural Economy" (Shanghai: Shenzhou Guoguang Publishing House, 1934), 320.
135 (America) John Commons, "Institutional Economics", trans. Yu Shusheng (Beijing: The Commercial Press, 1997), 95.
136 "Investigation of Peasants in Different Areas: Dangtu, Anhui", *The Eastern Miscellany*, 24, no. 16 (August 1927): 144.
137 Zhang Wentian, "Three Questions on Rural Work", in *Selected Works of Zhang Wentian* (Beijing: Hongqi Press, 1999), 447–448.
138 Hou Jianxin, "Population Migration and Labor Employment in Central Hebei Province in the 1930s and 1940s", *Journal of Northeast Normal University*, 3 (2002): 60.
139 Li Yining, "The Origin of Capitalism: A Study of Comparative Economic History" (Beijing: The Commercial Press, 2003), 14.
140 Luo Rongqu, "A New Theory of Modernization – The World's and China's Modernization Process" (Beijing: The Commercial Press, 2004), 331.
141 Qin Hui and Su Wen, "Pastoral Poetry and Rhapsody: Reconsideration of Guanzhong Model and Premodern Society" (Beijing: Central Compilation & Translation Press, 1996), 80.

Historical rural social structure changes 257

142 Zhang Youyi emphasized in his article "Reassessment of China's Land Rights Distribution in the 1920s and 1930s" that "From the 18th century to the beginning of the twentieth century to the 1920s and 1930s, the distribution ratio of land rights between the landlord class and the peasant class has not changed much". See *Anthology of Agricultural History in Ming Dynasty, Qing Dynasty and Modern Times* (Beijing: China Agriculture Press, 1997), 90.

143 Guo Dehong, "Research on Land Issues of Modern Chinese Peasants" (Qingdao: Qingdao Publishing Group, 1993), 62.

144 Yang Muruo, "A Glimpse of Rural Society in Shanxi", *New Countryside*, 2 (July 1933): 5.

145 According to Shanxi Provincial Institute of History, *Shanxi General History* (vol. 8) (Taiyuan: Shanxi People's Publishing House, 2001), 555–556. Contents: Survey in some villages in Pingding and Yu County: Landlords and rich peasants occupied 31.5 percent; Survey in 101 villages in Lingqiu and Guangling: Landlords and rich peasants occupied 27.85 percent; Survey in 20 villages in 9 counties, such as BeiXing County in Northwestern Shanxi: 60.8 percent; Survey in 123 villages in Licheng, Lucheng and other counties in Taihang District: 20.24 percent; Survey in some villages in 5 counties, including Qi County and Taigu in Jinzhong: 15.5 percent; Survey in 20 villages in 4 counties, including Wanquan and Quwo in Jinquan: 24.36 percent. (Author's note)

146 (America) Zhou Xirui, "Revolution in the 'Feudal Fortress': Mizhi, Yangjiagou, Shaanxi", ed. Feng Chongyi and Goodman, *North China Anti-Japanese Base Area and Social Ecology* (Beijing: Contemporary China Publishing House, 1998), 42, 43.

147 (America) Zhou Xirui, "Revolution in the 'Feudal Fortress': Mizhi, Yangjiagou, Shaanxi", 43.

148 Zhang Wentian, "Zhang Wentian's Collection of Investigations in Shanxi and Shaanxi", 95.

149 "Collected Materials of United Front Policy of Western Shanxi District Party Committee (II) People's Living Burden" (1941), Shanxi Provincial Archives, file number: A22 / 4/2/1.

150 "Collected Materials of United Front Policy of Western Shanxi District Party Committee (II) People's Living Burden" (1941), Shanxi Provincial Archives, file number: A22 / 4/2/1.

151 "Examples of Changes in the Life of Each Household in Each Class", "Collected Materials of United Front Policy of Western Shanxi District Party Committee (II) People's Living Burden" (1941), Shanxi Provincial Archives, file number: A22 / 4/2/1.

152 Fan Yuwen, "Overview of Peasants' Life in Three Counties in the Border of North Shanxi", *New Countryside*, 24 (May 1935): 21.

153 "Party Committee of the Western Shanxi District of the Communist Party of China (January, 1942), Understanding of Zhao Village of Xing County Experimental Branch" (Date unknown), Shanxi Provincial Archives, file number: A22 / 1/4/1.

154 "Collected Materials of United Front Policy of Western Shanxi District Party Committee (II) People's Living Burden" (1941), Shanxi Provincial Archives, file number: A22 / 4/2/1.

155 "General Situation of the Masses and Fighting against the Enemy in Donggou Village, Wuxiang County" (1941), Shanxi Provincial Archives, file number: A181 / 1/36/1.

258 *Historical rural social structure changes*

156 Liang Nong, "Depletion of Yanzhu Village, Shouyang County, Shanxi", *New China*, 2, no. 9 issue (September 1934): 78.
157 Yin Xuan, "The Current Stage of the Rural Economy in Villages of Middle Shanxi", *Chinese Countryside*, 2, no. 11 (November 1936): 74.
158 Liu Dapeng, "Liu Dapeng's Diary", 491.
159 Ma Songling, "To All Leaders of the Ten-Year Construction Plan", *New Countryside*, 6 (November 1933): 1.
160 Edited by Shanxi Provincial Institute of Historiography, "General History of Shanxi" (vol. 7), 238.
161 Liu Dapeng, "Liu Dapeng's Diary", 477.
162 Regarding the cause of the "universal poverty" in rural China in the early twentieth century, the author plans to write an article in the future and study it separately. (Author's note)
163 "Investigation Report of Duanjiagou Natural Village, Baode County" (1942), Shanxi Provincial Archives, file number: A137 / 1/3. See also: Xi Chao, "Wage Labor in Rural Areas of Henan", *The Eastern Miscellany*, 31, no. 18 (September 1934): 68.
164 Reporter, "Peasant Issues and China's Future", *The Eastern Miscellany*, 24, no. 16 24 (August 1927), 2.
165 Huang Xiaoxian, "Survey of Peasants in Haimen", *The Eastern Miscellany*, 24, no. 16 (August 1927): 24.
166 Yan Cuda, "Villages in Northwestern Hubei", *The Eastern Miscellany*, 24, no. 16 (August 1927): 45.
167 Gu Fen, "The State of Peasants in Quzhou, Zhejiang", *The Eastern Miscellany*, 24, no. 16 (August 1927): 56.
168 Fan Yuwen, "Overview of Peasants' Life in Three Counties in the Border of North Shanxi", *New Countryside*, 24 (May 1935): 14.
169 "Summary of Reasonable Burden in Pingbei County in 1941" (1942), Shanxi Provincial Archives, file number: A / 191/1/39/1.
170 Zhao Dehua, "The Living Conditions of Peasants in Jingjing", *The Eastern Miscellany*, 24, no. 16 (August 1927): 96.
171 There were also cases in the south, such as Wujin County, Jiangsu; "Among the 700,000 peasants, there are land-holding peasants ; who are also tenant peasants are so-called semi-tenant peasants. The boundaries between tenant peasants and farm laborers are not very clear, and the number of those surveyed is difficult to be accurate too". "Investigation of Peasants in Different Places · Wujin, Jiangsu", *The Eastern Miscellany*, 24, no. 16 (August 1927): 105.
172 (Soviet Union) A.B. Bakulin, "A Chronicle of Wuhan in the Period of Chinese Revolution (1925 – note of the Chinese Revolution of 1927)", trans. Zheng Houan, Liu Gongxun and Liu Zuohan (Beijing: China Social Sciences Press, 1985), 32.
173 "Summary of Reasonable Burden in Pingbei County in 1941" (1942), Shanxi Provincial Archives, file number: A191 / 1/39/1.
174 For example, in Tangjiaji Village, there were originally four hired laborer households. Two households were turned into poor farmers because, due to enemy raids, no one hired them, and their lives were affected. See "Class Relationships and Their Changes in Tang Jiaji Village" (1942), Shanxi Provincial Archives, file number: A141 / 1/118/2.

Historical rural social structure changes   259

175 For example, in 1936, because each of the two middle peasant households in the Tangjiaji Village sent a son to join the army, the labor force was tight. They previously employed short-term laborers. Since last year, they have hired long-term laborers, and then they became rich peasants. See "Class Relationships and Their Changes in Tang Jiaji Village" (1942), Shanxi Provincial Archives, file number: A141 / 1/118/2.

176 Sheng Cheng, "Investigation of Peasants in Different Areas: Dangtu, Anhui", *The Eastern Miscellany*, 24, no. 16 (August 1927): 143. Huang Xiaoxian, "Survey of Peasants in Haimen", *The Eastern Miscellany*, 24, no. 16 (August 1927): 25.

177 Huang Xiaoxian, "Survey of Peasants in Haimen", *The Eastern Miscellany*, 24, no. 16 (August 1927): 25.

178 Gong Jun, "Investigation of Peasants in Different Areas · Wujin, Jiangsu", 24, no. 16 (August 1927): 106.

179 Gong Jun, "Investigation of Peasants in Different Areas · Wujin, Jiangsu", *The Eastern Miscellany*, 24, no. 16 (August 1927): 106.

180 Zhang Jiafu, "The General Life of Peasants in Central Shanxi", in Qian Jiaju, "Proceedings on Chinese Rural Economy" (2nd ed.) (Beijing: Zhonghua Book Company, 1936), 380.

181 Qiu Zongyi, "Investigation of Peasants in Different Areas · Yexie, Songjiang, Jiangsu", *The Eastern Miscellany*, 24, no. 16 (August 1927): 127. According to the survey, "those – land-holding peasants or tenant peasants – who need this kind of farm laborers either have much land and they cannot take care of them, or they have no men in their family".

182 Zhang Jiafu, "The General Farm Life in Central Shanxi", in Qian Jiaju, "Proceedings on Chinese Rural Economy" (2nd ed.) (Beijing: Zhonghua Book Company, 1936), 380.

183 Sheng Cheng, "Investigation of Peasants in Different Areas: Dangtu, Anhui", *The Eastern Miscellany*, 24, no. 16 (August 1927): 143.

184 Wu Baoshan, "Investigation of Peasants in Different Areas: Jurong, Jiangsu", *The Eastern* Miscellany, 24, no. 16 (August 1927): 116.

185 Tian Gengyuan, "Investigation of Peasants in Different Areas: Hefei, Anhui", *The Eastern Miscellany*, 24, no. 16 (August 1927): 132–133.

186 Tian Gengyuan, "Investigation of Peasants in Different Areas: Hefei, Anhui", *The Eastern Miscellany*, 24, no. 16 (August 1927): 147

187 Mao Zedong, "Investigation of Xunwu", *Anthology of Mao Zedong* (Beijing: Hongqi Publishing House, 1999), 227.

188 Fan Yuwen, "Overview of Peasants' Life in Three Counties in the Border of North Shanxi", *New Countryside*, 24 (May 1935): 12.

189 Liu Dapeng, "Liu Dapeng's Diary", 501.

190 "Survey of Employers in Yangjiapo Village", "Yang Dezi" (1942), Shanxi Provincial Archives, file number: A88 / 3/32/3.

191 Liu Qingru, ed., "Chorography of Guantao County" (vol. 6: "Etiquette and Customs"), a stereotype edition in 1936, see also: Zhang Peiguo, "Modern Land Management in Villages of Shandong Province: Customary Description and Institutional Analysis", *Eastern Forum*, 2: 85.

192 "Classes in Northwestern Shanxi" (1943), "Collected Materials of the United Front's Policy", Shanxi Provincial Archives, file number: A88 / 3/32/3.

193 (America) James·C·Scott, "The Moral Economics of Peasants: Rebellion and Survival in Southeast Asia", 215.

260 *Historical rural social structure changes*

194 Social mobility is an important area in Western sociology. Part of the purpose of Western social sciences' discussion of intergenerational mobility is to see how modern and free this society is. So-called social mobility, according to the definition of the *Encyclopedia Britannica*, refers to "the movement of individuals, families or groups from a social hierarchy or stratification system. If the movement involves only changes of position, especially occupation, but not in social class, it is called 'horizontal mobility'. And if it involves a change in social class, then it is called 'vertical mobility'. This mobility involves 'upward mobility' and 'downward mobility.' Pitirim Sorokin, a famous sociologist who laid the foundation for the theory of social mobility, published the book *Social Mobility* in 1927. Comments and criticisms of the book can be found in the book review of Rudolf Heberle. Rudolf Heberle, "Social Mobility by Pitirim Sorokin" *American Journal of Sociology*, 34 (1928): 219–225. (Author's note)

195 Mike Savage, "Social Mobility and Class Analysis: A new Agenda for Social History?", *Social History*, 19 (1994): 69.

196 Yu Lin, "Review of Chinese Agricultural Production Relationship", *Chinese Countryside*, 1, no. 5 (February 1935): 8; Hong Zhong, "The Struggle Against Rich Peasants in the Countryside", *Red Flag*, 62 (December 1929), 3. "Eliminating rich peasants" was also an important task of the socialist revolution after the founding of New China. Therefore, "the party and the country will never allow rich peasant economy to develop without restrictions". See He Zai, "Talking about Eliminating Rich Peasant Economy", "The Glory of Yan'an" (Xi'an: Shaanxi People's Publishing House, 1993), 140. (Author's note)

197 Zhu Xinfan, "Relationships and Characteristics of China's Rural Economy" (Shanghai: New Life Publishing House, 1930), 267, 257, 259, 243, 256–257.

198 Related studies include: Qu Yanjia, "On the Party's Policy to Rich Peasants During the Second Revolutionary Civil War", *Research on Modern History*, 2 (1982); He Bingmeng, "On the Party's Policy to Rich Peasants in the Land Struggle", *Research on Modern History*, 1 (1986); Wang Jianke, "Evolution of the Party's Policies to Rich Peasant in Various Periods", *Jiangsu Social Sciences*, 2 (1992); Xu Xiuli, "Chinese Communist Party's Policy to Rich Peasants in the 1950s", in "Transition of the Times – Proceedings of the International Conference on 'China in 1949'", compiled by the Institute of Modern History of the Chinese Academy of Social Sciences (Sichuan People's Publishing House, 2002). Studies on the rich peasant policies of the Communist Party in different historical periods include: Wang Guohong, "On the Party's Policies on Rich Peasants during the Second Revolutionary Civil War", *Qilu Journal*, 4 (1981); Li Shaoming, "On Middle Peasants and Rich Peasants in the Land Reform Period", *The Journal of Chinese Social and Economic History*, 4 (1987); Xu Li, "On the Party's Strategies to Rich Peasants in the Land Struggle", *Historiography Research in Anhui*, 4 (1988); Lu Rong Shun, "A Probe into the Issue of Rich Peasants", *Suzhou University Journal*, 4 (1989); Ye Dexian, "On the Changes of the Party's Policy to Rich Peasants during the Agrarian Revolutionary War", *Inner Mongolia Normal University Journal*, 4 (1990); Lin Sulan, "On the Evolution of Our Party's Rich Peasant Policy", *Hangzhou University Journal*, 4 (1994); Qin Hongyi, "The Chinese Communist Party's Rich Peasant Policy in Four Stages", *Seeker*, 1 (2005), etc. Related theses include: Wang Haojun, "Understanding and Policy Evolution of the Chinese Communist Party on the Rich Peasant Class", master's thesis, School of Marxism, Jilin University, 2005;

Yang Song, "The Chinese Communist Party's Theoretical Policies on the Rich Peasants during the Agrarian Revolution", master's thesis, School of Marxism, Southwest Jiaotong University, 2004; Yang Feirong, "Mao Zedong's Use of the Rich Peasant Concept and Its Definition (1925–1933)", *Studies on Mao Zedong Thought*, 4 (1997), etc. (Author's note)

199 Liao Shiyi, "Agricultural Ladder in China", *Agriculture Newspaper*, 12, no. 3 (June 15, 1947), 2–4.

200 The author collected a part of the "Registration Form of Class Composition" during the period of the "four cleans" movement. These materials were basically completed in the mid-1960s. The registration form took a household as a unit. It required a detailed record of the economic status of the family at the time, and a "description of family history" to register the situation of grandparents and parents. Although the content is relatively brief, it can roughly reflect the context of family intergenerational development and change. (Author's note)

201 Wang Yuesheng, "A Survey of the Changes in the Number of Children of Peasants' Families in Southern Hebei: 1930s-1990s", ed. Huang Zongzhi, *Rural China*, the 3rd Series (Social Sciences Academic Press, 2005), 102.

202 Ding Ling, "The Sun Shines on the Sanggan River" (Shijiazhuang: Huashan Literary Press, 1995), 6.

203 "Registration Form of Class Composition", Ci County Archives Collection, Class Archives, file number: 95 / 12-13 / 8.

204 "Registration Form of Class Composition", Ci County Archives Collection, Class Archives, file number: 95 / 12-13 / 7.

205 "Registration Form of Class Composition", Ci County Archives Collection, Class Archives, file number: 95 / 12-13 / 7.

206 "Registration Form of Class Composition", Ci County Archives Collection, Class Archives, file number: 95 / 12-13 / 7.

207 "Changes in Class Relationships and Land Ownership in 5 Villages of Xing County and Lin County" (April 1945). Archives of Shanxi-Hebei-Shangdong-Henan Border Region Transportation Bureau, Shanxi Provincial Archives, file number: A90 / 2/199/1.

208 Zhang Youyi, "A Trivial Discussion on the Historical Materials of the Germination of Agricultural Capitalism in China", in *Anthology of Agricultural History in Ming Dynasty, Qing Dynasty and Modern Times* (Beijing: China Agriculture Press, 1997), 273.

209 Gu Shiling, "Poverty and Peasant Issue in China" (Shanghai: People's Book Company, n.d.), 108.

210 Zhang Jiafu, "The General Life of Peasants in Central Shanxi: An Account for the Peasant Households in Rural Bankruptcy", in Qian Jiaju, "Proceedings on Chinese Rural Economy", *Series of Books in Republic of China* (2nd ed.) (35), (Shanghai: Shanghai Bookstore, 1989), 380.

211 Ma Ruomeng, "Chinese Peasant Economy – Agricultural Development in Hebei and Shandong (1890–1949)", 261

212 Edited by Zhang Youyi, "Modern Agricultural History of China" (2nd ed.) (Beijing: SDX Joint Publishing Company, 1957), 303–304.

213 Zhou Rongde, "Classes and Mobility in Chinese Society – A Study of Gentry Identity in a Community" (Shanghai: Xuelin Press, 2000), 246.

214 (America) Huang Zongzhi, "Small-Scale Peasant Economy and Social Changes in North China", 74–78.

262 *Historical rural social structure changes*

215 (America) Yang Maochun, "A Chinese Village: Taitou, Shandong", trans. Zhang Xiong et al. (Nanjing: Jiangsu People's Publishing House, 2001), 129.

216 Wang Yuesheng, "Research on the Family Separation in South Hebei Province in the 1930s and 1940s", *Research on Modern History*, 4 (2002): 179.

217 (America) Huang Zongzhi, "Small-Scale Peasant Economy and Social Changes in North China", 174.

218 Wang Yuesheng, "Social Changes and Changes in Marriage and Family: Rural Areas in Southern Hebei in the 1930s-1990s" (Beijing: SDX Joint Publishing Company, 2006), 309.

219 "Registration Form of Class Composition", Ci County Archives, Class Archives, file number: 95/15 / 7-8.

220 Yang Chunchun, "A Village in China: Taitou, Shandong", 129.

221 Lu Huilin, "The Pattern and Changes of Rural Social Differentiation in China before and after the Revolution: Findings from Community Studies", in Institute of Social China Academy of Social Science, *Chinese Sociology* (vol. 3) (Shanghai: Shanghai People's Publishing House, 2004), 118.

222 Free mobility refers to the change in personal social status caused mainly as a result of special reasons. Structural mobility refers to large-scale changes in class, class structure or regional population distribution caused by production technology and social transformation and revolution. Wang Xianming, "The Social Mobility of Modern Chinese Gentry Class", *A Study of History*, 1993, no. 2, 81.

223 (America) Huang Zongzhi, "The Rural Class Struggle in the Chinese Revolution – The Expressive and Objective Realities from the Land Reform to the Cultural Revolution", *Rural China* (vol. 2) (Beijing: The Commercial Press, 2003), 74.

224 Yang Maochun, "A Village in China: Taitou, Shandong", 36–37.

225 Ma Ruomeng, "Chinese Peasant Economy – Agricultural Development in Hebei and Shandong (1890–1949)", 146.

226 Yuan: "A Survey of Economy in a Village of Hebei Province", *Chinese Economy*, 2, no. 7 (August 1934): 1.

227 (America) Han Ding, "Turn Over – A Revolutionary Record of a Village in China", trans. Han Jing and others (Beijing: Beijing Press, 1980), 52.

228 Lei Dian, Hong Chen, "Sun Dawu – Born for Peasants: The Efforts and Introspection of a Peasant Entrepreneur" (Beijing: China Social Sciences Press, 2004), 43–44.

229 Wang Xianming, "Hired Laborers in Shanxi in the Early twentieth Century", *A Study of History*, 5 (2006): 115.

230 "Registration Form of Class Composition", Ci County Archives, Class Archives, 95 / 12-13 / 7.

231 Jin-Sui Suboffice Information Research Unit, "Materials of Rural Land and Class Change – Based on a Survey of Twenty Villages in Nine Counties in the Old Base Areas" (June 1946), Shanxi Provincial Archives, Archives of the Jin-Sui Suboffice of the CPC Central Committee, file number: A21 / 3 / 14/1.

232 Prefectural Administrative Office of Central Hebei, "A Preliminary Investigation of the Rural Class Situation and the Burden Situation of Different Classes in the Central Hebei After the Land Reform" (March 1947), Archives of the Prefectural Administrative Office of Central Hebei, Hebei Provincial Archives, file number: 5/1/672/1.

233 Lvliang District Chorography Compilation Committee: "Chorography of the Lvliang Prefecture", 111.

Historical rural social structure changes   263

234 Prefectural Administrative Office of Central Hebei, "A Preliminary Investigation of the Rural Class Situation and the Burden Situation of Different Classes in the Central Hebei After the Land Reform" (March 1947), Archives of the Prefectural Administrative Office of Central Hebei, Hebei Provincial Archives, file number: 5/1/672/1.

235 Prefectural Administrative Office of Central Hebei, "A Preliminary Investigation of the Rural Class Situation and the Burden Situation of Different Classes in the Central Hebei After the Land Reform" (March 1947), Archives of the Prefectural Administrative Office of Central Hebei, Hebei Provincial Archives, file number: 5/1/672/1.

236 Shanxi-Chahar-Hebei Border Area Finance and Economics Office, "Investigation Materials on National Economic Affordability of People in 9 Villages, 7 Counties in Central Hebei and Ji-Jin" (August 1947), Shaanxi Provincial Archives, Archives of Shaanxi-Gansu-Ningxia Border Region Taxation Bureau, file number: 8/6/18.

237 Shanxi Provincial Archives, "Compilation of Data about Taihang Party History" (vol. 3) (Taiyuan: Shanxi People's Publishing House, 1994), 125. Wuxiang County Chronicles Compilation Committee Office, "Wuxiang County Chronicles" (Shanxi People's Publishing House, 1986), 295.

238 (America) Glensky, "Social Stratification", trans. Wang Jun et al. (Beijing: Huaxia Publishing House, 2005), 264.

239 Zhang Youyi, "Reassessment of China's Land Rights Distribution in the 1920s and 1930s", in *A Collection of Agricultural History in the Ming and Qing Dynasties and Modern Times* (Beijing: China Agriculture Press, 1997), 79.

240 "Anthology of Mao Zedong" (vol. 4) (Beijing: People's Publishing House, 1991), 1441.

241 Tian Wenbin ("Collapse of Petty Peasants in Hebei", ed. Qian Jiaju, "Proceedings on Chinese Rural Economy", 253) wrote: Among "the rich peasants and landlords with land of more than 50 mu", as the survey of ten representative villages in Baoding (joint investigation conducted by the Academia Sinica and the Peiping Social Research Institute in 1930) said, "The rich peasants occupy an average of 56 *mu* of land per household, while the landlords occupy an average of 58.5 *mu* per household. The poor peasants and farm laborers occupy an average of less than 7 *mu*". Wang Yijin said in "The Rich Peasant and Its Business" (*Chinese Economy*, 4, no. 7 (July 1936): 1 (text page)) that, "those with more than 50 *mu* of land are rich peasants". While the survey data in Tunliu County, Shanxi Province, shows that: 380 rich peasant households occupy 38,000 *mu* of land, which means that every household occupies 100 *mu* of land on average. (Gao Miao, "The Rural Economic Situation in Tunliu County, Shanxi Province", in Qian Jiaju, *Proceedings on Chinese Rural Economy*, 576.) (Author's note)

242 Feng Hefa, ed., "On China's Rural Economy", "Republic of China Series" (2nd ed.) (35) (Shanghai: Shanghai Bookstore, 1989), 229.

243 See Zhang Youyi, Zhang Youyi, "A Trivial Discussion on the Historical Materials of the Germination of Agricultural Capitalism in China", in *Anthology of Agricultural History in Ming Dynasty, Qing Dynasty and Modern Times*, 278–279.

244 Rural Rehabilitation Committee of the Executive Court, ed., "Survey of Villages in Jiangsu Province", "General Notices" (Beijing: The Commercial Press, 1933), 2; Rural Rehabilitation Committee of the Executive Court, ed., "Survey of

264 *Historical rural social structure changes*

Villages in Shaanxi Province", "General Notices" (Beijing: The Commercial Press, 1934), 1.

245 Li Feng, "The Development Process of Commercial Capital in the Rural Cotton Weaving Handicraft Industry in Hebei in the Past Fifty Years", *Chinese Countryside*, 1, no. 3 (December 1934): 73

246 Wang Yijin, "The Rich Peasants in Jiangsu and Their Management", *Chinese Economy*, 4, no. 7 (July 1936): 10 (text page).

247 Wang Yijin, "The Rich Peasants in Jiangsu and Their Management", *Chinese Economy*, 4, no. 7 (July 1936): 9 (text page).

248 Wang Yijin, "The Rich Peasants in Jiangsu and Their Management", *Chinese Economy*, 4, no. 7 (July 1936): 11 (text page).

249 Li Fangchun, " 'Turnover' and 'Production' in the Land Reform in the North – A Discourse on the Modernity of the Chinese Revolution – A Retrospective Study of Historical Contradictions", in Huang Zongzhi, editor-in-chief, *Rural China*, the 3rd Series (Beijing: Social Sciences Academic Press, 2005), 249.

250 Zhang Wentian, "Develop New Capitalism", ed. Zhang Wentian, Anthology Biography Group and Others, "Anthology of Zhang Wentian's Survey of Heibei and Shaanxi", 324.

251 He Zai, "On the Elimination of Rich Peasant Economy", in *The Glory of Yan'an*, (Xi'an: Shaanxi People's Publishing House, 1993), 141.

252 Lin Sheng, "On the 'Rich Peasant Economy'", *Shanghai "Chinese Construction"*, 3, no. 14 (December 1948), 3.

253 Since the new century, the research and discussion on the landlord in academic and theoretical circles has formed the deconstruction of its historical interpretation and historical orientation from multiple aspects. See Lu Heng, "The Evolution and Significance of Landlord Formation in a Century", *Academic Forum*, 4th issue, 2006; Wang Renhong, "Landlords: A Difficult Topic for 100 Years", *Book House*, 8th issue, 2010. The article "Today and Yesterday – A Discussion on the Social and Historical Issues of China" states that the opposition between "landlord" and "peasant" cannot explain the basic social divisions under the system of the Qin and Han dynasties in China, but people have been parroting that saying. The author believes that this problem was thoroughly analyzed in Wang Yanan's "Chinese Bureaucratic Politics Research" 50 years ago (see *Well-Read*, (vol. 1), 1998). Liu Chang's paper "Revolution in the South of the Yangtze River: Communist Party and Countryside in the South of the Yangtze River, 1927–1945" (*Rural China*, the 1st Series (Beijing: The Commercial Press, 2003) and Yang Kuisong's paper "Landlord Issues in the Context of Land Reform in New China" present the complexity of the landlords' living conditions from different perspectives (*Historical Review*, 6th issue, 2008). However, academia has not yet developed a deep understanding of the historical situation in which the consciousness of real right was changed to class discourse and has a lasting influence on the historical process of modern China.

254 "The Eulogy of Premier Zhao", Tao Changshan et al., eds., "The First Chronicle of the National Federation of Peasants' Associations" in May of the second year of the Republic of China, ed. Shen Yunlong, "The 87th Series of Modern Chinese Historical Materials", 49–50.

255 Mao Zedong, "On Rural Investigation" (September 13, 1941), *Anthology of Mao Zedong's Rural Investigation* (Beijing: People's Publishing House, 1982), 24.

Historical rural social structure changes 265

256 "On the Class System of China", *The Eastern Miscellany*, 1, no. 6 (June 1904), "Voice of Society", 106.

257 Li Wenzhi, ed., "Materials of Modern Chinese Agricultural History" (vol. 1) (1840–1911) (Beijing: SDX Joint Publishing Company, 1957), 344.

258 Feng Guifen, "Persuade the Gentry with the Theory of Average Rich", Xianfeng three years, "Xianzhitang Manuscript" (vol. 9), 23–24, ed. Shen Yunlong, "Modern Chinese Historical Materials Series Sequel" (vol. 79) (Taipei: Wenhai Publishing Company, 1995), 929.

259 Hu Sijing, "Tuilushu Manuscripts" (vol. 3), 3; ibid., 323.

260 Li Wenzhi, ed., "Materials of Modern Chinese Agricultural History" (vol. 1: (1840–1911) (Beijing: SDX Joint Publishing Company, 1957), 1.

261 Gong Zizhen, "Discussion on Setting Provinces in the Western Regions", *Complete Works of Gong Zizhen* (Shanghai: Shanghai People's Publishing House, 1975), 106.

262 Bao Shichen, "Four Techniques for Civilians to Make a Living" Pan Jinghan proofed, first half of 4th volume "Talking about Bao-jia" (Beijing: Zhonghua Book Company, 2010), 129.

263 Li Wenzhi, "Materials of Modern Chinese Agricultural History" (vol. 1: 1840–1911) (Beijing: SDX Joint Publishing Company, 1957), 749.

264 Li Wenzhi, ed., "Materials of Modern Chinese Agricultural History" (vol. 1: 1840–1911), 339.

265 The land seller is stated in the contract as the seller, the owner, the abandoner, the original owner or the original proprietor. The land buyer is called the buyer, the recipient or the proprietor. ibid., 51.

266 Quoted from "Collection of Chinese Articles" (vol. 474) (September 11, in the 32nd year of Guangxu Emperor), *Modern Agricultural History of China*, the 1st Series, 319.

267 Zhang Zhijue, comp., Meng Qingxuan, composer, Republic of *China's Annals of Li County* (vol. 3), Industrial Records, Agriculture, the 28th Year of the Republic of China, China Chronicles Series Hunan Province (Taipei: Chengwen Publishing Company), 75–76.

268 "The Revolutionary Strategy of the Chinese Alliance (1906)", vol. 1 of *The Complete Works of Sun Yat-sen* (Beijing: Zhonghua Book Company, 1981), 297.

269 "Speech in Tokyo Newspaper of Civilian's Anniversary Celebration Conference", December 1906, 329.

270 "Speech at the Farewell Dinner for Members of the Nanjing Alliance" (April 1, 1912), *The Complete Works of Sun Yat-sen*, vol. 2: 320.

271 "Speech to Parliamentarian Journalists in Guangzhou" (June 9, 1912), ibid., vol. 2: 371.

272 "Speech to Parliamentarian Journalists in Guangzhou" (June 9, 1912), vol. 2: 372.

273 "Three Principles of the People" (1919), *The Complete Works of Sun Yat-sen*, vol. 5: 193.

274 "Three Principles of the People" (1919), *The Complete Works of Sun Yat-sen*, vol. 5: 193.

275 Ibid., 194.

276 Liang Qichao, "Speech in Public Schools in China" (March 10, 1920), ed. Li Huaxing and Wu Jiaxun, *Selected Works of Liang Qi* (Shanghai: Shanghai People's Publishing House, 1984), 740.

266 *Historical rural social structure changes*

277 "Three Principles of the People" (1919), *The Complete Works of Sun Yat-sen*, vol. 5: 194–195.

278 Reporter, "Peasant Issues and the Future of China", *The Eastern Miscellany*, 24, no., 16 (August 1927), 3.

279 The Central Propaganda Committee, "Proceedings of the 1st, 2nd, 3rd and 4th National Congress of the Chinese Kuomintang" (printed the 23rd year of People's Republic of China), ed. Shen Yunlong, *The 98th Series of Modern Chinese Historical Materials* (Taipei: Wenhai Publishing Company, 1996), 56–57.

280 The Central Propaganda Committee, "Proceedings of the 1st, 2nd, 3rd and 4th National Congress of the Chinese Kuomintang", ibid., 56–57.

281 "Resolution of the Peasant Movement of the Second National Congress of the Chinese Kuomintang" (September 1926), "Chinese Modern Revolutionary History Materials Series", "Data of the Peasant Movement during the First Revolutionary Civil War" (People's Publishing House, 1983), 32.

282 Chinese Modern Revolutionary History Materials Series, "Data of the Peasant Movement during the First Revolutionary Civil War" (Beijing: People's Publishing House, 1983), 84

283 "Resolution of the First Peasant Congress of Hunan Province" (December 1926), "Data of the Peasant Movement during the First Revolutionary Civil War", Chinese Modern Revolutionary History Materials Series, "Data of the Peasant Movement during the First Revolutionary Civil War" (Beijing: People's Publishing House, 1983), 403.

284 Gan Naiguang, "Why the County Magistrates of the Gentry's Regiment Oppose the Peasant Association", *Chinese Peasants* (vol. 10) (1926), 3.

285 Ke Ming, "Analysis of the Issue of Gentry", *Chinese Peasants* (vol. 10), 9.

286 Deng Liangsheng, "The Obstacles of the Peasant Movement – The Gentry Class", pointed out: Most urban gentries are frustrated soldiers, politicians, elders of former Qing dynasties, compradors; rural gentries are evil landlords, inferior local ruffians, and boring semi-intellectuals. *Chinese Peasants*, 10: 15.

287 Chinese Modern Revolutionary History Materials Series, "Data of the Peasant Movement during the First Revolutionary Civil War" (Beijing: People's Publishing House, 1983), 10.

288 "Declaration on Peasants at the Third Plenary Session of the Second Central Executive Committee of the Chinese Kuomintang" (March 1927), ibid., 46.

289 "This resolution was drafted by a committee organized by five people: Lin Zuhan, Mao Zedong, Chen Gongbo, and a Mr. Wang". Except Chen Gongbo, "the other four are all Communists". See Zhu Xinfan, "China's Rural Economy Relationships and Their Traits" (Shanghai: New Life Publishing House, 1930), 2.

290 "National Revolution and Peasant Movement – Preface to 'Peasant Issues Series'", ed. Literature Research Office of the Communist Party of China Central Committee: vol. 1 of *Mao Zedong Anthology* (Beijing: People's Publishing House, 1993), 37.

291 Ibid., 38.

292 The Central Propaganda Committee, "Proceedings of the 1st, 2nd, 3rd and 4th National Congress of the Chinese Kuomintang" (printed the 23rd year of People's Republic of China), ed. Shen Yunlong, *The 98th Series of Modern Chinese Historical Materials*, 84.

Historical rural social structure changes 267

293 Deng Liangsheng, "Obstacles to the Peasant Movement – The Gentry Class", *Chinese Peasants*, 10 (December 1926): 18.
294 Chinese Modern Revolutionary History Materials Series, "Data of the Peasant Movement during the First Revolutionary Civil War" (Beijing: People's Publishing House, 1983), 3.
295 Wu Tiefeng, ed., "Peasants in the Unconventional Period" (Shanghai: Shanghai Zhonghua Book Company, 1936), 4.
296 Guo Fan, "Methods of the Peasant Movement", Chinese Modern Revolutionary History Materials Series, "Data of the Peasant Movement during the First Revolutionary Civil War" (Beijing: People's Publishing House, 1983), 600.
297 Reporter, "Peasant Issues and the Future of China", *The Eastern Miscellany*, the 24, no. 16 (August 1927): 3.
298 Chinese Modern Revolutionary History Materials Series, "Data of the Peasant Movement during the First Revolutionary Civil War" (Beijing: People's Publishing House, 1983), 37.
299 Ibid., 33.
300 John Fitzgerald, trans, Li Gongzhong and Li Lifeng, "Awakening China: Politics, Culture and Class in the National Revolution" (Beijing: SDX Joint Publishing Company, 2004), 265.
301 Arif Derek, "Revolution and History: The Origin of Chinese Marxist History, 1919–1937" (Nanjing: Jiangsu People's Publishing House, 2005), 50.
302 Chinese Modern Revolutionary History Materials Series, "Data of the Peasant Movement during the First Revolutionary Civil War" (Beijing: People's Publishing House, 1983), 38.
303 Arif Derek, "Revolution and History: The Origin of Chinese Marxist History, 1919–1937" (Nanjing: Jiangsu People's Publishing House, 2005), 49.
304 John Fitzgerald, trans. Li Gongzhong and Li Lifeng, "Awakening China: Politics, Culture and Class in the National Revolution" (Beijing: SDX Joint Publishing Company, 2004), 119.
305 Arif Derek, "Revolution and History: The Origin of Chinese Marxist History, 1919–1937", 24.
306 Zhu Zhixin, "On the Parallel of Social Revolution and Political Revolution", ed. Shao Yuanchong, *Collected Works of Zhu Zhixin*, the 66th Series of "Modern Chinese Historical Materials Series" (Taipei: Wenhai Publishing Company, 1980), 12.
307 John Fitzgerald, trans. Li Gongzhong and Li Lifeng, "Awakening China: Politics, Culture and Class in the National Revolution", 500–501.
308 Chinese Modern Revolutionary History Materials Series, "Data of the Peasant Movement during the First Revolutionary Civil War", 49.
309 Ibid., 54.
310 Ibid., 57.
311 Deng Chumin, "Outline of New Politics", "Republic of China Series" (1st ed.) (21) (Shanghai: Shanghai Bookstore, 1989), 25.
312 Deng Chumin, "Outline of New Politics", "Republic of China Series" (1st ed.) (21), 28.
313 Ibid., 47.
314 Reporter, "Peasant Issues and the Future of China", *The Eastern Miscellany*, 24, no. 16 (August 1927): 1.

268 *Historical rural social structure changes*

315 "Notice of the Fourth Army Command of the Red Army in January, 1929", see vol. 1 of *Collected Works of Mao Zedong*, 52.

316 Li Dazhao, "My View of Marxism", *Anthology of Shou Chang*, the 1st series of the Republic of China Series (Shanghai: Shanghai Bookstore, 1990), 124.

317 Li Dazhao, "From Vertical Organization to Horizontal Organization", *Anthology of Shou Chang*, 190.

318 See vol. 1 of *Collected Works of Chen Duxiu* (Beijing: Foreign Languages Press, 2013), 613, 449.

319 "On Rural Investigation" (September 13, 1941), *Collected Works of Mao Zedong Rural Investigation* (Beijing: People's Publishing House, 1982), 22.

320 "On Rural Investigation" (September 13, 1941), *Collected Works of Mao Zedong Rural Investigation* (Beijing: People's Publishing House, 1982), 22.

321 "Oppose Book Worship" (May 1930), Document Research Office of the Central Committee of the Communist Party of China, *Collected Works of Mao Zedong Rural Investigation* (Beijing: People's Publishing House, 1982), 5–6.

322 "Xunwu Investigation" (May 1930), ibid., 131.

323 Engels, "Karl Marx's 'Critique of the Political Economy'", *Selected Works of Marx and Engels* (vol. 2) (Beijing: People's Publishing House, 1973), 122.

324 Wang Donglin, "Political Consultation between CPC and KMT in Chongqing Liang Shuming Calls for the End of Civil War", China.com.cn, on December 13, 2007.

325 Liang Shuming, "The Problem of Chinese Social Structure", *Village Construction*, 6, no. 3 (September 16, 1936): 15.

326 Wang Donglin, ed., "Liang Shuming's Q & A" (Wuhan: Hubei People's Press, 2003), 158.

327 Marx, "Introduction to 'Critique of Hegel's Philosophy of Right'", *Selected Works of Marx and Engels* (vol. 1) (Beijing: People's Publishing House, 1973), 9.

328 "The Chinese Revolution and the Communist Party of China" (December 1939), *Selected Works of Mao Zedong* (vol. 2), 633.

329 "The Chinese Revolution and the Communist Party of China" (December 1939): Focusing on the "Objects of the Chinese Revolution", *Selected Works of Mao Zedong* (vol. 2), 638.

330 "Pay Attention to Correcting 'Leftism' Errors in Land Reform" (November 29, 1947), *Selected Works of Mao Zedong* (vol. 4), 322.

331 Zhang Sizeng, "Description of the Changes of Agricultural Conditions in a Bandit Area", *Yi Shi Daily*, "Countryside Weekly", November 24, the 23rd year of the Republic of China, p. 3, (11th) edition.

332 "Speech at the Enlarged Meeting of the Central Committee of the Communist Party of China in Yangjiagou" (December 25, 28, 1947), *Selected Works of Mao Zedong* (vol. 4), 322.

333 Various statistics about landlords vary widely, but are not reliable. "Because rich peasants often concealed the areas of their land during the survey or deliberately said that they had betrayed land in the past five years, while the poor peasants often reported relatively accurate numbers". See "Rural Survey of Henan Province", "General note" (Shanghai Commercial Press, 1944), 25. Tao Xisheng also stated in "Analysis of the History of Chinese Society" that "according to the information published by Tan Pingshan at the Hankou Land Commission, 5 percent of the peasant households occupied 42 percent of the land, while the households that had 1 to 10 *mu* of land accounted for 44 percent of the total

peasant households, they only occupied 6 percent of the land. But then Mr. Gongsun pointed out that the statistics were completely false. The estimates of the East Asian Association of Japan were exactly the opposite of the statistics of the Communist Party. They indicated that peasants that had below 10 *mu* of land accounted for 42 percent of the land, and peasants that had above 100 *mu* of land accounted for 6 percent. See Tao Xisheng, "Analysis of the History of Chinese Society" (Shanghai New Life Publishing House, 1929), 43–44.

334 "On New Democracy", *Selected Works of Mao Zedong* (vol. 2), 692.

335 "Investigation about Rural Areas" (September 13, 1941), Document Research Office of the Central Committee of the Communist Party of China, *Collected Works of Mao Zedong Rural Investigation* (Beijing: People's Publishing House, 1982), 26.

336 "Foreword and Postscript of the 'Rural Investigation'" (October 1937; March and April 1941), *Collected Works of Mao Zedong's Rural Investigation* (Beijing: People's Publishing House, 1982), 15.

337 "Speech at the Enlarged Meeting of the Central Committee of the Communist Party of China in Yangjiagou" (December 25, 28, 1947) (vol. 4), 335.

338 "Oppose Book Worship" (May 1930), Document Research Office of the Central Committee of the Communist Party of China, *Collected Works of Mao Zedong Rural Investigation* (Beijing: People's Publishing House, 1982), 6.

339 "Oppose Book Worship" (May 1930), Document Research Office of the Central Committee of the Communist Party of China, *Collected Works of Mao Zedong Rural Investigation* (Beijing: People's Publishing House, 1982), 7.

340 "Xunwu Investigation" (May 1930), *Collected Works of Mao Zedong Rural Investigation*, 173.

341 The Fifth Congress of the Communist Party of China has clearly stated that the land must be completely redistributed under the principle of equalization of land ownership to solve the land issue. To achieve this step, the land must be owned by the nation [...] Land nationalization is indeed the basic principle of the Communist Party's party platform on peasant issues. Chinese Modern Revolutionary History Materials Series, "Data of the Peasant Movement during the First Revolutionary Civil War" (Beijing: People's Publishing House, 1983), 54.

342 Compiled by the Economic Society, "Chinese Economics" (Beijing: The Commercial Press, 1910), 23.

343 "On the Parallel of Social Revolution and Political Revolution", *Collected Works of Zhu Zhixin*, 25.

344 Li Yu, "The Opposition between Officials and People: He Sees through the System of the Qin and Han Dynasties – Reading Wang Yanan's 'Research on Chinese Bureaucracy'", 4.

345 Wu Tiefeng, ed., "Peasants in the Unconventional Period" (Shanghai: Shanghai Zhonghua Book Company, 1936), 4.

346 According to the" Tianjin Agricultural Investigation Report" (1931), the contents of the survey materials on pages 8–34 are tabulated.

347 Zhao Gang, Chen Zhongyi, "History of Land System in China" (Beijing: New Star Press, 2006), 179.

348 Ibid., 314.

349 Wu Tiefeng, ed., "Peasants in the Unconventional Period" (Shanghai: Shanghai Zhonghua Book Company, 1936), 2–3.

270 *Historical rural social structure changes*

350 Tao Changshan et al., eds., "The First Chronicle of the National Federation of Peasants' Associations" in May of the second year of the Republic of China, edited by Shen Yunlong, "The 87th Series of Modern Chinese Historical Materials" (Taipei: Wenhai Publishing Company), 48.

351 Tao Changshan et al., eds., "The First Chronicle of the National Federation of Peasants' Associations" in May of the second year of the Republic of China, edited by Shen Yunlong, "The 87th Series of Modern Chinese Historical Materials" (Taipei: Wenhai Publishing Company), 59.

352 "A Survey of the Rural Areas of Henan Province" (Beijing: The Commercial Press, 1944), 30.

353 Wu Bingruo, "The Situation of Peasants in the Huaihe River Basin", *The Eastern Miscellany*, 1927, 24, no. 16: 52.

354 Feng Zigang, ed., "Investigation of Rural Areas in Lanxi" (Hangzhou: Hangzhou National Zhejiang University, 1935), 85.

355 Ibid., 99.

356 Ibid., 116

357 Feng Zigang, ed., "Investigation of Rural Areas in Lanxi", 123.

358 Feng Zigang and Liu Duansheng, ed., "Social Research Report on Rural Areas of Nanyang" (Dawn Publishing House), 1934, 38.

359 (France) J. Cazeneuve, "Ten Concepts of Sociology", trans. Yang Jie (Shanghai: Shanghai People's Publishing House, 2003), 172–173.

5 Historical changes in the structure of rural power

The powerful forces formed by the social structure could only be eliminated through the transformation and reconstruction of the social structure, and simple institutional changes and violent activities had a limited role to play in this. After victory in the War of Resistance against Japanese Aggression, the CPC launched the agrarian revolution and the policy of village election, and the new rural authority, mainly consisting of model workers and talents, gradually controlled the rural political life. Meanwhile the political influence of the traditional authority was greatly weakened. This fundamentally transformed the rural social structure and pointed out the social conditions the gentry power relied on for existence, and eventually the traditional village gentry disappeared from the power structure in rural society. For Chinese rural society, especially for the traditional power structure in rural areas, the withdrawal of the village gentry truly marked the end of an era.

From scholar-gentry to power-gentry – an investigation centering on the change of gentry power in the late Qing dynasty and the early Republic of China

With changes in social structure and institutions in the late Qing dynasty and the early Republic of China, the structure of rural social power was also in the process of undergoing frequent changes and reconstruction. Different from the development trend of the traditional era, the reconstruction of local power took place in the name of "civil rights" from the start and was no longer restricted by the balance between imperial power and gentry power. However, it was not difficult to find that the gentry power reflected by the New Deal of Hunan implemented in 1898 and by the Peasant Movement in Hunan in 1927 showed completely different values. This was certainly affected by the degeneration of the gentry class, but also related to changes in social structure and reconstruction of interest subjects.[1] However, the "historical memory" of the traditional gentry, in the process of reconstructing the social or power structure, had a potential but not an underestimated effect. The kind of "historical memory" embedded in the social-power structure,

272 *Historical changes in rural power*

to some extent, led to the trend of overthrowing the gentry class that the era called for and thus created specific situations of rural changes in the Great Revolution period.

From occupying the most important position among four kinds of people to a situation in which all gentry were bad

At the end of the 1920s, when the Great Revolution swept the rural society, the political trend of overthrowing the gentry class was recognized by the society, and it had become a call of the times due to its characteristic "collective memory". The third plenary session of the Kuomintang Central Executive Committee announced openly that it would reconstruct its power at the village level.

> Therefore, a revolution needs great changes in rural areas. There must be a great change in each rural area so that local tyrants, evil gentry, landlords breaking the law and all counter-revolutionary activities would be eliminated under the power of peasants. The rural regime was transferred from the hands of local tyrants, evil gentry, landlords breaking the law and all counterrevolutionaries to the hands of peasants.[2]

Meanwhile, it would combine its political appeal with peasants' interest appeal. "The Kuomintang will, standing on the side of peasants on behalf of the democratic forces, fight against local tyrants, evil gentry and landlords breaking the law on behalf of the feudal forces".[2] The tenth issue of the magazine *Chinese Peasants* published a comment on the theme of "overthrowing the gentry class",[3] and announced this revolutionary appeal to the whole society.

Though there were obvious differences in class nature and political stand between the CPC and the Kuomintang, both parties shared the same stance on the issue of overthrowing the gentry power. "As far as the Chinese revolution and transformation were concerned, apart from the Communist Party of China, the Kuomintang and etatist parties also aimed to overthrow local tyrants and evil gentry".[4] As for the CPC's early understanding of the rural social class relationship system, the gentry class was regarded as the object of revolution. Since 1926, the rural revolutionary movement organized by the Communist Party and aimed at "bringing down the evil gentry" had been in full swing in Hunan and Hubei Provinces, and had moved toward the stage of violent struggle. In some counties of Hubei Province, a bloody hard struggle happened "owing to the embezzlement of public funds by local tyrants and the evil gentry". In Hubei Province, peasants destroyed the Bureau of Banning Tobaccos and asked for the cancellation of the likin. In some places, conflicts occurred between peasants and the army who received bribes from the evil gentry.

Historical changes in rural power 273

The peasant associations is planning to directly put local tyrants and evil gentry on trial. Lots of local tyrants and the evil gentry fled to Changsha or Hankou [Hunan].

The property of local tyrants and the evil gentry who were killed or arrested and the property of landlords who were fleeing would be confiscated and arranged by the peasant associations. Peasants relentlessly punished those oppressors. Many counties put local tyrants and the evil gentry on trial. Because of the victory of struggles against local tyrants, the evil gentry and landlords, the village regime of most counties in the above regions was in the hands of the peasant associations [Hubei].[5]

After the revolution of 1911, the word "revolution" had become a main topic and even a new tradition of the era. It was also called a revolutionary era. The political appeal that the revolution had not yet succeeded could be interpreted as a revolutionary choice of overthrowing the gentry to some extent (The gentry was called the spawn of feudalism).[6] "If two or three revolutions occurred and no success was achieved, it would reveal that the status of local tyrants and the evil gentry was not undermined".[7] Since the late Qing dynasty, although on the whole,

village gentry played a leading role in promoting democratic "autonomy", they were still regarded as the spawn of feudalism, because from the perspective of both the Kuomintang's regime and the Communist Party's political position, feudalism and local autonomy had same demands.[8]

The "collective memory" of the gentry class by the Kuomintang and the Communist Party pointed out a concrete revolutionary object for the rural peasant movement:

At present, half of the traditions of the patriarchal society were still preserved in rural areas. Those pedantic scholar-gentry were of high status and held power in their hands, so they were held in awe by peasants. Therefore, we must expand our campaign against the evil gentry, so that everyone can understand that the evil gentry are an enemy of peasants.[9]

Hence the direction of the "great revolution" in rural areas, which began in the 1920s, was quite specific and clear.

The peasant movement was still in the name of "civil rights" and aimed at overthrowing the gentry class. "Only if the political foundation existing for more than 4,000 years that local politics had been built on the gentry class was broken could democratism proposed by the prime minister [Sun Yat-sen] be realized in rural areas".[10] However, ironically, the political practice of modern civil rights also began with promoting gentry power. In 1898, when Hunan Province implemented the New Deal, Liang Qichao proposed that "gentry

274 *Historical changes in rural power*

power should be promoted before promoting civil rights, and that academic society should be the first one to promote gentry power. Though it was not prevailing in China, it was an unchanged truth".[11] At that time, academic society was the main force for constructing local gentry power, as Tan Sitong stated:

> each province set up a general academic society, and each local government and prefecture set up a branch of the general academic society. Those branches were affiliated with the general academic society. Documents distributed by the academic society should be received by local gentry, each branch should recommend their scholar to the general academic society and the society would evaluate them by their quality and ability. According to this, the academic society performed the same functions as a parliament.[12]

At least for the local political reform carried out in Hunan Province, the gentry power was not only regarded as the specific content of civil rights, but promoting the gentry power almost became the historical starting point of implementing the New Deal:

First, the Southern Academic Society was the place where the gentry gathered to discuss political affairs. The Southern Academic Society was established in Changsha in February 1898. As Tan Sitong observed, "if there was no academic society, there was no way to learn new knowledge".[13] The Southern Academic Society was the general society in the province and all the other society in local areas was affiliated with it. Accordingly, the Southern Academic Society was endowed with the nature of a local parliament.

> The Southern Academic Society played an important role in promoting the New Deal in the whole province, and though it was an academic society, it also had the same size as a local parliament. At first, the governor would choose ten scholars as the president of the Southern Academic Society, and then those ten scholars would choose other scholars to join the society as members. Each county and prefecture must have three to ten members. The Southern Academic Society was the same size as the House of Commons, the schools where officials received education were the same size as the House of Lords, and the New Policy Bureau was the same size as the central government. All those organizations would delegate their power to the gentry like a mother giving her love to her son.[14]

"The local gentry in Hunan Province would try to establish such a system to realize local autonomy"[14], and create a trend of carrying out reform.[15]

Second, the Department of Security helped the gentry exercise their executive power. "The Department of Security delegated its power to the gentry and common people and promoting civil rights is a long-term plan, which was the most prominent characteristics".[16] The Department of Security was

Historical changes in rural power   275

mainly responsible for carrying out the New Deal in local areas. As Tan Sitong stated, "The Department of Security dealt with all kinds of political affairs and had jurisdiction over local areas".[17] As far as certain functions were concerned, those of the Department of Security were similar to those of the Bao-jia Bureau in the past, but the power subject had fundamentally changed, which meant "the so-called Department of Security today was the Bao-jia Bureau in the past, but its power was different from the officials' and the gentry's".[18] To avoid the shortcomings of traditional political reform, the gentry in Hunan Province made great efforts to build a foundation for implementing the New Deal in an institutional way and

> make the operation of the department of security known to the general public, but later common people were afraid that the officials just regarded it as mere formality. Therefore, the gentry participated in the operation of the department to make sure it would exist forever.[19]

In fact, the New Deal, with the gentry power as basic content, had been preserved to some extent even after the coup. "All were left undone after the coup, but the Department of Security still existed thanks to the gentry's and the common people's efforts. This was also a civil right".[20] When the New Deal was abolished (the imperial court asked Zhang Zhidong to fulfill this task), "local gentry and common people thought that it was a good thing and that it could protect the their well-being and remove dangers. Thus, they still followed their original path and continued to do so". "Only the department of security existed".[21] To some extent, this witnessed the influence of gentry power.

"Civil rights" is not an abstract concept but always has a very specific historical connotation. When civil rights prevailed in modern China, gentry power was its substantive content. As Xiong Xiling observed, "the gentry were representatives of common people".[22] This actually captures the "collective memory" of a particular generation. So it was in the gentry Wang Xianqian's memory. When the Southern Academic Society was founded in January 1898, Wang Xianqian was strongly in favor of this movement. He said, "it is impossible that all scholars in the world share same opinions. But if they have a common goal, they can establish schools of their own and learn from each other. This also interprets the meaning of professional commitment and team work". He also "thought highly of the *Xiang Newspaper* established by Tan Sitong and Tang Caichang, and held that the newspaper covered lots of news, so it was conducive to enlightening common people".[23] Even after the coup, the local political situation in Hunan Province still centered around the gentry power. The so-called struggle between the old force and the new force was more reflected in the division of power between the old and the new gentry.[24]

For the two important symbolic historical events in Hunan in modern China, the collective memory of the gentry class was quite different. We can

276 *Historical changes in rural power*

Table 5.1 Comparison of collective memory about gentry between the reform movement of 1898 and the Great Revolution

Time	The Reform Movement of 1898	The Great Revolution
Evaluation	The gentry were representatives of people.	The gentry were enemies of people.
Status	The gently were backbone force in saving the country.	The gently are supporters of great powers and warlords.
Function	The gentry promoted social progress.	The gentry set up obstacles to revolution.
Objective	To promote civil rights through promoting the gentry power.	To guarantee civil rights through overthrowing the gentry power.

make a comparison between them by choosing different key words about collective memory in different times, as shown in Table 5.1.

In less than 30 years, how did the "historical memory" of the gentry form such a striking historical contrast? It is certainly not difficult for us to understand the main interests of this "historical memory" (The social forces that dominate speech or public opinions had undergone a historic shift from the traditional gentry to new intellectual groups), but had the characteristics of public opinion and embodied the "sociality" of memory in a certain sense. Obviously, the two historical events had different demands for "civil rights", one starting with promoting the gentry power and the other aiming to overthrow the gentry power. The question is, what was the historical shift between the two events? How did the gentry change from occupying the most important position among four kinds of people to being seen as bad people? The memory of this historical evolution is fragmented and incomplete, and this is precisely the lost part of collective memory characterized by major events. Historical research should "regard historical materials as social memory remains". In the face of historical materials, researchers should always be vigilant: Who do these memories belong to? "How are they are created and used?" and "How they are preserved and forgotten?" "At the same time, it is also necessary to extensively study the neglected social and historical memories of various edges. Only the combination of exemplary history and marginal history can arouse complete social memory and reflect the truth".[25] Therefore, to search for memories that can present the historical process between the collective memories of the two major historical events is the key to understanding the issue and the necessary link to construct a reasonable historical understanding.

"Public memory" in the expansion of the gentry power

"'Social memory' refers to all 'memory' preserved and circulated in a society through various media".[26] But social memory has different directionality in

Historical changes in rural power 277

social groups, and the selectivity of its memory is also obvious. In the reform movement of 1898, the gentry class who dominated the reform of the local political system in Hunan was also the leading force of public opinion. Thus, the appeal for civil rights tended to reflect the interests of the gentry. The "collective memory" in this event undoubtedly embodied the gentry's own appeal and value judgments. Then, in the historical process of "promoting civil rights" guided by "promoting gentry power", what about people's interest and appeal? Especially in the relationship between the gentry and the common people, or in the historical process of adjusting the interests of the gentry and the common people, common people's "historical memory" of the gentry power is more worthy of our attention.

> Different groups at different levels, such as a family, a region, a class, a nation, and the whole human race, retain their historical record of past life in different ways [...] And the nature and content of this memory also varies from time to time, or a memory may consciously be suppressed and forbidden, or it may consciously be advocated and promoted. But most of them are an unconscious memory of past life. In any case, they are not purely personal memories and preservation of certain events, because they show us the existence of social memory.[27]

What is more difficult is that the people do not have the power and the ability to dominate and control public opinions, nor do they have the conditions to express their interests in a systematic way. Their "collective memory" is only expressed in twists and turns through various mass uprisings. Of course, this memory is very fragmented and irregular.

Shortly after the reform movement of 1898, the Qing government carried out the New Deal, and it still followed the trend of promoting the gentry power to advance civil rights when putting local autonomy into trial use. The expansion of the gentry power was not only reasonable in the era but also legitimate. An election was held for the first time by the consultative council in 1909. "It turned out that many electees were between the ages of 40 and 45, and the gentry accounted for a large part of them".[28] At the end of the Qing dynasty, 82 people were elected as members of the council in Hunan Province, most of whom were the gentry according to Zhang Pengyuan's guess.[29] The expansion of the gentry power in Hunan Province was like what Cen Chunming described at his memorial, that is,

> Establish the Institute of Autonomous Studies and select 270 qualified gentry. Since local autonomy was looked upon as a part of law and politics, the government rented the places of existing law and politics schools and the gentry schools to set up classes. Preachers and controllers would be carefully chosen from the teaching staff of the mentioned two kinds of schools.

278 *Historical changes in rural power*

At the beginning of the preparation, it was hard to coordinate the relationship between electing the gentry and allocating funds.[30]

It was not difficult to see that the history in which "local officials asked the gentry to assist them when making preparations for anything since the Taiping Rebellion occurred in Hunan Province" could be rewritten with the help of this institutional change. Therefore, with the historical causes of local power structure in Hunan Province and the support of the New Deal, the situation occurred in which "common people in Hunan Province began to show less respect to officials and the gentry held a lot of power in their hands". "Hence it happened occasionally that a county office was besieged by a crowd of people, and thus rites and laws were totally abandoned".[31]

However, it was also in the institutional changes caused by promoting the gentry power that mass uprisings in grassroots society happened frequently and thus the social life was in a serious disorder. What is more, the suddenly intensifying conflicts between the gentry and the common people had become the prominent characteristic of the whole era of the New Deal. According to the statistics of *Chronicle of Mass Uprisings in the Late Qing Dynasty*, the number of conflicts between the gentry and the common people continued to rise after 1906, reaching its peak in 1910. This evolution was always accompanied by the development of the New Deal. In terms of the "List of Yearly Preparations" issued by the Qing government, by 1905 the New Deal had been carried out across the board, and by 1908 it had begun to take shape: the consultative council began to make preparations for putting local autonomy into trial use and issued the *Constitution on Local Self-government in Cities, Towns and Villages*, and the reform in education, finance and law had also been conducted successively. In 1908, the regulations for the financial clearance were issued, simple spelling textbooks and books that citizens must read were edited, laws were revised and so on. By the end of 1908, the implementation of the New Deal had entered its seventh year, and after the political reform of local autonomy had been carried out for three years, the corresponding mass uprisings occurred frequently and conflicts between the gentry and the common people intensified. This suggested a historical or institutional correlation between the two sides.[32] Wei Guangqi also paid attention to this issue in his study and especially noted that

> the local organizations controlled by the new official-gentry collected taxes from peasants and petty dealers and forcefully distributed property. By doing so, the official-gentry would fill their own pockets with public funds. This had been a ubiquitous phenomenon from the late Qing dynasty to the early 1930s.

[Hence] the earliest social revolts against the expansion of "gentry power" were large- and small-scale mass uprisings launched by the masses at the bottom of the society in the late Qing dynasty and early Republic of China.[33]

Historical changes in rural power 279

Then, what kind of collective memory do the masses at the bottom of the society have for this historical process of "civil rights" dominated by the thriving gentry power? Since massive events of destroying schools happened in Wuxi, Jiangsu in 1904, many other events of destroying schools and beating the gentry also occurred in Yizhou, Shandong Province; Leping, Jiangxi Province; Kuizhou, Sichuan Province; Guangdong Province; and other places. Some comments on such shocking events were also published in *Oriental Magazine*, such as "After the event of destroying schools in Wuxi, such events also happened in Sichuan, Jiangxi and even Guangdong today". "The reason for these events was the collection of taxes".[34] Common people "tended to refuse to pay taxes after the riots in Wuxi and Guangdong".[35] Therefore, the gentry were directly affected in such mass uprisings. When the gentry all over the county took on the responsibility of establishing schools, which was an important affair of local autonomy, the gentry, who had once occupied the most important position among four kinds of people, were placed in the position where direct conflicts would occur between the interests of the common people and the gentry. After investigating the events of destroying schools and beating the gentry everywhere, *Oriental Magazine* suggested that

> Now the officials play the role the gentry originally played, so we gather together to fight with the gentry to resist changes. The so-called changes are caused by incidents of destroying private schools. Therefore, with regard to the causes of the incidents, we know that it was plebs that destroyed private schools, but they did not make troubles in schools on purpose. In fact, since the officials oppressed plebs too frequently, the latter wanted to give vent to their anger by destroying private schools.[36]

This at least indicated that the direct reason for the transformation from antagonism between the officials and the common people to conflicts between the gentry and the common people rested in the institutional changes of "the officials playing the role the gentry originally played". It was reported by the *Newspaper of People's Appeal* on June 18, 1909, that

> since the implementation of the New Deal, taxes were collected more frequently. Due to lack of money for establishing [...] and supporting the police stations, taxes should also be levied on shops selling pork, chicken and duck, tiles and bricks, tobacco and alcohol and small stores that were exempted from paying taxes before.[37]

The *Newspaper about Public Opinions* even made a critical comment on the New Deal and "criticized it as a downright lie to deceive people and extract people's wealth".[38] The interest conflicts between villagers and schools also triggered the destroying of schools to some extent. When the property of temples was allocated as funds for running schools, some people with vested interests could no longer touch these assets, and thus their personal

280 *Historical changes in rural power*

interests were damaged. As a result, they sowed discord among the villagers, making the contradictions more complex and even leading to bloodshed. For example, more than a thousand people in Cixi, Zhejiang, wanted to burn all the teaching staff of schools to death after hearing that schools intended to confiscate the land of a church. Furthermore, villagers in Suian, Zhejiang, vented their anger on schools due to the soaring price of rice.[39] The implementation of local autonomy and the New Deal depended on local tax collection. "Establishing a school would cost a huge amount of money. At the beginning, public funds would be used to cover its expense, but later money would be extorted from people. Under such circumstances, corrupt officials would benefit from it". "Universal education was based on establishing schools everywhere and the latter was based on fundraising".[40] By 1910, the events related to destroying schools had come to a climax, and thus constituted one of the main contents of mass uprisings in the late Qing dynasty.

In addition, the census and even nailing door plates, which had nothing to do with establishing schools and were closely linked to the New Deal, were also strongly opposed by common people. A special article was published in *Oriental Magazine* to publicize the significance of the household survey for the establishment of a modern country, and it held that the

> household survey was not only relevant to education and banning tobacco, but was also of significance for checking the population all over the country, determining election precincts, autonomous system, who had rights, who should bear responsibilities, who would serve in the army, and collection of national taxes and local taxes when the government drew up a constitution, formed a parliament and issued the autonomous system.[41]

However, the villagers had a strong suspicion about the survey, triggering a series of mass uprisings. In March 1910, peasants in Danzhou, Guangxi, resisted the household survey, beat the county magistrate to death and burned down the local government office; in Henan Province, "The county magistrate of Mi County, whose surname was Xu, focused his attention on raising money to carry out the New Deal since he assumed office last year, which annoyed the gentry and common people"; and all peasants in the county opposed the tax collection for implementing local autonomy, and nearly two thousand peasants entered the county and finally burned down the county office. Afterward, massive mass uprisings also happened in Yizhou (today it is Yi County of Hubei Province) directly affiliated with the central government, Ye County in Central China. Consequently, the autonomous bureau and secondary schools were burned down. Some people also required the county magistrate to return the grains originally stored in official granaries, and executed a member of the autonomous bureau. Other people asked the local government to stop collecting taxes for implementing local autonomy or to stop implementing local autonomy.[42]

Historical changes in rural power   281

When the concept of "civil rights" was put into the practice of implementing the New Deal or local autonomy, the gentry power became the most basic force of the era. "Almost all members working in the government offices of states, prefectures and counties were the gentry". The contemporary people made a comment that "those who carried out the local autonomy did not truly support local autonomy, and the gentry took advantage of the New Deal to make things worse".[43] As soon as the historical process of "local autonomy" led by the gentry unfolded, the people at the bottom of society formed a "collective memory" completely different from that of the gentry class. In this regard, we can only find out the basic characteristics and interest orientation of people's "collective memory" from the successive events of "mass uprisings" in various places:

First, the public's "collective memory" or interest appeal presented by those mass uprisings indicated that the conflict between the gentry and the common people lay not in the New Deal itself, but in such excessive infringement of people's interests by the expansion of the gentry power that it even imperiled people's basic conditions for survival, although the implementation of the New Deal was the direct cause of the conflict. For example, in the North Mountain regions of Shaanxi, local people "had no idea about the New Deal and regarded imposing a tax on sheep as a disastrous thing, so they had no choice but to gather together to fight against the local government".[44] The villagers' feeling was that "when the New Deal had not been conducted, people was still able to live a peaceful life. However, now the police station and schools were under construction, and all the money spent was raised from common people".[45] From the case of the rice riot in Changsha in 1910, we can distinguish the different interest orientations of the gentry and the common people in mass uprisings: the old gentry of Hunan Province took full advantage of the conflict caused by the New Deal and attempted to seize all rights controlling the local New Deal from the hands of the new gentry. The conflicts between the gentry of Hunan Province concentrated on the local New Deal itself. For example, Kong Xianjiao, the head of the old gentry, took this opportunity to request that the commissioner of Hunan Province stop carrying out the New Deal. "Kong and Yang [Kong Xianjiao and Yang Gong] did this to oppose the New Deal".[46] What the common people complained about was that local officials and gentry "deceived people, issued numerous orders and spent money like water in the name of implementing the New Deal. And people did not benefit from it at all". Instead,

over the past ten years, the taxes collected from people today have been twice or three times as many as those in the past. Owing to the burden, peasants who could merely support themselves before do not have enough clothes to wear or enough food to eat today, and thus suffer a lot from coldness and starvation. [...] at that time, accusations against "mobs" for their hostility toward schools and damage to education were just a rumor.[47]

282 *Historical changes in rural power*

In 1910, the civil corps of Laiyang in Shandong Province also reflected the same fact:

> The gentry had been the common people's enemies for a long time. In recent years, the village gentry were responsible for the implementation of the New Deal and ignored public opinion. Therefore, the common people bore grudges against the gentry and planned to fight against them.[48]

Thus, as far as mass uprisings were concerned, the New Deal was their cover, and tyrannical governance was their essence.

> In recent years, the New Deal was in full swing, and the gentry entered the government office at will and even availed themselves of this opportunity to pursue private ends. As a result, the gentry were despised by the common people and the common people also had many complaints about the local government.[49]

Some conflicts between the gentry and common people seemed to stem from people's ignorance and superstition. For example, villagers in Yizhou (today it is Yi County of Hubei Province) directly affiliated with the central government went to the city to pray for rain in periods of drought, only to find that all the statues of Buddha in Kaiyuan Temple had been destroyed by the autonomous bureau, so villagers "believed that the drought was caused by members of the bureau and the police for their destroying the statues of Buddha". "As a result, they flooded into the autonomous bureau and the gentry escaped after witnessing the scene. The villagers were so furious that they burned down hundreds of rooms of the autonomous bureau and secondary schools".[50] But the immediate reason was that the villagers believed that the conditions for their basic survival (like the drought caused by the gentry's destroying statues of Buddha) were damaged by the gentry.

Therefore, in the face of the historical process of promoting the gentry power after the reform movement of 1898, and especially after the implementation of the New Deal, the "collective memory" of the gentry showed the trend of addressing local social affairs with the gentry as a representative of civil rights, thus making modern gentry power expand on an unprecedented scale. By contrast, the gentry in traditional times "only played a leading role in various temporary local public affairs", and "did not preside over and participate in regular and subjective political, economic and cultural activities such as tax collection, litigation, public order, agriculture, industry and commerce, education, etc.". "They had no regular organization, or they did not systematize themselves through some permanent institution". "However, everything changed in the mid-nineteenth century, especially after the early twentieth century". In particular, after the Qing government's implementation of local autonomy, "the scholar-gentry were not only able to set foot in

Historical changes in rural power 283

economic and cultural fields, but also further in the political field, and openly created another source of public power apart from official governance". The local gentry "took part in local politics in a systematic and institutional way and mainly handled public affairs related to local education, industry, finance and so on".[51] It was in the process of institutional changes that a social situation formed in which "today local autonomy was not actually autonomy but official governance, and in my view, it was the combination of official governance and gentry governance".[52] Another trend was presented in people's "collective memory" in which the class of scholar-gentry

> wanted to take the opportunity to benefit from it and attempted to control everything in order to put their subordinates in certain positions. Given this, lots of bureaus were built. Those officials took advantage of the New Deal to do harm to common people's well-being.[53]

With the help of institutionalized bureaus and offices,

> local tyrants and the evil gentry made use of their official positions, wealth and power to collude with the officials, cover up the crime committed by bandits, take control of bureaus of civil corps and rural politics, embezzle public funds and oppress the common people. What they did was similar to feudal separation.[54]

Thus, the historical process of "promoting civil rights" through "promoting the gentry power" evolved into intensifying conflicts between the gentry and the common people.

Second, people's "collective memory" reflected extremism and violence related to the contradictions or conflicts between the gentry and the common people, and thus the "evil gentry" had become a word with the characteristics of the times, which people used to refer to the scholar-gentry class. "After the implementation of the New Deal, taxes were levied on various kinds of items". Before 1900, "the annual amount of taxes was less than 30 million taels of silver", and by 1909, "in the process of liquidating local finance, it proved that each province collected taxes of 43.96 million taels of silver". "Some places arbitrarily collected taxes in the name of the New Deal".[55] The local gentry who undertook the task of implementing the New Deal were responsible for collecting money from common people, thus forming a direct conflict with the interests of common people. When autonomy was carried out in Xuanhua directly affiliated to the central government,

> those working in the police stations in Xuanhua were the local gentry, which would lead to many problems, and they took their cue from the powerful when dealing with cases. Those unreasonable and evil gentry knew that most police officers were local people, so they looked down upon them in the depth of their hearts.[56]

284 *Historical changes in rural power*

In the process of tax collection, as long as local officials and the gentry or autonomous institutions engaged in malpractice and exploitation, the common people would be boiling with resentment. At that time, someone indignantly revealed that "they always collected taxes in the name of local autonomy and filled their own pockets with public funds".[57] Therefore, the conflict between the gentry and the common people often broke out in an extreme form. For example, in Zhexi, "villagers had grievances over the gentry, and only after destroying the houses of the gentry and government clerks would they be happy".[58] In the process of the household survey in Jiangxi, since there was a dispute, a local gentry "came forward to intervene, but local people beat him hard without any reason".[59] In November 1910, "villagers caused troubles" in Suichang, Zhejiang Province, and "they criticized the head of the study encouragement office, and claimed that they wanted to kill him. Then they went to the member's house and looted and destroyed it".[60] Events related to beating the gentry happened more frequently. "Local people had more and more violent actions. They beat the gentry, destroyed their houses and looted everywhere, so that the officials and gentry who fell victim to the violence fled into cities and dared not go home". Local people wanted to kill the gentry.[61] Such events in Taizhou, Jiangsu Province, were the most shocking ones. "A rich gentry in the city, whose surname was Chu, was hung up and beaten by villagers. The latter also used fire to burn him, so that Chu fainted many times".[62] From the slogan "Fighting against the officials and killing the gentry" put forward by common people in Yangshan, Guangdong Province, in 1904, to the slogan "Destroying schools and killing the gentry" was put forward by villagers in Fengtai directly affiliated with the central government when they gathered together to formulate stipulations in 1909 (Villagers in Yuanzhou, Jiangxi also made a request of "entering the city to destroy schools and kill the gentry"),[63] to the slogan "the officials drove the common people to rebellion and the gentry drove people to death"[64] put forward by people in Quanzhou, Guangxi, in 1910, all of these reflected a relatively general trend that conflicts between the gentry and the common people turned into extreme and violent ones step by step.

In more than two years from 1909 to 1911, riots directed at local autonomy spread across the country's 15 provinces. Thirty-seven riots occurred in Jiangsu, fifteen riots occurred in Jiangxi, five riots occurred in Zhejiang and three riots occurred in Guangdong and Guangxi respectively.[65] Many gentry as investigators, clerks and boards of director of the autonomous bureau were beaten by villagers, and the autonomous bureau was also destroyed. With the intensification of social contradictions at the grassroots level, the Qing government also felt unprecedented pressure and thus the imperial court issued an edict in July 1910 to rebuke local officials, which stated, "We have known that some incompetent officials in some prefectures and counties did not have contact with their superiors and local people, and cared little about administrative affairs like money raising and just entrusted those affairs to local gentry. Some of them only cared out their own interests and embezzled

Historical changes in rural power 285

public funds". Consequently, common people "began to have little confidence in them and even spread rumors. As a result, mass uprisings happened".[66] The social situation of the late Qing dynasty was almost affected by both the New Deal and mass uprisings: on the one hand, local scholar-gentry actively advertised that the New Deal was beneficial to the development of China and caused no harm at all. Even if common people could not accept it for the present, it must be promoted. The gentry, holding a banner of civil rights and with power in their hands, played a leading role in dealing with local social public affairs and exercising public power, which led to the gentry's power expanding; on the other hand, the promotion of the New Deal and the thriving gentry power did not elicit positive responses at the grassroots level, especially in rural areas, but received widespread indifference, discontent and resistance from common people. What is more, "more and more rumors were circulating, and people were boiling with resentment".[67] In the "collective memory" of people at the bottom of the society, the concept of "evil gentry" had replaced the title of "gentry". For example, "all affairs about the New Deal were controlled by several gentry".[68] Mass uprisings "should not be attributed to one factor and none of the local ruffians and the evil gentry could get away from their crime". "Who villagers abhorred was the officials, the evil gentry and local ruffians".[69] Doubtless, the term "evil gentry" had in fact evolved into a "collective expression" of the rising gentry power.[70]

Third, the "collective memory" of the people formed repeatedly in "mass uprisings" had gradually gained extensive public attention, thus forming a kind of "social memory" with the characteristics of the times. This memory, accompanied by the historical process of "mass uprisings" and "conflicts between the gentry and the common people", had been repeatedly formed and strengthened, which constituted a historical turning point between promoting the gentry power in the reform movement of 1898 and "overthrowing the gentry power" in the Great Revolution. In the constitutional structure of traditional imperial power and gentry power, compared with the absence of "civil rights", the advocacy of "civil rights" is undoubtedly a valuable symbol of the era when the traditional society turned into the modern society. From the promotion of the gentry power the reform movement of 1898 to the expansion of the gentry power in the period of the New Deal, the banner of "promoting civil rights" had always been held. Even after the reform movement of 1898, the historical trend of the local political reform with the gentry as the main body reflected no fundamental changes, but the gentry power was greatly enhanced in the implementation of the "New Deal" or "local autonomy" by the Qing government in the later period.

> When each province carried out local autonomy, local governors entrusted the task to officials at the prefecture and the county level, and then the latter entrusted it to the village gentry again. Those wise and impartial gentry often dared not take the responsibility, and those unqualified scholars played tricks to become one of the clerks, councilors and members of a

286 *Historical changes in rural power*

board of directors, and finally they occupied most of those positions. Most unqualified scholars had no idea about constitutions and the principles of autonomy, but oppressed people in the name of implementing local autonomy, carried out local autonomy in a hurry without a sound plan, paid attention to the surface of things instead of their essence, made use of official authority to bully others, made profits for themselves under all sorts of pretexts, or even colluded with police officers and conspired with governors to make excuses for gaining profits.[71]

Thenceforth, the traditional value orientation of "the gentry as the hope of a town and the scholar as the head of four kinds of people"[72] had disappeared, and a gentry-ruled (different from "self-governance")[73] society formed, which had a social structure different from that of the traditional times. Thus, it became a specific historical stage between "promoting the gentry power" and "overthrowing the gentry power".

Shortly after the implementation of the New Deal, *Ta Kung Pao* made an interesting comment on the historical prospect of "gentry power", titled "On the Gentry Power".

There was no gentry power in civilized nations all over the world, and whether the gentry power was thriving depended on the complexity of local affairs and the local gentry's influence. Just as a county magistrate could not rule on people within hundreds of miles on his own, officials were busy enough with various affairs like criminal cases, tax collection and lawsuits and had no energy to take care of other matters. Therefore, they had to ask the gentry for help. Under such a circumstance, the gentry power began to develop after the implementation of the New Deal. Since then, mediocre officials were not qualified to take up a position as an educator or policeman or to participate in implementing local autonomy. As a result, officials had to put the gentry in an important position, just as the saying goes, "A competent person should hold more power in his hand". Thenceforth, the gentry power was much more thriving.

However, would the political concept of promoting the civil rights through promoting the gentry power be realized? Would the gentry's power put local autonomy into practice? Regarding those questions, the comment of *Ta Kung Pao* did not give certain answers and indicated that "whether the thriving of the gentry power was a good thing or not lay in the effect the gentry power brought". At least, from the situation reflected by mass uprisings at that time, in which conflicts between the gentry and common people became more intense, the intention of civil rights advocated by promoting the gentry's power was subject to public suspicion. The article titled "On the Gentry Power" had predicted two prospects of the gentry power:

One prospect was that

after the gentry power was thriving, the gentry would try to play their role as representatives of local people. If people's opinions could not

Historical changes in rural power 287

be heard by high-ranking officials, the gentry would speak for them; if affairs about people's well-being remained to be handled, the gentry would handle them immediately; if competent officials were unable to deal with all cases, the gentry should assist them because the gentry were officials' assistants. No other people were as familiar with local affairs as native people. In this way, the foundation of autonomy could be laid and so could the foundation of constitutionalism.

The other prospect was that

> after the gentry power was thriving, the gentry played the role of representatives of officials. Officials would do their utmost to pursue personal gain with the help of the gentry, and they would arbitrarily oppress and exploit people with the help of the gentry. The gentry would help officials do more evil things and the gentry would become more vicious by relying on officials' power and position. Both of them did things at their will and committed all kinds of atrocities. In this way, the gentry served as flunkeys for officials.

Actually, after the New Deal had been carried out for only six years, *Ta Kung Pao* showed its concern about promoting gentry power: "The concern did not rest in whether the gentry power would be thriving, but in what results it would bring about. People showed both happiness and fear about the future!" The present situation of the construction of social power at the grassroots level had already revealed the trend of history:

> Thanks to the gentry, schools became officials' private schools, and police officers served as yamen runners in ancient times. The gentry and officials did not truly put the New Deal into practice but took advantage of it to pursue for private interests. Today, it is quite common that gentry power begin to develop. However, the thriving gentry power in China is not always a thing to be happy about. Since constitutionalism is impossible to realize, people begin to count on the realization of autonomy, and then they find that autonomy is also impossible to realize, and thus they begin to rely on the expansion of the gentry power. Though people today talk about it as the past history, the good gentry at that time felt disappointed, even hopeless, about the situation.[74]

When the new generation of intellectuals gradually became the social elites and dominated public opinion, the memory of "destroying schools and killing the gentry" accumulated by people at the bottom of the society in the historical incidents of "conflicts between the gentry and common people" naturally became the historical basis for them to reconstruct the social-power structure:

> Now that the gentry became the enemies of peasants, only if the political foundation existing for more than 4,000 years on which local politics had

288 *Historical changes in rural power*

been built on the gentry class, was broken and a radical transformation was made could the policy of direct civil rights be put into practice at the minimum level.[75]

Therefore, the historical process of "promoting civil rights" through "promoting the gentry power" historically evolved into the history of "realizing civil rights" through "overturning the gentry power".

Power-gentry in social reconstruction

Although in history, "the gentry power did not thrive in an enlightened era", under the pressure of imperial power, "the gentry power began to decline after Emperor Qianlong and Jiaqing came to the throne successively. Therefore, gentry power did not develop along with the evolution of autocracy". In this regard, it was due to the institutional change in which "all affairs related to the New Deal in local areas were handled by the gentry" that "the gentry power began to thrive".[76] In the historical process of replacing the old system with a new system and reconstructing social power, the promotion of gentry power obtained an unprecedented historical opportunity. The New Deal not only meant the demise of an era of "old politics", but also marked a change in the entire sociocultural epochal characters. Its epochal characters were just as Liang Qichao described: "Today's China is in a transitional period. Therefore, the status quo of China today, like a boat, drifted off the coastline and floated in the middle of a sea, which meant it couldn't reach any shore of both sides".[77] At the same time, the social interest relationship and social power structure were in the process of constant differentiation and reconstruction, and the gentry class as the intermediary of the officials and common people in the history gained an opportunity in the era of "promoting civil rights" and played an indispensable role in assisting officials in implementing the New Deal. Therefore, gentry power would certainly thrive in this transitional era.

The social interests and power structure of the "transitional period" were in the midst of drastic changes and reconstruction. There is no doubt that the status, position and relations with local social interests of the gentry who lived at the center of local public power and public affairs in the process of reconstructing society were far from those of the gentry in traditional times. In traditional times, "the gentry should not intervene in local public affairs to avoid being accused of controlling the government".[78] The gentry had not been endowed with institutional power, but had the natural authority established by the local society, thus having flexible and broad power space in the social field between officials and the common people.

In the structure of the tripartite interest relationship between officials, the gentry and the common people, though the gentry played a role as the "intermediary of officials and common people", at least in public interest of the community, there was more consistency between the gentry and the common people. During the reign of Emperor Tongzhi (1862–1875), officials collected

Historical changes in rural power 289

taxes on tribute grains in the middle reach of the Yangtze River. With the help of clan organizations, the gentry and plebs in the rural society worked together to fight against the feudal government. In some areas a kind of situation formed in which, in rural areas, people from clan organizations

> often gathered together to revolt against the officials, flaunt their superiority and bully the weak. Ancestral halls were the places where they assembled and hid themselves. If one committed crimes like murder and theft and then fled to a village protected by powerful people, it was difficult to capture him.[79]

However, in the construction of the New Deal after 1901, on the one hand, the replacement of the old system with a new system led to changes in and reconstruction of the inner structure of the gentry class, broke the original checks and balances of power and eventually triggered the sharp reversion of the gentry-people relationship in local society. On the other hand, the gentry class itself also became drastically divided. "The multi-directional movement of the gentry class not only gradually lost its original status and no longer constituted a specific feudal hierarchy, but also tended to be divided by the increasingly refined new social profession".[80] Thus the internal cohesion of a stable social class had been dispelled by the changing society.

After "a chain of institutional changes"[81] brought about by the New Deal, the structure of social interests and relationships was also reconstructed. The powerful class occupying the local public power in the reconstruction of social power obviously did not have the characteristic of the traditional gentry class taking "scholar" as the basic constituent element.

First, the character of the gentry had been completely weakened. This can be demonstrated by the study by Wei Guangqi, who said that

> with the implementation of local autonomy, the role of traditional gentry in handling local public affairs had been replaced by a new group. The new group was made up of leaders of various agencies responsible for carrying out the New Deal and autonomy, including members of the county council, leaders of some bureaus like the Education Bureau, the Police Station, the Industrial Bureau and the Financial Bureau, chairman of the chamber of commerce, chairman of the peasant association, chairman of the educational academy, head of the local security bureau, administrators of various districts and townships and schoolmasters of primary and secondary schools.

These people were called "scholar-gentry" by people in the society. However,

> in our view, the traditional gentry were a group of high social status. They relied on their official title gained through an imperial examination and

290 *Historical changes in rural power*

reputation as a bureaucrat to become distinguished personages. And the new gentry was a group with power in their hands, and their basic identity was the authority in current public organizations, so we called it the new gentry class.[82]

The traditional fame of these so-called "new gentry" did not win an advantage, but their educational background and control of local public power and public affairs were the important factors of their power. In the local "gentry power" structure, most of the gentry had once received education in new-style schools. For example, among 14 directors of the study encouragement office and education bureaus in Wan County directly affiliated to the central government from 1908 to 1928, 11 of them once received education in new-style schools, 1 of them gained his position through the imperial examination and 2 of them received education in new-style schools and took part in the imperial examination. In Gaoyi County, which was directly affiliated with the central government, 14 leaders of the Department of Education from 1906 to 1929 all received education in new-style schools and studied abroad. The new official gentry lacked an identifiable cultural background and "they were just a group with power".[83] People showed different attitudes toward the scholar-gentry and the new gentry:

If a young man from a rural area became *xiucai* through the imperial examination and came back his hometown for the first time, not only were his family members excited, but his villagers from the same village and neighboring villages would come out to welcome him several miles away from his village. Since then, villagers would always follow the *xiucai*'s orders. Even if he had done something wrong, nobody dared to berate him. Those new gentry thought that they should have equal status as the old scholars, but the former were less respectable than the latter from villagers' perspective, because villagers did not know whether the new gentry had received education or not. However, the elder people were afraid of the powerful. Thus, they might show less respect for the new gentry, but were still scared of them.[84]

Second, the control of local social public power and the possession of public resources constituted the basic condition of local gentry power. Regarding the institutional changes since the late Qing dynasty, "All affairs about the police, security, schools, farming, roads, bridges, dykes and dams, firefighting, sanitation, poverty alleviation, hospitals were all handled by autonomous bureaus".[85] They certainly fell into the control of the local gentry. Later, various kinds of bureaus that kept changing within the political system of counties laid down the main institutional basis for the formation of gentry power. For example, after 1912, a public funds bureau was established.

Its duty was to manage the county's local revenue, expenditure and special donations. Most of its members were local gentry who served as informal

Historical changes in rural power 291

officials and it was essentially run by local people and supervised by officials. The director general was selected by local gentry and reported the candidate to county magistrate for nomination.

What is more, the so-called bureau of commerce, the industrial bureau and the tobacco banning bureau were also "under the control of local gentry, and the director general dealt with local industry and administration under orders of the county magistrate".[86]

During the first 20 years of the twentieth century when a new system replaced the old system. "The village gentry took up the position as district directors, they were recognized by the county magistrate, and entered the council and participated in political affairs through election in the name of autonomy". Even funds for supporting the police station were raised by district directors or police directors (most of them were the gentry), and the gentry made use of "economic leverage" to indirectly control the police and even achieve the purpose of indirect manipulation of rural society.[87] Along with the process of the institutionalization of gentry power, that is,

when the New Deal was implemented as early as the late Qing dynasty, some gentry who were in charge of a certain affair in some places, had acquired the right of holding a plenary session to discuss administration of the prefecture and county.[88]

All local organizations were "just ones which served local scholar-gentry".

Some people recalled the local conditions in Song County in Henan in the 1940s, and stated that those who had taken up the position as senior officers were regarded as "the first-class gentry", those who had taken up the position as directors of the education department of the county government were regarded as "the middle-class gentry", and those who had taken up the position as head of a district, prefecture and town, or head of a security team were regarded as "the village gentry".[89]

Apart from the institutional public power, the gentry also controlled local public resources and other affairs, such as school-owned lands, lands used for building charitable institutions, lands used for building ancestral halls, public grain stocks and public funds.[90]

There was a kind of landlord who managed ancestral property, temples and its property. Those who managed such public lands were actually in the minority, so they easily became local tyrants and evil gentry and the landlord class, which was especially required by the country.[91]

The ancestral fields of the clan and the temple fields of the rural areas were also public lands. The temple fields attached to Buddhist and Taoist

292 *Historical changes in rural power*

temples were not public lands themselves, but since the implementation of the New Deal in the late Qing dynasty, quite a few of them had also been incorporated into school-owned lands. Therefore, we have seen from the documents about peasant associations movement in Hunan and Hubei provinces and Guangdong Province during the National Revolution that the temple fields were also usually defined as public lands.[92] According to Liu Yongtai's study, the average area of public lands in various counties in Hunan Province in 1934 and 1935 was more than 44,000 *mu* and 32,000 *mu* respectively. The effect of public property on the status of the power-gentry was self-evident. It was not only an important economic pillar for the organization of a civil corps, but also a small number of people who had power over public property could manipulate the economic and political institutions in rural areas.[93] Even they presided over the sacrificial rituals of the clandestine tribunals and controlled theocracy, and used sacred symbolic capital to justify their own power and authority. The power-bearers whitewashed their violent nature by pretending to communicate with God in the course of the sacrificial ceremony.[94] The ancestral temple and the local temple were both the center of clan or village power and the symbol of its authority. For the same clan, the clan power was the power of the village, and the ancestral hall was its executive body. The number of ancestral halls as a symbol of clan rights could be said to be almost proportional to the distribution of clan fields. For example, in Liling County, Hunan Province, every 881 people possessed an ancestral hall, whereas in Xiaolan Town, Zhongshan County, Guangdong Province, every 31 people possessed an ancestral hall. The ancestral halls of Hunan province were less binding on its people than those of Guangdong.[95]

> Each county in Hunan Province had various kinds of public property. Each clan had ancestral halls, the branch of each clan had house property and temples also had property of their own. Bridge associations, road associations, private or community-run schools charging no tuition, orphanages and so on all had land property. Those big ones could collect rents worth several thousand *dan* of grains and the small ones could collect rents worth dozens of *dan* of grains.[96]

However, "the so-called public land rent, was superficially the revenue of public institutions but it actually flowed into the pocket of the rich gentry".[97] Moreover, the trend of privatization of public property was accompanied by the development of the gentry.

> From the end of the nineteenth century to the beginning of the twentieth century, in the process of commercialization and the change of political system since the New Deal, market logic replaced the ethics of "public", and the public property and sacrificial rituals declined rapidly.[98]

Historical changes in rural power 293

In principle, it was forbidden to sell public lands, but under the influence of commercialization, a third of public lands were sold in the late 1920s.[99] Grains in public granaries were also sold for cash and it turned into usurers' capital, and warlords and local tyrants bought by force or seized public fields, public funds and grains. Therefore, in general, the decline of public property in the early days of the Republic of China was obvious. According to an investigation report of the autonomous investigation office of each county in Hunan Province, 60 percent of the sacrificial property in You County was used as school funds, and the rest was stolen and sold by their managers. All ceremonies and rituals were abandoned. The sacrificial rituals held in communities, altars and temples were all abolished.[100] Therefore, public property and the establishment of rural power relations based on "public" ethics began to undergo structural changes. At the same time, the young people from a peasant family who mastered new knowledge and thoughts were grouped into regional youth groups or student federations to launch local political struggles. Especially because they revealed the immorality of rural power holders who controlled public resource management institutions and sought private interests, they stood against rural power holders. This also accelerated the change in rural power relations. Therefore, Liu Yongtai believed that the decline of public property and the court and the emergence of modern intellectual youth from peasants' families were respectively the structural and main factor in the development of the peasant associations in the 1920s.[101]

Third, gentry power had been incorporated into the power within the "system". The traditional gentry's participation in local affairs was approved by the government, and not realized through the formal system or the inherent political mechanism of their local village community.[102] The characteristic of the traditional gentry power lay in its localism. However, the establishment of deliberative bodies at all levels had greatly expanded the activity space of the gentry and "made them go out of rural communities to provinces and turn from informal forces to formal legislatures".[103] The local gentry's power space was also expanded. According to the *Constitution on Local Self-Government in Cities, Towns and Villages* issued in 1908, the duties of Members included dealing with such matters related to schooling, hygiene, roads, engineering, agriculture, industry and commerce, charity and poverty relief, and public business, as well as fund-raising and other matters that had always been handled by the gentry.[104] The expansion of gentry power not only included the recognition and supplementation of the original power, but also the control and manipulation of the new public power in modern times. Once "they had taken control of these Western-style bureaus and other institutions, they could completely control the power of the countryside".[105] The system construction of the "New Deal" with modern characteristics, "was the development of democratic political mechanism, which provided a new opportunity for the gentry to exercise power and exert influence in a more formal political way".[106] In addition, the various new types of associations, groups and other

294 *Historical changes in rural power*

types of power organs were also one of the important content of the institutionalization of the gentry power. Chambers of commerce, agricultural associations, school boards and various semi-official bodies had been established to promote the development of industry and commerce. The gentry controlled those institutions, especially the chambers of commerce. With the help of the institutionalization of the New Deal, modern gentry power had entered the "system" and become an important content of the new social-power reconstruction.

Based on the above statement, we can outline the basic situation of the evolution of "gentry power" in the late Qing dynasty and early Republic of China: The local power structure underwent a historic shift from scholar-gentry to power-gentry. The New Deal and a series of institutional reforms had brought more of a legal basis for the expansion of gentry power, and led the traditional gentry who held local public power secretly to become the "power-gentry" who were known to the public.

However, in spite of this historic change, especially regarding the variation in the powerful forces in rural society, the social and cultural identity was lagging behind, which can be seen from the mixed use of various titles for the gentry, such as corrupt gentry, greedy gentry, hypocritical gentry, bad gentry, cunning gentry,[107] the gentry as bad as villains,[108] apart from the "evil gentry". Sun Yat-sen pointed out that in the Republic of China "those who took up the position as a county councilor were the evil gentry, rogues, and local ruffians. It was also those people who handled local affairs. So just imagine how badly they might perform in implementing autonomy in counties".[109] This reflected to a certain extent the evolution of the "scholar-gentry" to the "power-gentry". At that time, titles like "power-gentry" or "powerful gentry" appeared in newspapers.[110] For example, "In Hunan Province, some powerful gentry refused to pay back the grains".[111] However, the society did not reach a consensus on the those titles. Instead, the "historical memory" of "gentry" as a specific social-cultural symbol was still widely recognized and internalized in the changing social structure.

As we know, "the status of the gentry was acquired through the acquisition of scholarly honor or official ranks, scholarly attainments, academic titles and official posts, and whoever belonged to such status would naturally become a member of the gentry's group". Among them, the elements of "shi" related to "scholarly attainments and official ranks" were their most prominent and fundamental characteristics. "Scholarly honor or official ranks, scholarly attainments, and academic titles were all used to indicate the educational background of the person of this status. Official posts were generally provided only for those whose educational background had been certified through examinations". The imperial examination system was a related institutional support for it.[112] This determined that the scholar-gentry was the most stable and central structural part of the gentry class, although the identity acquired by other means, such as donations and military exploits, also belonged to the gentry class. However, the local gentry in the early years

Historical changes in rural power 295

of the Republic of China did not mainly have the qualifications and identity of the "scholar", and its scope was very wide and complex, including "local officials, scholars and celebrities, community leaders, local armed leaders, big businessmen, big landlords and even rich farmers and other complicated groups".[113] In the areas directly affiliated with the central government studied by Wei Guangqi, the heads of the local "New Deal" and the autonomous organs were composed of "county council members, the speaker of the council, the heads of the educational bureau, the police, the industrial and financial bureaus, the heads of the chamber of commerce, the peasant association, the educational council, and local security regiment, the heads of various districts and townships and the principals of primary and secondary schools". They were not characteristic of the traditional gentry, but "because of the social role they played as the traditional gentry, they were still called the 'scholar-gentry' by the local society".[114]

Therefore, the gentry as "historical memory" is not only a social and cultural symbol, or just "historical information", and it has actually become a cultural element of social reconstruction. "'Scholars' used to be the ruling class, and the head of each class. Since China established connections with Western countries, their status began to be undermined gradually".[115] Faced with the changing social structure and the local power-gentry class, the society still regarded the power-gentry as scholars, but they were totally different.

> There were two classes of scholar-gentry in the Republic of China. People in the one class, forced by the current situation, had to temporarily retire from their positions as the warlords, bureaucrats, politicians and so on, but once they seized a chance, they would resume their original positions. On the one hand, they could collude with the imperialists to oppress and exploit the people; on the other hand, they could become capitalists, big landlords and scoundrels to control everything by monopoly, and could make use of public opinion to expand their forces. People in the other class were local celebrities; they first catered to people in every aspect, took positions in people's communities, vaunted each other or boasted about themselves to raise their own status. The scholar-gentry had no professions or official posts, but when they failed, they could retreat to the status of celebrities and wait for a chance to make a comeback. People were afraid of losing their jobs or unemployment, but the scholar-gentry retired from their positions as bureaucrats, politicians and so on, or did not get a good opportunity to become bureaucrats and politicians.[116]

Without local public power or public resources, the impact of mere scholarly fame on local society had become negligible.

> A conventionally upright gentry understood that he had lagged behind, and suffered political oppression that have never happened before. If he was able to give priority to the interests of the people of the community,

296   *Historical changes in rural power*

and unwilling to offend the peasants or just very kind, he would rather retire.[117]

The gentry in "historical memory" formed a striking contrast with the gentry in the reconstruction of society.

"Gentry" as a long-standing and widely recognized social and cultural symbol, has become a relatively stable "historical memory". Although the grassroots social power structure changed in the late Qing dynasty and early Republic of China, and the power subject had been transformed from traditional "scholar-gentry" to "power-gentry", the gentry title as a part of "historical memory" was embedded in the reconstructed social power system, and the mutated "power-gentry" was still recognized by the society as "the gentry".

The gentry's absence in interest demand

In an article titled "The Gentry Students" and published on *Ta Kung Pao* in 1909, it was stated that

a gentry did not have a large amount of family property or a job. But he was good at playing politics, so he could start from scratch, enter the county office at his will to make acquaintance with officials, and exploit people to fill his own pockets. His neighbor's son once studied in Japan, and after coming back, he took his diploma obtained in Japan to join in the imperial examination and eventually became *jinshi*, a successful candidate in the examination, and held a key post in the academic circle. Having witnessed the situation, the gentry thought of studying abroad as a shortcut to advancement in his status. Therefore, he exchanged everything he exploited from people for money and made preparations for studying abroad. Unfortunately, he squandered his money to indulge in sensual pleasure abroad and finally had to go back home because he could not afford his tuition fee. His villagers came out to welcome him over ten *li* away from the town and gave him a warm round of applause, exclaiming "Long live the Gentry Student!" Such gentry students made acquaintance with officials, established connections with academic associations, made use of official funds to build schools, set up a clique to pursue selfish interests and did all manner of evil. Thus, there was another kind of vermin in the academic circle. Today, the country has made preparations for building a constitutional government, and each province set up a consultative council. A gentry was so shameless that he was elected as a member of the council for occupying a place among officials. How sad it was![118]

This might be a typical case, but the historical process was of universal significance in which the traditional gentry participated in local political affairs

Historical changes in rural power 297

with the help of their new academic qualifications and turned into the power-gentry in the replacement of the old system with a new one. This process, of course, unfolded in tandem with the differentiation of the gentry.

In 1923, Ye Dehui, who was living in Changsha, also described the differentiation of the local gentry and the gentry power change based on one aspect in the "Academic Notes of Xi Park". This "frank and informative" diary showed that the local gentry in Hunan Province gained more power after the reform movement of 1898.

> Most of issues related to reforms and that the central organs cared about had not been addressed yet at those meetings with the commissioner and the senior gentry present. Only my mentor [Ye Dehui] talked with confidence and composure, and pointed out the crucial issues. Successive commissioners listened to his advice patiently and immediately took measures. Because a rumor spread outside that the gentry in Hunan had too much power, so that four gentry whose surname was Wang, Zhang, Ye and Kong respectively, controlled the provincial politics, those officials who did not grow up in Hunan would always believe the rumor by mistake and try to combat and suppress those gentry. However, having worked with the gentry for a long time, those officials found the gentry treated others with sincerity and were satisfied with their capabilities of resisting foreign aggression and bearing responsibility for what they said. *Wenxiang*, a title granted to an official with both an academic background and military exploits, was criticized for setting up schools and constructing roads and being impeached by other officials, but he quoted what my mentor Ye Dehui said and what the gentry in Hunan did to defend himself. From this, it could be seen that my mentor Ye Dehui was well-known in the imperial court.[119]

In Hunan Province, there was a phenomenon indeed that "the gentry were more influential than county officials!"[120] However, with the replacement of the old school system with a new one and the emergence of new knowledge groups, the local "gentry power" also changed. That is to say, "since the reform, most of the senior gentry in Hunan had quit the scene".[121] According to Zhang Pengyuan's research, the new intellectual elite in Hunan Province grew rapidly and replaced the traditional gentry as the dominant force in local society. "The new elite in the consultative council accounted for 20 percent of the total, while they accounted for almost 64 percent in the congress. How rapidly they developed!" The influence of the traditional gentry gradually declined".[122] Moreover, the power-gentry took advantage of the New Deal to brazenly scramble for gains with the common people.

> They vied with each other to exploit mines, and the poor became rich overnight and showed off among the villagers. Since all of them pursued profits, disputes arose over the ownership of mountains and

298 *Historical changes in rural power*

lands. Villagers had no power to rely on, so they turned to the gentry working in provincial organs for help. They invited the gentry to form a partnership and guaranteed their safety. Therefore, most of the gentry in Hunan Province became rich or suffered a setback because of mine exploitation.[123]

The rise and fall of the "power-gentry" and "scholar-gentry" were the basic situation of the evolution of the local social power structure in the late Qing dynasty and early Republic of China. This situation also showed the decline of the traditional gentry and the loss of their dominance in discourse.

"After the Revolution of 1911, the gentry class was greatly impacted, and the influence of the gentry in local governments and local affairs had been weakened". Luxun wrote in his book *The True Story of Ah Q*, that

> At that time, *juren*, a successful candidate in the imperial examinations at the provincial level, were greatly affected. Since the government did not order the return of stolen money or goods, a *juren*'s family members felt desperate and cried. What is more, *xiucai* from the Zhao family went to town to notify the local government about a crime, but his pigtail was cut by bad revolutionists and he also paid 20,000 bucks. Therefore, his family was drowned in sadness too. Since then, they gradually became old fogies.[124]

This reflected the drop in the status of the rural gentry from one side. Even though some had proposed the restoration of the gentry system, from the perspective of public opinion at that time, the traditional gentry were regarded as anachronistic "relics of the former dynasty". For example, *Ta Kung Pao* once published articles containing these highly ironic words:

> The local gentry was recruited to assist local officials with political affairs. The task was heavy and important, so the qualification of local gentry should be examined carefully and strictly; otherwise, those petty people were likely to make up a number without active work. Therefore, some rules should be specified and used to examine the gentry: (1) An official of the Qing dynasty or a senior official of the Qing dynasty who retired in his old age; (2) an old man of noble character and high prestige in the Qing dynasty; (3) people with filial piety and integrity recommended from 1909 to 1912 in the Qing dynasty; (4) people who preached the good deeds of Yao and Shun and the doctrine of Confucius and Mencius; (5) an old pedant who served as a private teacher; (6) a white-haired old man who reached a ripe old age.[125]

After the Revolution of 1911, the traditional gentry's fame, educational background and status had lost institutional support and legitimacy. Their social and cultural authority and community leadership status were bound to be questioned by the new system, especially by the new learning youth group.

Even at the level of everyday life in rural societies, the epochal nature and depth of such challenges or conflicts deserved attention. In the peasant movement of Guangdong in 1925, the young people who received new education positioned the gentry as

> old fogies of the Qing dynasty, namely bureaucrats who resigned from office. Their ideology and behavior were all contrary to the democratic system. There is no comparison between them. Members of the peasant association were revolutionaries and the gentry were counterrevolutionary people. Therefore, they were quite different.[126]

Regarding the event of the distribution of school fields in Sha County, Fujian, traditional scholars had to share those fields with graduates from new-type schools at all levels, which aroused the opposition of young people receiving new education. Those young people regarded scholar-gentry with traditional fame as "anti-revolutionary and pedantic and they should be eliminated by modern times. How dare they share school fields with us? They were shameless and unrighteous".[127] Obviously, the traditional gentry did not have the advantage of a "theory of law" for the new era, and the label of "the spawn of feudalism" or of "old fogy of the Qing dynasty" was doomed to mark the traditional gentry and it was difficult for them to get rid of it. Therefore, when the young with new knowledge became the leading force of public opinion or discourse in the Republic of China, the interests of the traditional gentry were basically ignored, and the "historical memory" of the "good gentry", in contrast to the "bad gentry", was almost lost. Although the gentry was seen as a whole social class, even in the chain of institutional changes after the implementation of the New Deal, the "good gentry" still existed and had some influence on the society. According to the record of Xiong Xiling, the reason for the Rice Riot in Changsha in 1910 was that "the power was controlled by petty people", "but there were still good gentry who were impartial and wise and revered by common people".[128] But the power and influence of the gentry were being weakened greatly.

> Those who should have inherited the status of a gentry chose to leave. As a result, some unqualified people would substitute for them, the quality of the gentry would be reduced, and the sacred prestige of the gentry in the past was gradually damaged.[129]

The social situation was also getting worse.

> Most talents in the Republic of China went along two wrong paths: as politicians and as members of a parliament. Politicians made use of political trickery to sow discord and members of a parliament took advantage of their party to consolidate their own force. Both of them pursued private interests. However, those incorruptible and intelligent talents had no choice but to live like a hermit.[130]

300 *Historical changes in rural power*

In the rural society of Hubei, "the so-called scholar-gentry, also mostly with politeness and righteousness, bore their own responsibility like working out rules for villages, preaching classic works, reviving farming and sericulture, and organizing security groups. Local people benefited a lot from those good gentry's deeds". However, compared with the "power-gentry", "these traditional scholar-gentry could not assume a post in rural areas; and in the past, most of them were simple and honest, and talented, but later they changed".[131] Since the social situation changed, "the scholar-gentry class had lost their power and influence, and most of them were ignored by the society. Those who were impartial chose to retire from the world".[132]

> The governance of a country depended on recruiting talents, and only good gentry had the ability of helping officials govern the country well. If experienced and prudent gentry were not put in an important position, common people might have no confidence in the government. If some unqualified gentry were put in an important position, they had no ability of handling mass uprisings. Thus, I felt concerned about villagers' future.[133]

"The gentry did not care about common people, and the latter grumbled at the gentry's incompetence. The gentry and common people had no trust in businessmen".[134] Such a situation showed that the existence and behavior of good gentry could not attract public attention, and their existence and function were almost obscured by the power-gentry in the reconstruction of social power. Of course, it was also related to the historical process that a group of intellectuals with new knowledge had replaced the scholar-gentry in terms of discourse dominance in the change of social structure. "The rise of a new type of commercial port groups with new political consciousness weakened the importance of the gentry in the social structure of China".[135] As the

> rural power relationship began to undergo structural changes, due to building schools around China since the Republic of China, young people from a peasant family who mastered new knowledge and thoughts were grouped into regional youth groups or student federations to launch local political struggles. [...] The emergence of the modern intellectual youth was respectively the structural and main factor of the development of the peasant associations in the 1920s.[136]

Thus, new intellectual youth tried to express their own interests in the social reconstruction, and by mobilizing common people, the "social memory" of the "power-gentry" magnified, while the memory of traditional gentry, especially the good gentry, were selectively ignored. Of course, this was only one aspect of the problem.

"Collective memory was always linked to reality; memory was always specific, subjective and emotional, and always associated with a particular

Historical changes in rural power 301

group".[137] So, when the Kuomintang's efforts to rebuild national-state power in the 1920s penetrated largely into rural society, they met with stubborn resistance from the powerful class (power-gentry) in rural areas. The rural regime in Hunan was basically controlled by defense groups, "which only cared about their own interests". "The gentry in those groups possessed guns to protect themselves, and did not help or support each other". Though the gentry's control of branches of defense groups in each district was supposed to be "approved by the county government superficially", the power of the county government was impracticable, making it difficult to truly go deep into the rural society.

> Each group administered in its own way, and each branch took charge of civil and criminal proceedings without obeying the orders given by the head office. So those groups were too large in size to perform their functions effectively. Among the people, eight directors of eight districts were called "eight dukes". Just imagine how arrogant they were at that time.[138]

In Foshan, South Sea County, Guangdong Province,

> some public financial groups had been carved up by the evil gentry, retired bureaucrats, and old fogies of the Qing dynasty, and they also forcibly occupied others' property and kept it for their own. The party department had sent someone to the warehouse to supervise and check the property. An evil gentry refused to cooperate with him. [...] In Zhongshan County, an evil gentry controlled the sand protection bureau, and took this opportunity to oppress peasants and disrupt the party governance.[139]

This had given rise to strong resistance against the Kuomintang's power penetrating the grassroots society. Many county and township party officials were beaten and even killed by local gentry and merchants.[140] There would definitely be interest conflicts between the existing rural power and the grassroots power the Kuomintang attempted to rebuild. In most counties,

> all leaders of organizations below the county level were elected by a minority of people, and the election had nothing to do with the government, so it was difficult for the government to carry out its decree without the help of these leaders or directors.[141]

"There were lots of civil corps in villages, the directors assumed the post as township head and they had more power than county governments". This existing power structure was a thorny problem that the national government had to face when it tried to rebuild its state authority. "A county government without the help of the gentry class was just like a crab without claws and could not make any progress".[142] When the Kuomintang made great efforts

302 *Historical changes in rural power*

to construct the state power and penetrate into the rural society, breaking the power control of the gentry became a prominent problem: "at present, to address the issue of county administration was to revoke the privileges granted to the gentry and the notable, and to cancel the gentry meeting to prevent local tyrants and the evil gentry from monopolizing rural politics".[143] "The Kuomintang strove to launch the national revolution, and the local tyrants and evil gentry set it up and destroyed it by every possible means". Therefore, "local tyrants and evil gentry were sinners for the Kuomintang".[144] So, the choice of the Kuominting in the era was that "it will, standing on the side of peasants on behalf of the democratic forces, fight against local tyrants, evil gentry and landlords breaking the law on behalf of the feudal forces"[145].

The Communists at the time were mobilizing the peasants to "overthrow the gentry!" This political view was basically in line with that of the Kuomintang. By April 1927, the Communist Party had organized an agricultural association in 63 counties in Hunan alone, with 5 million members and nearly 10 million peasants.[146] By bringing down the "local tyrants and evil gentry", the relationship of rural power had even been thoroughly reformed.[147] Unlike the Kuomintang, the Communists not only regarded the gentry as a class but also delineated a broader scope. They thought "most of the gentry were noblemen, or *juren* or *xiucai* who received education and gained an official rank in the Qing dynasty, or entered the intellectual circle by obtaining a diploma".[148] Here the reference to the "gentry class" had been extended to all wealthy people or intellectuals, which meant that

> they were probably bourgeois (they did not necessarily own real estate, but an inexplicable qualification has made them have enough food and clothing). They were also intellectuals, and because of their sluggishness, and the status of inheritance, they often supported old ideas and the old system.

They served as consultants, counselors and people who ran errands, through which they gained money. Moreover, they also recommended the head of bureaus of likin and county magistrates, published newspapers with a special allowance, engaged in legal cases, embezzled official property and pretended to raise money in the name of charity and education. They did all of this to ask for money.[149]

This was another interpretation of the slogan "Man with land were rich, and all gentry were evil".[150]

Therefore, from the "conflicts between the gentry and common people" in the late Qing dynasty to the contradiction between the new intellectual youth and the traditional gentry in the Republic of China, from the confrontation between the Kuomintang regime and the power-gentry in the rural society to the contest between the peasant movement organized by the Communist Party and the gentry power, the direction of history had indeed remained unchanged: bringing down the gentry class had become a widely recognized call in the reconstruction of the social-power structure in the new era. Thus,

Historical changes in rural power 303

the historical process of "promoting gentry power" would eventually end up with the historical choice of "bringing down the gentry".

"Historical memory" is not merely an account of the past or the history, especially when it is a "collective memory" and recognized by society. Halbwachs, who first proposed the concept "collective memory", emphasizes in particular the presentness of historical memory. He thinks that the "past" in people's minds is not objective and real, but a kind of social construction. Memories always exist after the object of memories becomes a thing of the past. How people construct and describe the past depends to a large extent on their current ideas, interests and expectations. Memory is the object different groups of people compete for and an indicator of their power relationship. Mainstream culture tends to control the resources of memories, and to suppress different cultures, so an important means of cultural struggle is to preserve a kind of memory different from mainstream cultural memory or what Foucault calls "counter-memory".[151] Judging from the different "historical memory" of the gentry class in the late Qing dynasty and the early Republic of China, it did lie in the social life itself, and it could not be separated from the social life process and social structure, or it had been internalized as one of the elements of social reconstruction. Since the late Qing dynasty, the different "collective memory" about the gentry class not only presented the "selective memory" or "memory loss" of different interest subjects, but also this "historical memory" had become a factor, which was recognized by the society, in reconstructing the social power and interest relationship.

The historical change of rural power structure: a case study of the northwest Jin (Shanxi Province) base areas during the War of Resistance against Japanese aggression

During the War of Resistance against Japanese Aggression, the CPC established extensive anti-Japanese base areas in various rural areas. These bases were not only the rear bases for the War of Resistance, but also the "democratic experimental ground" for the CPC to actively explore the rural governance model. From the point of view of "state power construction", it was also an attempt to extend the state power downward and try to integrate the rural society into the formal regime system. However, the adjustment and reform of any political system could not be accomplished overnight. In the process of establishing and adjusting the new political system, how did the people outside the system enter the new system, in other words, how did the peasant class in the base areas step onto the rural political stage? This part takes the northwest base areas of Jin as an example, and tries to give an overview of this issue.

Revolutionary mobilization and the re-establishment of rural power

In the early days of the War of Resistance against Japanese Aggression, there coexisted two regimes. On the one hand, because of the Japanese attack on

304 *Historical changes in rural power*

the counties in northwest Jin, the old county chiefs had fled. Yan Xishan agreed to send members of the CPC as Commissioner of the Association of Sacrifice and National Salvation to assume the post as the county governor and so on, and mobilized the masses to reelect the county power. On the other hand, the political power in the areas under the control of Yan Xishan's forces was largely in the hands of the old bureaucrats, and even if the political power had been reorganized under the name of the Association of Sacrifice and National Salvation, the work had also been subjected to lots of obstacles. At this time, influenced by the situation, the focus of the work was on the county level and above, but the system of dividing places into villages was still used in villages and it was once prevailing in Yan Xishan's reign. The main village had a village head and village deputy, and subordinate villages also had their own heads like *lvzhang* or *linzhang*. "Serving as village chief was a duty, and the village chief was a respectable gentry".[152]

> The head of subordinate villages were not elected by people but appointed by the head of the main village. Prior to the appointment, one or two persons shall be recommended by the former *lvzhang* or *linzhang* and then approved by the village head.[153]

"Instead of solving problems for the villagers, the *lvzhang*'s job was mainly to deal with taxes and distributions for the governments of higher levels. And the *linzhang* was just the *lvhzhang*'s assistant".[154]

The new regime was built from early February 1940 to September of the same year. "In this period, due to the unclear policy, there was a phenomenon of 'leftism' in the work, and the government just built special offices, counties, districts, villages, and equipped them with cadres".[155] During this period, although the village regime also held a village election, "this election did not exert great influence because it did not make any change in administrative institutions of villages, and it was not democratic and solemn".[156] Only some of village heads were replaced, but most of the *lvzhang* and *linzhang* were not. Part of natural villages "added a representative between *lvzhang* and *linzhang*, that is, deputy *lvzhang*".[157] However, "as a result of this election, some of the landlords and gentry in the village regime were removed, and some of the progressives among the masses took part in the village regime".[158] After the second administrative meeting in September 1940, the construction of the regime in the northwest Jin stepped onto the road of formalization.

The mass organization construction was important content of the base area construction, and also the main content of the political work during the period of establishing the base areas in the northwest Jin. The mass organizations in the base areas of the northwest Jin were established under the leadership of the Association of Sacrifice and National Salvation and Federal of War Action. The two organizations were nominally established by the parties in accordance with the principle of the united front, and the

Historical changes in rural power 305

actual leadership was in the hands of the Communist Party. The Association of Sacrifice and National Salvation was founded in 1936 and had been transformed into an organization for the Communist Party and Yan Xishan to work together. After the outbreak of the war of resistance, the Association of Sacrifice and National Salvation sent a large number of personnel to the guerrilla areas to serve as county governors through legal means, laying the foundation for the development of the base areas. At the same time, it also went deep into the rural areas and built its own organizations.

The Association of Sacrifice and National Salvation also cooperated with the Federation of War Action to develop organizations such as the Rural Peasants' Rescue Association, the Women's Rescue Association, the Youth Rescue Association and the Self-Defense Forces to train cadres when developing these organizations. It was in the second half of 1938 that the Association of Sacrifice and National Salvation and the Federation of War Action went deep into the bottom of rural areas to develop those organizations. At that time, the process of establishing various groups and organizations was relatively simple, and the higher authorities sent people to the natural villages to hold meetings and register the villagers, and finally an organization was established. After the "north Jin incident", although those organizations were reorganized, most of them only reregistered members and elected cadres. Moreover, during this period, the activities organized by these organizations themselves were rare and their main task was to work with the government.

The establishment and development of grassroots political organizations in base areas and mass organizations required a lot of cadres to lead them, so training cadres became an important content of basic-level construction.

In order to make the best use of the various resources of the rural society, the CPC had to train and cultivate the local people and mobilize their enthusiasm to give full play to their respective abilities and influence in the rural society. This would not only reduce the party's political costs, but also made it easier for rural people to accept its leadership. Local cadres were both officials and native people, so the masses were "closer to them than to the ordinary officials".[159] Cadres could learn from the masses about many village affairs and people's inner understanding, and the masses also wanted to know the policies and information of government departments through these cadres. Renjiawan village head Ren Bude "upheld justice, worked hard, so local people revered him", and ordinary people especially wanted to inquire about some official news from him, such as requisitioning grain, expanding troops, sharing the burden of a payment among villages, the enemy's situation and so on, because people thought that he was an official with a wide range of knowledge and a broad horizon. Moreover, they were also willing to discuss with him some of their own unsolvable problems, because he was a native and everything could be done easily.[160]

In the base areas, the CPC mainly trained and cultivated local cadres through Party organizations and various mass organizations. After the

306 *Historical changes in rural power*

Association of Sacrifice and National Salvation was founded, the CPC, in the name of the united front,

> looked for and trained activists among the members of the association, and absorbed them into the Party. The Party's branch and the association's branch were jointly established, and it was publicly called the branch of the Association of Sacrifice and National Salvation, and it secretly completed the task assigned by the party and developed and strengthened anti-Japanese democratic forces.[161]

At the same time, the association opened up cadre training courses to train a large number of secretaries for the association in villages. For example, in Xing County, the branch of the Association of Sacrifice and National Salvation held three training courses. "Most of the trainees in the second and third phases were assigned to the districts and villages to serve as secretaries of the association, while some remained at the county level as heads of the branches and mass organizations".[162] In the process of establishing various organizations, governments and organizations at all levels also selected outstanding personnel from the villages and trained them. The trained cadres were not well-off in life, and most of them were middle peasants and poor peasants, but had strong abilities, a wide range of contacts and great social influence. After the training, they learned more ways to deal with problems, and improved their own ability to do things. Ordinary villagers thought those trainees had seen the world, especially those who worked in political organizations and mass organizations above the administrative village level, and were regarded as "officials" and had certain authority. But they also had many shortcomings, such as doing things arbitrarily, reluctantly listening to others' opinions, committing the crime of corruption, and displaying selfishness, indifference to the interests of the masses and so on.

Because of the limited organizational strength of the CPC in its early days, the selection of rural grassroots cadres was deeply influenced by the traditional way in the past. In ancient China, the official organs of state power only extended to the county level, and the organs below the county level were ruled by clans and the scholar-gentry. Since the Republic of China, the superstructure had been turned from feudal autocracy to democratic republicanism; however, the political pattern of rural areas changed very little, and each region, driven by the state power, strengthened the traditional mode of rural governance – the *Baojia* system and the system of *Lvzhang* and *Linzhang*. In the northwest Jin region, when Yan Xishan carried out the reform in villages, the system of dividing places into villages was implemented. The village heads and *lvzhang* and *linzhang* were appointed by their superiors. The villagers, who had long been immersed in such a political environment, did not have ideas and consciousness about democratic elections, but responded with indifference. After the outbreak of the War of Resistance, various organizations in rural society were established one after another. However, because of the

Historical changes in rural power 307

traditional inertia and formalism in the work of the higher authorities, the establishment of organizations at the bottom of the society was also informal, for an organization was established after simply registering villagers and designating leaders.

Influenced by past experience, ordinary people regarded the leaders of natural villages and mass organizations as people doing enforced and unpaid work for the government[163] and were unwilling to participate in it. Moreover, the superior staff did not do their job well to improve people's awareness and enthusiasm for participation, and some practices precisely strengthened the rural people's empirical understanding. The selection of the chairman of the Zhongzhuang Village Peasants Salvation Association fully proved this. The association was founded in July 1938 with the help of the Association of Sacrifice and National Salvation. When the association was founded, it seemed that the chairman of the Zhongzhuang Village Peasants Salvation Association was elected by people, but Liu Kangche was designated as the chairman in advance. "People thought the chairman must join the army", and then Liu Kangche joined the army in 1940. "The new chairman was decided by the village head and Liu Xiaoyu on Heiyukou Street, and the next day it was approved on a caucus (Liu Xiaoyu served as the chairman)".[164]

A large number of archival materials proved that, on the whole, the leaders of mass organizations mostly lived a well-off life. Although most cadres could perform their duties, cooperate with and support the work of the Party and the government, some of them did not take care of poor families, or were slack in their work, so that many common people did not know about those organizations' duty. Although the latter was in a minority, they also had a negative effect on the implementation of the Party's rural policy and left a bad impression on people.

In short, due to various factors, some shortcomings had been exposed in the process of establishing the rural grassroots political organizations and mass organizations.

Village selection: transformation of the rural regime system

As mentioned earlier, there were many shortcomings at the beginning of the establishment of the anti-Japanese regime, which affected the Communist Party's carrying out work in rural areas. Therefore, the CPC hoped that through village elections, the grassroots regime would be completely reformed, and that through democratic elections, people would be mobilized and democratic politics would be practiced. At the same time, through village elections, the isolated and scattered mass organizations would become an organic community based on small groups, and "good people" would become leaders of a village to prevent "bad people" from taking power. However, cadres and people had different opinions about who was a "good person" or a "bad person". In order to select satisfactory candidates, the Communist Party controlled the elections in various ways and used the class struggle to

308 *Historical changes in rural power*

mobilize the masses. However, "within rural areas, the class-rule relationship in the rural daily life was much more vague".[165] Class struggles had not been widely recognized and accepted by people at the bottom of society. A complex relationship had formed between leading cadres on behalf of the government, candidates and the common people. If the cadres and people shared a same goal, the election would be easier; if there was a deviation, there would be contradictions, which to a certain extent affected the image of the Party, the operation of the regime system and the political identity and participation of the people, and had a negative impact on the development of various undertakings in base areas. This had been shown in village elections.[166]

There were also many shortcomings in the operation of the "village election" regime. In order to fully reflect democracy and make ensure the smooth implementation of elections, the administrative office of northwest Jin passed the "Village Elections Regulations" and the "Village Regime Organization Regulations" at the second executive meeting. But whether the regulations could achieve the desired purpose lay not only in the regulations themselves but also in the people who implemented them. The results of the elections showed that a large number of the old regime personnel and those promoted by the Communist Party in the district and village regimes were retained, while the leading cadres of the county regime were mostly revolutionary young people with no practical experience, so their combination could not but affect the administrative efficiency and practical effect of the regime. This could be clearly reflected by both working methods and content.

According to the "Village Regime Organization Regulations" issued by the administrative office,

> The highest power organ of the administrative village is the village national assembly, and the village representative conference is the highest power organ of the village regime after the closing of the national assembly, and its members are composed of representatives elected by citizens in each natural village. The village representative conference can exercise all the power of the village national assembly.

The village public office shall be the executive organ of the village regime and shall have a village head.
The village head shall lead the work of the committees, and handle all affairs in the village. He is the representative of other directors and acts as village chief executive. He shall be responsible to the higher-level government, the national assembly and the village representative conference.[167]

However, in fact,

> The villagers' representative of each natural village has been selected, but the village representative conference is still formed yet, resulting in the present situation that there is a representative and no representative conference, so that only representatives of each natural village are led by the

Historical changes in rural power 309

village public office and are responsible to the village public office, while no village public office is led by the representative conference or no village public office is responsible to the representative conference.[168]

The leadership of the district over the administrative village and the administrative village over the natural village was mostly achieved through the meeting of increasing cadres. "The organ that really determines all major issues is not the villagers' congress but the meeting of increasing cadres.[169]

The higher authorities had arranged some work in a certain period, generally called "central work" or "urgent work"[170]. After the work was carried out, the first step was the message conveyed by the comrades sent by the district or the work group. The way to convey messages was to hold a meeting o, increasing cadres in the administrative village. Members who attended the meeting were to be "composed of village heads, chairmen of committees and representatives of natural village heads" as stipulated in the regulations".[171] However, a wide range of people would attend the meeting, including

all the cadres of the village public offices who were separated from production, members of the committee, the ministers of the armed forces committee, the secretary of the anti-Japanese united army, the secretaries and ministers, the chief representatives, directors of the co-operatives, accountants and the cadres who were not on the job now, active figures in the village and a few active party members in natural villages.[172]

After the messages had been conveyed, those representatives and directors would return to their own natural village. If there were many people from superior work groups, they would follow the representatives to each natural village so as to assist them in their work; if the number of people from work groups was adequate, they would write an outline and hand it over to each cadre of an administrative village like the village head, the director of the armed forces committee, the secretary of the anti-Japanese united army and so on. The cadre would arrange work according to the outline.[173]

In the natural village, the civic assembly was the highest authority in the village, and it was held at any time to solve all the matters in the village. But the investigators learned that in Zhongzhuang, because there were too many meetings, and it would cost a lot of time, a whole family were not willing to spend all the time attending those meetings. In the present rural society where a family was the economic unit, one person could represent the whole family's opinion. Therefore, the most important person in a family would attend the civic assembly and women were rarely present (unless women were required to be present), and old men could also not attend the civic assembly.[174]

The meeting of increasing cadres of administrative villages, the caucus of natural villages, and the civic assembly were regarded as three links

310 *Historical changes in rural power*

for completing all the work. Once there was work, they would be held in order and were called the "trilogy" of work.[175]

During the meeting, the cadres at all levels disregarded the know-how and understanding of the masses.

As a result, the comrades from superior work groups used lots of terms and new words and finally became "preachers", the village cadres became "listeners" in the "church" and the representatives of village directors became "people running errands" in the "church" and the work plan became "a bible".[176]

The administrative village cadres took the assigned task and outline to natural villages, and

repeated what they had heard at the caucus. They were loyal preachers, and their listeners were not qualified. People who went to church knew that they were going to hear stories from the Bible or worship God, but those who attended such meetings did not know why they came to the meetings and what the speaker was talking about.[177]

In the poverty-stricken northwest Jin regions, people's living standards were very low and unable to be improved, so it was difficult for people to guarantee supplies for the war. In order to persevere in the War of Resistance, and safeguard the interests of the people, the local government had taken various corresponding measures, such as lending grains and money for development and production, reducing rent and interest, streamlining the military and administrative structure to lessen the burden on people and organizing people to take part in spring plowing, mutual assistance, spinning yarn and so on. Through these measures, the local government helped the masses solve difficulties in production and life, so that "developing the economy and ensuring supply" became the starting point and destination of the policy of base areas.

But like everything else, the CPC and its government experienced a lot of twists and turns and made some mistakes in implementing these policies. This was particularly evident in the early days of the grassroots regime operation. Investigators of Xiping Village keenly discovered that

many work were seen as important by the superiors and enjoyed great popularity among people and cadres, such as poverty relief, cultivating land for others, spring ploughing, mutual assistance, spinning yarn, establishing cooperatives, new literature, rent reduction, mobilizing the masses, organizing all kinds of people and so on. However, in Xiping, the masses and cadres attached little importance to them and even thought it was futile to do so.[178]

Historical changes in rural power 311

This phenomenon did not only exist in a few villages, but was reflected in the survey records of several villages collected by the author.

In the process of reducing rent and interest in Gaojia Village, "only the work of reducing rent was actually completed", and people doing the work did not show the enthusiasm that the superiors had expected. This had a lot to do with the attitude and working style of the work groups and grassroots cadres. The village cadres were already familiar with the situation, but because the work group controlled everything, the village cadres only ran errands.[179] Thus, village cadres did not care about their own work, and both the work groups and cadres did not regard lessening the burden on peasants as the aim of reducing rent. "According to the cadres, the aim was to mobilize the masses and make the public grain work proceed smoothly".[180] Rent reduction had completely become a "stepping-stone" for public grain collection.

It was a very complex task to collect public grain (i.e., public grain to save the country), as the amount of the levy was determined based on the grain output and class status of each household. Classifying class status had been carried out many times before, and there was no objection, but how to determine the output and income of each peasant was very difficult. It was precisely in the process of rent reduction that cadres wanted to understand the economic income of each household in depth and prepare for the work of collecting public grain. At first, they asked peasants to report their own output.

The peasants, in order to emphasize the amount of the rent they had paid, reported very low grain yields, thus facilitating the cooperation of the landlord and tenant peasants in understating the output. In the tenant's view, delivering public grain was a major issue, and rent reduction was not a top priority.[181]

Self-employed peasants also reported low yields in order to deliver less public grain. In the "acquaintance society" in rural areas, no one was willing to come forward to tell on others, because if others understated their yield, he could do the same. Thus, it was beneficial to himself. In this way, collecting public grain in terms of peasants' reports did not help complete the task assigned by the superiors. The work groups had no choice but to adopt a standard output approach, which had a significant impact on the work of rent reduction.

The tenants in Gaojia Village were generally indifferent, for some of them paid less rent than the group had calculated; some of them were flexible rent and the rent of the tenants was a little more than the original rent after the work group's calculation. Some tenants had already paid their rent, saying "it was difficult to get meat from a cat's mouth and it was just in vain".[182]

312 *Historical changes in rural power*

Heroes and model workers: reconstruction of the new authority in the rural areas

The regime in the anti-Japanese base areas was a regime "combining the anti-Japanese war with the democratic system". The government in the anti-Japanese base areas had two functions: one was to launch, organize and lead the anti-Japanese war; and the other was to implement democratic politics in the base areas. In the leadership of the War of Resistance against Japanese Aggression, the efforts made by the northwest Jin base areas were obvious to all, but in the implementation of democratic politics, the northwest Jin base areas were still mainly in the stage of constructing and improving the system in the first two years. Although an anti-new bureaucracy inspection was carried out in March 1941, the overall outlook had not been greatly improved, especially in the rural grassroots regime. The central government had acutely observed that these problems still existed to varying degrees in the base areas. Thus, in 1942, the central government decided to carry out the rectification movement in the base areas.

On May 30, 1942, the Party Committee of the Western Jin District of the CPC issued the Instructions on Rectifying the Three Phenomena in the Northwest Jin. From June 1942 to 1944, the rectification movement in the northwest Jin was launched vigorously by the various departments of the Party, government and people. Through rectification, cadres' theoretical level and ideological awareness had been raised, and they had played an important role in improving the work of various departments.

At the same time, the quality of cadres had been improved through various training courses and on-the-job education methods. Among them, a large number of long-term education was on-the-job education. The administrative offices were to organize study committees and set up branches in special districts and counties. The cadres of counties and districts studied the "Theory of New Democracy", held seminars regularly and distributed the results to cadres of each district and village for reference. For village-level cadres, each county and district would make them assemble for training, educational training and winter training. They would learn about the Chinese characters, village elections, public grain, decrees and so on, and at last there would be a summary of their training and those cadres were to take an examination.

At the same time, in order to solve the economic difficulties of the base areas and bring the peasants who had been separated from the regime for a long time into the regime, various forms of movement had been carried out by the governments at all levels in the base areas, such as spring plowing, summer hoeing, autumn harvest, winter learning, exchanging labor, spinning yarn, rent and interest reduction, debt clearance, anti-corruption and so on. The government at all levels promoted the outstanding talented person and the advanced model in the movement, and established them as the backbone of the leadership, and "improved the centrists and laggards with the help of those talents, and then continuously promoted the activists in the struggle and replaced the

Historical changes in rural power 313

unqualified and corrupt person with those activists".[183] As American scholar Mark Selden observed, "If long-term development depends on the initiative of peasants and the joint action of the community, then practical encouragement and stimulation must be given. One way to solve this problem is to use model workers as leaders and models".[184] Among the various movements carried out in the base areas, the movement that had the biggest influence on the replacement of the rural power structure and achieved the most remarkable results was the model worker and hero movement combined with mutual assistance in labor exchanging and spinning yarn, the cooperative movement and so on.

Organizations of mutual assistance in labor exchanging and spinning yarn were established and advocated to solve the difficulties of rural economic development in border areas after 1942. Because of the invasion and plunder by the Japanese invaders, the agricultural means of production in base areas, especially farm cattle, were scarce, and the labor force was generally reduced, resulting in a situation in which people had difficulty cultivating land and reclaiming wasteland. Industry and commerce were also affected by the war at this time, and they were in decline, so the base areas lacked clothing and food. In order to address these difficulties, government departments actively encouraged people to produce food and clothing to meet their own needs, and people in the base areas organized production, exchanged labor and cooperated with each other in spinning yarn, so as to provide food and clothing for people and the army. At the same time, this policy was consistent with the new democratic economic theory of the CPC. From Mao Zedong's perspective, in China's rural areas, "individual economy has existed for thousands of years, and a family is a production unit. This scattered individual production, is the economic basis of feudal rule, so that the peasants themselves are stuck in permanent poverty. The only way to get rid of this situation is achieving collectivization gradually, and the only way to achieve collectivization, according to Lenin, is establishing cooperatives". Therefore, if a cooperative is established, "no matter what it is called, no matter how many people a unit consists of, no matter what kind of tools people exchange to help each other, no matter what conditions they live in, no matter how much time it lasts", "in short, as long as people voluntarily participate in (must not be forced) collective organizations providing mutual assistance, it is a good thing". "In the anti-Japanese base areas in North and Central China, such collective production cooperatives providing mutual assistance should be widely organized on a voluntary basis by people".[185] In 1944, more than 130,000 people in the Jin-Sui border areas participated in exchanging labor for mutual assistance. Various types of cooperatives had increased to 777, with 4,626 members. In 1945, in addition to the new expansion of mutual assistance in agriculture, there were 285 large cooperatives.[186] Xing County, the capital of the Jin-Sui border areas, took the lead in exchanging labor for mutual assistance. According to Xing County's statistics in 1945, "At that time, there were 13,000 people in the county and more than 10,000 in the mutual assistance group".[187]

314 *Historical changes in rural power*

A large number of excellent workers, cooperatives, model villages, model people and so on emerged in the productive work. Most of these activists were poor peasants and farm laborers at the bottom of rural society before the war, and lived in extreme poverty, but many policies since the establishment of the new regime changed their economic situation, improved their social status, stimulated their enthusiasm for productive work and prompted them to participate in mass organizations or construction of the grassroots regime. With the extensive development of various undertakings and movements in the base areas, they began to show their own talents in rural areas. Some were elected directly by the village and entered the political organizations, some joined the CPC and became members or leaders of grassroots branch organizations, and others took the "third path", leading the masses in developing production and carrying out their construction work, and became the leaders of the mass organizations, mainly including the Rural Peasants' Rescue Association, the Women's Rescue Association, the armed forces committee, guerrillas and so on. Because they were members of the ordinary villagers, and had a closer relationship with people, their leadership was easily acceptable to people. Moreover, they also proposed many organizational forms of production suitable for rural areas, which helped them continuously raise their status among common people.

In order to enhance the enthusiasm of the people's organizations to exchange labor and help each other, the border government had also actively taken measures to give material and spiritual rewards to villages and organizers that had made achievements. This was fully reflected in the conditions for elections for the model hero in March 1943 and August 1944. The main condition for one to be chosen as a model worker of 1943 was "that under the same conditions of labor, he also increased agricultural output by 15 percent", and "participation in labor mutual assistance to increase production" was only a subsidiary condition of the "main condition". The main condition for a woman to be chosen as a female model worker also depended on her achievements in spinning and weaving. "To influence and promote others to participate actively in the labor force with their own enthusiasm and exemplary role" and "to participate actively in the organization of mutual assistance" were only the subsidiary conditions of the election.[188] However, the basic condition for being elected as a model worker in 1944 was that "in addition to their own efforts to increase production, he must also play an exemplary role in contacting people and helping them increase production, and in organizing people and prompting people to participate into production". The condition for a woman to be elected as a female model worker was also that "she should do her best to spin and organize people to help each other". Accordingly, the primary condition for one to be elected as a hero or model was organizing and prompting people to help each other.[189] (Emphasis added; and the difference can be seen in words and sentences.)

All kinds of honorary titles like heroes, models and so on had become important political capital of activists in rural political life. With the expansion

Historical changes in rural power   315

of their social life network, they had frequent contacts and a closer relationship with administrative personnel at the upper level, so the political capital they possessed was expanding. They stepped onto the political stage with a new attitude, assumed the post of executive directors of villages or leaders of mass organizations and became the main characters in rural political life. Even a part of higher-level model workers such as county-level or border area-level model workers had more power than village-level leaders and guided the work of the whole administrative village regime and mass organizations. A total of 29 model workers attended the fourth conference of outstanding workers at the level of border areas in Xing County, and all were, without exception, the organizers and leaders of various labor exchange groups and cooperatives in their administrative villages. In this way, a core figure emerged in the rural society who was the leader of the grassroots organizations, the organizer of labor exchange and mutual assistance groups, and the model worker. He was regarded as the "new authority" of the rural society.

In the War of Resistance against Japan, the governments of Shaanxi-Kansu-Ningxia, Jin-Sui, Shanxi-Chahar-Hebei, Shanxi-Hebei-Shandong-Henan and other base areas trained a large number of such village leaders. The Jin-Sui border region held a total of four conferences for model workers and heroes. For the first conference, 80 people were elected as model workers or heroes; for the second conference, 103; for the third conference, 130; and for the fourth conference, 791.[190] Twenty-nine people from Xing County attended the fourth conference for model workers or heroes. Yangjiapo had 30 village-level model workers, 7 county-level model workers and 5 border area-level model workers in 1944.

In 1944, anti-Japanese base areas behind enemy lines started a series of partial counteroffensives against Japanese aggression, and the economic conditions and the social environment were greatly improved. After several years of rent-reduction campaigns, people lived a better life and their awareness of political participation was growing. At the same time, the Jin-Sui administrative office decided to conduct village election campaigns in the entire border areas in the spring of 1945, so as to attract a variety of heroes, model workers and activists emerging from the masses to take part in the regime, improve village political institutions, inspect the regime from bottom to top, give full play to public opinion and promote democracy, improve all aspects of our work and make the village regime more closely linked to the masses.

The division of citizen groups for village elections in 1945 was different from that in 1941. In 1941, for the village election, ten natural villages were divided into one group and people could form a group freely, while in 1945, a citizen group for the village election was mainly a labor exchange group or a textile group, and there was no need to divide them. In this way, the labor exchange group and the textile group were not only economically mutual assistance groups, but also grassroots political groups. The leaders of the grassroots regimes chosen by citizen groups based on these organizations could be seen as the new authority playing three roles at the same time.

316 *Historical changes in rural power*

At the same time, in the view of the party and government at a higher level, "heroes, models and various kinds of activists were chosen by people, and they were organizers and promoters of various types of work in rural areas. They had a close relationship with people". "All people with such characteristics should be elected".[191] "These good people should be elected in accordance with the method of election and chosen to enter the village regime by a democratic and voluntary election of the masses to strengthen its function".[192] Therefore, the Party and government also encouraged and supported the election of model workers in various ways. The election results showed that the policy of the CPC was effective and successful.

Among the six trial villages in Xing County,

> of the eight elected village heads and deputy village heads, four were heroes and models at all levels, two were secretaries of peasant associations and one was the manager of peasant associations. Of 191 new directors, 105 were heroes and models, as well as cadres of the peasant associations and armed forces committees. Many of them were leaders of labor exchange groups.[193]

In Weijiatan, "people believed that Kang Chengzhong, as a model worker, efficiently led two labor exchange groups, opened up 40 *shang* (a land measure equal to 15 *mu* in most parts of the northeast and three or five *mu* in the northwest) of flood land, solved the land issue for poor people and actively led people to plant cotton. Kang Guiying and three other women made great efforts to develop the textile industry for women, and they were also friendly to the Chinese army". In the village election, "Kang Tongzhu, as a village-level model, was elected as village head, Kang Chengzhong, as a border area-level model, was elected as deputy village head, and Kang Guiying, Zhao E'er, Jia Huachan and Liu Maochan, as models for women, were elected as representatives of the village".[194] "Of the county's newly elected village heads and deputy village heads, there were 18 heroes or models, and of all directors, there were 148 heroes or models". Most of the losers were people who were slack in their work, selfish and self-centered, and stubborn and cunning. Of 11 people who were not elected as directors in Heiyukou, four of them were slack in their work, two of them were selfish with unclear accounts, three of them were partial and two of them had bad manners".[195] Some of them had long served in the regime system, and in particular, developed a self-concerned, opportunistic, arbitrary style and habit in the old regime. In Ciyaogou, someone recommended Mao Ti to the government, but a widow said, "Mao Ti once treated common people in a terrible manner. How could we count on him to do good things for us?"[196] Consequently, Mao Ti failed to be elected.

Through village elections in 1945, the structure of rural political power changed dramatically. The new authority in rural areas, with the model workers and heroes at all levels and the leaders of mass organization as the main body,

Historical changes in rural power 317

gradually controlled the rural political life, and the political influence of the traditional authority, just like the afterglow of sunset, faded further.

To sum up, the change of power at the grassroots level in the anti-Japanese base areas is not accomplished overnight, and it went through a long process. In the early days of the War of Resistance against Japanese Aggression, the CPC used the banner of the anti-Japanese united front as a cover for organizing mass organizations such as the Rural Peasants' Rescue Association, the Women's Rescue Association, and the armed forces committee to attract the people at the bottom of rural areas to participate in the anti-Japanese cause and enhance their status. However, after all, mass organizations were not the regime, and they did not have the authority and legitimacy of the regime, even if the huge network formed by these organizations extended to the various fields of rural society. In the early days of establishing base areas, people's understanding of mass organizations was vague or even negligible, which limited the development of mass organizations and the improvement of the social status of leaders of those organizations. There was no major change in the structure of rural power.

With the development of the situation of the anti-Japanese war, the CPC controlled and initially transformed the regime. In order to carry out democratic politics, improve administrative efficiency, obtain all kinds of materials needed for the war of resistance, and mobilize the masses to join in the war of resistance, base areas conducted village elections universally and tried to fundamentally transform the grassroots regime. However, in fact, after the village election, the village grassroots power still took the old regime personnel as the main body, and those who stepped onto the administrative stage after the village election were in a subordinate position. In order to solve difficulties in the work, and bring peasants who had been separated from the regime for a long time into the regime, various forms of movement were launched in the base areas to develop the economy and stimulate people's consciousness and enthusiasm for political participation. Moreover, activists at the bottom of the society were promoted to serve as leaders of various rural undertakings. Among all movements, the most influential and effective one was the election of model workers and heroes. Through this movement, new authority figures emerged in rural society who played the role of the leader of the grassroots organizations, the organizer of labor exchange and mutual assistance groups, and model workers, and they gradually played the leading role on the rural political stage and "functioned as a link between rural areas and the upper leadership", "promoting the solidarity of the community and transforming the rural society".[197] In contrast, the traditional authority figures' economic status in the new situation was declining constantly, and their political and social influence further faded, and they had to follow others' leadership in rural areas.

On the whole, the replacement of the personnel of the grassroots organizations in the base areas was successful, which resulted in the leading role of the grassroots power in the rural society changing fundamentally.

318 *Historical changes in rural power*

Before the War of Resistance, the standards for holding public office in rural areas were: "first, one should be qualified (rich and powerful); second, one should be literate; third, one should be free and know how to deliver a speech before people".[198] By 1945, the standards for holding public office were: "the essential condition was that one should take the lead in rent reduction and production, and help the poor live a well-off life. Literacy and eloquence were not valued by people, because they thought being eloquent was no good".[199] This indicates a great transformation in the ideological understanding of ordinary villagers. This transformation not only accelerated the change in the leading role of political power at the grassroots level, but also drove the reconstruction of the overall social structure of rural areas. In turn, the reconstruction of the social structure strengthened the transformation of people's ideology, traditional ideas were gradually subverted, and the new ideology is gradually accepted. Since then, rural society began to play its part in history completely.

Notes

1 Relevant research: Wang Qisheng, *Evolution of Rural Power Structure in the Republic of China*, in Zhou Jiming, Song Dejin, *History of Chinese Society* (Wuhan: Hubei Education Press, 2000), 549–590. Wei Guangqi, *Official Governance and Autonomy – China's County System in the First Half of the 20th Century* (Beijing: The Commercial Press, 2004); Xu Maoming, *Scholar-Gentry and Society in Regions South of the Yangtze River* (Beijing: The Commercial Press, 2004); Zheng Qidong, *Rural Society in North China in the Transitional Period* (Shanghai: Shanghai Bookstore Publishing House, 2004), 37. Past research on the gentry class and social structure in the late Qing dynasty and the early Republic of China mainly focuses on the effect of the abolishment of the imperial examination system, the formation of new gentry caused by the obstruction of upward mobility channels and so on, and carried out analyses of the degeneration of the gentry class in the Republic of China. However, this static analysis has not yet shown the complexity of the historical evolution of the gentry class from occupying the most important position among four kinds of people in the late Qing dynasty to a situation in which all gentry were bad in the Republic of China. Most importantly, it fails to reveal the historical truth of repeated interaction among various interest subjects in this huge change. (Author's note)
2 "Announcement to Peasants at the Third Plenary Session of the Second Central Executive Committee of the Chinese Kuomintang" (March 1927), in *Documents of Peasant Movement during the First Civil Revolutionary War* (Beijing: People's Publishing House, 1983), 46.
3 See *Chinese Peasants*, ed. Ministry of Peasants, Central Executive Committee of the Chinese Kuomintang, issue 10, October 1926.
4 (Japan) Tadao Tanaka, *National Revolution and Rural Issues* (vol. 1), trans. Li Yuwen into Chinese (Beijing: The Commercial Press, 1927), 70.
5 (Soviet Union) A.B. Bakulin, *The Record of Wuhan during the Great Revolution of China (note of the Great Revolution of China from 1925 to 1927)*, 11, 142, 167.
6 Huang Qiang, *New Edition of Trial of the Bao-jia System in China* (Zhengzhong Publishing House, 1935), 278. It was recorded that "the Bao-jia system should

Historical changes in rural power   319

be adopted in order to prevent the resurrection of the spawn of feudalism". In the case about school fields in Fujian Province, *xiucai* were regarded as "anti-revolutionary and pedantic and they should be eliminated by the times". See "Provisions on the conversion of the public fields originally used by the clans to subsidize the students who took part in the imperial examinations to the school fees of the children studying in the clans", Sha County Archives, case file of 1938, vol. 156, p. 36. (Author's note)

7 Ke Ming, "Analysis of the Issue of the Gentry", *Chinese Peasants*, 10 (October 1926): 10.

8 (Australia) John Fitzgerald, *Awakening China: Politics, Culture and Class in the Nationalist Revolution*, trans. Li Gongzhong into Chinese (Beijing: SDX Joint Publishing Company, 2004), 249.

9 *Documents of Peasant Movement during the First Civil Revolutionary War* (Beijing: People's Publishing House, 1983), 276.

10 Gan Naiguang, "Why the County Magistrate of the Gentry's Civil Corps Opposed the Peasant Associations", *Chinese Peasants*, 10 (October 1926), 5–6.

11 Liang Qichao, "What Hunan Province Should Do", in *Selected Works of Liang Qichao*, ed. Li Huaxing, Wu Jiaxun (Shanghai: Shanghai People's Publishing House, 1984), 75.

12 Cai Shangsi, Fang Xing, *Complete Works of Tan Sitong* (revised and enlarged version, vol. 2) (Beijing: Zhonghua Book Company, 1981), 438.

13 Tan Sitong, "Preface by the Qunmeng Association", in *Complete Works of Tan Sitong* (revised and enlarged version, vol. 2), 430.

14 Liang Qichao, *The Record of Reform Movement of 1898* (vol. 8), *Reform Movement of 1898 (1)* ed. Association of Chinese Historians (Shanghai: Shanghai People's Publishing House, 1957), 300–301.

15 Tan Sitong, *The Third Institute of Governance, Empathy*, the 4th section of *Governance*, See Cai Shangsi, Fang Xing, *Complete Works of Tan Sitong* (revised and enlarged version, vol. 2), 437–438.

16 Wu Tianren, "The Transcript of Huang Gongdu", see *A Sequel of Modern Chinese History Series* (vol. 68), ed. Shen Yunlong (Taipei: Wenhai Publishing Company, 1979), 166.

17 Tan Sitong, note about the Officials' and Gentry's Discussion about the Department of Security, *Complete Works of Tan Sitong* (revised and enlarged version, vol. 2), 427.

18 Liang Qichao, *The Record of Reform Movement of 1898* (vol. 8), "Appendix II The Situation about Hunan and Guangdong", See *Reform Movement of 1898 (1)*, 302.

19 Tan Sitong, note about the Officials' and Gentry's Discussion about The Department of Security, *Complete Works of Tan Sitong* (revised and enlarged version, vol. 2), 426.

20 Liang Qichao, *The Record of Reform Movement of 1898* (vol. 8), "Appendix II The Situation about Hunan and Guangdong", See *Reform Movement of 1898 (1)*, 303.

21 Wu Tianren, "The Transcript of Huang Gongdu", see *A Sequel of Modern Chinese History Series* (vol. 68), Shen Yunlong, 147.

22 Xiong Xiling, The Fourth Bill for Dealing with Problems arising in Hunan, see Zhou Qiuguang, *Collected works of Xiong Xiling* (vol. 1) (Changsha: Hunan Education Publishing House, 1996), 349.

320   *Historical changes in rural power*

23 Qiu Tao, "Wang Xianqian's Annual Deeds from 1895 to 1899", *Documents of Modern History*, no. 96 (Beijing: China Social Sciences Press, 1999), 266.

24 Xiong Xiling said,

> when the school was built last year, Liang Zhuoru was recruited as a teacher. Zhang Yushan and Wang Yi were happy about this. In order to welcome Liang, Zhang and Wang decided to have actors perform operas in the Zengzhongxiang Ancestral Hall and also invited the gentry to join in them. They were very polite and considerate. However, Liang Zhuoru went back to Shanghai due to his illness in spring this year, and it was a pity that he had no chance to say goodbye to everyone. If Liang had stayed in Hunan, there would have been such a change.

This might be an explanation. See "A Memorial submitted to Chen Baojian about schools of political affairs" (July 15, 1898), Zhou Qiuguang, *Collected Works of Xiong Xiling* (vol. 1), 73.

25 Wang Mingke, "Historical Facts, Historical Memory and Historical Mind", *Historical Research*, 5 (2001): 139–141, 138.

26 Wang Mingke, "Historical Facts, Historical Memory and Historical Mind", *Historical Research*, 5 (2001): 139–141, 138.

27 Sun Dezhong, "Research on Social Memory Problems", *Philosophical Trends*, 3 (2003): 17.

28 Fei Zhengqing, Liu Guangjing, *The Cambridge History of China* (vol. 2) (Beijing: China Social Sciences Press, 1985), 390.

29 Zhang Pengyuan, *Early Progress Made in Hunan's Modernization* (Changsha: Yuelu Press, 2002), 153.

30 "A Memorial submitted by Cen Chunming, a commissioner in Hunan Province, about setting up the Institute of Autonomous Studies for implementing local autonomy", *Historical Documents about Preparation for Implementing Constitutionalism in the Late Qing Dynasty* (vol. 2), ed. Department of Ming and Qing Archives of the Palace Museum, 749–750.

31 Koetsu Fujiya, Rao Huaimin, *A Compilation of Historical Documents about the Rice Riot in Changsha* (Changsha: Yuelu Press, 2001), 44, 95.

32 Wang Xianming, "The Gentry Class and Civil Corps in the Late Qing Dynasty – The Causes and Historical Trend of Conflicts between the Gentry and Common People", *Modern Chinese History Studies*, 1 (200): 23, 30.

33 Wei Guangqi, Wei Guangqi, *Official Governance and Autonomy – China's County System in the First Half of the 20th Century*, 369.

34 Comment: "Does Destroying Schools Become a Common Practice?", *Oriental Magazine*, 1, no. 11 (November 1904): 78.

35 Comment: "Many Rebels Destroyed Schools", *Oriental Magazine*, 1, no. 9 (September 1904), 66.

36 Comment: "Does Destroying Schools Become a Common Practice?", *Oriental Magazine*, 1904, 1, no. 11: 78.

37 Ma Hongmo, *Selections of the Newspapers about People's Call, Appeal and Independence* (1) (Zhengzhou: Henan People's Publishing House, 1982), 188.

38 (America) Joseph W. Esherick, *Reform and Revolution in China – The 1911 Revolution in Hunan and Hubei*, 138–141.

39 "Records about Destroying Schools", *Education Magazine*, 2, no. 5, quoted from Yang Qifu, "Review of Villagers on Destroying Schools in the Period

Historical changes in rural power 321

of Implementing the New Deal of the Late Qing Dynasty", *Fujian Forum*, 5 (2002): 97.

40 Liu Dapeng, *Diaries Written in Tuixiang Study*, 158.

41 "Issue of Household Registration Survey", *Oriental Magazine*, 4, no. 4 (April 1907), 149, 151.

42 Zhang Zhenhe, Ding Yuanying, *Chronicle of Mass Uprisings in the Late Qing Dynasty, Documents of Modern History*, no. 49 (Beijing: China Social Sciences Press, 1982), 91–108.

43 "The Gentry Were Public Enemy"; See *Selected Works of Comments in the Ten Years before the Revolution of 1911* (vol. 3), ed. Zhang Zhan and Wang Renzhi, 303.

44 Ma Hongmo, *Selections of the Newspapers about People's Call, Appeal and Independence* (1), 188.

45 "Ye County of Henan Province sent the troops because people gathered in crowds", See *The Revolution of 1911* (vol. 3), ed. Association of Chinese Historians (Shanghai People's Publishing House, 1957), 435.

46 "Records of Turmoil in the Capital of Hunan", *Oriental Magazine*, 7, no. 5 and 6 (1910).

47 Koetsu Fujiya, Rao Huaimin, *A Compilation of Historical Documents about the Rice Riot in Changsha*, 286.

48 A memorial submitted by Governor Chen Kuilong, about the civil corps in Lai County and Hai County of Shandong Province, *Documents of Modern History of Shandong* (vol. 2), ed. Jinan Branch of Association of Chinese Historians, 49.

49 A memorial about Sun Baoqi's (the commissioner of Shandong Province) investigation of the civil corps in Lai County and Hai County according to the imperial edict, *Documents of Modern History of Shandong* (vol. 2), 53.

50 "The Record of the Great Events in China", *Oriental Magazine*, September 1910, 99–100.

51 Wei Guangqi, *Official Governance and Autonomy – China's County System in the First Half of the 20th Century*, 356, 357.

52 Ming Sun, "Discussion about Local Autonomy", S*elected Works of Comments in the Ten Years before the Revolution of 1911* (vol. 3), 413.

53 Comment: "Does Destroying Schools Become a Common Practice?", *Oriental Magazine*, November, 1904, 78.

54 "An Important Declaration of the Peasants' Association in Guangdong Province", see *Compilations of Historical Records of the Republic of China* (Series 4 (1)) ed. Chinese Second Historical Archives (Nanjing: Jiangsu Ancient Books Publishing House, 1991), 578.

55 Cai Meibiao, *General History of China* (vol. 12) (Beijing: People's Publishing House, 2007), 207.

56 Han Yanlong, *Modern Chinese Police History* (vol. 1) (Beijing: Social Sciences Academic Press, 2000), 177–178.

57 Chuzo Ichiko, "The Role of the Gentry: A Hypothesis", qtd. from Joseph W. Esherick, *Reform and Revolution in China – The 1911 Revolution in Hunan an Hubei*, 133–134.

58 "Records: Famine Hit Villagers in Zhexi", *Oriental Magazine*, September 1910, 220, 221.

59 "Records: The Event of Household Survey in Jiangxi", *Oriental Magazine*, September 1910, 222.

322 *Historical changes in rural power*

60 Wentian, "Villagers in Shunsui, Zhijiang Cause Troubles", *Oriental Magazine*, November 1910, 160.

61 Records: "A Sequel to the Record of Household Surveys in Jiangxi Province", *Oriental Magazine*, August 1909, 275.

62 Wentian, "The Record of the Great Events in China", *Oriental Magazine*, April 1910, p. 60.

63 Records: "Note of Villagers in Fengtai Affiliated to the Central Government Refusing to Pay Taxes", *Oriental Magazine*, October 1909, 349–350; Records: "A Riot of Villagers in Yuanzhou, Jiangxi", *Oriental Magazine*, October 1909, 365–367.

64 "The Recent Situation of a Riot Caused by Bandits", *Oriental Magazine*, July 1910; See *Chronicle of Mass Uprisings in the Late Qing Dynasty* (vol. 2), *Documents about Modern History*, 4 (1982), 103.

65 Feng Zhaoji, "Social Repercussions of Military Reform in the Late Qing Dynasty", *A Study on the Modern History of China Abroad* (vol. 22), 192.

66 *A Memoir of the Qing Dynasty* (vol. 60) (Beijing: Zhonghua Book Company, 1985), 661–662.

67 Association of Chinese Historians, *The Revolution of 1911* (vol. 3) (Shanghai: Shanghai People's Publishing House, 1957), 401.

68 Wentian, "The Record of the Great Events in China", *Oriental Magazine*, August 1910, 99–100.

69 Records: "A Civil Corps in Danyang", *Oriental Magazine*, August 1909, 270–272.

70 "A Field Investigation Report on the Incident of Laiyang Done by Shandong People Association in Modern Beijing", in which the gentry who controlled public power in local areas were called "evil gentry", see *Documents of Modern History of Shandong* (vol. 2), ed. Jinan Branch of Association of Chinese Historians, 5–27.

71 *Historical Documents about Preparation for Implementing Constitutionalism in the Late Qing Dynasty* (vol. 2), ed. the Department of Ming and Qing Archives of the Palace Museum, 757.

72 Tian Wenjing, Li Wei, *The Affairs of Prefectures and Counties in a Royal Edict·The Gentry* (Guangzhou: Yangcheng Publishing House, republished in 1873), 32.

73 Zhao Ruheng, *The Theory and Practice of Local Autonomy* (Shanghai: Huatong Publishing House, 1933), 17.

74 Opinion: "On the Gentry Power", *Ta Kung Pao*, June 2, 1907.

75 Gan Naiguang, "Why the County Magistrate of the Gentry's Civil Corps Opposed the Peasant Associations", *Chinese Peasants*, 10th issue, pp. 4–6.

76 Opinion: "On the Gentry Power", *Ta Kung Pao*, June 2, 1907.

77 Liang Qichao, A Theory of a Transitional Era, in *Selected Works of Liang Qichao*. ed. Li Huaxing, Wu Jiaxun (Shanghai: Shanghai People's Publishing House, 1984), 168.

78 Wang Xianming, *The Gentry of Modern times – The Destiny of a Feudal Class*, 59.

79 Tao Shu, "Details on the Situations in Various Regions of Jiangxi Province and on the Situations of Bandits", see *Selected Works of Tao Shu* (vol. 25), quoted from *Studies of the Officials, Gentry and Merchants in the Modern History of China*, ed. Zhang Kaiyuan et al., 388. As is indicated in Zhang Zhongli's study, the gentry shouldered the responsibility of promoting development of and protecting the interests of their own hometowns. In front of government officials, they spoke up for the interests of local areas. If their interests were opposite, the gentry would criticize, and even oppose or resist the government's administration. See *Chinese*

Gentry – A Study of Their Role in Chinese Society in the 19th Century, ed. Zhang Zhongli (Shanghai: Shanghai Academy of Social Sciences Press, 1991), 50, 51, 67. (Author's note)

80 Wang Xianming, "The Social Mobility of the Gentry Class in Modern China", *Historical Research*, 2 (1993): 94.

81 That is, a change in one system leads to a change in another system, and finally leads to a series of changes of the whole system. From the implementation of the New Deal in the late Qing dynasty to the abolishment of the imperial examination, local autonomy, the reform of the official system, the constitutional movement and even the end of the imperial system and the rise of republicanism, all of these constituted interrelated and interlocking reforms. (Author's note)

82 Wei Guangqi, *Official Governance and Autonomy* – China's County System in the First Half of the 20th Century, 360.

83 Wei Guangqi, *Official Governance and Autonomy – China's County System in the First Half of the 20th Century*, 360–361.

84 "Annals about Etiquette and Custom", in *Annals of Ba County* in the Republic of China, qtd. from Wei Guangqi, *Official Governance and Autonomy – China's County System in the First Half of the 20th Century*, 362.

85 Title: "Cities Which Could Put Local Autonomy into Trial", *Oriental Magazine*, September, 1906, 191.

86 Local Chronicle Compilation Committee of Hubei Province, *Chronicles of Hubei Province·Regime* (Wuhan: Hubei People's Press, 1996), 136; see (The Soviet Union) A.B. Bakulin, *The Record of Wuhan during the Great Revolution of China (note of the Great Revolution of China from 1925 to 1927)*, 32, 77.

87 Cong Hanxiang. *Villages in Hebei, Shandong and Henan Provinces in Modern Times* (Beijing: China Social Sciences Press, 1995), 58.

88 Wei Guangqi, *Official Governance and Autonomy – China's County System in the First Half of the 20th Century*, 364.

89 Literature and History of Song County (vol. 1), 20–21, see Wei Guangqi, *Official Governance and Autonomy – China's County System in the First Half of the 20th Century*, 381.

90 *Annals of Xiangtan County from 1871 to 1908*, "Table of Public Lands" (vol. 2), and "Chronicles of Rituals and Ceremonies" (vol. 7) (Chengwen Publishing House, 1970), 233–267, 581–582, 601. *A Sequel of Annals of Dazhi County from 1871 to 1908*, "Chronicles of Construction" (vol. 4), and "Chronicles of Schools" (vol. 5) (Taipei: Chengwen Publishing Company, 1970), 51, 86.

91 (Japan) Tadao Tanaka, *National Revolution and Rural Issues* (vol. 2), 9.

92 "Records of Members of Institute of Peasant Movement Who Attended the Class", see *Collection of Historical Documents of Guangdong Revolution from 1923 to 1926* (internal data) (Central Archives and Guangdong Provincial Archives, 1982), 230; Deng Yasheng, "Living Conditions of Peasants in Huang Mei", *Peasants Movement in Hubei Province*, 1st issue, 1927, 28–29.

93 Although the data indicates a distinction between "public land" and "community-owned land", both are "non-state-owned" and "non-private" land. In this sense, we can say that both belong to public lands. Liu Yongtai, "Issues of Public Property and Tribunals during the Period of National Revolution – A Comparison between the Peasant Movement of Hunan and Hubei Provinces and of Guangdong Province", in *Studies on Republican China*, ed. Center for the History of Republican China of Nanjing University, issue 5 (1999): 6, 7. (Author's note)

324 *Historical changes in rural power*

94 Emily M. Ahern, *Chinese Ritual and Politics* (Cambridge: Cambridge University Press, 1981), 77–92.

95 Liu Yongtai, "Issues of Public Property and Tribunals during the Period of National Revolution – A Comparison Between the Peasant Movement of Hunan and Hubei Provinces and of Guangdong Province", in *Studies on Republican China*, ed. Center for the History of Republican China of Nanjing University, issue 5 (1999), 7.

96 "Peasants in Hunan", *The Guide Weekly*, issue 181, 1905.

97 The Central Archives: *Compilation of Documents of the Second to Sixth National Congress of the Communist Party of China* (Beijing: People's Publishing House, 1981), 235.

98 Liu Yongtai, "Issues of Public Property and Tribunals during the Period of National Revolution – A Comparison Between the Peasant Movement of Hunan and Hubei Provinces and of Guangdong Province", in *Studies on Republican China* ed. Center for the History of Republican China of Nanjing University, issue 5, 7.

99 Zhang Youyi, *Data on Agricultural History of Modern China*, issue 2, 70.

100 *Note on an Investigation in Various Counties of Hunan Province* (vol. 2), 1931, 126, 135.

101 Liu Yongtai, "Issues of Public Property and Tribunals during the Period of National Revolution – A Comparison between the Peasant Movement of Hunan and Hubei Provinces and of Guangdong Province", in *Studies on Republican China*, ed. Center for the History of Republican China of Nanjing University, issue 5, 8.

102 Feng Zhaoji, "Social Repercussions of Military Reform in the Late Qing Dynasty", *A Study on the Modern History of China Abroad* (vol. 22), 180.

103 Wang Xianming, *The Gentry of Modern Times – The Destiny of a Feudal Class*, 303.

104 "Constitutional Compilation Bureau Examining the *Constitution on Local Self-Government in Cities, Towns and Villages* and Working out the Election Constitution", see *Historical Documents about Preparation for Implementing Constitutionalism in the Late Qing Dynasty* (vol. 2), ed. Department of Ming and Qing Archives of the Palace Museum, 728–729.

105 (America) Guy Salvatore Alitto, *The Last Confucian: Liang Shu-ming and the Chinese Dilemma of Modernity*, trans. Wang Zongyu, Ji Jianzhong into Chinese (Nanjing: Jiangsu People's Publishing, 2011), 229.

106 Feng Zhaoji, "Social Repercussions of Military Reform in the Late Qing Dynasty", *A Study on the Modern History of China Abroad* (vol. 22), 182.

107 "Summary of Shanxi's Achievements", see Zhou Qiuguang, *Collected Works of Xiong Xiling* (vol. 2), 1658.

108 Yu Zhongdi, "Life Issues and the Class of Scholar-Gentry", *China Youth*, 80 (May 1925) (Beijing: People's Publishing House, Photocopy in 1966), 443–444.

109 Chen Xulu, Hao Shengzhao, *Collected Works of Sun Yat-sen* (Shanghai: Shanghai People's Publishing House, 1990), 37.

110 Jifenzi: "On the Fear of the Powerful Gentry", *Ta Kung Pao*, December 20, 1909, (2nd ed.).

111 Xu Yubing, "The Investigation of Feudal Land Taxes in China", *Oriental Magazine*, May 1934, 64; "Summary of Shanxi's Achievements", see Zhou Qiuguang, *Collected Works of Xiong Xiling* (vol. 2), 1658.

Historical changes in rural power   325

112 Zhang Zhongli, *Chinese Gentry – A Study of Their Role in Chinese Society in the 19th Century*, trans. Li Rongchang (Shanghai: Shanghai Academy of Social Sciences Press, 1991), 1.

113 Wang Xianming, "Variation of the Constituent Elements of the Gentry and Rural Power – Take Northeast Shanxi and Central Shanxi in the 1930s and 1940s as an Example", *Modern Chinese History Studies*, 2 (2005): 252.

114 Wei Guangqi, *Official Governance and Autonomy – China's County System in the First Half of the 20th Century*, 360.

115 Wang Zaoshi, "Social Changes after China Establishing Connections with Western Countries", *Oriental Magazine*, January 1934, 31.

116 Yu Zhongdi, "Life Issues and the Class of Scholar-Gentry", *China Youth*, 80 (May 1925), 443–444.

117 Wu Han, Fei Xiaotong, *Imperial Power and Gentry Power* (Shanghai: Shanghai Bookstore, 1949), 128.

118 "The Gentry Students", *Ta Kung Pao*, January 6, 1909, 2nd ed.

119 Cui Jianying, "Academic Note of Xi Park", see *Documents of Modern History*, no. 57 (Beijing: China Social Sciences Press, 1985), 107.

120 "On the Gentry", see Xu Zaiping, Xu Ruifang, *40 Years of Historical Materials Declared at the End of the Qing Dynasty* (Xinhua Publishing House, 1988), 242.

121 Cui Jianying, "Academic Note of Xi Park", see *Documents of Modern History*, no. 57, 141.

122 Zhang Pengyuan, *Early Progress Made in Hunan's Modernization (1860–1916)*, 168.

123 Cui Jianying, "Academic Note of Xi Park", see *Documents of Modern History*, no. 57, 143.

124 *Selected Work of Luxun* (vol. 1) (People's Literature Publishing House, 1973), 415.

125 Jue Mi, "A Parody of Qualifications Used to Examine the Recruited Gentry", *Ta Kung Pao*, March 25, 1915, 14th ed.

126 Sima Wentao, Major Events of the Kuomintang and the Guangdong Peasants Movement (1924–1927) (Sequel 1), Editorial Group of Modern Historical Documents, Institute of Modern History of Chinese Academy of Social Sciences: *Documents about Modern History*, no. 96 (Beijing: China Social Sciences Press, 1999), 234.

127 See "Provisions on the conversion of the public fields originally used by the clans to subsidize the students who took part in the imperial examinations to the school fees of the children studying in the clans" (1938), Sha County Archives, file number 156/ 36. (Author's note)

128 "A memorial submitted to Yang Wending, who assumed office recently, for accusing the former commissioner Cen of being slack in his work", see Zhou Qiuguang, *Collected Works of Xiong Xiling* (vol. 1), 352.

129 Shi Jing, "The Successor of the Gentry", see Wu Han, Fei Xiaotong, *Imperial Power and Gentry Power* (Shanghai: Shanghai Bookstore Publishing House, 1991), 171.

130 Xiong Bin, *A Strategic Approach to Northern Hubei*, printed by Xiangyaodao Office, May 1924, collected by Hubei Annals Library, 29.

131 Department of Civil Affairs of Hubei Provincial Government, *An Overview of County Administration of Hubei Province·Introduction*, 1934, 10–11.

132 *An Overview of County Administration of Hubei Province*, "Zhijiang County", 1039.

326 *Historical changes in rural power*

133 Yi Suo, "Yellow Embroidered Ball", see A Ying, *Literature Series of Late Qing Dynasty* (vol. 1) (Beijing: Zhonghua Book Company, 1982), 168.
134 Yi Suo, "Yellow Embroidered Ball", see A Ying, *Literature Series of Late Qing Dynasty* (vol. 1) (Beijing: Zhonghua Book Company, 1982), 353.
135 Fei Xiaotong, *Chinese Gentry* (Beijing: China Social Sciences Press, 2006), 132.
136 Liu Yongtai, "Issues of Public Property and Tribunals during the Period of National Revolution – A Comparison Between the Peasant Movement of Hunan and Hubei Provinces and of Guangdong Province", in *Studies on Republican China*, ed. Center for the History of Republican China of Nanjing University, issue 5, 8.
137 Shen Jian, "The New Development of French History", *Historiography Quarterly*, 3 (2000): 81.
138 Zeng Jiwu, *Note on an Investigation in Various Counties of Hunan Province*, 1931, 23.
139 Sima Wentao, "Major Events of the Kuomintang and the Guangdong Peasants Movement (1924–1927)" (Sequel 2), Editorial Group of Modern Historical Documents, Institute of Modern History of Chinese Academy of Social Sciences: *Documents about Modern History*, no. 97 (China Social Sciences Press, 1999), 230.
140 "The 3rd District of Foshan City Was Destroyed by Scoundrels", *Guangzhou Republic Daily*, September 12, 1925, 11th ed.; "Investigation of the Demolition of Fengshun County Party Department", December 16, 11th ed.; "Yangjiang County Governor Beat up the County Party Branch Steward", January 5, 1926, 11th ed.
141 *An Almanac of Hunan Province*(6th ed.) "Politics", 1936, 113.
142 Ke Ming, "Analysis of the Issue of the Gentry", *Chinese Peasants*, issue 10, 11–12.
143 "Resolutions on Issues of County Administration", *Hankou Republic Daily*, March 23, 1927, qtd. from *Documents of Peasant Movement during the First Civil Revolutionary War*, edited by the People's Publishing House, 486.
144 (Japan) Tadao Tanaka, *National Revolution and Rural Issues*, 60.
145 "Announcement to National People at the Third Plenary Session of the Second Central Executive Committee of the Chinese Kuomintang", see (The Soviet Union) A.B. Bakulin, *The Record of Wuhan during the Great Revolution of China (Note of the Great Revolution of China from 1925 to 1927)*, 230.
146 "The True Situation of the Hunan Peasant Movement", *Guide Weekly*, June 1927, 2190.
147 Zeng Guicheng, "The Experience and Lessons the Party Learned from Leading the Peasant Movement in Hubei during the Revolutionary Period", *A Study of the History of the Communist Party*, 4 (1986); Liang Shangxian, "The Rise of the Kuomintang and the Guangdong Peasant Movement", *Modern Chinese History Studies*, 5 (1993).
148 Bu Yuan, "The Gentry Class Should Be Overthrown", *China Youth*, 5, no. 124 (June 1926), 667.
149 Shun Sheng, "Chinese Gentry:, *China Youth*, 1, no. 17 (February 1924), 5–6.
150 It is recorded in *Memory and Study* by Li Weihan that in his report, Mao Zedong "proposed the slogan 'Man with land were rich, and all gentry were evil', which was widely circulated for a time and was written on flags everywhere, thus exerting great influence". (Beijing: The Communist Party Historical Document Press, 1986), 103. (Author's note)

Historical changes in rural power   327

151 Halbwachs M., "Individual Consciousness and Collective Mind", *American Journal of Sociology*, 44, no. 6 (May 1939), 812–822.
152 "Collection of Materials for the Construction of the Political Power of the West Jin District Party Committee – Village Selection", File No. A22-1-4-1 (This article is collected in the Archives of Shanxi Province; the following is no longer noted).
153 "Xiping Government's Democratic Movement Organization and District Village Leadership", File No. A141-1-91-1.
154 "Zhaojiachuankou investigation materials (2) village regime", File No. A141-1-129-1.
155 Writing Group of Financial and Economic History of Jin-Sui Border Area, *Documents Compilation of the Financial and Economic History in the Jin-Sui Border Area* (General ed.) (Taiyuan: Shanxi People's Publishing House, 1986), 265.
156 *Documents Compilation of the Financial and Economic History in the Jin-Sui Border Area* (General ed.), 323.
157 "Huayuangou Village Regime and its Upper and Lower Leadership Relations", File No. A141-1-123-1.
158 *Documents Compilation of the Financial and Economic History in the Jin-Sui Border Area* (General ed.), 323.
159 "Seven Party Members of Renjiawan", File No. A141-1-119-2.
160 "Seven Party Members of Renjiawan", File No. A141-1-119-2.
161 The CPC Baode County Organization History Collection Office, *Organization History of Baode County of the CPC (Report)*, 1986, 4.
162 History Research Institute of Shanxi Province, *Selected Historical Materials of Shanxi Association of Sacrifice and National Salvation* (Taiyuan: Shanxi People's Publishing House, 1996), 419.
163 "The Regime Investigation of Ji Village of Tangjia", File No. A141-1-125-1.
164 "Materials about Zhongzhuang Mass Organizations", File No. A141-1-110-1.
165 Xu Yong, *Unbalanced Chinese Politics: A Comparison between Cities and Villages* (Beijing: China Radio Film and TV Press, 1992), 70.
166 Regarding village elections of 1941, see Han Zhenguo, "An Analysis on the Regime Structure of 'Village Selection' in the Early Anti-Japanese War", *Academic Bimestrie*, 1 (2005).
167 "Organs of the Regime", File No. A22-1-5-1.
168 "Huayuangou Village Regime and its Upper and Lower Leadership Relations", File No. A141-1-123-1.
169 "Huayuangou Village Regime and its Upper and Lower Leadership Relations", File No. A141-1-123-1.
170 "Renjiawan's Village Regime (attaching the political attitude of various classes)", File No. A141-1-114-2.
171 "Shanxi Provincial Administrative Office, Improve the Village Regime (1939)", File No. C1-39.
172 "Huayuangou Village Regime and its Upper and Lower Leadership Relations", File No. A141-1-123-1.
173 "Renjiawan's Village Regime (attaching the political attitude of various classes)", File No. A141-1-114-2.
174 "Materials about Zhongzhuang as a Natural Village", File No. A141-1-107-1.
175 "Village Regime of Liuye Village and Mass Organizations", File No. A22-1-20-2.

328　Historical changes in rural power

176 "Renjiawan's Village Regime (attaching the political attitude of various classes)", File No. A141-1-114-2.
177 "Renjiawan's Village Regime (attaching the political attitude of various classes)", File No. A141-1-114-2.
178 "Organization of Xiping Regime and Leadership in Districts and Villages", File No. A141-1-91-1.
179 "Investigation Materials of Gaojia Village in Xing County – Regime", File No. A22-1-15-1.
180 "Renjiawan's Village Regime (attaching the political attitude of various classes)", File No. A141-1-114-2.
181 "Investigation Materials of Gaojia Village in Xing County – Regime", File No. A22-1-15-1.
182 "Investigation Materials of Gaojia Village in Xing County – Regime", File No. A22-1-15-1.
183 *Selected Works of Mao Zedong* (vol. 3) (Beijing: People's Publishing House, 1991), 898.
184 (America) Mark Selden, *China in Revolution: The Yenan Way Revisited*, trans. Wei Xiaoming and Feng Chongyi into Chinese (Beijing: Social Sciences Academic Press, 2002), 248–249.
185 *Selected Works of Mao Zedong* (vol. 3), 931–932.
186 Zhang Guoxiang, *History of Anti-Japanese War in Shanxi* (vol. 2) (Taiyuan: Shanxi People's Publishing House, 1992), 480–481.
187 History Research Institute of Shanxi Province, *Shanxi Agricultural Cooperation* (Taiyuan: Shanxi People's Publishing House, 2001), 663.
188 Conditions for Being Elected as a Model Worker in 1943, *Anti-Japanese War Daily*, March 20, 1943, see Writing Group of Financial and Economic History of Jin-Sui Border Area and Shanxi Archives, *Documents Compilation of the Financial and Economic History in the Jin-Sui Border Area* (Taiyuan: Shanxi People's Publishing House, 1986), 161–162.
189 "Conditions for Being Elected as Labour Heroes, Combat Heroes, Militia Heroes and Model Workers in the Jin-Sui Border Region in 1944", *Anti-Japanese War Daily*, August 26, 1944.
190 Regarding the statistics of *Anti-Japanese War Daily*, January 9, 1945, and "Name List of Outstanding Personnel", January 10, 1945, see Wang Xianming, *The Gentry of the Changing Times – the Gentry and the Change of Rural Social Structure (1901–1945)* (Beijing: People's Publishing House, 2009), 431.
191 History Research Institute of Shanxi Province, *Construction of Regime in Jin-Sui Revolutionary Base Areas* (Taiyuan: Shanxi Ancient Books Press, 1998), 313.
192 History Research Institute of Shanxi Province, *Construction of Regime in Jin-Sui Revolutionary Base Areas*, 330.
193 Shen Yue, "Summary of Trial Selection in Six Administrative Villages in Xing County and How to Carry Out Universal Election Campaign in the Future", *Anti-Japanese War Daily*, May 17, 1945.
194 "The Election of Weijiatan Village in Xing County Ended, and Male and Female Models Were Elected", *Anti-Japanese War Daily*, May 9, 1945.
195 Administrative Office in the Jin-Sui Border Area, "The Summary of Village Election (in March, 1946)", File No. A89-1-20-4.

196 Administrative Office in the Jin-Sui Border Area, "The Summary of Village Election (in March, 1946)", File No. A89-1-20-4.
197 (America) Mark Selden, *China in Revolution: The Yenan Way Revisited*, 260.
198 "Investigation Materials of Sang'e Village Regime", File No. A141-1-110-3.
199 Administrative Office in the Jin-Sui Border Area, "The Summary of Village Election (in March, 1946)", File No. A89-1-20-4.

6 Rural crisis in the 1930s and countermeasures

The historical fact that cannot be ignored is that the "rural crisis" in the 1920s and 1930s was not only a problem of the rural society itself, nor a sudden phenomenon in this historical period, but also a result of the continuous accumulation of negative effects caused by the socially economic and political changes in the transformation from traditional to modern society under the impact of external forces in modern China.

Discussion on the rural crisis in the process of urban-rural deviation

The research on the rural crisis in modern China has been involved in the investigation of rural China in the 1920s and 1930s, but the disclosure of its nature and the discussion of the underlying causes is not in-depth, and is mostly limited to listing the factors.[1] Therefore, "it is difficult for us to integrate and analyze the rural societies they describe", "without sufficient contrast, it is difficult to find dynamic links and laws".[2] In recent years, many scholars have written about the "agricultural crisis" in the 1930s.[3] They believe that the underlying cause of the agricultural crisis was the decline in the overall level of agricultural productivity since modern times[4] or "it was greatly influenced by the economic crisis of capitalist world beginning in 1929"[5] and so on. But in general, it did not go beyond the scope of the factors discussed in the 1930s (except for the different focus or perspective).

It is important to emphasize that most of the previous discussion aimed at identifying specific cases, phenomena and their characteristics, and presenting them in a way that would help explain the causes and features of the rural crisis. However, there is no further research on the logical and causal relationship between specific cases, phenomena and characteristics. Worse still, some analyses of the particularities of rural crisis have been based on overgeneralizations of social crises since the start of the modern era, leading to the imperceptible dilemma that cause and effect were inversed, and presentation and essence were reversed. In modern China, where changes are intense and the development is extremely unbalanced, if the topic is not locked into a specific field or scope, in fact, a variety of cases and factors will be chosen at random to construct scholars' own interpretation. Obviously, this research path and interpretation are far from the historical facts and academic purpose. Therefore, it may be a feasible research path for understanding the rural crisis in modern China to limit the topic to a "controllable" category and construct a reasonable explanation system based on the inevitable connection between its cause and effect.

Analysis of the causes of rural crises

In the 1920s and 1930s, China's rural society was full of chaos and misery. "The rural political power was controlled by the gentry, or monopolized by the evil gentry. There was no possibility of improvement for peasants' economic condition, so they had to sink into poverty and ignorance".[6] The life of peasants lacked basic security. Since the era of the Republic of China, because of civil wars and the New Deal, the taxes on farmers had been far heavier than before. Therefore, there was a kind of extremely reactionary exclamation among the peasants: "it's better to live in the era of autocracy because the Republic of China has brought us too much pain".[7] Although this is a kind of extreme expression full of emotion, it reveals the resentment of farmers for social status. Someone in those days pointed out,

> Since the founding of the Republic of China, China's politics, economy, society, education and so on have turned into a mess. The ordinary people who are worried about the country are all anxious and shouting: "China's crisis is coming!" China's crisis does not lie in the nation's low morale, nor its people's lack of the virtues of etiquette, but originates from the gradually shaken foundation of the rural economy with a tendency toward bankruptcy. The political revolution in history involved many social or background factors, and it can be said that most of them are based on the rural economic bankruptcy.[8]

In terms of appearance, the rural crisis seems to be the basic condition or historical premise of the peasant uprising and rebellion in the traditional era. Previous researchers have reached a consensus on this view. "Fundamentally, the peasant uprising of the Taiping Heavenly Kingdom is a major outbreak of cyclical crises in traditional villages. It is rooted in the extreme poverty of the vast number of people under the aggravation of land annexation and taxation". "The inherently insurmountable contradictions in traditional Chinese land system is the root cause of the sluggish development of ancient Chinese society, which has made China linger for a long time in the cyclical crisis of chaos".[9] However, the rural crisis in the 1930s presented a more complex appearance and more characteristics of the times. "Agricultural China has begun to enter the era of industrialization and commercialization, so the plight of farmers is even greater than before".[10] People of the time call it rural collapse, agricultural panic, rural decay, agricultural bankruptcy and so on,

332 *Rural crisis in 1930s and countermeasures*

but that is just a summary of one aspect. In fact, the rural crisis at that time was a comprehensive crisis and a kind of "rural collapse".[11] It not only led to "all rural areas falling into danger" under the circumstances of a sharply ruptured economic foundation, the increasingly poor living conditions of people and misery beyond the subversion of a nation, but also raised "the severity of the rural problems to the highest level – an urgent state".[12] It was an overall crisis caused by political chaos, economic bankruptcy, social disorder and a cultural anomaly.

Judging from the signs of the rural crisis, people observed the current situation from different perspectives and thus had different views. At that time, there were several representative standpoints. Wu Juenong believed that the most visible examples of peasants' miserable life were seven kinds of phenomena: insufficient land allocation, peasant food panic, peasants living poverty, low peasant income, frequent disasters, urban industrial and commercial influence, and oppression by local capitalists.[13] Qian Yishi put forward that "China's rural areas have been sinking into the abyss of bankruptcy every day!" The signs of bankruptcy are as follows: First, the area of cultivated land gradually shrinks. Second, the number of self-cultivated farmers decreases, while the number of tenant farmers increases. Third, the price of agricultural products falls. Fourth, the rural finance dries up. Fifth, farmers leave their hometowns and flee from villages. Moreover, "the five signs of bankruptcy" with long-term historical characteristic "cannot disappear in a short time. Unless there is any great 'change', these five signs will probably remain for a period of time".[14] Dong Ruzhou put forward that "the current crisis in China is a shaking of the rural economic foundation", and the bankruptcy of the rural economy is mainly manifested by the gradual decline of peasant household registration (disasters, industrialization and urbanization), the increase of wasteland, the reduction of agricultural harvests, uneven land allocation, increased land rents, heavier land grants and taxes, the oppression of usury, and the suffering of farmers. "The average total annual income of current Chinese farmers rarely exceeds two hundred *yuan*. Most of them can get one hundred *yuan* or more, but few will receive only dozens of *yuan*".[15] Through the analysis of different appearances of the rural crisis, it is not difficult to identify their similarities: "They all think that China's rural economy will reach the final crisis of its collapse. The bankruptcy of rural China and the poverty of farmers are an ironclad facts".[16] Its most prominent manifestations are the fleeing of farmers, the decline of agriculture (or the desolation of farmland), and the bankruptcy of rural areas, which have caused the precarious situation of a "rural decline and economic slump".[17]

So what caused the outbreak of the rural crisis in China in the 1930s? Scholars have put forward various theories, and J. L. Buck, a professor at Jinling University who carried out a survey of China 's farm economy for many years, believed that it was mainly due to the small size of the farm area, weak productivity, dense population, excessive labor, shortage of farmers' savings, unprepared water conservancy, inconvenient transportation, less forest reserves and lack of credit organizations. Therefore, he advocated population control, fair land rent, improvement of transportation agencies, credit systems, agricultural technology, water conservancy and so forth. Wang Zhixin, a rural cooperation expert, believed that it was due to an adverse social impact, and he advocated that relief in rural areas should pay attention to the entire spectrum of rural social problems and start with rural autonomy problems. The economist Ma Yinchu believed that the main reason for the outbreak of rural crises in China was the backward family thought and large population. He advocated improving the thought of people and solving the population problem. Public education expert Gao Yang believed that it was because of a disruption in law and order, traffic obstruction, water conservancy in disrepair, opium cultivation, shortage of organizational ability, knowledge and skills, and morality. Therefore, he advocated starting with the maintenance of law and order, organization of traffic, water conservancy and refusal of opium income. The next step was to promote cooperative organizations, set up farmers' banks, popularize rural people's education, combine research and the extension of technical guidance, and enable intellectuals to guide farmers. Female leader Yu Qingtang believed that it was mainly due to 15 factors, including severe taxes, insufficient cultivated land, dense population, high interest rates, shortage of agricultural funds, bad agricultural tools, expensive wages, unfair sales, non-increasing sideline businesses, insufficient agricultural products, frequent disasters, oppression of local tyrants and the evil gentry, excessive superstition, inconvenience of transportation, shortage of educational opportunities and so on. It is advisable, in her opinion, to start with administrative affairs. In terms of common administrative affairs, she advocated abolishing all taxes, developing transportation and building water conservancy. For educational management, the government should focus on rural education, promote agriculture and implement labor education, which enables farmers to receive education and students to join the production activities. The intellectual class mostly worked in the countryside, and they paid attention to peasants' suffering, psychological communication, the introduction of scientific methods, the increase of production, improvement of peasants' lives and the ability of farmers' organization, and so on.[18] The reasons were numerous and various. The author has summarized them roughly into several categories, and found that the causes proposed by people at the time include the following aspects:

First, the cause of agricultural technology. It is mainly reflected in the following aspects: Stagnation of farming technology, frequent famines in previous generations (see Zhu Kezheng's statistics), and the tracking of peasant riots (see Xue Nongshan's *The History of Chinese Peasant Movement*) are chronic panic manifestations.[19]

> After analyzing the main causes of rural bankruptcy in our country, we find out that it is not only because the water conservancy is not yet flourishing, but also the land has not been cultivated well, which is also one of the important reasons.[20]

334 *Rural crisis in 1930s and countermeasures*

At the beginning of the crisis, "most people thought that the decline of agriculture was the direct cause of the current rural economic bankruptcy".[21] Rasiman, an expert on the League of Nations, also believes that

> the land is sufficient for farmers, instead of less land and more farmers, according to statistics of population and land in the whole country. Therefore, the problems of land management and operation are more urgent compared with that of land distribution.[22]

Among them, the "law of decreasing land remuneration" is also one of the most popular arguments, that is, "under certain technical conditions, more capital and labor invested cannot increase the benefits in proportion".[23] After the Kuomintang determined its capital would be in Nanjing, it also chose the "technical cause" to express its position, claiming that the backwardness of the economy "was due to the imperfection of China's production technology. After the opening of the sea embargo, China's economy encountered a great deal of resistance under the attack of external forces". It definitely stipulated the national government's basic plan for coping with the crisis, that is, the four guiding principles on the construction of the national economy: the best use of labor, the best use of land, the best use of goods, and the smooth logistics. "If our country can realize these four goals, then China will become a prosperous and powerful country".[24]

Second, the cause of the land system. It is believed that "rural areas tend to go bankrupt every day due to internal causes and external pressures", while the "existing land relation in China is the most important subjective condition of such a crisis, and at the same time the crisis has complicated the land problem in China".[25] Undoubtedly, land inequality and the tenancy system do not work alone, but have "close relations" with smallholder management, production technology, flood and drought disasters, miscellaneous taxes, war gangsters, and local tyrants and the evil gentry.[26] Therefore, "weak agricultural productivity and the fact that most farmers are often hungry because of insufficient production are the basic characteristics of China's chronic agricultural panic in recent years".[27] The main reason stems from land ownership and its tenancy system, that is, "the exploitation of tenancy, which can be regarded as one of the biggest sticking points in the destruction of rural areas in Jiangxi Province".[28]

Third, the cause of imperialist aggression. It is mainly reflected in the following viewpoints:

> Our country is based on agriculture, and farmers account for more than eight-tenths of the total population. The country's finance is also based on agricultural products. Since the Opium War, the imperialist aggression has continued to increase the bankruptcy in rural areas, which is an inevitable fact in the decline of the country.[29]

Rural crisis in 1930s and countermeasures 335

"Imperialist aggression in China affects the rural areas, which is an international factor in the collapse of the rural areas". The author has also verified from a comparison of foreign trade, such as "comparing the foreign trade over the past eight years from the 14th to the 21st of the Republic of China" (unit: a thousand maritime customs taels). It shows that "except for the 16th year of the Republic of China, the amount of trade deficit has been increasing year by year. By last year, the amount of exports had exceeded only half of that in the previous year, while the amount of trade deficit exceeded 556 million taels, breaking previous records".

> In the past few years, food and beverage products have accounted for 30 percent of imported goods, and the amount of raw materials in output products has been greatly reduced. The amount last year was less than half of that in the 14th year of the Republic of China. When the phenomenon existed in an agricultural country, how could rural areas avoid tending to collapse?[30]

Therefore, "the imperialists [...] control the major commercial ports along our coast through their agents to dominate and exploit our rural areas, which has led to the deformed phenomenon of urban expansion and rural depletion today".[31] Among them, the author's arguments are mainly based on "the invasion of mechanical products in the countryside instead of handmade products", "tariffs without autonomy, and the severe dumping policies of foreign surplus agricultural products, which have prevented domestic agricultural products from being sold".[32] "In fact, the first impetus for the collapse of China's rural economy was the imperialist economic aggression".[33]

Fourth, the cause of internal corruption. Some commentators have summarized the rural crisis as follows: "Unemployment and fleeing are both manifestations of farmers' losing their living means and the premise of rural turmoil". But the direct cause is that

> due to harsh and miscellaneous taxes, farmers flee from villages, which is the most obvious phenomenon. They donate land to others, but no one dares to accept it. No one wants to buy houses or furniture and so on, so poor farmers have to abandon the land and leave their hometowns. Meanwhile, another consequence of harsh and miscellaneous taxes has increased rural unemployment.[34]

According to the "external cause theory" based on the aggression of the great powers, some people believe that the main cause of "rural decline" is "corrosion and worm erosion".[35] Some commentators said, "Now we hear grumbling and complaints everywhere when visiting in the countryside. What they curse and hate is not the imperialists or local tyrants and evil gentry, but the government, officials and the army".[36] After the Revolution of 1911,

336 *Rural crisis in 1930s and countermeasures*

"China encounters challenges of politics in disarray, numerous soldiers and gangsters, heavy taxes, peaky and tired peasants, and strong desire of leaving villages. Rural bankruptcy has become a major and tragic phenomenon today".[37]

Although the above summary has limitations, it can basically reveal the main arguments of people of the time. Meanwhile, according to the outlines of subsequent academic studies, it is not difficult to find out that today's basic position of people's understanding and interpretation of the rural crisis is still included in the scope of the above arguments (a more universal proposition is to integrate the above elements to form a "comprehensive cause theory"[38]), especially affecting and guiding the opinion of the CCP scholars in the historical process at that time:

> As long as you are not blinded by the subjective interests of a certain social class and do not observe things with prejudice, it is impossible to neglect the true reason for China's rural economy and even the bankruptcy and decline of the entire national economy, that is, imperialist aggression and feudal exploitation. With this basic concept, it is not difficult to draw a conclusion that fighting against imperialist aggression and eradicating the feudal forces in the country is the main point to solve all social problems in China.[39]

However, the various aspects and causes of the above-mentioned "rural collapse" or "rural crisis" are actually descriptions or revelations of the social conditions of modern China. They construct a cognitive framework on the social nature, international status and characteristics of modern China at a macro level rather than put forward an absolute argument on the "rural crisis" itself. Therefore, the reasons or theoretical explanations at the macro level seem to be good (in principle), but they conceal the historical nature and the real cause in scientific rules (academically), which makes in-depth exploration of the problem remain at the level of general description.

The process of urban-rural deviation

The above-mentioned arguments, which seem reasonable, have failed in revealing the essence of the problem, or have not directly demonstrated the problem itself. The rural crisis is an unexpected, gathering, destructive and urgent crisis erupting in a specific time and conditions. In the general historical process, it is only a special problem in the entire historical process. It is a matter of timeliness and does not have the features of normality: In this sense, the crisis of peasants' uprising and riots caused by peasants' bankruptcy periodically in the traditional era is not a rural crisis but a social or political crisis. Therefore, if its particularity and specific causes cannot be revealed, then the discussion of the problem is essentially meaningless like itching in the boots.

Rural crisis in 1930s and countermeasures 337

First, whether it is agricultural technology, the land system, internal corruption, the view of a "combination of imperialist aggression and feudal exploitation" or other causes, they are actual explanations for the social crisis in modern China or the reasons for the backwardness of modern China. The rural crisis erupted in the 1930s, but the above factors formed or existed at least during the Opium War. The time can be tracked back even earlier as far as agricultural technology and land systems are concerned. "Since the prevalence of private land ownership in rural China, there has been a long-term collapse of land. The merger of land is extremely prevalent, and the disparity between the rich and the poor is also increasing day by day". The land system and the various regulations attached to it have always been a chronic illness in Chinese history. "It is certainly true in history and still true in all provinces now".[40] Therefore, the above-mentioned causes or aspects revealed may be an explanation path for a social crisis or the nature and status of modern Chinese society, but they cannot be an effective explanation for the rural crisis in the 1930s.

Second, modern China faced various crises after the Opium War, including a frontier crisis, anti-missionary riots and a war crisis. They were closely related to the political crisis and the social crisis of modern China, which caused modern China to suffer from both internal and external troubles. As a basic element, imperialist aggression was a problem that always existed since the Opium War, and the imperialist force or influence existed more prominently in commercial ports or metropolises. How did it become the direct cause of the rural crisis in the 1930s? Moreover, the triggering of the rural crisis has its own inherent rules and tendency, and it is not necessarily related to externally driven imperialist aggression (though it is not unrelated to modern China). Because in the course of the development of Western capitalism, the rural crisis or agricultural panic has not been avoided, "the process of rural bankruptcy in western Europe in the eighteenth century" was "a due product of the industrial revolution".[41] With the prosperity of industry and commerce, the result is a concentration of people in the city and the barren countryside. Therefore, the problem of food production emerged consequently in Britain, Germany, France and Japan. After the end of the European war, the Western "domestic politicians all advocated the movement of returning to agriculture" as the "spirit of the times",[42] and began to take measures in the countryside. In the process of industrialization, modernization and urbanization, rural crisis is still inevitable in Europe and the United States. In the United States, "from 1920 to October 1930, the price of American agricultural products fell by more than 40 percent, causing unprecedented agricultural panic".[43] According to a report by the US Central Bureau of Investigation in the 1920s,

> it has been proved that the rural youth entering universities even double that of in cities. In the past ten years, as many as over 1.5 million people have left the countryside according to the US Department of Agriculture.

338 *Rural crisis in 1930s and countermeasures*

> Those are all farmers from the countryside who run directly to the city, except for the people of the villages and towns.[44]

In the 1930s, the agricultural crisis in the United States continued to get worse. "The falling price of agricultural products has become increasingly radical since 1930, which indicates the situation worsens over time". Even in a disaster-free year, most farmers in the United States "cannot pay taxes on their annual income".[45] According to the statistical table of "farmers' net profits or losses" in the "statistics of agricultural bookkeeping" (World Association of Agricultural Affairs) of European countries, more than ten countries (Denmark, Switzerland, Austria, Czechoslovakia, Poland, Latvia, Estonia, Finland, Norway, Sweden) have different degrees of "continuous recession in agriculture" or "farmers' bankrupt".[46] Therefore, the argument based on the factor of "imperialist aggression" is not reasonable enough to explain the causes of rural crisis.

Third, the rural crisis is obviously not just a problem of declining agricultural productivity or harvests, because the Chinese villages at that time were trapped in a desperate situation in which a bad or good harvest would both bring disasters".[47] For example, logically, most farmers would celebrate with joy the big harvests throughout the country in 1932. But in fact, the result was opposite because the price of food was so low that farmers had exacerbated their poverty. In that year, many counties along the Yangtze River basin (like Jiangsu Province) had high yields, "which exceeded 5 to 20 percent of previous yields on average". "Between spring and summer, the price of japonica reaches thirteen to four *yuan* per *dan*, but it will fall to less ten *yuan* until the new grain grows. So far, the price has decreased to eight or nine *yuan*".[48] Therefore, the picture of

> "cheap grain and heart-broken farmers" is just a simple description of the peasants' life in the agricultural panic. At present, the sharply declining price of agricultural products in China is the result of this illusion. Meanwhile, the falling of agricultural products has become a basic sign of China's agricultural panic.[49]

Previous interpretations have failed to effectively explain the causes of the rural crisis and reveal the historical essence of this crisis. The rural crisis that broke out in the 1930s was not social crisis caused by the long-standing tension between people and land in the traditional era, the feudal landlords' land ownership, and the low efficiency and corruption of the government and bureaucrats under the autocratic system (it presents the survival crisis of farmers, which cannot be defined as the rural crisis). Compared with the traditional society, its historical essence and internal causes have specific characteristics of the times.

The modern rural crisis, in the final analysis, is a kind of crisis involving the rapid decline of rural society accompanied by the process of industrialization and urbanization. "As far as the evolution of human society is concerned, there are villages first and then cities, and cities are evolved from villages". However,

> cities, falling behind the countryside, have made considerable progress in cultural undertakings and activities due to the development of industry and commerce, convenient transportation, as well as the location of political institutions. In a densely populated area, the faster the progress of industrialization and urbanization, the higher the cultural standards and the better the material enjoyment. In rural areas, the relatively slow reform of agriculture and conservative society has caused a deficient material life and a monotonous spiritual life.[50]

Under the orientation of industrialization and modernization, there is no doubt that "the fundamental change in the industrial sector is the development of cities". Therefore, the rural crisis is a kind of crisis with a specific location corresponding to urban development or urban prosperity. "People in the rural areas are industrious in production all year round and fully supply the living expenses to the urban people until they are exhausted. As a result, cities are becoming more prosperous and rural areas are declining". "From the city to the countryside, the ties between agriculture, industry and commerce are cut off"; "the metropolis presents a morbid prosperity"; "the rural areas go bankrupt one after another".[51] Therefore, the epochal nature of the rural crisis is embodied in "the product of modern civilization", that is to say, "although rural problems change with the times and places, it cannot be denied that they are the product of modern civilization when we examine their essence". Because of the occurrence of rural problems, "it must be based on the development of national economy or international economy to a certain extent".[52]

> The rural crisis is not just economic bankruptcy but the decline of the rural society-culture as a whole. Although a large number of farmers "voluntarily leave the village, they cannot bear the economic distress and toilsome work".[53] "Unemployment" and "lost land" are also undoubtedly "the two fundamental problems" in rural China.[54] "The way that China's rural areas tend to collapse day by day can be felt by the anxious people who know even a little about the social situation". "The main source of diseases in China's rural areas is poverty", which leads to ignorance and weakness. Due to ignorance and weakness, the degree of poverty has increased, and then rural China is in a state of bankruptcy".[55] However, the appearance of "rural economic bankruptcy" presented by "poverty" is very serious, and it is only one aspect (or even the most basic aspect) of the problem, which cannot reveal the core content of the modern rural crisis. It is undeniable that the current rural problems in China include two important meanings: on the one hand, it is crucial to sense the tide of

340 *Rural crisis in 1930s and countermeasures*

modern rural problems to adapt to the world environment on the track of modern civilization for making preparations for diverse field construction. On the other hand, the maintenance of the traditionally agricultural management mode is necessary to protect small and medium-sized agriculture and preserve the spirit of the rural common society so as not to repeat the same mistakes as European and American capitalist countries do.[56]

Therefore, "the rural issue has become the most serious problems in China at present, and gradually turns into the overall goal and target of politics, economy and education".[57] In the process of institutional changes since modern times, although "political facilities are becoming more prosperous and rural systems are not established, but there is neither a basis for self-government nor measures for the implementation of policies".[58] The setting and construction of the rural political system is always backward and deficient so that life disorder and social chaos often appear in rural society more frequently. For example, in the Xingtai village of Hebei Province in the 1930s,

with the emergence of a bankrupt rural economy, declining industries and disturbing bandits in these days, the rural areas are in an unsettled state where bandits run across the countryside. They not only rob the wealthy villagers, but also the educational institutions. The robbing of the wealthy landowners and businessmen results in great destruction to the industrial sector.[59]

In addition, "eighty or ninety percent of Chinese farmers are illiterate, most of whom are in the countryside".[60] In recent times, for one thing, "rural schools in various places have not embarked on a proper track. China's rural education cultivates hooligans, tyrants, gentry and bandits". For another thing, "when it comes to rural education institutions, it is a great fortune to have even a small-size school. A large number of children are sent to private schools and entrusted to ignorant intellectuals. The teaching quality is inferior compared with urban education due to its disadvantages related to the learning environment. They offered courses that were no different from those offered in schools in the cities. But none of them taught students anything they really needed to know to live a productive life in the rural areas". Therefore, "the rural economy has fallen like a tide, and all social, political, and educational undertakings built on economy have collapsed".[61] Therefore, the rural crisis in modern times is not just an economic problem, but a problem of "extreme cultural imbalances" after "the destruction of the old social structure of China".[62]

It is true that the decline of China's rural areas is the decline of the whole society and the bankruptcy of China's rural areas is the bankruptcy of the whole society.

integral depression and bankruptcy in society. It is both a material and spiritual decline, as well as an economic and cultural bankruptcy. Economic and educational issues urgently need to be resolved, and other aspects or parts of the society have the same difficulties.[63]

Meanwhile, the rural crisis is the inevitable result of the collapse of the traditional development model of urban-rural integration. It is another negative effect of urban development and prosperity. "China's cities are currently in the ascendant, and urban culture is also developing rapidly. But the countryside is still isolated and desolate. This is the so-called abnormal development of Chinese society".[64] In the course of historical evolution,

Agriculture moves automatically or passively with the social-economic evolution, and its movement has a certain law. With the development of productivity, agriculture gradually separates industry from its internal development, causing urban prosperity and its opposition against rural areas; therefore, the historical driving force of society has transformed from the rural to the urban areas. The immature industry turned out to be a subordinate of agriculture, but agriculture later became its subsidiary. Through this affiliation, agriculture was continuously exploited by industry and lost its brilliance.[65]

Therefore,

in the developing process of Chinese cities, the countryside is not only trapped in desolation and depression, but collapsed at a further level. After the invasion of international capitalism, the industrial sectors in China have been changed. On the one hand, the forces of international capitalism have penetrated into the country. On the other hand, new types of industry and commerce have gradually developed. Under these circumstances, rural areas speed up the collapse from a desolate and isolated state. Thus, the urban and rural areas, one stepping forward and one backward, form a kind of deformation.[66]

However, in the traditional era, Chinese society-culture was integrated between the urban and rural areas. "All cultures are mostly from the countryside, but also for the countryside, including the legal system, etiquette, industry and commerce".[67] There are few differences between urban and rural buildings and other aspects of daily life.[68] Even the printing industry is integrated between the urban and rural areas.[69] As Fei Zhengqing, an American sinologist, says, until modern times, "China's privileged elite still tries to maintain a rural foundation close to the natural state. In the countryside, small traditions did not clearly separate values from the big traditions of urban elite".[70] Urban and rural cultures are integrated, and talents are always inseparable from the grass roots. As the old saying goes, the so-called "officials

342 *Rural crisis in 1930s and countermeasures*

originate from gentry and officials retire as gentry".[71] This summarizes the characteristics of the social-cultural integration model in traditional Chinese urban-rural society in a vivid and typical way.

However, in the process of modernization-oriented institutional changes, urban education gradually developed, and rural education fell far behind. With the construction of the "new learning" centered on cities, the educational system of China underwent significant changes. Jingshi University, high schools, specialized colleges, industrial colleges, normal colleges and so on, are all located in Beijing, provincial cities or other important cities. Secondary schools are located in the Fu (an administrative region covering major cities), Ting (similar to counties), and autonomous prefectures, and even primary schools are located in prefectures and counties. Rural schools account for only 10 percent of the total number of schools nationwide.[72] Even nearly 80 percent of agricultural schools serving rural communities are located in urban areas.[73] Taking 1931 as an example, there were a total of 103 junior colleges and universities nationwide, including 22 in Shanghai, 15 in Peking, and 8 in Guangdong. The universities in these three cities alone accounted for 44 percent of the total number. There were a total of 75 universities and independent colleges across the country, and most of them were built in big cities, including 12 in Peking, 16 in Shanghai, 6 in Guangzhou, and 5 in Tianjin, accounting for more than half of the total.[74] In terms of student numbers, there were 27,506 college students in six cities, which were Peking, Nanjing, Shanghai, Guangzhou, Hangzhou, and Wuchang, accounting for about four-fifths of the total number. The phenomenon of university education being concentrated in a few large cities is truly surprising.[75] In the late Qing dynasty and the early Republic of China, there were about 100,000 villages and 1 million rural communities in China.[76] Based on this calculation, there were 178,847 primary and secondary schools nationwide in 1922, with an average of one school in every six villages. In 1931, there were 262,889 primary and secondary schools nationwide, with an average of one school in every four villages.[77] Taking Hebei Province as an example, by 1928, about one-fourth of the villages still had no primary schools, and the figure in some counties even reached over 70 percent. As a result, a reversed flow of talents in rural and urban areas appeared. "The visionary men in the villages were constantly running toward the cities; those in the counties toward the provincial capitals, and those in other provinces toward the capital and commerce and trade ports".[78] "And the flow is increasingly becoming a one-way migration".[79] As a result, modern cities, which gradually became new-style education, wealth, industrial and commercial centers, and absolute political centers, progressively formed dominant advantages over the countryside. The integration model of social culture in urban and rural areas in the traditional Chinese era has been cracked. "Most educators only know urban education, and had no understanding of rural education".[80] The historical accumulation of urban and rural divergent development since modern times has

Rural crisis in 1930s and countermeasures 343

become the deep cause of the rural crisis. For modern Chinese villages, the direct consequences are obvious:

First,

> as for the development of the industry, of course, it also caused the acceleration of the rural collapse. The cash in the countryside was sent directly by the local tyrants and landlords to the factories or banks in the cities, or collected by the bureaucratic warlords and indirectly sent to the factories or banks in the cities, which robbed almost all the wealth in rural areas. This is one way to accelerate the collapse of the areas. In addition, farmers gradually moved from villages to cities after a number of factories in the cities had been built day by day. Over time, the rural population had decreased. This was another factor leading to the collapse of rural areas. At the same time, though many people in the rural areas rushed to factories in the cities, the signs of destruction in the countryside revealed an increasing number of people in idleness rather than a decreasing number in agriculture. This is a strange phenomenon in China. China's developed factories cannot absorb the surplus population in the countryside, but turn the people who were engaged in farming into surplus people.

"The most difficult problem in modern China is that there is almost no accommodating ability for the surplus rural population".[81]

After rich rural households and their capital flowed into the city unidirectionally,

> the most obvious result of the decline in rural areas was the outflow of silver coins in the mainland. Farmers had barren lands or low-price farm products, which led to a decrease in income. It is necessary to get products from the market due to the limited output. Rich rural households either migrated to cities because of numerous bandits or refused to invest in farming due to the failure of a good harvest. Therefore, rural savings gradually flowed into cities. This led to a great trade deficit and cash concentration between villages and towns, towns and cities, and cities and commercial metropolises.

this resulted in a continuous "financial concentration of cities, indicating indirectly the state of rural financial depletion". As a result, "the depletion of the rural economy has reached its peak".[82] Moreover,

> warlords just understood the trend and marched toward cities from villages. In recent decades, people in the villages have become poorer day by day, while those in the cities have become richer every day. This is the reason why the warlords now have to seize cities and even to occupy ports.

344 *Rural crisis in 1930s and countermeasures*

The collapsing villages provide the landlords with land rents and a surplus labor force; the developing cities offer taxes and loans to the warlords. In the process of rural collapse and urban prosperity, the warlords are getting mature and flourishing naturally.[83]

Second, the inherent strength and norms that sustain the rural society and culture have been shaken. As people of the time said, "it is another question to judge whether China's feudal society is good or bad. However, there is an influential group maintaining social order in the society, which is not easy to shake. That is the tradition of respecting the aged and the wise. The oldest person in a village can be a gentry who judges the right and wrong words and behaviors in the community. He can also direct everything and everyone must obey his orders. In addition to the condition of being the oldest, if someone has academic achievements, he can also be a gentry and has the right to be a local leader". In the process of institutional changes since modern times, "if it is urgent to abolish a system, we must have a better new system to replace it, but we have never had such a system". "Even though the old system was shaken, a new system was not created, leading to turbulence in the society. Now the facts had told us about the result that the new gentry replaced the old gentry, namely, the new gentry were neither famous sages nor experienced elders. They were unable to win everyone's trust and act as pillars in the society. It is so-called seeing its harms before benefits".[84]

Third, social inequality is very serious between urban and rural areas, and it continues to develop. Fu Baochen said emotionally,

> One day, I happened to chat with a foreign friend. He said, "the restlessness of Chinese society is due to three inequalities: One is that the rich take advantage everywhere, and those who have no money suffer everywhere; the second inequality is city dwellers always get benefits, and the rural people often get into trouble; the third inequality is that men are superior and women are lagging behind".[85]

The "three inequalities" distinguishing urban areas from rural areas represent a social problem that has only gradually formed since modern times, and its characteristics of the times are very obvious.

> The abnormal development of urban and rural areas is related to the imbalance in cultural standards and affects the progress of the whole country. From the perspective of equal opportunity, equal enjoyment, and democratic politics, this phenomenon should not exist. Rural life must be improved, and the rural society must be transformed. This is the only way that all parties will agree to adjust this abnormal phenomenon.[86]

From the perspective of the historical process in modern times, the rural crisis is not actually a crisis of the village itself. Rather, it is a crisis of the

Rural crisis in 1930s and countermeasures 345

overall decline of rural society, economy and culture caused by the deviating development of urban and rural areas in modern times.

> The opposite of urban development is the collapse of the rural areas. The facts that accelerate the collapse of the rural areas are also the facts that make the cities develop. China's urban development in recent decades has definitely destroyed rural areas. The acceleration of collapse has contributed to the development of the city, and that is an undeniable fact in the past few decades.[87]

Therefore, it is impossible to discover the historical nature of the rural crisis in modern times without revealing the contradictions in the evolution of "urban-rural deviation" in modern industrialization, urbanization and in modernization.

The epochal characteristics of the rural crisis

The rural crisis occurring in the 1930s had its unique epochal characteristics, and its features of a "developing crisis" were prominent. It was a historical process in which rural society had become marginalized, impoverished and disordered following the cracking of the traditionally developing mode of urban-rural integration caused by the process of industrialization, urbanization and modernization.

> The abnormal development of the cities like Tianjin in the north, Shanghai in the middle, Guangzhou in the south, and Hankou in the middle, and so on, attracts rural labor who are concentrated in the city, resulting in a shortage of talents in the rural areas.[88]

The so-called developing crisis was not only a crisis in the development of "urban-rural deviation", that is, "rural destruction and urban development, which run counter to each other. It is a way of social changes in modern China",[89] which also presents the decline of rural society in the process of "modernization". The so-called "inevitable trend of rural development due to the industrial revolution and development of industry and commerce"[90] indicates that it is a companion of the developing process of modernization. "The prosperity of North China has been presented in Beijing and Tianjin. In recent years, the political center has changed and residents have moved southward. Therefore, the falling price of daily items has become a common phenomenon".[91] The "developing crisis" is complex and diverse, and full of contradictions and conflicts. It is difficult to illustrate all the features in this book, but a few of them can reflect the general characteristics.

First, the historical development guided by industrialization, urbanization and modernization in modern times is generally based on the sacrificing of the rural areas. "In modern history, the thriving of new industries and cities

346 *Rural crisis in 1930s and countermeasures*

everywhere is at the expense of rural labor".[92] To some extent, the causes and consequences of the rural crisis depend on the progress and speed of development. "This kind of development is governed by its own characteristics, which will make the exploitation on the peasants even stronger. It also causes the contradiction between cities and villages to get more complex".[93] At the other end of "the pathology of prosperity in metropolises" is "the continuous bankruptcy in villages". "As a result, cities have become more prosperous and villages have been declining".[94] Consequently, "the prosperity of urban areas shows a new sign of rural bankruptcy".[95] For example, in Guangxi and Zhejiang provinces, "the construction of highways and aviation has made rapid progress in recent years, but its benefits to peasants' life are still questionable. An executive director in Guangxi Province made comments on the 'negative effect for farmers' in terms of road construction through the compulsive buying of lands. In 1934, an airport was built in Banrong County, Jiangdong Region, Zhuji City, Zhejiang Province. "The most fertile land in Banrong was enclosed and confiscated and no farming was allowed". "Over three thousand farmers went bankrupt since then and asked for justice everywhere in tears".[96] No wonder people have deep worries: "when the phenomenon exists in agricultural countries, how can we stop rural areas from collapsing?"[97]

The factor leading to the prosperity of cities also "attracts funds and farmers from rural areas into the urban areas, which imposes direct destruction on villages. As is the case with bank capital, this has gradually taken shape in recent years. Cash circulating in the rural areas gradually is transferred to banks, and then from banks to the business sector. As a result, the business sector shows positive signs, but the rural areas show low morale. In short, the fact is that China's urban development in recent decades has precisely destroyed the countryside. The acceleration of collapse in rural areas has contributed to the development of cities".[98] The depletion of rural finance, which is a major symptom of the rural crisis, is not actually a crisis of finance itself, but a phenomenon that has emerged along with the development of modern financial industries. For example, the banks, of which "12 banks were set up in 1928, 6 banks in 1929, 11 banks in 1930, and 11 banks in 1931", presented their degrees of development. That is, "the expansion of urban finance" not only depended on the development of the banking business and an increase in profitability, but also on the rise in land prices in Shanghai". From 1926 to 1930, "the increase in the value of real estate in Shanghai in five years was 2 billion taels of silver, which included the half profits in 1930". Especially after the September 18th Incident, in the process of accelerating the collapse of China's rural areas, "those with a certain amount of assets in the countryside moved to metropolises, which caused the abnormal development of surplus the urban financial and rural financial deficit. This trend is sufficient to prove that urban expansion is resulting from "the intensity of rural bankruptcy".[99] "The facts in the past few decades have proved it".[100] This is a basic trend in historical evolution since modern times.

Second, a "developing crisis", a kind of location crisis concentrated in the countryside, is also reflected in changes in social structure or social stratification, and disturbs the population change between urban and rural areas.

> Peasants must leave villages and migrate to cities. The rich still enjoy their comfortable lives, while the poor are turned into factory workers. As a result of the destruction of rural organizations, the national foundation is gradually shaken. [...] Rural bankruptcy today is becoming increasingly fierce,[101]

but the other side is "the progress of industry and commerce and urban development".[102] Correspondingly, the changes in the social hierarchical structure are also obvious. "On the one hand, the old landowners were falling, and on the other hand, the new landlords emerged. These new landlords include soldiers and officials with a strong political background or businessmen who have a close relationship with urban capital".[103] Therefore, although the deprivation suffered by farmers is directly related to the landlords, it is more prominently reflected in the urban-rural location differences, that is, the strong oppression of commercial capital or usury capital in cities (or with urban background).

> The decline of the sideline industries in rural areas can directly drive small-scale peasants into a hopeless situation. With the invasion of commercial capitals and usury capitals in the rural areas, all agricultural products are involved in the vortex of commodities, and farmers are gradually getting poorer.[104]

As a result, people even thought that "the enemies of the peasants at this stage are industrialists and businessmen". Because of the general trend of the times, "the industrial economy has great pressure on the agricultural economy in most countries".[105] Poor peasants in modern China

> not only suffered from low-price exploitation, but also they were almost plundered by commercial capitalists compulsively. [...] When the owners sold their properties or products at half price, it was inevitable they would lose more profits and go enter the path of bankruptcy.[106]

Third, the price gap between the rural and urban areas formed by the development of industrialization and urbanization was also a direct factor in accelerating the rural crisis. "In general, the rise in the price of industrial products has always been faster than that of agricultural products; hence, the price gap between the them has taken shape". With the advancement of the modernization process in recent times, villages as a whole, suffering from "the increasing prices, are still the victim of the urban economy". Facing rising prices, "the only way for farmers to defend their interests is to automatically

348 *Rural crisis in 1930s and countermeasures*

reduce their purchasing power. If farmers are stubborn about their original consumption, they will certainly go bankrupt". In Chongqing, from 1939 to 1940, "when agricultural products doubled in price, industrial products tripled or quadrupled in price. The same situation is also found in Chengdu". Businessmen "used abundant funds, diverse business technology, and favorable conditions such as market intelligence to absorb agricultural products in large quantities and hoard them for high prices".[107] In this regard, the inevitability of the trend had universal significance rather than being a consequence of modern Chinese history. At that time, the Western world was also in the predicament of the agricultural crisis.

> From 1932 to 1933, although the recession had reached the fourth year, agriculture was still at the top of the difficulties without any improvement. The problem of farmers in the world had focused on the fundamental problem of price. [...] The prices of major agricultural products fell continuously in the middle of 1932.[108]

As shown in Table 6.1.

"The focus of price problems on agricultural products is actually an imbalance between the price changes of industrial products and agricultural products. It is the reason why farmers are trapped into an unprecedented tragedy". "If the situation was same in industry, the products of the workshop like foodstuffs and various raw materials would also lower prices. Then the purchasing power and economic status of farmers might not fall to the present level".[109]

Because modern China was in the special historical stage of "semicolonial", this world crisis was only manifested as an "agricultural crisis" (economic level) in the West, while in China it was manifested as a wider and deeper rural crisis (comprehensive crisis). Meanwhile, facing the predicament of an economic crisis, Western countries could transfer the crisis to China through the advantages of dumping commodities. "In the last three decades, major grains like rice, wheat and flour have begun to be imported into China in large quantities".[110] However, China could only passively suffer the impact from the international market so that China's falling prices in agricultural products never ceased since 1931 under the impact of foreign agricultural dumping".[111]

Deep causes of the rural crisis

In addition, "universal poverty" was also one of the characteristics of the Chinese rural crisis in the 1930s. This rural crisis caused by the development of "urban and rural deviation" is completely different from the characteristics of "polarization" formed by the concentration of land or wealth in traditional society, and presents a unique evolution process of "universal poverty". According to a survey by the Beijing Ministry of Agriculture and Commerce, from 1914 to 1918, the number of farmers decreased by 15.64 million with

Table 6.1 Falling prices in Canadian and US agricultural products

Canada	Price Comparison	1926	1931	1932	America	Price Comparison	1926	1931	1932
	Crops	100	56.3	48.3		Crops	100	64.8	48.2
	Daily Necessities	100	80.0	78.8		Industrial Products	100	73.0	68.4
	General Wholesale Prices	100	72.1	75.7		General Wholesale Prices	100	71.1	64.9

Source: *Food Policies of Countries in the World*, ed. Grain Bureau of Japan's Ministry of Agriculture and Forestry, 33.

350 *Rural crisis in 1930s and countermeasures*

an average annual decrease of 4 million. The cultivated land decreased by 26387 million *mu*, and the wasteland increased by 497.37 million *mu*.[112] Obviously, "class differentiation" (that is, the evolutionary trend oriented by the concentration of land or wealth) cannot offer an effective and reasonable explanation between the facts of "decreasing farmers", "reducing arable lands" and "increasing wastelands".

> In a country with a severe shortage of cultivated land, the sadness of "more vacant lands by numerous people", "investing on lands by fewer people", and "increasing supply of land and decreasing demands" shows that the agricultural crisis at that time was already serious.[113]

In *Rural overview of Lincheng County in Hebei Province*, the author described the situation in 1934: "the distribution of farmlands had no extreme disparity in Lincheng, so there was no formation of landlords except for the difference between rich farmers and poor farmers". The crisis did not stem from the polarization of land concentration because the land purchase tends to be "vacant even though it was inexpensive or almost free in recent days".[114] Xu Shilian's research also shows that during 1926, the average annual minimum living costs of Chinese families (five persons) were about 125 to 150 *yuan*. Based on this figure, the poor in China accounted for 30.7 percent. Another statistic (Roche York, that is York)

> speculates that the total number of poor people in China (including the extremely poor and the poorest) accounted for 50 percent of the population. In other words, the incomes of half of China's population were below the minimum living standard every year.[115]

Zhu Qihua's statistics on the economic conditions of the population in the 1930s showed that the population below the poverty line accounted for 93.7 percent (including the urban population). "All the provinces in the country are struggling with the fate of total collapse. No province can be a little easier (for all provinces, the division of differences has been eliminated)".[116] This undoubtedly shows a picture of severely "universal poverty" in rural China around the 1930s, rather than "polarization" in the general sense.

In 1935, Yan Xishan also stated in his documents submitted to the national government: "the Shanxi rural economy has been totally bankrupted in the past years, which leads to 90 percent of villages trapped in poverty and the same proportion in rural households".[117] The squire Liu Dapeng also recorded in his diary the decline of the rural depression in Jinzhong city of Shanxi Province in the 1930s. He said,

> in the past, there were many wealthy households in the village with a total of 2,000 households and magnificent buildings. At present, the village is in great depression and there are only hundreds of households. Most

Rural crisis in 1930s and countermeasures   351

villagers are poor, and 80 or 90 percent of those sell houses and properties for living. No rich farmers live there.[118]

"Everyone sighed for their poverty".[119] "The term 'farmhouse bankruptcy' is a new term now, which means that a farmer fails to protect his assets. On this occasion, farmers' poverty and financial crisis have reached their extremes, which causes slack agriculture and worse living standards". What's worth noticing is that, as Liu sighed, "those who are going bankrupt will become poorer if no one buys their properties".[120] The phenomenon of "the unwanted properties" shows that it is not the concentration of "wealth transfer" presented by "polarization", but a decline in the overall sense. The overall decline of "universal poverty" and "polarization" are completely different evolutionary trends.[121]

But that does not mean that Chinese rural areas in the 1930s did not have a "survival crisis" based on the contradictions between man and land and class differentiation in the traditional era. In fact, people of the time also recognized it from different perspectives: "political revolutions in history were involved in social background, and it can be said that most of them were based on the bankruptcy of the rural economy".[122] The frequent occurrence of peasants' survival crises in the traditional era and its inherent relation to the periodical turbulence of Chinese history constitute a structural problem in the traditional Chinese society. In a sense, it is "an original problem since ancient times, but a more typical one in these days".[123] It is not a product of modern times, nor does it have the characteristics of the times in the modern sense. However, the rural crisis in the 1930s was completely different. It was a holistic crisis in which the survival crisis and the developing crisis coexisted and co-constructed; even under a certain condition, a "'developing crisis' had been passed on and gradually aggravated the survival crisis of the rural people. It caused endless and ever-increasing civil changes in rural society". In the face of the epochal rural crisis, the exploration of various solutions also surpassed the traditional mode of thinking and underwent changes with the character of the times.[124]

The interweaving and isomorphism of the survival crisis and the developing crisis made the occurrence and impact of China's rural crisis in the 1930s lasting and far-reaching. Later generations felt a dreadful pain when recalling China's rural crisis in the 1930s:

China's rural economy has completely collapsed. From the perspective of farmers, the number of self-cultivated farmers is decreasing and the number of tenant farmers is increasing. Thus, more farmers are leaving villages. With regard to cultivated lands, disasters such as flooding, draught, military destruction, opium planting, yearly increasing wastelands and so on, coupled with the falling price of agricultural products over the years and the shrunken market, have promoted the collapse of the rural economy. The collapse of the rural economy seems to be endless. It is related to the

352 *Rural crisis in 1930s and countermeasures*

entire spectrum of political, economic and social issues in the country, and farmers are not the only group that have suffered the great pain.[125]

Therefore, the analysis of the rural crisis became the responsibility of academia or society. As far as the background of the world economic crisis was concerned, the rural crisis in China was obviously not an isolated phenomenon. Therefore, it is necessary to interpret it in terms of the trends of the world economic crisis or the trends of imperialist aggression. However, on the one hand, China's rural crisis was not just the "Chinese manifestation" of the world economic crisis. On the other hand, the reason why this kind of world economic crisis was more concentrated and extensively reflected in the rural areas (there was no so-called urban crisis), can be certainly enumerated from multiple angles and levels for proof, but that explanation ignores the revelation of the inherent characteristics and characteristics of the times of the rural crisis.

Therefore, through an analysis of various complex aspects and factors, it can be found that the reason why the rural crisis occurred in the 1930s was due to a deep cause of its historical accumulation, that is, the historical process of urban-rural deviation since modern times, because there is a historical correlation between the rural crisis and the historical process of industrialization and urbanization.

Traditional Chinese society is full of social crises and social turmoil, as well as corresponding political crises, but they have not been concentrated in rural society with its geographical characteristics. "From the perspective of the coordinated exchange between urban and rural areas in the past, China is a model of stability. The problem of a sharp division between urban and rural areas has not become very obvious". Therefore, "Chinese cities cannot be attractive to both the poor and the rich like magnets. Cities differ from villages in only a few respects".[126] From 1912 to "the early 1920s, China's national bourgeoisie was at full capacity and cultivated a new generation of entrepreneurs engaged in industrial production and wage employment".[127] With the advancement of urbanization,

the growth of modern enterprises in coastal cities is just one aspect of the prosperous development of enterprises. It is undoubtedly the most significant aspect. From 1912 to 1920, the growth rate of China's modern industry reached 13.8 percent.[128]

The proportion of modern industry in the total output value of industry and agriculture also changed significantly "from 4.9 percent in 1920 to 10.8 percent in 1936".[129] It was "when the 'golden age' of Chinese national industry and commerce came", that "accelerated urbanization came with economic prosperity. The annual growth rate of the urban population has greatly exceeded the total population growth rate".[130] This reflects

Rural crisis in 1930s and countermeasures 353

an epochal development. During the nineteenth century, the total urban population in China grew at a very slow rate. Its growth rate was roughly the same as the growth rate of China's total population. However, from 1900 to 1938, the urban population growth clearly accelerate with the rate almost doubling that of the total population. In particular, the high growth appeared in the six largest cities in China: Shanghai, Beijing, Tianjin, Guangzhou, Nanjing, and Hankou, and "in the 1930s, the population growth rate was 2 percent–7 percent per year".[131] In the late 1930s, cities with a population of 1 million to 2 million increased by 33 percent; cities with a population of 100,000 to 500,000 increased by 61 percent, and cities with a population of 50,000 to 100,000 increased by 35 percent.[132] It can be said that "after 1900, the rise of urban factories and the proletariat in the European sense created such a movement", that is, "the movement of rural poor families toward the core area".[133] The reverse moving process, which had lasted for 30 years, was actually the accumulation process of the energy explosion of the rural crisis.

However, the development of modernity led to the reversal of the urban-rural integration process in the traditional era. With the trends of industrialization, urbanization and modernization, China's "urban-rural deviation" trend took place gradually.

The development of this situation extended the gap between urban gentry and businessmen and the dominant social celebrities. At the same time, it also widened the gap between urban and rural areas, forcing rural areas to provide funds for various urban undertakings. Taking Jinan City as an example, the cost of maintaining a police force responsible for health, public transportation, law and order, and firefighting came from provincial revenues and urban taxes. The two revenue sources were almost equal in amount.

By the end of 1928, "the modern economic sectors had experienced a new period of prosperity again".[134] That is to say, by the 1930s, with the development of modern China's industrialization, urbanization and modernization, the negative effects of the "deviation between urban and rural areas" had become very prominent.

The profound contradiction caused by the development of "urban-rural deviation" was not only manifested between the metropolises and the villages, but also presented an acute tendency in counties. A typical example was the situation of division, conflicts and change between "urban gentry" and "rural gentry" in Wenshui County, Shanxi Province, in the 1930s.[135] Zeng Yaorong's research also showed that the Yongding Riot in western Fujian in 1928 was "essentially a concentrated reflection of the urban-rural opposition caused by the development and change of modern urban-rural relations". "Its occurrence reveals the fierce resistance of the rural areas and farmers to modern cities".[136] Therefore, this kind of urban-rural contradiction and conflict can be described as omnipresent and sharp.

354 *Rural crisis in 1930s and countermeasures*

The aforementioned is the reason of the era that fundamentally determines the sharp decline in the status of rural areas, agriculture and peasants.

> In ancient times, the Chinese people valued agriculture rather than industry and commerce, so the status of peasants was high and the lives of peasants were also comfortable. However, in later years, with the development of commerce and industry, the status of commerce and industry gradually improved. The former artisans now became engineers and manufacturers, and the former sordid merchants now became commercial-family capitalists. But for farmers, their lives were deteriorating day by day, and their status was declining every day. They were oppressed and ridiculed by compatriots of other classes.[137]

There is no doubt that local apportionments, which directly cause rural social turmoil and agricultural distress, also intensified with the emergence of modernization, as it was observed that "in recent years, the demand for funds is very high to cover the numerous new policies". "Local apportionments of fees need not be reported to the provincial government and are not restricted by laws". Thus, "those local officials who are without conscience determine the amounts of apportionments randomly and attain a lot of benefits for themselves because of this official rights".[138] The various taxes and fees in the name of the "new policies" added to the burden of farmers and endangered the farmers' living conditions fundamentally.

Furthermore, from the late Qing dynasty until the Republic of China, the modern nation-state authority had been in the process of reconstruction, and the state authority was in dislocation to adjust and control the interests of rural society. It had increased the costs of reconstruction of the rural social order and slowed down the process of eliminating the rural crisis. The Nanjing National Government had formally completed the reunification of China, but "the annual military costs and debts on average have exceeded more than 70 percent of the total annual expenditure in the past 30 years. However, the fact that the military expenditures of the provinces have not yet been included"[139] shows that it had not really established the social identity of the national authority. Therefore, "the survival problem now facing Chinese society is even more urgent than it was 30 years ago [1901]".[140] Even with regard to the issue of additional taxes that had a profound impact on the survival of farmers, the actions of the National Government were still "inadequate".

> In the first year of the Republic of China, there was a restriction that the proportion of additional taxes should not exceed 30 percent. In October, the 17th year of the Republic of China, although the National Government promulgated eight pieces of laws and decrees restricting land taxes, unfortunately, the decrees turned out to be invalid pieces of paper. Worse still, the laws would almost add one or two new items every year".[141]

Rural crisis in 1930s and countermeasures 355

It can be said that the construction and operation of modern government agencies actually increased the intensity and strength of gathering resources from the rural areas. Especially when the Nanjing government "abandoned all fiscal power over the agricultural sector that created 65 percent of gross national product, it meant giving up any effort to undertake a thorough reform on the unfair land-tax system".[142] The increasing burden on farmers and the disorder of rural society were closely related to this. The results obviously exacerbated the process of polarization between urban and rural areas. "Isn't that a contradiction? On the one hand, the villages are extremely sluggish in development, but on the other hand, the cities have developed by leaps and bounds".[143] Due to the historical contradiction, coupled with the triggering of the world economic crisis and the promotion of various factors mentioned above, the rural crisis showed "the collapse of a rural economy covering a population of more than 300,000 like a overwhelming flood".[144] Thus, it led to the destruction of "rural organizations and the gradual shaking of the national foundation".[145] The formation and evolution of the rural crisis in modern China was indeed the historical result of the aggregation of many factors. However, the convergence of various factors or causes is not an obviously accidental "coincidence". It is the inevitable evolutionary trend of the modern urban and rural development process. "The changes in history are amazing. It is history that can tell us the truth; history can increase our self-confidence, and history can point out an infinitely bright road ahead us".[146]

The evolution of rural crisis and its countermeasures

The rural crisis in the 1920s and 1930s rapidly evolved into a comprehensive social crisis. After the 1920s, the rural issues in China developed into the focus of general social concern.

> The rural issue has now become the most serious problem in the country. It has not only determined social turmoil or stability, but also the future of the Chinese nation, the survival of 40 million people. However, it is also threatened by the collapse of the rural areas.[147]

In fact, the destruction of the developing mode of urban-rural society-cultural integration and the serious disconnection of urban-rural social development in the traditional era are also one of the results of China's industrialization and urbanization process in modern times. This revealed its basic trend since the start of the "New Deal" in the late Qing dynasty. In response, Michael Gasster did a study on this topic from another angle:

> Farmers before 1900 often rebelled and got slaughtered, but these resistances never caused a vast movement that fundamentally changed Chinese society. After 1900, the large-scale movement expanded to the peasants by the 1920s. Their struggle of survival became part of China's

356 *Rural crisis in 1930s and countermeasures*

struggle for modernization. As a result, China's modernization struggle began to take root in the rural areas.[148]

The complex and sharp social contradictions at the beginning of the twentieth century suggested the structural conflict formed by the differentiation of urban and rural interests. The rural crisis in China had emerged even though it would take some time to become the focus of social attention. After 1901, the modernization-oriented institutional changes made progress gradually, and the disintegration process of the traditional Chinese social-cultural structure accelerated. But the new structural system and national authority failed to be established simultaneously, thereby increasingly, social disorder and grassroots social upheaval were endless. In the process of increasingly frequent and violent social conflicts and contradictions, an endless rural crisis emerged in the 1930s.

Research on the rural crisis has already been involved in the investigation of Chinese rural areas in the 1920s and 1930s, but most of the discussions on the reasons for its formation were limited to enumeration.[149] Thus, "it is difficult for us to visualize the rural societies they describe".[150] "Without sufficient contrast, it is difficult to find dynamic links and Law".[151] In recent years, many scholars have also written about the "agricultural crisis" in the 1930s.[152] It is believed that the underlying cause of China's agricultural crisis in that period was the decline in the overall level of agricultural productivity since modern times.[153] Li Jinzheng tried to start from the perspective of the poverty of the peasants and its causes, and analyzed seven factors that led to the peasants' poverty, that is, land inadequacy, low productivity, depression of domestic handicraft industry, an inferior position in commodity exchange, rural financial exhaustion and usury, tax exploitation, and natural disasters and human disasters. Among them, insufficient cultivated lands, low agricultural productivity and frequent natural and human disasters were the most important causes of farmers' poverty.[154] But the extended question is, what are the dominant causes among these factors? Or where do these factors come from? In addition, we must ask whether these factors emerged accidentally in the early twentieth century or were the inevitable result of historical evolution and so on. These questions need to be further discussed later. Further discussion suggests that the enumeration of these factors is not enough to explain the formation of the rural crisis, and perhaps reveals that these factors may not be the deep cause of the rural crisis from another perspective. In his book *Small-Scale Peasant Economy and Social Changes in North China*, Huang Zongzhi discussed the evolutionary characteristics of the modern small-scale peasant economy. He believed that

> the world economy has not caused the collapse of the small-scale peasant economy, but promoted the small-scale peasant economy to move forward along the original path of changes. The patterns and principles of changes in the twentieth century are almost same as in the past. The

Rural crisis in 1930s and countermeasures   357

cultivation of industrial crops has increased the incomes and costs of small-scale farmers, which led to their differentiation.[155]

However, Huang Zhu also went on to say, "while the small-scale peasant economy in Western Europe was undergoing the development and transformation of capitalism, the small-scale peasant economy in China was getting gradual involution". And "these differences" "also contributed to the rural crisis of the large-scale peasant movement in the nineteenth and the twentieth century".[156] The contradictions discussed here are obvious: because there is no "economic collapse of small-scale peasants", "the rural crisis" could not actually be testified. Meanwhile, was "the increasing involution of small-scale farmers" the root cause of the rural crisis or the "rural crisis" itself? This is also worth discussing. Huang Zhu's argument only focuses on "involution" itself, and it is reasonable to fail to delve into the rural crisis. However, this also suggests that the issue still has value for further discussion.

Obviously, it is significant in theory and practice to promote our current modernization and the theoretical development of the "new rural construction", if we understand and reveal the epochal characteristics and deep causes of the rural crisis in this period from the perspectives of history and science, and summarize and condense various coping methods and measures.

Continuation and variation: the historical evolution of rural social conflicts

Since the twentieth century, the rural social order had become more turbulent and chaotic. At the beginning of 1901, the endless "mass uprisings" originated from the bottom of the society, "which almost broke out everywhere in any time". The revolutions, together with the so-called "New Deal" of the Qing dynasty, constituted the social interaction between the upper-class elite and the lower-class civilians of the late Qing dynasty.[157] According to current research results,[158] from the first lunar month of the 28th year of the Guangxu emperor in power (1902) to August of the 3rd year of the Xuantong emperor in power (1911), by the eve of the Revolution of 1911, there were a total of 1,028 civil revolutions in the country (Ma Ziyi counted more than 1,300 cases[159]).

The annual incidence of civil revolutions in the late Qing dynasty exceeded tens, hundreds or even thousands of times in figures compared with that in the middle of the Qing dynasty, which also increased significantly compared with the time before and after the Sino-Japanese War.[160]

In terms of years, the civil revolutions mainly emerged in 1906 (133 cases), 1907 (139 cases), 1909 (116 cases), 1910 (217 cases), and 1911 (108 cases). Unlike the trend of major contradictions between "officials and civilians" (that is, the general characteristics of "compulsory government and people's

358 *Rural crisis in 1930s and countermeasures*

opposition") in the traditional era, the trend of "civil revolutions" in the new century showed the unique complexity and multidirection of "structural" social contradictions from the beginning. One trend that deserves special attention is that the "gentry-civilians conflicts" in the tide of civil revolutions became increasingly frequent and intense.[161]

In the late Qing dynasty, grassroots social disorder became more frequent. On the one hand, the basic tendency was the opposition between the state and society. On the other hand, it presented the opposition between the rural power and rural civilians. The establishment of the Republic of China after the Revolution of 1911 did not fundamentally resolve the basic social contradiction. Instead, the rural local power and stratum strengthened and expanded their own power constantly by virtue of revolutionary changes. "Bandits have frequently appeared since the Republic of China was established". "In the mid-fifteenth year of the Republic of China, there had been few places which had not been destructed and plundered by bandits". Rural societies were chaotic, and the bandits colluding with soldiers had caused a great damage to the rural community. When describing the living conditions of peasants in Northern Anhui Province (the 16th year of the Republic of China), Zhang Jiehou believed that bandits, wars, bad directors and grassroots officials were the biggest banes.[162] According to the *Suzhou Communication* of the *Minli Journal* of February 1, 1912, after the recovery of Suzhou, in order to raise soldier's pay and provisions for the military governments, the "Land Association" in Suzhou (organized by squires and landowners) set up the Rents and Grain Collection Bureau to strengthen its authority on levying rents on farmers and to forcibly collect rents from villagers through military force.[163] In January 1918, *New Youth* published *Peasants in ZhenZe County*, which described the changes in local power caused by the revolution. Zhang Zuyin believed that the establishment of the Republic of China indicated the inspection department of the Qing dynasty for capturing and penalizing peasants was eliminated. However, "landlords feared that there were no laws or organizations to intimidate the peasants, and thus they established an organization, that is, the Land Association".[164] Traditional gentry or local power organizations had made great progress "on the occasion of the Revolution of 1911 and the Republic of China with the help of revolutionary changes". "Although the names of these organizations are various, their purposes are same, that is, gathering forces aimed at dealing with the anti-rents of the farmers".[165] According to the "Local Communication" of *Shun Pao*, in the ten years after the Revolution of 1911, the Land Association in Suzhou has never concealed its activities, and even" expanded the scale and its members".[166] This shows the basic trend of rural social contradictions and conflicts that continued to intensify after the Revolution of 1911. At the same time, the new regime of the Republic of China was not accepted by the inherent power of the rural areas. For example, in 1914, the gentry in Wu County of Jiangsu Province often resisted the county government in the name of the whole community.

Rural crisis in 1930s and countermeasures   359

"Since the recovery of Wu County, there has been the establishment of the Land Association. All affairs related to loans from water transportation and tax increase shall be contacted by the Association".[167] In May, 1922, the governor of Taicang County, "together with the county committee, once invited gentry to discuss the loans of water transportation in winter". Surprisingly, there were "no local gentry attending the conference".[168] As a result, the loan plan was ended without any discussion.

The development of the "Land Association" actually reflects the basic trend of the continuous intensification of rural mass uprisings. In response to the strengthening of the "community" organizations of the gentry, the rejection and resistance of the rural people had intensified and gradually "organized". In 1917, farmers in the Jinshan Region of Jiangsu Province formed a "One-Mind Association". The rules and regulations of the organization are as follows:

> Everyone who joins the association must follow the rules. First, they must pay land rents after the winter solstice. Second, whether the farmland is fertile or barren, the rents will be returned to the association for one *yuan* per *dan*. Third, if the renter is found to have repaid it privately, those who have not repaid the money will be punished by confiscating money and grain. Those who have already repaid are penalized ten times of money, and the funds will be kept by the head of the agency, which will be used as rents or food supply for those who get the barren lands. Otherwise, the organization has the right to remove their houses.[169]

In the villages around the Jiangnan Region (south of the Yangtze River), the trend of "mass uprisings" led by anti-rentalism had intensified.

> In the Songjiang Region, all villages gathered solemnly with beating gongs and refused to repay the rents. The Justice Town in Kunshan city confronted a serious debate and quarrel between soldiers and civilians because of the collection of land rents. In the Xixiang County of Qingpu Region, the crowd gathered to make trouble for the local organization, while villagers in the Zhoupu county of Nanhui Region demolished the houses of gentry. It is difficult to understand such ridiculous behaviors in various cases.[170]

Even in the town of Pingwang, Wujiang Region, hundreds of villagers "gathered with farming tools and flocked to a rental storehouse. They dragged the owner out and beat him to the last breath, and then threw the person into the river until he was drowning".[171] In addition, farmers in Xietang, Weiting, Waikuatang and other places also set up various organizations to "propose repaying the rents through documents, and removed the houses of rent collectors".[172] The "mass uprisings" in the rural areas actually spread all over the Jiangnan Region.[173]

360   *Rural crisis in 1930s and countermeasures*

Relevant documents also record that since 1914 (to 1932), there had been at least eight "mass uprisings" in the houses of the county government and the main officials of various institutions with the scale of over 2,000 people characterized by burning and destroying in Yangzhong County of Jiangsu Province.[174] From 1926 to 1927, rent-reduction movements took place in Jiangyin, Wuxi, Chongming, and so on. Land-occupation movements by farmers in Songjiang Region, Shatian County of Qingpu Region, and anti-rental movements in Xuzhou City, Rugao County, and Jiangbei Region also emerged in this year. Furthermore, there were events such as the destruction of the police station and the deportation of the governor by peasants in Yixing County, the Jiading civilians' killing of local tyrants and evil gentry, as well as struggles against the exploitation of the gentry by heavy profits in different places. "Every campaign must involve thousands of people".[175] Around 1932, there were hundreds of incidents of rice-grabbing, rich-household robbing and anti-rental movements in Jiangsu, Zhejiang, Hubei and other provinces, and there were over a thousand white-haired farmers who participated in anti-rental movements. Did this no "prove that the revolts in the countryside had reached a serious level?"[176] It can be seen that social contradictions and conflicts in rural China were in a state of intense tension throughout the early twentieth century.

Some scholars have pointed out that "the actual burden on farmers had been increased by four or five times compared with the original amount in the early twentieth century in Henan Province". In the reforming process of the "New Deal" at the beginning of the twentieth century, local gentry and supervisors created a new way of "local funds-raising", "causing the farmers to bear much more burden than that of farmers in the late Qing dynasty".[177] "The gentry and local ruling class actually control the local bureaucracy of the county that presents the grassroots power of the Central Province, and use it to strengthen their dominance over the peasants".[178] Obviously, after the Republic of China began, rural social contradictions and conflicts had not been resolved or slowed down, but became more serious and universal. Around the 1920s, the social crisis of "mass uprisings" and "gentry-civilians conflicts" in the rural areas continued to develop, and eventually triggered the boom of the "peasant movements" with the goal of overthrowing local tyrants and gentry.

During the Republic of China, especially in the 1920s and 1930s, there was no systematic and comprehensive statistical data on the "mass uprisings" in rural society. However, according to the statistical data on peasant turmoil in *Oriental Magazine*, rural social conflicts or incidents were still in a rising state. This trend is shown in Table 6.2.

Among them, the number of tenant-peasant revolts and participants reached the highest point in 1929 (the 18th year of the Republic of China). See Table 6.3.

It is particularly noteworthy that after 1927, the peasant movements began to be strongly oppressed by the Kuomintang government, but the sharp rise in the anti-rental trend of the rural population remained steady. "Some news on revolts of anti-rental and anti-debt in the rural areas has often been heard".[179]

Rural crisis in 1930s and countermeasures 361

Table 6.2 Statistics of tenant farmers in the Republic of China

Year (Republic of China)	Tenant-Peasant Revolts	Participants (Attendance and Estimated Number)
11 (1922)	11	18,112
12 (1923)	11	19,870
13 (1924)	9	18,564
14 (1925)	17	29,738
15 (1926)	19	30,926
16 (1927)	18	29,686
17 (1928)	25	38,800
18 (1929)	46	108,462
19 (1930)	20	24,530
20 (1931)	21	45,975
Total	197	374,663
Average	19.7	37,466.3

Source: Cai Shubang, *Research on the Trend of Chinese Peasant Farmers in the Past Decade*, *Oriental Journal*, 30, no. 10 (May 1933), 31.

Table 6.3 Evolving trend of tenant-peasant revolts

Year (Republic of China)	Revolts	Participants
11 (1922)	11	18,112
12 (1923)	11	19,870
13 (1924)	9	18,564
14 (1925)	17	29,738
15 (1926)	19	30,926
16 (1927)	18	29,686
17 (1928)	25	38,800
18 (1929)	46	108,462
19 (1930)	20	24,530
20 (1931)	21	45,975
Sum	197	37,4663
Average in Each Year	19.7	37,466.3

The number of revolts exceeded the average number of 19.7 in this statistical period for three consecutive years. There were 46 revolts at the peak in 1929. Moreover,

the trend had changed from negative to positive with fewer suicides in the second five years than in the previous five years. However, anti-rental incidents in the second five years were two or three times more than those in the previous five years, and the number of riots had increased significantly.[180]

See Table 6.4.

362 *Rural crisis in 1930s and countermeasures*

Table 6.4 Classification of tenant-peasant revolts

Classification Year	Suicide	Escape	Prosecution	Anti-Tax	Anti-Rent	Rice-Grabbing, Rich-Household Robbing	Petition	Demonstration	Riots and Others
11(1922)			3	2			3	3	1
12(1923)	2			1			6	1	6
13(1924)			1	1	1		3		2
14(1925)	2		1	1	3		6	2	5
15(1926)			2		1		6	1	10
16(1927)			2		2	1	3	2	11
17(1928)			3	1	1		12	1	11
18(1929)	1	2	3	2	7	2	13	1	22
19(1930)	1		3	1	3	2	4		6
20(1931)	1		5		1	1	13	1	9
Total	7	2	23	9	19	6	69	12	83
Average	3%	0.9%	10%	3.9%	8.3%	2.6%	30%	5.2%	36%

Note: 11–20 refer to the eleventh year to the twentieth year of the Republic of China.

Rural crisis in 1930s and countermeasures 363

Although "China's peasants do not have an identical feature to form a homogeneous group, there is a process of class differentiation in the villages, but it also ends with the falling of agriculture and the decline of productivity".[181] Farmers had made a great contribution to social change, but they were repeatedly recorded in the history of the past hundred years. From "after the Gengxin Period (1901), the heavy taxes and years of hunger resulted in farmers' livelihood being trapped in the low-income lands". Thus, farmers rushed to respond to the riots when someone proposed to launch a war against the government. "In other words, the problem of farmers' livelihoods has not been solved".[182] By the 1920s, the organized or "quasi-organized" movements of peasants' resistance such as the

> Red Gun Association, Green Gun Association, Yellow Sand Association, Broadsword Association, Lianzhuang Association, and so on, were organized semi-publicly or in secret. The number of members could reach tens of thousands or even hundreds of thousands. In addition, the unorganized peasant riots could happen at any time, such as the conflict between farmers and the army in Anyue County of Sichuan Province with over 2,000 farmers' deaths, and the surrounding of the county government by farmers due to anti-tax revolts in Yuxi, Luoyang and other counties in Henan. In Jiangsu Province, thousands of farmers gathered and destroyed the house of the town head for opposing the doorplate and house taxes.[183]

The situation was sufficient to prove that the social contradictions and conflicts of interest in rural China had accumulated for a long time, which would cause inevitable social crises.

Furthermore, it is not difficult to determine that the continuity of the contradictions and conflicts in the rural society in the early twentieth century was closely related with the terrible living conditions of villagers caused by the expansion of the interests of local powers. Generally speaking, class conflicts between landlords and peasants occurred from time to time, but no major contradictions had been formed because the rural society itself had not experienced large-scale class differentiation. (Details will be explained later.) The "gentry-civilians conflicts" that had developed since the end of the New Deal in the late Qing dynasty still constituted the main mode of civil revolutions in rural areas since the Republic of China, such as the villagers' riots targeting corrupt officials and evil gentry in Leting County, Yutian County, Yangliuqing County, Guangzong County, Yaliji and so on in the northern Zhili District in the late 1920s.[184] In particular, in 1927, the conflicts between the organized "peasant's association" and "the gentry in the organizations such as the Congress and the Education Bureau" in Yutian County, expanded into military actions several times.[185] In the early years of the Republic of China, "there were several unorganized peasant movements in Hubei Province". What attracted more attention was the occurrence of the

364 *Rural crisis in 1930s and countermeasures*

"rich-household robbing in sixty-nine counties",[186] which extended the "mass uprisings" to almost the whole province. Peasants in Huangmei opposed Shi Nanping, the evil gentry, and "held demonstrations of more than 5,000 people and destroyed the Shi Nanping's house successfully. All these movements emerged in the era of the Beiyang Warlords. Although unorganized, their revolutionary spirit is really impressive".[187] The same case appeared in the rural power structure in Puyang Village of Henan Province: "Before 1920, the rural government was still in the hands of talents, candidate officials, clan leaders, and a small number of landowners. With a small number, businessmen were poor and in low social status".[188] In the political trend in which "the gentry's superior status" was elevated by local warlords, they had taken more public positions in the "local autonomous institutions" and controlled local military forces.[189] Therefore, in short, the oppression of the peasants comes from anti-revolt organizations and gentry.

> They treat the gentry as horrible tigers that will eat people suddenly. They can endure humiliation from the gentry, and the latter can also allocate their property. If their widows remarry, they will give betrothal gifts to the gentry. When they sell the properties, a proportion of incomes should be given to the gentry too.[190]

Wu Dakun made a detailed analysis of the causes of the civil turmoil in Suzhou: At around 10 o'clock on the night of October 20, "four or five hundred farmers outside Lou Men first started their action. With gongs in hand, they rushed to set fire to the houses of township heads and the rent collectors". Similar incidents soon took place in about five or six towns and villages. "Because of the vast area and the large number of peasant participants, although the police and security teams shot at them, the peasants continued to incite riots everywhere, and the situation was very urgent at the moment".[191] The provincial government had to pacify the rebellion with military force at last. "However, there were forty or fifty households, that is, one hundred and forty-five houses destroyed in the revolts. As owners, rent collectors lost almost hundreds of thousands *yuan*. The cause of the 'civilian revolt' was different findings of the investigation on the agricultural reduction of crops. The result by the deputy of the township chief and the rent collector was far different from that of farmers. Then peasants demanded a resurvey". Farmers' anger toward rent collectors "resulted in the unlucky incident". But the far-reaching cause of the incident was not so simple. According to Liu Erxiu's (a local inspector) documents to the police station, "the incidents' occurrence may be related to farmers' grievances toward rent collectors in past days". Villagers' resentment probably came from at least four aspects: "First, landlords rely on rent-collecting officials who are capable of suppressing farmers and getting more rents. Second, landlords get their rents according to collectors' data. (The owners do not know where their lands are.) Third, the dwelling houses of collectors were previously burned by the villagers, and the owners built

Rural crisis in 1930s and countermeasures 365

new ones later under the sponsorship of two dimes (at that time) per acre. Fourth, the reason for the burning of houses results from collectors' partiality to the surveys of investigators. Therefore, farmers gathered to burn their houses to release their hatred". Moreover, this was not an occasional incident. "The collector's house had been burned twice in the late Qing dynasty and the seventh year of the Republic of China, and this was the third time". From this, we can know how outrageous he was in ordinary times. It is enough proof to reveal the serious confrontation between the villagers and the local power. "There is no fixed salary for rent collectors, but most of them are very wealthy, which shows they usually gain extra benefits through rent collection". "Because of the daily grievances, the revolts spread through most of the Suzhou region quickly in a short time". "Except for the original desire for revenge, there is no demand for the reclamation and rent adjustment".[192] Although the incident had to be pacified, "the reasons for the revolt in Suzhou are still there".[193] Therefore, similar civilian uprisings continued to appear. According to the *Xi Paper*, the rice-plundering incidents in Wuxi (the twentieth year of the Republic of China) had reached 25 times in a month, as shown in Table 6.5.

The newspapers published "only 20 or 30 percent the actual number of rice-plundering incidents".[194] "Because of extreme hunger, these villagers began to rob food or have meals in rich households. In recent days, the wave of rice plundering can be seen several times in a day".[195] "They are good farmers who are rushing for sacred survival!" The frequency of civilian riots is "undoubtedly the most obvious manifestation of the bankruptcy of the rural economy".[196] "According to recent studies, most of the spontaneous peasant disturbances in modern China are resistance to the governments' taxes rather than anti-rental behaviors against landlords".[197] The confrontations and conflicts between the grassroots forces and the villagers, and the inexorable expansion of the gentry's power and the deterioration of the basic living conditions of the villagers were the leading causes of rural social conflicts and large-scale civilian riots.

Table 6.5 Statistics of rice-plundering incidents

Districts	The 1st District	The 6th District	The 7th District	The 8th District	The 9th District	The 10th District	The 17th District
Duration	June 7	June 4	May 11–June 10	June 1–June 7	May 19	June 2–June 7	June 2–June 4
Rice-Plundering Times	1	1	11	2	1	7	2
Average	—	—	Once/three days	—	—	Once /a day	—

366 *Rural crisis in 1930s and countermeasures*

Underlying causes: fracture of the urban-rural integration process

So what were the underlying causes of the continuous disorder and social conflicts in rural society since the twentieth century? In the past, people usually attributed them to drastic social structural changes or class divisions, but this deductive attribution was too general and superficial and failed to reveal complex and diverse historical truths. The problem is that the changes in modern rural society had not been synchronized with the changes in urban society. Even at the end of the Qing dynasty and the beginning of the Republic of China, there was serious turbulence of the rural society and constant social conflicts arose, and its basic social structural mode did not seem to have undergone a "structural" change. Even in Jiangsu Province where the land was relatively concentrated, the changes in the rural social structure were not obvious. "According to the data, the agricultural stratum in Jiangsu Province had not changed much since the Republic of China. The few changes showed that the promotion of the peasants had failed".[198] Zhang Youyi's research indicated that from the early Kangxi Period (the 5th to 15th year of the Kangxi Period) to 1949, the ratio of landowners (including rich peasants) to farmers' land occupation in the Suzhou region was almost stable at 65:35 in these 270 or 280 years. "It seems that the inevitability of the continuous concentration of land rights under the ownership of landlords in people's assumptions has not been confirmed here".[199] For a long time, "at least since the Song dynasty, the transfer of land rights was mainly undertaken through the sale and purchase method. Occupants relying on political power were only an exception". In rural China, the flow of "recurrent land rights [...] included both scattered and concentrated form".[200]

> In general, there is a certain normality in the class distribution of land rights, that is, the ratio of landlords' and peasants' lands is generally stable. By the early 1930s, from 1931 to 1936, the average ratio of tenants to total farmers was only 30.33 percent. The percentage of tenants after more than 800 years had hardly changed and remained almost a constant. It seems that the long-term trend of continually concentrated land rights in people's mind did not actually emerge or have the possibility of existence.[201]

In general, there were no specific standards for distinctions between rural social classes or strata, most of which were overlapping and fuzzy. "Land-holding peasants with tenant features (the so-called semi-tenant peasants), tenant peasants and farm laborers, and so on, cannot be defined clearly; therefore, the number of surveys is also difficult to be accurate".[202] Furthermore, there were some similar characteristics between landlords and land-holding peasants.

Rural crisis in 1930s and countermeasures 367

The so-called landlords included many land-holding peasants, some of whom leased most of their lands to tenant peasants and left a small part of lands for self-employment. Therefore, few of them can be regarded as pure landowners. The same case was suitable for land-holding peasants, farm laborers and tenant peasants. Consequently, land-holding peasants can be landlords or farm laborers; farm laborers turned into land-holding peasants or tenant peasants; tenant peasants changed into land-holding peasants or farm laborers. It is not possible to cover all cases.[203]

Until the 1920s and 1930s, Chinese rural society was still in a traditional social structure mode with land-holding peasants as the major part. According to the continuous systematic survey of *Oriental Magazine* at that time, the structure of rural social strata is shown in Table 6.6.

The areas covered by the survey data is certainly limited, but it is quite extensive and representative, which can generally show the overall situation of the rural social structure.

First, class divisions in rural society are finite, and the standards are unclear. There are intersections and infiltrations between the various classes and strata in the rural areas, and the boundaries between classes and strata are not fixed and frequently change. For example, in Taicang County, Jiangsu Province, most of the landowners were not grasping rentiers but "small-scale farmers with many lands who cultivate lands themselves". "There is no crack in class consciousness between the landlords and the tenant peasants".[204] In Yin County, Zhejiang Province, "there were many landlords cultivating their own lands, while land-holding peasants took a part-time job as tenant farmers, or landlords as tenant farmers".[205] The survey data showed that the social structure of many villages in the Jiangsu and Zhejiang regions "gave priority to land-holding peasants rather than pure landowners. Landlords sometimes worked as land-holding peasants; tenant peasants sometimes also worked as land-holding peasants, and land-holding peasant farmers sometimes worked as landlords and tenant farmers too. The boundaries between them were not very clear". "On some occasions, farm laborers can become tenant farmers, and they can change their positions with each other. It was not permanent, and their distinctions were imperceptible".[206] In the villages in Dangtu County, Anhui Province, "there was no obvious difference between land-holding peasants and landlords".[207] Another complex situation, that is,

> the tenancy relationship-the opposition between landlords and tenant farmers (such as in Jinzhong Region, Shanxi Province) [,] was very vague in the region. The farming there was close to extensive agriculture, costs and labor salaries were relatively low, but the burden of paying taxes was heavy. So instead of renting it to others, it was more advantageous to run their own business. Except for the farming households without sufficient labor forces, they were not willing to rent to others.

Table 6.6 Status of rural social strata

Type percent Districts	Landlords	Land-Holding Peasants	Semi-Tenant Peasants	Tenant Peasants	Farm Laborers	Total
Wujin County, Jiangsu Province	1.4	7.0	35.21	45.07	11.27	100
Jurong County, Jiangsu Province	2	73		6	19	
Jinjiang County, Jiangsu Province	3	50		35	12	
Shatian County	1	4		95		
Taicang County	10	40	25	15	10	
Surrounding Shanghai	1	2	5	35		
Songjiang County,		30		60	10	
Yin County, Zhejiang Province	5	3		36	46	
Dangtu County, Anhui Province		35		50	15	
Guangshan County, Henan Province	< 20	About 4	4	70	2	
Dangyang County, Hubei Province	1	20		25	5	

Source: *A Survey of Peasants' Living Conditions in All Areas: Excerpts from Essay.*(*Oriental Magazine*, August 1927.)

Rural crisis in 1930s and countermeasures 369

Therefore, "being landlords here almost emerged in small households where men went out for business or only women and children stayed at home, while those permanent tenant-farmers were local large landlords". Thus, in terms of rural social contradictions or conflicts, the relationship between landlords and farmers was not a particular phenomenon. "The more obvious opposition lay in villagers to village heads and small-scale farmers to usurers".[208] Without doubt, this does not mean that there is no hierarchical identity relationship in rural society. For example, the relationship between landlords and tenant farmers in the rural Guangshan of Henan Province was "originally a kind of contractual tie, but in practice they had a master-servant-like obligation and right, which suddenly turned into a subordinate relationship. Now the landlords have the privilege of enslaving and governing tenants randomly, which cannot be violated or resisted!"[209] However, the division of hierarchy identity in the traditional era does not have the characteristics of class differentiation in modern society.

Second, the rural social structural relationship was not fixed. Although it was constantly changing, a large-scale social class differentiation had not been formed. In many villages, "small-scale landlords probably worked as land-holding peasants, and it was also very common for large-scale landlords to cultivate lands by hiring their own farmers".[210] The rural social structure and its hierarchical relationship did not form a stable, fixed structure, but a relatively active dynamic structure. The structural proportions of landlords, land-holding peasants, semi-land-holding peasants, tenant peasants and farm laborers

> were constantly changing. Farm laborers can become tenant peasants; tenant peasants can also become semi-land-holding peasants; semi-land-holding peasants can become pure land-holding peasants, and land-holding peasants can change into other types of peasants. As the native saying goes: "A land probably is occupied by eight hundred owners in one thousand years". You can imagine that how rapid and frequent the change is.[211]

For example, in Dading County, Guizhou Province, in the short period of one year, the natural power of floods and droughts can make landowners become land-holding peasants; land-holding peasants become tenant peasants, or tenant land-holding peasants become landowners, and landowners become tenant peasants". In rural society, it is possible for land-holding peasants to change into other types from time to time".[212] Therefore,

> the class differentiation of Chinese peasants is still vague and not pure. But from the perspective of the differentiation process (one end generates the rural bourgeoisie – rich peasants, and the other end gives birth to the rural proletariat – farm laborers.), there are many transitional strata among ordinary peasants, including middle peasants and poor peasants.

370 *Rural crisis in 1930s and countermeasures*

The so-called middle peasants can be extended into "minimum-scale peasants" and "small-scale peasants" based on the analysis of class (level). "Minimum-scale peasants" are close to farm laborers (hired workers) who can be defined as "semi-proletarian".[213]

A survey conducted by the National Government in the provinces of Hebei, Jilin, Shandong, Henan, Shanxi, Shaanxi, Jiangsu and Anhui in the 1920s (1917 to 1920) showed that the dynamic changes in the stratification of farmers were the following: The number of small-scale farmers owning 10 to 30 acres had increased, and the number of middle farmers owning 30 to 50 acres also tended to increase. "Although landowners of 50 acres, 100 acres, and over 100 acres in the Zhili Region (now in Hebei Province) and Henan Province had a tendency of increasing, the figures had a tendency of reduction in general".[214] This was roughly similar to the Japanese statistics: more than 70 percent of farmers owned 10 to 30 acres of lands, and 70 percent of Chinese agricultural industries were managed by small-scale farmers.[215] "During the 20 years from 1912 to 1932, the population increased by 12.20 percent, and its growth rate was slower than the previous period". But "it is worth noting that in the same period, that is, the 19 years from 1914 to 1933, the cultivated land increased by 12.52 percent, which maintained the same growth rate as the population, or even slightly skipped it".[216] "If we use stricter standards for information collection, there is no reliable evidence so far to support the argument that lands are gradually concentrated in the hands of minority people".[217] These data show that the rural social structure had not undergone drastic differentiation. "The increase in small-size farming and the decline of large-size farming are similar to equal land rights",[218] though the extremely decentralized small-scale farming had a detrimental impact on China's economy and society.

Since modern times, especially in the early twentieth century, in fact, Chinese society showed the trend of urban-rural evolving division. That is, the social structure of cities had undergone drastic social differentiation and changes, and new structural elements were rebuilding social life. However, there was no large-scale structural change and differentiation in Chinese rural society. Changes in people's social status or living standards were basically limited to changes in the homogeneous structure, and qualitative changes in the social structure were rare; however, changes in rural families' economic status were volatile. On the one hand, landowners often "lost their families' wealth before the third generation managed business". On the other hand, small-scale farmers were likely to become rich. "A cow, 30 acres of land, a wife, children and a comfortable life are not a dream even for a hired worker. Even in the Hutian area "where lands were more profitable than that in other regions",[219] small-scale landowners with less than 20 acres still owned more than 30 percent of the lands. "In Suzhou, where land rights were relatively concentrated, the lands of small-scale landowners still had a major share, let alone the other areas".[220]

Rural crisis in 1930s and countermeasures 371

In the Qing dynasty, all kinds of super-economic coercion by landlords against tenant farmers in Suzhou can be traced back to the Southern Song dynasty. The question was whether land distribution was further concentrated in Suzhou where landlords had dominant power, from the Southern Song dynasty to the early Qing dynasty. Until now, we have not had enough historical data to confirm its more concentrated features.[221]

Zhao Gang calculated the Huizhou's land data with a Gini coefficient in the Ming and Qing dynasties. The results showed that the Gini coefficient in the early years of the Republic of China had decreased to 0.3–0.4, which was much lower than over 0.5 in most areas during the Qianlong Period.[222] This can be confirmed from another aspect, which is that the rural society in the late Qing dynasty and the early Republic of China was far from reflecting the formation of a sharp polarization and the dynamic trend of a heterogeneous structure.

Obviously, the drastic changes of the social structure in modern China are more concentrated in the urban and rural location structure rather than the rural class structure. The drastic changes in the social structure of modern China occur with the changes in the economic structure. From the emergence of China's modern economy in the 1980s, since the year 1920, with 60 years of development, all modern economic output, including foreign capital, bureaucratic capital, and national capital, accounted for less than 8 percent of the national economy according to the estimations of economic-history scholars.[223] That is, more than 90 percent of the national economy was still old-style agriculture and handicrafts, and the majority of the country's population still survived in the small-scale peasant economy, which treated families or clans as the main production units. In terms of social structure, the bourgeoisie and workers are the main forces of modernization, but the groups are not only small-sized in China but also restricted by traditional ideas. From the perspective of location structure, new economic relations and even social structural changes usually occur in places such as commercial-port cities and regionally central cities, which consequently forms a dual pattern of social culture in modern China, that is, the process of urban-rural deviation under the trend of industrialization and urbanization. Almost all of the huge structural changes in the new mode of production and the new way of life have taken place in urban society. Among them,

> mechanized transportation is of course a completely new factor. As a result, in the half century from the early 1840s to the early 1990s, new port cities (such as Hong Kong and Shantou) emerged and other port cities also developed amazingly, including the attractive cities, Shanghai and Tianjin.[224]

Without doubt, the massive reconstruction of the new urban system marks the beginning of the historical changes in the modern social structure.

372 *Rural crisis in 1930s and countermeasures*

"The development of Shanghai is second to none in modern Chinese urban development. Due to its important port status, modern industries had emerged with the development of foreign trade and the expansion of the concession. The diverse international goods and commercial business were booming, and the scale of the city was expanding rapidly. At the beginning of modern times, Shanghai (1852) had a population of more than 500,000, or less than 600,000".[225] The establishment of Chinese and foreign enterprises in Shanghai causes a large number of people who have lost their livelihood due to poverty, natural disasters and wars to enter Shanghai. According to statistics, the number of workers in Shanghai had reached 36.22 million in 1894, which ranked first in the country. By the 1930s, the population of Shanghai had reached more than 3.4–3.5 million.[226] The modern era of "new industry" originated in Shanghai, which eventually led to structural changes in Shanghai. "The simple machinery industry driven by manpower had been destroyed by the new trend and disappeared in the country".[227] "When the Qing dynasty collapsed and ended in the 3rd year of Xuantong Emperor (1911), there were more than 90 large-scale factories in Shanghai". Shanghai's industrial development had been more rapid since the Republic of China. "From the first year to the twentieth year of the Republic of China, 2,177 new factories were built in this city".[228] As a result, Shanghai, the original "small county by the sea"[229] had finally undergone a structural historical change. By the early years of Guangxu Period, it had been "quite prosperous", characterized by "numerous ships near the Yangtze River and convenient transportation in all directions".[230] Modern roads, foreign carriages, ships and newspapers such as *Zilinxi Daily*, *Shun Pao*, Chinese and Western newspapers, and multinational communiqués and so on fundamentally changed the "small coastal county". "A comprehensive view of the situation in Shanghai indeed presented a modern trend".[231]

At the beginning of modern times, the urban economy in Tianjin was still dominated by workshop crafts and household crafts. The establishment of Tianjin Machinery Bureau by Chonghou in 1867 marked the beginning of modern industry in Tianjin. Since the beginning of the New Deal in the late Qing dynasty, Tianjin's urban development had been particularly rapid. In the "New Deal" reforms characterized by an "inclusive atmosphere", government-owned enterprise enterprises such as the Zhili Headquarters of Technology Association, the High Industrial Academy, the Exhibition Center of Industrial Products, the Internship Workshop, the Industrial Promotion Workshop and the Silver-Dollar Bank and so on., were founded in succession. Meanwhile, gentry and merchants in Tianjin raised funds to set up private enterprises such as towel factories and tooth powder factories one after another. By 1911, there were 134 factories in Tianjin. After the establishment of the Republic of China, a number of large-scale factories appeared in Tianjin, such as Danhua Match Company (1913), Jiuda Refined Salt Company (1915), Hengyuan Spinning Mill (1916), Huaxin Spinning Mill (1920), Rongli Soda Plant (1922) and other large-scale industrial enterprises.

In 1934, the Social Bureau conducted the first survey of Chinese-invested industries in Tianjin, of which there were 1,233 industrial enterprises with a total capital of 30.053 million *yuan*.[232] Tianjin connected foreign trade and modern industry with traditional handicrafts and commerce. In spite of the late development of modernization, it had become the fastest urbanizing city in modern North China. According to survey data in the 1930s, the annual output value of modern industry in Tianjin were 7,450 *yuan*, ranking third after Shanghai and Guangzhou.[233] One feature of the structural changes in this urbanization process was the urbanization of the rural population. As a result, the total population of Tianjin grew rapidly from 198,000 in the 1840s to 1.237 million in 1935 (urban population).[234] Qingdao was a fishing village with hundreds of residents in the middle of the Guangxu Period. In 1879, it gradually became a small town after the chief soldiers of Dengzhou stationed there. After the opening of the port, Qingdao soon established Chinese and foreign industrial enterprises such as spinning, cigarettes, machine manufacturing and oil refining. From 1915 to 1927, 37 industrial enterprises with a total capital of 7590.1 *yuan* had been established and maintained production in Qingdao.[235] In the nine years from 1919 to 1927, 42 national capital enterprises were established.[236] In 1902, Qingdao's population was only 14,905, but by 1933, it had grown to 436,772.[237] From the growth of population in the above major cities, we can see the rapid increase in population urbanization. Table 6.7 shows the general situation of urban industrialization in the country in the 1930s.

With the development of industry and the improvement of industrialization standards, the level of urbanization in this period had also greatly improved. An important indicator for measuring the level of urbanization is the change in the proportion of the total urban population to the total population of the country, but it is obviously very difficult to determine this in the absence of more accurate demographic data. In this case, an effective approach is to reveal changes in the level of urbanization through changes in the number of cities in different periods and different population scales. The related statistics show that before 1924, 3 cities in China (Shanghai, Guangzhou, Beijing) had a population of 1 to 2 million; 6 cities (Hangzhou, Tianjin, Fuzhou, Hong Kong, Suzhou, Chongqing) 50,000 to 1 million; 41 cities 100,000 to 500,000; and 83 cities 50,000 to 100,000.[238] By 1937, one city (Shanghai) had reached a population of more than 2 million; 4 cities (Beijing, Guangzhou, Tianjin, Nanjing) 1 to 2 million; 5 cities (Hankou, Hong Kong, Hangzhou, Qingdao, Shenyang) 50,000 to 1 million; 66 cities 100,000 to 500,000 with an increase of 61 percent; and 112 cities 50,000 to 100,000.[239] In comparison, cities with a population of 1 to 2 million had increased by 33 percent; cities of 500,000 to 1 million had decreased by 17 percent; cities of 100,000 to 500,000 had increased by 61 percent; and cities of 50,000 to 100,000 had increased by 35 percent.

Among the above cities, Shanghai, Tianjin, Wuhan, Chongqing, Qingdao, Zhengzhou, Shijiazhuang, Tangshan and other cities had become typical

Table 6.7 Comparison of industries in 12 cities across the country in 1933

Regions	Number of Factories	Percent	Capital (Million yuan)	Percent	Number of Workers	Percent	Net production value (Million yuan)	Percent
National	18,676	100	48,468	100	789,670	100	138,662	100
Shanghai	3,485	19	19,087	40	245,948	31	72,773	46
Tianjin	1,224	7	2,420	5	34,768	4	7,450	5
Beijing	1,171	6	1,303	2.6	17,928	2	1,418	1
Guangzhou	1,104	6	3,213	6.6	32,131	4	10,157	6
Wuhan	787	4	2,086	4	48,291	6	7,330	5
Nanjing	687	3.6	748	1.5	9,853	1	2,344	1.7
Chongqing	415	2	734	1.5	12,938	1.6	1,049	0.8
Fuzhou	366	2	261	0.5	3,853	0.5	777	0.4
Wuxi	315	1.7	1,407	3	63,764	8	7,726	5
Shantou	175	1	219	0.5	4,555	0.6	408	0.3
Qingdao	140	0.7	1,765	4	9,457	1	2,710	2
Xi' an	100	0.5	16	0.03	1,505	0.2	41	0.03

Source: Wei Yingtao, *The Urban History of Chongqing in Modern Times* (Sichuan University Press, 1991), 209. The industrial capital figure of Guangzhou seems to be wrong, and it is correct based on the original table.

Rural crisis in 1930s and countermeasures   375

representatives of the rapid population growth in commercial port cities, new emerging transportation hub cities and industrial and mining cities during this period. Shanghai had a population of 2.641 million in 1927, which in 1930 increased to 3.145 million and rose again to 3.702 million in 1935.[240] The population in 1935 increased by 40 percent compared to that in 1927. In 1982, Tianjin's urban area had a population of 1.12 million, which increased to 1.237 million in 1935, and 1.254 million in 1936.[241] The population increased by 3 percent in 1936 compared to that in 1928. Sanzhen City, Wuhan, had a population of 850,000 in 1928, which exceeded 1 million in 1930 and reached 1.29 million in 1935.[242] In 1935, it increased by 52 percent compared to that in 1928. Chongqing had a population of 208,000 in 1927, which increased to 253,000 in 1930 and 471,000 in 1936, with an increase of more than double within 10 years.[243] In 1927, Qingdao's urban (including only the first and second police districts and the two subsidiary police stations of the large and the small harbors in Haixi) population had reached more than 92,000, which were 19,615 households. In 1932, the urban (roughly including the first, the second, the third and the fourth police districts) population had amounted to over 241,000, more than 49,000 households.[244] The population in 1932 increased by 162 percent compared to that in 1927. Zhengzhou had 20,513 households with 81,360 people in 1928, which increased to 22,433 households with 95,482 people in 1930, and 27,892 households with 124,377 people in 1934.[245] The population in 1934 increased by 53 percent compared to that in 1928. Shijiazhuang's population was about 40,000 (including Xiumen Town) in 1926, and it increased to 63,000 in 1933.[246] The number grew by 58 percent in 1993 in contrast to that in 1926. Tangshan had a population of about 48,000 in 1926, which reached 150,000 in 1931. It had a population of about 78,000 before 1937.[247] The population had increased by 63 percent before 1937 compared to that in 1926. Although the above statistics are not very accurate, the rapid development of urbanization during that period is indeed an indisputable fact.

The process of modern urbanization resulted in profound changes in China's social structure. In the early twentieth century, the transition from traditional Chinese society to modern society entered a "chain institutional change" stage, in which not only the self-sufficient natural economy began to disintegrate, but also the different social ranks including scholars, peasants, workers, businessmen and others that originated from the traditional society were affected by the commodity economy and split up. The impact of the wave began to differentiate. After the twentieth century, especially after the abolishment of the imperial examination system, the traditional scholar-gentry class differentiated dramatically, and many enlightened gentlemen began to plunge into "freelance" work. Companies, enterprises, businesses, newspapers, societies, self-government and even new troops became their "arena".[248] As a result, new social groups appeared in the reconstruction of society, such as "gentry business", academia, intellectuals, military and so on. Moreover, the drastic changes in the social stratification and the structural changes in social

376 *Rural crisis in 1930s and countermeasures*

relations were basically historical phenomena that had accompanied urbanization, industrialization and modernization. By the end of the Qing dynasty and the beginning of the Republic of China, many modern specialized occupations were already available in the cities. The modern social structure had achieved a new reconstruction through fierce differentiation and flow. For example, the results of the 1919 occupation survey in Jiangsu Province showed that the industrial and commercial population and other urban laborers accounted for nearly 20 percent of the total population of the province. Civil servants, employees and freelancers became the newly emerging occupational groups in the city, accounting for 0.252 percent of the population of the province. Students and apprentices accounted for 3 percent of the province's population, while labors in industry, business, education, fishery and other professions accounted for 35.2 percent of the province's occupational population. The traditional social stratification and structure of scholars, peasants, workers and businessmen no longer existed. "This means that the industrial structure of urban society had undergone historical changes in the late Qing dynasty and the early Republic of China".[249] With the acceleration of China's modern urbanization process, the traditional social stratum in which scholars, peasants, workers and businessmen were the mainstays had been replaced by newly emerged social stratum. The urban social structure had formed three major social stratum: middle class, industrial workers and urban poor people. In addition, the stratification and structure of the various strata were constantly changing due to the intricate division of labor in the society. The middle class is a multilayered, multi-identity and highly mobile group in modern urban society, including industrial and commercial workers, middle and senior professionals and freelancers. There are four main social sources of businessmen and industrialists: compradors and chief executives of modern foreign-funded enterprises, new-style businessmen, new-style intellectuals and old-style businessmen. Therefore, the middle class, industrial workers and urban poor people – the three social classes resulting from urban social changes in the late Qing dynasty and early Republic of China – changed the original social composition with different roles and restructured the modern social relationship system. In the urban area where urbanization and modernization coexisted, the capital-based social production and lifestyle had been formed, occupational and class stratification with the characteristics of the era had begun to appear, and society was also undergoing fierce differentiation as well as a new restructuring process.

Since the twentieth century, the dual characteristics and trends of China's social structure and social stratification have more profoundly interpreted the basic pattern of modern urban-rural separation and the era characteristics of social contradictions and conflicts.

> The biggest economic crisis in China in recent years has been urban expansion and rural shrink. I disconcertedly find that there is too much cash circulating in the city, so I can only focus on the speculative cause

Rural crisis in 1930s and countermeasures 377

such as public debt and land, while the lowest productive capital in the rural areas of the mainland is not available, either. I am really out of money![250]

This should be an important historical prerequisite for our in-depth analysis of rural social contradictions and conflicts.

The characteristics of the era: the formation of the "double crisis"

Endless rural social contradictions and conflicts are not an isolated phenomenon. They represent the universality and severity of the disorder of social life. In fact, they are both a precursor to the arrival of the rural social crisis in China in the 1920s and 1930s and a historical boost to the outbreak of the rural crisis. The rural crisis, in the traditional society, refers to the survival crisis of farmers, which is manifested by the stagnation of agricultural production development and the persistent poverty of farmers and those struggling on the margins of survival. Judging from the appearance, the rural social crisis is the basic condition or historical prerequisite of the peasant uprising and rebellion in the traditional era. The Taiping Rebellion can be said to be the result of the sharpening of the traditional rural crisis. In previous studies, when we talked about the cause of the Taiping Rebellion, we overemphasized the aggression and exploitation of Western capitalist countries, which did not fully comply with historical facts.

We cannot simply attribute everything to the result of foreign aggression and give the role of internal causes secondary importance. In fact, China's foreign trade volume, foreign debt interests and foreign-invested enterprise income were quite low, whether according to the average population or against the ratio of gross domestic product. Moreover, the domination of imperialism over China can only function through internal factors.[251]

This revolt was the total outbreak of a long-term accumulation of traditional rural crises, and it was a repetition of the rules of cyclical chaos in traditional Chinese society. It was rooted in the long-standing tension between people and land in Chinese society, the land ownership of feudal landlords and the inefficiency and corruption of government and bureaucracy under the autocratic system. However, the rural crisis of the 1920s and 1930s had more complicated historical causes and connotations of the times. "The agricultural-oriented China has begun to enter the era of industrialization and commercialization, so the plight of farmers is even greater than before".[252] Compared with the traditional rural crisis, it has a characteristic of a new era. At that time, people might also call it rural collapse, agricultural panic, rural withering, agricultural bankruptcy and so on, and this is just to summarize one aspect of it. In fact, the rural crisis at that time was a comprehensive and profound social crisis. It was a kind of "overall collapse of the rural areas".[253] It not only

378 *Rural crisis in 1930s and countermeasures*

made "all rural areas fall into danger" with the situation that "the economic foundation is ruptured rapidly, the people's lives are becoming increasingly difficult, and its misery is even worse than the destruction of a nation", but also "elevated the seriousness of rural problems to its highest level, making it urgent to solve the problem". For Chinese villages, "both a poor harvest and a rich one are disasters", and "it is a state of all wrong directions".[254] It is an overall crisis caused by political chaos, economic bankruptcy, social disorder and cultural anomaly.

> Since the founding of the Republic of China, China's political, economic, social and educational aspects have become a mess. Generally, those who are worried about the country must shout at the top of their lungs: "China's crisis is coming!" [...] China's crisis is definitely not because the spirit of the nation is low, nor is it because the people lack the virtues of etiquette and integrity, but because the foundation of the rural economy has gradually shaken, and it is on the verge of bankruptcy. The political revolution in history had social background more or less, and it is safe to say that most of them are based on the bankruptcy of the rural economy. [...] We must clearly recognize that the current crisis in China is shaking of the rural economic foundation.[255]

From the signs of the crisis, the rural crisis first manifested itself as the bankruptcy of the rural economy, which is, "First, the peasant household registration is gradually decreasing (famine, industrialization and urbanization); second, the wasteland is increasing; third, the agricultural harvest is decreasing; fourth, the uneven distribution of land; fifth, the land rent is increasing; sixth, taxes are heavier; seventh, the oppression of usury; eighth, the suffering of farmers' lives". The decline of the rural economy is not just a problem of agriculture. Rural sideline industries and handicrafts have also fallen into bankruptcy. "Everything is being drawn to the newly emerged industries, so the big rural family disintegrates and the population concentrates in the city". "Within sixty-five years (1863–1928), the foreign goods imported into our country have shockingly increased by 26 times. (Import index was 8.13 in 1863, 209.8 in 1928–1913 – using 1913 as a standard)". A large number of women workers "flew into the city, either as weavers, or helpers or prostitutes. This is in the various towns in the south of the Yangtze River, especially the places near Shanghai".[256] Of course, the result of the rural economic bankruptcy was the farmers' bankruptcy, "Now the average annual total income of Chinese farmers rarely exceeds two hundred *yuan*, which is generally about one hundred *yuan*, and the least is no more than ten *yuan* [...] (the market prices rose 20–30 percent after the disaster)".[257] According to surveys in rural areas near Peiping and Anhui, "the average annual income of farmers is one hundred and thirty *yuan*, 80 percent of which is below the limit of one hundred and fifty *yuan*", "Many families cannot keep their relatives around any more because of oppression [...] In the

Rural crisis in 1930s and countermeasures 379

case of Zhili [...] their income is often 20 or 30 percent less than what is necessary for life"[258]. According to the survey data from Hunan in 1933, 6.8 percent of the population was adequately clothed, only 28.0 percent were basically fed, 53.7 percent were underclothed, and 2.4 percent were unemployed and exiled.[259] At that time, the proportion of Chinese farmers' food expenditure still accounted for more than 62 percent (whereas in America it was two-fifths in the same period). The poverty is beyond words!

Second, it is also manifested as the escape of the agricultural population, that is, the continuous occurrence of leaving the village. The case investigation of *Oriental Magazine* stated:

> In 1927, there were more than 50 farmers in Ergong Village of Anxi's rural areas, while in 1933, there was a sudden decrease of four-fifths, and only 11 families remained. In 1934, it was even more pitiful! The number has reduced to only five households. As far as the county is concerned, before the Tongzhi Military Disaster in the Qing dynasty, there were more than 2,400 rural households. In 1921, there were over 900 households. In 1933, there were no less than 700 households left. When they investigated again in 1934, it was said that there were only 600 households or so in the whole county [...] In many villages in Anxi, people were mostly gone, so the countryside was quite deserted. Japanese scholars had compiled data on peasants leaving villages around the end of the 1920s.[260]

Even this extremely incomplete data showed a surprising rate of leaving villages: among them, Zhanhua, Shandong, was 8.7 percent; Zunhua of Zhili, Tang county, Handan, and Yanshan were respectively 2.65 percent, 4.55 percent, 1.82 percent, and 8.72 percent, and the overall leaving rate was 4.52 percent.[261] According to data from the *Agricultural Situation Report*, the number of farmers leaving the villages in Hebei, Shandong and Henan in the 1930s could reach 529,000, 883,000, and 788,000 respectively.[262]

Third, it is also manifested as a shortage of rural finance and the phenomenon of rural shrink.

> The collapse of the rural areas and the concentration of capital in the cities have led to the expansion of industrial and commercial capital in the cities, while the absence of rural capital has forced the bankruptcy of three-quarters of the country's population. The destruction of purchasing power makes commerce and business wither. The influence of a credit crunch and financial panic overpowers day by day. No one knows when this will come to an end.[263]

The Nanjing government "issued public bonds amounting to 100,000 million *yuan*" within five years to repay military expenses incurred by banks (no more than 60 million *yuan* based on China's liquid capital (liquidity)), but "the result of issuing a large amount of public debt was that all liquid capital was

380 *Rural crisis in 1930s and countermeasures*

mostly absorbed into the city, the rural finance was in shortage at one time, and the phenomenon of lopsided development appeared. On the other hand, the city was flooded with silver goods, and even the price of silver slumped". Therefore it "accelerated the failure of the rural economy".[264]

Fourth, it is even more manifested in the trend of urban-rural divergence in new-style education. Education in the traditional era and its system was an urban-and-rural integrated development model. In China, "most of its culture is from the countryside, and it is designed for the countryside. The legal system, etiquette, industry and commerce are all in consistent with this rule".[265] There is very little difference between urban and rural buildings and other aspects of daily life.[266] Even the printing industry is integrated between urban and rural.[267] As the famous American sinologist Fei Zhengqing said, until modern China, "people of higher social class still tried to maintain a rural foundation close to its natural state. In the countryside, the minor traditions did not significantly separate from the mainstay traditions of the upper society in the urban areas".[268] Urban and rural cultures were integrated, and the intellectuals were always connected with the grassroots. After the new learning system came into being, the government focused more on the urban schools and ignored the countryside. Urban education gradually developed, but rural education was left far behind. Later on, the construction of the "new learning" focused on cities. Not only had there been a significant change in the educational system of China as a whole, for example, Beijing Normal University Halls, higher schools, specialized schools, industrial schools, teaching schools and so on, all clustered in Beijing, provincial capitals or other important cities, but secondary schools were also basically located in various cities. Middle schools were generally set up in the regions of prefectures, halls, and Zhili Prefecture. Even elementary schools were also located in prefectures and counties. Rural schools accounted for only 10 percent of the total number of schools nationwide.[269] Even around 80 percent of agricultural schools, which aimed at serving rural society, were located in urban areas.[270] Taking the year of 1931 as an example, there were a total of 103 occupational schools and universities nationwide, 22 of which were in Shanghai, 15 in Peiping and 8 in Guangdong. The universities in these three cities alone accounted for 44 percent of the total. There were a total of 75 universities and independent colleges across the country, most of which were built in Beijing and other big cities, including 12 in Peiping, 16 in Shanghai, 6 in Guangzhou and 5 in Tianjin. The above 39 schools accounted for more than half of the total sum.[271] In terms of the number of students, there were 27,506 college students in six cities, which were Peiping, Nanjing, Shanghai, Guangzhou, Hangzhou and Wuchang, making up four-fifths of the total. The phenomenon that university education was concentrated in a few large cities is truly surprising.[272] At the end of the Qing dynasty and the beginning of the Republic of China, there were 100,000 villages and 1 million rural communities.[273] Based on this, there were 178,847 primary and secondary schools

Rural crisis in 1930s and countermeasures 381

in the country until 1922, with an average of only one school in every six villages. By 1931, there were 262,889 primary and secondary schools across the country, and there was only one school in every four villages.[274] Taking Hebei Province as an example: about a quarter of primary schools had not yet been established by 1928, and some counties without primary schools even reached over 70 percent. As a result, a reversal of the flow of talents in rural and urban areas appeared. "Those more ambitious intellectuals in the countryside were constantly rushing to the cities, the side counties to the provincial capitals, and the provinces toward the capitals and the commercial ports".[275] "And this flow is becoming more and more a one-way migration".[276] As a result, modern cities, which were gradually becoming the center of new learning, wealth, industry and commerce, and of course politics, had gradually formed an absolute advantage over the countryside. As one of the most institutional changes with the characteristics of the era – "the ancient method of education had also been replaced by the school system". However, the new social problem caused by this was "the school system is adapted to and emerges from the requirements of capitalism [...] so, if a country wants to transplant capitalism to its own country and make it grow, it must set up schools to produce a large number of employees in production technology and management".[277] This new education, which was known as the "product of industrial civilization", aimed to develop educated workers, company employees and state officials. However, it was "in the air and unrealistic" for rural society and it fueled the trend of an outflow of rural elites. There would be no talents for local communities because they were all driven to the outside world,[278] because, "unfortunately, Chinese society is still a pre-capitalist society, Chinese production organizations are still about handicrafts and natural agriculture". "Schools cultivate graduates batch by batch every year, and these graduates have no place to make a living". Therefore, it also "trapped China in civil strife".[279]

"Whichever direction you look – none of the social, economic, political and educational aspects are dynamic. It can be said that we are dead halfway or mostly".[280] The whole village was in a full crisis. "In short, today's rural China is in entire bankruptcy with an overall economic foundation breakdown".[281] However, this overall crisis did not manifest itself with a characteristic of polarization, but presented a basic trend of "universal poverty". *Yishi Newspaper* once recorded the real situation of the life of a rural landlord in Daming County, Hebei Province (as shown in Table 6.8).[282]

Statistics show that the landlord of this ten-member family owned 171–160 acres of land, the management of which was also almost in debt. According to a survey by the Ministry of Agriculture and Commerce of Beijing, the number of farmers in the industry decreased by 15.64 million households from 1914 to 1918, with an average annual decrease of 4 million households; the farming land decreased by over 263,870,000 *mu*, and the wasteland increased by more than 490,730,000 *mu*.[283] Obviously, "class

382 *Rural crisis in 1930s and countermeasures*

Table 6.8 The real life of rural landowners

Year	Income	Expense	Comparison	
			Deficit	Gain
1928	655.40	1,275.04	619.64	
1929	699.90	929.92	230.02	
1930	1,281.54	1,275.93		5.61*
1931	1,383.76	1,488.20	104.46	
1932	1,874.90	1,955.58	80.68	
1933	1,739.20	1,589.85		150.02
Sum	7,634.70	8,513.85	874.17	
Aver-age	1,275.45	1,418.97	146.52	

Note: The original chart mistakenly reversed the figures of "deficit and gain" in 1929 and 1930, which is corrected now after calculation (Author's note).

differentiation" (that is, the evolution trend oriented by land or wealth concentration) cannot provide an effective and rational theoretical explanation between the facts of "farmers decreasing", "farmland decreasing" and "wasteland increasing".

> In a country with severely inadequate cultivated land, it is a really pathetic situation in which 'more people want to give up lands and fewer people invest in land' and 'the land supply is increasing while the demand is decreasing'. This shows that the agricultural crisis at that time was already rather serious".[284]

These data actually are a typical revelation of a fact that China's rural areas fell into an extremely serious trend of "general poverty" around the 1930s rather than "polarization" in the general sense. "All the provinces in the country are struggling with the fate of total collapse, with no provinces an exception (The standards of misery are actually not so much different among provinces)".[285] Zhu Qihua's statistics on the population and economic conditions in the 1930s can be used as supplementary explanation from another angle (as shown in Table 6.9 below).[286]

The population below the poverty line at that time accounted for 93.7 percent (including the urban population). There is no doubt that this portrayal is a vivid picture describing severe "universal poverty".

The squire Liu Dapeng also detailed in his diary the situation of "universal poverty" in Jingzhong Village of Shanxi in the 1920s and 1930s. Liu Wei was the director and a local celebrity of the Jinci Chamber of Commerce, but "he has too many family members to feed when the market price is extremely high, so he is often in shortage of food and has to loan to make a living".[287] Moreover, many wealthy families in the Jinzhong area could hardly escape

Rural crisis in 1930s and countermeasures 383

Table 6.9 Classification of the poor population

On the Edge of	Population	Percentage
Preference	5,000,000	01.3
Standard	20,000,000	05.0
Poverty	75,000,000	18.7
Hunger	250,000,000	62.5
Death	50,000,000	12.5
Sum	400,000,000	100

Note: Estimated by 400 million people, their economic status can be divided into five categories.

this tragic fate. For example, the diary recorded the situation of Liman Village:

> This village used to be a place of magnificence with arrays of rich families
> [...] but it went to its doom during the Guangxu period. The houses have
> no buyers so everyone is earning their living by demolishing the entire
> house and selling bricks, wood, and stone to distant villages. Year by year,
> 70–80 percent of the village has been destroyed, and the situation is more
> than bleak, making it too hard to cast sight to.[288]

In the past,

> the village had a large number of rich households with a total of 2,000.
> The high-rise buildings were splendid [...] but now, Liman Village is
> devastated with only a hundred households and most of them are in
> poverty. Eighty to ninety percent of the families make their living by
> demolishing and selling their big houses. There is no rich household in
> sight.[289]

"All the households are sighing about their poor life, and none of them are rich".[290] Obviously, this kind of "pervasive miserable image" of overall decline happened more concentratedly in wealthy "big households".

> In recent years [...] the number of peasants fleeing from their villages
> has been increasing, and the barren land has a tendency to expand every
> year [...] It has caused a general stagnation of the economic life of the
> province, and it has made it more tricky for the poor farmers to cope
> with.[291]

Yan Xishan also described in his submission to the National Government (1935) that "the rural economy of Shanxi has totally broken down for years [...], nine villages out of ten are in poverty and nine out of ten families are in need".[292] Liu Dapeng described the miserable condition of the local village and said, "The word 'rural bankruptcy' is a new term now, which means that a farmer is in such a failure that he cannot keep his assets. This is a time when people are extremely poor without any money, the agriculture is stagnant and there is no way for survival". What is particularly worthy of deep thinking is that Liu sighed, "It means that even though you want to go into bankruptcy, there's no one to buy what you have. Thus we can see the dilemma of farmers".[293] The phenomenon of "no one buying property" fully reveals that this was not the concentration of "wealth transfer" shown by "polarization" but a decline in the overall sense. Even in the affluent Jiangnan region, the decline of landowners is very obvious. For example, the landowner's (Wuxi) land ownership was only three-tenths of that in the heyday (Jiaqing period), and the pawn and silk business were almost stagnant.

> After 1927, it declined even more drastically. The largest landowner today only owns 900 acres of land, compared with the 3,000 or 4,000 acres of good land held by large landowners in the early Qing dynasty, which is like the difference between day and night.[294]

The overall decline in "universal poverty" and "polarization" are clearly completely different evolutionary trends.[295]

Therefore, it is not difficult to determine that the rural crisis in the twentieth century is completely different from the rural crisis in the traditional era. Its causes are based on the evolutionary accumulation of traditional social contradictions on the one hand, and based on the process of industrialization, urbanization and modernization on the other hand. The creation and accumulation of new contradictions present the dual characteristics of the crisis of survival and development.

> The plight of our rural life is not a phenomenon that only occurs today. However, in recent years, it has been oppressed by capitalists, industry and commerce, and internally by political disturbances and corrupt officials. So there is basically no more future for our rural life.[296]

The rural social order was in chaos, and public security had broken down. Therefore, farmers could not survive, and they either became bandits, or concentrated in cities – thus causing the abnormal *landflucht* phenomenon, which leads to abnormal metropolitan development.[297]

> The history of China in the last century is a history of the destruction of Chinese villages: the first half of the period followed the path of modern urban civilization to study the West and destroyed the Chinese countryside; the second half of the period was again the trend of modern cities against the trend of modern urban civilization and the destruction of the Chinese countryside.[298]

The rural crisis and the urban-rural divergence development trend since the twentieth century followed each other, and they were mutually reinforcing.

Historical dilemma: different rescue paths

The Qing government had also responded to rural social conflicts and their crises since modern times, but

> looking over the measures taken by the late Qing government to save the countryside, we know it only set up several nominal farming schools and model experiment factories besides the reclamation of wasteland and relief from disasters. These institutions had little impact on agricultural production, and because of a lack of talents and difficulties related to finance, it was hard to make great progress. At the same time, due to the decline of the countryside and the ignorance and conservativeness caused by it, new technologies and new methods rarely spread in the countryside, and the result could only be no improvement in the countryside, while the government's exploitation of farmers continued to increase.[299]

In addition, as mentioned earlier, the modernization process of modern China was initiated by the demonstration and stimulation of Western civilization, and the Qing government started to solve the crisis of its own making. Of course it lacked the various prerequisites on which modernization can proceed smoothly. When the rural society was in crisis, farmers' own survival became a problem, and it was impossible to offer any advantages to modernization construction from the aspects of funds and markets. In this predicament, if we cannot engage in modernization on the basis of fostering or nurturing rural development forces, we may be in danger of exhaustion. After the peasants uprising was suppressed, the Qing government started modern enterprises featured in their study of foreign techniques, but they did nothing to solve the rural crisis. Especially in the "New Deal" period, with the development of large-scale modern undertakings and institutions, rural society had become a source of income to maintain the "New Deal" under severely disordered conditions. The costs and unbearable burdens of modernization reform had been passed on to villagers. Therefore, the "development crisis" was transferred and the rural people's survival crisis was gradually aggravated. As a result, there was an endless and intensifying "revolt of people" in the rural society. It was these "rebellions" of invincible peasants that made the Qing government become like "a crumbling house on the verge of falling". It can be said that it was impossible for the weak bourgeoisie to overthrow the rule of the Qing dynasty so quickly without a preview of the peasants' resistance in various forms across the whole country. After the Wuchang Uprising, Sichuan was almost "full of fraternity bonds", forcing constitutionalists to

386 *Rural crisis in 1930s and countermeasures*

declare independence, and the local governments in many provinces were controlled by the party. Lenin once pointed out, "If the masses' revolutionary sentiment were not flourishing, Chinese democrats would not be able to overthrow China's old system and would not win the Republican system".[300] Many political events in the late Qing dynasty were more or less related to the rural crisis. Facing traditional rural crises (such as the Taiping Rebellion), the Qing government adjusted its policies to respond effectively and succeeded. However, in the face of the modern rural crisis (that is, the dual crisis of survival and of development) since the "New Deal", the Qing government failed to form an effective countermeasure, and eventually went to its doom in the wake of the civil commotion.

The historical changes of the 1911 Revolution and the founding of the Republic of China provided an opportunity for the release of the accumulation of rural social contradictions and conflicts, but did not refer to the problem itself. Even "when the Manchurian Qing Dynasty broke down, democratic politics could still not be established, and China's politics became more chaotic". The whole society "was in a tangled mess that cannot be straightened out".[301] Rural social contradictions and conflicts continued to develop, which not only triggered the rise of the peasants movement in 1926, but also finally led to the general outbreak of the rural crisis in the 1930s. Faced with the frequent turbulence and crisis in rural society, how can we relieve the predicament, rebuild the order of rural social life and eliminate the endless rural social conflicts? The strategies and measures adopted by the National Government, social groups and Communists at the time were different and can be roughly divided into the following categories:

I. Government-Led Countermeasures at the Socio-Technical Level. Since the end of the Qing dynasty, countermeasures to seek remedies for the rural crisis have become one of the important contents in Sun Yat-sen's thoughts, but he mainly proposed to start from two aspects: equalization of land rights and improvement of agricultural technology. After the 1920s, the National Government of Nanjing put Sun Yat-sen's idea of equalization of land rights and improvement of agricultural technology into practice. Regarding the measure of equalization of land rights, the National Government quickly stopped implementing it due to great resistance. In agricultural technology improvement, continuous efforts were being made. For example, from 1933 to 1937, the National Government successively established the Central Agricultural Laboratory, the National Rice and Wheat Improvement Institute, and the Central Cotton Production Improvement Institute. The main work of these agencies was to introduce American cotton seeds, improve wheat and rice varieties, and experiment with pesticides and chemical fertilizers. However, the Anti-Japanese War soon broke out, and certain organizations were eliminated. During the eight-year Anti-Japanese War, only the Central Agricultural Laboratory remained.

Rural crisis in 1930s and countermeasures 387

For a rural social crisis that is intertwined with a survival and development crisis, the practical effect of this response at the socio-technical level is extremely limited, even for the persistent gentry conflict in the countryside and local power manipulation. The heavy taxes and miscellaneous taxes were not practically affected, either.

> The grass-root powers collect taxes of varied categories. Although the central and local governments have repeatedly applied for injunctions to simplify the complicated ones in order to reduce the burden on people and prevent disturbance, what had been accumulated is hard to relieve. [Local powers often] make up categories to avoid restrictions or increase recruitment without approval. The taxes income had already surpassed the legitimate tax demand, and it is very difficult to overcome and eliminate this improper behavior. As a result, the government officials get wealthier while the people are at a loss. Thus, rural bankruptcy, and the industrial and commercial decay occurred.[302]

II. Rural Society – Cultural Restructuring Strategy Oriented by Social Forces. Liang Shuming believed that because Chinese society was a special society with ethical standards and professional separation, cultural imbalances caused by cultural conflicts between China and the West since modern times had been the main reason for China's decline. Under the impact of Western culture, the Chinese ethical standard had been lost, and the inherent good traditions had been completely destroyed. The Chinese had begun to "focus on themselves, understate ethical relations, look for rights and avoid obligations. Individualism or making society a priority, neither of them was successful, and it was stuck in a dilemma". So how to counter with China's decline? Liang Shuming pinned his hopes on "rural construction", and believed that only through "rural construction" can we save the countryside and rejuvenate China. In 1924, Liang Shuming declared that he was awakened, found a real solution to Chinese social and political problems, and began to try rural construction. Liang Shuming advocated "township governance" in Guangdong and tried "village governance" in Henan. In 1931, with the support of Shandong Provincial Chairman Han Fuzheng, he launched and carried out a "rural construction campaign" in Zouping, Shandong, for seven years. The rural construction campaign carried out by Yan Yangchu in Dingxian, Hebei, was a little different from this. In the autumn of 1923, Yan Yangchu established the General Association of Chinese Civilian Education Promotion Association in Beijing as the director-general. Through arduous social surveys, Yan Yangchu found that although the problems in rural China were numerous, the most fundamental ones were the four basic problems of "ignorance, poverty, weakness, and selfishness". To comprehensively reform and build Chinese society, we must overcome these four problems. To this end, Yan Yangchu proposed the

"Four Educations" concerning literature and arts, livelihood, health and citizenship, and the "three major education methods" of school, society and family to heal the four shortcomings of "ignorance, poverty, weakness and selfishness" of the Chinese. Yan Yangchu's "Universal Education" campaign in Ding County, Hebei, had a profound impact at home and abroad. In 1943, on the 400th anniversary of Copernicus's birth, representatives of more than 100 universities and research institutions in the United States selected Yan Yangchu as one of the "ten great men with the most revolutionary contributions in the modern world", and he was listed with the great scientist Einstein. However, the rural construction movement dominated by social forces was experimental on the one hand, and the trial area was limited on the other hand. It was not able to continue to develop and form a global plan to deal with the rural crisis. In the end, Liang Shuming himself had to admit that "rural construction has to depend on the political power, and the so-called rural movement does not stir the rural areas at all".[303] In response, Zhu Qihua commented, "The problem of China's rural economy is a problem of the fundamental social system, and it cannot be solved by branched improvements". Therefore, the Universal Education Movement in Ding County and the Rural Construction Movement in Zouping, Jiangsu's Mass Education Campaign and Yan Xishan's "Public Ownership of Land in Village" can be regarded as a "landlord's self-rescue campaigns" – fundamentally, these self-rescue campaigns did not make any difference, either.[304]

III. The Communist Party's Land Revolution Policy in Base Areas. After experiencing a series of setbacks, the CPC turned the focus of the revolution from the city to the countryside, and found a path suitable for the land revolution in China's rural areas in the course of the revolution, thus providing a basis for resolving the rural crisis. In the War of Resistance against Japan, the anti-feudal democratic revolution and the national revolution against Japanese imperialist aggression were closely combined, and the "May 4th Instructions" was promulgated to make a timely change to the policy of confiscating landlord land and belongings to farmers as rent reduction and interest reduction. At that time, the rural crisis was alleviated to the greatest extent, and the enthusiasm of the people was mobilized. "The land owned by farmers is not enough. This is a fact, but with their own land, farmers no longer need to pay land rent, and their poverty is immediately lessened". There is no doubt that "a government that firmly grasps the issue of land does not need to worry about foreign imperialism and chaos in the country because it has the trust and satisfaction of 500,000 villages".[305] At the same time, the Communist Party of China had completely reformed and restructured the rural grassroots government, basically eliminating the direct cause of the conflict between the local power and the villagers (that is, the ongoing contradiction between the gentry and plebs). This was also with the strong support of the vast number of farmers, so that the Communist

Rural crisis in 1930s and countermeasures 389

Party of China had a realistic and reliable force to achieve national independence and social progress and eventually – the victory of China's revolution.

However, the relief of the rural survival crisis is not equal to the delimitation of the development crisis. The deeper cause of the crisis was only temporarily covered during the revolution.

In the early twentieth century, the rural social order was turbulent with conflicts continuing, and deteriorated to a worse condition. The reason why it came into being had surpassed the traditional "circular rules of polarization due to land concentration and civil grievances because of political corruption". In addition to the existing crisis of traditional social contradictions, it had added the new contradiction caused by the deprivation of rural areas under the process of industrialization, modernization and urbanization, namely the development crisis. In the process of modernization, modern cities, which are both the focus of industry and commerce and, of course, the political center, gradually formed absolute advantages over the countryside, resulting in a reversible flow of rural and urban talents. "More ambitious intellectuals in the countryside continue to run to the city, those from other counties run to the provincial capital, and those in provinces run to the capital and trade ports".[306] "And this movement is becoming more and more a one-way migration".[307] This new education of "products of industrial civilization" was "unrealistic" for rural society, and it accelerated the trend of rural elite exodus, which had ruined and expelled talents from rural communities.[308] The problem is that this historical process has a long history. The historical accumulation formed by it only burst out suddenly under the synergy of various factors. This is the cause of the era that fundamentally determines the sharp decline in the status of rural, agricultural and peasant status.

In ancient times, Chinese people valued scholars and agriculture, but looked down on commerce and industry, so peasants were noble and the lives of peasants were also very satisfied. However, recently, with the development of commerce and industry, the status of commerce and industry had gradually improved. Former artisans had become engineers and manufacturers, while former market gurus had become commercial family capitalists. But farmers, their lives were deteriorating day by day, as well as their status. They were oppressed and ridiculed by fellows of other social ranks.[309]

There is no doubt that local apportionments, which directly caused rural social turmoil and agricultural distress, had also intensified with the emergence of modernization, just as "in recent years, there have been many new policies and the need for funds is high", "local apportionments of fees need not be reported to the province and were not restricted by laws". Thus, "those local officials who were without conscience increased the charge and attained

390 *Rural crisis in 1930s and countermeasures*

large a fortune". Its various fees for the "New Deal" "were more extracted from the people".[310] In particular, all kinds of donations and taxes other than the designated ones were "collected mostly by local authorities as local taxes. In addition, local tyrants and gentry were financially bullying folks".[311] The various taxes and fees in the name of the "New Deal" added to the burden of farmers and worsened their living conditions.

The various negative effects of the divergent development of urban and rural areas had profound and dramatic impacts on rural society, such as reversing the trend of urban and rural land prices. The Kuomintang had been in power for ten years, and the Land Law had been promulgated for five years. However, "the land speculation is popular, and the value added from the land is obtained without effort. Any tax has never been levied on some houses worthy of 3,000 *yuan*, but the monthly rent collection can reach 40 to 50 *yuan*. It means they can receive interest more than 2 percent [...]. In the past five years, the landlords of Nanjing who occupied an acre of land could receive 2,100 *yuan*, and if they occupied ten acres of land, they could receive 21,000 *yuan*, and they did not need to do anything". The urban-rural separation in the trend of land price was so alarming. "For example, the price of land at Nanjing Xinjiekou had increased at a rapid rate. Setting 1927 as a standard, it had risen to 2307.0 percent in 1932. In other words, the price had increased by 23 times".[312] The land price of Shanghai in 1930 rose twice as much as that in 1916.[313] However, land prices in rural areas continued to decline. For example, the price of land in Tangshan, Nanjing (in 1933), had fallen sharply. The reason was "a decrease in farmland income and a higher city profit". This point "shows the significance that the fall in land prices not only represents the decline of the rural economy, but also represents the greater degree of industrialization and urbanization in the region".[314] Therefore,

> the situation in the countryside has changed greatly from the past [...] Now, most of them are poor peasants except in the vicinity of the city. Their desire is just to maintain a simple life – having a proper meal to feed their family. It is not that they do not want to live better than that, but that they do not have this possibility![315]

It was this mutual transformation and influence of the development and survival crisis that had led to the deepening and continuous extension of the rural crisis at a deeper level. However, issues at this level never attracted enough attention.

Moreover, from the late Qing dynasty until the Republic of China, the modern nation – the state authority – had been in the process of reconstruction since the dissolution of the traditional royal family-state, and the state authority's adjustment and control of the interests of rural society had been basically in a state of carelessness. This had increased the cost of reconstruction of the rural social order and slowed down the process of eliminating the rural crisis. The National Government of Nanjing formally realized the

Rural crisis in 1930s and countermeasures 391

"unification" of the country, but "the military and debt costs have averaged more than 70 percent of the total annual expenditure in the past 30 years; and the military expenditures of the provinces have not yet been included".[316] The facts showed that it had not really established the social identity of a national authority. Therefore, "the whole question of survival now faced by Chinese society is more urgent than it was 30 years ago [1901]".[317] Even with regard to the issue of surcharges that had a profound impact on the survival of farmers, the National Government's actions were still "inadequate".

> In the first year of the Republic of China, there was a restriction that surcharges must not exceed 30 percent. In October 1928, although the National Government passed a law regulating that there were eight input methods restricting the collection of land grants and donations [...] Unfortunately, this order is nevertheless a piece of paper. Even worse, it is necessary to enlist one or two new subjects every year.[318]

The main source of finance to ensure the operation of modern government agencies was undoubtedly the rural areas. "The proportion of taxes collected from rural areas each year is much higher than the currency collected from towns". But "most of this money is for public purposes. In cities and towns, we can see the method used by the gentleman-banker-merchant group to transfer the tax burden to the poor peasants".[319] An obvious consequence of the process of urban-rural divergence is that the government "looked for a way through taxation" that would pass the crisis "on the verge of fiscal bankruptcy" into a rural crisis.

> Only one type of tax or military tax will be able to accelerate rural bankruptcy. No province in China can exempt military taxes. In the last ten years, more than half of the counties in China had military assessments, especially in the Yellow River Basin. [...] The impact of tax increases is like a vortex. First it increased the land rent. Over the past ten years, the land rents for tenant farmers in the provinces without disasters or wars in China have increased by 50 percent to 100 percent.[320]

In this context, the overwhelmed farmers deserted their lands and escaped.

> Large arable land has recently become wasteland. In the seventh district of Wuchuan County near the railway and the capital of Suiyuan, no less than 29,000 acres of land were deserted in 1932. In the south of the provincial capital of Shaanxi, 10 percent to 18 percent of the total farming lands are currently uncultivated. China's agriculture is indeed in a state of depression.[321]

Most of the measures taken by the social forces to help the rural areas were "actually superficial, which not only failed to save the farmers' livelihoods,

392 *Rural crisis in 1930s and countermeasures*

but also further increased the farmers' suffering".[322] Thus, in spite of the fact that there were at least 37 groups (1932),[323] that is, organizations and institutions, established from the New Countryside Movement, they were just experimental and actually provided no remedy for the situation.

Profound historical reflections

In short, the various countermeasures at that time had relatively limited effects, and focused more on solving temporary difficulties; thus, they failed to find an overall solution. Of course, history cannot be reversed, but the historical experience and lessons it integrates can mirror the future: First, farmers had not been led to the track of independent development; instead, they were in a state of negative and passive dependence. Most political parties and groups had positioned farmers in a place of opposing or setting back modern development, and thus regarded them as "poor, weak, stupid, and sick", or "to be reformed" and "to be liberated". They never made the farmers the priority of social development. On the one hand, a compulsory promotion model from top to bottom was formed; on the other hand, farmers had developed a strong dependency [on the institutions that were imposed on them], and lacked the will to explore new ways of doing things.

Second, the farmers themselves had tremendous creativity, and had the ability and drive to transform the existing state and create their own lives. Regardless of the state, political party or social groups, if the active role of farmers was not fully mobilized and the contradictions and conflicts between farmers and local power could not be adjusted in a timely and appropriate manner to an oriented and moderate social order, the occurrence of social crises was inevitable. What was more important was that the state or the power directly faced the endless demands of personal interests, resulting in an overwhelming dilemma of "rescue" everywhere. The development of society, especially in a rural society with vast areas and scattered settlements, should depend more on social forces themselves. The state should play the role of arbitration and final determination in conflicts between society and individuals, and between society and society, rather than intervening directly in society itself. This will make the social interests and conflicts lose the buffer space and opportunities.

Third, when the traditional social mechanism had failed, a new social mechanism was not successfully set up. "China's farmers are not only loosely organized, but also tend to collapse".[324] A village or peasant without a "social organization" can neither form a "synergy" for development nor make sure of its direction. There were countless directions and interests of millions of individual farmers, so the state had no ability to face each farmer directly. Without a sound rural social body, the cost of governance for the country would be multiplied or uncountable.

Rural crisis in 1930s and countermeasures 393

The land policy implemented by the Communists relieved the farmers' survival crisis to a certain extent. At that time, it was extremely necessary and most desired for Chinese farmers in a crisis of survival to obtain a piece of land that belonged to them, so that they could do their best to mobilize their production enthusiasm. However, the redistribution of land itself could not solve the rural problems – the modern rural crisis characterized by a survival and development crisis. Even landowners often faced bankruptcy and also faced a constant survival crisis. Throughout the period of the Republic of China, "'bankruptcy of a farmhouse' is a new term now, which means that the peasant family failed and could not conserve their property".[325] But in the long run, "bankruptcy of a farmhouse" or "rural crisis", neither is the product of class division in rural society but the product of a trend of "universal poverty" in society.

There is no such thing as extreme poverty and rich in rural China. Naturally, there is not too much disparity in different classes, so the class of the peasants cannot be defined. What is a well-off peasant family today may go bankrupt the next day; or a poor farmer in red today turns out to be a farmer of medium or superior degree a few years later, which is often the case in rural China.[326]

For example, "There were 1,300 villagers, 36 large and small shops [...] and most of them were high buildings in Beibao Village, Taigu County, Shanxi, sixty years ago". Now (1935) "there are only 60 families found in the broken ruins".[327] In the past 60 years, the appearance of a country in a village is so different! This is the same as witnessed by the squire Liu Dapeng:

At this point, Manli Village is totally obsolete. There are only 200 households, all of which are poor. There are 80 to 90 percent of people who sold off pavilions to make their living. Rich households are nowhere to be found. Compared to what the village used to be, you will find it really upsetting.[328]

Ding Wenzao described the rural situation in Suiyuan as

selling wives and sons is ubiquitous. Wherever you go, it is broken and destroyed. The tears of peasants have not yet dried up, and economic organizations have basically gone bankrupt [...] the flourishing large villages with 500 households in the past are now just a small village with 40 to 50 households. The small villages with less than 50 residents in the past are only left with collapsed houses and ruins that have become historical relics [...] Half of the affluent families that used to own miles of lands are now destitute. The self-cultivated farmers who made a living by hard work in the past are now inevitably in a situation of hunger and can not settle down and make life by themselves.[329]

Obviously, depending on "the equalization of land" policy to confront the rural crisis that was generated from the survival and development crisis was not a long-term remedy. The issue concerning agriculture, rural areas and farmers re-emerged in the modernization process of contemporary China, which also illustrates the epochal characteristics of this issue.

The historical process of the differentiation, contradiction and conflict of rural social interests in the early twentieth century allows us to profoundly reflect on history. History warns us that the core of the China issue is the peasant issue. "Every social disturbance in China's history and every dynasty's change has arisen from the instability of farmers' lives. Peasants always participate directly in every revolution in China".[330] The core of the peasant problem was the land issue, and the complexity of the land issue and the differentiation of interests caused by it were not a simple problem of "the equalization of land". "The peasant problem is the mystery of China. If this problem can be seen through, China's future is half guaranteed".[331] We really should keep this in our minds!

The formation of the theory of an "agriculture-oriented country" at the beginning of the twentieth century

At the beginning of the twentieth century, the complex and sharp social contradictions had already suggested the structural conflict formed by the differentiation of urban and rural interests. Social issues in rural China had also begun to emerge, although it would take some time before they became the focus of social attention. Usually, ideas lag behind life. The focus of social thought will not be on those contradictions until social problems or contradictions are fully revealed. However, we can still see the origin and sprouting of the theory of Chinese rural construction with the characteristics of the era within a limited chapter.

Since China at the beginning of the century was still undergoing the "great changes that had not happened for thousands of years" and under the powerful impact of the Western port trade policy and the insightful Chinese people's "business against business" thinking, the traditional Chinese policy of "emphasizing agriculture and restraining business" was finally replaced by the policy of "emphasizing business". In the ups and downs of the modern Chinese ideological trend, conflict between business advocacy and the traditional Chinese ideology of agriculture was inevitable, which triggered a decade of dispute over "a nation of industry and commerce" or "a nation of agriculture". Although neither side of the debate published a comprehensive and systematic theoretical treatise, we can see it in the statements published in the newspaper, *Ta Kung Pao*, and *Oriental Magazine* and get their basic points. In this lasting ideological debate, the discussion of rural development theory centered on agricultural issues gradually became an extremely important topic, and thus became the source of theoretical research on rural social issues in China throughout the twentieth century.

Rural crisis in 1930s and countermeasures 395

Revising farming politics and revitalizing agricultural science

The rise of business-oriented thinking in the late Qing dynasty greatly influenced the traditional national policy of agriculture-based thinking in China. In addition, the establishment of the Ministry of Commerce and the prosperity of the chamber of commerce in the late Qing dynasty finally shifted the focus of social development and national policy in the direction of "industry and commerce". Therefore, when people of insight who paid attention to rural issues in China in the early twentieth century attached importance to agricultural development and emphasized agriculture as the country's basis, they were regarded as having "inappropriate" theoretical thinking. Of course, the value of a thought or theory is never judged by the single standard of a "trend". The long-term academic orientation and theoretical guidance it contains are the social wealth full of enlightenment. In this regard, we need historical vision and insightful ideas.

As early as 1901, Zhang Zhidong and others pointed out in the "Political Report on Farming under Jiangchu's Two-System Military Policy" that

> China builds the country with agriculture because its vast land with the mild climate is far better than that in Europe, and it is most suitable for agriculture. Therefore, someone in the Han dynasty once proposed that agriculture was of the greatest benefit. Agricultural products are the foundation to enrich a country and its people. Without the foundation of agriculture, there is no support for the development of industry and commerce.[332]

In 1902, the governor of Hubei and others separately stated, "Agricultural production is the foundation of national power, while food and clothing are the stuffs that satisfy its people".[333] In an article titled "Large Scale of Cultivating Silkworm Industry to Boost Profits" published in *Shun Pao* in 1904,[334] the author also stated he believed that "China has fertile land and a mild climate. Since ancient times, everything in China has been from agriculture, no matter the things collected from people or the daily used among people".[335] Therefore, it was suggested that silk should be cultivated to make a profit. In 1906, the translator of the article "Agricultural-Oriented Thought in the United States" also stated it was believed that

> China has always been an agricultural country, but it is becoming commerce and industry-oriented now because of the discussion of scholars. This is actually a loss of their living foundation. In a word, people should know the geography of their own country. China is a continent, which is suitable for farming and agricultural orientation, just like the United States. It is not the same as the insular Britain or Japan. Why should we admire others and learn the superficial aspects of them?[336]

396 *Rural crisis in 1930s and countermeasures*

In 1907, the president of the Zhili Provincial Agricultural Association emphasized once again the importance of agriculture in China in a speech:

> Since Gengzi Negotiation (1900), China has lost a huge amount of money, so people began to realize the importance of running enterprises, which, however, is a bit late because the ownership of roads and mines has been lost and cannot be recovered, and commerce and industry are not mature to be prosperous all at once. However, agriculture is an advantaged enterprise of our country and all of it belongs to China. According to the economic theory, the labor is cheap when the land is wide.[337]

At the beginning of the founding of the Republic of China, Chen Jintao, minister of finance, expounded in an article on the important position of agriculture and forestry in the prosperity of the country:

> As far as I am concerned, the principle of a powerful country should be oriented to people, the laws that are good for them and sufficient food to feed them. From ancient times to the modern era, the strength of the country and the rise and fall of commerce all depend on the condition of agriculture. Therefore, the first thing that the ancient scholars taught people is about the sufficiency of food. If the country is going to be strong and powerful, agriculture and forestry should be highly thought of.[338]

People of insight who are concerned about China's agricultural improvement and development have not limited the discussion to a one-dimensional emphasis on the importance of agriculture, but have further explored theoretically how to apply the fundamental effect of agriculture. To develop agriculture and revitalize the countryside, we must not only do our best to help the poor but also revise farming politics. As early as 1901, Luo Zhenyu proposed that "the main points of agricultural politics are about nine aspects", that is, "establishing agricultural officials", "examining agricultural affairs", "rewarding the cultivation of wasteland", "inspiring agricultural science", "promoting forestry", "prospering animal husbandry", "promoting marine profits", "developing manufacturing", and "holding competitions".[339] In that same year, Zhang Zhidong and others also emphasized, "To make a fortune today, the first thing is to revise farming policies".[340] In 1912, at article titled "The Origin of the Agricultural Promotion Association" also held that

> Reading and studying all the historical records and inspecting the whole world, I found that there is no country that can have their industry and commerce advanced and its people stand at the top of the world if its farming is not vitalized.[341]

To revise farming policies, it is necessary to train a large number of agricultural talents. Therefore, the promotion of agricultural science is also essential.

Rural crisis in 1930s and countermeasures 397

For example, Zhang Zhidong and others pointed out in a memorial, "If you want to revise farming policies, you must first develop agronomy".[342] In an article titled "The Discussion on Developing Agronomy" the author also stated the belief that "Today, China wants to practice Western laws, and makes it a fundamental basis of specializing in Western knowledge. However, the root of China lies in the revitalization of agronomy". Therefore, it made establishing agricultural schools one of the major points of developing agronomy.[343]

It is said that Zhang Zhijun of Nanpi has set up a farming school in Hubei, [...] if the government can understand Zhang Zhijun's ideas and lead every province to follow his suit, China will benefit from this and be rich and strong, though it is in destitute now.

Another example is Luo Zhenyu, who also believed that "all of the enterprises come and develop from its basic knowledge. Chinese agronomy, however, has been forgotten for a long time. It is appropriate to build as many schools as possible to teach people about it".[344]

In addition, the Association of Agricultural Revitalization also became a desirable choice for people of insight who think about these problems. For example, in 1903, Hou Dianying put forward that "the country is based on the people, and the people are based on food. Therefore, it is the first priority to establish an association of agriculture". He also drafted Article 32 in the memorial of the Ministry of Commerce. His purpose is still to make agriculture the basis of becoming rich and strong. "The purpose of this meeting is to open up the wisdom of the people, gather the strength and feelings of the people so that the country can be rich and strong by revitalizing farming".[345]

In addition to theoretical thinking around agricultural issues, people also have some theoretical thinking about other rural problems. For example, an article specifically discussed the issue of setting up town officials:

Then how should we deal with it? We can only carry out the traditional official system again. The land of one village should be divided between the city and the town. People who live in the part that is placed in a town are farmers. It is proposed to designate an official who is familiar with farming and farmers. All of the trenches should be unclogged, farmlands inspected, trees planted, chickens and other livestock raised, silk promoted and vegetables and fruits transported. Everything should be in correspondence to its suitable conditions and meet people's needs. The official should educate the farmers and supervise the on-goings.[346]

Obviously, it is rare to be able to go beyond specific agricultural reforms and raise theoretical issues from the height of an era. Therefore, the emergence of "the era of agricultural war" theory naturally reveals its unusual significance and value. The author of the article "The Strategy of Farming in China" emphasizes that "China should defeat Western Europe by an

398 *Rural crisis in 1930s and countermeasures*

agricultural war" is "the most important viewpoint and the most reasonable principle", and believes that

> since the Chinese Reform, China has reformed in many ways aiming to be stronger and powerful. This is indeed a great opportunity for China's future. But the policies advocated by everyone vary. Some people propose to set up as many schools as possible, some say we should build more roads and dig more mines, some demand that military power is essential, and others suggest that commerce and business are priorities. Among the four groups of ideas, agriculture is the urgency that needs to be focused on even though the development of commerce and business is important, too. [...] The solution for now is to set up a Ministry of Agriculture that specializes in agriculture. Western Europe defeats China through commerce and industry, and China should in turn defeat Western Europe through agriculture. This is the most reasonable.[347]

For the "Era of Commercial War", which has become a social consensus since the Westernization Movement, this theory can be described as an opposite trend. Although it has not yet won the trend of time, it has raised the issue of "agriculture" to the height of "era concept", which is indeed far-fetched.

Taking a comprehensive look at the theoretical issues of China's rural development during the first 20 years of the twentieth century, it is not difficult to find that its discussions mainly focused on specific agricultural issues, and less on the perspective of the times and development. This situation would only change after the rural issues became more prominent later.

The viewpoint that agriculture, industry and commerce are equally important

At the beginning of the twentieth century, discussion on the theoretical issues of rural social development was launched against the background of the intertwined trend of mercantilism and traditional thought on agriculture in the late Qing dynasty. Within the ten years from the publishing of "On Self-Improvement"[348] at beginning of 1901 to the end of the Qing dynasty in 1911, published discussions in newspapers were increasing, and their views can be roughly divided into three main categories: business-based theory, agriculture and industry-based theory and agriculture-based theory.

The inertial development of the mercantilist trend of thought in the late Qing dynasty placed the business-oriented theory in a prominent position in the discussion during this period. An article titled "Mining Theory", published on January 9, 1901, started with a straight comment: "Based on today's situation, isn't mining a priority for being rich and powerful?"[349] It has

Rural crisis in 1930s and countermeasures   399

placed the development of mining in an important position. However, an article titled "On the Revitalization Opportunity for Chinese Crafts", published on December 29, 1901, asserted that the four domains of scholars, farmers, industry and commerce should be interrelated and help one another. "None of them should be overlooked". Nonetheless, industry and commerce were still in fact in a crucial position. The article stated that

> anyone who is a little bit familiar with current affairs today should know that the first aspect where foreigners compete with us is in business. If you want to beat your enemy, you should guarantee the scale and the accuracy of your business.[350]

A 1904 article titled "On Developing Commerce to Make a Country Powerful" stated that

> the leaders in China have an urgency to build a rich and powerful country nowadays. Businessmen and women are the key in any powerful country, at home or abroad, now or in ancient times. In the ancient times, the powerful countries had advantages over the pastoral industry, while in recent times they have an edge in agriculture. But now in modern times, commerce is the guarantee of a strong country. The profit and loss of commerce is interrelated with the security of a country, so the source of a country's strength is promoting business. [...] We should know that when business is prosperous, the people are rich; when people are rich, the country is strong. Wealth is the foundation of power. The business people in our country should shoulder their responsibilities. Businesses, regardless of their scale, are all closely related to the country. A profit of one cent is one boost of our country's strength. One more place to stand in the business world is one more gain of glory for our country.[351]

In contrast to the previous two articles, two essays titled "On the Future of China's Industry", reprinted by *Oriental Magazine* in 1904, and "China Should Be an Industrial Country", published in *Shun Pao* in 1906, have a stronger industrial and commercial color. The author of former essay pointed out that "Now is the era of the most intense industrial competition. Those who are on the mainland cannot build and protect their country if they fail to develop their industries through all their efforts".[352] The author of latter essay stated that

> when I say that China will have to be an industrial country in the future, it is exactly the same as if I say that the United States cannot help but be an industrial country today. This is an irresistible and reasonable trend. So it is obvious that the policy of developing and vitalizing enterprise aims at establishing a powerful industrial country.[353]

400 *Rural crisis in 1930s and countermeasures*

During this period, the emphasis on agriculture and industry was quite popular, too. In 1902, Cen Chunxuan and others realized that

> what stirs the desire and satisfies the demands of people all over the world are agriculture, industry and commerce. People need these to make their living, and these different aspects promote one another not just from recent years or only the Western countries but very ancient times.[354]

"Agriculture, industry and commerce are the foundation of prosperity; thus, they should be revitalized at any time".[355] In an article titled "Request for the Revitalization of Farming from Ministry of Commerce", published in the *Shun Pao* in 1903, it was clearly stated that

> we think that the preliminary steps to develop commerce should be making it a great priority to advocate for local products. Therefore, only when agriculture, industry and commerce are all needed and interrelated to one another can all ranks of enterprises be prosperous and promising.[356]

In 1907, "this is an era of agriculture, industry and commerce war"[357] was stated in the article "On the Reasons for China's Holding Agriculture Competition". After this slogan, *Agricultural and Commercial Newspaper* also successively published articles with titles such as "On the Inappropriate of Preference among Agriculture, Industry and Commerce"[358], "On the Rich Should Not Overlook Agriculture, Industry and Commerce", "On the Poor Should Definitely Not Overlook Agriculture, Industry and Commerce"[359] and so on, in 1908 and made further comments concerning this view.

The establishment of the Republic of China in 1912 overthrew the feudal monarchy of China that had lasted for thousands of years, and cleared the way for the development of capitalist industry and commerce. Therefore, in the early years of the Republic of China, the theory of establishing a nation through business was quite overwhelming. Subsequent periodical articles with titles such as "Encouraging Commerce" and "The Fundamental Remedy for Famine" and so on, contained some comments on the theory of founding the nation through business. For example, "Encouraging Commerce" argues that "commerce is between farmers and merchants. Agriculture without industry cannot become agricultural products, and commerce without industry cannot bring out the value of products. Both agriculture and commerce depend on industry"[360], while "The Fundamental Remedy for Famine" asserted that

> in a word, if our country wants to avoid hunger, it is necessary to revitalize industry and commerce, so that people can commit themselves to them. If so, I believe China will no longer have such a famine in one or two decades.[361]

Rural crisis in 1930s and countermeasures 401

In this period, there were still commentators who insisted that agriculture, industry and commerce should be given an equal push, among whom the theory on the four separate parts of agriculture, forestry, industry and commerce is still worthy of attention. The author of "Thoughts on Having Four Divisions of Agriculture, Forestry Industry, Commerce and Business" believed that

> China is an agriculture-based nation, just like the countries of the Western Europe establish their countries by business. China has adhered to the old system for thousands of years. Although we focus on agriculture, we never give much consideration to the quality of the soil, the solution to floods and droughts, and the role of artificial machines, let alone the focus on our abundant forest, the quality of industry and the profits made from exchanges and commerce. We regard them as dispensable. That is why China is poor and weak. To be rich and strong, agriculture and forestry should be separated from industry and commerce. Also, agriculture and forestry should be further separated and so should industry and commerce.[362]

The trend of mercantilism in modern China and the rise of its "Business Theory" and "Business-oriented Theory" is are timely theories formed during industrialization or modernization. From the 1860s when the "business-oriented theory" gradually formed in the Westernization period, to the 1920s, its social practice has been for nearly half a century. Although it has been practiced for decades, the target of "making the nation rich and the army strong" is still far away. The thought of certain time periods is, of course, subjected to the harsh test of the time periods' practices. Therefore, the questioning of reality, of course, leads to questioning and criticism of thought or theory. Discussion of the founding of the country reflects the historical necessity of the development of social understanding. The changes in the domestic situation after the founding of the Republic of China did not provide more room for the theory of founding the nation through industry and commerce, especially after Yuan Shikai's death in 1916. The domestic warlords were engaged in a turbulent situation, and the people were struggling. The actual dilemma made the "Dispute on the Construction of the Nation" begin to develop in a direction conducive to the theory of an agriculture-based nation.

As early as 1903, Yuan Shikai, governor of Zhili, put forward that "even though commerce is important in making us rich and strong, the trade and transportation of it all depend on agricultural products and the manufacture of industry. Agriculture and industry are indeed the root of commerce".[363] This comment emphasized the status of agriculture. In the same year, the Ministry of Commerce also pointed out in a memorial that "the Ministry of Commerce thinks it is of great importance to advocate agricultural products. The foundation of business is industry, and the foundation of industry is agriculture. Therefore, it is inevitable to revitalize farming or else the foundation

402 *Rural crisis in 1930s and countermeasures*

will collapse".[364] The "Report from the Farming Community of Yangxin County to the Industrial and Commercial Bureau", published in *Journal of Agriculture* in 1905, emphasized that

> if we want to revitalize our society, we must first develop education, and the education should be about agriculture. The Western countries always attach great importance to industry and commerce. However, either the manufacturing of industry or the trafficking of business is all from agriculture.[365]

The article "On the Principles of the Relationship between the Two Sectors of Agriculture and Commerce", published in 1910, emphasized that "since the twentieth century, commerce has been the foundation of the country, but agriculture is actually the foundation of commerce [...] agriculture should always be ahead of commerce".[366] In 1912, Chen Jintao proposed in the "Request for Establishing Branch Bank for Revitalizing Farming from Chen Jintao, Minister of Finance" that "The first thing that the ancient sages taught people is about sufficiency of food. The rich and powerful countries all began from developing agriculture and forestry".[367] "Promoting Farming",[368] published in *Ta Kung Pao* in 1916, and "Suggestions on Establishing Agriculture University",[369] published in *Ta Kung Pao* in 1920, once again recited their proposal for an agriculture-based country. Compared with the above two pieces, Lv Ruiting's "Advisory on Agricultural Nation" is more systematic and complete.

In summarizing the theoretical discussions on the relationship between agriculture, industry and commerce in the first 20 years of the twentieth century, it is not difficult to find that this discussion can be broken down into two stages. Although each stage has the theory of establishing a nation based on agriculture, or on industry and commerce, or on agriculture and industry, the focus is quite different. The advantages of the theory of establishing a nation based on industry and commerce at the previous stage are obvious. In particular, the publication of the "Advisory on Agricultural Nation" in 1920 marked that the idea of an "agriculture-based nation" will begin to have a unique significance for the era and value in future historical choices.

Proposal of the theory of an agriculture-based nation

Lv Ruiting's "Advisory on Agricultural Nation" clearly stated that "if you want to revitalize industry, you must set that principle first. If you want to set that principle, let us examine the national conditions". According to China's various situations, he thought that it is a world agricultural power with a vast area, fertile land and mild climate. Agricultural products occupied an extremely important position in its exports. Before World War I, agricultural products accounted for about 80 percent of total exports. Although they declined during World War I, they still accounted for 70 percent. Based on the above-mentioned national conditions, Lv Ruiting believes that

> if we can pay attention to silk cultivation and carry out agricultural policies, we will maintain some balance in input and output even if we cannot pay off foreign debts. When our country becomes a little wealthier, and the people's livelihood is a little bit more recovered, we will start mining and promoting and revising commerce and industry. So the country must become stronger gradually and there will not be any problem about land and our large population.[370]

The author listed ten major reasons for establishing an agriculture-based country: history, geography, politics, economy, finance, statistics, military, customs, health, and population of the country. The above ten reasons can be roughly summarized into six aspects: history, geography, politics, economy, customs and health.

The political reasons for an agriculture-based country, as summarized by Lv Ruiting, actually include the third and seventh item in the above list of ten reasons. Specifically, it includes three aspects. One is the political thought of Confucius that people are of principal significance and so is food. From Confucius, to Mencius, to Guan Zi, Xun Zi, Shang Yang, Li Zheng, Lu Buwei, Sima Qian, Xuan Cuo, Dong Zhongshu and so on, all politically advocated the establishment of the country through agriculture. The second is realistic political doctrine and practice. This point contains three aspects. One is based on the doctrines of Powell, a doctor of American agronomy; a scholar named Lear, a politician named Rabelo; Athenian historian Courchos; and Japanese agronomy doctor Nito Todo. They think that agriculture can resist extreme thoughts. The second aspect is based on the claims of Greek Socra, the French Surrey, Shiryou, the British Momson and so on. They think that agriculture can reinforce patriotism. The third aspect is based on the relevant theories of Japan, Britain and France, which state that agriculture can promote local autonomy. The third is the close relationship between agriculture and military. There are three reasons for this. One is that food shortage is the most terrifying event in wartime, and the other is that agriculture is less affected by war. Third, agriculture is the source of a powerful military.

The economic reasons for establishing the country through agriculture actually include the economic, financial, statistical, and population aspects that were listed by Lv Ruiting, which are the focus of this book. Among them, "the fourth economic reason" first pointed out that the economic policy of a country should focus on developing its land, and then gave some evidence of the gradual decline of Rome, Spain, Portugal, the United Kingdom and Germany, which are industry- and business-oriented countries, while the United States and Denmark grow rich day by day because they are agriculture based. He proved the argument that "those who build

404 *Rural crisis in 1930s and countermeasures*

their country with industry and commerce will find it hard to maintain, though it is easy to become rich and strong in the beginning, but those who build their country through agriculture make slow progress but have a solid foundation". The "fifth fiscal reason" considered that the state finance is derived from rent taxes, and the source of China's rent taxes is basically equal to agricultural products. "Today's agricultural administration is still naive and agriculture is underdeveloped [...] There is no other way than to focus on agriculture and increase tax sources. If you can implement appropriate management, the taxes can be increased".[371] The "sixth statistical reason" pointed out that China has chosen to establish a country based on industry, commerce and agriculture, and "not only rely on noble ideals, but also to seek common facts". To this end, the author draws from several aspects such as European grain production and consumption statistics, China's output of agricultural products, China's five major commodities (beans, cotton, seeds, tea, raw silk), which are the world's necessities, and introduces a large number of statistical data and tables to demonstrate that the theory of an agriculture-based country is based on a large number of facts and is in line with China's reality. The "tenth population reason" discussed two points of view: "Agriculture can increase the population" and "Agriculture can distribute the population".

Lv Ruiting's explanation for the customary reasons for establishing an agriculture-based country is also quite detailed. He quoted Guan Zhong's famous sayings: "Social class, moral standard, honesty, and dignity are the four dimensions of a country. If these four dimensions are not practiced, the country will be in its doom", and "Only when food is sufficient can people learn about etiquette, and only when clothing is warm can people feel honor". He also combined some real examples at all times and in all over the world, believing that agriculture can make filial piety last forever. "As is the true throughout both China and foreign countries in ancient and modern times, this idea is ubiquitous, the same and eternally changeless".[372] Specifically, there are eight influences of agriculture on customs, namely, "reward people of filial piety", "reward people who are diligent and thrifty", "reward people who save money", "cultivate a conservative nature", "cultivate a moderate nature", "cultivate a practical nature", "develop the thought of art", and "develop a noble personality". In addition, the author also analyzed the relationship between agriculture and health in the "ninth reason of health", which is quite new.

After detailing the reasons for establishing an agriculture-based country, Lv Ruiting summarized the book briefly by explaining the relief policy of Germany recorded in *Asahi Shimbun* of Osaka, Japan.

> After the failure of Germany, the Germans were still trying to save their country through policies concerning agriculture. On the contrary, China does not focus on agriculture and does not plan to build an

agriculture-based country though it is a naturally agricultural nation and it is in destitution now. Will the people who discuss national affairs take this aspect into consideration?[373]

Although Lv Ruiting's *Advisory on Agricultural Nation* is no more than 30 pages, with somewhat sketchy arguments, and cannot be called a "magnum opus", the book could as well be described as a valuable work because of the wide range of time and countries it covered. Also, it contained many reasonable pieces of evidence that are combined with the "national situation". "Advisory on Agricultural Nation" is undoubtedly of classic significance for the inspection of a country establishing theories and the choice of a development path. In a sense, it forms the starting point of the thought of rural construction in history, which deserves our best attention.

In "Dispute on the Establishing of the Nation" in the early twentieth century, three main points of view could be found: industry and commerce-based theory, agriculture and commerce-based theory, and agriculture-based theory. In the 1920s and 1930s, the debate continued, and the three opposing views were also formed. Among them, the "urban industrialists", represented by Wu Jingchao and Chen Xujing, strongly advocated the relief of the countryside through the development of cities. The school of rural construction represented by Liang Shuming and others advocated the relief of cities through the development of rural areas, and set agriculture and rural areas as the basis for China's social transformation. Harmonists represented by Chang Yansheng, Dong Shijin, Xu Shilian and Deng Feihuang advocated equal emphasis on agriculture and industry. In the early 1940s, "Dispute on the Establishing of the Nation" was once again "raised" as an "obsolete issue", and formed three main schools: the agriculture-oriented country, the industry-oriented country, and the agriculture- and industry-oriented country. These different groups carried out their discussion on some very specific questions concerning the prerequisites for China's development, whether it was agriculture or industry that could support China's Anti-Japanese War and the future of China.

The above facts fully show that from the beginning of the twentieth century to the 1940s, the content and viewpoint of the country were obviously inherited. Although the emphasis of the debates in each period was different, the core content was how to deal with the relationship between agriculture, industry and commerce. There were mainly three types of opinions: agriculture oriented, industry (commerce) oriented, and agriculture and industry (business) oriented. As "Dispute on the Establishing of the Nation" ran through the entire early twentieth century, it had a very important position in the formation and development of China's rural construction ideas. Therefore, the birth of the theory of an "agriculture-based country" in the early twentieth century undoubtedly influenced the development and the trend of rural construction ideas profoundly.

406 *Rural crisis in 1930s and countermeasures*

Notes

1 For example, Chen Zuiyun classified them into ten causes, that is, port opening, agricultural imports, agricultural commercialization, heavy taxes, land concentration, unfair land rents, usury loans, corrupt officials and greedy gentry, political corruption and intensified famine, and continuous civil wars. See Chen Zuiyun's "Countermeasures for the Revival of Rural Areas", "Peasant Issues and the Future of China", *Oriental Magazine*, July 1933, 113 (Author's note)
2 See Li Peilin, Sun Liping, Wang Mingming et al., *Survey of Rural Society in China, Chinese Academics and Society in the twentieth Century* (Sociology Volume), (Jinan: Shandong People's Publishing House, 2001), 159, 137.
3 Xiang Yucheng, "Analysis of the Causes of the Agricultural Crisis in the 1930s – on the Decline of Agricultural Productivity in Modern China", *History of Chinese Agriculture*, 4 (1999); Zhang Xike, "A Preliminary Study of the Roots of China's Agricultural Crisis in the 1930s", *Journal of Jining Teachers College*, 2 (2003).
4 Xiang Yucheng, "Analysis of the Causes of the Agricultural Crisis in the 1930s – on the Decline of Agricultural Productivity in Modern China", *History of Chinese Agriculture*, 4 (1999).
5 Xu Dixin and Wu Chengming, *History of Chinese Capitalism* (vol. 3), 335.
6 "Declaration of the Policies on the Second National Congress of the Kuomintang: Stop the Local Tyrants and Evil Gentry from Monopolizing the Village Government! Support the Autonomous Group of Farmers!" See Tadao Tanaka's *National Revolution and Rural Issues*, 27.
7 Wen Gongzhi, *Research on the Problems of Chinese Peasants* (Shanghai: Shanghai Sanmin Bookstore, 1929), 22–23.
8 Dong Ruzhou, "Bankruptcy of China's Rural Economy", *Oriental Magazine*, December 1932, 14.
9 Zhang Fuji, Lu Yuanquan, "A Brief Discussion on the Rural Crisis in Modern China", *Historical Monthly*, 1 (1999): 107.
10 "Peasant Issues and the Future of China", *Oriental Magazine*, August 1927, 3.
11 Gu Mei, "Construction of Rural Areas and Transformation of Rural Education", *Oriental Magazine*, November 1933, 6.
12 Chen Zuiyun, "Countermeasures for the Revival of Rural Areas", *Oriental Magazine*, July 1933, 112.
13 Wu Juenong, "The Peasant Problems in China" (1926), see Chen Hansheng, Xue Muqiao, Feng Hefa, *Chinese Rural Areas Before Liberation* (vol. 2) (Beijing: China Prospect Press, 1985), 26–28.
14 Qian Yishi et al., *China's Rural Issues* (Beijing: Zhonghua Book Company, 1935), 3–6, 17.
15 Dong Ruzhou, "Bankruptcy of China's Rural Economy", *Oriental Magazine*, December 1932, 20.
16 Qian Jiaju, "Relieving Rural Poverty and Urban Expansion", see Chen Hansheng, Xue Muqiao, Feng Hefa, *Chinese Rural Areas Before Liberation*, 2nd Series, 400–402.
17 Zeng Jikuan, "How to Solve the Problems in China's Rural Areas", *China Construction*, 8, no. 5 (November 1933): 10. Similar views including "agricultural withering", "rural bankruptcy", and "farmers' misery" can refer to Xu Qin, "Exploring the Wanjiabu Experimental Area", *Rural Area*, 1, no. 2 (December 1932), 77 (Author's note)

Rural crisis in 1930s and countermeasures   407

18 Li Jinghan, *China's Rural Issues* (Beijing: The Commercial Press, 1937), 121–123.

19 Qian Junrui, "China's Agricultural Panic and Land Problems", see Chen Hansheng, Xue Muqiao, Feng Hefa, *China's Rural Areas Before Liberation*, 2nd Series, 177.

20 Dong Xiujia, "How to Develop China's National Economy in the Future", see *Theory and Practice of the National Economic Construction Movement* comp. Propaganda Department of the Central Executive Committee of the Chinese Kuomintang, 1936, 88.

21 Dong Xiujia, "How to Develop the National Economy of China in the Future", see *Theory and Practice of the National Economic Construction Movement*, 88.

22 "Report of the Lytton Commission", 42 and 31, see Chen Hansheng, Xue Muqiao, Feng Hefa, *Chinese Rural Areas Before Liberation*, the 2nd Series, 186.

23 See Xue Muqiao, "The Fundamental Causes of Poverty", see Chen Hansheng, Xue Muqiao, Feng Hefa, *China's Rural Areas Before Liberation*, the 2nd Series, 267.

24 Lin Sen, "The Importance of National Economic Construction", in *Theory and Practice of National Economic Construction Movement*, 1936, 31 and 28.

25 Qian Junrui, "Land Issues of China at the Present Stage", see Chen Hansheng, Xue Muqiao, Feng Hefa, *China's Rural Areas Before Liberation*, the 2nd Series, 198.

26 Shen Changye, "My Opinions on Rural Construction", *Guo Wen Weekly*, 13, no. (March 1936), 24.

27 Qian Junrui, "Land Issues of China at the Present Stage", see Chen Hansheng, Xue Muqiao, Feng Hefa, *China's Rural Areas Before Liberation*, the 2nd Series, 194.

28 Yu Duo, "How to Improve the Rural Areas of Jiangxi Province", *Rural Areas*, the 1, no. 1 (December 1933), 53.

29 Fang Xianting, "Rural Construction and Anti-Japanese War", *Rural Construction*, 1st issue, September 1938, 1.

30 Wang Zhenxin, "Opinions on the Current Crisis and Relief in China's Rural Areas", *Rural Areas*, 1, no. 1 (November 1933), 4.

31 Li Zhujiu, "Trivial Words on Reviving Rural Areas and Improving Agriculture", *China Construction*, 8, no. 5 (November 1933), 95.

32 Li Younong, "Rehabilitation of Jiangxi Rural Areas", *China Construction*, 8, no. 5 (November 1933): 25–26.

33 Ding Da, *The Collapse of Cphina's Rural Economy* (Shanghai: Shanghai Union Bookstore, 1930), 27.

34 Gu Meng, "Rural Areas of Hebei Province in the Process of Collapse", *China Economy*, 1, no. 4 (April 1933), 66.

35 Chen Guojun, "My Opinions on Reviving Rural Areas", *China Construction*, 8, no. 5 (November 1933), 1–2.

36 Zhong Xiuqiong, "Prerequisites for Improving Rural Areas", *Rural Areas*, 1, no. 2 (December 1932), 56.

37 Liu Yuncou, "Agricultural College of the Agricultural Association of the Ministry of Agriculture and Rural Renaissance", *China Construction*, 8, no. 5 (November 1933), 57.

38 Li Jinzheng believes that the seven factors leading farmers to live in poverty are as follows: inadequate land, low productivity, gloomy handicraft industries, a weak position in commodity exchange, depletion of rural finance and usury, tax exploitation, natural and human disasters. Among them, insufficient farmland, low agricultural productivity and frequent natural and human disasters are the most important reasons leading to farmers' poverty. See Li Jinzheng's *Poverty and*

408 *Rural crisis in 1930s and countermeasures*

Related Factors of Farmers' Life in North China in Modern Times, A Probe into the Socio-Economy of China's Rural Areas in Modern Times (People's Publishing House, 2004), 216–230 (Author's note)

39 Sun Yefang, "The Way for Rural Workers", from *Several Theoretical Problems Concerning Chinese Society and Its Revolutionary Nature* (Beijing: China Social Science Press, 1985), 142.

40 Zhou Gucheng, *Changes in Chinese Society* (Shanghai: Shanghai Bookstore, 1989 photocopy), 188, 194.

41 "Publishing Speech of China's Rural Economic Papers", see Qian Jiaju's *China's Rural Economic Papers, Republic of China Series*, 2nd version (35) Economics (Shanghai: Shanghai Bookstore, 1989), 2.

42 *Construction of China's New Rural Areas*, comp. Wang Junsheng (Beijing: The Commercial Press, 1937), 7–8.

43 Xue Muqiao, "The Basic Causes of Poverty", see Chen Hansheng, Xue Muqiao, Feng Hefa, *Chinese Rural Areas before Liberation*, 2nd Series, 267.

44 "The Inference of Recent Rural Education Problems in the United States", see Chen Xia and Fu Qiqun, *Selected Works of Fu Baochen's Education Theory*, 242–244.

45 *Food Policies of Countries in the World*, ed. the Grain Bureau of Japan' s Ministry of Agriculture and Forestry and trans. Cao Chensi et al. (Beijing: The Commercial Press, 1937), 41.

46 *Food Policies of Countries in the World*, ed. the Grain Bureau of Japan' s Ministry of Agriculture and Forestry, 35, 39.

47 Youxin, "Does Low-price Grain Hurt Farmers?", *Oriental Magazine*, November 1932, 1.

48 Jiang Junchen, "A New Attitude on China's Agricultural Panic in 1932 – Harvest and Disasters", see Chen Hansheng, Xue Muqiao, Feng Hefa, *Chinese Rural Areas before Liberation*, 2nd Series, 380, 390.

49 Qian Junrui, "The Life of Chinese Farmers in the Current Agricultural Panic", from *Chinese Rural Areas before Liberation*, 2nd Series, 201.

50 "General Review of Rural Construction Movement", see Chen Xia and Fu Qiqun, *Selected Works of Fu Baochen's Education Theory*, 84.

51 Zhou Gucheng, *Changes in Chinese Society*, 7, 45–47.

52 Zeng Jikuan, "How to Solve China's Rural Problems", *China Construction*, 8, no. 5 (November 1933): 9.

53 Li Hongyi, "Improving Agricultural Tools and Rejuvenating Rural Areas", *Rural Areas*, 2, no. 3 (December, 15, 1934): 51.

54 Ren Zheming, "The Fundamental Problems of China's Rural Economy", see Qian Yishi et al., *China's Rural Issues*, 22, 32.

55 "Declaration of the Establishment of the Commune", *Rural Areas*, 1, no. 1 (November, 15, 1933): 91.

56 Zeng Jikuan, "How to Solve the Problems in China's Rural Areas", *China Construction*, 8, no. 5 (November 1933), 12–13.

57 Zhang Qiwen, "The Decline and Rescuing Methods of China's Rural Economy", *Rural Areas*, 1, no. 3 (January 1934), 59.

58 Xing Zhenji, *General Introduction to the Outline of Shanxi's Rural Administration*, Ten-day Journal Office of Shanxi's Rural Administration, 1929, 8.

59 Ti Si, "The Status Quo and Improvement of Rural Public Order in Hebei Province", *Zhongzhi Monthly*, 1, no. 2 (November 1934), 91, 94.

Rural crisis in 1930s and countermeasures 409

60 "Why We Need Rural Civilian Education?" See Chen Xia and Fu Qiqun, *Selected Works of Fu Baochen's Education Theory*, 2, 25

61 *Rural Revival and Rural Education Movement*, edited by Jin Lunhai (Beijing: The Commercial Press, 1934), 35, 34.

62 "China's Politics in Despair: the Unestablished State Power", comp. Academic Committee of the Chinese Culture Academy, see *The Complete Works of Liang Shuming* (vol. 2) (Jinan: Shandong People's Publishing House, 2005), 213.

63 Li Jinghan, *China's Rural Issues* (Beijing: The Commercial Press, 1937), 125.

64 Zhou Gucheng, *Changes in Chinese Society*, 85.

65 Lan Mengjiu, "The Road to Rural Revival", *China Construction*, 8, no. 5 (November 1933), 44.

66 Fu Baochen, "General Review of Rural Construction Movement", see Chen Xia and Fu Qiqun, *Selected Works of Fu Baochen's Education Theory*, 86.

67 Liang Shuming, "The Theory of Rural Construction", see *The Complete Works of Liang Shuming* (vol. 2), 150.

68 (America) Gilbert Rozman, *The Modernization of China*, 660.

69 Zhang Ming, *Eighty Years of the Rural Road* (Shanghai: Shanghai SDX Joint Publishing Company, 1997), 220.

70 (America) Fei Zhengqing, ed., *Cambridge History of the Republic of China*, (vol. 1), trans. Yang Pinquan et al. (Beijing: China Social Sciences Press, 1993), 33.

71 "Documents of Jiangsu Academic Council", 84, see Wang Xianming, *Modern Gentlemen: The Historical Fate of a Feudal Class*, 157.

72 Tao Xingzhi, "The New Trend of Normal Education", see *Complete Works of Tao Xingzhi (1)* (Changsha: Hunan Education Publishing House, 1986), 167.

73 (America) Gilbert Rozman, *The Modernization of China*, 551–563.

74 (Japan) Akigorou Taga's, *Historical Materials of Modern Chinese Education* (Taipei: Wenhai Publishing Company, 1976), statistics on pages 770–777.

75 Education delegation of the League of Nations: "Report of Education Delegation of the League of Nations (1931)", see *Modern Chinese Historical Materials Series* (3rd version), ed. Shen Yunlong (vol. 108) (Taipei: Wenhai Publishing Company, 1966), 160–161.

76 The world-renowned agricultural economist Dr. Do. L. Butterfield visited China in 1921 and found that there were at least 100,000 villages and 1 million rural communities in China. (Author's note)

77 "The Second Annual Statistics of China Education": In 1922, there were 177,751 national schools and elementary schools, 1,096 middle schools; in 1931, there were 259,863 national schools and elementary schools, and 3,026 middle schools. (Author's note)

78 Pan Guangdan, "Comments on Rural Education", see *Pan Guangdan's Anthology*, ed. Pan Naigu and Pan Naihe (Beijing: Guangming Daily Press, 1999), 371–378.

79 (America) Kong Feili, *The Rebellion and Its Enemies in the Late Chinese Empire*, 238.

80 "Introduction to the Curriculum in Chinese Rural Primary Schools", see *Selected Works of Fu Baochen's Education Theory*, ed. Chen Xia and Fu Qiqun, 46.

81 Zhou Gucheng, *Changes in Chinese Society*, 87–88.

82 Yu Duo, "How to Improve the Rural Areas of Jiangxi Province", *Rural Areas*, 1, no. 1 (November 1933), 53.

410 *Rural crisis in 1930s and countermeasures*

83 Zhou Gucheng, *Changes in Chinese Society*, 89, 90.
84 *Report on the Experimental Area of Rural Service (1)*, ed. Zheng Yanfen (Guangzhou: Publishing Department of National Sun Yat-sen University, October 1936), 10.
85 Fu Baochen, "The Reality of Rural Women's Lives in Our Country and Our Responsibility", in *Selected Works of Fu Baochen's Education Theory*, ed. Chen Xia and Fu Qiqun, 197.
86 Fu Baochen, "General Review of Rural Construction Movement", in Chen Xia and Fu Qiqun, *Selected Works of Fu Baochen's Education Theory*, 402.
87 Zhou Gucheng, *Changes in Chinese Society*, 181.
88 *Rural Revival and Rural Education Movement*, ed. Jin Lunhai, 48.
89 Zhou Gucheng, *Changes in Chinese Society*, 314.
90 Zhou Gucheng, *Changes in Chinese Society*, 163.
91 Compilation Committee *of Chinese Economic Yearbook of the Ministry of Industry*, ed. *Chinese Economic Yearbook Sequel*, chap. 16, "Price and Living Expenses" (Shanghai: Commercial Press 1935), 4.
92 Qian Junrui, "Introduction to Chinese Rural Areas", from *Chinese Rural Areas before Liberation*, the 2nd Series, 8.
93 Qian Junrui, "The Life of Chinese Farmers in the Current Agricultural Panic", from *Chinese Rural Areas before Liberation*, the 2nd Series, 199.
94 Lan Mengjiu, "The Road to Rural Revival", *China Construction*, 8, no. 5 (November 1933), 47, 45.
95 Zhou Gucheng, *Changes in Chinese Society*, 181.
96 *Hua Nian Weekly*, 3, no. 48, refers to Qian Junrui, "The Life of Chinese Farmers in the Current Agricultural Panic", from *Chinese Rural Areas before Liberation*, the 2nd Series, 205.
97 Wang Zhenxin, "Opinions on the Current Crisis and Relief in China's Rural Areas", *Rural Areas*, 1, no. 1 (November 1933), 4.
98 Zhou Gucheng, *Changes in Chinese Society*, 181.
99 Qian Jiaju, "Relieving Rural Poverty and Urban Expansion", *Chinese Rural Areas Before Liberation*, the 2nd Series, 407, 409.
100 Zhou Gucheng, *Changes in Chinese Society*, 181.
101 Dong Ruzhou, "A Review of the Problems of Chinese Peasants off Villages", *New China*, 1, no. 9 (May 1933), 7.
102 Zhang Qiwen, "The Decline and Rescuing Methods of China's Rural Economy", *Rural Areas*, 1, no. 3 (January 1934), 163.
103 Qian Junrui, "Land Issues of China at the Present Stage", *Chinese Rural Areas before Liberation*, the 2nd Series, 196.
104 Feng Hefa, "Agricultural Management in China", *Chinese Rural Areas before Liberation*, the 2nd Series, 563.
105 "Analysis and Solutions to Chinese Rural Problems", in Ru Chunpu, *Analysis and Solutions to Chinese Rural Problems* (vol. 1) (Peking: Zhendong Book Company, 1934), 128.
106 Feng Hefa, "Agricultural Trade of Chinese Farmers", *Chinese Rural Areas before Liberation*, the 2nd Series, 574.
107 Zhang Xichang, "Whether the Rural Economy Is Prosperous under the Rising Prices", *Chinese Rural Areas before Liberation*, the 2nd Series, p. 536.
108 *Food Policies of Countries in the World*, ed. Grain Bureau of Japan's Ministry of Agriculture and Forestry, 31.

Rural crisis in 1930s and countermeasures 411

109 *Food Policies of Countries in the World*, ed. Grain Bureau of Japan's Ministry of Agriculture and Forestry, 32.

110 Chen Hansheng, "China's Development in the Past Three Decades", *Chinese Rural Areas before Liberation*, the 2nd Series, 129.

111 Qian Junrui, "Land Issues of China at the Present Stage", *Chinese Rural Areas before Liberation*, the 2nd Series, 201.

112 *Documents on the Peasant Movement during the First Civil Revolutionary War*, comp. People's Publishing House, p. 11.

113 Wang Fangzhong, "A Preliminary Study on the Fall of Rural Land Price in the 1930s (before the War of Resistance against Japan)", *Research on Modern History*, 3 (1993): 214.

114 Xue Cunren, "A Survey of Rural Areas in Lincheng County of Hebei Province", see Qian Jiaju's *China's Rural Economic Papers*, 2nd version (35) Economics (Shanghai: Shanghai Bookstore, 1990), 496, 497.

115 Xu Shilian, *Discussion on Several Social Issues in China* (Beijing Bookstore, 1929), 64, 69.

116 Zhu Qihua, *A Perspective of China's Rural Economy* (Shanghai: Shanghai China Research Bookstore, 1936), 3–4, 54.

117 *General History of Shanxi Province*, comp. Shanxi History Institute (vol. 7), 238.

118 Liu Dapeng, *Diary Written in Tuixiang Room*, 491.

119 Liu Dapeng, *Diary Written in Tuixiang Room*, 286.

120 Liu Dapeng, *Diary Written in Tuixiang Room*, 477.

121 Wang Xianming, "Rural Workers from Shanxi Province in the Early Twentieth Century", *Historical Research*, 5 (2006): 115.

122 Zhu Xie, "The Heavy Land Tax and the Decline of the Rural Economy", *Oriental Magazine*, 30, no. 22 (November 1933), 7–8.

123 Zhou Gucheng, *Changes in Chinese Society*, 224.

124 Wang Xianming, "The Evolution and Countermeasures of Rural Social Conflicts in the Early twentieth Century", *Journal of Huazhong Normal University*, 4 (2012): 11–12.

125 Huang Fuguang, "Analysis of the Collapse of China's Rural Economy" (one of the 3rd graduation theses, National Wuhan University, supervisor Ren Kainan), 1933, 121–122.

126 (America) Gilbert Rozman, *The Modernization of China*, 209, 208.

127 (America) Fei Zhengqing, ed, *Cambridge History of the Republic of China (1912–1949)* (vol. 1), 735.

128 (America) Fei Zhengqing, ed, *Cambridge History of the Republic of China (1912–1949)* (vol. 1), 737.

129 *Modern History of China (1840–1949)*, ed. Wang Xianming (Beijing: China Renmin University Press, 2011), 529.

130 (America) Fei Zhengqing, ed., *Cambridge History of the Republic of China (1912–1949)* (vol. 1), 736, 740.

131 (America) Fei Zhengqing, ed., *Cambridge History of the Republic of China (1912–1949)* (vol. 1), 36.

132 *Modern History of China (1840–1949)*, ed. Wang Xianming, 532.

133 (America) Pomeranz, *The Great Diversion: Economic Development in Europe, China, and the Modern World*, 234.

134 (America) Fei Zhengqing, ed., *Cambridge History of the Republic of China (1912–1949)* (vol. 1), 744, 809.

412 *Rural crisis in 1930s and countermeasures*

135 Wang Xianming, *The Gentry in an Era of Change – The Gentry and the Changes of Rural Social Structure (1901–1945)*, 363.

136 Zeng Yaorong, "Resistance and Compromise: The Development of Modern Urban-Rural Relations and the Rural Revolution – A Case Study of the Yongding Riot in 1928", *Research on the History of the Communist Party of China*, 11 (2011): 85, 86.

137 Yang Kaidao, "The Causes and Solutions of Rural Life Decline in China", *Oriental Magazine*, August 1927, 5–6.

138 Cheng Shutang, "The Increasing Problems of Rural Assessed Contributions", *Oriental Magazine*, December 1935, 54.

139 Qian Jiaju, "China's Finance in the Last Thirty Years", *Oriental Magazine*, January 1934, 123.

140 Xu Dixin, "The Livelihood of Peasants in Rural Bankruptcy", *Oriental Magazine*, January 1935, 56.

141 Xu Yushui, "A Survey of land taxes in China", *Oriental Magazine*, May 1934, 57.

142 Fei Weikai, "The Economic Trend of the Republic of China", qtd. from Luo Rongqu's *New Reviews on Modernization: The World and China's Modernization Process*, 327.

143 Qian Jiaju, "Relieving Rural Poverty and Urban Expansion", *Chinese Rural Areas before Liberation*, the 2nd Series, 408.

144 Xu Zhengxue, "Rural Issues: A Study of the Causes of Rural Collapse in China – Preface" (Nanjing: Research Association of Chinese Rural Rejuvenation, 1934), 2.

145 Dong Ruzhou, "A Review of the Problems of Chinese Peasants off Villages", *New China*, 1, no. 9 (May 1933): 7.

146 Qian Yishi, "A Review of the Modern Chinese Economy", see Chen Hansheng, Xue Muqiao, Feng Hefa, *Chinese Rural Areas before Liberation*, 1st Series (Beijing: China Prospect Press, 1985), 533.

147 "Introduction to Chinese Rural Economics Papers (Preface)", ed. Qian Jiaju, *Republic of China Series*, 2nd version (35), Economics (Shanghai: Shanghai Bookstore, 1990 photocopy), 1.

148 Michael Gasster, *China's Struggle to Modernize* (New York: Alfred A. Knopf, 1983), 4.

149 For example, Chen Zuiyun classified them into ten causes, which are port opening, agricultural imports, agricultural commercialization, heavy taxes, land concentration, unfair land rents, usury loans, corrupt officials and greedy gentry, political corruption and intensified famine, and continuous civil wars. See Chen Zuiyun, "Countermeasures for the Revival of Rural Areas", "Peasant Issues and the Future of China", *Oriental Magazine*, July 1933, 113. (Author's note)

150 See Li Peilin, Sun Liping, Wang Mingming et al., *Survey of Rural Society in China, Chinese Academics and Society in the twentieth Century* (Sociology volume), 159.

151 See Li Peilin, Sun Liping, Wang Mingming et al., *Survey of Rural Society in China, Chinese Academics and Society in the twentieth Century* (Sociology volume), 137.

152 See Xiang Yucheng, "Analysis of the Causes of the Agricultural Crisis in the 1930s – on the Decline of Agricultural Productivity in Modern China", *History of Chinese Agriculture*, 4 (1999); Zhang Xike, "A Preliminary Study of the Roots of China's Agricultural Crisis in the 1930s", *Journal of Jining Teachers College*, 2 (2003).

Rural crisis in 1930s and countermeasures 413

153 See Xiang Yucheng, "Analysis of the Causes of the Agricultural Crisis in the 1930s – on the Decline of Agricultural Productivity in Modern China", *History of Chinese Agriculture*, 4 (1999).

154 Li Jinzheng, "The Poverty of Farmers in North China Since Modern Times and Its Related Factors", from *Socioeconomic Analysis of Rural China in Modern Times*, (Beijing: People's Publishing House, 2004), 216–230.

155 (America) Huang Zongzhi, *Small-Scale Peasant Economy and Social Changes in North China*, 141.

156 (America) Huang Zongzhi, *Small-Scale Peasant Economy and Social Changes in North China*, 301.

157 For details, see Wang Xianming, "The Gentry and 'Civilian Revolts' in the Late Qing Dynasty – the Historical Trend and Epochal Causes of Gentry-Civilians Conflicts", *Research on Modern History*, 1 (2008), 21–33.

158 See Zhang Zhenhe and Ding Yuanying, "The Chronology of the Civil Revolutions in the late Qing Dynasty", from *The Modern Historical Documents*, comp. the Documents Editing Group of Modern History, Modern History Institute of the Chinese Academy of Social Sciences, 3 and 4 (1982); *Historical Documents of Civil Revolution Archives in the Ten Years before the Revolution of 1911* (vols. 1 and 2), compiled and selected by the First Historical Archives of China and the Department of History of Beijing Normal University (Beijing: Zhonghua Book Company, 1985); Du Tao, "Review of the Research on the Civil Revolutions in the Last Ten Years of the Late Qing Dynasty", *Fujian Forum*, 6 (2004), 70–74

159 Ma Ziyi, "The Unprecedented Peak of the Civil Revolutions – Analysis of the Cases of the Civil Revolutions in the Ten Years before the Revolution of 1911", *Journal of Shanghai Jiaotong University* (Philosophy and Social Science ed.), 5 (2003), 66.

160 Ma Ziyi, "The Unprecedented Peak of the Civil Revolutions – Analysis of the Cases of the Civil Revolutions in the Ten Years before the Revolution of 1911", *Journal of Shanghai Jiaotong University* (Philosophy and Social Science ed.), 5 (2003), 66.

161 Wang Xianming, "The Gentry and 'Civilian Revolts' in the Late Qing Dynasty – the Historical Trend and Epochal Causes of Gentry-Civilians Conflicts", *Research on Modern History*, 1 (2008), 21–33.

162 *Chinese Rural Economic Documents*, ed. Feng Hefa, 491–493.

163 Qiu Jianli, Li Xuechang, "A Preliminary Study of the Land Association in Jiangnan Region in the 1910s and 1920s", *Historiography Monthly*, 5 (2010): 23.

164 Zhang Zuyin, "Peasants in ZhenZe County", *New Youth*, 4, no. 3 (January 15, 1918), 226.

165 Qiu Jianli, Li Xuechang, "A Preliminary Study of the Land Association in Jiangnan Region in the 1910s and 1920s", *Historiography Monthly*, 5 (2010): 23.

166 Qiu Jianli, Li Xuechang, "A Preliminary Study of the Land Association in Jiangnan Region in the 1910s and 1920s", *Historiography Monthly*, 5 (2010), 24.

167 "Local Communications· Suzhou· Preparations of the Sixiang land Association Branch", *Shun Pao*, November 22, 1921, 11th edition.

168 Qiu Jianli, Li Xuechang, "A Preliminary Study of the Land Association in Jiangnan Region in the 1910s and 1920s", *Historiography Monthly*, 5 (2010): 26.

169 "Local Communications· Jinshan· Recent News on Reduction of Taxes in Case of Barren Land", *Shun Pao*, December 7, 1917, 7th ed.

170 "On the Villagers' Anti-rental Trend", *Shun Pao*, January 3, 1912, 2nd ed.

414 *Rural crisis in 1930s and countermeasures*

171 "Another Anti-Rental Trend in Su County", *Shun Pao*, February 11, 1912, 6th ed.

172 "Troubles of Rent Collectors from Tenant-Peasants", *Shun Pao*, December 24, 1911, 4th ed.

173 Qiu Jianli, Li Xuechang, "A Preliminary Study of the Land Association in Jiangnan Region in the 1910s and 1920s", *Historiography Monthly*, 5 (2010), 26.

174 Xu Yushui, "A Survey of Land Taxes in China", *Oriental Magazine*, May 1934, 64.

175 *Selected Archives of Peasant Movements in Jiangsu Province*, comp. Jiangsu Provincial Archives (Beijing: Archives Press, 1983), 61.

176 Xu Dixin, "The Livelihood of Peasants in Rural Bankruptcy", *Oriental Magazine*, January 1935, 54.

177 Wang Tianjiang, "Modern Usury in Rural Henan", *Research on Modern History*, 2 (1995), 36–37.

178 (Japan) Takashi Mitani, *Secret Associations and the Chinese Revolution*, 62.

179 Li Yan, "Research on the Political Structure of Rural China", *China Rural*, 1, no. 10 (July 1935), 40.

180 Cai Shubang, "Research on the Trend of Chinese Tenant Farmers in the Past Decade", *Oriental Magazine*, May 1933, 31.

181 Wang Zhongming, *The Peasant Problems and Movements in China* (Shanghai: Pingfan Publishing House, 1929), 114.

182 Wang Zhongming, *The Peasant Problems and Movements in China*, 266.

183 Wang Zhongming, *The Peasant Problems and Movements in China*, p. 302.

184 (Japan) Tadao Tanaka, *Chinese Agricultural Economic Data*, Wang Fuquan (Shanghai: Dadong Book Company, 1934), 313–322.

185 (Japan) Tadao Tanaka, *Chinese Agricultural Economic Data*, 315.

186 *Domestic Peasant Movements before the 16th Year of the Republic of China*, Zhejiang KMT Party Headquarters (publishing house unknown, publishing time unknown), 52.

187 *Domestic Peasant Movements before the 16th Year of the Republic of China*, Zhejiang KMT Party Headquarters, 52.

188 Zhang Youyi, *Agricultural History Data of Modern China*, the 3rd series, 381.

189 Wang Tianjiang, "Modern Usury in Rural Henan", *Research on Modern History*, 2 (1995), 43.

190 Wu Bingruo, "The Living Condition of Farmers in the Huaihe River Basin", *Oriental Magazine*, August 1927, 44.

191 Wu Dakun, "Recent Peasant Revolts in Suzhou", *Oriental Magazine*, January 1935, 83.

192 Wu Dakun, "Recent Peasant Revolts in Suzhou", *Oriental Magazine*, January 1935, 84.

193 Wu Dakun, "Recent Peasant Revolts in Suzhou", *Oriental Magazine*, January 1935, 84.

194 *Chinese Rural Economic Documents*, ed. Feng Hefa, 423.

195 *Chinese Rural Economic Documents*, ed. Feng Hefa, 423.

196 *Chinese Rural Economic Documents*, ed. Feng Hefa, 425.

197 Zhang Ruide, "The Development and Crisis of China's Modern Rural Economy – Note (93)", from *A Collection of Papers on the History of Rural Economy in Modern China* (Institute of Modern History of Academia Sinica, 1989), 739; Du Zanqi (America), *Culture, Power and State – Rural Areas of North China in 1900–1924*, 244.

Rural crisis in 1930s and countermeasures 415

198 Liu Hebei, "Traditional Financial Regulations in Jiangsu Province (1912–1937)", from *A Collection of Papers on the History of Rural Economy in Modern China* (Taipei: Institute of Modern History, Academia Sinica, 1989), 688.

199 "A Survey on Three Volumes of Land Register Books in Changzhou County of Jiangsu Province in the Early Years of Kangxi Period", from *The Collection of Agricultural History of the Ming and Qing Dynasties and Modern Times*, comp. Zhang Youyi (Beijing: China Agriculture Press, 1997), 75.

200 "Reassessment of China's Land Distribution in the 1920s and 1930s", from *The Collection of Agricultural History of the Ming and Qing Dynasties and Modern Times*, comp. Zhang Youyi, 88.

201 "Reassessment of China's Land Distribution in the 1920s and 1930s", from *The Collection of Agricultural History of the Ming and Qing Dynasties and Modern Times*, comp. Zhang Youyi, 89.

202 "A Survey of Peasants' Living Conditions in All Areas", "Excerpts from Essays", "Wujin County in Jiangsu Province, *Oriental Magazine*, August 1927, 105.

203 "A Survey of Peasants' Living Conditions in All Areas", "Excerpts from Essays", "Jurong County in Jiangsu Province, *Oriental Magazine*, August 1927, 116.

204 "A Survey of Peasants' Living Conditions in All Areas", *Oriental Magazine*, August 1927, 123.

205 "A Survey of Peasants' Living Conditions in All Areas", *Oriental Magazine*, August 1927, 133.

206 "The Living Conditions of Peasants in Quzhou County of Zhejiang Province", *Oriental Magazine*, August 1927, 56.

207 "A Survey of Peasants' Living Conditions in All Areas", *Oriental Magazine*, August 1927, 145.

208 Jiafu, "The Normal Life of Farmers in Central Shanxi Province – A Settlement Account for the Farmers in Bankruptcy", *Tianjin Yishi News*, p. 3, July 13, 1935, 11th edition; *Rural Weekly*, issue 71, July 1936.

209 "A Survey of Peasants' Living Conditions in All Areas", *Oriental Magazine*, August 1927, 137.

210 "Farmers in Haimen County", *Oriental Magazine*, August 1927, 25.

211 Yan Zhongda, "The Rural Areas in Northwest Hubei", *Oriental Magazine*, August 1927, 44–45.

212 Yang Wanxuan, "Farmers in Dading County, Guizhou Province", *Oriental Magazine*, August 1927, 16.

213 Zhang Youyi, *Agricultural History Data of Modern China*, 2nd series (Beijing: SDX Joint Publishing Company, 1958), 433.

214 Sa Mengwu, *A Sociological Study of Chinese Social Issues* (Shanghai: Huatong Publishing House, 1929), 163.

215 Sa Mengwu, *A Sociological Study of Chinese Social Issues* (Shanghai: Huatong Publishing House, 1929), 159.

216 "Reassessment of the Population and Cultivated Land in Modern China", from *The Collection of Agricultural History of the Ming and Qing Dynasties and Modern Times*, comp. Zhang Youyi, 23.

217 Zhang Ruide, "The Development and Crisis of China's Modern Rural Economy", from *A Collection of Papers on the History of Rural Economy in Modern China* (Taipei: Institute of Modern History, Academia Sinica, 1989), 734.

218 Zhang Ruide, "The Development and Crisis of China's Modern Rural Economy", from *A Collection of Papers on the History of Rural Economy in Modern China*, 164.

416 *Rural crisis in 1930s and countermeasures*

219 Qian Yong said: "Among the three counties of Wu Region, there were more than hundreds of thousands of hectares in Hutian where lands were more profitable than that in other regions" (*Lv Garden Compendium of Ruminations and Commentaries, Hydrology Volume, Societal Participation*), from *The Collection of Agricultural History of the Ming and Qing Dynasties and Modern Times*, comp. Zhang Youyi (Beijing: China Agriculture Press, 1997), 73.

220 "A Survey on Three Volumes of Land Register Books in Changzhou County of Jiangsu Province in the Early Years of Kangxi Period", from *The Collection of Agricultural History of the Ming and Qing Dynasties and Modern Times*, comp. Zhang Youyi, 73.

221 "A Survey on Three Volumes of Land Register Books in Changzhou County of Jiangsu Province in the Early Years of Kangxi Period", from *The Collection of Agricultural History of the Ming and Qing Dynasties and Modern Times*, comp. Zhang Youyi, 74.

222 Zhao Gang, *Traditional Land Distribution in Rural China* (Beijing: New Star Press, 2006), 65–70.

223 Xu Dixin and Wu Chengming, *History of Chinese Capitalism* (vol. 2) (Beijing: People's Publishing House, 1990), 1051.

224 (America) Shi Jianya, *Cities in the Late Chinese Empire*, 262.

225 "Shanghai Research Materials", ed. Shanghai News Agency, from *Modern China's Historical Materials* – 3rd Series, ed. Shen Yunlong, 42nd edition (Taipei: Wenhai Publishing Company, 1988, photocopy), 577.

226 "Shanghai Research Materials", ed. Shanghai News Agency, from *Modern China's Historical Materials* – 3rd Series, ed. Shen Yunlong, 42nd edition, 753.

227 "Shanghai Research Materials", ed. Shanghai News Agency, from *Modern China's Historical Materials* – 3rd Series, ed. Shen Yunlong, 42nd edition, 698.

228 "Shanghai Research Materials", ed. Shanghai News Agency, from *Modern China's Historical Materials* – the 3rd Series, ed. Shen Yunlong, 42nd edition, 699–700.

229 Ge Yuanxi, "A Thriving and Prosperous Story in Shanghai", from *Modern China's Historical Materials* – the 3rd Series, ed. Shen Yunlong, 42nd edition., 23.

230 Ge Yuanxi, "A Thriving and Prosperous Story in Shanghai", from *Modern China's Historical Materials* – 3rd Series, ed. Shen Yunlong, 42nd edition, 23.

231 "Shanghai Research Materials", ed. Shanghai News Agency, from *Modern China's Historical Materials* – 3rd Series, ed. Shen Yunlong, 42nd edition, 548.

232 *The History of Modern Tianjin City*, ed. Luo Shuwei (Beijing: China Social Science Press, 1993), 505.

233 *Modern Economic and Social Studies in the Bohai Rim*, comp. Zhang Limin et al. (Tianjin: Tianjin Academy of Social Sciences Press, 2003), 268.

234 *Modern Economic and Social Studies in the Bohai Rim*, comp. Zhang Limin et al., 452.

235 Wang Shouzhong, Guo Dasong, *The Modern History of City Changes in Shandong Province*, 476.

236 Wang Shouzhong, Guo Dasong, *The Modern History of City Changes in Shandong Province*, 478.

237 Wang Shouzhong, Guo Dasong, *The Modern History of City Changes in Shandong Province*, 660.

Rural crisis in 1930s and countermeasures 417

238 Ruan Xiang, et al., *The First Chinese Yearbook and Population* (Beijing: The Commercial Press, 1926), 54–55.

239 Gu Chaolin et al. *Urban Geography of China* (Beijing: The Commercial Press, 1998), 76.

240 Xin Ping, *Discovering History from Shanghai – the Shanghain Citizens and Their Social Life in the Process of Modernization 1927–1937* (Shanghai: Shanghai People's Publishing House, 1996), 40.

241 Luo Weiwei, *The History of Modern Tianjin City* (Beijing: China Social Science Press, 1993), p. 457.

242 Pi Mingyu, *The History of Modern Wuhan City* (Beijing: China Social Science Press, 1993), 660.

243 Kui Yingtao, *The History of Modern Chongqing City* (Chengdu: Sichuan University Press, 1991), 398.

244 Zhao Qixiu, Yuan Rongsou. *The Records of Jiaoao* (Taipei: Chengwen Publishing Company, photocopy edition 1968), 231–276. Ministry of Industry, Bureau of International Trade. *China Industry Journal (Shandong Province)* (C), (Beijing: The Commercial Press, 1937), 9–10.

245 Liu Yanpu, *Contemporary Zhengzhou Urban Construction·Appendix* (Beijing: China Architecture & Building Press, 1988), 336. Chen Yanya, *Inspection of Northwest China*, Declaration Hall, 1937, 472.

246 Jiang Pei, Xiong Yaping, "Railway and the Rise of Shijiazhuang City 1905–1937", *Research on Modern History*, 3 (2005), 185.

247 Wang Xianming, Xiong Yaping, "Railway and the Development of Inland Newly Emerging Towns of North China 1905–1937", *Research on the History of China's Economy*, 3 (2006), 15; Cheng Changzhi. "A Brief Introduction to Tangshan Towns", *Municipal Administration Review*, 3, no. 14 (July 1935), 12; Beining Railway Administration, *Report on Economic Investigation along the Beining Railway*, 1937 (Taipei: Publishing Company, photocopy edition 1989), 1247.

248 Wang Xianming, "The Differentiation of the Scholar-Gentry Class in Modern China", *Social Science Front*, 3 (1987), 168; Wang Xianming. "The Social Mobility of Modern Chinese Scholar-Gentry Class", *Historical Research*, 2 (1993), 92, 94.

249 Li Mingwe, *Research on the Social Ranks of Chinese Cities in the Late Qing Dynasty and Early Republic of China (1897–1927)* (Beijing: Social Sciences Academic Press, 2005), 96.

250 Peng Xuepei, "Bird's Eye View of the Renaissance Movement of Rural Areas", *Oriental Magazine*, January 1935, 4.

251 "Attach Importance to the Internal Causes of China's Modern Economic Backwardness – A Discussion on the Central Clues of China's Modern Economic History", in Zhang Youyi, *History Collection of Ming, Qing and Modern Agricultural*, 3.

252 Reporter. "The Peasant Problem and China's Future", *Oriental Magazine*, August 1927, 3.

253 Gu Yi, "Construction of Rural Areas and Transformation of Rural Education", *Oriental Magazine*, October 1933, 6.

254 "Will Cheap Crops Devastate Farmers? ", *Oriental Magazine*, "Oriental Forum", November, 1932, 1.

255 Dong Ruzhou, "Bankruptcy of the Chinese Rural Economy", *Oriental Magazine*, December 1932, 14.

418 *Rural crisis in 1930s and countermeasures*

256 Zhu Xi, "The Heavy Land Tax Surcharge and the Rural Economy Declination", *Oriental Magazine*, November 1933, 7–8.

257 Dong Ruzhou, "Bankruptcy of China's Rural Economy", *Oriental Magazine*, December, 1932, 20.

258 "The Narratives of Marlen and Tyler of the Huayang Donation Association", see Li Shuqing, "The Poverty Level of Chinese Peasants", *Oriental Magazine*, January 1935, 78.

259 Meng Weixian, "The Peasantry Life beside the Dongting Lake", *Oriental Magazine*, April 1936, 116–117.

260 Gengfu, "Anxi's Man-Made Disasters and Natural Disasters", *Oriental Magazine*, May 1936, 109.

261 Quoted from Wang Yinhuan, *Research on the Problem of Farmers Leaving Villages in Hebei, Shandong and Henan* (China Social Publishing House, 2004), 5.

262 "The Investigation of Farmers in Every Province by Li Village (Appendix 2)", *The Report of Agriculture Situation*, 4, no. 7 (July 1936), 173. Quoted from Wang Yinhuan, *Research on the Problem of Farmers Leaving Villages in Hebei, Hebei and Henan* (Beijing: China Social Publishing House, 2004), 7.

263 Lin Hecheng, "What Should China's Agricultural Financial System Be?", *Oriental Magazine*, April 1936, 57.

264 Zhu Xie, "Heavy Land Tax and the Decline of Rural Economy", *Oriental Magazine*, November 1933, 7–8.

265 Liang Shuming, "The Theory of Rural Construction", in *The Complete Works of Liang Shuming* (vol. 2) (Jinan: Shandong People's Publishing House, 2005), 150.

266 (America) Gilbert Rozman, *The Modernization of China*, 660.

267 Zhang Ming, *Eighty Years on Rural Road*, 220.

268 (America) Fei Zhengqing, *History of the Republic of China* (Beijing: China Social Sciences Press, 1993), 33.

269 Tao Xingzhi, "New Trends in Teaching Education", *Complete Works of Tao Xingzhi* (One) (Changsha: Hunan Education Publishing House, 1986), 167.

270 (America) Gilbert Rozman, *The Modernization of China*, 551–563.

271 Akigorou Taga, *History of Modern Chinese Education* (Taipei: Wenhai Publishing Company, 1976), 770–777.

272 See League of International Education Expedition: *Report of the League of International Education Expedition*, 1931, in Shen Yunlong, *Modern Chinese Historical Materials*, Series 3, vol. 11 (Taipei: Wenhai Publishing Company, 1988 photocopy).

273 Dr. Do. L. Butterfield, world-renowned agricultural economist, visited China in the last ten years of the Republic of China and surveyed that there were at that time at least 100,000 villages and 1 million rural communities (Author's note)

274 "Second Statistical Yearbook of China's Education": There were 177,751 national schools and elementary schools and 1,096 secondary schools in the 11th year of the Republic of China, whereas there were 259,863 national and primary schools and 3,026 secondary schools in the twentieth year. (Author's note)

275 Pan Naigu, Pan Naihe's *Selected Works of Pan Guangdan*, Series 3 (Beijing: Guangming Daily Press, 1999), 371–378, concluded in Pan Guangdan, *On Rural Education*.

276 (America) Kong Feili, *Rebellion in the Late Chinese Empire and Its Enemies*, 238.

277 Sa Mengwu, *Sociology of Chinese Social Issues* (Shanghai: Huatong Publishing House, 1929), 130.

Rural crisis in 1930s and countermeasures 419

278 Fei Xiaotong, "Landscaping under Erosion", in *Reconstruction of the Native Land*, 72, the 3rd Republic of China Series (Shanghai: Shanghai Bookstore, 1991 photocopy). Pan Guangdan, "Education without Principles", in Pan Naigu, Pan Naihe, *Selected Works of Pan Guangdan*, 3rd Series, 430–433. Liang Shuming, "Distress in My Heart", in Bao Shu, *Essence of Liang Shuming's Academic Essence* (Beijing: Beijing Normal University Press, 1988), 450–453. All of the above mentioned the problem. (Same as cited later)

279 Sa Mengwu, *Sociology of Chinese Social Issues* (Shanghai: Huatong Book Company, 1929), 131.

280 Yang Kaidao, "The Reason for Rural Life Failure in China and Its Solutions", *Oriental Magazine*, August 1927, 5.

281 Zhu Jingzhou, "Gansu's Trade Overview in the Recent Three Years", *Shun Pao*, May, 15, 1935, quoted from Zhu Qihua, *Perspective of China's Rural Economy* (Shanghai: Shanghai China Studies Bookstore, 1936), 64.

282 Ci Fan, "Family Economy of a Landlord", *Tianjin Yishi Newspaper*, p. 3, June 2, 1934, 11th edition, *Rural Weekly*, 13th issue.

283 People's Publishing House, *Information of the Peasant Movement during the First Civil Revolutionary War*, 11.

284 Wang Fangzhong, "A Preliminary Study of the Fall of Rural Land Price in the 1930s (before the War of Resistance against Japan)", *Research on Modern History*, 3 (1993), 214.

285 Zhu Qihua, *A Perspective of China's Rural Economy* (Shanghai: Shanghai China Studies Bookstore, 1936), 54.

286 Zhu Qihua, *Perspective of China's Rural Economy*, 3–4.

287 Liu Dapeng, *Tuixiangzhai Diary*, 228.

288 Liu Dapeng, *Tuixiangzhai Diary*, 242.

289 Liu Dapeng, *Tuixiangzhai Diary*, 491.

290 Liu Dapeng, *Tuixiangzhai Diary*, 286.

291 See Ma Songling, "To the Ones who Plan the ten-year Construction", *New Countryside*, 6 (1933).

292 The research college of history collection in Shanxi Province, *General History of Shanxi* (vol. 7), 238.

293 Liu Dapeng, *Tuixiangzhai Diary*, 477.

294 Feng Hefa, *China Rural Economics*, 417.

295 Wang Xianming, "Shanxi Rural Workers in the Early Twentieth Century", *Historical Research*, 5 (2006), 115.

296 Wu Juenong, "The Peasant Problem", *Oriental Magazine*, August 25, 1922, 7–8.

297 Zhu Xie, "Land Tax Surcharge and the Rural Economy Declination", *Oriental Magazine*, November 1933, 7–8.

298 Gu Yi, "Construction of Rural Areas and Transformation of Rural Education", *Oriental Magazine*, October 1933, 6.

299 Zhang Fuji, "The Rural Crisis and the Evolution of China's Political Structure in the Last Century", www.LEGAL-HISTORY.NET, August 29, 2004. *Journal of Shandong Normal University*, 3 (1996), 19.

300 Lenin, *China's Nationalism and Populism* (vol. 2) (Beijing: People's Publishing House, 2012), 293.

301 Wang Zaoshi, "Social Changes after the Contact between China and the West", *Oriental Magazine*, 1934, 40.

420 *Rural crisis in 1930s and countermeasures*

302 Chen Mingyuan, "Abolition of Miscellaneous Taxes", *Oriental Magazine*, January 1934, 211.

303 Liang Shuming, *The Theory of Rural Construction · Appendix* (Binzhou: Zouping Rural Bookstore, 1937), 1.

304 Liang Shuming, *The Theory of Rural Construction · Appendix* (Binzhou: Zouping Rural Bookstore, 1937), 1.

305 Chen Hansheng, "The Land Revolution of China" (25th, 1948), in *Chen Hansheng Works Collection* (Beijing: The Commercial Press, 1999), 332.

306 Pan Guangdan, "On Rural Education", in Pan Naigu, Pan Naihe, *Work Collection of Pan Gungdan* (Beijing: Guangming Daily Press, 1999), 371–378.

307 (America) Kong Feili, *The Rebellion and Its Enemies in the Late Chinese Empire*, 238.

308 See Fei Xiaotong, "Hometown under Erosion", in *Homeland Reconstruction*, 72, "Series of Republic of China", 3rd Series (Shanghai: Shanghai Bookstore, 1991 photocopy). Pan Guangdan, "Education without Principles", in Pan Naigu, Pan Naihe, *Selected Works of Pan Guangdan*, 3rd Series, 430 -433. Liang Shuming, "Distress in My Heart", in Bao Shu, "Essence of Liang Shuming's Academic Essence" (Beijing: Beijing Normal University Press, 1988), 450–453. These have been discussed previously. (Same as cited above)

309 Yang Kaidao, "The Causes of the Decline of Rural Life in China and Its Solution", *Oriental Magazine*, August 1927, 5–6.

310 Cheng Shutang, "Aggravating Rural Charging", *Oriental Magazine*, December 1935, 54.

311 Party Branch of Zhejiang Province, Chinese Nationalist Party, *(Before 1927) The State of Peasant Movement in China* (Publisher is unknown, and publication date unknown), 9.

312 Zhu Xie: "Is the Land Ownership Public? Does the Government Implement VAT?", *Oriental Magazine*, December 1935, 22, 23, and 26.

313 Wang Shuhuai, "The Land Price of Jiangsu Province", in *The Collection of Modern Chinese Rural Economic History Papers* (Taipei: Institute of Modern History, Academia Sinica), 200.

314 Wang Shuhuai, "The Land Price of Jiangsu Province", in *Historical Essays of the Modern Chinese Rural Economy*, 202.

315 Huang Zhuyi, "A Perspective of the Present Situation of Farmers in Northern Sichuan", *Oriental Magazine*, August 1927, 36

316 Qianjiaju, "China's Finance in the Recent 30 Years", *Oriental Magazine*, January 1934, 123.

317 Xu Dixin, "The Livelihood of Middle and Bottom Class Farmers in the Rural Bankruptcy", *Oriental Magazine*, January 1935, 56.

318 Xu Yushui, "A Survey of China's Land Tax", *Oriental Magazine*, October 1933, p.57.

319 Chen Hansheng, "Revealing China's Political Farce" (January 13, 1932–July 9, 1932), in *Chen Hansheng Collected Works*, 144.

320 Chen Hansheng, "Chinese Farmers under the Rule of Nationalist Party", in *Collected Works of Chen Hansheng*, 182.

321 Chen Hansheng, "Chinese Farmers under the Rule of Nationalist Party", in *Collected Works of Chen Hansheng*, 184.

322 Xu Dixin, "The Livelihood of Middle and Bottom Class Farmers in the Rural Bankruptcy", *Oriental Magazine*, January 1935, 56.

Rural crisis in 1930s and countermeasures   421

323 Shao Yuanchong, "The Evolution of Chinese Social Construction in the Past Thirty Years", *Oriental Magazine*, January 1934, 32.

324 Zou Bingwen, "The Way to Solve the Problems in China's Rural Areas", *Oriental Magazine*, January 1935, 16.

325 Liu Dapeng, *Liaoxiangzhai Diary*, 477

326 Gu Shiling, *China's Poverty and Peasant Issues* (Beijing: Public Book Company, Shanghai-Nanjing Branch, publishing date unknown), 108.

327 Yin Xuan, "The Current Stage of the Rural Areas in Zhonglu, Shanxi", *China Rural*, 2, no. 11 (1936): 74.

328 Gu Shiling, *China's Poverty and Peasants Problems*, 492

329 Yi Shuangqiu, etc. The third selection of educational reference materials. *Theory and Practice of Rural Education* (Shanghai: Educational Translation and Edition Publishing House, 1935), 4.

330 Reporter: "The Peasant Problem and China's Future", *Oriental Magazine*, August 1927, 1.

331 Reporter: "The Peasant Problem and China's Future", *Oriental Magazine*, August 1927, 1. Yi Shuangqiu et al., The third selection of educational reference materials. *Theory and Practice of Rural Education* (Shanghai: Educational Translation and Edition Publishing House, 1935), 4.

332 "Political Report on Farming under Jiangchu's Two-System Military Policy", *Journal of Agriculture*, 162nd issue, in Jiang Yasha, Jing Li, Chen Zhanqi, *Compilation of Early Chinese Agricultural Journals* (vol. 7) (National Center for Reproduction of Books and Documents, 2009), 673.

333 "The Document of the Official of Hubei Deal with the Local Farming", *Journal of Agriculture*, 188th issue, in Jiang Yasha, Jing Li and Chen Zhanqi, *Early Chinese Agricultural Journal*, vol. 10 (National Center for Reproduction of Books and Documents, 2009), 11.

334 "Report from Magistrate Xu Jiahe, Anlu Prefecture, Zhongxiang County", *Journal of Agriculture*, 188th issue, in Jiang Yasha, Jing Li and Chen Zhanqi, *Journal Compilation of Early Chinese Farming*, vol. 10, 15

335 "Large Scale of Cultivating Silkworm Industry to Boost Profits", *Shun Pao*, August 17, 1904, first edition.

336 "The Physiocracy of the US", *International Communiqué*, 208 (1906), 61.

337 "Speech Draft of Zeng Fangbo, President of Zhili Agricultural Association", *Ta Kung Pao*, May 15, 1907, first edition.

338 "Report on Asking for Financial Support to Establish a Branch Bank for Agriculture and Cultivation by Chen Jintao, Minister of Finance", *Shun Pao*, March 13, 1912, first edition.

339 Luo Zhenyu, "Explanation on Agricultural Politics", *Journal of Agricultural Science*, 162nd issue, in Jiang Asha, Jing Li and Chen Zhanqi, *Compilation of Early Chinese Agricultural Journals* (vol. 7), 125–128.

340 "Political Report on Farming under Jiangchu's Two-System Military Policy", *Journal of Agriculture*, 162nd issue, in Jiang Yasha, Jing Li and Chen Zhanqi, *Compilation of Early Chinese Agricultural Journals* (vol. 7), p. 673.

341 "Origins of Agricultural Promotion Association", *Industrial Magazine*, July 1912, 5.

342 "Political Report on Farming under Jiangchu's Two-System Military Policy", *Journal of Agriculture*, 162nd issue, in Jiang Yasha, Jing Li and Chen Zhanqi, *Compilation of Early Chinese Agricultural Journals* (vol. 7), 673.

422 *Rural crisis in 1930s and countermeasures*

343 "Discussion on the Prosperity of Agriculture", *Shun Pao*, February 10, 1901, first edition.

344 Luo Zhenyu, "Explanation on Agricultural Politics", 162nd issue, in Jiang Yasha, Jing Li and Chen Zhanqi, *Compilation of Early Chinese Agricultural Journals* (vol. 7), 126.

345 "Request Higher Official to Boost Farming by Scholar Hou Dianying, Qufu County", *Journal of Agriculture*, 263rd issue, in Jiang Yasha, Jing Li and Chen Zhanqi, *Compilation of Chinese Early Agricultural Journals* (vol. 14), 4–5.

346 "Discussion on Nominating the County Officials", *Shun Pao*, January 10, 1902, first edition.

347 "The Declaration of China's Farming War", *Ta Kung Pao*, March 28, 1905, 2.

348 "Declaration of Self-Improvement" was published in *Shun Pao* on January 1, 1901. The author emphasized: "If you want self-improvement, you must first get rich. The way to get rich should be the top priority of financial management. Financial management should first focus on the sources. Plenty of sources are the guarantee of eternity. If not, those with clever appearances always fail in the end. Where is the source? Products property should be the base. Although China's products are abundant, people do not know how to make use of them. So outsiders get a profit from what we have". "In other words, the provinces should open up minerals, and establish schools, which is especially what is needed for China's self-improvement. These are all of the task of self-improvement nowadays". (Author's note)

349 "On Mining", *Shun Pao*, January 9, 1901.

350 "On the Chance of the Revitalization of China's Handicraft", *Shun Pao*, December 29, 1901, first edition.

351 "The Theory of Promoting Business for a Powerful Country", *Oriental Magazine*, the 3rd issue, volume 1, May, 1904, p.41.

352 "On the Future of China's Industry", *Oriental Magazine*, the 10th issue, volume 1, December 1904, p. 165.

353 "On the Rationality of an Industrial China", *Shun Pao*, August 3, 1906, 2nd edition.

354 "Request for Revitalizing Agriculture and Commerce from Shanxi Governor Cen", *Journal of Agriculture*, in Jiang Yasha, Jing Li and Chen Zhanqi, *Compilation of Early Chinese Agricultural Journals* (vol. 9), 491.

355 "Request for Establishing Farming School from Hu Fuyu", *Journal of Agriculture*, in Jiang Yasha, Jing Li and Chen Zhanqi, *Compilation of Early Chinese Agricultural Journals* (vol. 9), 431.

356 "Request for the Revitalization of Farming from Ministry of Commerce", *Shun Pao*, December 5, 1903.

357 "On the Reasons of China's holding Agriculture Competition", *Ta Kung Pao*, July 24, 1907.

358 "Agricultural and Commercial Newspaper", 47th issue, September 25, 1908, in Shanghai Library. *Journals Catalogue of Modern China* (vol. 2) (middle) (Shanghai: Shanghai People's Publishing House, 1979), 2242.

359 "Agricultural Industry and Commerce", *Shun Pao*, 48th issue, October 5, 1908, in Shanghai Library. *Journals Catalogue of Modern China* (vol. 2) (middle), p. 2243.

360 "Encouraging Commerce", *Ta Kung Pao*, July 2, 1916.

361 "The Fundamental Relief Solution to Famine", *Oriental Magazine*, October 1920, 13.

Rural crisis in 1930s and countermeasures 423

362 "Thoughts on Having Four Divisions of Agriculture, Forestry Industry, Commerce and Business", *Ta Kung Pao*, August 30, 1916, 3.

363 "Direct Supervisory Report on the Local Product Inspection", *Journal of Agriculture*, 246th issue, in Jiang Yasha, Jing Li and Chen Zhanqi, *Compilation of Early Chinese Agricultural Journals* (vol. 13), 251.

364 "On Revitalizing Farming from Scholar Hou Dianying of Qufu County", *Journal of Agriculture*, 263rd issue, in Jiang Yasha, Jing Li and Chen Zhanqi, *Compilation of Early Chinese Agricultural Journals* (vol. 14), 3.

365 "Report from the Farming Community of Yangxin County to the Industrial and Commercial Bureau", *Journal of Agriculture*, 294th issue, in Jiang Yasha, Jingli and Chen Zhanqi, *Compilation of Early Chinese Agricultural Journals*, (vol. 15), 491.

366 "On the Principles of the Relationship between the Two Sectors of Agriculture and Commerce", *China Business Association Journal*, 6th issue, May 1910, qtd. from Zhu Ying, *Modern Chinese Businessmen and Society* (Wuhan: Hubei Education Press, 2002), 267.

367 "Request for Establishing Branch Bank for Revitalizing Farming from Chen Jintao, Minister of Finance", *Shun Pao*, March 13, 1912, first edition.

368 "Promoting Farming, *Ta Kung Pao*, in "Persuasion of Farmers", *Ta Kung Pao*, March 23, 1916, 1.

369 "Suggestions on Establishing Agriculture University", *Ta Kung Pao*, February 12, 1920, 2.

370 Lv Ruiting, "Advisory on Agricultural Nation", *Beijing Daily*, 1920, 1.

371 Lv Ruiting. "Advisory of Agricultural Nation", 6–7.

372 Lv Ruiting, "Advisory of Agricultural Nation", 25.

373 Lv Ruiting, "Advisory of Agricultural Nation", 33–34.

Index

administrative villages 85, 89, 99–100, 103, 109–112, 309, 315, 328
anti-Japanese national united front 88, 93
Association of Agricultural Revitalization 397
autocratic imperial power 1
average land rights 231

Bao-jia Bureau 63, 275
Bao-jia system 13, 39, 61–65, 67–9, 71–8
Book of Family Names 151

chain of institutional changes 289, 299
civic assembly 309
civil corps 16, 18, 26, 31–2, 34–7, 39–42, 57, 71, 74–7, 282–3, 292, 301, 319–322
civil rights 72, 82, 231, 271, 273–77, 279, 281–83, 285–86, 288
compradors 234–35, 266, 376
conflicts between the gentry and plebs 1–2, 4, 12–4, 18, 20–1, 23–4, 36, 38, 44
conservatism 6
constitutional movement 41, 323
Constitution of Five Powers 44
Constitution on Local Self-government in Cities, Towns and Villages 26, 62, 72, 141, 278, 293, 324
contradiction between officials and plebs 2

democratic experimental ground 303
democratic republicanism 1, 44, 306
destroying schools and killing the gentry 2, 284, 287
directors of civil corps 16
Dispute on the Establishing of the Nation 405

Downward Mobility 202–04, 206, 208, 213–15, 218, 221–23, 225

economic leverage 291
employment relationship 85, 166, 169, 171, 173, 176, 180, 188, 192, 194–96, 250, 253
equal distribution of land 94, 95, 101, 109, 114–16
equalization of land ownership 231, 269
era of gentry governance 21

farm laborer 85, 87, 90, 93–4, 98–109, 110, 113, 115, 165, 167–8, 176–180, 188–191, 192–5, 197, 216, 225, 235–6, 242–3, 248
feudal and semi-feudal system of exploitation 94, 105, 110, 112
Federal of War Action 304–5
First Civil Revolutionary War 55, 57–8, 118–9, 319, 411, 419

gentry drove people to death 24, 52, 284
gentry power 2, 9, 14, 16–8, 23, 25, 27, 32, 33, 37, 39, 42, 54, 56–7, 271–9, 281–3, 285–8, 290–1, 293–4
gentry working in civil corps 16
group of high social status 289
grain stored in grain stock 8
grass-roots level 7

historical materialism 239
household surveys 18–20, 36, 50, 322
horizontal surveillance 69
horizontal mobility 211–13, 260
Hunan and Hubei provinces 9, 11, 13, 24–5, 28, 31, 34, 39–41, 47–8, 52–6, 58, 61, 62, 65, 70–1, 80, 83, 272, 292, 323–24, 326

Index

imperial examination system 42, 149, 294, 375
industrialization 128, 129, 131–133, 135, 138, 142, 150, 159–161, 196, 331, 332, 337–339, 345, 347, 352, 353, 355, 371, 373, 376–378, 389–390, 401
innovation 6, 68, 84
institutionalization 14, 160, 24, 291, 294
institutionalization of gentry power 291
intrageneration mobility 199, 200, 204, 213–215, 219
intergenerational mobility 204, 209, 211, 213, 219, 260

Jin-Sui Border Area 84, 85, 87, 88, 90, 93, 94, 102, 107–110, 112–13, 115–16, 121–27, 221, 313, 327–29
Jin-Sui suboffice 95, 96, 107, 108, 123–26, 221, 222, 262

land extraction and compensation 101
land-holding peasants 85–7, 93, 109, 165, 167–68, 176, 189–190, 194–195, 197, 202, 236, 243–48, 258–59, 366–69
land occupation 90, 93, 95, 97–105, 123–24, 189, 221, 225, 229, 235, 245–46, 250, 366
land reform 84, 87, 94–108, 110, 112–16
land reform working groups 95
land relation 84, 85, 89, 90, 94, 97, 100, 102, 105, 107, 109, 116, 122, 334
liquidation struggles 97
local autonomy 8, 16, 17, 26, 28, 29, 31, 40, 49, 50, 52, 54, 55, 63, 65, 70–4, 78, 81, 82, 118, 119, 121, 273, 274, 277–286, 289, 320–323, 403
local gentry power 9, 274, 290
local property depository departments 27, 43
local public power 288–290, 294, 295
local tyrants and the evil gentry 2, 31, 272–73, 291, 302, 335, 360, 406

marginalized people 3
Mass Uprisings 1–6, 9–14, 18–20, 24, 32, 34, 38, 44–7, 50–2, 56, 277, 278–282
mass uprisings in Changsha 10
mass uprisings in Laiyang 11, 47, 56
May 4th Instructions 95, 107, 112, 388
meeting of increasing cadres 309

middle peasants 85–7, 90, 93, 94, 96, 98–107, 109–115, 176–180, 186, 190, 193–194, 203
modernity of state power 83

national government 64, 67–9, 71–4, 77–8, 82–3, 117, 134–35, 141–42, 150, 161, 185, 247, 255, 301, 334, 350, 354, 370, 383, 386, 390–91
natural villages 85, 97, 99–103, 109, 250, 258, 304, 305, 308–09, 315
New Deal 1–2, 5–8, 12–4, 16–24, 26, 28–30, 32, 34, 38, 40–1, 46, 51–2, 61–2, 68, 129, 132, 149, 271, 273–75, 277–289, 291–95, 299, 321, 323, 331, 355, 357, 360, 363, 372, 385, 386, 390
new gentry class 290
new-style schools 148–155, 157, 158, 290
normalization 16
northwest Jin (Shanxi Province) 303–04, 306, 308, 310, 312

officials drove plebs to rebellion 52
old-style private schools 148–150, 161–162
operational farmers 216–217
Outline of the Land Law of China 97, 223

Paying Taxes in Laiyang to the Rice Riot in Changsha 6
peasant association for anti-Japanese national salvation 88
pests and two moths 7
polarization theory 189–190
police system 13, 62–3, 68–9, 118
Populism 15, 419
power subjects 7, 84
powerful gentry 16, 18, 21, 24, 30, 294, 324
production cooperatives 313
protective brokerage 43–4
public interests of society 7
public power 7–8, 18, 21–3, 35–6, 40, 53, 70, 283, 285, 288–91, 293–295, 322

rectification 312
reforming systems 7
rent and interest reduction 88–91, 94–5, 97, 100, 109, 223, 312

426 *Index*

Revolution of 1911 1–2, 4, 11, 24, 26,
    30–4, 36, 38–40, 44–8, 50–2, 54–9, 68,
    117, 163, 167, 237, 273, 298, 321–22,
    335, 357–58, 413
Revolutionary League of self sacrifice
    for national salvation 88
rich peasants 85–7, 89, 90, 93–109,
    112–15, 126, 146, 166, 168, 176–77,
    189–191, 194, 196–98, 200–03, 206,
    208–213, 215–19, 221
ruling crises 6
rural crisis 330
rural hired laborer 164–66, 168, 170,
    187, 194, 196
rural public property system 1
rural society 1, 2, 14–5, 18, 23, 31, 40,
    52–4, 61–4, 68–71, 73, 76, 78, 81,
    83–5, 87, 97, 105–07, 114–16, 148–151,
    153–58, 169, 173, 176, 179, 180, 183,
    191–92, 194–96, 198, 215–19, 222, 223,
    226–28, 240, 244, 256–57, 271–72, 289,
    291, 294, 300–03, 305–06, 309, 314,
    315, 317–18, 330–31, 338, 340,
    344–45, 351–52, 354–55, 360, 363,
    366–67, 369–371, 380–81, 385–87, 389,
    390, 392–93, 396, 406, 412

Security Bureau 63, 289
security group 10–11, 300
semi-old base areas 96, 100–03, 105, 109
September 18th incident 346
Sino-Japanese War 2, 129–130, 166, 357
small-scale peasant economy 199,
    207–08, 216, 249, 253, 261–62, 356–57,
    371, 413
social invisible web 81
special taxes 26
structural imbalance 2
structural mobility 216–18, 262

Taiping Rebellion 9, 16, 24–5, 28, 30, 32,
    34, 39–40, 278, 377, 386

Ta Kung Pao 58–60, 162, 286–87, 296,
    298, 322, 324, 325, 394, 402, 421–23
tax farming 44
tenancy relationship 85, 87, 89, 90, 166,
    194–367
Three-character Classic 151
Three Principles of the People 38,
    44, 265–66
turmoil in Hunan Province 9, 20, 51

Universal Education 161–62, 280, 388
Upward Mobility 199, 200, 201, 205–07,
    211, 213–19, 223–25, 260, 318
urban and rural deviation 348
urbanization 128–29, 131–32, 138, 140,
    142, 196, 332, 337, 339, 345, 347, 352,
    353, 355, 371, 373, 375–76, 378, 384,
    389, 390

vagrants without means of production 3
vertical mobility 211, 260
village election 271, 304, 307, 308,
    312, 315–17
Village Elections Regulations 308
village governance 53, 58, 387
village national assembly 308
village public office 308–09
"Village Regime Organization
    Regulations" 308
village representative conference
    308
village union 9

War of Liberation 87, 94, 116, 121,
    126
War of Resistance Against Japan 87–9,
    121, 137, 159, 177, 183, 189–190, 217,
    250, 271, 303, 312, 315, 317, 388,
    411, 419
well-field system 232, 238, 243
Westernization Movement 128–130, 132,
    398